For Jenny, Steve, Kristen,
and all of tomorrow's leaders.

# Preparing for Leadership

# PREPARING FOR LEADERSHIP

## LEADERSHIP

### A Young Adult's Guide to Leadership Skills in a Global Age

ROBERT B. WOYACH

GREENWOOD PRESS
Westport, Connecticut · London

In order to keep this title in print and available to the academic community, this edition was produced using digital reprint technology in a relatively short print run. This would not have been attainable using traditional methods. Although the cover has been changed from its original appearance, the text remains the same and all materials and methods used still conform to the highest book-making standards.

**Library of Congress Cataloging-in-Publication Data**

Woyach, Robert B.
    Preparing for leadership : a young adult's guide to leadership
skills in a global age / Robert B. Woyach.
      p.    cm.
    Includes bibliographical references.
    ISBN 0-313-28602-7 (hc : alk. paper)—ISBN 0-313-29053-9 (pb :
alk. paper)
    1. Leadership.    I. Title.
HM141.W693   1993
303.3'4—dc20       92-45076

British Library Cataloguing in Publication Data is available.

A hardcover edition of *Preparing for Leadership* is also available from the Greenwood Press imprint of Greenwood Publishing Group, Inc. (ISBN 0-313-28602-7).

Library of Congress Catalog Card Number: 92-45076
ISBN: 0-313-29053-9 (pb)
      0-313-28602-7 (hc)

First published in 1993

Greenwood Press, 88 Post Road West, Westport, CT 06881
An imprint of Greenwood Publishing Group, Inc.

Printed in the United States of America

The paper used in this book complies with the Permanent Paper Standard issued by the National Information Standards Organization (Z39.48-1984).

P

**Artwork Acknowledgments**

Computer-generated Drawings: Lizabeth Alecusan

Interpretive Drawings: Tom Crane

# Contents

# Preface

Several years ago a young Vietnamese immigrant to the United States by the name of Viet Lee came to me with a problem. He had been elected student body vice-president at his high school. As vice-president, he was in charge of a committee on student activities. Viet had chaired the committee for only two months, but he was already frustrated and disillusioned. "They don't do what I tell them," he complained. "They have no discipline. They do not care if anything gets done!"

Viet was looking for advice on how to run a more effective meeting—on how to get his group to be more "disciplined." Unfortunately, Viet, like many before him, was looking in the wrong place. What his committee lacked was not discipline. Nor was his a problem of technical meeting skills. Viet knew how to plan an agenda. He knew all about parliamentary procedure. What he did not know about was *leadership*. He had no idea that "discipline" came from caring about the work of the group. He had no idea that caring came from commitment to a common vision, motivation, and ultimately empowerment.

This book is written for Viet and for all the Viets across the United States. Its purpose is to help you understand *what* leadership is and what it takes to develop your abilities as a leader. What does it take? Basically four things:

- MOTIVATION. Leaders are people who want to accomplish something. They want to make a difference in the lives of others. Leadership is never aimless. It reflects a commitment to something. That something may be a big social issue, or it may just be keeping some group alive. In part, preparing for leadership involves finding that mission—finding the motivation to lead.

- INVOLVEMENT. Great causes or small, the things that leaders try to achieve arise from their involvement in the world—their involvement with other people. In fact, many experts on leadership regard leadership development as a process of expanding your horizons through time. Today you may be involved in a club whose members are only from your school. Tomorrow the group in which you exercise leadership may have members from throughout the whole community. Someday you may exercise leadership in a statewide, a regional, or even a national organization. Some of you will inevitably exercise leadership in a group or on issues that involve people all around our world. In part, preparing for leadership requires that you get involved, and that you look for new and more challenging ways to be involved throughout your life.

- SELF-CONFIDENCE. To become involved in ever-wider arenas, indeed to exercise leadership wherever you are, you must be willing to take risks. You must be willing to put your name and your ego on the line. You must be willing to let other people think you are wrong. Most of all, you must be willing to risk failure. All leaders do fail, sometimes. If you do, you must have the self-confidence to pick yourself up and try again. Preparing for leadership involves gaining the self-confidence necessary to take these risks.

- SKILL. Finally, the difference between success and failure in leadership is ultimately tied to your leadership skills. Many different ideas exist of what these skills are. The model of leadership in this book is based on the work of scholars and leaders at The Ohio State University's Mershon Center. Unlike most models of leadership you will find, it is specifically developed to help leaders in the civic arena: in community groups that depend on the commitment and efforts of volunteers. It stresses precisely those skills of envisioning, motivation, and empowerment that Viet Lee needed to succeed as a school leader and will one day need as a community leader.

This book owes much to the thought and the work of others. Dr. Charles F. Hermann and Dr. Margaret G. Hermann along with the rest of the Mershon Center's Public Leadership Seminar helped develop many of the ideas. The many leaders, young and old, associated with the Columbus Council on World Affairs and the International Student Leadership Institute provided many of the real-world experiences upon which this book is based. Special thanks go to George Grantham and Ingeborg Burck, whose insights, example, and support have made this book possible.

Anyone can exercise leadership. It does not matter if you are young or old, assertive or quiet, a man or a woman. In fact, because both young men and young women will be tomorrow's leaders, the pronouns *he* and *she* are used interchangeably throughout this book. However, no model of leadership, no book on leadership can make you a leader. To become a leader you must take the ideas and models you have learned and put them into practice. If this book can give you a little more self-confidence, a little more vision, and a little better understanding of the skills that leaders must have, it will have accomplished its vision. Ideally it will have played a small role in launching you on your path toward leadership in this global age.

# Preparing for Leadership

# 1

## Leaders and Leadership

Miriam Witt was a high school student in Germany. She had a gift for learning languages and already spoke English and French. But Miriam wanted more: she wanted to learn Spanish. Spanish was not taught at her school, although there were teachers who could teach it, and students like Miriam who wanted to learn it.

Most of us face situations like Miriam's at some point. There is something we think ought to be done, but we cannot do it alone. In such a situation we have three options: we can ignore the issue; we can complain about the situation and hope *someone* does something; or we can exercise leadership, and try to get something done.

This book is for people who choose the last option: leadership. Its purpose is to help you begin developing the skills necessary to exercise leadership in today's world. In the process, it may make you think about leadership and about yourself in new ways. But before we look in detail at the skills that can make you an effective leader, we need to look more closely at what we mean by leadership and what it means to learn leadership.

### WHAT IS LEADERSHIP?

A famous political scientist once said that leadership is among the most highly studied of subjects and yet remains among the least understood. His remark has much truth to it. Leadership is a complicated thing. It exists in every society. Every one of us has experienced it. Yet most of us have only the vaguest idea of what it is. Even scholars have a hard time defining leadership exactly. Over the past few decades, they have come up with over 350 different definitions!

## Images of Good Leaders

Our ideas of leadership usually reflect our experience. Leadership is what the "good leaders" in our lives have done, or the opposite of what the "bad leaders" have done.

Who comes to your mind when you think of a "good leader"? What are the traits that make that person a good leader? The following are answers that high school students from the United States, Germany, France, Canada, and the Netherlands gave to these questions. Which of these examples come close to your image of a good leader?

- HANS DIETRICH GENSCHER (German politician)—he is concerned about the good of the nation; he gets things done; he is ethical.
- COLONEL GOLDSMITH (army officer)—you have to respect him because he treats you with respect; he has a good sense of humor and a way of keeping up morale.
- MY PARENTS—they raised me . . . gave me my values.
- ROBERT DOLE (U.S. politician)—he is such a well-rounded person; he understands what is going on around him.
- JOHN NAMEY (high school teacher)—he knows his material; he gets you to go along just through his enthusiasm and vitality.
- SHANNON SAUNDERS (high school student)—she was able to get everything done, at the same time she got people to work together; she worked so hard you wanted to work with her.

This list shows how common our experience with leadership is. Leaders are all around us—in our families, our schools, and our local communities as well as in distant capitals. The list also reveals how complex our image of leadership is. We know good leaders when we see them, but it is hard to say exactly what makes a person a good leader. Moreover, the things that make one person a good leader may be quite different from the things that make another person a good leader!

What makes a leader "good"?

## Leaders Are What Leaders Do

One way to understand leadership is to look at what leaders do. That itself is not easy. Leaders in business firms or national governments do different things than leaders in schools and small organizations. Even within one of these settings, leadership is a complex affair. (The 350 different definitions of leadership reflect just how complex leadership is.) However, there are some basic ideas about leadership with which most people agree.

*Leaders point the way.* The modern notion of "leader" comes from a Middle English word that meant "to guide." That simple phrase says a lot about what leadership is and what it is not. Look back at the list of "good leaders" who were suggested by the European and North American students. Each one of these people was a guide. Each one, from fellow students to political leaders, gave his or her group (family, nation) a sense of direction, a sense of purpose or mission.

A shared sense of purpose is critical to any group of people. It helps hold a group together; it transforms a mere collection of people into a "group." One of the most important things leaders do is to help groups develop a common sense of purpose. Remember, however, that leaders are *guides*. Groups depend on leaders to help the group shape its vision. But there is a difference between controlling a group and leading it— between giving the group its vision and helping the group see its vision. Leaders should not impose their personal visions on others. When they do—as in religious cults and dictatorships—the results can become dramatic examples of bad leadership!

***Leaders help groups get things done.*** In the eyes of most people, leadership involves helping a group to get things done by helping the group work together. This simple idea actually has three distinct and challenging aspects:

- Getting people to *work.*
- Getting people to work *together.*
- Getting *the things people need* to get something done.

Leaders get people to work. Everyone who exercises leadership faces the challenge of how to motivate people. How can I get David to help organize a church fair? How can I get Sarah to play harder on the soccer team? If groups are to get things done, they need leaders who can motivate people to work!

But leaders must go beyond individual motivation. Leaders get groups to work *together!* This requires a shared sense of purpose, but it also requires skill at building teamwork. Groups need leaders who can help people to cooperate, to make group decisions, and to resolve conflicts that arise within the group.

Finally, leaders must go beyond the group itself. Most groups need the support of people outside the group to accomplish anything. They need things like meeting space, money, and permission to hold public events. To get outside support, groups need leaders who can help make the group known and respected by others. They need leaders who can advocate their visions and ideas. They need leaders who can cooperate with other groups without compromising their own group's goals.

*A model of leadership.* These basic tasks provide a model of what leadership is all about. They also serve as a guide to the skills that new leaders should try to develop. Those skills are:

- Shaping Visions and Goals—Envisioning
- Helping Groups Make Decisions—Consensus-seeking
- Resolving Conflicts—Negotiation
- Motivating Members—Creating Rewards
- Getting Recognition for the Group—Creating an Image
- Getting Respect for the Group—Gaining Legitimacy
- Attracting Support and Defending the Group—Advocacy
- Cooperating with Other Groups—Coalition-building

This book takes a detailed look at these tasks and at how to do them well. But many would argue that leadership is more than a set of tasks and skills. It is a relationship among people. Understanding that relationship is critical if you are to exercise leadership effectively.

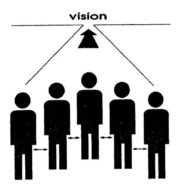

How do leaders help groups?

## Leaders, Followers, and Authority

It is all too easy to see leadership as something that an individual has. People routinely say things like "Karla is a leader" or "Greg has leadership ability." That can be very misleading. Leadership does not rest within a person. It is a relationship among people.

***Followers make leaders.*** No matter how dynamic, articulate, insightful, and knowledgeable a person may be, if she is stranded alone on a desert island, she cannot exercise leadership. You only become a leader when other people *accept* your leadership, when they choose to *follow* your leadership.

In this sense the term *follower* is misleading. Followers are not passive. They do not simply respond to what "leaders" tell them to do. In fact, by accepting or rejecting the leadership attempts of others, followers actually choose their leaders. People choose particular leaders for many different reasons. In some cases they choose leaders who bring out the best in them. In many cases they choose leaders who empower them as followers. Only rarely do people choose leaders who take away their freedom and their power.

***Authority cannot substitute for leadership.*** This is an important reason for not confusing leadership with authority. We often refer to a person in authority as "the leader" of the group. The student council president is "the leader" of the student body. The principal is "the leader" of the school. What we mean is that we expect this person, because he or she is in a position of authority, to exercise leadership.

All too often, however, people in authority begin to think they can use their authority (their right to make certain decisions) as a substitute for leadership (guiding and helping the group to work together effectively). That can cause problems.

In his presidential letters, John Kennedy mused that the hardest lesson he had to learn as president was that his success depended, not on the enormous authority of his office, but on being a skillful leader! Kennedy wanted Americans to commit themselves to visions of racial equality, a strong defense, and an expensive quest to conquer space. He quickly learned that he could not order the Congress or the American people to accept these visions and work toward them. He had to let other people exercise leadership by shaping the goals. He had to exercise leadership himself by persuading still others to support these goals and by motivating them to do what was necessary to achieve them.

The formal leaders of school and community groups have far less authority than the president of the United States. Not surprisingly, they also find that authority alone cannot make them successful.

- Authority can get people to do some things at some times, but
- It cannot get people to commit themselves to the group's goals or to work together effectively.

Accomplishing these things requires leadership.

## CAN ANYONE LEARN TO BE A LEADER?

Over the centuries, many people have wondered why certain people become leaders and not others. They have wondered whether it takes some kind of charisma or some special inborn personality traits to exercise leadership effectively. More recently, people have even suggested that leadership comes about as a happy accident. People with just the right skills happen to be in just the right place at just the right time— and voilà! History records another example of great leadership! Whether leaders are born or made by the times, these two ideas share a common assumption: leadership is not something that can be learned.

### Is There a Leadership Personality?

For many years the "personality" approach dominated thinking about leadership. People believed that some individuals were "born leaders." They had that special mix of personality and physical traits that made other people look to them for leadership.

*Charismatic leaders.* Students of leadership focused on personality because the success of many historic leaders seemed to come from an elusive quality that people called "charisma."

Charismatic leaders are people whose personality and physical presence automatically attract the confidence of others. We find these "charismatic" leaders so compelling that it is hard, if not impossible, not to give them our permission to exercise leadership.

One of the most charismatic leaders in modern times was Charles de Gaulle. De Gaulle, a French general during World War II, went on to become the president of his country. De Gaulle's imposing physical stature, his speaking ability, and his regal bearing all added to his charisma. In the United States we have also had charismatic leaders. Some, like Martin Luther King, Jr., and John Kennedy, have led people in positive directions. Others, like the evangelist Jim Jones, have led people in very negative directions.

*There is no one leadership style.* Charismatic leadership does exist. You may even know a charismatic leader yourself. The real question, however, is whether you *need* to have a particular "charismatic" personality in order to exercise leadership effectively.

The answer to this question is a resounding "No!" Even charismatic leaders do not necessarily have similar personalities. Indeed, in many cases what makes charismatic leaders effective may be the happy coincidence of their personality and the needs of the people they lead! One of the reasons why the French people rallied around Charles de Gaulle was their need for a symbol of stability and greatness at a time of great national peril. De Gaulle may not have seemed so charismatic had the French people not needed someone with his specific qualities!

Personality does influence leadership. An outgoing, assertive person may feel more comfortable exercising leadership in highly visible ways. A quieter person may not. However, *a person's ability to exercise leadership does not depend on having the right personality*. Years of research have failed to uncover any single set of physical traits or personality traits that mark successful leaders.

### Can You Learn to Be a Leader?

The fact that there is no one leadership personality, however, does not necessarily mean that leadership can be learned. As with De Gaulle, successful leadership may involve being in the right place at the right time.

***The right skills for the times.*** Many of the people we think of as great leaders (Abraham Lincoln, Winston Churchill) were not charismatic. They did, however, have the right skills for their times.

Abraham Lincoln might well have gone down in history as one of the world's most frustrated politicians had he relied on his charisma. Even as president of the United States, he seemed unimpressive to many people of his time. Yet Lincoln, like Churchill a century later, was able to provide the right kind of leadership for the times. Circumstances brought out a greatness that was not otherwise apparent.

The fact that great leaders seem to emerge from special circumstances has led some people to think that leaders emerge by happy coincidence. To them, good leadership happens when a person with certain traits finds himself or herself in a situation that requires just those traits. In this sense leadership cannot be learned: it just happens.

Can a democracy ever have too many leaders?
(Bill Day—*Detroit Free Press*, Tribune Media Services.)

*Preparing for leadership.* The idea that effective leadership happens by accident states the relationship between skills and context backward.

The situation does determine what a leader will be called on to do. A group that seems to be going nowhere needs a leader who can help it identify new goals and get it moving. A group whose members seem unmotivated needs a leader who can get people involved. A group torn apart by conflict needs a leader who can help resolve the conflict. Each situation calls for a particular skill, and different people may be more or less capable of exercising these skills.

- Exercising leadership effectively means using appropriate skills—at creating goals, at motivating people, at resolving conflicts—to meet the specific needs of your group.

However, each of these skills is just that: a skill. People learn skills. They learn them through study—including the observation of others who have those skills. Ultimately they learn them through practice—by trying to apply what they know about the skills in real leadership situations. The effort you put toward preparing for leadership—toward developing a tool kit of leadership skills—will determine how successful you will be in responding to the leadership needs of any one group at any one time.

Not only *can* leadership be learned, it *must* be learned. Very few of us are effective leaders right from the start. Most of us have to learn how to lead, and most of us learn by making mistakes! So if you want to learn leadership, the first step is to give yourself permission to lead—and permission to learn by failing every now and then.

## DO WE NEED MORE LEADERS?

Even if you want to be a leader and are convinced that leadership can be learned, you may doubt whether you have an opportunity to exercise leadership—or to practice leadership skills. As you look around you, it may seem that there are quite enough leaders already! Here too, however, reality is not what most people think.

### Groups Benefit from Having Many Leaders

In societies like ours, there are far more opportunities to exercise leadership than there are leaders. In fact, *democratic societies cannot have too many leaders*. Nor do you need to be an officer of a club, class, or student council. If you look closely at the most successful groups, you will find that many if not most of their members exercise leadership in one way or another.

Sharon was captain of the Worthington High School girls' soccer team. The job carried heavy responsibility. The captain was expected to be "the leader" of the team. She was expected to help motivate other players and to get the team working together. She guided younger players on the field and helped the coach find ways to adapt to the strategies of other teams. This year Worthington's team was good; a state title was not out of the question.

But Sharon was not the only person who could exercise leadership on the team. Other players could also help motivate the team so they believed they could win a state title. Other players could even suggest new plays and encourage less enthusiastic players to try harder. The

Worthington soccer team made it all the way to the championship game. They did it in part because of Sharon's leadership. But they also succeeded because Sharon was *not* the only one who exercised leadership!

### Disruptive versus Authentic Leadership

The idea that a group should have many leaders troubles some people. It suggests images of chaos—of people "leading" the group in different directions, of everyone talking and no one listening. An old proverb says that "Too many cooks spoil the broth." Does having too many leaders ruin the group?

Most' of us have seen or been part of groups that lacked a sense of direction or the discipline to work together. We would be mistaken, however, to see those groups as having had too many leaders. In reality, they had too *few!*

*Authentic leaders.* Authentic leaders are people who constantly try to balance personal, group, and community interests so that all three are better off. They place the good of the group on a par with their own self-interest. They try to find success for the group in ways that benefit the overall community. A group cannot have too many people who exercise leadership in this spirit.

Martin Luther King, Jr., was an example of an authentic leader in the fullest sense. He did not see the civil rights movement as a way to force his will on other people. He did not put his personal interests ahead of the interests of the movement. At the same time, Martin Luther King, Jr., had strong ideas of what civil rights meant and how they could be won. He would not abandon those values simply to forge agreement within the group.

King also tried to be an authentic leader by balancing the interests of his group—African-Americans—with those of the society as a whole. Many Americans believed that the civil rights movement pitted the interests of the black minority against the interests of the white majority. King refused to accept that idea. He reaffirmed the interests of the wider community by placing black civil rights squarely within America's broader vision of itself. He challenged white Americans, not to give African-Americans a break, but to live up to their own highest values of freedom and equality. By doing that, he argued, we would unleash the full potential of all Americans.

Authentic leaders like King sometimes make us uncomfortable. They often make trouble. But they do so because they believe it will lead to a better community as well as serve the interests of their group. The following example shows just how effective a group can be when it has many authentic leaders.

*A leaderful group.* Lori, David, Mary Anne, Mary Lynn, Bob, and Ed were six young professionals who were taking part in a community leadership program. As part of the program, they had to do a group project that would benefit the community. The six agreed to do a project on "The Image of Columbus."

The group's first meeting was held at Lori's office. No one chaired the meeting, but Lori started things off by talking about her ideas for the project. She suggested several things, including a series of interviews with community leaders, a survey of Columbus residents, and a survey of people outside the city. After Lori had finished, Dave began talking about the dynamic images other cities had created. With a confused look on his face, Bob wondered aloud what the group actually meant by an "image." It seemed that the word included everything from a logo or a theme like "Indianapolis: The Sports City" to a complex description of the community's quality of life and business climate.

The group talked for a long time. They tried to clarify what they meant by an image. They brainstormed ideas for projects. After a while Mary Anne realized that Ed had been very quiet. She asked him what he thought. Ed hesitated, but only for a second. The group, he said, seemed to agree on several things. Most importantly they seemed to agree on the need to learn more about how other cities had gone about creating and promoting their images. If we know more about that, Ed continued, we might be able to help Columbus improve its image. Mary Anne smiled as the head of everyone present nodded in agreement.

When Ed finished, Lori suggested that the group survey people in about 20 other cities to find out about their images and how they had been created. Everyone agreed. A list of cities was quickly drawn up. Questions for the survey were brainstormed. Bob volunteered to draft a letter that would be sent to the people to be interviewed and to type up a list of interview questions. Mary Anne suggested that the Central Ohio Marketing Council might be interested in the project and volunteered to contact them. Lori volunteered to contact the Chamber of Commerce and get an up-to-date list of contacts in the cities on the list. The meeting broke up on an enthusiastic note.

For the next six months, the group continued to meet, reporting progress, refining their goals, and bolstering each other's commitment to what turned out to be a time-consuming project. No one was ever appointed chairperson. No one was in authority. No one was in control of the group. Still, the group completed its project successfully and on time.

The study group had no one in authority, but it did have leaders. The group would never have defined its task if Lori had not helped shape the agenda or if Bob and Ed had not helped focus it. Nor would the group have succeeded if Mary Anne had not ensured that everyone was brought into the discussion and committed himself to the decision. Finally, the group would not have completed its work if all its members had not taken personal responsibility for achieving some part of the task.

- *That ultimately is what leadership is all about—taking responsibility for the success of the group.*

The study group had many leaders, and that is why it succeeded!

*Inauthentic leaders.* Groups cannot have too many authentic leaders. They can, however, be destroyed if they have too many inauthentic leaders. What is an inauthentic leader? How do you recognize one? Inauthentic leaders do not walk around with scarlet *I*'s on their shirts. Too often you only know them when their damage is done.

Inauthentic leaders typically seek their own personal interests at the expense of the group. The most common inauthentic leader is the "egotist," who is looking only for what she can get out of a group. Now, all people participate in groups in part for selfish reasons. However, egotists have no regard for the interests of the group at all. They want the recognition of the group or the gratification that comes from controlling others. When they get what they want, everything goes fine. However, when they do not, they disrupt the group until they get their way.

Other inauthentic leaders seek the group's interests at the expense of the community. Adolf Hitler was such a leader. He claimed to want what was best for the German nation. But only for *some* Germans—not Jews or people who disagreed with him. And his vision of what was good for Germany was crafted at the expense of other Europeans. Luckily, the tragic examples of inauthentic leaders like Hitler are exceptional. Unfortunately, inauthentic leadership itself is not. Learning how to deal with inauthentic leaders—to protect the group from them, or to harness their energy and turn them into authentic leaders—is one of the great challenges of leadership.

# 2

# *Exercising Leadership in a Global Age*

Leadership is always exercised in some place—in a club, a business firm, a neighborhood, a school—and through some role—as president, respected friend, new member. Taken together, our place and role determine the challenges we will face as leaders and the opportunities we will have. The president of a small school club faces different challenges than a large city mayor, although both exercise leadership. A club president has different opportunities than a new member, although both can be leaders.

Today the context in which we all exercise leadership has changed. We live in an age like no other in history: a global age. People all around the world have become so dependent on each other that:

- We are touched every day by the actions and decisions of people in other countries, and we touch their lives;
- We must cope with more diversity and complexity in our lives than any past generation; and
- We can know with confidence only that the world we leave to our children will be vastly different from the world our fathers and mothers are leaving to us.

This global age has very real consequences for exercising leadership. For one thing, it has expanded the community with which we must be concerned if we are to be authentic leaders. The world has become our stage even if we exercise leadership in a seemingly small and remote part of it. Similarly, this diverse, complicated, and ever-changing world has made a new, participatory style of leadership a necessity if we are to be effective.

## AUTHENTIC LEADERS THINK GLOBALLY

In many respects today's world has become a global village. People of all countries depend on each other for the basic necessities of life. Events and decisions on one side of the world affect people living on the other.

In a global village, authentic leaders must not only balance their personal values and interests with those of their group and their local community; they must balance these interests with those of the global community. The balancing of personal, group, and community interests has never been easy. Conflicts routinely arise among the interests of the individual, the needs of the group, and the good of the community. But this balancing of interests is all the more challenging when the community encompasses a world of different cultures and sometimes violent conflicts. It requires that leaders be able to think globally.

### See the Connections

At a minimum thinking globally requires that leaders see the connections between the world they experience directly and the wider world. To see those connections, you have to look beneath the surface of things. You must use your creative insight to see connections that others may miss and to understand what those connections mean.

*Global activities.* The evidence of our global connections is all around us. Have you taken a good look at the foods available in a local grocery store? How about the clothes and other things you use every day? If you have looked closely, you have some idea of the extent to which you depend on people in other countries. A grocery store in Minnesota is well stocked with fresh fruit even in mid-December because it can get fruit from Mexico, South America, and even Africa. A shoe store in Texas has the latest French styles, and the newest Brazilian imitations. A department store in Connecticut sells wine from France, radios from Japan, sweaters from Italy, and computers from Korea. Nor is the United States unique. Most people in the world today are part of a global economy.

*Hidden connections.* Not all of our global connections are easy to see, however. Each one of the foreign-made products in your home represents a whole chain of international connections. The clock-radio that woke you up this morning may have been assembled in Brazil by a Japanese company. It may contain parts made in Taiwan or Korea. It was probably shipped from Brazil in a Swedish-built ship, licensed in Liberia, and insured by Lloyds of London. The captain may have been British, the crew mostly Pakistani. In other words, the global connections we see are but the tip of an enormous iceberg.

*Interdependence.* These chains of global connections are important because our lives depend on them. We enjoy a higher standard of living because corporations can locate factories in and buy goods from countries with low production costs. We also enjoy a wider range of styles and have higher-quality goods. Markets in other countries create jobs for us as well. Americans have long considered themselves independent of world trade, but today one job in five depends on imports or exports.

Because of this dependence, events and decisions in any one country have an impact—good or bad—on people in distant places. It also means that many of the problems we face have their origins in our global connections. Homelessness, for example, is usually seen as a local or perhaps a national problem. Yet, homelessness around the world is directly related to the global economy.

In many of the countries of Africa, Asia, and Latin America, homelessness results from contact with Europe and North America. A hundred years ago these people would have lived in extended families in rural areas. There would have been little if any homelessness. Today people flock to cities, where they have neither families nor homes. Why? Most go in search of the jobs that come from world trade. The problem is that there are not enough jobs for everyone.

Even in the United States homelessness reflects the changing world economy. As we have become more globally connected, traditional jobs have disappeared. New skills are needed. Many of the homeless are people ill equipped for the jobs that are available and pay living wages. Some are ill equipped for the pace of change, or the insecurity and disconnectedness of modern life—which again reflects our global age.

What does it mean to "think globally"?

We can only do something about problems like these if we understand what causes them—if we see their global connections.

## See the Big Picture

Thinking globally also means being able to see the big picture, that is, being able to look at things from the viewpoint of the world as a whole.

*A shared fate.* In a global age, people around the world share a common future. This has become abundantly clear in the case of the environment. In recent years we have become aware of such problems as global warming, nuclear waste, acid rain, and depletion of ozone in the upper atmosphere. We have become concerned about the disappearance of tropical rain forests and soil erosion in key farming regions. The future of the entire planet depends on what we do about these problems. Yet, no one person or no one country acting alone can deal effectively with them.

*Global and local perspectives.* Our shared interest in solving issues like these means that it pays to look at them from a global perspective. Our shared fate means that we have a common interest in minimizing global warming or stopping ozone depletion. We will all suffer from higher cancer rates if the ozone is lost, or from the social, economic, and political consequences of global warming.

At the same time, having a global interest in solving a problem does not mean that we all have the same interest in how it is solved. How, for example, will the costs of saving the ozone be shared? Saving the ozone layer will require us to use fewer of the chemicals called chlorofluorocarbons or CFCs. The more industrialized countries use the most CFCs—in everything from aerosol cans to refrigerators and air conditioners. But limiting the use of CFCs in the more industrialized countries will do little good if people in less developed countries increase their use of them. Everyone must cut back if the ozone is to be saved. However, limiting the use of CFCs in less developed countries creates one more obstacle to their economic development! Some people in these countries see a requirement that they stop using CFCs as unfair. In other words, while we all have an interest in saving the ozone, we have different interests in how it is saved.

A global thinker does not ignore these differences in order to see the big picture: the global perspective. A global perspective takes these conflicts, ambiguities, and complexities into account. In looking for the big picture, a global thinker looks for ways to resolve the conflicts and to bring the ambiguities and complexities into better focus. Remember, being an authentic leader means *balancing* the needs and interests of self, group, and community—not ignoring some in favor of others.

### Accept Responsibility and Power

Perhaps most importantly, thinking globally requires that leaders accept the responsibility and power to act on behalf of the global community. To a young adult, this may seem impossible. Are you ready to deal with real world issues? Can you really make a difference? There is little reason to think globally if doing so will have no impact.

The truth is, however, that you can have an impact. The case of a student group at the Crossroads School in St. Louis shows what we mean. The students, mostly sophomores and juniors, had attended an environmental symposium featuring the French oceanographer Jacques Cousteau. The experience inspired the students to do something to address the problems of pollution and the wasteful use of resources.

After considering various alternatives, the group decided to launch the "Think Ecology" campaign. The heart of the campaign was an aluminum recycling project. Permission was gotten from the principal. Barrels were placed at strategic places around the school. Posters were hung on bulletin boards. The entire school community was encouraged to commit itself to the recycling effort.

The students at Crossroads School demonstrated their ability to think globally in several respects:

- They spoke for their local, national, and global communities when they recognized the need to control pollution and resource waste.

- They looked for and found connections between their daily activities and this global problem.

- In these everyday connections they found a realistic response which contributed to solving an enormously complex problem.

· Most importantly, they took responsibility for acting on a problem far greater than they alone could solve.

They recognized that, *even though they alone could not solve the problem, by working on a piece of it they could contribute to the solution.* They accepted the responsibility to act despite the limits of their power.

Many of the global problems we face require actions like those of the students at Crossroads School. They are enormous and complex problems. They cannot be solved by any one person or country. Yet, they can only be solved if people like us are willing to do something to solve them. They require us to think globally and to act locally, to balance our interests with the needs of the world. In short, they require us to be authentic leaders in a global age.

**CALVIN & HOBBES**

What does it take to be a good leader in a global age?
(Calvin and Hobbes copyright 1990 by Bill Watterson. Dist. by Universal Press Syndicate. Reprinted with permission. All rights reserved.)

## PARTICIPATORY LEADERSHIP

Living in a global age requires leaders who think about leadership in a new way. In a global age leadership can no longer mean "taking control" or "telling people what to do." A global age calls for a new kind of participatory leader.

Participatory leaders try to involve and to empower group members to do the work of the group. They do not see themselves as being in charge or in control. They see themselves as stewards of the group, responsible for taking initiatives, identifying issues, and structuring activities so that the group can do its work effectively.

Participatory leadership is not easy. It is far easier to tell people what to do than to get people to agree on a common cause and a common course of action. But highly directive leaders are far less effective than participatory leaders in coping with the key challenges of today's world:

- Increasing diversity,
- Rapid change, and
- Growing alienation.

## The Challenge of Diversity

Try to imagine being ten years old again and living in Southern California. Is the idea appealing? A warm, sunny climate. Beautiful ocean beaches to the west; rugged, picturesque mountains to the east. Southern California is a large, cosmopolitan community in which almost anything you can imagine is available. For over a generation Americans have seen it as an ideal place to live.

Now consider that you are a ten-year-old Cambodian refugee! Suddenly Southern California is a more difficult place in which to grow up. Most people speak English or Spanish, and they think you have a strange accent. School used to be easy, but now the subjects you liked most are hard because you do not understand the teacher. Your father is having a hard time finding a job, even though he was a respected doctor in Cambodia. Everywhere you look you are reminded that you are a stranger, even though what you want most is to make this new country your home.

*Increasing diversity.* Places like Southern California are on the front lines of one of the most important trends of our times. Thousands of immigrants, seeking a better life, come to the United States every year. Nor are we unique. In Germany, Berlin's Turkish population is second only to Istanbul's. From Spain to Sweden as well as from Boston to San Diego, immigration is making our local communities look increasingly diverse, like our global community.

Nor is immigration the only reason for increasing diversity. Technology is another. From instantaneous satellite communication to modern modes of production and transportation, we depend on very sophisticated technology to make our world work. Developing and maintaining this technology require specialization. The Renaissance scholar, who knew all there was to know about every topic in the world, has vanished. Today even the most educated people must know very much about very little.

Diversity can create serious problems for leaders. When most people in a community or group have a common background, they tend to agree about what can and must be done. When people have different cultural heritages or technical specialties, they tend to see problems in different ways. They may be affected differently by the problems. They may not speak the same language—even if they all use English! Thus they are more likely to disagree.

Diversity can lead to creativity or conflict.

*Managing diversity creatively.* With the wrong leadership, diversity can destroy a group by creating conflicts and misunderstandings. With the right leadership, a diverse group can be more successful at problem-solving than a homogeneous one.

Diversity means that group members have a variety of skills and knowledge to contribute to the group. In a diverse group innovative ideas can emerge as contrasting ways of thinking collide. The value of having diverse people *work together* is a lesson that corporate America has learned. The auto companies once let design engineers, marketing specialists, and production employees work separately. The results were often disastrous. Design engineers created cars that no one wanted, even though the marketing people knew what consumers would buy. Production workers spent long hours fixing problems the design engineers could have prevented had they understood what it was like to work on the assembly line. Now the auto companies bring all these specialists together from the start. As a result, production costs are down, quality is up, and cars are more in line with consumer tastes.

Making the most of diversity requires that people be allowed to participate in governing as well as doing the work of the group. Being part of shaping the group's vision and making its decisions also increases a person's commitment to the group—even if the group ultimately acts in ways the person does not prefer. Giving people a legitimate say in their group is what participatory leadership is all about.

### The Dizzying Rate of Change

Frank Shiraldi grew up in a steel town in the 1960s. Steel making was the heart of Frank's community. His father, like the fathers of virtually all his classmates, worked in the steel mill. Like their fathers, the young men of Frank's town looked forward to a future making steel.

Today there is no steel mill in Frank's hometown. The old mill could not compete with mills in Japan, Germany, Korea, and a host of other countries. When the steel mill closed, the town almost died. Frank, along with many of his friends, had to find a job elsewhere. Their once secure image of the future turned to dust on lonely streets.

Change, like diversity, is a hallmark of our global age. People born in 1945 (not *really* that long ago) have in their lifetime seen the first nationwide television broadcast and the first man in space. They have witnessed the birth of the nuclear age and lived through the computer revolution. In today's world, change has become so constant that in a sense change has become the only constant.

*Change, uncertainty, and risk.* What kind of job will you have in the future? Where will you live? Who will your boss be? What languages will you need to know? These questions reflect one of the greatest problems with change: uncertainty about the future.

As the pace of change has quickened, the degree of uncertainty about the future has increased. The less similarity there is between the present and the future, the less confident we can be about the facts and assumptions we use to make our decisions. That increases the risk that we will make bad decisions.

The students in St. Louis who began recycling aluminum, for example, may be leading their school toward a better future. They may also be on the wrong track. Within 20 years new technology may eliminate the need to recycle aluminum. The St. Louis students may look back and wish they had recycled paper to save our forests!

Change means that the future is uncertain.

***Reducing uncertainty through participation.*** There is no way to eliminate the uncertainty that accompanies rapid change. Uncertainty can, however, be reduced and the risk of making bad decisions lessened.

The students in St. Louis, for example, can never be certain they are on the right track. However, they can try to get the best available information about the issue. They can get information on:

- The depletion of various resources,
- Pollution trends indicating the greatest problems,
- The economics of recycling various materials, and
- Existing recycling programs.

In most cases, participatory groups will be better able to get and use the information they need to make a good decision. No one person, however smart or knowledgeable, is likely to have more information than the group as a whole. Likewise, the more sources of information a group has, the more likely it is that distorted or inaccurate information will be discovered. By encouraging everyone to accept the responsibility of leadership, groups can avoid many of the pitfalls that change and uncertainty create.

## Global Living and Alienation

A hundred years ago people lived in smaller communities. They knew that distant events (wars and disasters) could affect them, but those effects were rare. Daily life seemed to be under the control of local people. Even if those people were business or political elites, they seemed accessible because they were close.

Our lives today seem quite different. Political power in a country like the United States seems to be centered in Washington, D.C., not our local community. Even decisions made in foreign countries seem to have more impact on our future than those made in our hometown. Power over our lives seems to be moving ever further away from us.

This sense of powerlessness has contributed to a growing alienation in our country. People who believe they have no power tend not to care about the public life of their communities, let alone their world. Some focus on their personal success, over which they still do have some control. Others simply find diversions. In the words of young people in the 1960s, they drop out.

The cure for alienation is empowerment.

*Participation and empowerment.* No magic cure exists for alienation. However, people who participate in civic groups—that is, groups that serve some community need—tend to be less alienated. They learn that they can make a difference. As a result they begin to care more about their communities. In other words, the best response to alienation is participation, which results in empowerment.

Empowering people means giving them a greater say in governing themselves, their groups, and their communities. The people of Eastern Europe were looking for this kind of empowerment when they toppled their communist regimes at the end of the 1980s. Like Abraham Lincoln, they believed in "government of the people, by the people, and for the people." Unfortunately, in the United States the part of this formula most often missing is government "by the people." To respond to alienation, we need leaders who empower rather than control people.

*Seeing members as stakeholders.* Empowering people in organizations requires a new approach to the idea of "followership."

Whenever we think of leaders, we automatically think of followers. If one person leads, then other people must follow. Yet, the heads of organizations who look at their members as followers routinely complain that no one ever takes any initiative; too few people work hard; not enough people really get involved.

The problem lies in our understanding of the role of follower. The very word *follower* is part of the problem. Followers seem passive; following seems uninteresting. Followers do not initiate activities or take responsibility. They react.

To get members more committed, involved, and enterprising, we need to help members see themselves as "stakeholders." Stakeholders take personal responsibility for the success of the group. They do not leave anything as important as leadership to those in authority. They exercise leadership along with those in authority, and sometimes in spite of them.

## Make Your Group More Skillful

As we will see throughout this book, participatory leadership is not easy. In fact, it is far easier for leaders to do things themselves or to try to use authority rather than leadership to get things done. Involving other people requires skills that leaders in the past did not always need—and many did not have. However, in our global age we need participatory leaders. To take advantage of the creativity that diversity makes possible, to deal with the uncertainty of change, and to respond to the problem of alienation, we need leaders who have the skill to empower, to energize, and to involve others.

You may not have these skills right now. Not all leaders are ready to be participatory leaders. Even if you do, you may belong to groups that are unable to work with you in participatory ways. Not all groups are ready to act as stakeholders! These groups represent what may be the greatest challenge for those who exercise leadership today.

From a practical point of view, leaders must deal with a group in ways that are appropriate to the abilities of the group. Groups that are not skillful at participation will have a hard time dealing with participatory leaders. *The key task of leadership in these groups is to make them more skillful at doing the work of the group in participatory ways.*

# 3

## Envisioning

Bob was ecstatic. He had just been elected president of the Latin Club. That honor was reserved for the best and the brightest. Over the next few weeks, however, the excitement began to wear off. Friends asked about his plans for the club. His answers were vague. He realized that he had no plans for the club. In fact, he had not even planned to *make* plans for the club!

A great many people find themselves in Bob's situation. As they rise to high offices within groups, others begin to look to them for leadership. In particular they look for a sense of direction, of purpose, of mission. In a word, they look to them for vision.

Visions are images of a future toward which a group strives. In a very real sense, a group's vision is its soul—the cement that holds the group together and makes it what it is. A group's vision sums up what the group is about. It gives the group a reason for being. Without a vision no group will survive for long. The process of creating and maintaining a group's vision—envisioning—may well be the most important challenge of leadership.

### MAINTAINING A GROUP'S VISION

All groups have or have had a vision. However, over time even the most successful groups can fail to maintain their visions for one reason or another. In fact, *the larger, more diverse, and more active the group, the easier it is for members to become caught up in daily activities and lose sight of their common vision.*

Leaders should routinely check the state of their group's vision. The election of new officers or other times of change can be good opportunities for this. But there is no wrong time. Nor are there wrong leaders. Even new members can exercise leadership by checking the state of the group's vision.

## Check the Vision

In Bob's case, it did not take much imagination to realize that before he could make plans for the Latin Club, he needed to check his own thinking about the club's vision. He began with what seemed like a simple task. He found a quiet place, sat down with paper and pen, and tried to answer one simple question: Why does the Latin Club exist?

***Visions come in many shapes.*** If you ask yourself why the groups to which you belong exist, you may find that it is not a simple task at all. Your answer, if you have one, may take any number of shapes. The vision of a group, after all, depends on the group and on the leader who puts that vision into words. Here are some examples of visions:

- The Worthington High School soccer team had a vision of winning the state championship. The dream was vivid. Members would close their eyes and see themselves kicking the winning goal, holding aloft the trophy, and waving to the cheering crowd.
- The Michelemakinac Preservation Society envisioned a future in which the history of their area was a vital part of the present. They were committed to preserving the past by recreating the dress, skills, and lives of seventeenth-century frontier settlers.
- The vision of the American civil rights movement was eloquently expressed in Martin Luther King, Jr.'s, famous ''I Have a Dream'' speech. In that speech Dr. King painted a vivid and stirring picture of an America in which a person would be judged on the basis of her values and abilities, not her race, and in which people of different backgrounds could still call each other brother and sister.

***What makes visions great?*** Despite their differences, these three visions share basic qualities that make visions great. Like the soccer team's vision, they each:

Envisioning.

- Describe a future that seems achievable and yet challenges people to accomplish things they never have before.

Like Martin Luther King, Jr.'s, vision of racial equality, they each:

- Excite people or touch important feelings so that people want to contribute their time and energy to the group.

Even the Preservation Society has this kind of vision, at least for its members. That is an important point. What makes a vision exciting, challenging, and relevant to me may not seem very exciting, challenging, or relevant to you. Like beauty, great visions lie in the eyes of the beholder.

*Your vision or the group's vision?* When Bob tried to write down why the Latin Club existed, he came up with the following:

To give people interested in Rome and ancient history a chance to be together.

That vision seemed a little weak, but at least it was a vision. It helped to define what the Latin Club was all about.

However, the fact that *Bob* had a vision for the club was not enough. If this was a vision for the group, the whole group had to share it. So Bob began to talk with some of his friends.

What he found came as a surprise. It seemed as if the others belonged to different clubs! Most could not answer the question. One even admitted that he had only joined because it would look good on his college applications.

## Look for Lost Visions

Most of us know of groups that appear to be going nowhere. Members may take part in the group's routine activities, but there is no commitment or enthusiasm. There is no sparkle in their eyes or excitement in their voices. In most cases, these are groups, like Bob's Latin Club, that have lost their vision.

Facing up to the fact that your group has no vision can be half the battle. Many people, especially those in positions of authority, may resist the idea. Once the problem is recognized, however, you can begin to solve it.

*Look for an existing theme.* In some cases a group's vision may be misplaced but not entirely lost. In these cases you may be able to renew a sense of vision by looking at the group's current activities. The group has continued for some reason. Perhaps the activities themselves contain a sense of mission that can rekindle the vision.

The Latin Club still met regularly and once a year they organized a Latin Day to recruit new students. Bob and his friends asked themselves whether these activities responded to some need that could serve as a focus for their vision. For Bob they did. The meetings met his need to be with people who shared an interest in the ancient world. However, not all his friends found this to be a particularly exciting, challenging, or relevant reason for having a Latin Club.

*Look for the new challenges.* In many cases groups lose their vitality because their former vision ceases to be relevant. Bob's Latin Club had been created to help students prepare for the National Latin Competition. The club had become an anachronism when students stopped taking part in the competition.

A club whose vision has fallen victim to changing times may renew itself by adapting its vision to the new times. Members of the Latin Club, seeing lower enrollments in Latin classes, may want to encourage greater interest in the language or in the classical world. In short, they may be able to forge a new vision by looking to the challenges that the group now faces. If they can discover those challenges and put them into words, they may be able to forge an exciting, challenging, and relevant vision for the group. This seemed a reasonable route for the Latin Club.

## Keep the Vision Alive

You may be luckier than Bob. Your group may have a vision. It may even have a great vision. Still, an important leadership task remains: keeping that vision alive. Here are some commonsense things you can do to keep the vision in your group alive.

*Communicate your excitement.* Use every opportunity you have to remind members of the group's vision and to communicate your enthusiasm for it. The group may remember without your help, but remembering the vision is not living it. You want members to commit themselves to the vision, not just to identify it on a multiple choice test!

*Recruit interested members.* How does your group go about recruiting new members? Do you seek out people who will share your vision? Many people join an organization because friends belong or because it will look good on their resumes or college applications. They may not know or care much about the group itself. In recruiting new members, try to reach beyond your circle of friends. Make sure people know what your vision is—then people who share the vision can come to you.

*Orient new members.* No matter how you recruit new members, you should orient them to the group. In the orientation, stress the group's vision and the expectation that members will actively work to achieve it. As soon as possible, involve new members in communicating the group's vision to others or in orienting new members. By having them communicate their own understanding of the group, you can encourage an even greater commitment.

Visions are the focus of a group's commitment.

## SHAPING NEW VISIONS

The more Bob and his friends talked, the clearer it became that the group needed a whole new answer to the question, Why does the Latin Club exist? It needed a whole new vision.

Shaping a new vision within an existing group or within a newly forming group involves essentially the same process. In both cases a genuinely effective vision is most likely to emerge informally, but with a great deal of effort.

## Why This War?

Dan Pekarske was an average high school student. He was not, however, an average guy. Dan liked to keep up with the world around him. He read a lot, and a lot of what he read bothered him. The year was 1965, and the United States was becoming more deeply embroiled in the war in Vietnam. Dan had no real reason to question that policy, but it still bothered him.

*Questions without answers.* In 1965 most Americans saw Vietnam as distant and unimportant. The costs of the war were not yet obvious. Few of Dan's friends would have thought much about Vietnam had it not been for him. He kept asking himself, and his friends, hard questions. Were we standing up to communism or replacing French imperialism? If we did not fight the communists in Vietnam, would we really fight them in San Francisco?

The more Dan talked with his friends, the more they began to share his unease. The pat answers of government officials became less convincing. By year's end Dan and his friends had become convinced that the war was a mistake. They began to believe that young Americans should not have to die in Vietnam, and that young Americans could put a stop to it. Dan's questions had led him and his friends to a new vision. That vision compelled several of them to become active in the new antiwar movement.

*Three steps to new visions.* Dan's experience says a lot about how new visions take shape. In particular it suggests three broad steps toward new visions that you must always pass through:

- Discovering the dream;
- Letting the vision mature;
- Challenging others to respond.

### Discover the Dream

Visions often begin with nothing more than a sense of unease or opportunity. There may be no obvious problem, no earth-shaking insight. There may only be a sense that something is missing. Even those causes which eventually seem so obvious—promoting racial equality, ending world hunger, cleaning up the environment—are usually not obvious until someone makes us aware of them in a compelling way. Discovering the dream in the welter of needs and opportunities that surround you is the first step in shaping a vision.

*Listen to the world around you.* Thomas Edison, one of the most prolific inventors in history, once told an admirer that coming up with new ideas was easy. He simply plucked them out of the air. In a sense Edison did just that. He did not bury himself in his workshop. He was aware of his society and of the work being done by other scientists. His ideas were often adaptations of their ideas.

Dan Pekarske was like Edison. His feelings about the Vietnam War did not come from some special insight or wisdom. They came from the world around him. Dan routinely read newspapers and magazines. He listened to presidential speeches. He became sensitive to the issue of the Vietnam War before his classmates because he was more in touch with his world. In general, people who are creative envisioners thirst after new information, new ideas, and new experiences. They collect information, even information they cannot use right away.

The people around you can be the most important source of this information. What things concern them? What things are important to them? Good envisioners are not only in touch with distant worlds. They are in touch with the world close at hand.

*Question your assumptions.* Dan Pekarske was ahead of his times in questioning the Vietnam War. But his foresight did not depend on special knowledge. It depended on a willingness to question ideas that most people took for granted.

Why do we do things the way we do? Does it still make sense to do them this way? Are there other alternatives? Do those alternatives make more sense? To be a creative envisioner, you must be willing to shake things up. You must be willing to give up cherished and comfortable ideas.

When Bob and his friends set about creating a new vision for the

Latin Club, their biggest obstacles were their assumptions. The greatest assumption was that the club was a "Latin club." Latin was in fact not what held the club together. Latin and Rome symbolized an interest in a world beyond the limits of their own place and time. Bob began to realize that vaguely as he listened to members. Some talked about the need to get students interested in the real world. Some said the club should provide a way for students who cared about the world to discuss important issues. These felt needs became the seeds for the club's new vision. But they could not take root until Bob and his friends shook off their old assumptions and looked at their club in a very new way.

## Let the Vision Mature

The best visions are not shaped by gurus on mountaintops or through public opinion surveys. They are shaped in dialogues among people. Dan Pekarske's unease about the war only took shape as he talked with his friends. He did not bring them a vision, fully formed. He brought questions. He *listened* as well as talked. He paid attention to his friends' feelings, not just the facts. A new vision for the Latin Club also came about only as people talked about the club and its problems.

Even well-defined needs do not translate immediately into compelling visions.

- You must find that special dimension of the need that people find most relevant.
- You must then find the words that express the vision in exciting and challenging ways.

One of the worst mistakes a leader can make is to rush through the process of shaping new visions.

*Talk it over.* Even the visions of important political leaders take shape through a long process of talking things over. Many people take part in that process, even if history portrays the final product as a single person's vision. In 1961, John F. Kennedy set his nation on a bold new course. He proposed that America put a man on the moon by the end of the decade. The vision, however, did not emerge easily. Nor was it the product of one man's mind.

Before he took office John Kennedy was concerned about the Soviet Union's apparent lead in space. Once in office he engaged a number of people in a dialogue about the problem. As they talked, a broader vision than anyone imagined began to take shape. The final vision was expressed as a challenge to the whole nation:

> We choose to go to the moon in this decade, and to do the other things, not because they are easy but because they are hard; because that goal will serve to organize and measure the best of our energies and skills. . . . The moon and the planets are there, and new hopes for knowledge and peace are there.

***Learn as much as you can.*** By giving the vision time to mature, leaders give themselves time to understand the vision better and to find the right words to express it. Tom Peters, a consultant on business leadership, suggests that envisioning requires five different kinds of "understanding."

- *Worldview.* To articulate an effective vision you must be able to see the broad strokes of an issue and its relationship to larger issues.
- *Depth perception.* At the same time, you need to see the important details of the issue. You must be able to move easily from the broad ideas, which give a vision meaning, to the details, which make it vivid to others.
- *Foresight.* Good envisioners project the vision into the future to see if it will become more or less relevant.
- *Hindsight.* They also project back into the history of the group to ensure that the vision fits with its evolving culture and with the capabilities of its members.
- *Peripheral sight.* Finally, an emerging vision must be judged in terms of its relationship to other groups. Are other groups competing with you? How will they react to your new vision?

This may sound like a huge task. However, envisioning, like the other leadership tasks, is rarely done by a single person. A great many people helped to shape John Kennedy's vision of the space program. No one person had the knowledge needed to create such a broad and exciting vision.

### Challenge Others to Respond

An old saying tells us, "Strike while the iron is hot." This is good advice for making horseshoes—and for envisioning. Effective visions take time to mature. However, when a group is ready to act, a leader must be willing and able to put the vision into words and challenge the group to accept or reject it.

Sometimes events over which you have no control become a catalyst for challenging the group to action. A dramatic oil spill may solidify a club's concerns over environmental issues. A church group may find a new vision as it struggles with the suicide of one of its own members. Catalytic events focus people's attention and feelings. They demonstrate the importance of the issue and the need to act. When catalytic events occur, leaders must take advantage of them. The moment will vanish as quickly as it appears.

For most groups, catalytic events never occur. In these cases, leaders must judge when the group is ready to respond.

- Are people talking about the issue on their own?
- Do members seem to believe that something *ought* to be done—
- That something *must* be done—
- That *we* should be doing something?

When group members begin convincing each other it is time to act, the iron is hot!

For Bob and the Latin Club, the signs were a combination of events. After almost two months of talking things over, Bob realized that his friends were saying the same things. They had convinced themselves that the school needed a group that could engage students in serious discussions about world affairs. Then, two new students asked Bob whether the Latin Club was planning to become a "world affairs club." For Bob the name put the emerging vision into focus. He raised the idea of changing the club's name and mission statement at the next meeting. The World Affairs Club of St. Nazianz School was born!

## MOVING FROM VISIONS TO GOALS

Once a group has committed itself to a vision, it is only halfway through the envisioning process. Visions bind groups together. They are the focus of people's commitment. Yet, visions can be fairly abstract. They describe a future toward which the group wants to move. To start moving, the group needs something more concrete. It needs a plan of action—a set of goals.

Martin Luther King, Jr., envisioned an America that lived up to its values of equality. But having that vision and moving toward it were two different things. The civil rights movement had to identify what equality would look like and the steps that would achieve it. They began by trying to eliminate segregation laws that prohibited African-Americans from using certain facilities. Then the movement turned its attention to antidiscrimination laws that could ensure equal access to housing and employment. These goals represented steps in a plan of action that would move the nation toward the vision of racial equality.

Goals provide a path toward the group's vision.

### Use Backchaining to Define Goals

How does one translate a vision into a meaningful set of goals? In many respects developing goals is an art. However, in recent years a number of highly systematic ways of setting goals have been developed. One of the best is called backchaining. *Backchaining* defines itself metaphorically: the process is like building a chain backward, one link at a time.

*A campaign against drunk driving.* SADD, Students against Drunk Driving, was formed around the vision that young people could save the lives of their fellow teens by encouraging the responsible use of alcohol. That was the vision, but how was that to be done?

In backchaining, a group starts with its vision and then identifies some *ultimate goals* by asking what the world would look like if the vision were achieved. These ultimate goals define the vision more precisely. They sort out the different aspects and implications of the vision. For SADD, some ultimate goals would include:

- More responsible attitudes toward alcohol,
- Peer pressure not to drink, and
- Increased awareness of the danger of drunk driving.

Once the ultimate goals are identified, the group must ask itself what must happen if each of these goals is to be achieved. For example, what must be done if young people are to become aware of the dangers of drunk driving? As the question is answered, a new tier of *intermediate goals*—new links in the chain—is formed. These goals may include the following:

- Students will have valid information about drinking and driving,
- SADD will have effective and informative materials, and
- A strategy will be designed to get students to pay attention to the information.

The backchaining process continues like this until the group has identified a shopping list of *short-term goals*—goals that can be worked toward now. You know you have reached the end of the chain when your short-term goals are:

- *Practical.* Good goals are doable; the group must agree that they can accomplish the goals before they start. In fact, some of the group's goals must be achievable fairly quickly, or members may lose faith!

- *Concrete*. Goals must be clear and specific so that anyone can see when you have achieved them. The World Affairs Club may have two goals: increasing student interest in world issues and discussing current world issues in social studies classes at least once per week. The second goal is more concrete because it is far easier to tell whether you have achieved it.

- *Controllable*. The best goals are also under the control of the group itself. Discussing world issues in social studies class may seem to be an important goal. However, teachers control the agenda of classes, not students. A better goal might be to organize a series of Issue Forums for students. The Forums would take more work, but the goal would be under the control of the club! The majority of any group's goals should be under its control.

Backchaining, like the shaping of visions, takes time. Goals that meet these criteria may emerge only after four or more rounds (links in the chain) have been finished.

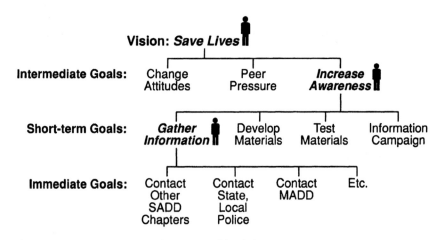

The stages of backchaining.

***Benefits and pitfalls.*** Backchaining can be a powerful planning tool. It allows the group to get involved in defining its goals, which usually increases member commitment. Backchaining can also give the group a far richer understanding of its goals. That can help the group adjust more quickly if things go awry. Finally, backchaining clearly shows the links between the goals and the group's larger vision. Seeing the whole chain, group members can easily explain how holding a raffle today will help to save lives tomorrow.

Backchaining can also be dangerous if it leads to overconfidence in the plan. Then, group members may fail to take advantage of unanticipated opportunities. They may resist the need for change if the plan begins to fail.

### Goals for Frankfurt American High School

Backchaining is not the only way to move from visions to goals. Other, less structured approaches can work as well.

***The Kransberg Connection.*** In the spring of 1986 a small group of student leaders at Frankfurt American High School in Germany envisioned a school in which the students could work meaningfully to improve the school community. They recognized that achieving their vision required getting as many students as possible involved. That in turn required a more concrete idea of what "school improvement" meant and a set of meaningful goals.

They set about identifying their goals through the "Kransberg Connection." They organized a three-day conference involving 75 formal and informal leaders. At the conference the students took a serious look at their school community. They completed individual assessments, listing what was right and what was wrong at the school. These assessments identified six areas which needed improvement: activities, beautification, communications, discipline, new students, and student unity. These areas were equivalent to backchaining's ultimate goals.

The 75 students then broke up into task forces which addressed each of the areas of school improvement. Each task force brainstormed a list of more specific goals, discussed the importance of each, and selected a practical set of goals on which to work during the year.

***The impact of Kransberg.*** The Kransberg meeting proved to be a good planning experience. The process of setting goals gave greater concreteness to the otherwise abstract vision of school improvement. By allowing the group to identify multiple goals, the organizers also allowed student leaders to see the vision of a better school in somewhat different ways. The different goals enabled students to find goals that interested them. Yet, the goals fit together because the group as a whole had to agree on them. So, despite the diversity, students still felt that they were working together toward a common vision.

# 4

## Consensus-seeking

Patti was getting angry. Dan and Kelly had been arguing about the group's new logo for 15 minutes. Dan wanted green on gold. Kelly wanted blue on green. It had become a test of wills, and Patti was sick of it. Here they were, arguing about colors when the group still needed to decide about the upcoming Earth Day Fair. Should they have their own booth? Should they share a booth with some other group? Or should they skip this year's fair? Time was getting away, and it looked as if the group would never get started.

All groups make decisions. They make decisions about their visions and goals, about what to do, and how to do it. In fact, most groups spend more time making decisions than anything else. How a group makes its decisions affects its ability to get things done. It also affects how members feel about the group.

### DECISION-MAKING BY CONSENSUS

Giving members a meaningful role in making meaningful decisions makes the group more effective. It also increases members' commitment. This is why consensus-seeking is the best way to make group decisions.

### The Case of the Earth Day Fair

When Patti's group finally did turn to the question of the Earth Day Fair, they used consensus-seeking to arrive at their decision. Patti led the discussion. She outlined the group's three choices along with arguments for and against each one.

The reason for participating in the fair was to attract the attention of people important to the group. Having their own booth would accomplish that goal best. But would it do so at a reasonable cost? There was a $50 exhibitor's fee, and that was a lot of money for the group. Sharing the booth, and the fee, with another group would help. But this would lower the publicity value of the booth. Finally, organizing and having members staff the booth throughout the fair would be a major undertaking. The group was small and had other things to do. Was the fair really the best investment of time, money, and people?

Patti then invited discussion by the entire group. It was soon clear that most of the members wanted a booth. No one seemed to favor sharing it with another group. Yet, some members questioned the whole idea. The group had just started a new campaign, CLEAN-UP. The campaign would take a great deal of time and effort over the next several months. Would the booth demand too much time of a small group?

The discussion went on for 30 minutes, but no one seemed to mind. They recognized that this was an important question. Patti herself kept:

- Asking new people to voice their opinions until everyone had said something;
- Summarizing what people were saying, to make sure everyone understood the issues involved; and
- Inviting members to think about alternative ways to get to the same goals.

In the end Kelly brought the group to a decision. The new CLEAN-UP campaign needed a big kick-off. No one had come up with a really exciting idea for it yet. What if the booth were used to kick off the campaign? The suggestion seemed so simple, yet it had not occurred to anyone.

The chairperson asked whether anyone objected to having a booth focused on the CLEAN-UP campaign. Her eyes scanned the group. No one spoke, but Dan was frowning. She asked Dan whether he had any reservations. "No," he said. "I was just wondering whether the color scheme for the booth should be green on gold, or blue on green!"

***Consensus means unanimous agreement.*** The experience of Patti's group was just one example of how consensus-seeking works. In practice consensus-seeking takes many different forms, depending on the issue and the group. It does not even have to happen in a formal meeting. What makes *consensus-seeking* special is the result. Consensus-seeking leads to a consensus decision, that is, a decision which *everyone* involved accepts as the best possible solution.

Consensus means unanimous but not absolute agreement.

Consensus does not mean that every member thinks the consensus decision is ideal. Members may only feel that the decision is the best one on which the group can agree. In the case of Patti's group, some members may still have *preferred* to have no booth at all. They accepted the decision because they believed it was good for the group, even if not the best possible option. Moreover, they recognized that the group could not agree on the option they preferred.

***Quality decisions and member commitment.*** If done well, consensus-seeking allows the group:

- To share all its available knowledge;
- To use that knowledge effectively to create new solutions that are in the best interest of the group as a whole; and
- To build member commitment to the decision and to the group.

To get the entire group to agree on a decision, all the arguments, information, feelings, concerns, values, hopes, and ideas that touch on the decision must be heard. Members must listen to those with whom they disagree as well as those with whom they agree. They must be willing to use new information and ideas and to modify their own opinions. Unless everyone is willing to do these things, it will be impossible to arrive at a consensus. This is why groups using consensus-seeking usually make better decisions than individuals deciding alone.

Consensus-seeking also promotes member commitment. There are no losers in consensus-seeking. Not only is every member heard, his key concerns and needs will have been taken into account. In other words, everyone contributes meaningfully to the ultimate decision. When that happens, no one loses, whether or not her preferred choice is accepted.

Making decisions for group members rather than with them can get leaders into trouble.
(Calvin and Hobbes copyright 1990 by Bill Watterson. Dist. by Universal Press Syndicate. Reprinted with permission. All rights reserved.)

**Why not vote?** Because voting requires only majority agreement, it is easier than consensus-seeking. It also does not encourage the kind of information sharing and synergy that consensus-seeking does.

If you only need a majority, there is no need to accommodate the entire group. Skilled vote managers aim at building a "winning coalition"—just enough votes to make up a majority. This allows them to make the fewest possible changes in their position and still win. Thus with voting you can ignore those people with whom you disagree. In fact, you want to ignore them! Putting together a winning coalition is easier if you include only those people whose position is closest to yours.

When groups routinely use majority voting, member commitment can suffer. Certain people whose ideas are "different" may routinely be ignored. These people will eventually resent the group since they have no influence over it. Ultimately they will lose interest, and the group will lose the benefit of their perspective. That can severely hurt the group if these people are out of step with the group today because they are in step with the trends shaping tomorrow!

## MAKING CONSENSUS-SEEKING WORK

As you might guess, getting everyone to agree on a decision can be both difficult and time consuming. Consensus-seeking works best when all of the members are more interested in finding the best decision for the group than in promoting their personal ideas. When issues evoke strong feelings, or when the group is particularly diverse, consensus-seeking can be extremely challenging or even impossible.

The example of Patti's group suggests several things that leaders need to do to help a group with consensus-seeking:

- Structure the consensus-seeking process.
- Ensure that the ideas and feelings of everyone, especially those who disagree, are adequately explored.
- Help to prevent disagreement from getting out of hand.
- Look for the linkages among ideas.
- Persist until a genuine consensus is forged.

### Structure the Process

Groups do not arrive at a consensus simply by talking. In fact, guiding a group through consensus-seeking is a little like conducting an orchestra. All the musicians have their distinct parts to play, but the orchestra needs a conductor to make sure those parts fit together into a whole. In consensus-seeking, the conductor keeps the discussion flow-

Consensus-seeking.

ing smoothly. She makes sure that the group has a clear sense of where it is going, how far it has gone, and how far it still has to go. A leader in a group must be more flexible than the conductor of an orchestra, since there is no written script to follow, but she still must:

- Help the group understand the decision being made;
- Make sure that everyone understands what is being said and how it all fits together;
- Manage what can be a very chaotic process of sharing ideas and information.

*Frame the decision.* When Patti began the discussion of the booth for the Earth Day Fair, she did an excellent job of ensuring that the whole group understood where it was going. She framed the decision by:

- Laying out the possible options as she saw them,
- Identifying key facts that touched on the decision, and
- Suggesting criteria for making the decision.

She did not recommend a particular option, although she did have a preference. She also avoided laying out the facts so that one option seemed better than the others. She wanted to give the group a common base so that they could talk together effectively. She also wanted to encourage members to think of creative options and important issues that she had not foreseen. Thus she wanted to avoid putting artificial limits on the discussion.

Groups only make better decisions than individuals if their discussion is open and not steered toward a particular end.

***Sum up agreements and disagreements.*** Patti did less well at helping the group keep track of how far it had gone and how far it still had to go. She could have done this by summarizing the emerging consensus from time to time.

Patti should have clearly stated the points of agreement in the group— as she understood them. She also should have stated the points of disagreement—those issues the group still had to resolve. This would have helped them keep track of the discussion without limiting it. For complex decisions, this kind of summing up is absolutely essential, or the group may talk for hours and still get nowhere.

***Restate ideas.*** Building a consensus requires that everyone in the group understand what people are saying. Do not assume that they do. Do not even assume that you do!

Patti frequently summarized what people said. Especially when someone made a long or complex statement, Patti immediately tried to restate it in new and simpler ways.

When you summarize the statements of others, you prove that you have been listening. You also test your understanding of what has been said and give the speaker a chance to set things straight if communication has broken down. Finally, you give other group members a chance to hear the ideas through a second perspective. In the process, you may clarify ideas that some people found vague. You may also reveal misunderstandings that could otherwise get in the way of building a consensus!

***Manage the chaos.*** When groups get involved in making decisions they care about, the flow of ideas can become chaotic. More than one person may talk at the same time. People may talk even if they have not been recognized by the chair. No matter how orderly the discussion, what one person says may have little relationship to things that others have said before them. As a result, ideas may be impossible to put together.

A little chaos is all right in most groups. At the same time, the flow of ideas must be managed or too much information will be lost. Patti used two techniques in her group:

- Whenever possible she made a point of linking new ideas to things that had been said previously. By making a simple comment before recognizing a new speaker, she helped the group see how the discussion was adding up.
- She also used a technique called "storyboarding." Whenever people had ideas that did not seem to fit the current discussion, she wrote them on sheets of paper and stuck them to the chalkboard where everyone could see.

As the discussion went on, people could refer to the posted sheets, reminding the group of ideas that might otherwise have been lost. When the discussion lagged, Patti had the group consider posted ideas that had received little attention. The storyboarding ensured that all ideas and concerns got the attention they deserved.

*Reward good consensus-seeking.* Consensus-seeking is hard work. Whatever your role in the group, you can and should encourage members to do a good job. Praise behavior that helps the group arrive at a good decision.

You should also be willing to criticize behavior that gets in the way of good consensus-seeking. Tell people you do not appreciate what they are doing. Be specific, and focus on the behavior, *not* the individual. Criticism like this can prevent inauthentic leaders from getting out of hand—particularly if the criticism comes from someone who does *not* have a position of authority in the group!

*Vote only as a last resort.* Voting (majority rule) is a far less effective way of making group decisions than consensus-seeking. In an imperfect world, however, voting does have its place. In some cases a group may simply run out of time. In others, you may sense that the group is becoming frustrated with its inability to reach a consensus. In these cases, it may be necessary to turn to voting and to risk alienating some members in order to prevent alienating them all.

Do not, however, let voting become the rule rather than the exception. If the group expects to vote, members may not give consensus-seeking a chance. They may stake out rigid positions because they know you will vote in the end. They may find subtle and not so subtle ways to limit participation. They will almost certainly ignore uncomfortable information. If you use voting regularly, you may lose the benefits of consensus-seeking. You will certainly make it more difficult.

## Explore the Differences

For most people, sharing ideas, feelings, and information is easy. But consensus-seeking depends on active listening as well. People need to hear others and to take their ideas and feelings into account. For most of us, this is more difficult. In consensus-seeking leaders should:

- Make sure that everyone is heard by the group;
- Force the group to deal with differences in fact and opinion;
- Prevent people from intimidating others and forcing them to agree.

*Encourage everyone's participation.* If everyone in the group must agree on a decision, then everyone should participate in the discussion. For vocal people, this is no problem. However, all groups have some quiet people. In some cases their lack of involvement represents a lack of interest. In many cases it represents an unease about voicing ideas and opinions.

Patti made a point of drawing people who had said nothing into the discussion. She asked what they thought about an idea, or whether they had anything to add. She did not force them to say anything, but she gave them the opportunity. Some people made important contributions when given this opening. Others still said nothing. But even these people saw that Patti valued what they had to say! That helped to build commitment.

Try to get quiet people involved early in the discussion, even if they have nothing to say. If you wait too long, they will stop listening. Then, even if they go along with the decision, they are unlikely to be very committed to it.

*Seek out differences.* To build a consensus, people must pay special attention to differences of opinion. Like Patti, you need to make sure that everyone in the group recognizes and understands that there are different possible options. Beyond that you should:

- Draw attention to any disagreements or conflicting information that you hear. Do not try to cover over disagreement for the sake of quick agreement.
- Ask whether anyone disagrees whenever the consensus is summed up. That can be more important than asking whether everyone agrees!
- Test the consensus yourself by disagreeing with ideas that everyone seems to accept. Agreement reached too quickly or too easily may result in bad decisions.

*Keep options open.* To keep people listening to each other, you also must make sure that they keep their options open. Patti was constantly listening to make sure that no one became personally identified with a particular idea. Once someone's ego was involved, he might find it hard to change positions without feeling that he had lost.

Early in the discussion, for example, Dan expressed support for sharing a booth at the Earth Day Fair. His statement seemed to express a real commitment to this option, and Patti wanted to prevent that. So she asked whether the really important thing was sharing a booth or getting exposure in a cost-effective way. Dan agreed that cost-effectiveness was his real goal. That reopened his options. Both Patti and Dan recognized that they could never build a consensus if he became a prisoner of his first preference.

*Guard against intimidation.* Consensus-seeking requires that everyone, including you, share ideas with the group. But beware. Sharing should be an open-minded process. For some people, however, sharing really means intimidation.

When people feel strongly about something, they usually try to persuade others to go along. Sometimes the effort is obvious. Sometimes it is subtle. They may act as if there is only one reasonable solution, or that any right-thinking person would agree with them.

Avoid this kind of intimidation in what you say. As importantly, try to prevent intimidation by others. Bring attempts at intimidation to the attention of the group. Had someone tried to force his ideas on Patti's group, she—or any other member—could have jokingly observed that she felt that she was being railroaded. Then she could suggest rethinking the question. By doing this she would:

- Make the group aware of what was happening,
- Show that someone was willing to resist, and
- Immediately get the group moving in another direction.

Most people dislike being intimidated. But even if they are aware of it, they need someone to organize a reaction against it. Otherwise, most people will simply go along, even if they resent what is happening!

### Keep Disagreement in Perspective

Consensus-seeking has a catch-22 at its very core. Good consensus-seeking requires that you bring points of disagreement into the open and freely discuss them. This can create conflict. But if the group gets caught up in conflict, people will stop listening to each other. In other words, unless you are careful, the very things that lead to good decisions can make consensus-seeking impossible! In consensus-seeking, therefore, leaders must be constantly aware of the level of conflict in the group and make sure that conflict does not get out of hand.

*Never personalize disagreements.* Have you ever been in a heated discussion, finished talking, and then felt as much as heard another person mutter, "What an idiot!"? When people who disagree become "idiots," the chances of reaching a consensus become dim.

One of the easiest ways to destroy group solidarity is to let disagreements over issues become personal conflicts between individuals. When disagreements arise in consensus-seeking:

- Focus the group's attention on the ideas and information. Agree with people, but disagree with ideas!
- Try to prevent disagreements from becoming centered around just two people. Get others involved as quickly as possible.
- Look for people who have alternative perspectives. Two-sided issues become personalized far more easily than three- or four-sided issues.

*Relieve tension.* No matter how serious the issue under discussion, a little humor can relieve tension and prevent disagreements from getting out of hand. Many a group has failed at consensus-seeking because members have taken themselves or their ideas too seriously. Making wisecracks about the group, the project, the issue, or even yourself can restore a calm and comfortable atmosphere when things get too intense.

At the same time, levity should not be disruptive. It should help the group relax, not get the group off track. Nor should the quips be aimed at another person. Tension in a group cannot be relieved at one member's expense.

*Remind the group of its goal.* If emotions do rise and humor seems out of place or ineffective, it can be useful to remind the group of its goal. People may feel strongly about decisions being discussed. You need to direct these feelings in the right direction: toward the good of the group. If you think emotions are getting too intense:

- Note that emotions are rising and take a break.
- When you come together again, remind the group that they are all on the same side, that their common goal is to make the best possible decision for the group, and that they will all be winners if they succeed.

## Look for the Linkages

Consensus-seeking reaches its full potential only if the group can link ideas and information in productive and creative ways. In Patti's group, Kelly was able to do this. The group may well have come to some agreement without his idea to focus the booth on the CLEAN-UP campaign. However, he was able to put ideas together to create a new option. His suggestion literally achieved what everyone agreed was best for the group.

The creative linking of information and ideas is called *synergy*. How consensus-seeking leads to synergy is summarized in the Johari Window. An individual has only so much information about any issue. Part of that information is explicit and understood. Part is unknown in the sense that its relevance to the issue is not clear. When people share their ideas and listen to others, the relevance of this hidden information may become clear. Likewise, by putting new information and ideas together, the group can literally develop new insights and knowledge about the issue. This kind of synergy is not always possible, but it is always desirable.

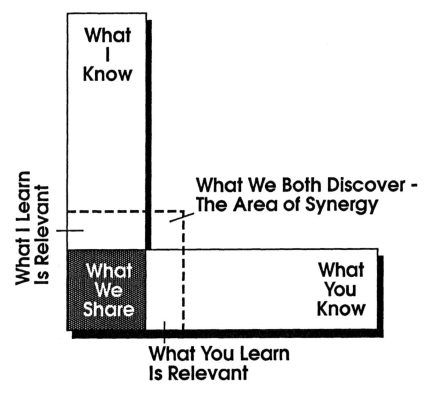

The Johari Window.

### Persist until a True Consensus Is Forged

Consensus-seeking takes persistence. Sometimes consensus can be built easily and quickly within a group. More often it cannot. The more controversial or complex an issue is, the more difficult it will be to build consensus. Skillful consensus-seekers guard against building a false consensus.

- Never change your mind or encourage others to change theirs just to prevent conflict or to reach a quick decision. Agreement should be genuine.

• If you sense that someone still has reservations about a decision, encourage her to voice those reservations.

Patti's group seemed to have built a good consensus around Kelly's suggestion. It would have been easy for the chairperson to welcome that decision and move on. She did not. One last time, she asked whether anyone disagreed. She saw nothing more than a frown on Dan's face, but she still asked him whether he disagreed with the decision. In essence, she was saying that it was more important that everyone agree than that the discussion be finished.

Had Dan disagreed, and had the group voiced its impatience with him, the chairperson would have reminded the group of its goal. As long as anyone in the group genuinely believes that a better decision is possible, a better decision may be possible. You should not reward stubborn people bent on preventing the group from taking action, but you should respect genuine disagreement. That takes patience, persistence, and common sense.

## WHEN CONSENSUS-SEEKING CANNOT WORK

Because of the synergy it creates, consensus-seeking usually leads to the best possible decisions for a group. Yet, there are times when groups should not be involved in consensus-seeking.

### Too Little Interest

Involvement in group decision-making can be a two-edged sword. Not all decisions are equal. People should only be involved in consensus-seeking if:

• They want to be involved;
• They have information that is critical to making a good decision; or
• They must help in implementing the decision.

The debate over the group's new logo was a case in point. Patti and a great many other members had no interest in the debate. Nor did they have anything important to contribute. The color scheme was largely a matter of opinion. Nor was their cooperation needed to create new materials using the logo. In other words, forcing Patti to be involved in making a decision about the logo could not lead to a better decision. It could, however, damage her commitment to the group. She felt she was wasting her time.

On the other hand, Dan and Kelly wanted to be involved. They felt that this was a very important issue. In situations like this, it is better to create a subgroup or committee to make the decision by coming up with a recommendation for the whole group. Dan, Kelly, and others who wanted to be involved could have been appointed to the committee, along with someone who could mediate between them. Consensus-seeking might still be appropriate within the committee, but not within the larger group.

### Fundamental Conflicts

Patti's group arrived at a consensus about the Earth Day Fair because everyone kept an open mind about what was best for the group. While there was disagreement, the group was never polarized. It was never divided by a fundamental conflict over values or goals.

But what if the group had been polarized from the start? Or what if the group had become polarized as the discussion progressed? If that had happened, the conflict might well have paralyzed the group. People who hold strong, conflicting views resist doing anything until the issue has been resolved *their way!* In a situation like this, consensus-seeking becomes impossible. Leaders must recognize what is happening and turn from seeking a consensus to resolving the conflict. The skill of resolving conflicts is called *negotiation*.

# 5

## Negotiation

We all have disagreements with other people. We disagree over what movie to see, what music to play, or who should get the first turn in a game. Disagreements—conflicts over what to do, when to do it, how to do it, who will do it, or why to do it—occur all the time. Disagreements like this can actually help groups make better decisions if they force group members to learn more about an issue.

However, if conflicts become too intense or personal, they can make consensus-seeking impossible. People take rigid positions and stop listening to others. They place a higher value on getting their way than on the good of the group. In the end, no matter who wins, commitment to the group suffers. In this situation the group can stay together and move forward only if the conflict is adequately resolved. Resolving conflict is what negotiation is all about.

### DECIDING WHEN TO NEGOTIATE

The word *negotiation* has been used to mean many things. For us, negotiation is the way groups make decisions in the face of divisive conflict. This approach to negotiation makes it look a little like consensus-seeking. The ultimate goal of both is a decision with which everyone can agree. *But in negotiation, the way you must get to an agreement is very different because of the conflict.* The skill of negotiation lies in knowing when to negotiate as well as how.

## How Much Conflict?

A group can use consensus-seeking to make decisions even when there is some conflict among members. In the last chapter, Patti's group needed to decide whether it would have a booth at the Earth Day Fair. Several values were in conflict, and members gave those values different priorities. Some members thought that publicity was important and wanted a booth; others preferred to put the group's limited time and money into a program that did more to achieve their vision.

However, the conflict did not destroy the group's effort to arrive at a consensus. No one took a rigid position. The disagreement was treated as a problem to be solved, not a competition between individuals. In the end, consensus-seeking led to a creative new idea—using the booth at the Earth Day Fair to promote the group's new CLEAN-UP campaign.

***The case of the marching band.*** Not all groups succeed at building a consensus in the face of conflict. Craig Shemenski faced just such a situation as president of his high school marching band.

The band had received three invitations to perform at events in distant cities, including one in California. Craig was excited about the trips. They promised to be fun. They gave the band a chance to go to some exciting places. What really attracted Craig, however, was that the trips would increase the band's prestige in the eyes of other students.

Craig had mentioned the invitations to a few of his friends, and they had been enthusiastic as well. He was just about to accept the invitation from the parade committee in California when the trouble started.

George and Mary, two band members, heard about the trips from one of the Band Board members. They wanted no part of them. They felt that the travel would take too much time, and that raising money to pay for the trips would be too much work. Like many others, they had joined the band in order to perform at Friday night football games, and that was all. At the next meeting of the Band Board, Mary and George demanded a chance to speak. To Craig's embarrassment they angrily denounced him and his decision to accept the California invitation.

***The need to negotiate.*** The situation Craig faced was typical of one requiring negotiation. The group was faced with a decision but neither George nor Mary was in a mood for consensus-seeking. Craig could have put the issue to a vote—he was sure he had enough board members on his side to win. But both of these options would leave George, Mary, and everyone who agreed with them unhappy. At the same time, Craig could not just give in. He and the majority of band members wanted to go on the trips. No matter what happened, it seemed that the morale of the band would suffer. That could discourage students from joining next year. Craig realized that the stakes in this conflict were high, and that his only option was to try to resolve the conflict through negotiation.

Whenever groups face a decision, the potential for conflict exists. These conflicts must be resolved through negotiation if:

- The individuals who disagree become personally identified with their positions, or
- They become so committed to their positions that they are willing to paralyze the group to get their way.

When this happens, consensus-seeking will not work. Someone has to shift the group from building a consensus to negotiating a solution to the conflict.

Negotiation.

## Bring Hidden Conflicts into the Open

In cases like Craig's, the need for negotiation is obvious. At other times conflicts within a group may lie beneath the surface. They seethe and simmer, perhaps never exploding into the open because the occasion never presents itself.

Through time hidden conflicts poison relationships within a group. Slowly but surely they erode the commitment of members. One of the most important ways to exercise leadership in situations like this is to force the conflict into the open. Give disaffected members the opportunity to voice their unhappiness. Force those in power to resolve the conflict in good faith.

Getting a group to recognize and resolve hidden conflicts can revitalize it. It can, of course, also destroy the group if the conflict is not handled well. But conflicts left to simmer under the surface will destroy the group anyway. It will simply take longer.

## CREATING A WIN-WIN ATMOSPHERE

Negotiation is a little like a three-act play. The three acts are the stages you must go through to arrive at a mutually agreeable solution. They include:

- Gathering intelligence,
- Creating a win-win atmosphere, and
- Getting to yes.

Unlike a three-act play, however, the three stages do not always take place in the ideal order. They almost always overlap with each other. Still, it is useful to think about them as distinct steps because each makes a unique contribution to success.

In the case of the marching band, the first step in the negotiation was to create a win-win atmosphere. *In a win-win atmosphere negotiators look for solutions that allow both sides to feel that they have won something.* In fact, win-win solutions are common. Unless one side can dictate a solution, the final decision usually has something for everyone.

However, when people get caught up in conflicts, the emotions they feel usually lead them to adopt a *win-lose* approach. Without any thought about the consequences, they try to get their way at the expense of the other side! Thus in most negotiations it is necessary at the outset to do things that encourage a win-win atmosphere.

To create a win-win atmosphere requires a careful balancing of firmness and collaboration. You must be firm enough to discourage win-lose behavior by the other side. At the same time, you must collaborate enough to show that you see the others as partners in problem-solving, not as adversaries to be defeated! Just how you balance firmness and collaboration depends on the relative strength of the other side.

## Accommodate the Weak

Sometimes, as in Craig's situation, you find yourself in a position of strength. Craig knew he could get his way because the majority of band members supported him. That made him stronger—at least for the time being. Craig's strength also helps to explain why Mary and George were so aggressive at the meeting. A sense of weakness or insecurity often encourages people to take an all-or-nothing, win-lose approach.

To encourage weak parties to adopt a win-win approach you must allay their feeling of insecurity by emphasizing collaboration. In particular you should:

- Stay out of the mud.
- Draw the line.
- Shorten the time frame.
- Put your cards on the table.
- Wave red flags.

*Stay out of the mud.* The most important thing you should do is resist aggressive behavior, especially name-calling and threats. At the Band Board meeting, Craig was angry and hurt. He wanted to lash out at George and Mary. But he did not. He let them vent their anger. Then he calmly and firmly said that name-calling would solve nothing. He had not realized that some band members were so strongly opposed to the trips.

At every point, Craig avoided antagonizing the other side. The worst thing he could have done would have been to join in the insults. That might have made him feel better. But anger and hard feelings do not encourage win-win solutions.

*Draw the line.* At the same time, Craig did not back down. He drew a line. He indicated that he:

- Understood what George and Mary were saying,
- Wanted to find a way to accommodate their needs, but
- Had no intention of simply giving in to them.

Craig tried to show that, while he did not want to force a decision on the two, he would not let them force a decision on him! If they were unwilling to negotiate seriously, he was willing to let the majority decide.

***Shorten the time frame.*** When you find yourself in a position of strength, you should try to shorten the time frame. Things change. Craig's position, for example, would have become weaker as time passed. If the decision was delayed too long, it would have been impossible to take the trips. George and Mary would win by default.

In this case, however, Craig faced a real dilemma. At the board meeting emotions were too high. The group needed a cooling down period. But how much time should he let go by? Had Craig wanted to lengthen the time frame, he might have suggested that the board meet again in a week. Because he needed to shorten the time frame, he decided to call an emergency meeting the next day.

***Put your cards on the table.*** In consensus-seeking, openness is critical to making good decisions. In negotiation, it is a two-edged sword. To get a win-win solution you must communicate what you want and why. At the same time, you can be hurt if you communicate too much. If you let the other side know your *minimum acceptable position* (that is, the worst solution you can still accept), that may become the only solution they will accept.

When Craig started the meeting on the next day, he shared his reasons for being interested in the trips—the fun, the excitement, and the prestige. He indicated that he was sure an agreeable solution could be found. But he did not suggest that he would be willing to take only one trip—the most fun, exciting, and prestigious trip—if need be.

***Wave a red flag.*** Finally, in order to encourage a win-win atmosphere it is often necessary to wave a red flag—that is, to remind the other side of the danger of win-lose negotiations.

Craig waved a red flag at both meetings. He reminded George and Mary that the band had a great reputation. It would be a mistake to let this disagreement destroy that reputation! At the second meeting, both George and Mary agreed.

Waving a red flag does three important things:

- It communicates your interest in the good of the group, including the other side.
- It helps to establish that both sides have some common ground despite the conflict.
- It gives you a chance to test the atmosphere of the negotiations. When you wave your red flag, does the other side agree, or do they ignore it? If they ignore or reject the flag, they are clearly playing by win-lose rules. If they agree, as George and Mary did, you may be able to start looking seriously for a solution.

## Stand up to the Strong

When the other side in a conflict is stronger than you, your emphasis must shift to firmness. You must convince them that they cannot win at your expense—even though they can. You must demonstrate your resolve through assertive actions. But be assertive, not aggressive. Assertive actions say that you will not be pushed around. Aggressive actions say that you will not cooperate. Being too aggressive may encourage the stronger party to play by win-lose rules and be done with you! In general you should:

- Refuse to go along.
- Buy time.
- Wave red flags.

***Refuse to go along.*** The ultimate power available to weaker parties is their right of refusal. George and Mary were a perfect example. They could not force the Band Board to reject the trips. They could, however, refuse to go along. They could quit or boycott the band. They could also threaten to make the conflict public, which might compromise any prestige the trips could bring.

By refusing to go along, weaker parties force the majority into a difficult and uncomfortable position. They may even change the balance of strength between the two sides. If enough members joined a boycott, even if still a minority, the trips might have become impossible.

Just how assertive you should be in your actions depends on the other side. You want to mirror their insensitivity to you. If they propose an extreme solution, you need to be equally extreme. But remember, your purpose is to make the other side take you seriously! Do not antagonize them. You want to wake them up to your needs. You want to encourage a win-win solution. You do not want to alienate them and destroy the group.

*Red flags and honesty.* Especially if you must take assertive actions, you should communicate your interest in the good of the group. Despite their weakness and anger, George and Mary should have waved a red flag of their own at the first Band Board meeting. Their name-calling would have had undesirable results had they goaded Craig into taking a win-lose approach!

Weaker parties also need to be very careful about not communicating too much. Craig needed to know why George and Mary were opposed to the proposed trips. He could not respond to their needs if he didn't know them! At the same time, Craig was willing to make a greater sacrifice for the good of the group precisely because he thought George and Mary's position was more extreme than it in fact was.

*Buy time.* When you are in the weaker position, you usually want to buy time. Too quick a decision will give the other side a victory at your expense. You want to put off a decision long enough to get the other side to negotiate in good faith. Of course, just how much time you buy depends on the situation. If time is not on your side, do not buy too much!

In the case of the marching band, George and Mary did not need to buy time. At the emergency meeting it was clear that Craig had no intention of dictating a solution. His behavior allowed and encouraged them to collaborate. That is why they agreed when Craig waved his red flag!

## Collaborate with Equals

When neither side is able to dictate a solution, a win-win approach becomes logical for everyone. However, negotiations between equals can be hard to recognize. The other side may well adopt a win-lose approach or a position of firmness simply because they misjudge the situation—or fear that you do. Either way valuable time is lost, feelings may be hurt, and group solidarity may suffer.

If you are negotiating with an equal but do not know if he will take a win-win approach, you should use the collaborative tactics of stronger parties and the delaying tactics of weaker ones:

- *Stay out of the mud.* You do not need to be highly assertive to block a decision.
- *Wave red flags.* You want to find out what approach the other side is taking as quickly as possible.
- *Buy time.* You want to give the other side time to size up the situation accurately.

You want to avoid:

- *Laying your cards on the table.* Until you are sure that the other side is adopting a win-win strategy, too much honesty can work against you.
- *Drawing the line or refusing to go along.* You do not need either tactic. It may simply antagonize the other side.

## GATHERING INTELLIGENCE

In a perfect world, gathering intelligence is the first step in negotiation. Good negotiators always learn as much as they can before they begin to negotiate. At a minimum they need to know:

- What values are at stake?
- What interests do the different parties think they have in the conflict?
- What approaches (win-win or win-lose) are the parties likely to take?

When a conflict takes you by surprise, as it did Craig, you have to gather intelligence as you negotiate. In any case, intelligence gathering continues throughout the negotiations. You need to be alert to changing conditions and positions.

## Clarify the Conflict

Understanding what values are at stake is critical. You cannot resolve a conflict you do not understand. To resolve the marching band conflict, Craig needed to understand that George and Mary objected to the time and effort required to make the trips—and to the fact that they had not been consulted on so important a decision. Once he understood this, he could look for a way to resolve the conflict.

Clarifying the values at stake can also have other benefits. It can:

- *Reveal unexpected shared values.* As they talked, Craig came to realize that George and Mary valued the prestige of the trips as much as he did. He also became more sensitive to just how much work the trips would require! This common ground laid the foundation for a win-win atmosphere and the ultimate solution to the conflict.

- *Suggest new ways of looking at the issue.* In the last chapter, Kelly's idea to use the Earth Day Fair booth to publicize the CLEAN-UP campaign only came when he stopped looking at the issue as a choice between two conflicting goals and started looking for ways to achieve both goals at the same time.

## Find out Who's Who

A negotiator needs an accurate guide to who's who in the conflict. Who is taking the different positions? Who is taking no position at all?

People who are sitting on the fence in a conflict can be vitally important. They may be able to calm things down if negotiations become too heated. They are also more likely to come up with creative solutions. They have the least stake in either side and the most stake in a win-win solution.

Similarly, the people who must be satisfied with any proposed solution may not always be obvious. In some cases the chief negotiators may be the "opinion leaders" for their side. But in other cases there may be less obvious opinion leaders working behind the scenes. These are the people who must be satisfied, but you must discover who they are before you can find a mutually acceptable solution.

You need to know who is taking what positions on the issue.

### Judge the Atmosphere

Finally, an important part of intelligence gathering involves judging the atmosphere. You must try to discover what approach the other side will take to the negotiations. Is the other side interested in winning, even at your expense? Or are they interested in finding a mutually acceptable solution? You can save yourself a lot of grief if you learn early on what approach the other side is taking.

## GETTING TO YES

In most conflicts there comes a point when both sides want to come to some agreement. At this point they should be willing to find a win-win solution. They should recognize that any solution will require that both sides get something out of the agreement!

Even at this point, however, negotiation will not look exactly like consensus-seeking. *Being willing to look for a win-win solution does not ensure that you will find one. One wrong step and you may destroy the win-win atmosphere!* Thus while consensus-seeking focuses on areas of disagreement and "conflict," negotiation tries to focus on areas of agreement. If you focus too soon on areas of conflict, you may well push the two sides back into rigid positions and stalemate.

You can improve your chances of success if you keep the following in mind:

- Divide and conquer the issue.
- Keep conflict in bounds.
- Encourage flexibility and creativity.

### Divide and Conquer the Issue

All issues and all conflicts have multiple dimensions. The best way to get to yes in a negotiation is to divide up the issue and to try to resolve the easiest dimensions first. In most cases these dimensions will reflect the values which the two sides share.

Craig's situation seemed straightforward. The conflict was about taking the trips. But, in fact, the issue involved two questions that allowed Craig to make decisions about easy questions first:

- Did everyone in the band have to make the trips?
- Did everyone need to help raise money?

Both sides to the band conflict had assumed that the decision was an all-or-nothing one. Either everyone would go or no one would. Either everyone would help raise money or no one would. But these assumptions were actually negotiable! Craig and his supporters might well have been willing to let some band members go on the trips but not help with the fund-raising. Likewise, both sides might have been willing to explore a smaller "traveling band" for members who wanted to go on the trips.

Dividing up an issue allows you to focus on the easier questions first. Even if both sides agree that having a traveling band will *not* work, they will have *agreed* on something! Establishing a pattern of agreement by tackling easy questions encourages the two sides to view each other as partners in problem-solving rather than as adversaries. It encourages greater flexibility when you get to the tougher issues.

Solve easy problems first.

## Keep the Conflict in Bounds

In negotiations disagreement can be impossible to avoid, even when dealing with fairly easy questions. It is an ever-present threat when you get to the harder ones. As in consensus-seeking, it is important to try to keep these conflicts within bounds. In this case, most of the techniques that are useful in consensus-seeking also work in negotiation. In particular you should:

- Prevent conflicts from becoming personalized. Avoid name-calling, threats, jibes, or anything else that will re-create an adversarial relationship.
- Try to relieve tensions before they get out of hand. Tell a joke on yourself or remind people of something funny from the past. If emotions begin to flare, ask for a cooling down period and try to smooth over feelings between meetings.
- Constantly wave red flags to remind negotiators that they share an interest in preserving the group and in resolving the conflict in a satisfactory way.

**Foster Flexibility and Creativity**

As in consensus-seeking, successful win-win negotiation requires flexible, creative thinking. Unfortunately, unlike consensus-seeking, negotiation rarely encourages such thinking. To get the creativity and flexibility you need, you must use special techniques.

- Float a trial balloon. Trial balloons are creative ideas that are offered as off the wall suggestions for resolving the conflict. Be ready to follow up on your trial balloon if the other side takes it seriously. But do not be disturbed if they do not. Trial balloons show that you are willing to be flexible and look for creative solutions.
- Offer a "straw man." Straw men are solutions that you know the other side will reject. Craig might propose having a traveling band even if he knows it cannot work. Then, when George and Mary argue against the idea, Craig can come around to their thinking. In the process Craig will have shown his flexibility.

Resolutions to conflicts most often result, not from brilliant new alternatives, but from changed perceptions of the existing choices. In the case of the band, all the members knew that they could resolve the issue by accepting the California trip and turning down the others. At the initial meeting, that would have seemed like a defeat for both sides! By the end of the negotiations, however, perceptions had changed. That solution now represented a victory for both sides. Encouraging flexible thinking and focusing on shared values can play a major role in changing perceptions!

Finally, during this stage of negotiation you should take every opportunity you can to reinforce the cooperative, win-win atmosphere. If the other side floats a trial balloon or offers a straw man, reward the effort. Treat both seriously, even if the specific solutions are not acceptable. You do not want to encourage unacceptable ideas, but you do want to reward the flexibility and creativity the other side has demonstrated.

## NEGOTIATION AND AUTHENTIC LEADERSHIP

You feel strongly about an issue; you are convinced you are right. You may even feel that the group would be better off divided and going separate ways rather than intact and going the wrong way! The result: you want to do whatever you can to win the argument and get your way.

Negotiation is the most difficult of the skills of leadership because it forces us to choose which is more important: getting our way or maintaining the group. Unfortunately, many people choose getting their way in situations like this. If they have strong personalities, or if their positions are strong, they may even win more often than not. But at what cost?

In most cases, were we completely honest, we would admit that no one can be certain about the best action or policy. We would also admit that maintaining good working relationships within the group is more important to achieving the group's vision than any one decision or action. While leaders should try to prevent groups from making bad decisions, they must also remember that authentic leadership is not the same as getting your way. Authentic leadership involves trying to maintain the commitment of the group in order to keep it moving toward its vision. Being able to resolve conflicts through win-win negotiations is critical to that task.

# 6

# Creating Rewards

It was all set. The famous marine ecologist Jacques Cousteau was coming to Quebec. He would also make a special visit to Charles de Gaulle High School, and Jean Paul was responsible for the welcoming ceremonies. Everything had to be perfect. That included the huge banner that, in Jean Paul's imagination, already hung across the stage of the school auditorium.

But who would make the banner? Henri was the best artist in the World Ecology Club, but he was also very busy. The banner would take many hours to make. Would Henri agree to do it? What would it take to get Henri interested in the project?

## CREATING A REWARDING GROUP

Jean Paul's dilemma will be familiar to anyone who has led a voluntary group. How do you motivate people to get involved? Most leaders, like Jean Paul, deal with motivation in a makeshift way. Faced with a job that must be done, they wonder how someone can be "motivated" to do it. This is a rather manipulative way to motivate people. It can also be ineffective. A more productive approach involves looking at how you can make your group routinely rewarding, so that people *want* to participate!

## An Informal Reward Audit

After the visit by Jacques Cousteau—a visit that went without a banner—Jean Paul decided to look at the problem of motivation systematically. He did a "reward audit" of the World Ecology Club.

A reward audit simply looks at who get rewards in a group and why they get them. Like a financial audit, a reward audit tries to see whether benefits (rewards) and costs (work) are balanced. Jean Paul planned to do his reward audit very informally. He would ask his friends some questions about the club. He would also take a hard look at his own behavior and the behavior of other group leaders.

Before he could start, however, Jean Paul had to know what to look for. He went back to some material he had received at a leadership workshop the year before. It described the kinds of rewards people get from groups, and how they are linked to higher commitment and participation.

*Human needs.* As human beings we have a variety of needs. The most basic are our physical needs:

- *Security and well-being* (which includes protection from the elements and from people who might hurt us, food, health care, and productive employment).

Almost as basic are our social needs:

- *Fellowship, solidarity, affection, and fun* (including a sense of belonging, love, enjoyment, and the support of others in difficult times).

Once these needs are met, people try to meet less basic needs:

- *Recognition, a sense of accomplishment, and self-esteem* (which reflect the respect of others and ourselves and which say that we are special or have done something worthwhile).
- *Power and influence* (which come from being able to affect what other people do or to have some control over the world around us).
- *Growth and fulfillment* (which come from learning new skills or from acquiring knowledge of any sort).

*Groups fulfill needs.* People do not participate in a group simply because of its vision. Over time a person's loyalty depends on the satisfaction he or she receives from being part of the group. When participation provides no satisfaction—that is, when participation does not meet a person's needs—interest in the group declines no matter how important its vision may be.

In a sense, all human needs are fulfilled in association with other people. However, some needs are clearly more relevant to a group like the World Ecology Club than others. No one belonged to the club in order to satisfy basic physical needs. These came from family and community. Basic social rewards like solidarity, fun, and affection were obviously more relevant. But the rewards that seemed most important to Jean Paul were those related to a sense of accomplishment, recognition, influence, and growth.

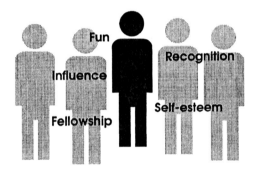

What needs does your group help people fulfill?

## Solidarity

Solidarity rewards—fellowship, identity, support, and fun—have been described as "hygienic" rewards. When they are absent in a group, people become dissatisfied. On the other hand, when they are present, they usually do no more than create a positive atmosphere. Rewards like affection and a sense of belonging may come only if you spend time with a group. However, they do not necessarily motivate high levels of participation. The best policy is to make hygienic rewards widely available to members, but only to members.

Jean Paul intended to take only a casual look at solidarity rewards. To his surprise, however, he found that these rewards were a problem for the World Ecology Club. He would have to pay much greater attention to them, if he was going to strengthen the club.

*Does the group build "team spirit"?* The best way for a group to provide fellowship, identity, and support is to have members do interesting things together. The sharing of success, failure, frustration, and joy creates bonds among people.

- Plan projects so that people work together cooperatively as much as possible, even if they seem to prefer working alone.

Organizing activities that involve competition can also build team spirit if those activities:

- Are recreational. Avoid direct competition between group members if the stakes (status, prizes) are high or if the activities are directed toward achieving key goals.
- Involve team rather than individual competition. Team competitions at least build bonds among team members.
- Pit the group against some other group, not member against member.

As Jean Paul thought about the activities of his club, he realized that he often missed chances to build team spirit. The group rarely did things together outside club meetings. When they did have a project, like the Cousteau visit, individuals or pairs of people took responsibility for the different tasks. They seldom worked as a group.

The banner for the Cousteau visit was an example. Henri was the best artist in the club. But did Henri have to make the banner alone? He could have designed the banner, and then a number of people, working under his direction, could have helped finish it. That kind of cooperation would have made the job easier. It might also have built a sense of identity and fellowship among the members.

*Does the group have fun?* The more closely he looked at solidarity rewards, the more convinced Jean Paul became that he was the source of the problem. To Jean Paul ecological issues were serious business. He really believed that if people wanted to have fun, they should join a social club! Unfortunately, many members were doing just that. Being part of the World Ecology Club had been fun under the last president. It no longer was.

The leaders of many groups share Jean Paul's problem. Some take their own responsibilities too seriously. They may feel that joking around or having fun with other group members lessens their authority. Other leaders take the group's vision too seriously. They can fail to see the humor in things or to find opportunities just to have fun.

Solidarity within a group is impossible if people cannot enjoy each other's company. So:

- Even if your group has a serious vision, do some things just for fun; and
- Even in the midst of serious business, welcome joking and other ways to keep the group's work in perspective.

The world can be saved by happy people just as easily as by serious ones.

You must satisfy members' needs before you can work toward your vision.
(Reprinted with special permission of North American Syndicate.)

## Accomplishment and Recognition

In his reward audit, Jean Paul took a close look at rewards related to recognition and accomplishment. To his relief, he found that the club was doing pretty well with these rewards.

***Does the group accomplish anything relevant?*** Groups give people a chance to do great things. Most of us have little power if we act as individuals. However, when we act as part of a group, we can change the world.

If a group has a relevant vision, and if it achieves its goals, it will give its members a profound sense of accomplishment. The greater the sense of accomplishment, the better members feel about themselves as individuals. The better they feel, the more they will want to contribute to the group's success in the future.

Jean Paul believed that the most important reason for belonging to the World Ecology Club was that it did important work. Everyone in the club and the school agreed. The club had an important vision (a cleaner, healthier world). It was doing relevant things to achieve that vision. In fact, the club had defined its goals very effectively. It had long-term and ambitious goals—like getting the school to adopt a new waste management policy. When people said the club was doing important things, they usually had these goals in mind. At the same time, there were easier, short-term goals—like holding a school rally on the environment. When people said the group was successful, they often had these goals in mind. The mix of large and small goals had been accidental, but Jean Paul saw how important it was:

- Groups should have some major, long-term goals that people see as important, but
- These should be balanced with easier, short-term goals that give members a steady stream of successes and prove that the group is accomplishing something.

Like solidarity rewards, the sense of accomplishment that comes from being part of a successful group may not lead to high participation. Just belonging to a respected group helps a person's self-esteem. Nonetheless, this sense of accomplishment is important. Most people lose interest in a group that does nothing relevant. Some people join groups primarily for the sense of accomplishment that group membership can provide.

***Do leaders give positive feedback?*** For most people a sense of accomplishment stemming from the group's success is a hygienic reward. More important are rewards that recognize personal achievements and personal contributions to the group. This kind of recognition says that the individual, as an individual, has done something important and worthwhile. It makes active members feel appreciated, and it gives less active members a reason to try harder.

One of the easiest and yet most important ways for leaders to recognize a person's efforts is to give positive feedback. Despite his problems with solidarity rewards, Jean Paul found that he was doing a good job in this regard. Members could count on him to:

- Tell people when they were doing a good job;
- Give people credit for the work they had done;
- Thank them publicly for their contributions to the group; and
- Mention awards or accomplishments achieved outside the group.

As importantly, when Jean Paul praised or recognized someone, he meant it—and the person knew it. He never exaggerated his enthusiasm for a person's accomplishments. He was totally honest about work: he never praised work that was not good enough; he never complimented work he did not like.

- Recognition is too important a reward to waste. Avoid praising everything and everyone for no reason, or your praise will soon lose its value.

***Do leaders share the limelight?*** Giving people the recognition they deserve goes beyond the feedback of group leaders. Giving opportunities for public recognition, that is, recognition from people outside the group, is usually even more important.

The World Ecology Club had never had much public recognition. It was rarely noticed in school and had never been noticed by the wider community—until now. The Cousteau visit had changed that. It had drawn a lot of attention to the club. Reporters had come to ask questions. A short article, with Jean Paul's picture, had appeared in the newspaper.

Everyone had assumed that Jean Paul, as club president, was responsible for persuading Cousteau to visit. The attention had made Jean Paul feel proud and important. He had even been honest with them. He had told the reporters that the real credit belonged to Marie. She had written to Cousteau and had followed up with telephone calls. Unfortunately, the reporters only half-heard. In the end it was Jean Paul's picture and not Marie's that had been in the newspaper.

When a group does something important, the formal "leader" usually gets the recognition. The attention is exciting and rewarding. But opportunities for public recognition do not come every day. When they do,

- Make sure that those people—and only those people—who deserve recognition get into the spotlight, and
- Resist the temptation to enjoy the spotlight alone even for a moment.

Jean Paul should have made sure that Marie was present when the reporters came. He should have let her answer their questions. Fame is usually fleeting; tomorrow will be too late. By not sharing the spotlight, Jean Paul had failed to give Marie the reward she deserved.

### Power and Growth

People who commit a lot of time and energy to a group often want more than a sense of accomplishment or recognition. Some want empowerment. They want opportunities to influence personally what goes on in the group or in the larger world. Some want enrichment. They want opportunities to learn new things and to grow intellectually or socially.

Through his reward audit Jean Paul found that several members saw power and growth as the most important rewards the World Ecology Club could offer.

***Do members have opportunities to exercise power?*** The ability of members to influence what goes on in the group or in the wider community depends on two things: how the group makes decisions and how leaders delegate authority.

- Rewarding groups gives members opportunities to make meaningful decisions in meaningful ways.
- Such groups also delegate meaningful and desirable tasks to their members.

When Jean Paul involved the group in making decisions, he was a skillful consensus-seeker. Members usually found the experience satisfying. But Jean Paul seldom recognized when the group ought to be involved. The Cousteau visit was an example. Jean Paul never asked the group whether Cousteau should be invited or what should be done for his visit. Everything was so obvious to him—including the banner he wanted across the stage. If he had involved the group in planning for the event, they may have agreed that a banner was needed. If they had, there might have been a banner even without Henri's help!

Jean Paul's track record on delegating authority was similar. He only delegated jobs to people he knew could do them well. As a result, he had come to rely solely on a few close friends. That limited what the club could do. It also took away what could have been an important reward. Delegating meaningful tasks to members helps build their sense of identity with the group. It gives them a sense of contributing to the group and of exercising power within it.

Delegation does, however, pose a dilemma for leaders. On the one hand, you want things done well. On the other, you cannot empower members unless you delegate real authority to them, whether you know they can handle the job or not. As he made his reward audit, Jean Paul realized that he was dealing with this dilemma in the wrong way. He was right in seeing that leaders take risks by delegating authority. However, he was wrong in seeing delegation as an all-or-nothing affair. He needed to see delegation, not just as a way to empower members, but as a way to help them grow!

*Does delegation promote growth?* People often participate in groups in order to learn new things or to improve their skills. Sometimes the only way to give them this opportunity is to give them responsibility for tasks you are not sure they can complete.

- Delegation should be used to promote the personal learning and growth of members. To do this,
- Leaders need to provide appropriate support to make sure that delegated tasks are completed successfully.

Delegation is not an all-or-nothing process. You can delegate more or less control over an activity. Just how much control you delegate should depend on the knowledge and self-confidence of the person to whom you are delegating the authority.

For the Cousteau visit, Jean Paul delegated the job of publicity to Annette. She knew what to do and how to do it. She was also completely confident that she could handle the job well. Under those circumstances, Jean Paul's style of *complete delegation* made sense. Annette should have been given more or less complete authority over the task. Anything less would have made the experience less empowering and less rewarding!

But what if Annette had been less sure of herself? She might have helped someone else do a similar project in the past. That experience might have given her the knowledge to do the job, but not necessarily the self-confidence. This situation calls for a *mentoring style* of delegation. Mentors do not tell people what to do. They provide moral support and are available to help people think things through. Mentors get involved only when called on. They may provide nothing more than positive feedback. But they are available. That can give a person an added sense of security.

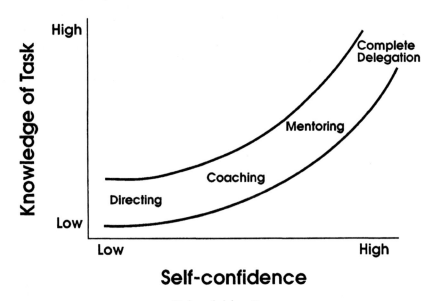

Styles of delegation.

A *coaching style* would have been appropriate if Annette had had less experience and knowledge. Like mentors, coaches do not provide detailed directions. They do, however, keep a more watchful eye on the project. They intervene to offer suggestions and insights even if not asked. When appropriate, they suggest how to improve performance. They warn of pitfalls and problems. In other words, coaches do not

merely provide moral support, they help teach the person how to perform the task well.

Finally, people with little or no experience need a *directive style* of delegation. For the Cousteau visit, Jean Paul decided to handle the printing of admission tickets himself. This would, however, have been a perfect job for a newer member like André. André was looking for ways to get involved, but he had no experience. If given responsibility for the admission tickets, he would have needed detailed instructions. He would need to know how to choose colors—because some colors were hard to read, and others were too easily forged. He would need to know what information to print on the tickets. He would need to know how to get estimates on printing costs. In other words, someone would have spent a considerable amount of time telling André how to get the tickets printed. But it would have been time well spent. André would have had a meaningful chance to exercise power within the group, as he completed the job and solved little problems along the way. He would also have learned how to do the job, so next time he could do it more independently!

*Are leaders models of commitment?* Delegation provides important opportunities for members to exercise power and to grow. In a very real sense, leaders cannot delegate too much. However, leaders can delegate for the wrong reasons.

If you have ever encountered a "dilettante" leader—one who expects a lot from you but does little work himself—you understand the danger in asking others to work when you seem to do nothing. Most people will feel abused if group leaders seem to be getting a free ride.

- While it is important to delegate tasks, it is equally important to model the kind of active commitment you expect from others!

Delegate in order to get things done, to share power, and to give members a chance to grow. Do not delegate merely to get out of work, or to get others to do jobs you dislike.

### Meet Personal Needs

All people have similar needs. However, not all people place the same value on particular rewards. Even if they do, people's need for any one reward is limited, and it changes over time. Just as you can

satisfy your need for food and water, you can satisfy your need for recognition, power, or even fun! As a result, what some people in a group find rewarding, others may not. What a person finds rewarding today may be unimportant to her tomorrow!

- Rewarding groups offer a variety of rewards to meet the different needs of different people; and
- The most important thing you can do to make your group rewarding is to give members the freedom to discover, express, and meet their unique personal needs.

Creating a group in which members can meet their personal needs requires flexibility and an openness to the initiatives of others. Through his reward audit Jean Paul began to realize that this was another of his weaknesses. After the Cousteau visit three of the newer club members had suggested some follow-up activities. Jean Paul and most of the people who had taken responsibility for the Cousteau visit were exhausted. They had no interest in starting anything new.

Now Jean Paul realized that his negative reaction to the trio had been a mistake. He could have encouraged them to spell out their idea and begin to work on it. By dismissing the idea, rather than using it as a way to get the three more involved in the club, he had missed a great opportunity to make the group more rewarding for them.

## PROBLEMS IN MOTIVATION

Motivation can and should be approached in a positive way—by creating a more rewarding group. In the long run, this approach will be more satisfying and more successful than any other. However, there is a negative side to motivation which must be recognized: the problem of free riders and the value of punishment and conflict in motivating people.

### Free Riders

No matter how rewarding your group might be, there will always be some people who take rewards without giving anything in return. These

people are free riders. They may get fellowship simply from coming to meetings and socializing with other members. They may get social recognition simply from belonging to a prestigious group. They are always available when benefits are passed around. They can never be found when work must be done.

*Free riders can reduce group solidarity.* Free riders are inevitable. The larger and more successful the group, the more free riders there will be. Some people are equal opportunity free riders—they behave the same in all groups. Others may be free riders only in your group, perhaps because you give certain rewards too freely.

Free riders really become a problem only if active members begin to resent them. At that point they break down the link between rewards and participation because they seem to get something for nothing. They also damage the commitment of active members who must bear more than their fair share of the group's burden. To protect themselves, active members may start looking for ways they too can take a free ride.

*Keep free riding to a minimum.* Free riders cannot be eliminated. But they can be held in check. The single most important way to limit free riding is to make sure that key rewards go only to those who deserve them. Recognition and power are most important in this regard. Know what is going on in the group so that you know who has done what. When projects are successful, congratulate those who have really contributed to the effort. Do not let free riders steal the spotlight or take advantage of special situations. If a reporter and photographer for the school newspaper come calling, try to ensure that the right people show up in the picture. When a decision must be made, do not let free riders have an unfair influence simply because they talk fast.

- Do not let free riders cheapen rewards like recognition and power by taking advantage of the situation.

## Punishment and Conflict as Motivators

Although most leaders focus on positive rewards when it comes to motivation, punishment and conflict can often be useful. Parents use punishment (spankings, grounding) to get children to obey. Teachers use punishments (poor grades, withholding of privileges) to get students to work harder. Managers in business firms use punishments (withholding of raises, criticism) to improve worker performance.

Conflict can also be used to encourage greater commitment to a group. When groups are attacked by outsiders, members often rally to their defense. They may be willing to make any sacrifice in order to ensure the survival and success of the group. Conflict within groups can also motivate people to contribute to, and thus defend, projects or people they cherish or respect.

The problem with punishment and conflict is that, while both can have positive motivational value, neither does much to improve relationships or long-term commitment. Students who receive nothing but criticism eventually give up. Employees who receive nothing but grief eventually seek other employers. Even the bond between parent and child eventually breaks down if punishments are constant, unfair, and never balanced by praise or other positive rewards.

Similarly, conflicts must be resolved at some point or morale will suffer. Once the conflict is resolved, its motivational impact fades rapidly. A group that depends on conflict to motivate commitment must bounce from one conflict to another, an emotionally exhausting life for everyone!

Punishment and conflict can be useful motivators at times. However, they are rarely the best basis for getting people to participate in a group. Positive rewards should be the bedrock of any leader's effort to encourage commitment and involvement.

# 7

# Creating an Image

As Marcia walked the last ten feet to the classroom door, she knew the Fulton High Spanish Club had a problem with its image. Marcia was on her way to a club meeting. She had just left a group of friends. They had teased her about the club before, but today the teasing had taken on a nasty tone. Marcia's friends were turning against her—all because they misunderstood the club!

Virtually all groups need the support or acceptance of people outside the group. A group like the Spanish Club needs a place to meet, so it needs the support of the principal. It needs to raise money for activities, so it needs the support of teachers, parents, and other students. Like all groups, it needs members, and members are hard to recruit or keep when people are harassed for being part of the group!

Getting support requires that people recognize and feel good about the group. This is why the image of a group is important. Creating a positive and well recognized image is the first step in building the goodwill that groups need to survive and prosper.

## THE CASE OF THE MISTAKEN IMAGE

In Marcia's case the image problem appeared to be one of survival. Fulton was a school with a problem, and the Spanish Club was caught in the middle of that problem.

Fulton was considered an inner city high school. A majority of the students were African-American. The sizable white minority was bussed in from other parts of the city. But the neighborhood around Fulton was changing, and Fulton was changing with it. A number of Hispanic families had moved into the neighborhood. As the number of Hispanic students rose, they had upset the delicate balance between blacks and whites, creating new tensions. Fights had broken out between a few troublemakers.

*Caught in the middle.* The Spanish Club had become a victim of the conflict. The club had always been small; it had never been well recognized. It had attracted only those students with a real interest in Spanish language and culture. As racial tensions rose, many non-Hispanic students began to see the Spanish Club as a group *for* Hispanic students. On the other hand, the Hispanic students avoided the club because it seemed to be dominated by non-Hispanics. Now members like Marcia were being harassed. Clearly the Spanish Club had to do something about its image if it was going to survive.

*What kind of image?* At the meeting Marcia described what had happened. Other members told of similar experiences. Brock suggested that the club needed to clarify its image—to let people know it was for all students.

Marcia wanted to go further. The real problem was the racial conflict, she argued. The Spanish Club was one of the few groups that might be able to mediate among the three groups.

The other club members agreed with Marcia's assessment—even the adviser, Mr. Cherry, who never seemed to agree with anything. They decided to start with the annual Spanish Week. The Spanish Club always organized the week's activities. This year some activities could focus on the cultural heritage of Spanish-speaking Americans, rather than Spain. Others could begin a dialogue among the student groups. Mr. Cherry even volunteered to invite someone to lead workshops on discrimination and tolerance. If their plans were going to succeed, however, something had to be done right away to start changing the club's image.

## PROJECTING AN IMAGE

Images are the mental pictures that we have of people and groups. Everyone projects an image of some kind. When people think of the

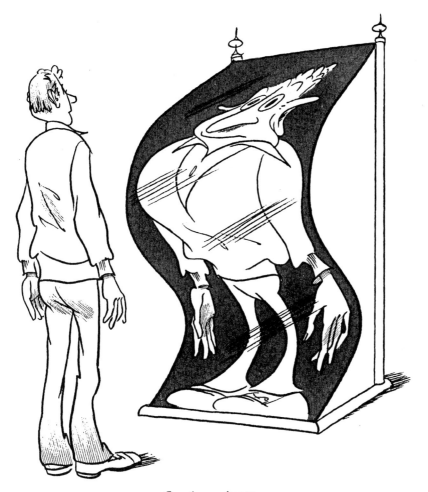

Creating an image.

Sierra Club, for example, the image "environmental group" comes to mind. In one sense this label says very little. Yet it *implies* many things about:

- The vision and goals of the group;
- Its values;
- The type of people who support and join it;
- Its relationships with other groups.

Creating an image involves finding and communicating an image that will persuade key people to support the group as it works toward its vision.

### Find the Right Image

Before Marcia and the Spanish Club could do anything about their image, they had to decide what image they wanted to project. However, the members themselves saw the group in different ways. As they talked, Marcia listed the four most common images:

- A group committed to cross-cultural understanding.
- A group open to students of all races and ethnic groups.
- A group committed to protecting the rights of all students.
- A group that could be a bridge among the different ethnic and racial groups.

All four images said similar things. Each also touched on a truth about the group. But which would be *best?* Each communicated a somewhat different image. As she thought, Marcia realized that the question of which image was the best—the right image—depended in large part on which audience was most important!

*Who is your audience?* When you try to create or change your group's image, you need to make sure that the image you create produces the desired reaction in the target audience. Calling the Sierra Club an "environmental group" may trigger a positive reaction in a high school student concerned about pollution. The same image may get a negative reaction from a corporation president who has been charged with polluting.

Unfortunately for the Spanish Club, the audience was not altogether clear. Some members argued that the student body as a whole should be the primary audience. Mr. Cherry thought that the teachers and principal were important. Marcia argued that the students who were looking for some way to solve the school's racial problem were the most important audience.

The Spanish Club decided to concentrate at first on sympathetic students and on teachers. That decision helped crystallize the image. These people were looking for a way to bring the school together. For them the image of a bridge seemed perfect. Among its members the Spanish Club bridged the divide of culture. It could also bridge the different groups at school and bring Fulton together again.

- To find the right image you must know what you hope to accomplish. Images, like visions, tell people who you are and what you are about.

- To find the right image you must also know your audience. The same image will mean different things to different people. Will the image be valuable in their eyes?

**BLOOM COUNTY**　　　　　　　　　　**by Berke Breathed**

Preconceived images affect how people interpret messages.
(© 1982, Washington Post Writers Group. Reprinted with permission.)

*Does the audience have a preconceived image?* The image of a bridge among the races and cultures at Fulton was good for the Spanish Club in another way. It responded to the chief misconceptions of the club that already existed.

Creating images is like giving people a set of lenses through which to view the group. Unfortunately, some people already have lenses which you need to take into account. In a sense, you need to fashion clip-on sunglasses which, when placed over the existing lenses, produce the desired image—without distortion or confusion.

The problem of preconceived images affects everyone. Many years ago the Exxon Corporation launched an advertising campaign using a Bengal tiger as a symbol of the company. The campaign slogan, "Put a Tiger in Your Tank," implied that people could gain the strength, agility, and beauty of the tiger by using Exxon gasoline.

The campaign was so successful that Exxon decided to use the same symbol in the Asian market. What they did not realize was that people in Southeast Asia viewed tigers differently than people in North America. Asians saw tigers as scruffy, dirty, and dangerous beasts. The last thing they wanted was to put one in their tank. The advertising campaign failed miserably because the new audience had a preexisting image that the image creators had failed to recognize!

If people have a preexisting image of your group, do not ignore it.

- How does your audience view the group now? Look for preexisting images that may cause confusion or distortion.
- How does the image you are trying to create fit with those preconceptions? Can you use the preconceptions to build a new image? Do you need to address preconceptions head-on to change them?

If you do not pay attention to preconceived images, whatever image you end up creating may be distorted or confused, with very unwelcome results.

### Communicate Your Image Creatively

People receive a great many messages. All day, every day, they are bombarded by messages about products, groups, people, and events. They receive so many messages, in fact, that they must screen some of them out simply to get anything done. People learn to pay close attention to some messages and barely hear others. Some messages are ignored altogether.

One of the greatest challenges that you face in creating an image is breaking through these barriers. The problem is particularly severe if the group has no image at present. To get attention, messages which communicate your image must catch people's eyes. They must stand out amid the noise of everyday life!

*Craft an effective message.* Several years ago a world affairs council in the Midwest took a hard look at its image. The council had publicized its many service programs for years. But few people paid much attention. When leaders asked for donations to support the council's work, people often said that they did not even know there was a local world affairs council!

The council's efforts to create an image had failed because it had no clear and effective way to communicate its image. A public relations consultant suggested that the group find a phrase that summed up what the organization was all about. After a few strategy sessions, group leaders found what they were looking for. In the future, the council would be known as "The Community's Window on the World."

The new slogan worked very well. It was catchy and easily remembered. Despite its simplicity, it contained the essence of the group's vision. As a "window on the world" the council would help increase international awareness in the community. Even its subtleties communicated something desirable. The council was a "window." It stood between the viewer and the world, but it would not distort what the viewer saw—a promise to be nonpartisan.

The council's new image got people's attention because it was communicated clearly and effectively. In general the best messages for communicating your image:

- *Are easily grasped.* Busy people only pay attention to relatively simple and easily understood messages. Try to communicate your image in simple phrases or a single sentence.
- *Project an attractive image.* A group's image lays the foundation for support of the group. The message should focus on that part of the image that will create favorable impressions.
- *Portray the group as unique.* People must choose from a wide variety of groups that ask for their support. More often than not they support the group that seems truly different in a positive way.

The Spanish Club's image of a "bridge among races and cultures" had these qualities. It was short and graphic. The words created a picture in people's minds that said it all! It was attractive—at least for those who wanted to solve the school's racial problems. Finally, it was unique. Fulton had problems precisely because no other group could bridge the differences among the racial groups.

***Select the best media.*** Creating an image in the minds of potential supporters clearly requires communication through some medium. Just what medium you use can be as important in conveying your image as the message itself.

Virtually anything can serve as a medium for communicating your image. A picture in the school or community newspaper can be worth a thousand words. But posters on bulletin boards, handbills, even graffiti on a wall are also used to communicate images. For many groups, word-of-mouth is the most important medium available. People's images are highly affected by what they hear from others.

The media you should use will depend on your answers to two questions:

- Which media can reach your audience most efficiently?
- Which media will communicate your message most effectively and accurately?

Posters can be great, if your audience actually looks at them. If not, they will be a waste of time. Mass media (newspapers, radio, even television) reach a lot of people, but they give the group less control over the message. Word-of-mouth can be a powerful way to reach people, but if someone else does the talking, it can also be dangerous.

The Spanish Club thought of several ways to get their image across to the students at Fulton High. Marcia suggested posters on all the school bulletin boards. Mr. Cherry suggested making presentations to other student groups and at the next faculty meeting. Anna, who worked on the school newspaper, thought she could get an article published.

After much discussion the group decided to make presentations to other student groups, even though it had been Mr. Cherry's idea. The posters and the newspaper article seemed like good ideas, but they might not reach the intended audience. On the other hand, the students who really cared about the school belonged to at least one club or organization. Talking to the other school groups would reach those students.

The group decided to put together a simple slide show about Spanish Week and to make presentations to any club that would invite them. Mr. Cherry agreed to arrange a presentation at the next faculty meeting. The presentations would show how Spanish Week could be used to bring Fulton together. The idea that the Spanish Club itself was a bridge among the school's races and cultures would also be mentioned several times. Posters and other things could come later. People would be more likely to notice them after the presentations.

***Beware of hidden messages.*** As the Spanish Club worked on its presentation and slide show, they became sensitive to the possibility that the medium itself could communicate unintended messages.

Even when you shine a light on your group, other people usually see little more than the shadow.

Brock was the first to draw attention to the problem. As they gathered slides, he began to wonder whether the slide show was artificial. The slides were mostly pictures of the school and students. Everyone knew what the school looked like. Would the group communicate something unfavorable by showing slides rather than just talking with the groups?

Mr. Cherry also noted that the composition of the teams making the presentations was critical. If the club wanted to create an image as a bridge among the racial groups, the teams themselves needed to communicate the image. They had to be made up of students from different racial groups.

Image makers all too often get the message right only to discover that the medium they use distorts or contradicts the image in some way.

- Look critically for any hidden messages your medium may be communicating.
- Test your message and medium by asking people to react to them. Listen for subtle cues that point to hidden messages and meanings.

***Be creative, but not too creative.*** Marcia and her friends decided to use a slide show precisely because they knew it would get people's attention. Simply standing in front of a group and talking seemed so ordinary. The slides would add a special dimension. If the show was done well, it would create added interest in what was being said.

Image makers constantly try to communicate their messages in new and different ways.

- Observe and use the creative ideas of others. Imitation is flattery.
- However, guard against falling in line with trends. Things that are creative and eye-catching today will become staid and boring tomorrow if everyone does them!
- Don't be afraid of your own creativity. Try to do things a little differently.
- But guard against hype as well. Too much creativity can be as damaging as too little if it distracts people from your message.

When creative messages and media get out of hand, that too becomes part of your image. People begin to see you and your group as more interested in getting attention than in communicating the truth. Once you get an image like that, people stop listening!

## PROTECTING YOUR IMAGE

Images are like gardens. The work continues even after they have been planted. Even groups with positive and well-recognized images must work to protect and maintain those images.

- Group leaders must be constantly attentive to the state of the group's image—at least among its more important supporters.
- People forget. Unless the group keeps itself in the public eye, its image will fade.
- Members represent the group in the wider community. They must pay attention to how their words and actions will affect the group's image.

### Take Soundings

The only way to stay in touch with the group's image is to take routine "soundings" among your key supporters. You should have a clear idea of the people on whom your group depends. For school groups it may be the principal and the key opinion leaders among the students (perhaps the captain of the football team or the president of the student council). For community groups it may be the president of a local corporation, a few prominent citizens, or people on the board of charitable foundations. Whoever these key others are, keep in touch with them. Try to find out how they feel about the group, and how their feelings are changing.

You do not need to do anything elaborate to take soundings. In fact, informal approaches often work best.

- Create opportunities to talk casually with significant supporters.
- If interesting new things are happening, mention the group and ask how they feel about recent projects or activities.
- If nothing noteworthy has been going on, listen to hear whether the other person brings up the group (that is a good sign). If not, let her know about things that may be coming up in the future.

Soundings both test the group's image and keep other people aware of the group.

### Get the Mass Media's Attention

One of the best ways for a group to keep its image in the public eye is to get attention in the mass media. An occasional article or picture in the school newspaper reminds people that the group is still there, and still doing good things. A story in the community newspaper can do even more.

Using the mass media in this way, unfortunately, is not easy. Anyone who has ever tried to persuade a reporter to cover some event knows that catching the media's attention can be very difficult. People in the mass media will not cover just any story. They want things that have human interest or significance for the wider community. These are the stories that sell newspapers.

Of course, you know that your group has human interest and that its activities are important. The challenge is to get people in the media to share that judgment. As often as not, the way to do that is not to try to convince them. Rather it is to look at your message through their eyes, and to be persistent.

- *Be helpful.* Ask yourself how you can both meet your need for publicity and help people in the mass media do their jobs! Can you tell your story in such a way that reporters and editors also find it interesting and important?
- *Prioritize your messages.* Like simple messages, simple approaches get people's attention. Decide which events or messages are most important and focus on them. If you emphasize a few simple messages, those messages may be communicated. They are also more likely to be communicated accurately and create a clearer image!
- *Be assertive and persistent.* Unfortunately, more people fail to get the attention of the mass media than succeed. But you increase your chances of success simply by being assertive and persistent. Remember, "The squeaky wheel gets the grease." Sometimes people will give you a hearing just to get rid of you. Sometimes they decide that your story must be good since you are so committed to telling it.
- *Cultivate relationships.* The only way to guarantee media attention is to cultivate a relationship with particular people in the media. Once you get the ear of a reporter or an editor, that person will always be willing to listen. He or she may disagree that you have a good story *this time,* but at least you will have had a hearing.

## Avoid Conflicting Images and Messages

In the 1960s, Martin Luther King, Jr., was the most visible figure in the American civil rights movement. For white Americans in particular, King was civil rights. As American involvement in the Vietnam War grew, however, King faced a dilemma. He felt that the war hurt African-Americans and distracted the nation's attention from pressing domestic problems. For those reasons he wanted to take a strong stand against the war.

Many of King's colleagues warned him against getting involved. Many shared his feelings about the war, but they feared that taking a public stand would hurt the image of the civil rights movement. Support for the movement was at a historic high. However, most Americans also supported the war effort in Vietnam. They saw the antiwar movement as unpatriotic. King's advisers feared that taking a stand would link the image of the civil rights movement with that of the antiwar movement. That could cost the civil rights movement thousands of supporters.

King's dilemma is a dramatic example of something that happens every day.

• The actions of group members are themselves messages that affect the group's image.

Even when a member's actions have nothing to do with the group, they may be interpreted as a message about the group. If Marcia receives an academic award, some people will think of the Spanish Club as a group of academically able students! If Brock gets involved in a food fight in the cafeteria, some people will wonder whether everyone in the Spanish Club is irresponsible!

• Responsible leadership means protecting the image of the group! Ask yourself what message your actions will send? Will that message promote the group's image or hurt it?

# 8

# *Gaining Legitimacy*

One of the most important aspects of a group's image is its legitimacy. Having legitimacy means that the group has the right to do the things it is doing . . . that it has the right to work toward its vision. In a democracy, of course, groups have the *right* to do whatever they want, as long as they hurt no one. However, when a group seeks the support of nonmembers, it needs more than a formal right. It needs legitimacy.

In the 1960s, when young Americans first demonstrated against the Vietnam War, one of the greatest obstacles they had to overcome was their lack of legitimacy. Many adults questioned whether young people could understand what was at stake in Vietnam. So they questioned whether young people had the right to participate in the debate over the war. Until young Americans established their legitimacy, their right to participate, their arguments and protests were not taken seriously.

Although legitimacy is part of a group's image, simply projecting the *image* of legitimacy is not enough. When it comes to legitimacy, image *must* reflect reality. Thus the skill of gaining legitimacy lies not in creating an image, but in assessing and in establishing a genuine basis for legitimacy.

## THE NEED FOR LEGITIMACY

The importance of legitimacy often becomes apparent only when a group lacks it. When new groups form or when existing groups try to do radically new things, people can ask troubling questions. Who are these people? What are they up to? Can I trust them? Even if they cannot put their concerns into words, they sense that something is missing. They sense the lack of legitimacy.

That was the situation in which Steven found himself. He did not know the word *legitimacy,* but he understood that he had a problem. He also understood that unless the problem was solved, a very important project might fail.

### A Suicide Hotline

Steven was the president of his church youth group. Every year the group did a service project. For as long as anyone could remember, they had raised money for overseas missions. Unfortunately the mission project had become routine. People had lost interest in it. This year Steven wanted to do more.

The previous spring, a nearby community had been shocked by the suicides of three young men. Steven knew that many students in his school were under stress. Some had talked about suicide at the time. He wanted his church group to do something to prevent a similar crisis in his community.

At the time of the suicides, Steven had read about a suicide hotline in another city that was staffed by volunteer teenagers. There was a Teen Center in Steven's city, but no suicide hotline. Steven envisioned helping the local Teen Center start a program, using young people from his group as the initial volunteers. He thought the Teen Center would understand the need for a hotline. He also knew they were too poorly funded and understaffed to start one on their own.

### A Question of Legitimacy

The parish youth group was excited about the idea. But when Steven mentioned it to his friend Kathy, she asked some unsettling questions. "What do you guys know about suicide prevention? Wouldn't you be scared if you got a call? What if the person committed suicide anyway?"

It was not Kathy's questions that bothered Steven. He had asked himself the same things. It was her attitude that bothered him. She seemed to say that a suicide hotline was too important and difficult for the youth group. Steven worried that other people, including officials at the Teen Center, would share those feelings. Somehow he had to establish his group's credibility.

*"God has also chosen me to speak to you about insurance"*

**We are most conscious of legitimacy when we fail to see it.**
(Reprinted by permission of the *Punch* Library.)

## ASSESSING THE GROUP'S LEGITIMACY

Although he did not know it, Steven was already on the right path toward gaining legitimacy. Kathy's questions had been the source of his concerns. But he realized that the most important people were the officials of the Teen Center. He also realized that the key question was whether his group would be seen as legitimate to deal with the issue of teen suicide.

Legitimacy is in the eyes of the beholder. What gives you legitimacy with some people may be quite irrelevant or even damaging with others. Legitimacy is influenced by the perspective of the other—that is, by her values, assumptions, and attitudes.

- In assessing your legitimacy, start by listing all the people whose support you need to accomplish your goals.

- Then ask how those people view you now. Do you already have some legitimacy in their eyes? How can your present legitimacy be used to establish legitimacy with respect to a new issue or task?

• Finally, ask what more you must do to make yourself legitimate. Which of the many possible *bases of legitimacy* must you establish if you are to be taken seriously?

As Steven thought about it, he realized that a number of people would be in a position to veto the group's work on the suicide hotline. First on the list were the church pastor and the parents of group members. If they did not approve, the group would not be allowed to go ahead. The church parishioners, while not directly involved, also had a stake in the project and its success. If they disapproved, the pastor might veto the program. Finally, the people at the Teen Center were obviously important.

### Look at Your Track Record

For established groups, the first place to look for legitimacy is in your track record. Beware, however, of blind spots. There are many different ways of looking at the same track record. A group may have had little or no direct experience with an issue, but the group's track record may still establish some basis for legitimacy.

*Do you have the knowledge to succeed?* The most important way to establish legitimacy in the eyes of the people on Steven's list was to demonstrate that the group had the knowledge to organize the hotline project successfully. The problem was that the group had no track record in this area. They knew nothing about teenage suicide, except that it was a serious problem. They had never organized anything as complex as the hotline would be.

• *Knowledge and expertise.* In general groups need the legitimacy that comes from knowledge or expertise. They need to demonstrate that they know what they are talking about or people will not listen to them.

• Expertise is, however, a narrow source of legitimacy. Knowing a lot about one thing may not give a group legitimacy when it comes to other issues. A group that knows all about zoning laws may not have legitimacy when it comes to teenage pregnancy.

In Steven's case, the group's track record did nothing to establish their knowledge or expertise on teenage suicide or suicide hotlines. Had Steven stopped there, that might have been the end of the story. However, he did not. Knowledge and expertise, after all, are learned. What you need is to be given the chance to learn. To be given the chance, two other sources of legitimacy can work, at least for a time.

*Do you have a record of success?* Steven's group did have experience raising money and organizing teen volunteers for fund-raising efforts. While these activities were not on a scale required for the hotline, they did demonstrate that the group could set a goal and achieve it.

- *Past accomplishment.* Groups that routinely succeed in one area will usually be given a chance to succeed in another.
- *Pattern of success.* It is not enough to have succeeded at something. People must expect you to succeed in whatever you try.

We see the importance of past accomplishment all the time. When student leaders want to get something done, they usually turn to people who have accomplished things in the past. That is why some students' time is overcommitted while others are never asked to do anything.

Past accomplishments are also relevant to groups. For many years the Nature Conservancy kept a low profile among environmental groups. The low profile helped the organization buy thousands of acres of land, which it turned into protected nature areas. However, when the group tried to expand into political action in the late 1980s, most people had never heard of it. However, the Nature Conservancy could establish a solid basis for legitimacy. "What organization has quietly bought up thousands of acres and protected them for future generations?" brochures asked. "The Nature Conservancy!" The message was simple and compelling. Here was a group that got things done! If you wanted to support a group like that, here was your chance.

While Steven's group had successfully raised money in the past, they had never attempted anything as complex as the effort they now envisioned. Their record established some legitimacy, but only some—perhaps not enough to get people to take them seriously when it came to the hotline effort. On the other hand, over the years the group had established another source of legitimacy: a reputation for being responsible and trustworthy.

Gaining legitimacy.

*Do people trust you?* Time and time again the youth group had demonstrated that it could be trusted to follow-through on commitments. Steven found that out when he talked with his parents.

As expected, Steven's parents were concerned about the group's ability to succeed. At the same time, they were surprisingly supportive. His father advised that they find out as much as they could about the suicide prevention programs in other cities. "If they can succeed with teenage volunteers, you can." He also praised the idea of working with the Teen Center. "They have a good reputation." If the Teen Center went along with the idea, most people in the community would see it as legitimate. Finally, his mother gave him a hug. "This is a very big project," she said. "It won't be easy. But you have always taken things like this seriously in the past. We trust you to be thoughtful about this."

When Steven talked with his pastor, he found that the group as a whole had established that kind of trust. The pastor was enthusiastic about the idea. He felt confident that the group would do a responsible job. That trust became an important part of the image the pastor later communicated to the director and board of the Teen Center.

- *Trust.* Although less powerful than either knowledge or accomplishment, trust is one of the most flexible sources of legitimacy. When people trust you, they will normally accept your right to work toward a variety of visions.
- *Does your group have a reputation for being dependable?* Do you routinely keep promises? Are you responsible and reliable?

Groups can establish a basic level of trust, and legitimacy, simply by creating a positive image of themselves. People trust the familiar. They assume the legitimacy of people and groups they recognize. However, trust based on familiarity has a weak foundation. It is easily lost if something brings your legitimacy into question.

**Is your group impartial or committed to the issue?** A group's track record can also establish two other bases of legitimacy that can be useful in certain situations: fairness and commitment. In a sense they are exact opposites.

- *Fairness.* A reputation for fairness will help groups that want to play a mediating or educational role. Fairness means that the group approaches issues with an open mind, willing to be convinced by the evidence and not by their preconceptions.

The League of Women Voters has a reputation for this kind of fairness. As a result, the group plays a critical role in many communities at election time. Both politicians and citizens see them as a nonpartisan source of information about candidates and issues.

- *Commitment.* The opposite of fairness is commitment. A group that seems willing to make incredible sacrifices to accomplish its goal can earn a great deal of legitimacy.

You may or may not agree with a committed group's goals or ideas, but you often cannot help but respect their commitment. Issue groups like Amnesty International, the antinuclear movement, and groups on both sides of the abortion issue are examples. These groups may or may not impress you with their knowledge. At the same time, you accept their legitimacy because they obviously care so much about their cause.
Neither of these sources of legitimacy was particularly relevant to

Steven's group. The suicide hotline did require commitment. However, like knowledge, commitment must be specific to an issue. Even if the youth group had demonstrated its commitment to religious causes, that would not necessarily demonstrate commitment to the suicide hotline. In fact, it could do the opposite. People might fear that a group committed to religious causes would use the suicide hotline to further its religious goals.

### Look at Your Membership

Even groups that have no track record may have a basis for legitimacy if they have members. A group's membership can be a source of legitimacy in two ways. First, the members may have individual track records that establish legitimacy. Second, the members taken together may be a source of power in dealing with an issue, or they may have a special stake in the issue.

***Do your members have good track records?*** When Steven looked at the youth group's members, he found some surprising things. Unknown to him, five of the members were already active with the Teen Center. All five had reputations as likable people and dependable volunteers. When he talked with the director of the Teen Center, he found that his pastor was also known and respected by the Teen Center board. The pastor and the Teen Center volunteers gave the group what is called the "halo effect." The group as a whole was taken more seriously because the board respected these people.

- *Association—the halo effect.* Groups, like individuals, are judged by the friends they keep. If members and supporters have legitimacy, the group itself gains legitimacy.

Even if the group has not established legitimacy through its track record, members may have. Individual members may have gained knowledge or expertise working with other organizations. They may be widely recognized for success on important projects, they may be highly trusted, or they may have reputations for fairness or commitment. It is not necessary for these people to be famous. They simply need to be seen as legitimate by those people whose support you need!

Community organizations routinely use the halo effect to establish their legitimacy. They often recruit an honorary board of trustees made up of respected or powerful people. These trustees may never become active in the organization. But by serving on the Honorary Board, they lend their legitimacy to the group.

*Do you have special resources or power?* The members of Steven's group might have contributed legitimacy to the group in another way had Steven thought about it. They might have been a source of power.

- *Power.* Power is the ability to influence events or to make things happen. Groups that have power gain legitimacy because they can credibly promise future accomplishments.

Groups can establish that they have power in many different ways. Powerful individuals can lend their power to the group. For example, one of the members of Steven's parish was also the head of a local charitable foundation. If that individual supported the project and could promise money for training volunteers and hiring professional supervisors, the youth group's legitimacy would have been much greater in the eyes of the Teen Center board. This kind of power is different from and more useful than the halo effect. It is not just the association of the individual that is important. It is his ability to give the group resources which it needs to get the job done.

The group's overall membership can also be a source of power—and legitimacy. Steven's group was relatively small. However, if it had been large, its size could have ensured that the suicide hotline would have plenty of volunteers. This too would have raised the group's legitimacy in the eyes of the Teen Center because the group's chances of success would be greater. Large groups do not always have more power than small groups, but they usually do.

*Do you have a stake in the issue?* Steven's group had one last important source of legitimacy to draw upon: their stake in the issue. As teenagers they could claim to be close to the problem of teenage suicide. It was their friends whom the hotline would serve. They could understand the problems other teens faced. As he explored suicide hotlines in other cities, Steven found that this was one of the best reasons for using teenage volunteers.

- *Stake in the issue.* How does the issue affect people like your members? Do they have a special stake in how it is resolved, in whether it is resolved?

In our democratic society, people who are affected by an issue usually have the legitimacy needed to act on it. They may not get exactly what they want, but other people almost always accept their right to participate.

The young Americans who protested against the war in Vietnam ultimately gained legitimacy in this way. They were the ones who were fighting and dying. Since they bore the chief burden of the war, they claimed a right to be heard when policy was shaped. That right was eventually recognized despite their lack of expertise. It was a major reason why 18-year-olds were given the right to vote.

There are many less dramatic examples of how a group's stake in an issue gives them legitimacy. Traffic engineers building a road may not think of asking people in the area what they think—until those people demand to be heard. Then the engineers will be hard-pressed to ignore them. They may even look for ways to change their plans to meet some of the group's concerns.

If you do establish legitimacy on the basis of your stake in an issue, however, do not rest on your laurels. Having a stake and being able to do something constructive are two different things. An initial grant of legitimacy based on your stake in the issue will last only so long. It will disappear quickly if you fail to deliver!

## ADDING TO THE GROUP'S LEGITIMACY

Legitimacy is like money in the bank. The more accomplishments or power a group has, the greater its legitimacy will be. A group can have more or less knowledge, it can have built up more or less trust, it can even have a greater or a lesser stake in an issue. A group cannot have too much legitimacy: it can only have too little. As a result, most groups continuously look for ways to add to their legitimacy.

### Recruit for Legitimacy

One of the easiest ways to add to a group's legitimacy is to attract members or supporters who give the group additional legitimacy. Steven

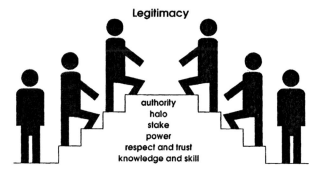

Build legitimacy on as solid and diverse a foundation as possible.

did not consider looking for new members for the youth group, but it happened anyway.

Soon after talking with his pastor about the suicide hotline, Steven heard from Kristen, whose family had just joined the parish. Kristen had been involved in a suicide prevention program in another city. She hoped to become involved in something similar again. The pastor had told her of Steven's efforts.

Kristen proved to be a valuable source of information when the group did its planning. She was even more valuable when it was time to talk with the board of the Teen Center. Her obvious knowledge and experience added considerably to the group's legitimacy.

- Recruit new members with legitimacy in mind. If you need knowledge, recruit people who have knowledge. If you need power, recruit people who have power. Recruit people whose halo effect adds to the legitimacy of the group.
- Just increasing the size of the group can add legitimacy since the number of members can be a source of group power.
- When you recruit for legitimacy be flexible. Advisers (like Steven's pastor), benefactors, or just "friends" of the group can all add to the group's legitimacy, not just members!

New groups sometimes experience a "chicken and egg" problem when it comes to recruiting members to gain legitimacy. Some people with legitimacy will decline your invitation if your group is unknown to them. Persistence can be important in these cases. Even if people reject the invitation at first, keep trying. Eventually someone with legitimacy will accept. When she does, or when the group has accomplished something—no matter how small—go back to the people who rejected your invitation at first. You may be able to turn a no into a yes once you have some basis for legitimacy.

### Expand Your Track Record

Ultimately the best way to add to your group's legitimacy is to build the kind of track record that creates trust: a record of accomplishment and relevant knowledge or expertise. You should build this track record with everything you do.

Steven's group realized this as they began to create support for the suicide hotline. Their pastor played a key role in persuading the Teen Center board to consider their proposal. However, it was the group's proposal itself that persuaded the board to take them seriously. The board was impressed with the work they had done to get solid information about other suicide hotlines. The youth group's subsequent help in fundraising, and its success in providing an initial core of volunteers, firmly established its legitimacy.

- When a group tries to build a track record, it should start with easy projects. They will help you build a foundation of knowledge and skill as well as a track record of accomplishment and trust.
- See every action, no matter how small, as part of your track record. Every action is part of the medium if not the message that communicates your image and your legitimacy to outsiders.

### Establish Authority

For any group, the ultimate source of legitimacy is authority.

- *Authority.* Authority is the right to make and implement decisions. It is the strongest but also the least available source of legitimacy.

Authority gives a group an assumed legitimacy which people outside the group rarely question. Student government has this kind of legitimacy. People accept its right to speak on virtually any issue that affects students because of its authority. If another organization gains the legitimacy to speak on behalf of the student body, it normally does so because of its track record and power—and because the student government has somehow defaulted on its right to speak for the students.

Any group can gain legitimacy based on authority over a specific issue or program. In Steven's case, the Teen Center could get authority to operate a suicide hotline from the city council. Once that authority was given, the Teen Center would be consulted on any activity related to teen suicide. Furthermore, if another group tried to establish a competing hotline, it would have a hard time gaining legitimacy for the effort.

Similarly, a school's International Club may be given authority to plan Earth Day activities by the student government or the principal. Unless that authority is taken away, most people will accept the club's right to plan the activities. Unless the club totally fails and Earth Day becomes a disaster, other groups will not usurp the club's rights. They may ignore the event, but they will not challenge the legitimacy that comes with authority.

### Protect the Legitimacy You Have

Benjamin Franklin once said that a penny saved is a penny earned. In a sense, legitimacy protected is also legitimacy gained. While adding to a group's legitimacy is always a good idea, it is even more important that group leaders protect the legitimacy that the group already has.

Every time you say or do anything in public, you and your group invest a little of your legitimacy. If the investment is successful, you gain additional legitimacy by adding to your track record. If it is unsuccessful, your overall legitimacy declines. If your investments never succeed, you can end up with no legitimacy at all.

There are many ways in which groups can lose legitimacy.

- People who fail to keep promises lose legitimacy by showing that they cannot be trusted.
- When past accomplishments are followed by a series of failures, you lose legitimacy because people begin to doubt that you will succeed in the future.
- People who have legitimacy based on knowledge cannot afford to be too wrong too often, or they will no longer be seen as legitimate.

After Kristen became involved in the suicide hotline project, she did much to protect as well as to establish the group's legitimacy. When a reporter from the local newspaper showed up at a meeting, Steven had Kristen answer most of the questions. She could deal with the practical issues more confidently and knowledgeably than Steven. Even though Kristen's name appeared more than Steven's in the final story, the group's legitimacy benefitted from putting her up front.

Even legitimacy based on so solid a source as authority can be lost. If a new teacher does not know his subject, teaches poorly, or grades unfairly, he will lose the legitimacy that comes with the role of teacher. If a government fails to meet the expectations of its people, it can lose the compliance and loyalty that come with legitimacy. The breakdown of communist governments in Eastern Europe in 1989 represented just such a loss of legitimacy. Those governments had consistently failed to meet the expectations of their people. Finally, the people had had enough. They not only stopped complying with government initiatives; they took to the streets to demand change.

# 9

## Advocacy

Michelle looked nervously at the noisy crowd. Advocacy was the part of the Youth Forums she hated. Dr. Bob said this was a good experience, but Michelle had her doubts.

Overall Michelle loved the forums. In the morning, small groups wrestled to reach a consensus on some foreign policy issue. This forum was about the North American Free Trade Agreement. Michelle felt her group had a great policy. In the afternoon, each small group had to advocate its policy to the entire assembly—over 100 students. Michelle knew that persuading the others to support her group would be hard, maybe impossible. But she was ready to try.

A respectful silence descended as Michelle took the microphone. Deep inside she knew that her opponents were sharpening their knives.

### THE USE AND MISUSE OF ADVOCACY

Everyone plays the role of advocate at one time or another. You use advocacy to convince your parents to give you money for a concert or to convince your friends to go to a particular movie. In other words, advocacy is a kind of persuasion. An advocate tries to move people to support his or her ideas or plans. Advocacy is a critical leadership skill. But there are times when advocacy is inappropriate.

### Advocates Hurt Group Decision-making

Most of us have argued for an idea within a group. That is fine as long as we keep an open mind to alternatives and encourage others to help shape and improve our ideas. In fact, a "devil's advocate"—someone who argues for an idea to get the group to take it seriously—can help a group make better decisions.

However, genuine advocacy contributes nothing to good decision-making. The value of group decisions lies in their ability to uncover hidden information and create new options. Advocacy does the opposite. Advocates want you to accept their ideas, not discuss them. They present solutions, not options. Advocates do not use disagreement to spur creativity; they oppose and discredit opposing ideas. In short, advocates are not *looking for* the best answer. They *already have* the best answer, and they want others to accept it.

### Advocacy Is Needed to Gain Support

The primary value of advocacy lies in relations with people outside the group. Advocacy becomes critical when the group needs the support of nonmembers.

When a group reaches to the outside community it often encounters people who reject its legitimacy or its ideas. It routinely encounters people who simply need to be persuaded to support it. After all, people outside the group have played no role in shaping its vision or goals.

### The Essentials of Advocacy

Leaders can be called on to use advocacy in a variety of settings and through a variety of media. They may meet with prominent people in one-on-one meetings or give interviews with news reporters. They may solicit support over the telephone or in meetings with small groups. Like Michelle, they may give presentations to large audiences. On the other hand, advocates may never see their audience. They may write letters to the editor or editorials. They may even advocate a group's vision or goals through posters or handbills.

These various settings and media all differ from each other. A leader who is skillful at one may find others next to impossible. At the same

Advocacy.

time, all these settings and media share some basic elements. Each requires that the advocate:

- Have a well-prepared argument;
- Understand how to appear personally appealing to an audience; and
- Know how to use the medium to relate to the audience.

The setting which poses the greatest challenge for most advocates is the one Michelle faced. At the Youth Forum Michelle had to speak to a large audience, of potentially hostile people, with little time for preparation. But the forums had taught Michelle some valuable lessons about advocacy.

## PREPARING YOUR ARGUMENT

Half the challenge of advocacy lies in preparing a compelling argument. At the Youth Forums Michelle had learned early on that:

- The heart of advocacy lies in answering the question, Why? You must give people reasons *why they should support you.*

Many inexperienced advocates merely describe *what* their ideas are. They never get to the question, Why? As a result they fail miserably.

At the forums, more experienced people like Michelle knew how to focus their arguments. They also knew that fashioning a compelling case was difficult. It required more than just good logic and a smooth delivery.

### Tailor Your Argument to the Audience

As an advocate your goal is to gain the audience's support. But you cannot make up their minds for them. To succeed you must appeal to them in a compelling way. To do that you must respond to the audience's specific concerns and needs.

This was difficult at the Youth Forums. Most of the students did not have deeply felt concerns about foreign policy. Yet, Michelle knew that the issues were related to students' concerns. In this case, the Free Trade

Agreement would have a great impact on jobs—both their parents' jobs now and their own jobs in the future. This was something about which her fellow students did care.

- You must address the concerns of your audience or you cannot hope to answer the challenges of your critics or calm the fears of your potential supporters.

The concerns of your audience may or may not be obvious. If you are talking to a neighborhood group about a proposed school project, you can assume they are concerned about its impact on the neighborhood. But people with children will have additional concerns that are not shared by people without children. To miss an important difference like this could lead to disaster just as surely as ignoring the audience's more obvious concerns!

**BLOOM COUNTY**                               **by Berke Breathed**

Advocates need to know their audience.
(© 1982, Washington Post Writers Group. Reprinted with permission.)

### Be Solid and Creative

Arguments can focus on the concerns and needs of the audience and still fail if they are not logically sound. Being logically sound depends on having the facts and putting them together in an effective way.

*Know and use the facts.* Michelle had learned that to be convincing she had to demonstrate that she knew what she was talking about. She had also learned that:

- Concrete information and examples do more than abstract concepts to demonstrate your knowledge and to buttress your arguments.

For the Free Trade Agreement, Michelle had figures that showed how the U.S. economy benefits from world trade. She could also show how much consumers would save if existing trade barriers were eliminated.
At the same time, Michelle had learned that:

- Facts can be overused. Most people find presentations that include too many facts confusing.

In her presentations, Michelle included just enough information to make her point without boring her audience with too much detail.
Finally, Michelle had learned the importance of knowing the facts that her opponents could use against her. For the Free Trade Agreement, she knew the estimates of how many jobs might be lost. These figures could have a big impact on her audience, so Michelle had decided to talk about them herself. That gave her a chance to raise questions about the data or to make counterarguments. In this case, she would indicate how many jobs might be gained and that the new jobs would involve higher skills than the lost jobs. In general, advocates must:

- Know and be prepared to respond to information that supports the arguments of others.

***Put ideas together effectively.*** Having all the facts in the world will not help if you put them together in a confusing, long-winded, or illogical way. Especially in settings like the forums, which involved impromptu public speaking.

- An advocate must be clear, concise, and logically consistent.

Michelle had heard a great many fuzzy arguments at the forums. She knew how unconvincing they were. She also knew how hard it could be to put together a clear and concise argument when an issue was complicated.
But Michelle was particularly sensitive to the danger of being self-contradictory. On more than one occasion, she had seen people put to-

gether really good arguments, only to lose it all by contradicting themselves when they answered questions.

- Even one self-contradictory statement can destroy the logic of an
  entire argument and cost you the support of an entire audience.

*Find a novel approach.* In many cases audiences that seem uncommitted are really looking for a reason to support the advocate. In these
cases the key to success can lie in finding a new way to look at your
argument.

At the Youth Forums, Michelle faced many people who remained
uncommitted to a policy, but who had been discussing the issue all day!
So she always asked her group to brainstorm new ways of presenting
their case. What kinds of arguments had the audience heard? How could
their argument be presented so that it looked new, different, or particularly insightful? She did not always find a novel approach, but time
spent looking for one was always well invested.

- If your audience has thought about the issue and remains uncommitted, you had better find a new way to present your case!

## Go Beyond Logic

Human beings are a jumble of logic, emotions, and ideals. To be
truly compelling, arguments usually must appeal to more than one side
of our nature. In many cases appeals to emotions or the relationship you
establish with your audience may be more important than facts and logic!

*Appeal to emotions, values, and needs.* In advocating her position
on the Free Trade Agreement, Michelle planned to appeal to her audience's emotions—to their hopes and fears for the future.

She would explain logically how much the United States depends on
free trade, but the real power of her argument would lie elsewhere. She
would paint a graphic picture of how her audience would be hurt without free trade—how they would find fewer jobs when they graduated,
how trade wars could result in hot wars, with young men dying on
distant battlefields.

- A message that appeals to emotions, ideals, hopes, fears, and needs has a better chance of gaining support than one based solely on logic.

## Human Nature

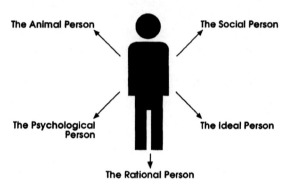

The Animal Person

The Social Person

The Psychological Person

The Ideal Person

The Rational Person

Advocates should appeal to many aspects of human nature.

*Establish a basis for rapport.* The Youth Forum also taught Michelle that appeals to emotions are not enough when you face a hostile audience. That was Michelle's greatest challenge. The other students had gone through a consensus-seeking process like hers, but they had come to different conclusions! While most might be uncommitted, some were now advocates for different policies. These people saw Michelle as an opponent. They were "inoculated" against her. They would listen only to find inconsistencies or to devise ways to defeat her.

Michelle cannot overcome this hostility completely. She can, however, mute it by establishing a rapport with her audience. The process begins with her argument. In her presentation she must establish a basis for common identity and common cause.

- If people see the advocate as somehow like them, they will want to agree if they can.

- People will also be more receptive if the advocate agrees with them about something relevant—even if that agreement involves only general principles.

Many things can be used to establish *common identity*. Michelle might remind her audience, "We are all students, so we understand each other!" or "We all live in this community, so we face the same problem here." In other cases, advocate and audience may have the same social or economic background. They may have worked in similar occupations. Even trivial things can establish a common identity with less hostile audiences. Do you all speak French? Have you all traveled to Greece? Have you all struggled with math?

- Weave examples of common identity throughout your argument. Tell stories about yourself or your group with which the audience can identify.

Michelle has an even better chance of breaking down her audience's resistance if she can establish *common cause*. At this forum, she decided to lead off her presentation by agreeing with her audience "that the real issue is jobs." She would agree that "a policy is only acceptable if it is in our best interest!" Establishing a common cause puts hostile people off-balance. They expect conflict, and here the advocate seems to be agreeing with them!

- The easiest way to establish common cause is to stress those points of your argument with which the audience already agrees.
- However, do not distort your argument to establish common cause. That could cost you the support of people who agree with you or who are uncommitted. Instead, establish common cause by appealing to some general, shared value.

Establishing a common identity and a common cause will usually not convince people who disagree with you. However, it can establish that you are a reasonable, well-meaning person. That may mute their hostility, and keep your chances of success alive.

## MAKING YOUR CASE

Adequately preparing yourself and your argument will lay a foundation for effective advocacy. But it will only lay the foundation. Even with good preparation, you must make your case effectively. Doing that will depend on your skill at using a particular medium. In face-to-face meetings, it also depends on your ability to:

- Establish a rapport with your audience,
- Deal with problems posed by the setting, and
- Stay cool in the face of attacks or interruptions.

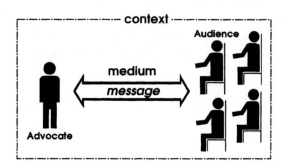

Advocates need to pay attention to every element of the communications cycle.

### Establish Rapport with the Audience

Establishing common identity and common cause with your audience creates a foundation for building an amiable relationship. Demonstrating that you know and care about their concerns adds to this foundation. However, an advocate must go beyond these things if she is to win support.

*Choose appropriate dress and style.* Most people want to believe advocates that they find attractive. But being attractive is not simply a question of being beautiful or handsome. It is largely a question of being appropriate, and it depends a lot on those superficial things, like dress and hairstyle, that create first impressions!

- Dress as formally or informally as your audience expects.
- Never dress less formally than your audience, or they may not take you seriously.

For the Youth Forums, Michelle had her mind on advocacy from the very start of the day. She picked out a dress that was nice but not too showy. She wanted people to notice her, but she did not want to distract them from what she said. Her haircut also said something about her personality, her tastes, and her values. She wanted them to say: "I am a reasonable person. I am someone you could like, someone you can trust and believe."

The Youth Forums also required Michelle to adjust her style of presentation. At the forums she had to give a formal speech. Michelle generally preferred a more informal style. Yet, she had learned the importance of interacting with her audience in a way that fit the setting. At her first forum, Michelle had tried to be very informal. She had simply stated her group's policy briefly and asked for questions. The strategy failed. Rather than establishing rapport with her audience, she lost control of the debate.

- When possible, choose or create a setting in which you are comfortable. That will allow you to pay more attention to your argument and unexpected things.
- If you cannot choose your setting, at least know what to expect beforehand and adjust your style to fit it. Be less formal in intimate settings or with small groups. Be more formal in large groups or with groups that expect formality.

Being too formal with small audiences or audiences that value informality makes you appear pompous and distant. With large audiences or audiences that expect more formal presentations, informality seems artificial or dishonest. In both cases you create a barrier between you and your audience rather than a rapport.

*Use your limits to build common identity.* One of the first lessons Michelle learned at the Youth Forums was to admit the limits of her knowledge. Some advocates try to trick audiences into believing that they know more than they do. That can work for a while, but beware. If you are caught in a lie, you will destroy any rapport you have established with your audience.

- People rarely expect an advocate to know everything. They will respect you for admitting your limits as long as you have command of the important issues.

There were, of course, times when people tried to use Michelle's lack of knowledge to embarrass her. At those times, recognizing the difference between important and peripheral issues was important. If people attacked her for not knowing peripheral facts, Michelle would politely say that the criticism was unfair—the issue raised was not the most important. *Then she would tell the audience what the really important questions were.* In the process she would get some sympathy for an unfair attack and demonstrate her knowledge of the core issues.

- If people challenge you because you admit ignorance of peripheral issues, use the attack to demonstrate your competence.

***Balance conviction and reason.*** Advocates are expected to hold firm on the essentials of their ideas. If you are talking primarily to people who already agree with you, the clearer and firmer your conviction the better. However, if you are talking to people who are uncertain, conviction must be balanced with reason or it can be a little frightening.

- Listen to your audience. If people question your position, build bridges to them as individuals but do not compromise or waver on your position. Show that you have considered the alternatives with an open mind, but have rejected them.

### Adjust to the Unexpected

Advocates who fumble around trying to find the next page of their speech are not convincing. Nor are advocates who know they have that information—but cannot find it right now.

- Experienced advocates always organize themselves and their materials to ensure that they have everything they need to back up their argument. They know exactly where things are so they can find them in an instant. No matter how well you prepare, however, you must be ready for surprises.

In fact, the purpose of a thorough preparation is not to give you a rigid plan. Rather it is to put you in a better position to adjust confidently when the unexpected does occur.

In public speaking, the unexpected generally takes one of three forms:

- An unexpected problem with the setting,
- An interruption, or
- Attacks from people who disagree with you.

In all three cases, if you react well, you can turn a difficult situation to your advantage.

*Adjust to the audience's physical state.* How people respond to an advocate will depend as much on their physical state as on the logical and emotional qualities of the argument. Advocates need to pay attention to their audience and the context and adjust accordingly.

At the forums, Michelle gave different kinds of presentations depending on the order in which she spoke. There were usually six speakers at the forums. If she were one of the first, the audience would be alert and interested. Her arguments would have to be good. If she were the third or fourth speaker, people would be getting tired. She would have to do something dramatic to get their attention and be remembered. If she were one of the last speakers, people would be restive. They would be more interested in going home than in listening to her. Appealing to emotions and ideals would be far more important than emphasizing facts or logic.

Michelle had the benefit of knowing how timing affected her audience. But in any situation you can tell how your audience feels by looking for nonverbal cues. If heads nod in agreement and questions are supportive, you know people are listening to the arguments. If eyelids droop or people fidget in their chairs, you need to find a more dramatic approach.

- If an audience has been sitting for a long time, invite them to get up and move around.
- If their attention is flagging, shorten and simplify your argument. Try to be more dynamic or shift to a more emotional appeal.

*Use a poor setting to build rapport.* An audience's physical state may, of course, depend on the setting itself. Youth Forums were usually held in a school auditorium. The chairs were uncomfortable, the lighting poor, the room either too hot or too cold. Michelle had little control over these things, but she had learned that she could use them to her advantage.

- If your audience is uncomfortable, try to do something about it. People are more likely to support an advocate who cares about them.

If you can do nothing about the problem, use it to establish a common cause.

- Portray the situation as something with which both you and the audience are struggling—"We have all been sitting here long enough."
- Sympathize with the audience and note your efforts to change things.
- Do not try to blame the problem on someone else, but never apologize for it yourself.

If you apologize, you accept responsibility. You give the audience permission to blame you. No advocate needs the added burden of being responsible for the audience's discomfort.

***Go with the flow if interrupted.*** Interruptions pose a problem because they distract the audience's attention from the advocate and her argument. Michelle may be building a strong, emotional appeal. But if a teacher's chair breaks in the back of the room, her audience's attention shifts to the comic image of the teacher on the floor. All the power of Michelle's argument is lost.

Michelle cannot totally recover from this kind of interruption. But she must regain the audience's attention and reestablish the flow of the argument as quickly as possible. That can be very difficult if the audience is uncomfortable or tired.

The best way to recapture an audience's attention is to make a joke about the interruption. After the teacher's chair breaks, Michelle should let the initial surprise wear off and say something like "People have disagreed with me before, but this is going too far!"

- A joke gives the audience both a chance and a reason to refocus their attention on the advocate. Just asking them to settle down or simply proceeding will give them the opportunity but not a reason.
- The joke also builds a bridge between the interruption and the argument. It literally takes the audience's thoughts from the interruption and leads them back to the discussion.

By turning the interruption into a joke, Michelle could regain control of the situation. More importantly, she could establish her competence as an advocate. That makes her even more credible.

*Use attacks to create sympathy.* Hostility, especially emotional attacks and heckling, poses the most difficult problem for any advocate. How you respond can strengthen your appeal or weaken it.

- In the face of a hostile question or emotional attack, stay calm. Try to project self-assurance and self-control.
- If the audience dislikes the attacker or her position, a strong verbal counterattack will show your strength and resolve.
- If the audience sympathizes with the attacker, it is better to hold your ground politely and hope for the best. If the attack continues long enough or if the attacker gets too hostile, most audiences will begin to sympathize with you.
- If a hostile question catches you off-guard, ask a question in reply. That will give you time to collect your thoughts. Do not, however, yield the floor to the attacker. Ask for clarification, not a defense.
- Another way to respond to hard or harassing questions is to answer a related question of your own choosing. Suggest that the attacker's question does not get at the real issue, and then ask your own question.

You can salvage your credibility if the audience believes the attacker does not know what he or she is talking about! When you are under attack, your goal is to get the audience to feel that you have been abused but have handled it well. Never create a situation in which the audience feels sorry for the attacker! No matter how difficult things may seem, keep in mind the "enigma of advocacy."

## The Enigma of Advocacy

The people who pose the greatest challenge to the advocate are those who disagree, especially those who are hostile. These people tend to be the most vocal. They are the ones who object to your ideas or who propose alternative ways of looking at the issue. In this sense, they are the most important part of the advocate's audience.

However, people who disagree with you are also the least likely to be persuaded by anything you say! In terms of the advocate's goal, the most important part of the audience are those who are uncertain and those who want to agree with you.

- *As an advocate you spend most of your time worrying about and talking to people who disagree with you. But the people to whom you are really talking are those who are uncertain or who already agree!*

No matter how good an advocate you are, people who disagree with you are still likely to disagree after the encounter. On the other hand, if you do a reasonable job, people who already agree will be strengthened in their support. You may even win the support of people who were uncertain. But you can do a *reasonable job* only by dealing successfully with the objections of those who disagree!

That is why muting the hostility of an audience is so important. You may not get hostile people to agree with you. But if they are off-balance, you have a better chance of making a compelling case in the eyes of the others.

# 10

## Coalition-building

Groups create images, gain legitimacy, and advocate their ideas in order to attract supporters. Unfortunately, groups cannot always get enough support. Sometimes the best planned images and the most skillful advocacy simply do not work. Sometimes even a powerful group cannot achieve its vision working alone. In these cases, groups turn to a final method for gaining outside support: coalition-building.

Coalitions are "groups of groups." Most communities have coalitions. The United Way is a coalition of social service agencies that joined together to raise money. In many communities an arts council does the same thing for groups like the symphony and the opera. A metropolitan church board may bring together the different religious denominations.

Coalitions even exist within schools. When the Spanish Club at Fulton High School (Chapter 7) set out to organize Spanish Week, they put together a coalition of groups concerned about the school's racial problems. In the process they learned a lot about the problems and pitfalls of coalition-building.

### LOOK BEFORE YOU LEAP

Groups often need to cooperate with each other to meet common needs or to achieve common goals. However, even coalitions with solid purposes and committed members can prove frustratingly difficult to create

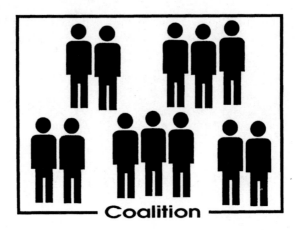

Coalitions are groups whose members are groups.

and maintain. No group should create or join a coalition without first assessing the need and the chances for success.

### Does the Coalition Meet Real Needs?

When the Spanish Club began thinking about Spanish Week, the idea of a coalition arose naturally. If Spanish Week were to become a schoolwide effort to deal with the school's racial tensions, other groups had to be involved in the planning. So the club decided to organize Spanish Week through a special Planning Committee, made up of representatives from the different student groups.

Marcia at first argued that every group in the school should be invited to join the Planning Committee. Mr. Cherry urged a more cautious approach. "Do you need all the groups?" he asked. "Might it make more sense to invite only the ones you really need?"

The club accepted Mr. Cherry's advice. The slide presentation would encourage all groups to find ways to do something about the school's racial problems. Decisions about whom to involve in the Planning Committee would come later.

*The hazards of coalitions.* Mr. Cherry's deliberate approach was a good one. As part of a coalition, groups often invest considerable time and energy in an effort over which they have limited control. That can lead to real problems:

- By taking up time and energy, coalitions make it harder for member groups to get other business done.
- Coalitions can hurt the image of a group or compromise its legitimacy if the effort fails or if other coalition members act improperly.
- Coalitions can compete with member groups for outside support.

*Judge the balance between costs and benefits.* Because coalitions can be risky, you must be sure that the potential benefits outweigh the probable costs. How will the coalition help your group? What are you expected to contribute to the coalition? Are the benefits worth the price?

For the Spanish Club, the need for a coalition seemed obvious. However, the decision to join the coalition was quite difficult for groups like the Radio Club. The Radio Club had no direct interest in Spanish culture or in international affairs. Even the school's racial problems were only of indirect interest because they had never touched club members directly. However, when Marcia and Brock gave their presentation, the Radio Club members strongly agreed that something needed to be done. When they were invited to join the Planning Committee, Radio Club leaders had to look seriously at the opportunity.

The question for the Radio Club was whether the costs of participating on the Planning Committee and organizing some activity for Spanish Week would be worth the possible benefits. The only direct benefits would be greater visibility and legitimacy within the school. Those benefits, however, were important. Very few people in the school knew about the Radio Club. Fewer still cared. The club always had trouble raising money for projects. Being part of Spanish Week might help, especially if the club did something really spectacular.

For the Radio Club, the costs of the coalition were certain. The benefits were only possible. Despite the risk, the Radio Club decided to join. They judged that the potential benefits were worth the costs, in part because they saw no better way to get the visibility and legitimacy they needed.

- The process of judging costs and benefits does not need to be precise, but it should be explicit.

Even a general sense of the costs, the benefits, and the balance between them can help you make a more reasoned decision about creating or joining a coalition.

## The Building Blocks of Successful Coalitions

In putting together the Planning Committee, the Spanish Club looked at several points that were important to successful coalitions:

- The commitment and competence of the organizing group;
- The compatibility and commitment of member groups; and
- The size of the coalition.

***Judge the coalition by its organizer.*** Coalitions can succeed only if an organizing group is both committed to and capable of making the coalition work.

Marcia was surprised when Mr. Cherry insisted on asking whether there was a committed, capable organizer for Spanish Week. After all, the Spanish Club was the organizer. However, when Mr. Cherry explained what he meant, the question made a great deal of sense.

- The organizing group must be willing to invest enough of its own time and energy into the effort to ensure success even if coalition partners prove unreliable.
- The organizing group must have the skills and legitimacy to make the coalition work.

The commitment of the Spanish Club seemed solid. While the decision to create a coalition had not been a conscious one at first, the effort seemed quite necessary now. Spanish Week was essential to the club, and there was no other way to make it succeed.

The club's ability to organize the coalition was another matter. Did the Spanish Club have the resources, skills, and legitimacy to make the coalition work? The club was small. Did it have the people needed to carry on the burden of the coalition if other groups failed to fulfill their commitments? The Spanish Club had no experience with coalitions. Were its leaders skillful enough at advocacy, negotiation, and consensus-seeking? Could they hold the coalition together and keep it working smoothly? Finally, the image and legitimacy of the Spanish Club had improved, but were they strong enough to lead a schoolwide coalition?

The Spanish Club decided to go ahead with the project despite these questions. However, they did so with their eyes open. Furthermore, by making the decision in this way, the group was forced to make *an ex-*

*plicit commitment to the coalition.* That proved valuable to Marcia and Brock, who represented the Spanish Club on the Planning Committee.

• Individuals who organize coalitions should always get an explicit, enthusiastic commitment from their own group. Do not take on the responsibility of coalition leadership unless you know your own group is behind the effort.

Coalition-building.

*Look for compatibility.* Once they had decided to go ahead, the Spanish Club began to look for suitable coalition partners. Mr. Cherry suggested three criteria. The first was compatibility. Compatible members make coalitions run more smoothly. But what does compatibility mean?

• Compatibility comes from having a common interest in the coalition. Even similar groups that have no common interest in the coalition may not be compatible.

To the Spanish Club, the French Club seemed a natural coalition partner. Marcia had been unable to arrange a presentation, but she had talked with Rachael, a friend who was in the club. Rachael wanted to get involved, and the French Club seemed compatible enough. It was, after all, a language club.

Unfortunately, the French Club was not compatible. Once the Planning Committee started, the French Club representatives caused nothing but trouble. They were against everything. Finally they insisted that the coalition change the focus of Spanish Week. They wanted to have an International Festival so that their activities could emphasize French culture and language! The proposal was rejected by the Planning Committee, and the French Club contributed little to the coalition thereafter.

Coalition partners can have diverse goals. In fact, every coalition partner asks itself the same questions: What are we putting into this coalition? What are we getting out of it? And each group has a different answer, at least in part. To be compatible, however, they must all accept the basic goals or purposes of the coalition. The French Club was interested in doing something about the school's racial problems. However, they had no interest in the primary purpose of the coalition: to organize Spanish Week.

***Look for commitment.*** Mr. Cherry's second criterion in looking at possible coalition partners was commitment. Even compatible coalition partners may do little to help the coalition unless they are genuinely committed to it. Groups often say they value the goals of the coalition so they will not be left out. Once inside, however, they feel no need to accomplish anything.

You can have confidence in the commitment of a coalition partner only if:

- The group must actively participate in order to achieve its goals, and
- The group has made an explicit decision to support the coalition.

The Radio Club proved to be a committed member for precisely these reasons. The Spanish Club had taken a calculated risk with the Radio Club. Everyone knew the Radio Club was drawn to the coalition primarily to gain visibility and legitimacy. What made the risk reasonable was the fact that *the Radio Club had to be active to get the visibility and legitimacy it wanted!*

Marcia and Brock did not know that the Radio Club had also gone the extra step. Club leaders had asked the club to make a consensus decision about joining the coalition. That gave the club an opportunity to sort out its options and to make sure that joining the coalition was the right thing to do.

In the end the risk paid off. The representatives of the Radio Club were model members of the Planning Committee. Moreover, during Spanish Week the Radio Club helped organize a workshop, Communicating across Cultures. They also set up a radio link during lunch hour with a club in Venezuela and let students talk to people there.

*Create the smallest coalition needed.* Mr. Cherry's last criterion surprised many of the Spanish Club members:

- Coalitions should be just as large as they need to be, and not one group larger.

When a group organizes a coalition for the first time, it naturally tends to aim big. Having more members means having more resources. Unfortunately, having more members also means having more trouble. Simply giving everyone a say is more difficult with ten members than five. The problems involved in making decisions grow exponentially larger as the number of participants rises.

- In general the question of *how large* a coalition should be is best answered by asking *which groups are needed to make the coalition a success.*

If the coalition's purpose is to make international clubs more visible, then the cooperation of all or most of the clubs with international interests may be desirable. If the coalition's purpose is to raise money to aid the victims of some disaster, then a few large groups may be quite enough.

In the case of Spanish Week, a few groups might have been enough if those groups were able to organize a week-long program of workshops and special events. Other groups could be invited to participate without necessarily being invited to be part of the Planning Committee. Unfortunately for the Spanish Club, one of the groups that seemed necessary to the coalition, the Student Council, was one of the greatest problems.

Spanish Week was supposed to begin a long-term, schoolwide effort to deal with the school's racial problems. If that goal were to be achieved, the Student Council had to be involved. It was the only group that could give the effort legitimacy and continuity.

But involving the Student Council posed a problem. The Spanish Club had no intention of turning Spanish Week over to another group, but could the Student Council be just a member of the coalition? In fact, representatives from the Student Council proved difficult at first because they thought they should be in charge of the project. They constantly competed with Marcia—who chaired the Planning Committee. They raised trivial objections to everything. Only when the effort seemed about to fail did the council members finally begin to play a more authentic leadership role.

In one sense the Student Council was one group too many for the coalition. In another sense, however, the Spanish Club had made the right decision. If the long-term goal of the project were to be achieved, a coalition without the Student Council would have been one group too small.

- Coalitions should be kept as small as possible. At the same time, they must include all the groups necessary to achieve their goals.

## Be Part of the Action

How can you know which groups may be compatible, or what benefits a group is trying to gain from a coalition? One way is to ask. The Spanish Club used their presentations to look for good coalition partners. They described the school's racial problem, invited groups to get involved, and listened for reactions.

A more effective way to know what is going on, however, is to be part of the action.

- The most effective coalition-builders are those people who are in constant contact with people of other groups—especially groups with similar visions and goals.

Being a part of formal and informal communication networks provides a lot of useful information. As a potential coalition organizer, you can learn what different groups do and why. You will know what a group can offer a coalition. You can find out which groups get along, and which groups do not. As a potential coalition member, you can learn which groups have the skills and legitimacy to be organizers. You will also become known to potential coalition organizers. That may create valuable opportunities in the future.

## MAKING THE COALITION WORK

Putting together a workable coalition is unfortunately only the prelude to coalition-building. Once you have a coalition, no matter how good it looks on paper, you still face the often daunting task of making it work.

Making a coalition work requires the same skills any group does. Coalitions must have a shared sense of purpose, so envisioning is required. Coalitions must make decisions and resolve conflicts, so consensus-seeking and negotiation are needed. Coalitions must get individuals to work together, so it is necessary to create rewards. However, the skill of coalition-building requires more, as the Spanish Club found out when the Planning Committee began to meet.

### Representation Creates Obstacles

Coalitions have special problems because they are groups of groups. The individuals who work in a coalition do not act on their own behalf. They represent other people, and as a result they usually behave differently than they would if acting on their own:

- In coalitions people must judge things not only by what is best for the coalition, but by what is best for their group.
- Representatives make decisions as if someone were looking over their shoulder. So they usually make conservative decisions.

Representatives try to avoid actions that may be criticized by their group. When in doubt, it becomes easier to say no. An opportunity lost is easier to blame on others than a disaster which you supported! Because representatives behave in these ways, coalitions can be very frustrating.

Marcia and Brock, who represented the Spanish Club on the Planning Committee, saw these problems clearly in the behavior of the other representatives. The Planning Committee seemed to talk endlessly without ever agreeing on anything. Every little detail seemed important to someone! Most people seemed more interested in protecting their group than in making Spanish Week a success.

But Marcia and Brock also appreciated what the other representatives faced. They had problems of their own. Fearful that the Planning Group would fail, or that someone would do something to hurt the Spanish

Club's hard-earned image, some club members insisted on reviewing every detail. That made it impossible for Marcia or Brock to make commitments at Planning Committee meetings!

### Let Groups Support the Coalition Their Way

Coalition leaders can help representatives gain a freer hand in the coalition by making sure that support for the coalition remains strong in member groups. In most member groups there will be some disagreement about the coalition. Some people will support it; others will not. Just which group is stronger will depend on two things:

- Is the group satisfying its needs and achieving its goals through the coalition?
- Are these benefits balancing the costs of participation?

If the balance between costs and benefits is meeting or exceeding expectations, you help and encourage the people who want to be involved. If the costs are too great or the benefits too small, you undercut your allies and create new pressures on the group's representative.

The best way to keep costs and benefits in balance is to find or create different ways for coalition members to support the effort. Representatives must be allowed to do things:

- Which require only the level of effort their groups are willing to support, and
- Which let the group achieve the goals it has set for itself within the coalition.

Coalitions with complex projects or long-term goals have an easy time doing this. An activity like Spanish Week was ideal. Many different activities were relevant. The Radio Club's link with people in Venezuela fit the theme of the week and showcased the club's unique skills and interests! The Student Council involved students in envisioning their preferred school in order to start organizing peer pressure against violence and racism. The school newspaper ran a series of articles on the contributions of Hispanic-Americans—including blacks who had grown up within Hispanic cultures. As long as an activity contributed to the basic theme, groups could define their involvement to suit their needs and capabilities.

• Allow coalition members to identify ways they can be supportive. Encourage creativity. Be genuinely open to the ideas they suggest.

Giving coalition members the opportunity to be creative is a must. The French Club did not want to put its efforts into a "Spanish" Week. However, it might have been possible to keep and increase their support by letting them propose some additional project. After all, Spanish Week was only the beginning of a long-term effort to deal with the school's racial problems. Inviting the French Club to take a leadership role in a next step might have silenced their objections to Spanish Week and encouraged them to support the coalition in the long run.

## Stroke and Stroke Again

You also help maintain group interest in a coalition by ensuring that individuals and groups get the recognition they deserve.

• Coalition members (individual representatives and their home groups) need to feel appreciated, particularly if their commitment is low or the resources they provide are important.

Showing your appreciation for, or "stroking," a group becomes especially important in times of conflict. When things get rough, a coalition member always has the option of leaving. If the group provides a critical resource, a little stroking will be absolutely necessary.

Marcia often got angry with John and Anna, the Student Council representatives on the Planning Committee. But she also knew she needed them. She could not let them take over the Planning Committee, which is what they wanted, but she could stroke them. She frequently talked with John and Anna after meetings. She let them know how important the Student Council was to the effort.

When the French Club suggested changing the theme of Spanish Week, Anna and John were their biggest supporters. Anna had almost shouted at Brock when he spoke out strongly against the idea. Afterward Marcia talked with Anna and asked her what was really important: doing something about racial tensions at the school or pushing aside the Spanish

Club? She noted that the whole Planning Committee would fall apart if Anna and John kept opposing everything. She needed their support. She also pointed out that the Student Council was the key to going forward in the future. It would have to take a leadership role after Spanish Week. The crisis helped clear the air. Anna and John saw their own role in a new light and became far more cooperative.

Stroking does not always smooth over conflicts and keep a coalition on track. But it is amazing just how important it can be.

### Respond to Dissatisfactions

Conflicts avoided are almost always less damaging to coalitions than conflicts resolved. Coalition leaders need to keep in constant touch with members, listening for dissatisfaction.

- Take informal soundings to find out whether members are satisfied with what is happening or problems are emerging.
- If you uncover dissatisfaction, do not jump to the defense of the coalition. Listen with empathy. Try to agree, even if you cannot act. Let the dissatisfied group know you hear, understand, and will *try* to do something if you can.

Coalition members are often jealous partners. They compare the benefits they receive with the benefits that others get. The need to respond to dissatisfactions is particularly great if a group feels it is not being treated fairly.

It is not necessary to treat all coalition partners the same. Some groups give more to the coalition than others. However, if a group feels it is not being treated fairly, it means their costs now exceed their benefits. If you want to keep the group in the coalition, you must find a way to restore that balance.

### Do Not Compete with Member Groups

The Planning Committee for Spanish Week did not face one last problem that confronts most active and successful coalitions. The more active the coalition and the longer it stays in existence, the greater the risk that it will begin to compete with member groups.

*Do not duplicate the work of members.* One of the most threatening things a coalition can do is try to take over the activities of its members!

A few years ago, the international groups in a large midwestern community decided to create an International Center. The center was supposed to allow the groups to meet basic needs such as photocopying more efficiently. In the long run it was hoped that the center would help the groups work together and get more visibility in the community. As she looked for ways to get the groups working together, the director of the new International Center decided to publish a *Directory of International Groups*. The *Directory* would increase visibility and be a service to the coalition. Unfortunately, one of the member groups was already publishing a directory! When the coalition tried to take over the effort, the threatened group not only objected but began to undermine the joint effort.

Assess all coalition plans or projects in the light of what members are doing. If a proposed activity is something a member group is currently doing or wants to do on its own, leave it alone. The best activities for coalitions are things that:

- Member groups would like to see done,
- They do not want to do themselves, and
- They do not want other member groups to do on their own.

*Keep the coalition in the background.* Coalitions can also compete with their member groups for the attention and support of outsiders. This inevitably happens if the coalition begins to conduct activities in its own name, rather than on behalf of its members.

There is nothing wrong with having ambitious plans for a coalition. Coalition leaders only get into trouble when their plans become more important than preserving the commitment and interests of member groups. Coalition leaders should always:

- Put the member groups, not the coalition, in the limelight, and
- Prevent outsiders from seeing the coalition as a group in its own right rather than as a cooperative effort among the member groups.

When the coalition does some project or activity, use it as an opportunity to promote the member groups. Keep the coalition in the background. In general the most successful coalitions try to be as invisible as possible. If you put the coalition up front, you inevitably lay the foundation for conflict.

### Persist until Trust Grows

Finally, making a coalition work requires considerable trust. Representatives can only work together if they believe that no one will take advantage of them or their group. Building trust takes time. It also requires that people have the opportunity to work together on successful activities.

Both cooperation and success are important. Merely working together—as when a coalition meets time after time and appears to go nowhere—builds frustration, not trust. Working together on activities that fail can dampen even the strongest commitment. The best approach is to start with smaller, easier activities and build up to riskier ones.

Of course, engaging the coalition in its own activities takes us back to where we started. The more active the coalition, the more member groups must invest in it. That makes it harder to keep costs and benefits in balance. It also makes it more difficult to prevent the coalition from competing with member groups. In other words, to make a coalition successful you have to walk a tightrope. Staying on that tightrope requires tremendous leadership skill!

# 11

## *Perspective-taking*

Shaping visions, seeking consensus, resolving conflicts, creating rewards—within groups these are all critical parts of exercising leadership. Creating images, gaining legitimacy, practicing advocacy, and coalition-building are essential to gaining support outside the group. How well you do these things, however, depends in part on other, underlying skills. Most importantly, it depends on your ability to:

- Listen to and understand other people;
- Uncover their unspoken assumptions, concerns, and needs;
- See the world as it appears through their eyes.

These are the elements of perspective-taking.

### LOOKING THROUGH THE EYES OF OTHERS

One of the first things young artists learn is that the appearance of things changes if you stand in different places. Depending on your point of view, or perspective, some features become exaggerated; others become hidden. Some things become clear, others clouded. Depending on your perspective, things can even take on different meanings. Standing atop a mountain, you see a forest, not trees. But when you are in the forest, all you see are the trees!

We all see reality somewhat differently because we all see it from our own unique perspective.

• A person's perspective is a complex mix of knowledge, feelings, experience, opinions, values, and assumptions.

We are keenly aware of some things that go into our perspective, especially our opinions and feelings. We may be unconscious of others, especially our most basic assumptions.

To exercise leadership effectively we need to be more conscious of our own perspective—and its limits! We also need to learn how to get inside the perspectives of others.

Miriam Witt, the German high school student who wanted a new Spanish program for her school, was keenly aware of the need for perspective-taking. To turn her vision into reality, Miriam needed the support of many people: the school's director, other students, and teachers. To get their support, Miriam needed to anticipate the objections teachers or the director might raise. She needed to find out how to make her proposal appealing to her fellow students. She had to identify the common ground between her ideas and those of the others. She had to calm fears, resolve conflicts, highlight areas of agreement, and build enthusiasm. All these things required her to understand why people reacted to her proposal as they did. They required her to see herself and her ideas *through their eyes*.

### Talk with the Other

Getting inside the perspective of another person is not easy. In most cases the best and easiest way to probe another's perspective is to talk with him—or more precisely to *listen to* him!

Miriam did just that with her fellow students and several of her teachers. She simply asked them what they thought about her proposal. Was a Spanish program desirable? Was it needed? Was it practical? Would students take Spanish if it were offered?

*Listen for opinions and feelings.* From her conversations, Miriam clearly saw how people felt about her idea. She also began to see that a lot more people had a stake in it than she had thought.

Most of the students did not have strong opinions. They did, however, have questions. Do other schools have Spanish programs? How would a Spanish program help me? Would having a Spanish program mean that other languages would not be taught, or that I would have to take Spanish?

The students' questions gave Miriam insight not just into their opinions, but into their emotional responses to her idea. Were they excited about it? Did they feel it was important, even if they did not want to take Spanish themselves?

The teachers looked at the potential Spanish program from a very different perspective. They raised far different questions. Who would teach the new courses? Would new teachers have to be hired? Was there money for new teachers or would some current teachers have to be let go? Would the Spanish program mean that fewer students would take French? (And how does the French teacher feel about that?) Would the money spent on a Spanish program mean that less could be spent in other areas of the curriculum?

- Talking with people will show you *how* people react to an idea and *how strongly* they feel.

It may seem obvious that you have to talk with people to find out these things. But especially in conflict situations, talking is what people usually stop doing.

*Search for assumptions and values.* In her conversations with both students and teachers, Miriam found that opinions and feelings surfaced quickly. Deeper assumptions and values did not.

In fact, Miriam found that people's deeper values often conflicted with their surface feelings. In some cases, these deeper values created grounds for agreement and support that were not obvious at first. Many teachers, for example, saw a Spanish program as threatening because it might take money away from their areas. At the same time, most teachers in principle wanted to give students as many opportunities for learning as possible. Later, when these teachers saw how many students wanted to take Spanish, they supported the new program despite their concerns.

Of course, hidden assumptions and values can also cause conflict. A person who holds unspoken prejudices against Spanish-speaking people may never agree to support Miriam's idea. Until Miriam understood the real reasons for the objection, however, she could never hope to deal with it.

Perspective-taking.

You need to look inside what people say to uncover hidden assumptions and values. Ask yourself:

- Which facts do people use, and which do they ignore?
- Which dimensions of the issue do they emphasize, and which do they leave out?
- Do they agree with some ideas or parts of the plan? Is there a pattern in what they like and what they dislike?

If you talk with several people who have very different perspectives on an issue or idea, you will get a better impression of the whole picture. That will help you *recognize* and understand the different perspectives.

## Look at a Person's Past

Sometimes you cannot talk with a person directly to learn her opinions and feelings. In many cases you will not want to talk with a person until *you know something* about her perspective! Miriam, for example, needed to get inside the director's perspective before talking with him. Unlike her fellow students and many of her teachers, Miriam could not approach the director until she was ready to answer his objections to her proposal. She could not do that until she understood his perspective.

In cases like these an individual's personal history or past behavior can help you predict his opinions, feelings, or reactions toward an issue or idea. People who have gone backpacking even once in their lives, and enjoyed it, are likely to have more empathy for environmental causes than those who have never experienced the wilderness. People who like to hunt regularly are more likely to oppose strict gun control laws than those who have never owned a gun. While past actions and words help you predict a person's perspective only imperfectly, they are better than nothing.

· Our past experience plays a role in shaping our perspective. Thus past actions and words can be a useful window on our perspectives.

Miriam had no direct knowledge of her director's past or that of her teachers. However, she had been a student in the school for two years. During that time she had observed the director, and she had had a number of different teachers. What she had seen and heard gave her some insight into their likely perspectives.

Miriam knew that some of the teachers spoke Spanish. They were likely to support her idea. At least one teacher had taught Spanish in another school. He too would probably support her, unless his workload would increase.

Miriam had had less contact with the director, so she knew less about him. But she tried to remember whether he had done anything that showed his support for language instruction. She did remember one occasion when the school had hosted visitors from Spain. She thought the director had had a role in arranging that visit.

Miriam could have received additional insight into the director's response to her idea if she had looked at general patterns in his behavior.

Did he usually support or reject student-initiated ideas? Had he ever said anything to suggest that the school's program needed to be expanded or strengthened?

*"Negotiate? What is there to negotiate?"*

**Roles can tell you a lot about how the world looks to others.**
(Reprinted by permission of the *Punch* Library.)

### Get inside the Person's Role

Talking with people or looking at their past words or actions will help you understand *what* their opinions and feelings are. Unless people are very open with you, however, even talking with them may not tell you *why* they hold those opinions or why they feel as strongly as they do. In most cases the best way to get more deeply inside a person's perspective is to look at his or her social roles.

- Our perspectives on issues and ideas are fundamentally influenced by our social roles—our jobs and our relationships to other people.
- Our roles influence our experiences, our knowledge, and many of the other things that shape our perspective.
- How people feel about a proposal also depends on how it affects their ability to perform relevant social roles or how it affects their status in those roles.

*Look for the impact on role performance.* The best way for Miriam to get inside her director's perspective before talking with him was to try to understand how her idea would affect him as director.

Miriam had never been the director of a school, so it was hard for her to imagine exactly how he would be affected by her proposal. But she did know something about his responsibilities, and that was the place to start.

- What responsibilities does the person have?
- How will your idea or vision affect her ability to fulfill those responsibilities—to do her job?

A school director has three critical responsibilities. First, he has to ensure that the school remains financially sound. Miriam's director would, therefore, be concerned about the cost of the program. Could it be run in a way that did not cost too much? Second, a director is responsible for the quality of the academic program. Miriam's director would be concerned about the effect of the program on the school's overall curriculum. He would welcome the program if it improved the school's academic standing. He would be concerned if it hurt some other program. Finally, a director must be concerned about morale within the school. Thus Miriam's director would be concerned with how the teachers, especially the French teacher, reacted to the proposal!

*Beware of changes in status.* The French teacher's reaction to Miriam's proposal demonstrated a second way in which social roles can affect a person's perspective.

The French teacher reacted very negatively to Miriam's idea at first. Yet, it seemed to Miriam that she had no direct stake in it. The French teacher could not teach Spanish, so her workload would not increase. Nor would students stop taking French, since French would remain one of the two languages required for graduation. However, as Miriam talked with other people, she began to realize that a vision may affect not only role performance but the status attached to a role.

- Could your idea or proposal make the person or the person's role more or less important in the eyes of others?

In Miriam's case, adding a Spanish program could have changed the relationship among the various foreign language teachers. Other teachers, who could teach both Spanish and another language, would suddenly be more valuable to the school than the French teacher. As a result, the French teacher might not be treated with the same respect. She might not be consulted as often by the director.

• Fears of losing status or hopes of gaining status can have a profound impact on a person's reaction to a new vision or idea, even if they are groundless and even if the person is only remotely aware of them.

For Miriam's French teacher, the fear of losing status was the single most important part of her perspective. Miriam had to calm that fear before she could hope to get the French teacher's support.

### Check with Third Parties

If you do not have firsthand knowledge of a person's background or any real understanding of her role, a final way to get insight into her perspective will be to talk to someone who does. In Miriam's case, the teachers at her school were a highly reliable source of information about the director. Some teachers had worked closely with him for a long time. They had seen his reactions to a wide range of issues. These teachers gave Miriam important insights into the objections he might raise and the concerns he might have.

*Handle information with care.* Beware, however. Third-party information must be labeled ''Handle with Care.'' The teachers knew a lot about the director, but they also interpreted and understood what they knew from their own perspective. Miriam had to look carefully at what they told her. What was fact, and what was opinion? How biased were the opinions likely to be? How did the teachers feel about the director?

• In general it is better to talk with people who know, like, and respect the person whose perspective you want to understand. People who dislike a person may not be dishonest, but they also may not really understand the other's perspective.

• You can more easily identify bad information if you talk with more than one source. What facts and impressions are shared by many people? The common threads may be reasonably accurate.

Unless you have tremendous confidence in a person's perspective-taking ability, always take what he or she says about another with a grain of salt.

*Use third parties to test your understanding.* Because perspective-taking can never be completely accurate, it pays to test your assessment of another's perspective before acting on it. Talking with third parties can be an excellent way to check on your understanding.

- Describe your emerging understanding to another person and get feedback. Do your ideas make sense? Can the other person see flaws? Does he or she see things differently?

While Miriam did not think her fellow students were a reliable source of information about the director, she did use them to test her understanding of his perspective before she met with him.

## MINIMIZING DISTORTIONS

You can never understand the perspective of another person *perfectly*. No matter how hard you try or how objective you try to be, you will always be influenced by mental barriers that distort your understanding to some extent. There are four barriers that make perspective-taking particularly difficult:

- *Frame of Reference.* We have little choice but to experience and understand the world though our own perspective. Our experiences, assumptions, values, and judgments create a lens that brings other people, events, and ideas into focus. They create a frame of reference for interpreting what things mean. They also cause us to read a little of ourselves into other people. That inevitably distorts our understanding of their perspective.
- *Stereotypes.* The real world and real people are very complicated. To make that complexity more manageable, we create stereotypes, which are like mental cubbyholes that simplify reality. When we

see something new, we put it into a cubbyhole. We then infer all sorts of things about it that are based on our stereotype. Stereotypes are useful—as long as they are not simplistic, and as long as we put new things in the right cubbyholes! But stereotypes can also distort our perspective-taking if we forget that no two things are ever exactly alike.

- *Prejudice.* Prejudice is an extreme form of stereotype. Prejudices are categories that are highly simplistic, highly charged emotionally, and rigidly protected. Prejudices can be positive or negative. They are extremely difficult to recognize in yourself and almost impossible to correct because prejudiced people resist experiences that might challenge or change their prejudice.

- *Generalization.* When we meet someone who is like us in some way, most of us automatically assume that the person is like us in other ways. Without thinking, we assume the person shares similar interests, needs, assumptions, and values. When we meet someone who differs from us in some obvious way—for example, someone who has a different skin color or different nationality—we assume that he has different interests, needs, assumptions, and values. Since these generalizations are made without thinking, we are often not even aware we have made them!

While you can never eliminate these barriers, there are things you can do to minimize the distortion they create.

*Recognize your feelings.* How you feel about a person has a profound impact on your ability to interpret his or her perspective accurately. How do you react to the person's appearance, to her physical movements and facial expressions, to his tone of voice? Simple things like this can have a great impact on how you think about and interpret the other's perspective.

- If your feelings about a person are positive, guard against generalization by consciously looking for ways in which the other's perspective *differs* from your own.

Continuously ask yourself whether you are imposing your own perspective on the other person.

*"Aha! Trying to buy us off with huge salaries and great working conditions, huh?"*

You must look beyond stereotypes to prevent conflict.
(Reprinted by permission of the *Punch* Library.)

The need to recognize your feelings is even more important if you react negatively to someone.

- If you have even mildly negative feelings, or see a person as very different from you, deliberately look for similarities between the other's perspective and your own.

If you have extremely negative feelings, you need to do more. The only way to change a strong negative bias is to work with the other on some problem that you have in common. Even then, unless you have some reason to respect the other as an individual, the contact may simply reinforce your prejudice. It is virtually impossible to understand the perspective of people if you are prejudiced against them.

*Make inferences consciously.* In order to get beneath the surface of a person's perspective and recognize hidden assumptions and values, we must make inferences. We must read between the lines of what they say. We must interpret the pattern of their actions. We must make assumptions about how our ideas or plans will affect their roles or status.

Making inferences is necessary. It is also the greatest source of error in perspective-taking. A while back, a Japanese student who was participating in an anti-American rally saw a Western-looking man passing nearby. The Japanese student approached the Westerner, who immediately assumed that he was being mistaken for an American. The Westerner also assumed that he would now be accosted by this anti-American Japanese.

The Westerner's inference was partly correct. The Japanese student did think the man was an American. His second inference was wrong. The Japanese protestor had no interest in discussing Japanese-American relations or in debating foreign policy. He was planning to go to the United States, and he wanted to practice his English!

The more inferences you make to understand the perspective of another, the greater the danger that your understanding will be wrong. That danger cannot be avoided. It can be controlled.

- Always separate inference from fact and keep them separated. What parts of your understanding are based on what another person has said or done? What parts are based on your *interpretation* of what they have done, or how they have done it?

- Whenever possible talk openly with people, and, if possible, go back and talk with them again if you uncover new questions.

*Make judgments carefully and slowly.* Leadership requires the ability to make judgments about the perspectives of others. Negotiation and advocacy in particular require that you be able first to understand another's perspective and then to recognize (judge) what is wrong with it from your point of view.

At the same time, leadership requires the ability to hold off judgments, especially in conflict situations, until you understand the other's perspective in its entirety. It requires that you judge the other's perspective, not the other.

In the 1970s Western environmentalists began criticizing Japanese fishermen for killing dolphins. The dolphins were often trapped in drift nets used to catch tuna. From the environmentalists' point of view, the dolphins were a higher form of animal that should not be killed without reason. The fishermen saw the dolphins as just another "fish," which unfortunately got in the way of their nets.

The conflict was an example of the need to make judgments, and the need to make them carefully and slowly. Some environmental activists labeled the Japanese fishermen insensitive or, worse, inhuman. They wanted to confront the fishermen and force them into changing their ways. Other environmentalists tried to look at the issue from the perspective of the fishermen. They learned to appreciate Japan's need for fish as a source of protein. They learned to appreciate the fishermen's need for a cost-effective way to catch fish. These environmentalists continued to see the killing of dolphins as wrong, but they began to build some common ground with the fishermen. They also began to look for solutions to the conflict that satisfied both, such as new types of nets and fishing techniques that could catch fish effectively but allow the dolphins to escape.

- Judgment is part of leadership; premature judgment is not. Quick decisions about people or about their perspectives are always based on inference, not observation.

Delay making judgments about another's perspective as long as possible. Only when you are confident that you really understand the other's perspective are you ready to judge that perspective.

- In making judgments, separate the person from his perspective. If your judgment has led you to condemn the person, it may be clouded by bias or even prejudice.
- If you judge another's perspective as totally wrong, your judgment is probably premature. Most people do not agree or disagree with you completely. Look further for the common ground.

Miriam could easily have made a quick judgment about the French teacher, who seemed to oppose her idea without giving it a fair hearing. However, when she finally realized that the French teacher's objections arose from a fear of losing her special status, Miriam actually began to sympathize with her. She also began to look for ways to reassure her.

***Expect the unexpected.*** When you try to understand the perspective of another, do not be surprised by surprises. Remember how hard it is to penetrate the perspective of another person, particularly when you have had little or no experience with her role. Keep an open mind and be ready to adapt your efforts to new revelations.

When Miriam finally did go to talk with the director, she was well prepared. She had answers for all his questions about the cost of the program. She could assure him that the students were behind the proposal and that many would take Spanish if it were offered. She could even assure him that a teacher on staff would gladly teach the new courses.

Miriam expected that the director would think carefully about her proposal, but she expected him to be supportive because of his personal contacts in Spain. However, Miriam had no way of predicting the director's actual response. He had, in fact, been looking at the language curriculum of several competing schools. They all offered Spanish. He himself had taken Spanish and had wondered why their school did not have a Spanish program. If he had had the time to pursue the matter, he told her, there would already be a Spanish program.

The director was as good as his word. Thanks to the groundwork she had laid, and the leadership she had exercised in mobilizing support for the new program, Miriam took Spanish when school started the next year.

# 12

# *The Group Context*

Leadership does not occur in a vacuum. It is a relationship among people. It occurs within groups of one kind or another. But those groups differ greatly. A scout post involves a small number of tightly knit people; the International Red Cross involves thousands of people spread across the world. Honor societies have strict rules and clear lines of authority; small groups of friends do not.

Despite all their differences, all groups need skillful leadership to survive and prosper. At the same time, the differences among groups affect how leadership can best be exercised in them. They create a context that influences how leaders must behave and determines which skills are most important.

## GROUP LIFE CYCLE AND NEEDS

All groups—whether they be formal or informal, large or small—go through a series of stages that can be compared to the life cycle of individuals.

- Like individuals, groups begin life unshaped—with the innocence, strength, and vigor of youth.
- If they survive the dangers of childhood, groups enter a period in which they search for a clear identity—a stage not unlike adolescence.

- Groups that survive the turmoil of adolescence achieve a stability and self-confidence typical of maturity.
- Finally, like individuals, groups ultimately lose their vitality. They enter a period of decline similar to old age. Unlike the life cycle of individuals, however, this process need not end in death. Guided by skillful leaders, it can produce reform and rebirth.

At each of these stages, groups face distinct challenges. They need leaders with a special mix of skills. If you understand where your group is within its life cycle, you may be better able to respond to its unique leadership needs.

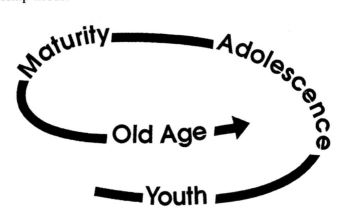

All groups go through a series of stages. At each stage the group faces distinct challenges.

### Youth: The Entrepreneurial Group

The early life of a group is an exciting time. The young group is entrepreneurial in the sense that it is full of promise and enthusiasm. Yet the young group is also extremely fragile. Its members have not yet established a commitment to or stake in the group, so even minor conflicts can tear it apart.

During this initial stage the group's leadership needs center on group-building. The group must:

- Bring together an initial cadre of members and gain their commitment;

- Define essential norms for decision-making and rewarding of members; and
- Gain at least minimal support from the wider community to ensure survival.

*Envisioning takes center stage.* Envisioning is the single most important leadership skill for the young group. The group's success at bringing people together depends on it. Yet, in young groups the effort to develop a common vision may not go very far.

Young groups are entrepreneurial precisely because they encourage experimentation. They have no norms limiting what should be done. They may have few norms defining who should do it. As a result, the diversity of their activities is often limited only by their resources—in particular by the number of members who have the self-confidence, energy, and vision to exercise leadership. As a result, diverse and even competing visions and goals may exist side-by-side.

This tolerance for diversity weakens the group in certain respects, but the group's survival often depends on it. Creating too clear a vision too soon may create conflicts that the young group cannot resolve. Too clear a vision may also limit the group's appeal to potential supporters. Finally, the precise features of the group's vision may need to change as creativity and experience combine to teach members what works best and what has the most meaning. Thus the diversity builds a broad foundation for the group's ultimate vision.

*The need for consensus and negotiation.* As long as a new group keeps active, the excitement of starting a new enterprise can mask the need for many other skills. Energized by the adventure itself, the group may have little need to worry about rewards. If diversity continues to be tolerated, the need for skillful consensus-seeking and negotiation may also be limited.

However, the young group will struggle with the need to live within its means. It will also struggle from time to time with conflicts that arise from its freewheeling nature. Since the lines of authority are unclear, there may be no way to resolve competition among members for desirable tasks, and no way to ensure that undesirable tasks get done. Members may fail to live up to each other's expectations because they see their roles and responsibilities in different ways. These conflicts may not happen often, but when they do, the fragility of the group means that skillful consensus-seekers and negotiators will be required to keep the group together.

*A limited need for outside support.* The young group faces a particularly difficult challenge when it comes to gaining outside support. Like all groups, young groups need support. Most do not have the resources to achieve even small successes. At the same time, unknown and having only a vague vision, the young group faces an uphill battle in creating an image and gaining legitimacy.

The difficulty of gaining outside support usually causes young groups to adopt a limited strategy. Considerable effort and creativity may go into gaining legitimacy, but because success is limited, relatively little effort may go into creating an image. The process of reaching out to the wider community often stops as soon as the group finds a few supporters capable of ensuring its survival. Since these supporters were probably predisposed to support the group, skilled advocates may not even be necessary.

In some cases depending on a few supporters can retard the group's progress to the next stage. Efforts to clarify the group's vision may be delayed lest they upset outside supporters. In other cases, external supporters can force a group to begin clarifying its vision before members are ready. When this happens, the move to the next stage of development can be very painful.

### Adolescence: The Conflictual Group

At some point, a group loses its willingness to try anything. Members begin to question who they are as a group. Potential supporters demand a clearer sense of the group's vision, and how it contributes to the larger community. Past supporters become more aware of competing groups and need reassurance that they have made the right commitment.

When the need to clarify things becomes strong enough, the group enters a period that is aptly named adolescence. The group's leadership needs center on the search for a unique identity. The group must:

- Find a clear and uniform vision and a consistent set of goals;
- Resolve the often intense conflicts that this process can create; and
- Build a firm foundation of support.

Adolescence is probably the most dangerous and challenging stage in the life of a group.

*The skills of envisioning and negotiation.* Even more than the young group, the adolescent group needs skillful envisioners. However, while envisioners in the young group can be entrepreneurs—blazing their own paths—envisioners in the adolescent group must also be consensus-seekers and negotiators.

As they search for identity, groups expect members to agree on a single vision. They expect well-defined goals, closely linked to that vision. They expect predictable and uniform norms. In short, the group no longer tolerates the diversity of youth. Hard choices must now be made, and with hard choices comes conflict.

Moreover, because these are choices about visions and goals, the group's stake in them is enormous. These are decisions about the very soul of the group. Skillful consensus-seeking can make the process easier by preventing small disagreements from erupting into divisive conflicts. However, the greater the group's diversity in youth, the more likely it is that genuine conflicts will have to be resolved in adolescence.

Moreover, once the process of forging a new, uniform vision begins, it must be completed. If not, members will drift away, unsatisfied because the group appears to be going nowhere.

*The need to expand the base of support.* Once they have found their identity, adolescent groups usually face the need to develop a larger base of support. In doing so, they face a unique challenge.

In their youth dynamic and successful groups may create complex and even contradictory images. As they reach out to new supporters in adolescence, they find that they must not only communicate a new image: they must dispel old and inaccurate ones.

Adolescent groups also soon find that they need people skilled in advocacy. In youth groups often stir up a great deal of trouble. They sometimes alienate powerful people who disagree with what they are doing. They just as often create resentment among other groups with which they compete, even groups with similar visions and goals. Since they have usually built only a narrow base of support, on reaching adolescence groups may find that they have few friends but many enemies. In fact, they may encounter more hostile audiences in adolescence than at any other stage in their lives.

*The need to resolve conflicts with past supporters.* Nor are possible conflicts limited to new supporters. Adolescent groups often become locked in conflicts with past supporters, putting even greater pressure on the negotiation skills of leaders.

The very effort to clarify a group's vision and goals will cause tensions with some past supporters. Some supporters will not like the choices made within the group. In some cases unhappy supporters will become more active in the group, reigniting the internal conflicts over the group's vision and goals. Other supporters will simply withdraw their support. Unless it is careful, the adolescent group can alienate old supporters before it finds new ones. If so, it may find that it has survived the internal conflicts of adolescence only to wither away for lack of resources and legitimacy.

## Maturity: The Stable Group

Not every group reaches maturity. Those that do have a clearly defined vision and have established a more or less routine set of goals. Thus in the mature group, the key leadership challenges shift from creating and building the group to maintaining and protecting it. Mature groups must:

- Maintain their visions;
- Keep members committed despite the routine nature of many of the group's activities;
- Protect the group's image and make sure that its base of legitimacy remains solid.

*Leadership within the mature group.* In the mature group, envisioning centers on keeping the group's vision alive. Consensus-seeking, if it has become part of the group's culture, will have become routine. The need for negotiation will remain, but it will primarily be required for resolving personal conflicts. Even motivation will become part of the routine of the group.

Unfortunately, the stability of the mature group is often its greatest enemy. It is all too easy to become so comfortable with the group's vision that no one sees its growing irrelevance. Too much consensus becomes more a threat to good decision-making than possible conflicts.

Even rewards can become so routine that they lose their motivational power. Thus the leaders of mature groups must continuously assess the health of their groups. They must listen for signs of trouble, and not be lulled by superficial stability. They must look into the future and see how relevant the group's vision, goals, and rewards will continue to be.

Leaders of mature groups should force themselves to look for ways to strengthen their groups. Mature groups ought to be able to make decisions in participatory ways. They ought to have strong reward structures that encourage growth in members. Yet, not all do. Those that do not often resist these kinds of changes. The success, self-confidence, and satisfaction of the mature group usually make change seem unnecessary, even undesirable. In mature groups, leaders may need to create conflict in order to get the group to reassess itself and consider alternatives!

*The need to maintain support.* As long as a mature group continues to work toward its goals successfully, its external leadership needs will reflect its overall stability.

With its image and legitimacy established, the mature group should have less need of advocacy—unless its vision is a controversial one. Yet, leaders must continue to monitor the group's image and respond to problems that emerge. They must ensure that the foundations for the group's legitimacy remain strong and relevant, despite changes in the wider community.

The leadership challenge that often takes on new relevance in the mature group is coalition-building. In their youth, most groups cannot afford to participate in coalitions. They have neither the legitimacy nor the resources to form them. In their adolescence, most groups become unattractive coalition partners. However, once a group reaches maturity, coalitions become the best path toward greater power, legitimacy, and visibility. Thus it is at this stage that groups are most likely to need leaders who are skillful coalition-builders.

## Old Age: The Declining Group

Mature groups can maintain a basic stability for years, even for generations. In fact, groups pass from maturity to old age primarily because of a failure of leadership, not the passage of time. Leaders may fail to notice that the group's long-standing vision is becoming less relevant, or that the rewards it offers are less desirable. Leaders may fail to see that the old sources of legitimacy are eroding and not being replaced. They may fail to notice that the group's image is fading among important supporters. In most cases, this process is a gradual one, marked more by apathy than by controversy or passion.

When a group begins the process of decline, it can do one of two things. It can die, or it can change. For some groups the wiser course is to accept the end. The basic leadership challenge in these cases is to make the process as painless and nondisruptive as possible. For many groups, however, old age need not mean the end. It may be an opportunity for a new beginning. For such groups, the leadership challenge centers on:

- Getting the group to recognize and respond to the decline;
- Recognizing the sources of the decline; and
- Reforming the group for a new age.

*Leadership in reforming groups.* The process of reforming is aptly named. Giving new vitality to an old group literally requires the rebuilding of the group and all the leadership skills that that entails.

The first challenge leaders of reforming groups face is the need to make members recognize the group's decline. Rarely do group members and leaders recognize the need for reform simultaneously. Leaders must help the group recognize that something is wrong and accept the need for change. It may be possible to accomplish this through a process of envisioning or consensus-seeking, but more than a little advocacy may also be required.

Once a group recognizes the need for change, it must go through the process of rethinking its vision. Unfortunately, even those members who recognize the need for change may disagree about what changes are needed, or about the direction change should take. Thus the reforming group may experience the same kinds of conflict that marks adolescence.

*Support within the community.* Most groups that have been in decline for a while also face the challenge of rebuilding their base of support in the community. That challenge can take several different forms.

In some cases the group's image in the community may have faded but not have been damaged. Few people may think about the group, or see its relevance, but once reminded they may have a positive image of it. In these cases, the challenge is not unlike that faced by young groups. The reforming group needs to get people's attention and to build a new base for legitimacy. It may not have to change existing images. In these cases, a rich history may prove useful. People are more likely to pay attention because the group has been known. They may be interested in helping to restore a once successful group to health.

In other cases the process of decline will give rise to a negative image in the community. Group members may not recognize the group's decline, but the community will. Irrelevance may actually become part of the group's image, a part that must be overcome before people will take it seriously! A group that establishes a bad track record as it declines will have to persuade people to give it another chance. In all these cases the challenge for the reforming group will be to persuade people to look at it in a new way. That may require extremely skillful advocates, not just creative image builders.

## GROUP CULTURE AND LEADERSHIP

You can assess the leadership needs of your group—and the skills that are most important to it—by looking at its stage in the life cycle. However, there are other aspects of the group context that set limits on how you as an individual can exercise leadership in the group. These aspects of the group can be thought of as the group's "culture."

A group's culture includes all the rules, behavior, and assumptions that the group uses to live and work together smoothly. Leaders should think of themselves in part as creators of a group's culture. In young groups leaders have a wide-ranging ability to create culture. They determine how the group will make decisions, how offices within the group will be organized, how information will be shared among members, whether leadership will be narrowly focused in a few people or widely spread among members. Even in mature groups, leaders can be creators of group culture by trying to make the group more participatory or by looking for new visions or goals.

In mature groups, however, there are many aspects of a group's culture over which leaders have little immediate control. You need to understand these aspects of the group's culture and to use them to your advantage. The most important of these cultural elements can be summed up in three questions:

- Who has authority and how seriously is it taken?
- Who has informal power within the group?
- How do people within the group communicate?

## The Group's Approach to Authority

All formal groups have some kind of structure. Special offices exist with specific responsibilities. The people who hold these offices have authority—the right to make decisions and act in the name of the group. The pattern of authority and the norms surrounding its use are among the most basic elements of a group's culture.

***Know the chain of command.*** In most cases you can learn about a group's pattern of authority by looking at its organization chart. The organization chart shows what the positions of authority are. It lays out a "chain of command" within which group members may be expected to operate.

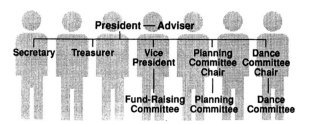

What can you tell about the pattern of authority in this group?

Ignoring a group's chain of command can be dangerous. Melissa, a new member of the Leadership Club, found that out the hard way. She knew the group was having financial trouble. She also had a great idea for raising money, which she discussed with several group members. They liked the idea, as did the whole club when she presented it at the next meeting. But then something unexpected happened.

Melissa did not know that the club had a fund-raising committee. No one had bothered to tell her because everyone assumed she knew. But when Melissa finished describing her plan, the president asked Carl, the chair of the fund-raising committee, to follow through on her ideas. Unfortunately, Carl was upset that Melissa had not gone to him first.

He felt that she had made him "look bad." For the next month, Melissa kept asking Carl about the project. He simply said that the committee was working on it.

In the meantime, Carl was busy convincing his committee and the club president that Melissa's idea would not work. He criticized Melissa as well. In the end, Melissa's idea got lost in the chain of command. So did Melissa. She began to feel unwelcome in the group and quit.

*Know the norms surrounding authority.* While most groups have formal lines of authority, not all deal with them in the same way. To understand how authority operates in the group completely, you need to go beyond the organization chart and look at how people actually treat authority.

In Melissa's group, the chain of command was considered very important.

- People expected tasks to be done according to the chain of command. That is why Carl got responsibility for Melissa's project and not Melissa.
- People in authority also guarded their rights carefully. Carl punished Melissa for violating the chain of command.
- Finally, the norm of authority was stronger than the norm of leadership. Most people accepted Carl's behavior—protecting his turf by blocking Melissa's idea—but not Melissa's—taking initiative but bypassing Carl.

If Melissa had understood the culture of the Leadership Club, she could easily have gone to Carl's committee with her idea. Then she could have exercised leadership and not made trouble.

*Violate norms by choice, not accident.* An old saying about authority advises that "it is often easier to ask for forgiveness than to ask for permission." In other words, if you want to do something new, it may be better just to do it and take the consequences. If you follow the chain of command, you risk getting nowhere.

At one time or another, most leaders choose to ignore the chain of command. They deliberately violate the norms of authority. This is no reason, however, not to know the group's chain of command and norms. Leaders cannot violate norms all the time. They need to pick their battles carefully. If they do not, they may lose their legitimacy and the opportunity to exercise leadership at all!

## Status and Informal Power

Authority is important because it affects how a group gets things done. Status can be important for the same reason. Individuals who have status, that is, who are respected by others, can often use that status to influence group members. These people will not show up on an organization chart, but they can be even more important than the formal "leaders" if you want to get something done.

*Negative leaders and informal power.* Viet Lee learned about informal power when he was elected student body vice president. Viet had only recently immigrated to the United States from Vietnam, and several people in the school resented both his academic and his political success.

One of those students was Don, who served on the Student Activities Committee that Viet chaired. Don resented Viet's success, and he resented Viet's behavior even more. Although Viet did not know it, Don was very popular with a certain group of students. The previous chair of the Student Activities Committee had always talked with Don about her ideas before going to the whole committee. She knew that if Don supported an idea, it would be accepted. If Don opposed it, it would not. Viet had never gone to Don about anything. In fact, sensing Don's attitude, Viet had avoided him. As a result, Don did everything he could to make Viet's life difficult. He disrupted meetings and mobilized people against Viet. With Don working against him, Viet had no chance of succeeding.

In many groups there are people whose status gives them a special influence over other group members. If you intend to exercise leadership within a group, it pays to know:

- Who has status?
- What kinds of influence does that status give them?
- Over which people do they have influence?
- What is the limit of that influence?

Had Viet known how important it was to have Don's support, he probably could have won him over. At least he could have tried.

### The Informal Communication Network

Communication is as basic to a group as authority and status. Unless members communicate with each other, a group will not remain a group for long. Communication is also fundamental to leadership. Leaders must communicate their ideas to the group; they must listen to the ideas and reactions of others. As they do in authority and status, however, groups differ greatly in the pattern and style of communication among members.

*Who talks with whom?* Every group has its own unique communications pattern. People talk with other people, but everyone does not talk equally with everyone else. They talk more with some people and less with others. The larger the group, the more complex and uneven this pattern will be.

Knowing who talks with whom in a group can help you get things done.

· How easily does information move around in the group?
· Are there cliques, that is, subgroups of people who talk almost exclusively with each other and not with the others?
· Are there people who are routinely left out of the network? Are there people who act as hubs of the network?

Not knowing the answers to these questions can cause problems. Cliques, for example, make it difficult to get information circulated in a group. If you want to engage the group in envisioning, you have to make sure you involve someone from each of the cliques. By contrast, in some groups certain individuals act as telephone operators. If you want everyone in the group to know something, all you need to do is tell that person and, presto, word gets around!

*The communication style.* Groups also differ in terms of their style of communication. You can learn the communication style of a group just by listening to people.

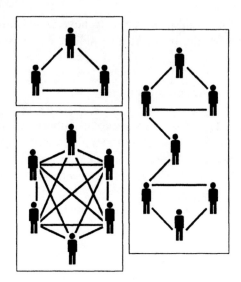

The pattern of communication in a group affects how a leader must communicate his or her messages.

- Are conversations open and friendly?
- Are people friendly on the surface, but also very superficial?
- Do people use a more formal tone to communicate with some people than others?

Not knowing a group's style of communication is a little like talking a different language or having a different accent. If you use a different style, you mark yourself as an outsider. Outsiders almost always have a more difficult time exercising leadership than insiders.

### The Need to Analyze Group Culture

Most people can follow the norms of groups to which they belong, even if they have not bothered to analyze them. When you have been part of a group for a while, its norms become familiar. Following them becomes almost second nature. New members of the group, like Melissa in the Leadership Club, can have difficulty with group norms. But once you feel comfortable in a group, you have probably learned its culture well enough to get along.

However, if you want to exercise leadership, you need to do more than just get along. You need to be willing and able to analyze a group's culture. On the one hand, you need to be able to analyze the culture of groups other than your own. Being able to understand how another group handles authority or status may be critical if you want to involve that group in a coalition. Knowing how the members of another group communicate with each other can help you to create an image or advocate your vision more effectively if you need the group's support.

To exercise leadership effectively, it is equally important that you be able to analyze the culture of your own group. Remember that leaders are culture makers, not just culture followers. A group that has difficulty accomplishing its goals may need better ways for members to communicate with each other. A group that relies too much on a few members may need a new chain of command, or different norms of authority. A group that cannot make decisions or take actions on its own may need to give less status and power to outsiders.

- Groups need leaders who can use all the leadership skills we have talked about in this book. But even skillful leaders may fail if the group's culture makes effective leadership impossible.

# 13

# *Your Leadership Style*

Peg sat back in the chair and tried to relax. The meeting with Chuck and Rebecca had stretched her to the limit. All Peg's careful planning seemed to have been for nothing. Chuck was the worst. He always took over discussions, his booming voice and self-confidence sweeping the group along. But Rebecca was maddening, too. She always went along, no matter what anyone said. But in truth, Peg was most disturbed about herself. She had not kept the group on track. Now things had worked out very differently than she had planned. The committee had adopted a proposal that Peg just knew could not work!

When people come together in groups they bring their ideas, knowledge, and skills with them. They also bring their personalities—the ways they typically behave in different situations. While there is no one leadership style, your personality does affect how you exercise leadership. The style of people like Chuck is to try to dominate groups. The style of people like Rebecca is to go along. People like Peg feel uncomfortable if things do not go precisely as planned because that is their style. Understanding your style can help you to understand your strengths and weaknesses as a leader better.

## INFORMATION PROCESSING STYLES

Our leadership style actually has two parts. The first is our *information processing style*—the way we put ideas together to understand things. There are four basic information processing styles:

- The Analyst
- The Pathfinder
- The Reactor
- The Dreamer

Each of these styles differs in the kind of information a person prefers to use and the way a person puts that information together to create meaning. As you read the descriptions of these information processing styles, look for the one that *most nearly* describes you. Do not be surprised, however, if you also identify with some aspects of the other styles—even styles that seem opposite to your main style.

## The Analyst

The Analyst is a no-nonsense sort of person. He prefers concrete information about specific situations to abstract concepts or vague generalities. Analysts put meaning into facts through systematic logic, carefully working things out from A to Z.

In a group that is deciding whether to sponsor an Earth Day Fair booth, an Analyst would want to know *the facts and nothing but the facts.* How much will the booth cost? How much money does the group have? How many members are available to work in the booth? He would take this information and logically sort it out until he had a clear sense of whether the booth would succeed or fail. He would not waste time on guesses. He would not be interested in preferences. He would not be sidetracked by emotional reactions to the situation.

*Analysts create and assess plans well.* In exercising leadership, Analysts make their greatest contribution in planning and management. People with this style have a mind for putting details together logically. They can lay out a detailed plan for recruiting new members or patiently balance the group's budget. They can put together an organization chart that clearly separates group activities and responsibilities. They can organize tasks and schedules in great detail.

Analysts help groups keep their feet on the ground and their heads out of the clouds. When a group is involved in envisioning, consensus-seeking, creating an image, negotiation, creating rewards, advocacy, or coalition-building, Analysts want the group to be practical and logical.

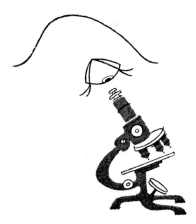

The Analyst.

They help ensure that visions are realistic and that goals are doable. They help ensure that the group's new image really does say something meaningful. They help pull backchaining and other strategic plans apart and find out whether one idea really does lead to another.

**They may miss the big picture and feelings.** The concrete, practical nature of the Analyst can have its drawbacks. Focused on the here and now, Analysts often ignore the bigger issues and the feeling side of things.

In planning the Earth Day Fair booth, an Analyst is unlikely to consider whether the booth would improve the group's image. Possibilities are not facts. The Analyst is also unlikely to ask whether the group *likes* the idea. His focus is on observable, measurable things. His only concern is whether the plan will work. Only if it becomes clear that the plan can only work if people *like* it will emotions become relevant.

The Analyst's tendency to neglect feelings does have its positive side. In negotiations and consensus-seeking, Analysts help the group concentrate on the facts and not the emotional side of the conflict. The Analyst will focus on the issue, not the people. That can prevent disagreements from getting out of hand.

**The chaos of group decisions can be frustrating.** When it comes to consensus-seeking and negotiation, the Analyst's preference for order and concreteness also has its positive and negative sides.

Because the Analyst likes to put information together in an orderly way, group decision-making can be very frustrating. In consensus-seeking ideas often flow in creative chaos. It can be hard to sort them out logically or to develop them in a systematic way. That can make the Analyst more than a little frustrated.

At the same time, the Analyst can keep the group on track. Analysts tend to be task-oriented. They continuously pull the group back to the decision at hand. The more creative and freewheeling the group, the more it may need an Analyst to ensure that it gets something done!

### The Pathfinder

Unlike Analysts, Pathfinders prefer working with abstract ideas. They like to generalize, and to use those generalizations to understand specific cases. They like to think about the possible, not just what is. They look for the big picture. They routinely take into account the less tangible issues—like the impact of an Earth Day Fair booth on the group's image.

Since Pathfinders like to work with abstract and speculative ideas, creativity comes easily to them. At the same time, like Analysts, they like to put their ideas together in an orderly, logical way. Their creativity is like blazing a new trail through the wilderness. It may be a path that no one has trodden before, but it is a *path*. One step flows logically from the last. One piece of the puzzle fits logically with the rest.

The Pathfinder.

*Pathfinders creatively link ideas.* Pathfinders can play a valuable role in envisioning, consensus-seeking, negotiation, and coalition-building because they see the big picture and yet can make all the pieces fit together logically. They look for the broader implications of decisions and actions. Thus in consensus-seeking and negotiation, they can identify new alternatives around which consensus can be built or conflicts resolved. They see the big picture of the group's purpose, so they can more easily identify visions and images which capture and communicate that essence.

Backchaining (Chapter 3) is the kind of planning process a Pathfinder can really enjoy. It begins with the big picture (the vision) and asks you to work logically and systematically backward toward specific goals. That is the epitome of the Pathfinder's approach to planning.

*Their logic can be limiting.* Like Analysts, Pathfinders are limited as well as aided by their logical side. New ideas tend to flow only from what is already known. You can rarely look to Pathfinders for radically different ideas. A Pathfinder might well realize that an Earth Day Fair booth could be used to publicize a new CLEAN-UP campaign (Chapter 4). Coming up with that idea requires a broad grasp of the group's overall interests and a creative but logical combining of ideas. But the final outcome simply flows from things that have already been suggested, not something entirely new.

Pathfinders also share some other limits with Analysts. They may find group decision-making frustrating because of its chaotic creativity. They often overlook the emotional side of things. As a result, even though they see the big picture, they may not always anticipate conflicts. They often cannot understand how other people can oppose their very logical ideas.

## The Reactor

Reactors share with Analysts a preference for concreteness. They tend to focus on the situation at hand, not abstract "problems like this." Like Analysts, Reactors also focus on the here and now. They tend not to look to the future.

Reactors, however, are radically different from both Analysts and Pathfinders in the way they put information together. Reactors do not rely on systematic, logical thinking to sort things out. As their name implies, they react to situations, ideas, and problems in a way that can best be described as random—at least to Analysts and Pathfinders. They often attach meaning to things on the basis of emotions, values, and ideals—the illogical aspects of human nature.

*Reactors add a human touch.* Reactors give a human touch to the work of groups. Because they respond to situations and ideas on the basis of more than logic, they tend to be more aware of emotions and values, either their own or those of others.

In consensus-seeking, it is the Reactor who is likely to broaden the discussion by asking how people feel or by expressing her own spontaneous reactions. Reactors help ensure that the arguments used in advocacy touch more than the logical side of an audience. They can often understand conflicts among negotiating partners which seem to make no sense to Analysts or Pathfinders because they are based on feelings, ideals, or emotions rather than reasoned differences.

Reactors can be of great value when it comes to creating rewards and generating excitement about visions and goals. Their enthusiasm about a vision—or about an image or any other decision—provides an important balance to the solid, but sometimes sterile, logic of the Analyst and Pathfinder. Their attention to psychological needs and rewards helps them see what is often most rewarding in a group.

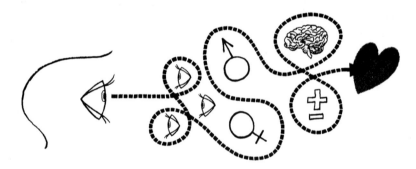

The Reactor.

*Reactors go beyond logic.* The fact that Reactors go beyond logic can be a strength when it comes to group decision-making and planning. They can often evaluate ideas, plans, and decisions with uncanny accuracy, and much more quickly than systematic thinkers. If their reactions are based on solid experience, they can get to the heart of a problem in a way that Analysts and Pathfinders cannot hope to duplicate.

At the same time, the Reactor's tendency to go beyond logic can lead to disaster if he has too little experience. In these cases a Reactor's feelings can be quite confused. Reactors can also become caught up in

false consensus. They support decisions which feel good. For most Reactors, an emerging consensus can be a compelling reason to feel good
about the decision!

*Group decision-making versus planning.* Finally, when it comes to
decision-making and planning, the Reactor thrives on the kind of chaos
that frustrates Analysts and Pathfinders. Indeed, Reactors contribute more
than their share to the chaos of group decision-making since their ideas
are not generated in a logical, systematic way. A Reactor may not even
notice that a freewheeling group discussion is chaotic. If he does, he
will value the chaos because it gives free reign to ideas and insight. It
is also less boring.

However, the Reactor's comfort with the chaotic group process has
its darker side. Caught up in the excitement of the situation, the Reactor
may not notice that a discussion is getting nowhere—until it is time to
leave and nothing has been decided. Moreover, once a decision is made,
the Reactor can be as uncomfortable with planning as the Analyst is
with freewheeling group discussions. Putting ideas together in a systematic way to achieve a predictable result will simply be too boring to
endure.

## The Dreamer

The last information-processing style is that of the Dreamer. Like
Pathfinders, Dreamers prefer to look at the big picture. They see things
in complex ways, with a past and a future. Like Reactors, Dreamers do
not depend on systematic logic to understand things. They also appreciate the emotional side of things and the values that underlie them.

A Dreamer's ability to think abstractly and to find meaning in random
ways gives her a unique ability to think in holistic terms. Dreamers do
not need to find the logical fit among all the parts of an idea. Small
contradictions or ambiguities that would distract Pathfinders do not dis-
turb Dreamers. So they can see the big picture in its complexity in a
way even Pathfinders cannot.

*Creative envisioners and planners.* The Dreamer's ability to think
holistically and to go beyond logic gives him an unparalleled potential
for creative thinking. These are the envisioners who can discover genuinely exciting, challenging visions that capture the feelings of people.

These are the decision-makers who can find the truly novel alternatives around which consensus can be formed, conflict resolved, or a group's image expressed.

The Dreamer.

Like Reactors, Dreamers also give a human side to the group. They can create visions that excite people and that touch basic feelings and needs. As advocates, they can create arguments that touch the psychological, emotional, and ideal sides of people. Sometimes Dreamers can even see emerging conflicts well before they erupt.

Dreamers are at their best when little or no structure is imposed on their thinking. They are not bothered by the chaos of group discussion. On the other hand, they are likely to find backchaining too structured and artificial. They would prefer a completely open process like brainstorming.

*An uncertain practicality.* Unfortunately, the dreams of Dreamers come at a price. Dreams, unlike paths, do not always lead anywhere. They are not always practical.

The ideas of Dreamers can sometimes be as absurd as they are creative. Thus Dreamers need help. They need Analysts to keep their feet on the ground and Pathfinders to ensure that their ideas are logically consistent. They need Reactors to test the relevance of their dreams to real people here and now. Dreamers contribute creativity; they often need help to stay relevant.

Likewise, Dreamers cannot be expected to plan the activities that will accomplish their dreams. They often cannot even organize their dreams into concrete, systematic visions that show others how to achieve them. Dreamers find systematic thinking too constraining. They find it hard to focus long on specific details. Thus, long before any plan is complete, the Dreamer will have moved on, distracted by some new idea or insight.

## ACTION TAKING STYLES

In addition to our information processing style, each of us has an *action taking style*. Our action taking style is the way we prefer to interact with other people. People have four basic action taking styles:

- The Playwright
- The Gamesplayer
- The Persuader
- The Facilitator

Each of these styles differs in terms of where people prefer to focus their energy and attention and in terms of whether a person prefers to control or to adjust to other people and situations. As with the information processing styles, you may identify with more than one of these action taking styles in one way or another.

### The Playwright

The Playwright likes to be in control of people and situations. He exercises control by carefully planning the situation and orchestrating the action from behind the scenes. Like his theatrical counterpart, the Playwright likes to write "scripts" for his group. His script lays out the plot (the questions to be asked, the decisions to be made, the actions to be taken). The script names the characters and spells out their roles (who in the group is included and how each contributes to the final outcome). His script even spells out the outcome of the play (the final decision).

Once the play has started, the Playwright prefers to sit on the sidelines and watch the action unfold. He hopes that all the actors will read the proper lines, do the proper things, and achieve the proper outcomes with little or no direct involvement by him. The Playwright even prefers that others get the attention when the play comes off as planned. Most comfortable behind the scenes, he shuns the limelight.

***Playwrights lay the groundwork.*** The hallmark of the Playwright is the need to be well prepared. This can be of great value to groups, especially when it comes to negotiation, advocacy, coalition-building, and creating an image.

Playwrights naturally try to create situations that lead to desired outcomes. In advocacy, they automatically try to see how the context and other factors will influence the audience. In negotiations and coalition-building they anticipate and create conditions that work in the team's favor. In crafting an image, they work hard to find just the right image and to craft messages that say just the right things. Just how Playwrights go about their planning depends on their information processing style. How successful they are depends on whether they understand the situation accurately.

The Playwright's need to be prepared can also protect the group from undesirable commitments. If some unexpected idea comes up, the Playwright will want to put off a decision. She will want to think about the implications on her own, unless her information processing style is random (Reactors and Dreamers). This can dampen a group's spontaneity, but it can also save the group from making bad decisions when excitement runs high.

***Decisions, conflicts, and coalitions.*** The Playwright's need to plan applies to group meetings and discussions, although sometimes with less desirable results. Going to a meeting "unprepared" would be unimaginable for a Playwright! She will try to understand the issue as completely as possible. She will plan how the issue should be presented and how the discussion should be led. She will know exactly what to say and when to say it to achieve the right outcome.

The Playwright's planning can prevent the group from wasting time

The Playwright.

on blind paths. It can also take away the benefits of group decision-making. The Playwright's script usually has a preferred outcome. If the Playwright is in control of the situation, she will mold what happens so that the group cannot help but come to that conclusion. If the group departs from the script, the Playwright will want to delay a decision, work out a new plan, and try again later. If the group makes a different decision than the Playwright planned, she may not accept the outcome.

Playwrights behave the same way when it comes to envisioning. They construct visions on their own. Only when the visions are complete do they get input from others. If new ideas do not fit easily into their plans, they tend to resist them.

*Playwrights create rewards.* The Playwright is often at his best, however, in assessing how rewards are distributed within the group. Playwrights will be more interested in developing rules or norms for giving rewards than in rewarding members personally. Even if he is sensitive to the need for emotional and psychological rewards, he may prefer to find impersonal ways to provide rewards. However, once a Playwright sets out to make his group rewarding, he will effectively plan things so that rewards are delivered and people are motivated!

## The Gamesplayer

Like Playwrights, Gamesplayers prefer to sort things out on their own—to plan everything out beforehand. Unlike Playwrights, however, they prefer to react to situations rather than control them.

Gamesplayers approach the world as they would a game. Planning, or sorting things out beforehand, is really a question of knowing what the game is, and what the rules are. The Gamesplayer wants to know who the other players are, and what their stake is in the game. However, Gamesplayers do not assume they can choose the game or set the rules. The purpose of planning is not to structure things so that a particular outcome occurs. The purpose is to know how to act appropriately so that once the game begins he will do the right things.

*Gamesplayers react slowly.* Gamesplayers can appear a little clumsy when it comes to consensus-seeking, negotiation, or advocacy. If the Gamesplayer has not anticipated a situation correctly—if he is playing the wrong game or by the wrong rules—like the Playwright he may not be able to adjust quickly to the unexpected situation. He may need to withdraw, reassess his strategy, and only then come back to try again. Spontaneity is as hard for the Gamesplayer as it is for the Playwright.

However, the Gamesplayer's need to be prepared does not stem from a need to control things. So the Gamesplayer can be a natural mediator in conflict situations. She will not try to control the outcome, only to deal effectively with the conflict. In consensus-seeking, the Gamesplayer is unlikely to subvert the group decision through her planning. If there is time to adjust to new ideas and if the group's norms encourage genuine consensus-seeking, the Gamesplayer will be a valuable contributor, trying to find a solution that represents a genuine consensus.

With friendly audiences, win-win negotiations, and friendly coalition partners, the Gamesplayer will also be an effective advocator, negotiator, or coalition-builder. However, when confronted with hostile audiences, win-lose negotiators, or coalition partners who want to take advantage of the group, the Gamesplayer may find it hard to succeed. He will not want to manipulate things in order to change the behavior of

The Gamesplayer.

others. He may not even really know what outcome he wants! Thus the Gamesplayer may be less able to get a satisfactory result for the group.

*Less enterprising but more inclusive.* Gamesplayers are less likely to take the initiative in creating rewards, envisioning, or creating images than are Playwrights. They have little interest in controlling their environment or manipulating other people. If left to their own preferences, they may see little value in trying to create visions, or in looking for ways to increase people's participation, or in developing images that attract their support.

On the other hand, if the Gamesplayer's role requires that he create visions, build images, or provide rewards, he will do these things very well. Most importantly, he will find it easy to use the ideas of others. The Gamesplayer will create visions on his own, but he will always ask himself how others will respond to them. When he gets their reactions, he will accept them even if they raise unexpected issues. Armed with this feedback, the Gamesplayer will go off to adjust his vision so that others can accept it. In short, given time to make adjustments on his own, the Gamesplayer will always search for decisions, visions, images, and rewards that are relevant to others and strengthen their commitment.

## The Persuader

Like the Playwright, the Persuader prefers to be in control of situations and people. However, unlike either the Playwright or the Gamesplayer, the Persuader prefers to work out ideas or problems by talking with other people rather than by going off by herself.

When the Persuader "talks things over," she is the one who does the talking. A Persuader exercises control by being at the center of things. Her style is to overwhelm the people around her. She takes charge and asserts her ideas or feelings. She does this even when she is not yet sure what she thinks or feels! In other words, in many cases the Persuader is trying to convince not only the people around her but herself as well!

*Natural advocates.* As their name suggests, Persuaders can be natural advocates. But their value to groups trying to gain outside support goes beyond advocacy. In communicating an image, gaining legitimacy, and even coalition-building, groups at some point need people who can state the group's ideas, vision, goals, needs, and preferences with self-confidence and resolve. This is the Persuader's natural style. Persuaders exude confidence and determination. They overwhelm the opposition. They cut protest short by not giving it a chance to get started. They convince the unsure and shore up the confidence of wavering supporters simply by the force of their style.

Unfortunately self-confidence and style are at times all the Persuader has. If left to his own, the Persuader can seem shallow to Playwrights and Gamesplayers, who usually work out ideas in greater depth regardless of their information processing style. Persuaders can also seem inconsistent. They may seem to advocate a particular course, convincing others simply because of their self-confidence and firmness. In the end, however, they may reject the idea themselves! Having worked through the logic of the idea, they may find it wanting, even though they have now convinced others of it.

*Problems with consensus and negotiation.* The tendency to act as an advocate can hurt Persuaders in situations requiring consensus-seeking and negotiation.

Because advocacy comes so easily, Persuaders almost automatically

The Persuader.

undermine consensus-seeking. The Persuader's style is not that of a devil's advocate but a real advocate. Others in the group can be swept along easily, and not necessarily in good directions. Persuaders can also find that their egos have become attached to arguments they do not really support. Then it can be hard for them to change positions without losing legitimacy.

Persuaders also find it hard to listen. In trying to control the situation, Persuaders often miss opportunities to get input and feedback from others. Thus even though the Persuader seems highly involved with the people around him, he may have a hard time assessing the situation accurately.

*Persuaders can reward others.* Finally, for the Persuader, the supportive pat on the back, the vocal congratulations, the smiling "job well done" come easily. So Persuaders can play a very valuable role in creating a rewarding group. While the Persuader may have a hard time assessing a group's reward system and may or may not be sensitive to how other people feel about things, he is comfortable giving rewards—especially the psychological rewards that require a personal, hands-on approach. The Persuader likes to be in the public eye even when it comes to rewarding others!

## The Facilitator

The last action taking style is that of the Facilitator. Like Persuaders, these people prefer to sort out ideas and problems by talking with other people. Like Gamesplayers, however, they feel little need to be in control of the situation. In fact, Facilitators do not even need to know the rules of the game. They can comfortably walk into an unstructured situation, without a clear agenda or goal, and work with people to define and achieve some eventual end.

***Facilitators build commitment and agreement.*** The Facilitator's strength as a leader results from his openness to others. In envisioning, consensus-seeking, and coalition-building, Facilitators naturally draw other people into the discussion. Thus they can play a critical role in building commitment to the group and its vision.

In envisioning, Facilitators use interaction with others to shape their own sense of the vision. Thus the eventual vision is likely to be seen as a group product and commitment is built as the vision emerges. In consensus-seeking and coalition-building, it is the Facilitator who will ask what other people think. It is the Facilitator who will explore the ideas of others. In coalition-building, the Facilitator will listen to what other groups need and will be able to create a coalition that brings mutual advantages to everyone. Facilitators, more than any of the other types discussed, are in touch with people and events around them.

***A distaste for taking and defending positions.*** The very strengths of the Facilitator suggest her weaknesses. Openness and the ability to draw people into the group work well in consensus-seeking and envisioning. They can be handicaps in negotiation or advocacy.

Without help from others, Facilitators have a hard time defining a clear position. Even when it is defined, they find it absurd to stick firmly to it. As a result, they can find advocacy a very difficult skill to master. They may also be at a disadvantage if negotiating partners decide to play by win-lose rules. In those situations, Facilitators may not be firm enough to get the other side to accept win-win rules.

Finally, while Facilitators can play a valuable role in coalition-building, they often need a counterbalance. Because of their openness to the needs and ideas of others, Facilitators may unwittingly invite coalition partners to take advantage of them, or to become free riders. The Facilitator wants to involve and include people. She is open to their ideas, interests, needs, and perspectives. She may, however, have a hard time asserting and defending her own interests or those of her group when that is needed.

The Facilitator.

## KNOWING AND USING YOUR STYLE

As you read the descriptions of the various leadership styles, you should have found both an information processing style and an action taking style which *more or less* describe you. Keep in mind the limits of these descriptions, however.

- The styles are generalizations. They describe any one individual only to a degree.
- The styles reflect tendencies and preferences, not absolutes. An Analyst may prefer working with facts but, given practice, feel comfortable with ideas and generalizations.
- All people are more complex than these styles assume. Even if a particular style seems to describe you perfectly, you are likely to have at least some traits associated with other styles—including *the opposite style.*

If you apply the categories too rigidly, either to yourself or to others, you may make embarrassing mistakes or artificially limit your own leadership potential.

These descriptions of the various leadership styles also demonstrate that there is no one leadership personality. Leaders have a wide range of styles. Every one has strengths. Every one has weaknesses. No one style even has a monopoly on a particular leadership skill. Persuaders are natural advocates, but Playwrights can better plan for situations requiring advocacy. Facilitators are natural consensus-seekers, but they need others to help protect them from false consensus. Dreamers may be natural envisioners, but they need help anchoring those dreams in reality.

If you recognized yourself in any of these styles, you may now have some insight into your own strengths and weaknesses as a leader. But now what? The challenge is to put all the pieces together to help you learn how to be a better leader.

# 14

## *Putting It All Together*

Appreciating your personal leadership style, understanding the leadership needs of your group, learning leadership skills—this is what it takes to prepare for leadership. By now, however, the prospect of learning leadership may seem a bit overwhelming. How can any one person hope to understand, learn, and do it all?

In reality, no one ever does put it all together completely. Perfection, however, is not the goal. Preparing for leadership means *working with your strengths and improving on your weaknesses*. It means becoming *increasingly sensitive* to the group's needs. It means using the qualities and the opportunities you have so you become *more skillful through time*. Nor is *preparing* for leadership something you do only as a young adult. It is something that continues as long as you live.

### ASSESSING YOUR STYLE

The place to start in developing your leadership abilities is with you and your leadership style. The last chapter described eight different leadership styles. Each of these styles has some natural strengths—skills with which you are probably more comfortable or can learn more easily. Each also has natural weaknesses—skills with which you are less comfortable or will learn more slowly.

Begin assessing your strengths and weaknesses by taking a second look at these styles. Which seem to fit you the best? Look for both:

- An information processing style (Analyst, Pathfinder, Reactor, Dreamer), and
- An action taking style (Playwright, Gamesplayer, Persuader, Facilitator).

No style will describe you perfectly. You may also find that more than one fits you to some extent. As you skim the styles, write down the characteristics (strengths and weaknesses) which best describe you.

Jennifer, Kristen, Eric, and Steve were four friends who went through this exercise. The four had very different styles. Their experience may help you.

The ingredients of leadership.

### Jennifer: The Pathfinder-Facilitator

Jenny was known to her friends as quiet, friendly, and very intelligent. Few saw her as a "leader," but she was the first one to whom they went if they needed help. Jenny saw herself as a logical thinker. She liked to be around people, even though she was quiet. What really set Jenny apart, however, was her keen but uneven awareness of others. She was honestly open to their opinions and ideas. Yet, she often failed to appreciate the emotional side of issues.

When Jenny looked over the leadership styles, she quickly identified her information processing style. She was a Pathfinder. She was less certain about her action taking style. The Gamesplayer fit somewhat, but she finally settled on the Facilitator. The combination of Pathfinder and Facilitator reconciled her logical style with her desire to pull in the ideas of others. Her final list of strengths and weaknesses looked like this:

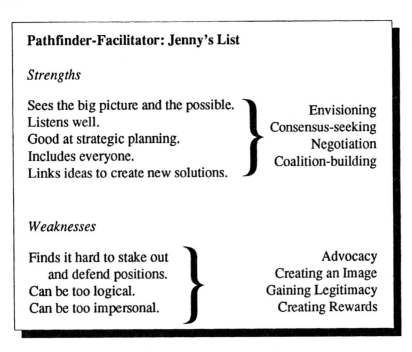

**Pathfinder-Facilitator: Jenny's List**

*Strengths*

Sees the big picture and the possible. ⎫   Envisioning
Listens well.                     ⎬  Consensus-seeking
Good at strategic planning.       ⎬   Negotiation
Includes everyone.             ⎭  Coalition-building
Links ideas to create new solutions.

*Weaknesses*

Finds it hard to stake out     ⎫     Advocacy
   and defend positions.       ⎬ Creating an Image
Can be too logical.           ⎬ Gaining Legitimacy
Can be too impersonal.      ⎭ Creating Rewards

Pathfinder-Facilitator: Jenny's list.

### Kristen: The Reactor-Gamesplayer

Kristen was Jenny's closest friend, but her leadership style was quite different. When Kristen looked at the leadership-styles, she settled on the Reactor and Gamesplayer. Kristen was a private person. She liked to figure things out on her own. But she was not a systematic thinker. She seemed to just know what people around her were feeling, what they would favor, and what they would oppose. She hated new situations because she never knew how to act. Yet, once she felt comfortable, Kristen was always very effective in groups. Kristen's list of strengths and weaknesses looked like this:

**Reactor-Gamesplayer: Kristen's List**

*Strengths*

People-oriented.
Sensitive to feelings and ideals.
Likes to be prepared.
Comfortable with disorder.
Flexible.
Includes others.

} Consensus-seeking
Negotiation
Creating Rewards
Creating an Image
Coalition-building

*Weaknesses*

Projects personal reactions onto others.
Can lead groups in the wrong direction.
Can be too flexible.
Can be slow to react.

} Gaining Legitimacy
Advocacy
Envisioning

Reactor-Gamesplayer: Kristen's list.

In reality, Kristen did not have a single leadership style. Some people, like Kristen, learn to fit their style to what seems needed at the time. The more experience they have with different situations, the more flexible they can be. So Kristen's list of strengths could have been expanded. But the one she came up with was still the best place for her to start.

## Steve: The Dreamer-Persuader

Steve's close friends could have described his style without reading the last chapter. Steve was a Dreamer. In a group, he always had the most imaginative, if not the most practical, ideas. He was also a Persuader. He had something to say about everything. He could monopolize any conversation if you let him. Actually, that was why Jennifer and Kristen liked him. There was never a dull moment when Steve was around. His list of strengths and weaknesses looked like this:

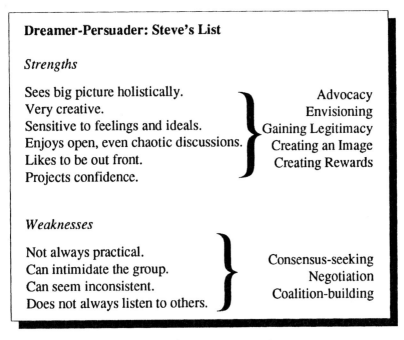

**Dreamer-Persuader: Steve's List**

*Strengths*

Sees big picture holistically.
Very creative.
Sensitive to feelings and ideals.
Enjoys open, even chaotic discussions.
Likes to be out front.
Projects confidence.

> Advocacy
> Envisioning
> Gaining Legitimacy
> Creating an Image
> Creating Rewards

*Weaknesses*

Not always practical.
Can intimidate the group.
Can seem inconsistent.
Does not always listen to others.

> Consensus-seeking
> Negotiation
> Coalition-building

Dreamer-Persuader: Steve's list.

## Eric: The Analyst-Playwright

In many ways Eric was the odd man among the four friends. For each of the qualities that best described the others, Eric was the opposite. Steve dreamed dreams. Eric was solid and practical. Kristen was always flexible. Eric always knew what he wanted and hated to change his mind. Jenny understood everyone. Eric often had no idea what other people were all about. Yet, when some project had to be done, everyone knew who could do it. Eric's list of strengths and weaknesses looked like this:

---

**Analyst-Playwright: Eric's List**

*Strengths*

Keeps group practical and on task.
Can fit details together effectively.
Likes to be prepared.
Keeps disagreements impersonal.
Does not change ideas easily.

} Creating Rewards
Advocacy
Negotiation

*Weaknesses*

Can be unwilling to take risks.
Tends to neglect feelings.
Tends not to see the big picture.
Finds it hard to be spontaneous.

} Envisioning
Consensus-seeking
Creating an Image
Gaining Legitimacy
Coalition-building

---

Analyst-Playwright: Eric's list.

## ASSESSING THE OPPORTUNITIES

Your list of strengths and weaknesses is the place to begin the quest to develop your leadership skills, not the place to end it. Once you know who you are, you can begin looking for ways to build on your strengths and to improve on your weaknesses.

- What opportunities do you have to exercise leadership? In what groups are you active? In what groups would you like to become active?
- What are the unique leadership needs of these groups? How do those needs match your leadership style?

### Look at the Available Groups

When Jennifer, Steve, Kristen, and Eric looked for interesting leadership opportunities, they focused on three groups. Each of the three was at a very different stage in its life cycle. Each had unique leadership needs.

*The Youth League.* The four friends had first met in their local church youth group. The group had a long history. Its purpose was to involve young people in the charitable, social, and religious life of the church community. The president, whose name was also Steve, had started a new initiative to help the Teen Center create a suicide hotline. However, for the most part the group did the same things it had done for years— a series of social events to match the seasons, a major fund-raiser for the missions, and a program to help with religious classes for younger children.

The Youth League was a mature group. What it needed most were leaders who could:

- Plan and manage the group's dances, picnics, hayrides, and other annual events.
- Create rewards to keep group members motivated.
- Resolve personal conflicts that arose from time to time.
- Maintain the group's image and legitimacy.

It needed solid, skillful leaders who paid attention to details.

Even though it was a mature group, the Youth League had a special need that called for a special skill. While the group valued mutual respect and individual responsibility, it had never used consensus-seeking to make decisions. The current president was the last in a long line of officers who had had no experience with participatory leadership. Some members wanted to change that.

*Junior Council on World Affairs.* The Junior Council on World Affairs struck all four friends as an old group. The council had been around for only six years, but it had fallen on hard times. Its only regular program, the Youth Forum, still attracted students, but the council itself was not thriving. Three years ago the group had had 30 members; now it had 10. Few of the 10 seemed committed to doing anything new or exciting. Whether the council could survive had become a real question.

The council needed leaders who could shake things up. It needed leaders who could:

- Give the group a new, more exciting image.

- Revitalize its vision; set new goals; create new programs that would rekindle the commitment of current members and attract new ones.

- Sell this new vision to their fellow students.

- Negotiate the conflicts that would inevitably be created by change.

*The Ecology Club.* The final group, the Ecology Club, was an adolescent group. Over the past few years the Ecology Club had done a number of interesting things. It had sponsored a recycling drive, participated in the Earth Day Fair, and brought in speakers on ecological issues. Unfortunately, none of the group's activities seemed to give it a focus—a vision uniquely its own. The lack of a shared vision was beginning to cause problems.

If it was going to survive, the Ecology Club desperately needed leaders who could guide it through the turmoil of adolescence. It needed someone who could:

- Find a focused vision for the group and put it into words.

- Resolve the conflicts that would emerge as the group struggled to find a uniform vision.

- Use consensus-seeking effectively, since the group had a strong commitment to participatory leadership.

- Find ways to make the group rewarding enough to put up with the turmoil and problems of adolescence.

## Match Opportunity to Style

Once you know your leadership style and your opportunities for exercising leadership, you can match opportunity to style. The best match will allow you to build on your core strengths and to improve on your strategic weaknesses.

- Building on your strengths means using and developing those skills with which you are most comfortable—which you can develop most easily.

A Persuader finds advocacy easy to learn because it is comfortable. So a Persuader should look for groups that need advocates in order to develop that skill to its fullest!

- Improving on your strategic weaknesses means developing some of the skills that are less comfortable but are too important to ignore.

A Persuader may find consensus-seeking uncomfortable. But recognizing its importance, she may look for a group that will provide a supportive environment for learning that skill.

None of the four friends found a perfect match between his or her style and the available groups. They did find some appealing opportunities.

*Eric chooses the mature group.* Eric was the first to select a group. Any one of the groups could have benefitted from Eric's planning skills and practicality. But from Eric's perspective, the Youth League fit his needs best.

For Eric a mature group like the Youth League offered a comfortable but challenging opportunity. The Youth League needed practical people who could handle management tasks. Any one of the group's program committees would have given Eric a solid opportunity to use and develop his planning skills. However, as a mature group, the Youth League was less likely to place great emphasis on those skills which were Eric's greatest weaknesses: envisioning and creating an image.

Unfortunately, the Youth League did not provide a good opportunity for Eric to develop his consensus-seeking skills. For that he needed a group that already used consensus-seeking and would reward rather than resist his efforts. Yet, the Youth League did give Eric a chance to improve on some of his strategic weaknesses. Eric wanted to challenge himself to look beyond the concrete and see the larger vision and goals. As a mature group, the Youth League needed leaders who could "keep the vision alive" by doing just that.

The Youth League also gave Eric an opportunity to work on coalition-building skills. In fact, Eric planned to get involved with the suicide hotline committee right away. The coalition was already set up and relations among the coalition members were good. Yet, Eric knew that coalitions are constantly challenged to build a consensus or negotiate issues. These were areas to which Eric brought certain strengths (impersonal approach to decisions), but in which he also had real weaknesses (involving others and being flexible). Thus Eric contributed something to the group and had the chance to grow personally. More importantly, the group provided a supportive atmosphere for working on his weaknesses. The positive relationships within the coalition would make it easier for Eric to learn new ways of working with people.

*Steve accepts the challenge of reforming.* The Youth League attracted Steve as well. But Steve wanted something more. For him, the Junior Council on World Affairs fit the bill. The council needed a Dreamer to find new directions for the group. It needed an advocate who could sell those dreams to others. In other words, it needed Steve!

The council also offered Steve an opportunity to work on his weaknesses. To resurrect the council, Steve would have to learn to listen better—to take the ideas, opinions, and feelings of others into account. He would have to try to develop a more flexible style—using advocacy to recruit new supporters but consensus-seeking and negotiation inside the group. The council could succeed if Steve stumbled a bit as he worked on consensus-seeking and negotiation. It could not succeed without his skills as envisioner and advocate.

*Jennifer faces a dilemma.* Like Steve, Jennifer was attracted to the Council on World Affairs. It needed envisioning, consensus-seeking, and negotiation skills—all of which she found comfortable. In the end, however, Jennifer decided that the Ecology Club was the group for her.

The Ecology Club needed an envisioner but not necessarily a Dreamer. The club needed someone to bring the several existing and partially competing visions together. It needed someone who could hold the group together in the process. In short, the Ecology Club needed a Pathfinder, who could build a logical, consistent vision from the many existing pieces, and a Facilitator, who could involve everyone in creating that vision.

At the same time, the Ecology Club would force Jennifer to work on strategic weaknesses. Jennifer would need to become more sensitive to the emotional side of issues. If she could see and appreciate emotions more quickly, her strengths (impersonality of a Pathfinder and listening skills of a Facilitator) could help the group work things out. The group would also force Jennifer to advocate creative solutions from time to time. That was the kind of controlled opportunity to develop advocacy that Jennifer needed.

*Kristen learns about herself.* Kristen faced a different kind of dilemma from her friends. As she looked at the three groups, she realized that each of them provided an opportunity to develop a different strength. The Youth League needed a planner, and Kristen could create logical, detailed plans if needed. The Council on World Affairs needed an advocate, and Kristen's work with the suicide hotline proved she was comfortable with that. The Ecology Club needed an envisioner and negotiator, and Kristen was pretty sure she could do that too. The result was eye-opening. For the first time Kristen realized just how flexible her style could be.

In the end Kristen decided to help Jennifer with the Ecology Club. An adolescent group seemed to need everything, and that appealed to Kristen. She also realized that she could complement Jennifer in important ways, especially when conflicts arose. Most importantly, she could help Jennifer take people's feelings into account. On the other hand, the Ecology Club would help Kristen add to her flexibility. She was becoming quite good at advocating ideas effectively in formal settings. However, she still found it hard to use advocacy in small groups. She also found it hard to react quickly to new ideas and to work through ideas logically. These were precisely the things that Jennifer did well.

*Look for the right match.* No one group is likely to provide a perfect home, no matter what your leadership style. At the same time, all groups have a variety of leadership roles and needs. Some roles will pose challenges that you can easily meet. Others will pose challenges that you will overcome only with great difficulty.

- Look for the roles which use your strengths but still challenge you to improve on your weaknesses.
- Work with your style; do not ignore it. Some skills can be strengthened with effort; others may elude you forever.
- Always look for a supportive environment for learning new skills. Avoid groups that make failure all but certain.
- Do not let other people lock you into a particular role just because you fit it well. Try new challenges. If that is impossible in your current groups, look for a new group.
- Most importantly of all, do not try to be all things to all people. No matter how skillful or flexible your leadership style, you will end up disappointing someone—probably yourself.

## Look to the Leadership Team

Truly effective leaders do not just try to improve their leadership skills. They learn to compensate for personal limitations by building effective leadership teams composed of people with complementary strengths.

Even Steve, whom people saw as a natural leader, needed others to complement his weaknesses. Steve had a genuine facility for advocacy. He was forceful, dynamic, and confident. But Steve's charisma was not always enough. Convincing other people sometimes required actions that Steve did not perform well. He did not enjoy doing the careful preparation that was often needed, and that Eric did very well. He did not find it easy to understand the feelings people had about an issue, which was something Kristen did well.

- You cannot and do not need to develop every leadership skill to become an effective leader. If you are willing to become part of an effective leadership team, you can accomplish things you could never hope to do alone.

*Clashes among leadership styles.* Bringing together people who have different leadership styles does not always result in teamwork. The different styles complement but also conflict with each other. You need to anticipate these conflicts to make the team work smoothly.

As a general rule, opposite styles clash with, as well as complement, each other the most. The opposite styles are:

- Persuaders and Gamesplayers.
- Playwrights and Facilitators.
- Reactors and Pathfinders.
- Analysts and Dreamers.

There are, however, some important exceptions. While Analysts are extremely uncomfortable with Dreamers, Dreamers often like to work with Analysts. Dreamers can be so incomprehensible to Analysts that they actually gain control over them. So, despite the Analyst's discomfort, the Dreamer may thrive in the relationship.

Similarly, Facilitators usually distrust Playwrights. However, the people whom Playwrights most distrust are Persuaders. To all the others, the Persuader can seem superficial, inconsistent, or too quick to act.

But to the Playwright, the Persuader seems dangerously naive—ready to lurch the group in all sorts of absurd directions.

*Containing unproductive conflicts.* Personality clashes can actually benefit a group. They keep people "on their toes." They force people to look at things from different perspectives! Knowing that an Analyst like Eric will challenge a poorly designed plan will make someone like Steve a little more careful. However, personality conflicts can get out of hand, and then they need to be contained.

- In many cases, simple awareness can prevent personality clashes from becoming unproductive conflicts. Just expecting a certain pattern of behavior—and knowing that the other finds any other pattern uncomfortable—can encourage tolerance if nothing else.

Tolerance, however, may not go far enough. In some cases, people can only work together for a time before conflicts surface. Leaders should be alert to these situations and should structure work so that people's styles complement each other without causing too much friction.

- Work with flexible, changing committees. Make it possible for Gamesplayers to help Persuaders prepare for a public relations campaign and then get out of the way when the time comes to do something.
- Watch for the signs of conflict—which may be more or less easy depending on your style! If you catch them early, you can usually prevent personality conflicts from causing too much damage.

## PREPARING TO LEAD IN A GLOBAL AGE

Young people who hope to exercise leadership as adults should take steps to prepare for leadership today. But preparing for leadership requires leading, not just reading. And when you start learning to lead, you will find that the preparation never really ends.

So do not be afraid to exercise leadership now, even if you feel "unprepared" for the challenge. You never will be completely prepared. In fact, if you feel too confident, you probably should get nervous. There must be something you have missed! No one has mastered all the intricacies of leadership. Everyone learns as he goes along. So do not be afraid to try. Give yourself permission to lead. Use every chance you have to develop your leadership skills.

As you do, struggle as well with the challenge of exercising leadership in a global age. Creating visions, making decisions, and resolving conflicts in ways that include others—even when they disagree with you—are essential parts of the leadership needed in a global age. Seeing your visions in the light of global needs and seeing ways to respond to needs that seem too complex for you to handle are also essential.

Just as you can never be completely prepared to exercise leadership, you can never be completely attuned to our global age. None of us is a global leader, but we are all involved in one way or another in shaping this global age. Do not let the enormity of the world stand in the way. Just as you must give yourself permission to lead, you must give yourself permission to be a global leader. There is no magic. There are no patented formulas for success. There are only the caring and the doing. To borrow a phrase from a once popular commercial, the next and most important step in preparing for leadership is for you to. . . .

"Just Do It!"

# Bibliography

Valuable books for further reading on leadership, leadership skills, and styles include the following:

Bennis, Warren. *On Becoming a Leader*. Reading, Massachusetts: Addison-Wesley, 1989.

Bennis, Warren and Burt Nanus. *Leaders: The Strategies for Taking Charge*. New York: Harper & Row, 1985.

Blanchard, Kenneth and Spencer Johnson. *The One Minute Manager*. New York: Berkley Books, 1982.

Cambell, David. *If I'm in Charge Here Why is Everybody Laughing?* Greensboro, North Carolina: Center for Creative Leadership, 1984.

Cribbin, James J. *Leadership: Your Competitive Edge*. New York: American Management Association, 1981.

Gardner, John W. *On Leadership*. New York: The Free Press, 1990.

Green, Madeleine F. *Leaders for a New Era*. New York: Macmillan, 1988.

Johnson, David W. and Frank P. Johnson. *Joining Together: Group Theory and Group Skills*. Third Edition. Englewood Cliffs, N.J.: Prentice-Hall, Inc., 1987.

Kouzes, James M. and Barry Z. Posner. *The Leadership Challenge: How to Get Extraordinary Things Done in Organizations*. San Francisco: Jossey-Bass Publishers, 1990.

Myers, Isabel Briggs with Peter B. Myers. *Gifts Differing*. Palo Alto, California: Consulting Psychologists Press, Inc., 1980.

Nanus, Burt. *Visionary Leadership: Creating a Compelling Sense of Direction for Your Organization*. San Francisco: Jossey-Bass Publishers, 1992.

Peters, Tom and Nancy Austin. *A Passion for Excellence: The Leadership Difference*. New York: Warner Books, 1985.

Roberts, Wess. *Leadership Secrets of Attila the Hun*. New York: Warner Books, 1987.

Zartman, I. William and Maureen R. Berman. *The Practical Negotiator*. New Haven: Yale University Press, 1982.

A good way to learn more about leadership is to read the biographies and autobiographies of people who have been effective leaders. Because they focus on a particular individual, these books often neglect the ways in which leaders mobilize and use the contributions of others. However, they can still be insightful and inspirational looks at leadership. Some good and less noticed works include the following:

Davidson, Margaret. *I Have A Dream: The Story of Martin Luther King.* New York: Scholastic Books, 1986.

Davis, Angela. *Angela Davis: An Autobiography.* New York: Bantam Books, 1975.

De Mille, Agnes. *Martha: The Life and Work of Martha Graham.* New York: Random House, 1991.

Diehl, Kemper and Jan Jarboe. *Cisneros: Portrait of a New American.* San Antonio, Texas: Coronoa Publishing Co., 1985.

Erikson, Erik. *Gandhi's Truth.* New York: W. W. Norton, 1969.

Gallen, David and Roger Goldman. *Thurgood Marshall: Justice for All.* New York: Carroll & Graf, 1992.

Geldof, Bob. *Is That It?—An Autobiography.* New York: Weidenfeld and Nicolson, 1987.

Jackson, Jesse. *Straight from the Heart.* Philadelphia: Fortress Press, 1981.

Jordan, Barbara and Shelby Hearon. *Barbara Jordan: A Self-Portrait.* Garden City, N.J.: Doubleday, 1979.

Kilian, Pamela. *Barbara Bush: A Biography.* New York: St. Martin's Press, 1992.

Lieberson, Goddard. *John F. Kennedy—As We Remember Him.* Philadelphia: Courage Books, 1988.

McKeever, Porter. *His Life and Legacy.* New York: Morrow Publishing, 1989.

Meer, Fatima. *Higher Than Hope: The Authorized Biography of Nelson Mandela.* New York: Harper & Row, 1991.

Meir, Golda. *My Life.* New York: G. P. Putnam's Sons, 1975.

Mother Teresa. *My Life for the Poor.* San Francisco: Harper & Row, 1985.

Parks, Rosa. *Rosa Parks: My Story.* New York: Dial Books, 1992.

Pascarelli, Peter. *The Courage of Magic Johnson: From Boyhood Dreams, to Superstar, to his Toughest Challenge.* New York: Bantam Books, 1992.

Rolbein, Seth. *Nobel Costa Rica.* New York: St. Martin's Press, 1988.

Roosevelt, Eleanor. *An Autobiography.* New York: Harper & Brothers, 1961.

Sadat, Anwar. *In Search of an Identity: An Autobiography.* New York: Harper & Row, 1978.

Scheader, Catherine. *Shirley Chisholm: Teacher and Congresswoman.* Garden City, N.J.: Enslow Publishers, 1990.

Sheehy, Gail. *The Man Who Changed the World: The Lives of Mikhail Gorbachev.* New York: Harper Collins, 1990.

Tames, Richard. *Helen Keller.* London: F. Watts Publishing, 1991.

Terry, Walter. *Alicia and Her Ballet Nacional de Cuba.* New York: Anchor Press, 1981.

Urquhart, Brian. *Hammerskjold.* New York: Harper & Row, 1984.

Young, Hugo. *The Iron Lady: A Biography of Margaret Thatcher.* New York: Farrar, Strauss & Giroux, 1989.

# Index

**About the Author**

ROBERT B. WOYACH is Senior Faculty Associate of the Mershon Center at The Ohio State University, where he is part of the Mershon Citizenship Development for a Global Age Program. Under grants from the Danforth Foundation and the Stanley Foundation he directed several projects on youth leadership. He is the author or editor of several books and numerous papers on global education and international relations.

BERNARD BERGONZI (Born 13.4.29,
London) is Senior Lecturer in English
at the University of Warwick.

A graduate of Wadham College, Oxford, he
taught in the English Department at
Manchester University from 1959 to 1966.

His publications include *The Early
H. G. Wells* (1961), *Heroes' Twilight*
(1965), *Innovations* (1968) (Editor), and
*The Situation of the Novel* (1970).

He has contributed to a large number of
English and American literary periodicals,
including *The New Statesman, The
Observer, Encounter* and the *New York
Review of Books.*

# HISTORY OF LITERATURE IN THE ENGLISH LANGUAGE

# HISTORY OF LITERATURE
# IN THE ENGLISH LANGUAGE

## Vol. 7 The Twentieth Century

# The Twentieth Century

EDITED BY BERNARD BERGONZI

BARRIE & JENKINS
London
In association with
Sphere Books Ltd

First published in Great Britain in 1970 by Barrie & Jenkins Ltd
2 Clement's Inn, London W.C.2

© Sphere Books 1970

A paperback edition of this volume is available from
Sphere Books

Set in Linotype Pilgrim

SBN 214 65083 9

Printed and Bound in Great Britain by
Hazell Watson & Viney Ltd,
Aylesbury, Bucks

# CONTENTS

## INTRODUCTION

This book has been compiled with a full sense of the difficulty of writing about the literature of the recent past. The literary historian who deals with earlier periods will be concerned to make fresh valuations and establish new connections, to redraw the map of his period in order to make it more accurate and more usable by the modern reader. Yet his basic landscape is, as it were, given and unchangeable: no more sixteenth century poems or eighteenth century novels are going to be written, no matter how much recent scholarship and criticism can deepen our understanding of the ones that already exist. But as one approaches the 'modern' end of the spectrum, valuations and questions of relative stature, even the choice of what to write about, become much more problematical, particularly when one is dealing with living authors who are still in mid-career. Notoriously, many earlier histories of literature which still have valuable things to say about the past tend to become useless and even absurd as they approach their *terminus ad quem*. One cannot absolutely exclude such a fate for the present volume: nevertheless, it has been compiled with certain assumptions in mind which seem to be commonly if not universally accepted.

As the twentieth century moves into its last third, it has become evident that its first three decades were a period of rich and brilliant literary activity, exemplified by those writers we now think of as the masters of the Modern Movement; with the death of T. S. Eliot in 1965 it was clear that this phase was concluded, and indeed much of its creative energy had been spent by 1930, the year in which D. H. Lawrence died. The nature of Modernism and the possible ways of defining the term are discussed in the opening chapter, which covers the period from 1900 to 1920. The greater part of this book concentrates on the Modern achievement, and there are detailed essays on the four great writers of our time whose stature, fifty years after they produced their most characteristic works,

9

seems unshakeably established: Yeats, Joyce, Lawrence and Eliot. In a fifth essay, on the fiction of the nineteen-twenties, Malcolm Bradbury discusses some of the lesser but still substantial masters of that remarkable epoch. The sense of major cultural catastrophe following the First World War, though not exclusively caused by it, dominates much of the writing of that time, and is independently remarked on by several of the contributors to this volume. It appears in such central works as Eliot's *The Waste Land*, Lawrence's *Women in Love*, Ford Madox Ford's *Parade's End*, and Yeats' *The Tower*.

The literature published since 1930 has been treated in a less extensive form, and with a few exceptions the discussion stops in 1960, in the hope of avoiding the embarrassingly rapid obsolescence that can overtake judgements made on immediately contemporary work. This may seem unadventurous, but in a book which aims at a fairly enduring degree of usefulness, such prudence seems justified. Inevitably, there are a few cases of overlapping, such as the early novels of Evelyn Waugh, which are treated by Malcolm Bradbury as important exhibits in his essay on the fiction of the twenties, and which are referred to again by Stephen Wall in an analysis which is centred on Waugh's later fiction. What each of these critics has to say seems to me, in different ways, so interesting and relevant that I have preferred to leave the overlap, rather than mutilate the argument of one or other of them in the interest of a somewhat factitious tidiness. Although the main emphasis in this volume is on fiction and poetry, G. K. Hunter surveys the course of English drama over the decades from 1900 to 1960, and provides a chronological list of major theatrical productions during this period. Andrew Bear's essay on popular fiction reflects the increasing recent interest in the relations between 'serious' literature and other cultural forms, while David Lodge's concluding essay on literary criticism establishes the large intellectual and educational context in which the discussion of literature has developed during the twentieth century.

# CHRONOLOGICAL TABLE

This table shows, in a severely selective form, significant public and literary events between 1901 and 1960. V indicates verse, F fiction, and P other prose works; there is a separate list of theatrical productions appended to G. K. Hunter's essay.

1901  Death of Queen Victoria. First wireless communication between Europe and America.

1902  End of Boer War. F: Arnold Bennett, *Anna of the Five Towns*; Henry James, *The Wings of the Dove*.

1903  Wright Brothers make first successful aeroplane flight. F: Samuel Butler, *The Way of All Flesh*; Joseph Conrad, *Youth*; James, *The Ambassadors*.

1904  Russo-Japanese War. *Entente Cordiale* between Britain and France. F: G. K. Chesterton, *The Napoleon of Notting Hill*; Conrad, *Nostromo*; Baron Corvo (Frederick Rolfe), *Hadrian the Seventh*; James, *The Golden Bowl*. P: A. C. Bradley, *Shakespearean Tragedy*.

1905  Einstein propounds first principles of Relativity. Abortive revolution in Russia. F: E. M. Forster, *Where Angels Fear to Tread*; H. G. Wells, *Kipps*.

1906  Liberal Government; Campbell-Bannerman prime minister. F: John Galsworthy, *The Man of Property*; Rudyard Kipling, *Puck of Pook's Hill*.

1907  V: James Joyce. *Chamber Music*. F: Conrad, *The Secret Agent*; Forster, *The Longest Journey*.

1908  Asquith prime minister. Old Age pensions introduced. F: Bennett, *The Old Wives' Tale*; Forster, *A Room With a View*.

1909  Blériot flies English Channel. V: Ezra Pound, *Personae*. F: Rudyard Kipling, *Actions and Reactions*; H. G. Wells, *Tono-Bungay*.

1910  Death of Edward VII, accession of George V. First Post-Impressionist exhibition in London. Stravinsky, *The Fire Bird*. V: W. B. Yeats, *The Green Helmet*. F: Bennett, *Clayhanger*; Forster, *Howards End*; Wells, *The History of Mr. Polly*.

1911  Parliament Act. V: Rupert Brooke, *Poems*. F: Conrad, *Under Western Eyes*; D. H. Lawrence, *The White Peacock*.

1912 Militant suffragette activity. Loss of the *Titanic*. Schönberg, *Pierrot Lunaire*. V: *Georgian Poetry* (anthology); Pound, *Ripostes*. F: Lawrence, *The Trespasser*.

1913 Proust, *Swann's Way*. Stravinsky, *The Rite of Spring*. F: Conrad, *Chance*; Lawrence, *Sons and Lovers*.

1914 Outbreak of First World War. V: *Des Imagistes* (anthology); Thomas Hardy, *Satires of Circumstance*; Yeats, *Responsibilities*. F: Joyce, *Dubliners*.

1915 Coalition Government; Asquith prime minister. Dardanelles campaign. V: Brooke, *1914 and other poems*. F: Ford Madox Ford, *The Good Soldier*; Lawrence, *The Rainbow*; Virginia Woolf, *The Voyage Out*.

1916 Lloyd George prime minister. Easter Rising in Dublin. Battle of Verdun. Battle of Somme. Death of Henry James. F: Joyce, *A Portrait of the Artist as a Young Man*.

1917 Revolution in Russia. USA enters war against Germany. V: T. S. Eliot, *Prufrock and Other Observations*.

1918 Peace treaty between Germany and Russia. German breakthrough on Western Front. Armistice, November. V: Gerard Manley Hopkins, *Poems* (ed. Robert Bridges); Siegfried Sassoon, *Counter Attack*. F: Wyndham Lewis, *Tarr*. P: Lytton Strachey, *Eminent Victorians*.

1919 Alcock and Brown fly Atlantic. Treaty of Versailles. F: Ronald Firbank, *Valmouth*; Virginia Woolf, *Night and Day*.

1920 League of Nations established. V: Pound, *Hugh Selwyn Mauberley*; Wilfred Owen, *Poems* (ed. Siegfried Sassoon); Yeats, *Michael Robartes and the Dancer*. F: Lawrence, *The Lost Girl, Women in Love*. P: T. S. Eliot, *The Sacred Wood*.

1921 Irish Free State. F: Aldous Huxley, *Crome Yellow*. P: Percy Lubbock, *The Craft of Fiction*.

1922 Bonar Law prime minister. Fascist revolution in Italy. Death of Proust. V: Eliot, *The Waste Land*; A. E. Housman, *Last Poems;* Isaac Rosenberg, *Poems* (ed. Gordon Bottomley); Yeats, *Later Poems*. F: John Galsworthy, *The Forsyte Saga*; Joyce, *Ulysses*; Lawrence, *England, My England*; Katherine Mansfield, *The Garden Party*; Virginia Woolf, *Jacob's Room*.

1923 Baldwin prime minister. Inflation in Germany. F: Bennett, *Riceyman Steps*; Huxley, *Antic Hay*; Lawrence, *Kangaroo*. P: Lawrence, *Studies in Classic American Literature*.

1924 Labour Government; Macdonald prime minister. Conservative Government; Baldwin prime minister. Death of Lenin; deaths of Conrad and Kafka. F: Ford, *Some Do Not*; Forster, *A Passage to India*. P: T. E. Hulme, *Speculations*; I. A. Richards, *Principles of Literary Criticism*.

1925 F: Ford, *No More Parades*; Huxley, *Those Barren Leaves*; Lawrence, *St. Mawr*; Virginia Woolf, *Mrs. Dalloway*. P: Yeats, *A Vision*.

1926   General Strike. V: Hugh MacDiarmid, *A Drunk Man Looks at the Thistle*. F: Ford, *A Man Could Stand Up*. P: T. E. Lawrence, *The Seven Pillars of Wisdom*; Yeats, *Autobiographies*.

1927   F: Lewis, *The Wild Body*; Woolf, *To the Lighthouse*. P: Forster, *Aspects of the Novel*; Lewis, *Time and Western Man*.

1928   Death of Hardy. V: Yeats, *The Tower*. F: Ford, *Last Post*; Huxley, *Point Counter Point*; Lawrence, *Lady Chatterley's Lover*; Lewis, *The Childermass*; Siegfried Sassoon, *Memoirs of a Fox-Hunting Man*; Evelyn Waugh, *Decline and Fall*.

1929   Labour Government; Macdonald prime minister. Collapse of New York Stock Exchange. Start of world economic depression. V: Cecil Day-Lewis, *Transitional Poem*; Louis MacNeice, *Blind Fireworks*. F: Galsworthy, *A Modern Comedy*; Graham Greene, *The Man Within*; J. B. Priestley, *The Good Companions*. P: Robert Graves, *Goodbye to All That*; I. A. Richards, *Practical Criticism*.

1930   Mass unemployment. Death of Lawrence. V: Auden, *Poems*; Eliot, *Ash Wednesday*; Stephen Spender, *Twenty Poems*. F: Lewis, *The Apes of God*; Sassoon, *Memoirs of an Infantry Officer*; Waugh, *Vile Bodies*. P: William Empson, *Seven Types of Ambiguity*.

1931   National Government; Macdonald prime minister. Japanese invasion of Manchuria. Death of Bennett. F: Anthony Powell, *Afternoon Men*; Woolf, *The Waves*.

1932   Roosevelt president of USA. V: *New Signatures* (anthology); Auden, *The Orators*. F: Huxley, *Brave New World*. P: F. R. Leavis, *New Bearings in English Poetry*; Q. D. Leavis, *Fiction and the Reading Public*.

1933   Hitler chancellor of Germany. V: *New Country* (anthology); George Barker, *Thirty Preliminary Poems*: Spender, *Poems*. F: J. C. Powys, *A Glastonbury Romance*.

1934   V: Dylan Thomas, *Eighteen Poems*. F: Waugh, *A Handful of Dust*. P: Wells: *Experiment in Autobiography*.

1935   Baldwin prime minister. Germany rearms. Italian invasion of Abyssinia. V: William Empson, *Poems*; Yeats, *A Full Moon in March*. F: Christopher Isherwood, *Mr. Norris Changes Trains*; L. H. Myers, *The Root and the Flower*.

1936   Death of George V, accession and abdication of Edward VIII, accession of George VI. Civil War in Spain. Deaths of Chesterton, Housman, Kipling. V: Eliot, *Collected Poems 1909–35*; Auden, *Look Stranger!* F: George Orwell, *Keep the Aspidistra Flying*. P: A. J. Ayer, *Language, Truth, and Logic*.

1937   Chamberlain prime minister. Destruction of Guernika. Japanese occupation of Pekin and Shanghai. V: David Jones,

*In Parenthesis*. F: Lewis, *The Revenge for Love*; Woolf, *The Years*. P: Orwell, *The Road to Wigan Pier*.

1938 Munich agreement. F: Samuel Beckett, *Murphy*; Elizabeth Bowen, *The Death of the Heart*; Laurence Durrell, *The Black Book*; Greene, *Brighton Rock*. P: Orwell, *Homage to Catalonia*.

1939 End of Spanish Civil War. Russo-German pact. German invasion of Poland, and outbreak of Second World War. Deaths of Yeats and Ford. V: Roy Fuller, *Poems*; Louis MacNeice, *Autumn Journal*; Thomas, *The Map of Love*. F: Isherwood, *Goodbye to Berlin*; Joyce, *Finnegans Wake*; Orwell, *Coming Up for Air*.

1940 Churchill prime minister. Fall of France. Evacuation from Dunkirk. Battle of Britain. Italy enters war as ally of Germany. V: Auden, *Another Time*; Yeats, *Last Poems and Plays*. F: Greene, *The Power and the Glory*; Arthur Koestler, *Darkness at Noon*.

1941 German invasion of Russia. Japanese attack on Pearl Harbor. USA at war with Germany, Italy and Japan. Deaths of Joyce and Virginia Woolf. V: Auden, *New Year Letter*. F: Woolf, *Between the Acts*.

1942 Hitler begins extermination of European Jews. Fall of Singapore. Battle of El Alamein. German defeat at Stalingrad. V: Fuller, *The Middle of a War*; Sidney Keyes, *The Iron Laurel*. F: Joyce Cary, *To Be a Pilgrim*.

1943 Conquest of Tunisia and Sicily. Invasion and surrender of Italy. V: Durrell. *A Private Country*; David Gascoyne, *Poems 1937–1942*. F: Henry Green, *Caught*.

1944 Invasion of France. Flying bomb and rocket attacks on London. V: Eliot, *Four Quartets*. F: Cary, *The Horse's Mouth*. P: Cyril Connolly (Palinurus), *The Unquiet Grave*.

1945 Death of Roosevelt; Truman president of USA. End of war in Europe. Labour Government elected; Attlee prime minister. Atomic bombs on Japan, and Japanese surrender. Nuremberg Trials. V: Auden, *For the Time Being*; Philip Larkin, *The North Ship*; Edith Sitwell, *The Song of the Cold*. F: H. Green, *Loving*; Orwell, *Animal Farm*; Waugh, *Brideshead Revisited*.

1946 First Assembly of United Nations. Death of Wells. V: Roy Campbell, *Talking Bronco*; Robert Graves, *Poems 1938–45*; Edwin Muir, *The Voyage*; Thomas, *Deaths and Entrances*. F. Larkin, *Jill*. P: Bertrand Russell, *History of Western Philosophy*.

1947 Nationalization of mines. Marshall Plan. Independence of India. P: Keith Douglas, *Alamein to Zem Zem*. F: L. P. Hartley, *Eustace and Hilda*; Malcolm Lowry, *Under the Volcano*.

1948 Assassination of Gandhi. Communist take-over in Czechoslovakia. Russian blockade of Berlin. State of Israel declared. V: Auden, *The Age of Anxiety*. F: Greene, *The Heart of the Matter*. P: Eliot, *Notes Towards a Definition of Culture*; F. R. Leavis, *The Great Tradition*.

1949 Communist Government in China. North Atlantic Treaty Organization set up. Devaluation of pound. F: Joyce Cary, *A Fearful Joy*; Aldous Huxley, *Ape and Essence*; C. P. Snow, *Time of Hope*; Angus Wilson, *The Wrong Set*. V: MacNeice, *Collected Poems 1925–48*; Muir, *The Labyrinth*.

1950 Korean War. Deaths of Shaw and Orwell. V: Auden, *Collected Shorter Poems*. F: H. Green, *Nothing*; Doris Lessing, *The Grass is Singing*; Angus Wilson, *Such Darling Dodos*.

1951 Conservative Government; Churchill prime minister. V: Keith Douglas, *Collected Poems*; John Wain, *Mixed Feelings*. F: Greene, *The End of the Affair*; Anthony Powell, *A Question of Upbringing*; Snow, *The Masters*.

1952 Death of George VI; accession of Elizabeth II. Eisenhower president of USA. V: Auden, *Nones*; David Jones, *The Anathemata*. F: Thomas Hinde, *Mr. Nicholas*; Powell, *A Buyer's Market*; Waugh, *Men at Arms*.

1953 Death of Stalin. End of Korean War. F: Beckett, *Watt*; Ian Fleming, *Casino Royale*; Wain, *Hurry on Down*.

1954 Geneva Conference on Indo-China. Outbreak of Algerian War. V: Thom Gunn, *Fighting Terms*. F: Kingsley Amis, *Lucky Jim*; William Golding, *Lord of the Flies*; Iris Murdoch, *Under the Net*.

1955 Eden prime minister. V: Auden, *The Shield of Achilles*; Donald Davie, *Brides of Reason*; William Empson, *Collected Poems*; W. S. Graham, *The Nightfishing*; Larkin, *The Less Deceived*; Spender, *Collected Poems*. F: Nigel Dennis, *Cards of Identity*; Golding, *The Inheritors*; Greene, *The Quiet American*; Powell, *The Acceptance World*; Waugh, *Officers and Gentlemen*.

1956 Revolution in Hungary. Anglo-French occupation of Suez. V: *New Lines* (anthology). F: Wilson, *Anglo-Saxon Attitudes*.

1957 Macmillan prime minister. Russian sputnik in orbit. Independence of Ghana. Death of Wyndham Lewis. V: George Barker, *Collected Poems*. F: John Braine, *Room at the Top*; Durrell, *Justine*; Powell, *At Lady Molly's*. P: Richard Hoggart, *The Uses of Literacy*; Frank Kermode, *Romantic Image*.

1958 First Aldermaston march. Overthrow of French Fourth Republic; De Gaulle back in office. V: John Betjeman, *Collected Poems*. F: Durrell, *Balthazar, Mountolive*; Murdoch, *The Bell*, Alan Sillitoe, *Saturday Night and Sunday Morning*; Wilson, *The Middle Age of Mrs. Eliot*. P: Raymond Williams, *Culture and Society*.

1959   Castro takes power in Cuba. Death of Edwin Muir. V: Robert
       Graves, *Collected Poems 1959*. F: Golding, *Free Fall*, Muriel
       Spark, *Memento Mori*; Sillitoe, *The Loneliness of the Long
       Distance Runner*.
1960   United Nations intervention in Congo. Kennedy president of
       USA. V: Auden, *Homage to Clio*; Muir, *Collected Poems 1921–
       1958*; Charles Tomlinson, *Seeing is Believing*. F: Amis, *Take
       a Girl Like You*; Durrell, *Clea*; Powell, *Casanova's Chinese
       Restaurant*; David Storey, *This Sporting Life*.

## THE ADVENT OF MODERNISM 1900–1920

### Bernard Bergonzi, University of Warwick

I

Until a few years ago, 'modern' literature might have been
equally well described as 'contemporary' or 'recent' or 'twentieth-century' literature, and all these terms would have been
understood in much the same way. But as our century moves
into its final decades, a refinement of critical language has taken
place: the word 'modern' is increasingly used to refer to a
particular period—that is to say, the years between 1900 and
1930—and the kind of writing that flourished at that time. It
has, in fact, become another descriptive term, like Augustan or
Romantic, to be freely used or misused by literary historians.
In its broadest sense the Modern Movement was international
and embraced all the arts: representative names would include not only Joyce and Eliot, but Proust and Kafka, Schoenberg and Stravinsky, Picasso and Diaghilev. Further developments of terminology have followed on this use of the word
'modern': Frank Kermode, for instance, has distinguished between the 'paleo-modernism' of the great innovators of the
early twentieth century, and the 'neo-modernism' of avant-
garde experimentalists of the present time (mostly in other
arts than literature, and in other countries than Britain), seeing
the latter as doing no more than work out implications already
present in paleo-modernist achievements. Another usage has
been suggested by Stephen Spender, who makes a distinction
between the Modern and the Contemporary: in literature the
Modern is marked by aesthetic concentration, imaginative intensity and boldness, a stress on individual sensibility, a corresponding indifference to purely social values, and a certain
contempt for the recent past (which may, however, be associa-

ted with attachment to a 'tradition' embodying the more remote past): the Contemporary writer, on the other hand, is
not very interested in artistic innovation. He is positively
involved with the world he lives in, is a serious commentator
on it and is inclined to activist and progressive social attitudes.
Such writing is perpetually in danger of declining into journalism. If Eliot and Pound and Joyce and Lawrence offer clear,
though sometimes conflicting, versions of the Modern, the
Contemporary can be represented by Shaw and Wells and
Galsworthy and the Georgian poets; and, for that matter, by
most living English novelists.

These distinctions have their uses, though they need to be
applied with tact and common sense. What is certain is that
the history of twentieth century English literature can now
no longer be understood in the relatively simple terms that
were current about thirty years ago. With the passing of time,
the events, seen in perspective, look more complex. The earlier
version, which is still extant in much critical writing, posits a
clear, decisive and successful literary revolution occurring in the
years following 1910: in poetry, the Georgians were over-
thrown by Eliot and Pound; and in the novel, the popular 'Contemporaries' like Wells and Bennett were superseded by such
dedicated Moderns as Lawrence and Joyce and Virginia Woolf
and, less certainly, E. M. Forster. Michael Roberts' introduction
to *The Faber Book of Modern Verse* of 1936—an important document in the history of twentieth-century literary taste—is an admirably comprehensive expression of the attitude in relation to
poetry: Roberts offers a detailed history and explanation of the
poetic revolution, but the underlying assumption is that the
revolution is firmly established. And in 1924, Virginia Woolf, in
an essay called 'Mr. Bennett and Mrs. Brown', presented an early
example of the opposition between Contemporaries and Moderns. The former were represented by such novelists as Bennett,
Wells and Galsworthy, whom she described as 'Edwardians';
she acknowledged their talents, but felt that their concern with
the superficialities of social existence prevented them from
being true artists. (A few years later D. H. Lawrence made
similar but sharper attacks on Galsworthy and Wells). Rather
confusingly, Virginia Woolf described the Moderns as 'Georgians', and included in their ranks Lawrence, Joyce, Forster,
Eliot and Lytton Strachey: the passing of time has made the
presence of Lytton Strachey in this list look surprising, but
otherwise Virginia Woolf's instinct was remarkably sure. Nevertheless, she was too much part of her age to see the true con-

figuration of its literature; her essay ends, 'I will make one final and surpassingly rash prediction—we are trembling on the verge of one of the great ages of English literature'. Virginia Woolf was, interestingly, both right and wrong. In John Holloway's words: 'The 1910–30 period was one of the great epochs of English literature. It stands with 1590–1612, or 1710–35, or 1798–1822. What has been written since then does not bear comparison with it for a moment.'[1] But Virginia Woolf did not realize that the excellence was all around her, and that in a few more years the creative energies of the Modern Movement would be largely exhausted. Thus, in 1924, the year in which she was writing, E. M. Forster published *A Passage to India*, and Ford Madox Ford brought out *Some Do Not*, the first volume of his *roman fleuve*, *Parade's End*. Two years before, 1922 had seen the publication of Joyce's *Ulysses*, Lawrence's *England, My England* and *Aaron's Rod*, Katherine Mansfield's *The Garden Party*; and, in poetry, Eliot's *The Waste Land* and Yeat's *Later Poems*, not to mention volumes by Hardy and Housman.

Seen from the 1960's the Modern Movement now looks like a creative explosion that produced some great and many excellent works in a short period of time, but which never established the decisive revolution that was once believed to have taken place; or not, at least, in Britain (the American situation is quite different). Modernism has had a marked effect on the idiom and methods of much subsequent literature; but at the same time it has provoked a considerable resistance and even a counter-movement. Graham Hough's *Image and Experience*, published in 1960, argues that much of the poetry of the Modern Movement was merely a detour from the true English tradition; a similar anti-modernist case was advanced, though more crudely, by Robert Conquest, in an attack on Ezra Pound published in the *London Magazine* in 1963, and in the introduction to an anthology, *New Lines II* (1963). Perhaps the most striking exhibit of all is a remark made in 1966 by Philip Larkin, the most admired English poet of his generation: 'one reader at least would not wish Hardy's *Collected Poems* a single page shorter, and regards it as many times over the best body of poetic work this century so far has to show'.[2] There is no room for ambiguity here: Mr. Larkin quite clearly regards Hardy as not only a better poet, but a much better poet, than either Eliot or Yeats. The counter-revolutionary assurance of this opinion is none the less striking for the quietness with which it is uttered. Extrapolating from Philip Larkin's remark, and picking up a number of critical hints from Graham Hough and Robert Conquest, one could, theoretically at least, construct an anti-modern 'native' English poetic tradition, in which Hardy would play a central role, where the Georgians would be of considerable importance, and where the true line of descent would include such names as Housman, Edward Thomas, Robert Graves, Edwin Muir and John Betjeman.

In practice, however, whilst such conservative attitudes offer interesting evidence about English cultural life, a considerable degree of eclecticism and pluralism remains evident: if the bold hopes of the revolutionaries of 1910 have patently not been fulfilled in any very permanent way, their achievement and example is not, in fact, to be dismissed as a mere detour. Modernist and traditionalist (or Contemporary) attitudes continue to co-exist in a state of fluctuating stasis.


## II

In this chapter I want to begin by considering the literary climate of the 1900's, to indicate some of the anticipations of Modernism, and its subsequent impact from 1910 onwards; of which year Virginia Woolf observed in 'Mr. Bennett and Mrs. Brown', 'in or about December 1910, human character changed'. I shall try to avoid using the model of a literary 'revolution' despite its attractive clarity and simplicity, since I think it is misleading. Rather than talk of a 'revolution', which suggests a single rapid change from one state of affairs to another, I prefer to see the advent of the Modern Movement as a series of foci or nodes, centred round influential individuals or groups, between which connections can be traced, but which cannot be seen to have effected absolute or lasting transformations. In recent years a great deal of valuable work has been done on early twentieth century literature, in the form of critical biography, editions of letters, and cultural history generally. Drawing on this material, and sharpening the focus somewhat, one can point to a number of separate incidents or encounters, spread over several years, which all played an important part in the emergence of a characteristically Modern literature. Thus, one can refer to the long arguments that used to go on between Joseph Conrad and the young Ford Madox Ford (then known as Hueffer) in a Kentish farmhouse in the early 1900's, when they would spend long hours agonizing over the art of fiction, frequently having recourse to the sacred text of Flaubert. Again, there was Jessie Chambers, sending in 1909 a batch of poems by an unknown young schoolmaster, D. H. Lawrence, to Ford, by now editor of the *English Review* and a man with a discriminating eye for new talent. There was the period spent together by Ezra Pound and W. B. Yeats in a Sussex cottage during the winter of 1913–14, when Yeats, who had influenced Pound's earliest poetry, submitted to learn from his junior about ways in which he could modernize his own verse. Most important of all, perhaps, was Pound's jubilant discovery, late in 1914, of a young compatriot living in London :

> He is the only American I know of who has made what I call adequate preparation for writing. He has actually trained himself *and* modernized himself *on his own*. The rest of the *promising young* have done one or the other but never both (most of the swine have done neither). It is such a comfort to meet a man and not have to tell him to wash his face, wipe his feet, and remember the date (1914) on the calendar.[3]

The young man was T. S. Eliot; with Pound's help, his 'Love Song of J. Alfred Prufrock' was printed in the American magazine *Poetry* in 1915, and thus one of the masterpieces of distinctively modern poetry saw the light; it had been begun as early as 1910—the year in which 'human character changed'— without any contact with the experimental literary movements that Pound was sponsoring in London. As a final illustrative fragment, there is Ford Madox Ford, serving as an over-age subaltern in the British Army during the First World War, and writing depressed letters from France about the humiliations he was undergoing; experiences which were, however, to be splendidly transmuted into literature when Ford came to write *Parade's End*, the finest novel by an Englishman to have emerged from the First World War.

What is striking about these incidents is that so few of the people involved were English : Conrad was Polish, and Ford was half-German (although he came increasingly to affect the role of a romantic High Tory Englishman); Yeats was Irish, and Pound and Eliot were Americans. This leaves only Lawrence as the representative of a truly English tradition, evident in literary terms in his admiration for Hardy. Lawrence was idiosyncratic in his modernity, and he was not at all in sympathy with the aesthetic ideals associated with Ford or Pound, or the writers they sponsored. The dominance of alien talents in the Modern Movement, whether Continental or Celtic or American, has given weight to recent attempts to erect an anti-modern native tradition, even though a major aspect of English literary culture has always been its eclecticism and openness to outside influences.

The first few years of the twentieth century were not marked by any decisive literary movements, although the sense of a new era was apparent. The death of Queen Victoria, occurring in 1901, at the very beginning of the new century, showed that an age had passed in a sense that denoted more than a simple change on the calendar. Frank Kermode, ranging widely, has offered reasons for seeing the year 1900 as having more than an arbitrary significance:

> In 1900 Nietzsche died; Freud published *The Interpretation of Dreams*; 1900 was the date of Husserl's *Logic*, and of Russell's *Critical Exposition of the Philosophy of Leibnitz*. With an exquisite sense of timing Planck published his quantum hypothesis in the very last days of the century, December 1900. Thus, within a few months, were published works which transformed or transvalued spirituality, the relation of language to knowing, and the very locus of human uncertainty, henceforth, to be thought of not as an imperfection of the human apparatus but part of the nature of things, a condition of what we may know. 1900, like 1400 and 1600 and 1000, has the look of a year that ends a *saeculum*.[4]

In English literature the dominant mood of the first years of the new century was compounded of relief that the onerously long reign of Victoria was finally over, and an impulse of limited revolt against the survivals of the Victorian spirit. The revolt was limited insofar as it was restricted to the themes and content of literature, and the attitudes consciously held by the writers: the remaking of sensibility and the radical changes of literary form associated with the Modern Movement were still several years in the future. One of the most interesting and influential literary examples of this revolt was Samuel Butler's *The Way of All Flesh*, a novel written in the early 1870's, but kept unpublished for many years. It finally appeared in 1903, after Butler's death, an anti-Victorian time bomb which exploded under some cherished idols of the previous era: fatherhood and the family and domestic pieties generally. *The Way of All Flesh* picked up and then influenced an existing current of feeling; in form it was a *Bildungsroman*, a novel which traced the growth and spiritual education of a young man, and its influence was to extend to Forster and Lawrence and Joyce, and beyond. The weak, cultivated, iconoclastic young hero,

22

whose rebellion is basically genteel, was to become a familiar figure in twentieth-century English fiction.

The novelists whom Virginia Woolf was to label 'Edwardian' manifested this mood of limited revolt, which was both directed at, and conditioned by, social attitudes: there was no trace of the metaphysical revolt against the nature of things that we find, for instance, in Dostoievsky's tormented heroes. The mood was effectively embodied in John Galsworthy's *The Man of Property* (1906), a novel of substantially greater merit than the later volumes of *The Forsyte Saga*. In this book, which is set in the heavily respectable upper-middle-class London of the eighteen-eighties, Galsworthy first introduced to the world the vast interlocking clan of the Forsytes, who were subsequently to become softened in the public imagination to a gallery of much loved and familiar faces. But Galsworthy's original imagination was satirical and, for its time, bold. The Forsytes, brooding over their property and the price of Consols, are shown in a cold, even derisive light. And no-one is depicted with sharper irony than the novel's central figure, Soames Forsyte, a rising solicitor in his thirties, tight-lipped, closely shaven and supercilious (in portraying him, Galsworthy seems to have made a classical embodiment of the Freudian anal-erotic type, complete with hoarding instinct). *The Man of Property* describes the break-up of Soames's marriage. For all his cold nature he is passionately in love with his beautiful, enigmatic wife, Irene; but she finds him repulsive. She falls in love with a young architect, Philip Bosinney, and their affair ends tragically.

The novel is centred on two pieces of highly expensive property: Robin Hill, the country house which Bosinney has designed for Soames, and Irene herself. Galsworthy establishes a parallel between them by showing Soames engaging in litigation with Bosinney over the cost of his house at the same time as he is losing Irene to him. Galsworthy emphasises the 'property' motif with some insistence: at one point Soames exercises his marital rights over Irene in what, it is implied, is a virtual rape, and this is later described as 'the greatest—the supreme act of property'. Galsworthy is better at social satire than in rendering scenes of passion, most of which are heavily melodramatic. But the satire is sufficiently prevalent and incisive to make *The Man of Property* one of the best novels to have been written in Edwardian England. Galsworthy draws the Forsytes as purely social beings: rather more than mere caricatures, but something less than deeply conceived fictional characters. They seem, in fact, to exist on the same plane of reality as their furniture and hangings, stuffed and gilded objects rather than authentic persons, impossible to imagine outside the oppressive physical setting of their tall, over-furnished houses in Kensington or Bayswater. It was this over-materiality that Virginia Woolf objected to, but Galsworthy was in fact exposing a particular social ethos, illustrating the process that Marxists call 'reification', in which persons or ideas or values are transformed into fetichistic objects. Yet he was unable to maintain his indictment: in later volumes of the *Saga* the Forsytes are sentimentalized, and Soames is transformed from a tragic villain into the admired and endorsed central intelligence of the novel. As Lawrence remarked, 'Galsworthy had not quite enough of the superb courage of his satire. He faltered, and gave in to the Forsytes'.

Of the other 'Edwardians', in Virginia Woolf's sense, H. G. Wells is the most interesting, but at the same time the hardest to keep in critical focus. Although he was in a genuine though uneven way a literary artist, he was increasingly determined to be much more than that, until in the course of a celebrated quarrel with Henry James in 1915, he wrote, 'I had rather be called a journalist than an artist, that is the truth of it'. As a young man in the eighteen-nineties, Wells had achieved popularity with his scientific romances, works which, as well as being splendidly entertaining, embodied a series of brilliant mythopoeic visions. By the turn of his century his reputation had grown so that he was the most celebrated man of letters in England, and Wells's tremendous energies sought outlets in several different fields at once. He went on to develop the vein of sentimental realism that he had exhibited in *Love and Mr. Lewisham* (1900), and during the following decade produced several realistic novels of a broadly Dickensian kind; of these, *The History of Mr. Polly* (1910) is the most complete artistic success, an enchanting work that celebrates its humble hero's successful desire to escape from the squalor and boredom of the contemporary world. At the same time, Wells was becoming increasingly interested in politics—he was for some years a dissatisfied member of the Fabian society—and in speculative sociology. His visions of the future, which, in the nineties, had been wholly pessimistic, now took on a brighter aspect, as Wells became convinced of the possibilities of radical improvements in the human lot, thanks to scientific discovery and large-scale social engineering. His *A Modern Utopia* (1905) is the first and best of a long series of imaginative projections of a

24

transformed future that Wells wrote at intervals during the rest of his life. It made a great impact at the time and still has a certain period charm. What is, perhaps, hard for a modern reader to recapture is the way in which Wells, during the 1900's, offered an imaginative and intellectual vision of escape to thousands of young people who desired above all to free themselves from the constricting remnants of Victorianism. A novel such as Wells's *Ann Veronica* (1909), about a young girl's search for fulfilment, at first in the suffragette movement and then in wholly personal terms, acquired a significance far beyond its slender literary merits.

In *Tono-Bungay* (1909) Wells made an ambitious attempt to write a long novel that would embody a large-scale social panorama, of Victorian comprehensiveness. Its central story is about a small-town pharmacist who makes a fortune out of a useless patent medicine; his success catapults him into the world of Edwardian high finance, in which, for a time, he cuts a great figure, until at length his fraudulent business methods are exposed and he dramatically tumbles to disaster. *Tono-Bungay* is a consistently entertaining work, which includes most of Well's current preoccupations : Dickensian comedy in the account of Teddy Ponderevo's humble origins and meteoric rise; science fiction, in the episodes that deal with the construction of a new kind of flying machine; the laboured analysis of marital problems; and a vivid employment of the sociological imagination in anatomizing the Edwardian plutocracy, a process comparable to Galsworthy's presentation of the Forsytes, though Wells is livelier if less scrupulous. The novel is more impressive as a sprawling social panorama than as a portrayal of the subtleties of individual behaviour, and to this extent it embodies Wells's characteristic strengths and weaknesses as a novelist. Nevertheless, it won the admiration of such a scrupulous critic as Ford Madox Ford, who serialized it in the *English Review*, and of the young D. H. Lawrence, who continued to regard it as a touchstone of Wells's fictional excellence when he attacked later books by Wells like *The World of William Clissold*. Even though it is far from being a novel of deliberate aesthetic concentration, *Tono-Bungay* has worn remarkably well.

Arnold Bennett is a less various figure, and more consciously a literary artist than either Galsworthy or Wells, and to this extent Virginia Woolf's attack is not wholly fair. But insofar as Bennett was a rebel, his rebellion was limited to questions of literary allegiance. In many respects, the history of the

Modern Movement in English can be directly related to the degree of literary openness to French influence. In the eighteen-nineties there had been a certain interest in such poets as Rimbaud and Laforgue, although their influence was not to enter the mainstream of English poetry until their 'rediscovery' by Pound and Eliot twenty years later. Similarly, in fiction the influence of Flaubert and Zola and Maupassant was already beginning to affect the complacent insularity of the late Victorian novel, and George Moore was an important channel of such influence. Bennett began his career as a novelist in the eighteen-nineties, at a time when literary relations between England and France were very close; his model was George Moore, and behind Moore the French naturalists themselves. He knew French well, lived for much of his life in Paris, and had a genuine feeling for French literature. It is, however, true that Bennett never acquired the concentration of those writers who were more centrally in the Flaubertian tradition and who regarded the novel as a supremely important literary form, such as James and Conrad and Ford. He was more in tune with the scrupulous naturalism of Zola. His immersion in the life of the Staffordshire pottery towns (the 'Five Towns') where he had grown up prevented him from ever giving total allegiance to the canons of extreme selectivity in fiction: his fascination with accumulated physical detail was too strong. And in his sense of humour and his awareness of the endless varieties of human eccentricity he was, perhaps despite himself, Dickensian.

Bennett was a man of prodigious energy, who wrote fiction on two levels: in addition to those carefully planned novels which he regarded as serious works of art, he produced a great many books of a frankly pot-boiling kind in order to make money. Of the former, *Anna of the Five Towns* (1902) remains a distinguished early example, a delicate character study whose mode of composition is deliberately selective. But it is *The Old Wives' Tale* (1908) which is generally and rightly thought of as Bennett's masterpiece, though it is a book in which we see his awareness of the French canons of novelistic art being swamped by his saturation in the physical presence of the world he is describing. *The Old Wives' Tale* is about the girlhood, adult life and old age of two sisters in the Five Towns, and it is a novel obsessed with the slow but inexorable passing of time: Walter Allen has described it as 'the most impressive record we have in English of life in time, of birth, change and decay', but adds that it is important to realize 'the simple basis of the novel, which is that of so many of the most moving lyric poems, that girls must grow old and beauty fade'. Although there are many exuberant passages in *The Old Wives' Tale*, the total impression it leaves is sombre, strongly marked by Bennett's conviction that there is not much one can do about life but endure it, whatever it may do to one. It was this quality that provoked Lawrence to protest: 'I hate Bennett's resignation. Tragedy ought really to be a great kick at misery'. This quality of resignation is also evident in *Clayhanger* (1910), another fine novel and a good example of the Edwardian *Bildungsroman*. Unlike Galsworthy or Wells, Bennett was not concerned to expose social abuses or deride any particular class or group; although he was capable of writing satirically, satire plays little part in his fiction. He wrote as an artist, without any other design than to render what he saw; and if the passing of the years has shown the limitations of his best novels with some clarity, nevertheless their survival as art seems assured.

There were, however, other novelists writing at the same time as Galsworthy, Wells and Bennett, who, though less acknowledged then, now seem of intrinsically greater importance on the map of twentieth-century literature. Henry James, for instance, though one of the greatest novelists ever to have written in English, can merely be mentioned in passing in this survey. Despite his long residence in England he must be considered as part of the history of American literature; and in any case the majority of his novels were written during the last three decades of the nineteenth century. After the turn of the century James published three long and intricate novels in which he turned again to the 'international theme' of his early novels, which dealt with dramatic collisions between innocent Americans and worldly Europeans; these were *The Wings of the Dove* (1902), *The Ambassadors* (1903) and *The Golden Bowl* (1904). These books have been much discussed during the past twenty years or so: many critics regard them as the peak of James's achievement, but there is not general agreement about their place in his work. Although the extreme intricacy of their style, reflecting the movement of a mind of almost unfathomable subtlety, combined with the remoteness of their subject-matter, make these novels difficult of access to the present-day reader, they have the spiritual penetration that characterizes the major works of the Modern Movement. Strange though they seem, James's immensely rich and cultivated Americans moving in a world without fixed points of connection or sense of community, anticipate the rootlessness and alienation that typifies so much present-day existence, as R. P. Blackmur pointed out some years ago:

> His own experience of 'America' and of 'Europe', where America had apparently moved faster than Europe towards the mass society, towards the disinheritance but not the disappearance of the individual, had moved him ahead of his contemporaries; had moved him to the nineteen-thirties when he began to be read seriously, and the 'forties when he got to be the rage, and now to the 'fifties when he seems, so to speak, an exaggerated and highly sensitized form of the commonplace of our experience . . .[5]

By the 1900's James had a respectable reputation, but his work aroused little public interest and his books did not sell at all well, a point to which he ruefully referred from time to time in his correspondence with the younger and far more successful writer, H. G. Wells. James carried the novel of aesthetic concentration, of selective presentation and total dramatization, to a point of great refinement, and his critical writings —particularly the prefaces he wrote for a revised edition of his own novels—have laid the foundation for much subsequent academic criticism of fiction. James was the supreme representative in English of Flaubert's conception of the novel as high art, although his own finely developed moral sensibility made him reject the inhuman element in Flaubert's aestheticism.

This concept of the novel was shared by Joseph Conrad, who is certainly one of the greatest English novelists, and at the same time one of the hardest to fit into convenient critical categories. His origins and background were romantically unlike those of most English men of letters: he was born in Poland, of a minor aristocratic family, and as a young man took to life at sea, beginning his career in French ships, but ending as a member of the British merchant service. He did not learn English until the start of his adult life. His career at sea brought Conrad many adventures, which were later recapitulated in his tales and novels: ironically, he has always had a considerable reputation as a writer of stirring yarns about the sea, even though such works are not among his most important books, and he was anything but a simple spinner of adventure stories. His first novel, *Almayer's Folly* appeared in 1895, when he was thirty-eight, and it was not until then that he left the sea and devoted himself to full-time writing. Conrad's books are written in an impeccable though somewhat unidiomatic English prose, but they are pervaded by a sense of values that is scarcely English. From his Polish origins Conrad drew certain strong convictions about the importance of chivalry, honour and reputation, which seem positively feudal when placed in a context of late-nineteenth century bourgeois society. His feelings about honour are well expressed in *Lord Jim* (1900), one of his best-known books, which is about a young ship's officer who deserts his post on an apparently sinking vessel, and spends long years as a wandering exile in the Far East, always conscious of his besmirched honour, which he finally redeems in a heroic death. Conrad's experience as an officer in the merchant service left him with a view of existence which concentrates on a small, enclosed world, where the supreme values are endurance, authority and fidelity. He had a thoroughly pessimistic view of existence, with little room for liberal optimism or progressive sentiments: the ship as an enclave of order and purpose was surrounded by the blind, hostile forces of Nature and chaos, which might at any time overwhelm it. Such a view of life has something in common with that of the existentialist philosophers, and it was very much in advance of its time in Edwardian England. Conrad had little belief in the staying power of Western civililization, and he shows the collapse of conventional Western values in *Heart of Darkness* (1902). This novella is set in darkest Africa, in the Congo, and it offers both an insight into metaphysical despair and an indictment of imperialism. The combination of metaphysical extremity and political understanding is unique in English fiction, and one has to look for anything similar to Dostoievsky, an author whom Conrad disliked—as he did everything Russian—but whose influence is apparent in another important novel, *Under Western Eyes* (1911).

In *The Secret Agent*, (1907), which is one of Conrad's most compelling books, all the constituents of his particular world are apparent. There is no vision of society as a whole, although we are very much concerned with questions of social action: the novel is about revolutionaries and an *agent-provocateur* in late-Victorian London. We are shown a number of illuminated scenes, standing out by contrast from the prevailing darkness: in Conrad's view of things, there is no reason to regard London as radically different from Central Africa. We see a meeting at the Russian embassy, a succession of scenes in a seedy backstreet newsagent's shop, used by the revolutionaries as a meeting place, a portentous encounter between a senior police officer and the Home Secretary at the House of Commons. Read simply as a thriller, *The Secret Agent* can still maintain a satisfying level of suspense, but even at a casual reading one sees that there is much more to it than that. If we are attentive we are left with a disturbing sense of human isolation, of the precariousness of any kind of organized society—even one as complacent as late-Victorian England—and of the absurdity of politics. There is also a surprising amount of dark comedy in the book, indicating a certain debt to Dickens; its total effect may be summed up in T. S. Eliot's phrase, 'tragic farce'.

By common consent, Conrad's masterpiece is *Nostromo* (1904), a long, very highly organized novel, in which it is not merely an individual or group that is focused on in isolation, but a whole country, the South American republic of Costaguana, locked between sea and mountains. Conrad presents Costaguana as a microcosm of contemporary civilization : it is dominated by a silver mine, and Conrad weaves the motif of 'silver' throughout his narrative. There are clashes between the local political interests, and the designs of Western capitalists who want to exploit the wealth of the mine. There are many characters : the title figure, 'Nostromo', is a dashing Italian overseer, a typical Conradian individual in his absorption with his own reputation, who is nevertheless not, in the end, exempt from the corrupting force of the silver; amongst other major characters there are Charles Gould, the owner of the mine, and the embodiment of an ideal of liberal capitalism, who lives only for the mine and the material advances he sees it as bringing to Costaguana; Dr. Monygham, who once betrayed his political associates under torture, and who spends the rest of his life a sardonic, broken figure trying to live down the shame of that betrayal; Captain Mitchell, a stupid, bluff, honest English seaman; and Martin Decoud, a French-educated intellectual, whose capacity for action is vitiated by a radical scepticism. As F. R. Leavis has pointed out, there is something of Decoud in Conrad himself, and running through the book there is a tension between Conrad's belief in the traditional virtues of order, fidelity and discipline, and a deeper underlying scepticism about the viability of any human values at all. In the honesty with which it poses these dilemmas, and in its stress on violence and insurrection and the reality of economic exploitation, *Nostromo* remains an astonishingly modern work: it seems to be far more about our world than the seemingly sedate one of the Edwardians.

Conrad was a master of fictional technique, who had studied long and arduously with the masters of the French tradition, and by all accounts he found writing agonizingly difficult. He undoubtedly lavished all his mastery on *Nostromo*, which Walter Allen has described as 'the most highly organized novel in English apart from perhaps the late James and Joyce's *Ulysses*'. The intricacy of Conrad's technique is evident in the difficult but justifiable manipulation of time sequence in the opening chapters, which marks a decisive break with Victorian narrative method. At the same time, there are clearly marked limitations to Conrad's range as a novelist: he could not, for instance, portray convincing women characters, and his attempts to introduce 'love interest' tend to be embarrassingly bad. Conrad's style was always conscious, even calculated, and at times it was liable to degenerate into an over-assertive rhetoric, where his sense of the strangeness and mysteriousness of life would be conveyed through a plethora of adjectives rather than directly enacted.

A writer who has affinities with Joseph Conrad is Rudyard Kipling: he too acquired a public following as a writer of exciting tales set in far-away places, although he was also a subtle, complex and disconcerting artist. Like Conrad, Kipling was deeply interested in the nature and significance of Imperialism, and although he was a committed believer in Britain's imperial role, he was never the crude unthinking jingo that popular sentiment sometimes made him out to be. Kipling also resembled Conrad in looking at English life with an alien eye: he was born in England, but spent the formative years of his adolescence and young manhood working as a journalist in India, and although the early books that drew on his Indian experience, like *Departmental Ditties* (1886: verse) and *Plain Tales from the Hills* (1888) quickly established him as one of the most admired young writers of his day, he was always something of an outsider in English life. Although Kipling wrote a great deal of highly accomplished verse, his literary reputation rests primarily on his short stories. Kipling early on showed a mastery of that exacting if limited art form, for which he had served two separate but parallel apprenticeships. His years as a journalist in India taught him the importance of precision and extreme economy in writing prose; but at the same time he was a keen reader of de Maupassant and other masters of French naturalism. It is only slowly and, as it were, reluctantly that critics have accepted Kipling as an important man of letters, and even now his final stature is problematical. Part of the difficulty is that although Kipling was a genuine literary artist, with a great devotion to his craft, he used his art, at times, to advance a view of experience that was highly illiberal, in ways that offended—and still offend—the sensibility of most reasonably enlightened modern readers. If his belief in imperialism was defensible in a theoretical way, there is something intensely jarring in the way Kipling advances his views, and the readers of his stories are often invited to endorse attitudes that are frankly brutal, and even cruel. Other major writers, admittedly, have been political and social reactionaries, but for the most part they have avoided Kipling's crude over-emphasis of tone and cheerful contempt for the liberal virtues. Yet this crudity represents only one side of Kipling's art: to see how capable he was of tenderness and human warmth, one need only read such a story as 'Without Benefit of Clergy', a moving, tragic tale about an English civil servant in India, his Indian mistress and their child. Kipling is a complicated writer, some of whose stories show a remarkable degree of obscurity and ambiguity; here he approaches the characteristically Modern taste for literature that needs explication in depth (which had been ironically glanced at in a *novella* by Henry James, 'The Figure in the Carpet', published in the nineties): Kipling's story, 'Mrs. Bathurst' is a particularly teasing example.

If Kipling's Imperialism had its vulgar side, it was at heart a pessimistic, even tragic vision; although he had become convinced by his Indian experience of the rightness and nobility of the Empire, he came increasingly to feel that the Empire was being betrayed by the slack and decadent inhabitants of modern England, and that, like the Roman Empire, it was doomed to pass away. Kipling embodied this conviction in a remarkable book, nominally intended for children, called *Puck of Pook's Hill*, published in 1906. Although it can still be read as an admirable children's book, *Puck of Pook's Hill*, which describes a series of magical visits back into earlier periods of English history, offers in essence Kipling's intense and sombre vision of the English past as it illuminated the English present. He identifies the Roman legionaries guarding Hadrian's wall with the young British soldiers defending remote corners of the Empire in India, largely forgotten by the indifferent population at home. Noel Annan has brilliantly analysed this book, concluding that Shaw's *Heartbreak House*, Forster's *Howards End* and *Puck of Pook's Hill* 'are the attempts by a socialist, a liberal, and a conservative to discern England's destiny'.[6]

The name of Ford Madox Ford has already occurred in this essay, both as a literary associate and collaborator of Conrad's, and as editor of the *English Review* between 1908 and 1910. He played an active part in Edwardian literary life, and was proficient in many kinds of writing: novels, poetry, biographies, travel books, *belles lettres*. For several years Ford's work in these fields was competent but not distinguished; what set him apart from other Edwardian men of letters was the intensity of his devotion to literature and art—an intensity that Ford could not always uphold when faced with the exigencies of earning a living by his pen—and his somewhat un-English discipleship to Flaubert and the other French masters. Ford's Edwardian fiction is not among his best work, but his *Fifth Queen* trilogy, about Henry VIII's Queen, Katharine Howard, which was published between 1906 and 1908, is a work of some distinction. It is vividly and dramatically written, and has few of the usual faults of historical fiction. But Ford was not to achieve his full stature as a novelist for a few more years. On his fortieth birthday, in 1913, he embarked on a novel which was to be as artistically fine as he could make it: this work was published in 1915 as *The Good Soldier* (despite the date, the novel had nothing to do with the war; Ford disliked this title, which was suggested by his publisher, and had originally intended to call the book *The Saddest Story*). This remarkable work is certainly one of the masterpieces of modern English fiction, a brief, tightly-wrought, formally very intricate story, about the adulterous entanglements between two rich families, the Ashburnhams and the Dowells, in their successive meetings in a German watering place during the 1900's. The subject matter may seem conventional, but the whole quality of the book is in the rendering; one critic has referred to it as the 'best French novel in the English language'. Despite its formal fascination, the core of *The Good Soldier* lies in its intense vision of the human condition, whose confusion and pathos are successively revealed in the intricate, minuet-like movements of Ford's couples. In this novel, form and content are completely at one, and the action unfolds through the successive discoveries made by the weak and duped narrator, John Dowell, and the kaleidoscopic changes they force on his consciousness. *The Good Soldier* shows what Ford was capable of in a constricted, intensive mode of fiction; later, in *Parade's End*, he turned to the large-scale fictional panorama.

## III

1910, even if it lacked the cataclysmic quality ascribed to it by Virginia Woolf, has several claims to significance. Edward VII died, and the accession of the new king, George V, brought the hope that a fresh start could be made after the conspicuous vulgarity and grossness associated with the Edwardian interlude. In the arts other than literature English insularity seemed at last to be breaking down: 1910 saw the First Post-Impressionist Exhibition, which showed what had been done by the new wave of continental painters, and in that year, too, Richard Strauss's operas *Elektra* and *Salome* were performed in London. In 1911 Diaghilev brought his Russian Ballet to London (it included in its repertoire several celebrated works by Stravinsky) whose brilliant union of diverse arts aroused astonishment and enthusiasm in audiences unaccustomed to regarding ballet as high art. In social and political matters the years between 1910 and 1914 were full of contradictions: a general sense of hope, and even of complacent optimism, was undercut by growing unrest at home, and a sense of increasing menace on the international scene. The fascinating but confused public climate of that time has been ably described in George Dangerfield's *The Strange Death of Liberal England* (1935).

This mixture of promise and confusion was apparent in an interesting novel published in 1910, E. M. Forster's *Howards End*. Forster was thirty-one when this book appeared, and he had already published three other novels, pleasant but slight books, which embody themes not confined to Forster's work: Cambridge as an ideal of civilization and enlightenment; the supreme value of personal relationships; the stuffiness, even deadness of conventional English middle-class life, and the importance of Italy as a source of personal liberation for the northern visitor. One of these novels, *The Longest Journey*, is in the form of a *Bildungsroman* visibly showing the influence of Samuel Butler's *The Way of All Flesh*; it is a mawkish book, which indicates Forster's weaknesses rather than his strengths. *Howard End* is a good deal better, yet one uses the word 'interesting' of it advisedly, for its cultural significance is greater than its purely literary merit. The epigraph of this novel consists of the two words 'Only Connect', which express the book's thematic aspiration. Forster shows contemporary England divided between the Wilcox family, who represent activity, commerce, Empire-building, the whole world of what one character calls 'telegrams and anger'; and the Schlegels, two highly cultivated girls of German origin, who embody the liberal ideals of sensibility, personal relations and love of art. A third element is sketchily represented by an unfortunate young clerk, Leonard Bast, whose aspirations to culture are patronized by the other characters, but whom Forster want us to see as the embodiment of the democratic future. (He is a very uncertainly and externally rendered version of a type that H. G. Wells had drawn with intimate knowledge in his own novels). Forster shows the division between these groups very effectively, but his attempt to discover—or impose—connections between them lapses, in the second part of the book, into melodrama and incredibility. Yet *Howards End* remains impressive as an attempt—in Noel Annan's words—'to discern England's destiny'. Forster uses the modest Hertfordshire country house which gives its name to the novel as a symbol of the continuity of English tradition; one can compare Wells's use of the much grander mansion, Bladesover, in *Tono-Bungay*, another novel to which Annan's phrase could be applied. Although he was sensitive to the unrests of the time, Forster's fictional technique was conservative; in many ways he remained a disciple of George Meredith. It was not until he published his fifth and last novel, *A Passage to India*, in 1924, that Forster made a radical step forward in the form of the novel, and achieved a new and remarkable aesthetic intensity and degree of tragic understanding.

The year 1911 saw the appearance of D. H. Lawrence's first novel, *The White Peacock*, an immature work, heavily indebted to Hardy and George Eliot, which gives only a limited sense of the later development of Lawrence's genius. Like Forster, Lawrence was depressed by the deadness of conventional English life, and was intermittently convinced of the liberating possibilities of Italian life for the northern consciousness—clearly brought out for instance, in a novel like *The Lost Girl*—but he was unlike Forster in having had a direct knowledge of the nature of industrial society. Lawrence's major novels, particularly *Women in Love*, also attempt in their own way to 'discern England's destiny', a topic that became almost obsessive with Lawrence during the black years of the First World War. But Lawrence's was a more individual vision than Forster's, less moulded by a conventional education and inherited cultural attitudes, and his total achievement as a novelist is of a far more impressive order: it will be discussed in detail in a later chapter.

The period extending from 1900 to 1914 was a good deal richer in fiction than in poetry. Most of the illustrious Victorian poets were dead by 1900; only Swinburne and Meredith survived in old age until 1909. Even the poets of the nineties, whose verse was more noticeable for manner than for matter, but who had possessed the limited virtue of a conscious attachment to style, tended not to live long into the new century: Wilde, of course, died in 1900, and so did Ernest Dowson; Lionel Johnson lingered on for another two years, before dying at the age of thirty-five. One of the most robust and interesting poets of the nineties was the Scotsman, John Davidson, a disciple of Nietzsche and a realistic observer of the urban scene; during the 1900's his poetry seemed to be developing, in its own way, towards the techniques of the Modern Movement, but he committed suicide in 1909.

Unquestionably, the one major poet to have been nurtured in the poetic circles of the nineties (though his roots were elsewhere) was W. B. Yeats; but the 1900's were a period when much of his energy went into work for the theatre, and his poetry was passing through a transitional period between his early work, with its immersion in the myths of the Celtic Twilight and symbolist imprecision, and the mature poetry that began to emerge in *The Green Helmet* (1910) and was more confidently present in *Responsibilities* (1914). It is the mature Yeats, whose work offers such an astonishing blend of the colloquial and the formal, the public and the aesthetic, who is accounted a great modern poet, even though his relationship to the Modern Movement is a somewhat oblique one. The most admired English poet during the Edwardian decade was Kipling, who was preoccupied with asserting the glories of Empire and at the same time berating the English for their indifference to defending Nation and Empire. In one of his most deeply felt poems on this theme. 'The Islanders', Kipling made his familiar attack on 'The flannelled fools at the wicket and the muddied oafs at the goal'. The imperialist theme was taken up by a variety of lesser poets, who lacked Kipling's idiosyncratic and essentially sombre vision. During the 1900's Thomas Hardy, who had gone back to poetry after the hostile reception of *Jude the Obscure* in 1896, was writing copiously though without attracting a great many readers. Hardy's reputation as a poet has grown slowly but surely during the forty years since his death, until it has reached a point where, as we have seen, Phillip Larkin can regard him as by far the best poet of the twentieth century: he has always been something of a poet's poet, who has influenced the work of W. H. Auden, C. Day Lewis, and John Betjeman, as well as Mr. Larkin himself. Whether Hardy really possesses the stature, however, to form the focus for an anti-Modern 'native tradition' in English poetry is doubtful, despite the claims of his admirers. Hardy had a splendid lyric gift, and his feeling for the humble tragedies and perennial failures of the human condition has an impressive warmth and decency. But he was also a remarkably clumsy poet, whose feeling for language, though laboured, was frequently inadequate to express his insights. He has, unquestionably, a personal and frequently appealing voice, and in the great bulk of his poetry there are a good number of successful poems. For several years Hardy was engaged on a vast epic-drama about the Napoleonic wars, called *The Dynasts*, which appeared in three sections between 1904 and 1908. A poet who has something in common with Hardy is A. E. Housman, who was a less prolific and a more perfect artist; he too uses themes from English rural life to express a pessimistic personal philosophy. Housman published *A Shropshire Lad* in 1896, and his *Last Poems* appeared in 1922; his finely chiselled verse links Housman with the nineties, and his concern with the English countryside gives him affinities with the Georgians, though his view of poetry was more fastidious than theirs.

The word 'Georgian' frequently occurs in discussions of modern poetry, nearly always in a perjorative sense. The Georgians are seen as a group of feeble versifiers, representing the last gasp of the great Romantic and Victorian traditions, who were shortly to be swept away by the truly Modern poets like Ezra Pound and T. S. Eliot. The facts are less straightforward. The Georgians certainly saw themselves as reacting both against Edwardian imperialistic bombast and the remains of the *fin de siècle* spirit. They were inclined to the small-scale, unpretentious treatment of familiar subjects, and a poetic diction that was unelevated and which might, on occasion, even be vigorously colloquial. They favoured simple English themes, as opposed to the exoticism of the nineties, and they were happy to appeal to a wide audience. The first of the Georgian anthologies, published in 1912, was, according to the editor, Edward Marsh, 'issued in the belief that English poetry is now once again putting on a new strength and beauty'. By degrees the concept 'Georgian' has come to seem applicable to more poets

than the contributors to the original Georgian anthology and
its successors, like Rupert Brooke, W. H. Davis, Walter de la
Mare, John Drinkwater, W. W. Gibson, Lascelles Abercrombie,
John Masefield, Robert Graves, and Siegfried Sassoon, among
others. Such poets as Housman, Andrew Young, Charles Sorley,
Edward Thomas, Wilfred Owen and Edmund Blunden can also
be regarded as broadly Georgian in spirit, and have all been
included in a modern anthology, *Georgian Poetry* (1962), edited
by James Reeves.

One recent critic, C. K. Stead, has seen the Georgians as
personifying the spirit of liberal cultural aspiration in the years
just before 1914, and has related them to the humane ideals
expressed in *Howards End* :

> The Georgians belonged to the new liberal intellectual group
> that grew steadily in numbers during the first decade of this
> century; and their type is perhaps best illustrated by the
> Schlegel sisters in E. M. Forster's novel, *Howards End*. They
> did not consider it bad taste (as the Wilcox type did in the
> same novel) to discuss social problems. They were willing
> to think of the Leonard Basts and the geranium sellers of
> the world as human beings worthy of consideration. Politi-
> cally they were 'affiliated with the then dominant Liberal
> party'; intellectually they asserted 'that this new Georgian
> age should begin clear of all the muddled notions of its
> amorphous predecessor'. The Wilcox type on the other hand
> were imperialists of the Tory, rather than of the new 'liberal
> imperialist' kind, and undoubtedly approved of Henry New-
> bolt's Trafalgar Day Odes in *The Times*.[7]

There is an engaging evocation of this state of mind in the
correspondence of Rupert Brooke. It did not last long, for the
ideals of the Georgians were shattered by the outbreak of the
First World War in 1914. There was a rapid transformation
of the Georgian poets into the 'war poets', and their cherished
ideals of English rural life were held in nostalgic tension with
the grim actuality of trench warfare. Rupert Brooke died early
in the war, on his way to Gallipoli, and was enshrined in the
popular imagination as a brilliant young culture hero. Other
victims followed during the next three years : Charles Sorley,
Edward Thomas, Isaac Rosenberg, Wilfred Owen. Other poets
fought and chanced to survive, like Siegfried Sassoon, Robert
Graves, and Edmund Blunden. All of them wrote poetry about
the war; Siegfried Sassoon's was the most celebrated, expressing
in angry, satirical verse a mood of bitter disillusionment about

the continued slaughter. The survivors returned to their memories in a more extended form in prose works published ten or more years after the end of the war, like Sassoon's *Memoirs of a Fox-Hunting Man* and *Memoirs of an Infantry Officer*, Graves's *Goodbye to All That*, and Blunden's *Undertones of War*. Of those who perished, Wilfred Owen is generally regarded as the most remarkably gifted: he was only twenty-five when he died, a week before the Armistice in 1918, and his fairly brief exposure to the conditions of the Western Front rapidly transformed him from a conventional versifier writing in a sub-Keatsian manner to a poet who showed a uniquely intense and wholly new poetic realization of the horrors of large-scale technological warfare. Owen's poetry is full of the pity of war, just as Sassoon's is full of its anger. The only victim of the war who approached Owen's achievement is Isaac Rosenberg, a Jewish private soldier from the East End of London, who was unlike most of the Georgians in being a conscious experimenter in verse techniques.

The Georgians, whether in their pre-war form or in their later guise as war poets, may have been literary innovators, but they were not revolutionaries. They were content to use familiar verse forms, with slight modifications of tone and diction. It is a paradox that the First World War, which had a cataclysmic effect on the settled patterns of English life, was directly encountered by poets whose poetic habits and modes of understanding were scarcely adequate—or often quite inadequate—to grasp the unprecedented modes of experience that they were forced to undergo. At the same time, the poets who were most deeply concerned with the remaking of English poetry—Pound, Eliot, Yeats—were able, by reasons of nationality or age, to remain aloof from the war. The refashioning of artistic form, and the associated new ways of looking at experience, which were already familiar in music and painting by about 1912, and were beginning to appear in the novel, were slow to enter into English poetry.

In any account of the advent of Modern poetry in English the name of Ezra Pound must take a central place: Pound arrived in London in 1908 as a young and quite unknown American poet and stayed until 1921; during those years he achieved considerable eminence in avant-garde circles as poet, critic and impresario of the arts generally. Pound's gifts as a poet were an exquisitely fine ear and sense of rhythm; an ability to project brilliant visual images; and a wide if somewhat disorganized reading in several foreign literatures, which he readily drew on to enlarge the possibilities of writing verse in English. His early poetry was an elegant pastiche of Browning and the Pre-Raphaelites and the poets of the nineties, and although he achieved a greater modernity of theme and manner, Pound was always an intensely literary poet who used other poetry—whether Latin or Provençal or Chinese—as a way of formulating his own feelings. In the words of A. Alvarez:

> He needs the framework of translation. It keeps his intellect and imagination at full stretch by providing for all the technical business whilst he sustains his understanding of the poem and the poet. Within those limits he recreates the feeling for himself. As a poet he moves, thinks and feels with the greatest ease and strength in other men's clothes.[8]

In Pound's two most successful poetic works, *Homage to Sextus Propertius* (1919) and *Hugh Selwyn Mauberley* (1920), he uses the figures of two poets as *personae* (or masks) behind which he can make a critique of contemporary English civilization: the first is the Roman poet Propertius, whose Latin verse is freely adapted rather than accurately translated by Pound; the second is an imaginary minor English poet of the eighteen-nineties, whose art has some affinities with Pound's own.

Even the best of Pound's poetry has a somewhat backward-looking air about it when compared with the work of innovators in the other arts; with, for instance, the music of Schoenberg, the paintings of Picasso and Braque, or the sculpture of Gaudier-Brzeska. The impression that Pound made on other artists in 1914 has been vigorously described by Wyndham Lewis; Pound and Lewis had collaborated in 1914 in the short-lived Vorticist movement, which aimed to unite the literary and pictorial avant-garde, and had published an iconoclastic magazine, *Blast*; but, as Lewis remarks, the painters were not greatly impressed with Pound's claims to modernity:

> Ezra Pound attached himself to the Blast Group. That group was composed of people all very 'extremist' in their views. In the matter of fine art, as distinct from literature, it was their policy to admit no artist disposed to technical compromise, as they regarded it. What struck them principally about Pound was that his fire-eating propagandist utterances were not accompanied by any very experimental efforts in his particular medium. His poetry, to the mind of the more fanatical of the group, was a series of pastiches of old French or old Italian poetry, and could lay no claim to participate in the new burst of art in progress. Its novelty consisted

largely in the distance it went *back*, not forward; in archaism, not in new creation. That was how they regarded Pound's literary contributions. But this certain discrepancy between what Pound said—what he supported and held up as an example—and what he did, was striking enough to impress itself on anybody.[9]

The division between poet and painters that Lewis describes was largely the result of the contradictions in Pound's temperament; but it also had larger implications. Stephen Spender, in *The Struggle of the Modern* (1963), has remarked that the collaboration of writers, painters and musicians in the years before 1914, though it produced some striking activity, mostly in Paris, was inevitably threatened by the fact that writers could not rival the really revolutionary innovations of the painters and musicians, since their medium, language, was inescapably rooted in the past.

Within the field of literature, however, Pound's importance was considerable, although it stemmed less from his example as a poet than from his tireless energies as editor, talent-scout and impresario generally. His sponsoring of Joyce, for instance, was a case in point: Pound helped to find a publisher for Joyce's book of short stories, *Dubliners* in 1914, and arranged for his first novel, *A Portrait of the Artist as a Young Man*, to be serialized in the *Egoist* in 1914–15 and to appear in book form in 1916. In poetry Pound launched the Imagist movement in 1912. The basic principles of Imagism were to present an experience itself rather than reflections drawn from the experience; to use words in an exact, economical fashion; to prefer the concrete to the abstract; and to attempt a high degree of sensuous immediacy, which in practice tended to mean high visual definition. These principles have become basic in much poetry deriving from the Modern Movement, though they have been rigorously upheld in American rather than English poetry. T. S. Eliot, in his influential critical notion of the 'objective correlative', which stated that a poet should not attempt to express emotion directly, but should project and embody it in some aspect of the external world, formulated a theoretical counterpart to Imagist practice. Nevertheless, these principles, or some of them, were not invented by Pound: poems of Imagist precision and high definition were written from time to time in the nineties and 1900's, by Arthur Symons and other poets, and there was a continued interest in the compressed small-scale forms of Japanese poetry, which tended to produce

Imagist effects when applied in English. In about 1908 the philosopher T. E. Hulme—whose aesthetic ideas had a considerable influence on the Modern Movement—wrote a handful of short poems corresponding with Imagist prescriptions, five of which were reprinted by Pound in 1912 as a postscript to his own book, *Ripostes*. In 1912 Pound saw the Imagist school as consisting largely of himself and two young protegees, Richard Aldington and H. D. (Hilda Doolittle); in 1914 an anthology appeared called *Des Imagistes*, which included the work of these three poets, together with several other contributors (including Ford and Joyce) whose work supposedly approximated to Imagist principles. Unlike the Georgians, the Imagists were not interested in a wide readership, and they were very open to French and other non-English influences. Yet the present-day reader who looks in an open-minded way at the first volume of *Georgian Poetry* and at *Des Imagistes* will probably be struck by the fact that both groups are noticeably derivative and literary, even following for the Imagists' taste for free verse and poetic condensation.

But despite all Pound's admirably energetic activity, the simple truth is that the really radical examples of the new poetry in English had been produced quite independently of Pound's example and influence. In 1910 a young graduate student of philosophy at Harvard began writing a poem, which he finished on a visit to Munich the following year: this poem was 'The Love Song of J. Alfred Prufrock' by T. S. Eliot, one of the truly seminal works of modern literature, which was to remain in manuscript for four more years. 'Prufrock' is both a poem of superb verbal assurance and a work in which traditional apprehensions of experience are dissolved and refashioned, in a way that has something in common with the work of the avant-garde painters of the time. This much is apparent from the poem's striking opening:

> Let us go then, you and I,
> When the evening is spread out against the sky
> Like a patient etherized upon a table . . .

and from the bizarre distortions of its protagonist's relation to the world:

> And when I am formulated, sprawling on a pin,
> When I am pinned and wriggling on the wall,
> Then how should I begin
> To spit out all the butt-ends of my days and ways?

At about the same time as 'Prufrock' Eliot wrote the 'Preludes', four harsh vignettes of urban life; though composed before Pound formulated the Imagist principles, they express those principles more effectively than anything produced by Pound and his admirers. Pound, discovering Eliot and his work late in 1914, was immediately struck by the genius of his young compatriot, and at once directed his celebrated energies to getting Eliot's poetry published. Eliot had formed a style and a method entirely on his own, largely derived from the creative interaction of his reading in Baudelaire, Laforgue, and the Jacobean dramatists, long before he met Pound, even though Eliot later allowed himself to come under Pound's influence and direction. Pound edited the first version of *The Waste Land* : the final version was dedicated to Pound as 'il miglior fabbro', which means 'the better workman'. Eliot may have been drawing just attention to Pound's technical accomplishment, to express his gratitude for Pound's encouragement and help. Yet there can be no doubt that Eliot was the finer poet, and the more profound explorer, whose place in twentieth century literature—and in English literature generally—is more firmly established than Pound's.

Pound met Eliot after the First World War had already broken out : the next four years were to see both a catastrophic waste of life and resources, and an incalculable shock to traditional English attitudes. It was during those years that some of the major achievements of the Modern Movement appeared : Ford's *The Good Soldier* and Lawrence's *The Rainbow* in 1915; Joyce's *Portrait of the Artist* in 1916; Eliot's *Prufrock and Other Observations* and Pound's *Homage to Sextus Propertius* in 1917. None of these works directly reflected the war, although Pound's poem looked at it obliquely : in 1922 Eliot published *The Waste Land* where history and personal vision were brought into the same focus.

## V

It may be objected that in this survey the word 'Modern' has been freely used without having been adequately defined; or that it has been used in various senses; sometimes to refer to a particular literacy period and the works written in it, sometimes to a particular set of attitudes and qualities. Now that a good many writers and works have been referred to, further attempts can be made at clarifying terminology, though a total clarity can never be achieved, since the difficulties are not ultimately lexical, but form part of the material being discussed. It should be apparent that what distinguished, say, Lawrence or Joyce or Eliot from Bennett or Wells or Rupert Brooke was an unwillingness to take anything on trust, whether a sense of the nature of reality or the nature of literary form. Uncertainty was emphasized by a conviction that there had been a radical break with established cultural traditions, and that new ones had to be formed, or older ones recovered. Nothing, in short, could be taken for granted. And since it was felt that twentieth century urban society was of an unprecedented complexity, the very nature of perception had to be reformed in order to cope with this complexity, whether it was environmental, intellectual, or moral. A new comprehensiveness had to be found in literature; in such things as the extension of diction and imagery to take in the full spectrum of contemporary reality (in ways that had already been indicated by Baudelaire and Flaubert). Literature had to be open to a variety of relevant foreign cultural influences, and so emulate the international quality of art and music. Opposed and even contradictory insights and attitudes had to be accommodated within the same work, by the techniques of ironic juxtaposition and superimposition. The inner life of man was to be given as much weight as the outer world, and the unconscious mind given its place, alongside, or underlying, conscious modes of thought as traditionally understood.

Having said as much, one must acknowledge that a number of crucial problems remain. In the first place, the effects of Modernism on English cultural life have been much less total than was supposed in the fairly recent past. With the salient exception of Lawrence, the masters of Modernism were foreigners or Celts, who discovered in England (or at least the English cultural ambience) an accommodating home whilst they pursued their literary discoveries; but its soil was not to be particularly fertile for later growths in the modern manner. So that by about 1930 the major creative phase of the Modern Movement was over. Already, in the nineteen-twenties, Thomas Hardy had told Robert Graves: 'vers libre could come to nothing in England. "All we can do is to write on the old themes in the old styles, but try to do a little better than those who went before us." '[10] If one uses vers libre as shorthand for all the Modern innovations of form and sensibility, then it is evident that some of the most admired practitioners of poetry and fiction in England in the last twenty years have followed his advice to the letter. In 1948, the late Sir Herbert Read, a dedi-

44

cated Modernist, complained, like Trotsky, that the revolution had been betrayed; he remarked of the young poets of that period, 'one can only conclude that these poets have never stood where we stand, nor seen what we see, nor felt as we feel'. In the next two decades many voices could be heard denouncing the excesses of Modernism as being no more than idle experimentalism and obscurantism, a wilful retreat into unintelligibility, now happily ended, with the recovery of the still unbroken native traditions of English fiction and poetry. (In a very different accent, and speaking out of a very different tradition, the Marxist critic Georg Lukács has complained that 'modernism means not the enrichment, but the negation of art', and asserted the continued viability and potentiality of the central traditions of nineteenth-century realism). There were complex historical reasons why the Modern Movement, which came very late to England—one can look, by contrast, at what had happened in French poetry or Russian fiction from the middle of the nineteenth century—did not put down roots and was never properly established as a living tradition. What was already here was, in a sense, too strong; to try to unravel this question further would involve one in wide-ranging speculations about the essentially conservative and innocent nature of English cultural life.[11] There is no equivalent in our literature to those scenes in Flaubert's *L'Education Sentimental* in which the hero goes about his private affairs with the noise of a revolutionary street battle coming from round the corner. Even the masters of Modern literature in English are, in a sense, less radical, less uncompromisingly subversive than those from countries where the crises of the public order have deeply affected private life : one may compare Baudelaire, Dostoievsky or Kafka with Eliot, Lawrence or Joyce. English literature remains, at heart, literary; which is perhaps both its limitation and its privilege.

45

# NOTES

1. *The Modern Age*, ed. Boris Ford (Harmondsworth, 1961), p. 92.

2. Philip Larkin, 'Wanted : Good Hardy Critic', *Critical Quarterly*, viii (1966).

3. *The Letters of Ezra Pound 1907–1941*, ed. D. D. Paige (London, 1951), p. 80.

4. Frank Kermode, *The Sense of an Ending* (New York, 1967), pp. 97–98.

5. R. P. Blackmur, *The Lion and the Honeycomb* (London, 1956), pp. 287–88.

6. Noel Annan, 'Kipling's Place in the History of Ideas', *Kipling's Mind and Art*, ed. Andrew Rutherford (Edinburgh and London, 1964), pp. 97–125.

7. C. K. Stead, *The New Poetic* (London, 1964), pp. 85–86.

8. A. Alvarez, *The Shaping Spirit* (London, 1958), p. 59.

9. Wyndham Lewis, *Time and Western Man* (London, 1927), p. 55.

10. Robert Graves, *Goodbye to all That* (Harmondsworth, 1960), p. 251.

11. I attempt to take this question further in *The Situation of the Novel* (London, 1970).

# BIBLIOGRAPHY

There is no comprehensive recent study of the literature of the early twentieth century, although Frank Swinnerton, *The Georgian Literary Scene* (London, 1938), contains a good deal of miscellaneous information and is still worth consulting. Richard Ellmann (ed.), *Edwardians and Late Victorians* (English Institute Essays 1959: New York, 1960) has assembled some useful material; his own contribution, 'The Two Faces of Edward' is outstanding. Samuel Hynes, *The Edwardian Turn of Mind* (Princeton, 1968), is an excellent account of the Edwardian intellectual climate, which treats, in passing, a good deal of literary material.

For discussion of Modernism as a cultural phenomenon, see Frank Kermode, *Romantic Image* (London, 1957) and *Continuities* (London, 1968), and Stephen Spender, *The Struggle of the Modern* (London, 1963). Richard Ellmann and Charles Fiedelson, jr., have edited *The Modern Tradition: Backgrounds of Modern Literature* (New York, 1965), a vast collection of international texts which traces the cultural and intellectual history of Modernism back to the eighteenth century.

C. K. Stead's *The New Poetic* (London, 1964) is a brilliant and indispensable account of the origins of modern poetry, S. K. Coffman, *Imagism* (Norman, Oklahoma, 1951) is still a standard work, and Robert H. Ross, *The Georgian Revolt* (London, 1967), is a well-documented history of the Georgian movement. James Reeves. in his Penguin anthology, *Georgian Poetry* (Harmondsworth, 1962) provides a representative selection of the school. The poetry of the First World War is discussed in John H. Johnston, *English Poetry of the First World War* (Princeton and London, 1964) and Bernard Bergonzi, *Heroes' Twilight* (London, 1965). Studies of individual poets include D. S. R. Welland, *Wilfred Owen* (London, 1961) and Michael Thorpe, *Siegfried Sassoon* (Leyden and Oxford, 1966). Brian Gardner (ed.), *Up the Line to Death* (London, 1964), and I. M. Parsons (ed.), *Men Who March Away* (London, 1965) are the two most recent anthologies of war poetry.

There are useful studies of personalities who were important foci of literary activity in Alun R. Jones, *Thomas Ernest Hulme* (London, 1960), Christopher Hassall, *Edward Marsh* (London, 1959) and *Rupert Brooke* (London, 1964), and Joy Grant, *Harold Monro and the Poetry Bookshop* (London, 1967). Wallace Martin, *The 'New Age' Under Orage* (Manchester, 1967), ranges more widely than its title might suggest, and is particularly good on the Imagist movement.

J. K. Johnston, *The Bloomsbury Group* (London, 1954), examines a remarkable group of writers; his account can be supplemented by Leonard Woolf's autobiographical volumes, *Sowing, Grow-*

47

*ing, Beginning Again,* and *Downhill All the Way* (London, 1961–7); and by Michael Holroyd, *Lytton Strachey* (2 vols., London, 1967–8).

Studies of the individual writers include the following:

### Arnold Bennett

Reginald Pound, *Arnold Bennett: A Biography* (London, 1952) and James Hepburn, *The Art of Arnold Bennett* (Bloomington and London, 1963) are both recommended.

### Joseph Conrad

Jocelyn Baines, *Joseph Conrad* (London, 1960). The standard biography. There are relevant critical discussions in F. R. Leavis, *The Great Tradition* (London, 1948), Douglas Hewitt, *Conrad: A Reassessment* (London, 1952), T. J. Moser, *Joseph Conrad: Achievement and Decline* (London, 1957), and A. J. Guerard, *Conrad the Novelist* (London, 1958).

### Ford Madox Ford

Douglas Goldring, *The Last Pre-Raphaelite* (London, 1948) and Frank MacShane, *The Life and Work of Ford Madox Ford* (London, 1965) are complementary biographical studies. There are good critical discussions in Richard A. Cassell, *Ford Madox Ford: A Study of His Novels* (Baltimore and London, 1962), and John A. Meixner, *Ford Madox Ford's Novels: A Critical Study* (Minneapolis and London, 1962).

### Rudyard Kipling

Charles Carrington, *Rudyard Kipling: His Life and Work* (London, 1955) is the standard biography. J. M. S. Tompkins, *The Art of Rudyard Kipling* (London, 1959) is a valuable critical study, and there is an excellent collection of critical essays in Andrew Rutherford (ed.), *Kipling's Mind and Art* (Edinburgh and London, 1964).

Much incidental illumination is shed on the period in the recently edited volumes of letters of such writers as Rupert Brooke, Arnold Bennett, Ford Madox Ford, James Joyce, D. H. Lawrence, Wyndham Lewis, Wilfred Owen, Ezra Pound, and W. B. Yeats.

J. I. M. Stewart, *Eight Modern Writers*, which is Volume XII of the *Oxford History of English Literature* (Oxford, 1963), contains long essays on Hardy, James, Shaw, Conrad, Kipling, Yeats, Joyce, and Lawrence, and provides extremely detailed bibliographies for each of them.

2

## W. B. YEATS

### Thomas Parkinson, University of California

To begin the 20th century with Yeats is to affirm its continuity with the preceding age and to consent to its special
flavour. By 1900, when he was thirty-five years old, he had
developed a style that he then took to be his very self; at the
close of his life thirty-nine years later, he was still restlessly
seeking a style adequate to his continuously developing self
and the historical flux of a world entering the agony of the
Second World War. Like other protean masters of modern art,
Stravinsky or Picasso, he underwent a succession of styles, out-
growing and casting aside a fully developed manner only to
return to it again to follow out its unrealized possibilities. Following his work from its beginnings, his belief that William
Morris was the happiest of poets and that Dante Gabriel Rossetti was a proper model, the cloudy tenderness and twilight
dimness, the early formulation of a theory of symbolism based
on his studies in Blake and in the occult, his aesthetic nationalism that resulted in the Abbey Theatre and *Kathleen ni Hou-
lihan*—it is possible to see general strands of continuity in
attitude and sector of experience chosen for poetic treatment
(for attitudes as much as experience were elected rather than
accepted). He exhibits also a deep conservatism in art and
politics that checks the tendency toward improvising and gives
his romantic interest in self-exploration a fixity and a rigour that
it would otherwise have lacked. 'Too soft' was a verdict that
Pound made on most work in the Symbolist tradition, and
though he did not complain of the softness of Yeat's later work,
its systematic symbology made it unpalatable to him. In fact,
for Yeats's immediate successors, notably Eliot and Pound, his

49

later poetry had no inventive relevance, though Pound's early poetry owes an evident debt to the style Yeats had established by 1900 and then refined and altered to such a point that the division between early and late Yeats has become a major critical puzzle.

Yeats presents the anomaly of a poet with two distinct accomplishments that can be associated with two historical periods often thought of as opposite. He is anomalous in other ways that make serious readers question his claim to be the greatest modern poet; he might better be described as a great poet writing in the modern period. Many of the intellectual and social concerns that obsessed intellectuals contemporary with him he found irrelevant; he had no use for the interests that were central to Shaw or Russell; he was indifferent to depth psychology and modern physics, and the issues raised by the Russian Revolution were secondary, in his attention, to those raised by the founding of the Irish Free State. While theologians agonized over the decay of religious faith and institutions, he was content to accept the tradition of heterodox mysticism as it came to him through the writings of Blake, Blavatsky, and Mathers and such organizations as the Theosophical Society and the Order of the Golden Dawn. The major developments in modern visual and literary art that have changed the general sense of artistic form and reference were antipathetic to him; he preferred the norms of the pre-Raphaelites. He seems, when so generally described, an intellectual provincial, committed to a minor aesthetic movement, a limited nationalism, and an eccentric religiosity.

Yeats himself was aware of the difficulties that his interests presented not only to his readers but to himself. In 1919 he wrote of the problem that, in his youth, his primary concern presented to him. 'Hammer your thoughts into unity'—this sentence persisted in his head:

> For days I could think of nothing else, and for years I tested all I did by that sentence. I had three interests: interest in a form of literature, in a form of philosophy, and a belief in nationality. None of these seemed to have anything to do with the other ...

The development of a coherent world view from these unpromising materials may be accounted a tribute to Yeats's genius, and in the later poetry he did so with an amazing vigor. Even in his youth he did manage to shape a style, a mode of thought and perception as well as a distinctive manner of writing and a special subject matter that allowed him to be, of all the poets who came to maturity in the 1890's, the only one who shaped a valid body of work:

I was unlike other of my generation in one thing only. I am very religious, and deprived by Huxley and Tyndall, whom I detested. of the simple-minded religion of my childhood, I had made a new religion, almost an infallible church of poetic tradition, of a fardel of stories, of personages, and of emotions, inseparable from their first expression, passed on from generation to generation by poets and painters with some help from philosophers and theologians. I wished for a world where I could discover this tradition perpetually, and not in pictures and poems only, but in tiles round the chimney-piece and in the hangings that kept out the draft. I had even created a dogma: 'Because those imaginary people are created out of the deepest instinct of man, to be his measure and norm, whatever I can imagine those mouths speaking may be the nearest I can go to truth.'

This statement suggests how he did in practice attain unity, whatever the theoretical problems that remained unsolved. His primary motives, and his main technical designs, as poet were dramatic and traditional. The tradition he created was, as he once phrased it, the tradition of himself, the special set of Irish mythology and history, caballism, and alchemy that he formed into a rich compelling structure; and beyond those external bookish forces, the accidents of his life that he transformed into essences, the dramatic figures he recognized in experience and presented in art.

One of the dangers for critics of Yeats is to take with such seriousness the difficulty of shaping vital forms from these materials that they ignore the art, the forms that grew from the shapes of experience into the permanent matter of the imagination. Few poets have taken their poetic substance from material so varied and odd as that with which Yeats worked; but complex as those materials are, inherently interesting as they are, they are of a different order of complexity from that of the finished works, the poems first but also the plays, the essays, the stories, the autobiographies. The materials, his life-long relation with Maud Gonne, the commanding figure of his father, Ireland in torment, the documents of neo-Platonism and Hermeticism, the complications of the Abbey Theatre, of the Hugh Lane controversy—these are in themselves interesting, so that it is possible for critics to think of Yeats's poems as footnotes to his spiritual, erotic, and political autobiography, but the poetry remains, dramatic always, but the lyric poetry primarily, as the very reason for interest in the biography. And would the political history of Ireland hold the attention it now does if Yeats had not written? This seems a large claim, but as Yeats once remarked, the great poet creates his audience, so that it is legitimate to add that he also creates an audience for his subject matter, his concerns, his origins.

\*

He began in Dublin, in 1865, son of the distinguished irascible painter, John Butler Yeats and his quiet withdrawn wife Mary Pollexfen Yeats. The only compliment, Yeats would later say, that ever turned his head was his father's statement that the Yeats family had ideas and no passions, '. . . but by marriage with a Pollexfen we have given a tongue to the sea cliffs.' The contrast between his mother, who exchanged tales with serving maids before the fire, and his father, who was so theoretical in his view of life that he gave his son a lecture on the principles of perspective rather than rushing him to an optometrist when the boy revealed that he could see out of only one eye—this contrast with all its complications remained central to Yeats's sensibility throughout his life. His characteristic vision of life was dual; whenever one concept entered his mind, another followed it in quick contrast, and his belief that 'Between extremities/Man runs his course' took its origins in the extremes of his childhood environment, the West of Ireland contrasted with the intellectual centres of Dublin and London, the emotional and cerebral life in direct opposition. This habit, as his autobiographical writings indicate, was life-long.

Yeats was raised as a bohemian with aristocratic predilections. He attended no university but at first attempted to follow his father's course as a painter. He wrote from childhood, and it is important that his earliest surviving writings tend with natural gravity toward dramatic form. His first book, *The Wanderings of Oisin*, in its original format, contained numerous dramatic poems, many of them suppressed in succeeding editions of his work, and even the long narrative title poem is in a form of rhapsodic dialogue. His second book of poems has as its title poem the play *The Countess Cathleen*, written expressly for Maud Gonne, who had entered his life at the time of the publication of *Oisin* in 1889.

The story of Yeats and Maud Gonne has been told in detail often enough to allow merely the briefest reference to its outline. His feelings for her were so serious that one has to say that few men have ever suffered for a woman as Yeats did for Maud Gonne. She was the trouble of his life; she was beautiful, cold, cruel, fickle, demanding, and it is hard to believe that she realized the extent of her unfairness and mischievousness. To say that Yeats loved her is too much and not enough. He adored her, devoted his personal and poetic energies to her service, allowed her to disrupt and muddy every clear valid relation he had with other women; and she was his escape from any other deep involvement. She took from him everything except his freedom, and that was what he most required. Whatever miseries his frustrations caused him, and they were great, they were probably less than he would have suffered in marriage to her, and more rewarding. This statuesque woman with the marble heart released a passion in him that allowed him to create in his poetry a figure that will have a practically endless life.

Yeats was the greatest love poet of the 20th century, and his poetry up to 1917 was dominated by the dramatic beloved that he shaped from his experience with Maud Gonne. The woman of the poems (or rather the chief woman, for there are other, more obliging women in the verse) is a figure with heroic stature and dedication to an ideal distinct from yet related to the poet's aspirations. She is aloof and austere, unyielding and powerful, beautiful and cold. Her beauty is unattainable, and her passion goes into abstract politics. She has none of the qualities, other than beauty and passion, that sensible men seek and admire in women: she is not generous, elegant, or affectionate. Nor does she have the abstract ideal features of the conventional poet's *inamorata*. She is busy; she has children; she ages; she participates in violent politics; she has bad taste in men; she is pathetically childlike; and she is extraordinarily brave to the point of foolhardiness. The women of other lyric poets are pale abstractions when seen against this vivid forceful figure.

The cruel beloved who walks like a goddess, spreads strife among men, and ignores her lover's suffering—she is a recognizable form in the literary imagination, and in the poetry Yeats wrote in the 1890's, he brought to bear on his work over a century's meditation on the figure of the demanding cold woman who appears so persistently in the literature and art of romantic Europe. She required devotion and was unmoved by it, and her impassive demands make her finally unattractive, so that one drama in Yeats's love poetry emerges

53

from a lifelong process of adoration that ultimately outwore its object and allowed him to see this goddess as a limited being. Once he had lived through this process he could move past the illusion to a physical reality, in the love poetry written after 1917, on which a new system of values in love could be explored.

That end was remote, and from 1889 to 1917, a primary motive of his lyrics was to contemplate and in effect create this figure: take the love poetry out of those volumes from *The Rose* up to the 1917 edition of *The Wild Swans at Coole*, and surprisingly little remains. If sex and the dead, as he would later remark, are the chief concerns of his work, the erotic impulse takes first place in the lyrics of his early and middle periods, and his entire early stylistic development as well as his changes in basic disposition toward experience are intimately evident in the love poetry. In *The Rose*, for instance, he formalizes his passion by historical analogy and hyperbole:

> Who dreamed that beauty passes like a dream?
> For those red lips, with all their mournful pride,
> Mournful that no new wonder may betide,
> Troy passed away in one high funeral gleam,
> And Usna's children died.

It is at once superb and fumbling, as is the entire poem. Within a few years he would not purchase rhymes with such archaisms as 'betide', and the tone of appositive explanation in the third line is awkward; but no other poet of his generation developed the mastery evident in the first and the two final lines. In this poem his impulse toward the heroic received a form adequate to his ambitions. His grand ambitions are the reach and limits of these early love poems, and they are alien to current readers largely because of their hyperbole. This generation tends to restrict hyperbole to satirical purposes; Yeats's style came from more generous habits. There is in these poems an overflow of impassioned tenderness that is always close to despair—despair at the remoteness of the beloved and equal despair at the limits of language, which can neither seduce nor adequately present the adored figure. Angels, saints, the Rosicrucian rose and lily, eternal beauty, the Virgin Mary—nothing is adequate to his passion. The beloved merges into an ideal realm where her features are lost.

She was to embody a generalized mood; the concern is with psychological states rather than any fixed being. The basic temper of the very early poems, the amorphousness of the woman, the separation of love from temporal existence, the search for the disembodied condition of white birds (souls) rather than men and women, the poet's sense that he is '. . . haunted by numberless islands'—the lyrics of *The Rose*, although more sophisticated in texture, extend the habits of vague longing that had dominated the poetry to 1889, when Maud Gonne entered his life. Maud Gonne gave fresh and particular emphasis to a predisposed mood; she tapped a reservoir of rich feeling and gave it an object.

The basic mood persisted in the poems written between 1892 and 1899 and collected in *The Wind Among the Reeds*. He was still tempted by Swinburnean rhythms, by the faded effects of tapestry, by the blandishments of the epithets mournful, sad, dim, and pale, and by a falsely imposed simplicity that was betrayed by the involuted syntax and complicated symbology. Part of the richness of *The Wind Among the Reeds* comes from the appearance of another tone in Yeats's love-poetry. In the book there are obviously two women, and although he attempted by editorial arrangement to minimize the potential drama of the divided image, one of the women is obliging, and the other continues the aloof demanding habits of the heroic beloved of *The Rose*.

At this point, while perfecting and bringing to a relative dead end the early style, the poetry moves toward the complexity and fullness that distinguish the body of his work. The constant figure of the demanding lover remains central, but a lighter, more human woman appears. This figure is also stylized, so that she seems to come from an unfinished room in *The House of Life*. These lines from Rossetti have the tepid air of *The Wind Among the Reeds*:

> Then loose me, love, and hold
> Thy sultry hair up from my face. . . .

But the amiable woman of Yeats's 1899 volume represents the most favourable aspect of the white goddess of the pre-Raphaelite dream. Her pallor and her long heavy hair are her chief characteristics:

> Beloved, let your eyes half close, and your heart beat
> Over my heart, and your hair fall over my breast,
> Drowning love's lonely hour in deep twilight of rest . . .
>
> ('He Bids his Beloved be at Peace')

55

... that pale breast and lingering hand
Come from a more dream-heavy land,
A more dream-heavy hour. than this;
And when you sigh from kiss to kiss
I hear white Beauty sighing, too ...

('He Remembers Forgotten Beauty')

The impulse of the poem is to find through sexual relations some reality beyond the senses, so that man and woman in love embody and evoke a force that transcends their nature. In Yeats's early poetry this belief is not placed in a perspective that includes ranges of being such as history, politics, and the dead; later, he would establish such a perspective.

The complication of experience and poetic method that marks *The Wind Among the Reeds* sets the stage for the more extensive development in the verse of Yeats's middle period, from *In the Seven Woods* (1903) to the first edition (1917) of *The Wild Swans at Coole*. The period from 1903 to 1917 is at once a defined body of work with a style and set of subjects that distinguishes it from the early and later work and a connective tissue between the early and late accomplishments. This becomes most strikingly evident when one contemplates 'Adam's Curse', a poem that begins with the characteristic dramatic utterance of the middle period, continues with the charm and tact that distinguishes the love poems of Yeats's work to 1917, and ends with a return to the cosmic suggestiveness of the earlier work:

We sat together at one summer's end,
That beautiful mild woman, your close friend,
And you and I, and talked of poetry.
I said : 'A line will take us hours maybe;
Yet if it does not seem a moment's thought,
Our stitching and unstitching has been naught.
Better go down upon your marrow-bones
And scrub a kitchen pavement, or break stones
Like an old pauper, in all kinds of weather;
For to articulate sweet sounds together
Is to work harder than all these, and yet
Be thought an idler by the noisy set
Of bankers, schoolmasters, and clergymen
The martyrs call the world.'

                                And thereupon
That beautiful mild woman for whose sake
There's many a one shall find out all heartache
On finding that her voice is sweet and low
Replied : 'To be born woman is to know—
Although they do not talk of it at school—
That we must labour to be beautiful.'

I said : 'It's certain there is no fine thing
Since Adam's fall but needs much labouring.
There have been lovers who thought love should be
So much compounded of high courtesy
That they would sigh and quote with learned books
Precedents out of beautiful old books;
Yet now it seems an idle trade enough.'

We sat grown quiet at the name of love;
We saw the last embers of daylight die,
And in the trembling blue-green of the sky
A moon, worn as if it had been a shell
Washed by time's waters as they rose and fell
About the stars and broke in days and years.

I had a thought for no one's but your ears :
That you were beautiful, and that I strove
To love you in the old high way of love;
That it had all seemed happy, and yet we'd grown
As weary-hearted as that hollow moon.

This poem already demonstrates the characteristic structure of such admired later poems as 'Among School Children,' moving from circumstantial reality through conflict to the rhapsodic apprehension of symbolic reality. The language ranges from colloquial to high rhetorical, and the tone from literal flat description to sardonic satire to enraptured passion. This remarkable range, even in so quiet and unpretentious a poem, was not within Yeats's powers until he had learned through his experience in writing for the theatre how to modulate language to give the impression of a voice with a body behind it. He learned, too, to set his widely suggestive symbols within a more extensive context, so that the contact between time and eternity, so often the implied subject matter of his early verse, could be overtly and effectively presented. This habit of composition came to engross his concern and dominate his style in lyric as in dramatic writing.

From 1899 to 1917, Yeats developed an idiom that allowed him greater range in his love poems and also the power to treat occasional and satiric public subjects. The love poems reached out to include moments of brief physical passion abstracted from the legendary beloved of the earlier poems, and to treat those affectionate relationships with women that Yeats found so crucial to his personal and intellectual well-being. A new boldness and a new denseness of reference came into his work. He continued his elegiac poems for Maud Gonne, and his poems of farewell to her ('Broken Dreams,' 'Fallen Majesty,' 'Her Praise,' 'The People,' 'His Phoenix,' and 'A Deep-Sworn Vow,' among others) appear in his work as implied dramatic sequences, thus foreshadowing a device that he would follow later in 'A Man Young and Old' and 'A Woman Young and Old.' As the love poems continue to develop, they exhibit a curious alternation of bitterness and wisdom, of isolation and familial connection, of regret and gratitude, that composes a very complex sense of the erotic and affectionate life. The poetic enterprise of Yeats from 1903 to 1917 was unique. The grandeur and comprehensiveness of the later poetry tend to blind readers into considering this middle period as transitional and, in effect, unsatisfactory. The occasional poems on the Hugh Lane controversy and on the Easter rising impose themselves on critics' attention because they require ancillary material for full reading. Yet there is in the simple lyrics of personal affection and passion an original poetic undertaking, showing a capacity for inclusiveness and candour in treating relations between men and women, a maturity, that is exceptional. The impressiveness of these poems comes from their emotional fullness, their inclusion of friendship, solicitude, intellectual comradeship, gentleness of manner and generosity of heart as elements appropriate to the bonds that unite men and women; and the impressiveness of these basic sweet human qualities is increased by their being presented in a scheme of life that does not deny lust, resentment, self-pity, and malicious disgust.

If we had only the poems written by Yeats up to the 1917 edition of *The Wild Swans at Coole*, we should think of him as essentially a poet of personal passion and affection. It is only from the retrospective position of the later work that 'The Magi' seems a more significant poem in his middle period than 'Presences' or 'Friends.' Taste shifts and changes, and as the revived interest in *art nouveau* makes Yeats's early work more accessible to this age, so the interest aroused by the personalist work of Sylvia Plath or Robert Lowell may make Yeats's middle period more attractive than it has been in the recent past. For like that of other major artists, Yeats's work has such variety that it is difficult to imagine a taste that would deny legitimacy to a great bulk of his poetry.

Yeats's life and work are so interconnected, and both so complex, that it is at once tempting and impossible to determine what precise effects rose from what precise causes. Maud Gonne, for instance, was as much the excuse as the cause for the elegiac tone of the early poems, and the tone of the middle period could be explained by a multitude of events: Yeats's direct involvement through 'Theatre business, management of men.' in public life, his close association with Ezra Pound, the technical demands of the theatre on his verse, the example of Synge, the embitterment that followed upon Maud Gonne's marriage, even simple impatience with the tone and texture of his earlier work, or a late but elaborate maturity. And the change that came to his work in 1917, the expansion of its subject matter, the sense of controlling mastery of reality, the recklessness of external judgement, the capacity for creating fresh personae—this too is subject to multiple explanation. His marriage to Georgie Hyde-Lees in 1917 brought a new stability and order to his life, as well as the learning and insight of that witty, sensitive woman; shortly after the marriage he referred to her as 'a perfect wife.' His diminished responsibilities at the Abbey Theatre after 1911 released his lyric energies and allowed him to make prolonged studies in philosophy, history, and occult phenomena. The events in revolutionary Ireland stirred him deeply and compelled him to examine his historical environment afresh. From 1912 on he was busy writing his autobiography, so that he was forced to look on the design of his life and find what destiny it embodied and proposed.

What these several activities have in common is concentration, bringing to a centre the numerous concerns that his youth had generated and opened to study. He was still, even as he would be on his death-bed, striving to hammer his thoughts into unity, and the personal and literary events of the period 1911 to 1917 granted him, and even demanded that he grasp, the opportunity to define a centre for his being, to bring his knowledge and experience to that centre and to radiate from it the energy thus compacted. The process was further accelerated by the collection of his work issued by Macmillan between 1922 and 1925, in which he could see—and often correct—the work that he had done to date. He lived in a process of defining and beginning, shaping the contours of his being to that moment and projecting beyond it yet another series of possibilities.

T. S. Eliot once remarked that a man wanting to write poetry beyond the age of twenty-six must develop a sense of history. The age is arbitrary, but the general idea is not. What Eliot had in mind was the necessity for the poet to move beyond the limits of his personal experience into the wider possibilities suggested by the experience of the race. Yeats had the good fortune in his Abbey years to be forced imaginatively into the position of a spokesman for other voices, and the legends of heroic Ireland had granted him an extension beyond his personal life. He had also learned an idiom, flexible, various, inclusive, that granted him a fine poetic instrument. And after his period of prolonged study, he could turn his technical abilities toward a wider subject, so that he could eventually say, 'I am a sixty years old man; it is 1925,' and know what both statements meant.

From this period of study and concentration came a document, *A Vision*, that has become for many readers a road-block against the study of Yeats's later poetry. One result is the *canard*, and it is that, that Yeats began as a simple direct emotional poet and became in his later years an eccentric, over-intellectual, difficult, obscure modern poet. His early and middle poetry, in both syntax and symbol, was often more obscure than the great bulk of the later work—the notes to the original edition of *The Wind Among the Reeds* were extensive and puzzling, and many of the poems in that volume are unintelligible without recourse to obscure books and curious personal associations. Although some of the later poems have this characteristic, the great bulk of them have a primary literal meaning that is perfectly clear, and often difficulties in one poem are soluble by reference to some other poem where the symbol in question is used in a clearer context. The best explanatory comment on a poem by Yeats is frequently another poem by Yeats, or his collected poems. There is a grand architecture to his work that gives it a scope parallel to that of an epic or an immensely inclusive novel, with the advantage of lyric intensity.

*A Vision* is a complex work of historical psychology. It is not a comprehensive theory of history; its substance is all drawn from the history of Western Europe with brief asides on Oriental culture and practically no reference to other elaborate cultures that have arisen throughout the geographical world. Its assumption is that all cultures, and all men, are fixed in the same general pattern, that this pattern can be divided into distinct historical epochs which in turn are associated with certain psychological types. Rather than the customary metaphor of the seasons, Yeats uses the 28 phases of the moon to represent the several historical phases, granting him more counters to manipulate and a corresponding greater complexity in historical and psychological judgement. Complications increase when it becomes evident that men are frequently, even usually, born out of phase; Shelley is assigned to Phase 17, Byron to Phase 19, while the Romantic Period comes early in Phase 21. Two phases, that of the full moon (15) and the dark of the moon (1) transcend the human condition—human life is not possible at full or dark of the moon. The human consciousness cannot exist without antinomies.

The problems raised by *A Vision* are too vast for the limits of this essay; it is possible only to suggest the function of this elaborate construct in Yeats's poetry. *A Vision* is perhaps best thought of as a construct in its own right, an extended philosophical work with certain poems closely related to it and even dependent on it for their meaning. Yeats himself created some mischief by expressing public scepticism about the objective importance of his system. When, first through automatic writing, then through trance-like speech, his wife began communicating the elements of the system, Yeats reports that he was so excited that he offered to give up his entire life to articulating the knowledge; but the communicating spirits replied that they had come to bring him metaphors for his poetry. This statement, which should be taken as a form of self-protective irony on Yeats's part, has had dismal results, chiefly a tendency on the part of critics to seek in *A Vision* an explanation of symbols that are, in the poetry, clear enough in meaning and function. This has resulted in having reasonably lucid poems obscured by the rich specialized vocabulary of *A Vision*. It might be more profitable to think of *A Vision* as being primarily concerned with the thought that Yeats wanted to *keep out* of his poetry, thought necessary to Yeats in making the poetry, a scaffolding but not necessarily part of the final structure. In the 'Introduction' written in 1928 and later, Yeats talks of Blake's fondness for the diagrams in Law's *Boehme*, '. . . where one lifts a flap of paper to discover both the human entrails and the starry heavens. William Blake thought those diagrams worthy of Michael Angelo, but remains himself almost unintelligible because he never drew the like. We can (those hard symbolic bones under the skin) substitute for a treatise on logic the *Divine Comedy*, or some little song about a rose, or be content to live our thought.'

The diagrammatic shapes of his system were 'stylistic arrangements of experience,' that helped him '. . . to hold in a single thought reality and justice.' But with that symbolic frame established, he could then live his thought and give it dramatic voice and body.

*A Vision* was thus liberating. It opened a large subject matter and granted him historical measures for the violent public life that burst out before him in the Ireland of Michael Collins and Kevin O'Higgins. It gave him imaginative ingress to the world of Periclean Greece, Augustan Rome, the Byzantium of Justinian, the Quattrocento. The historical pattern emerging from his studies, the revelations from his wife's automatic writing and speech, and his own imaginative projections from these sources—this allowed him to place and estimate events and persons. And it allowed him to continue his dramatic lyrics with the sense that there was no need for any general context in the poems themselves The results were a few cryptic lyrics, several poems in a new historical manner, and an extension and subtilizing of his earlier motives. The bulk of the poetry was not, however, so radically affected as one might at first believe; the basic change was in Yeats's morale, his confidence in facing the poetic problem. Many factors contributed to the concentration of power that would characterize the later poetry, and *A Vision* was one.

Of the poems that rose directly from the system of history, several have become so well-known that their very phrasing has passed over into the common idiom of English. Public men attempting to describe the urban crisis in the United States find themselves quoting 'The Second Coming':

> Things fall apart; the centre cannot hold;
> Mere anarchy is loosed upon the world,
> The blood-dimmed tide is loosed . . .

And though one's sense of the best and worst may shift, the cogency of these lines is widely admired: 'The best lack all conviction, while the worst/ Are full of passionate intensity.' This poem on 'the growing murderousness of the world' not only grew from his studies but in a sense extended them, gave them a new base. It was completed while *A Vision* was still in very rough outline form. The primary outline divides history into periods of almost equal length. The basic unit is the

62

millennium, and historical civilizations cover roughly two thousand year periods, divided into single millenia, which are in turn divided into five hundred year periods. 'The Second Coming' plays upon this basic idea and combines it with popular chiliasm only to reverse the expectations of the Christian and substitute for the expected saviour a rough beast, sphinx-like in its monstrosity. 'Leda and the Swan' shows the start of the second millennium of classical civilization, love and war, Helen and Clytemnestra, emerging from the intercourse of Zeus with Leda. Each new age begins with the impress of the superhuman on the human, and with the death of one civilization another enters the historical drama. They interpenetrate, each living and dying within the other. Opposition and conflict are the law of historical as of individual being. Momentary stasis is possible for a civilization (Byzantium), and for individuals the marriage bed is a symbol of the resolved antinomies—unfortunately, Yeats wryly remarks, man falls asleep. But unresolved conflict is the law of historical and personal being.

The intersection of cultures in Yeats's poetry may best be understood in his 'Two Songs from a Play.' The first song is a choral introduction to his prose play, *The Resurrection*, in which three of Christ's followers, a Hebrew, a Syrian, and a Greek, guard the eleven apostles who await the resurrection of Christ. Outside a Dionysian revelry takes place, but it is an ugly parody of the mysteries, with homosexuals acting female roles. The scene is described by the Greek, and arguments between him and the Hebrew touch upon the possibility—not acceptable to the Greek—that a god can take bodily human form. Before the action of the play, the chorus sings:

> I saw a staring virgin stand
> Where holy Dionysus died,
> And tear the heart out of his side,
> And lay the heart upon her hand
> And bear that beating heart away;
> And then did all the Muses sing
> Of Magnus Annus at the spring,
> As though God's death were but a play.
>
> Another Troy must rise and set,
> Another lineage feed the crow,
> Another Argo's painted prow
> Drive to a flashier bauble yet.
> The Roman Empire stood appalled:

> It dropped the reigns of peace and war
> When that fierce virgin and her Star
> Out of the fabulous darkness called.

The virgin of the first line is Pallas Athena who rescued the heart of Dionysus after he had been murdered by the Titans, and from that heart the god was born again. The Magnus Annus is the large historical cycle that a civilization lives through, and the closing line of the first stanza sadly foreshadows the activity of the play itself, in which the end of classical civilization is presented as a perverse play by the street revellers. At the close of the second stanza, the virgin Athena is replaced by the Virgin Mary, and the fabulous darkness of Christianity spreads over the world.

At the close of the play, the Greek is so shattered by discovering that the resurrected Christ does have a beating heart, that he too is reborn, that this, like the death of Dionysus, is myth become flesh, he cries out:

> O Athens, Alexandria, Rome, something has come to destroy you. The heart of a phantom is beating. Man has begun to die. Your words are clear at last, O Heraclitus. God and man die each other's life, live each other's death.

The gods are immortal men; men are mortal gods: they are, historically, alike perishable. The play concludes with the second song:

> In pity for man's darkening thought
> He walked that room and issued thence
> In Galilean turbulence;
> The Babylonian starlight brought
> A fabulous, formless darkness in;
> Odour of blood when Christ was slain
> Made all Platonic tolerance vain
> And vain all Doric discipline.
>
> Everything that man esteems
> Endures a moment or a day.
> Love's pleasure drives his love away,
> The painter's brush consumes his dreams;
> The herald's cry, the soldier's tread
> Exhaust his glory and his might:
> Whatever flames upon the night
> Man's own resinous heart has fed.

Reading the poems is helped by reading the play; and a

general knowledge of Yeats's historical system helps reading both play and songs. But there is nothing in the songs that demands much more specialized knowledge than could be provided by recourse to a sound reference book on mythology and some general sense of history. The tragic poignancy of the closing stanza demands the kind of generous objective feeling for the human fate that great art imposes on its audience—no more than that, and no less.

'Two Songs from a Play' appear in *The Tower* (1928) along with 'Sailing to Byzantium,' 'Nineteen Hundred and Nineteen,' 'Leda and the Swan,' 'Among School Children,' 'All Souls' Night,' and the remarkable sequence of lyrics 'A Man Young and Old.' This volume, appearing only a few years after Yeats had received the Nobel Prize, revealed to the critical and reading public that the Yeats of the Celtic Twilight and Abbey Theatre, the Yeats who in effect had received the Nobel Prize, had been transmuted into a new, harder, more inclusive, more objective, and more masterful poet. Sentiment had become passion, opinion conviction. The book also had a profound dramatic centre, growing from Yeats's capacity for moving through a variety of voices while retaining a tone of passionate conviction and commitment to the values of art, courage, love, friendship, and wisdom. Later, Yeats was to say that he was surprised at the bitterness of the book, but is it hardly bitter in any unrelieved sense. It is often harsh and vindictive in its tone, even sardonic, but this is relieved by outbursts of tenderness, pity, and awe. At times the poet seems to occupy an *optique* that is outside the human, but never inhumane.

The book is generally reckless in the best sense of the term : indifferent to eternal judgement. The poet treats his experience directly and fully, but with the freedom that grows from a capacity to look on his own being as a datum. The manuscripts of the poems show that they grew often from a very personal and pathetic situation or feeling to an austere and passionate one, as if the aim of the poetry were to release the inherent pattern of experience rather than follow its overt contours. Even in the details of prosody there is a sense of free indifference to merely conventional notions of form. 'Sailing to Byzantium,' for instance, uses off-rhyme with great frequency : young-song, dress-magnificence, wall-soul-animal; and other poems are equally free. Freedom without relaxation, with continued concentration and tension, is the norm of the verse, in dramatic structure, in symbolic use, in linear measure.

Here all the conflicts of Yeats's thought are brought to focus :

art and nature; youth and old age; man and woman; past and present; body and spirit; love and death; instinct and intelligence; passion and intellect; heart and soul; natural and supernatural; time and eternity. These primary contentions that had obsessed his being and his art and had been presented implicitly and obliquely in preceding work were here directly faced. The book has an air of definitiveness, accomplished finality. In part this comes from the book's subject, which could be phrased in a single sentence : I am a dying man in a dying civilization. The book shares in the sense of cultural crisis that distinguishes other poems of the same period, notably 'Gerontion,' *The Waste Land*, 'The Hollow Men.' Within this milieu of a disintegrating culture, however, *The Tower* presents the poet as the courageous contemplative man whose victory resides in his capacity for seeing such a world without blinkers and discovering within it those human values that make the reality of such terrible years not only endurable but in a real sense conquerable. None of the standard anodynes are called into play, and in 'Nineteen Hundred and Nineteen' Stoicism, Platonism, and cynicism are successively denied as possible responses to a world where there is no comfort to be found.

*The Tower* placed Yeats once again in his position as innovator but it showed that he was a poet capable of handling the problems that are thought of as particularly modern. His idiom was at once traditional and colloquial, capable of moving from the realistic opening of 'Among School Children,' with the nuns teaching in an actual school-room to the ultimate symbolic revelation of the tree as a sign of possible unity of being. He was capable of extrapolating from the Black and Tan terrors and the Irish Civil War those designs of violence that increasingly mark the 20th century. In technical skill and in historical understanding he had attained 'right mastery of natural things.'

There is in *The Tower* also a valedictory or testamentary tone, notably in the title poem : 'It is time that I wrote my will. . . .' The poet seems willing to settle for subjective isolation as the only solution to his problems, both personal and historical. The book closes with just such an assertion :

> Such thought—such thought have I that hold it tight
> Till meditation master all its parts,
> Nothing can stay my glance
> Until that glance run in the world's despite
> To where the damned have howled away their hearts,
> And where the blessed dance;

Such thought, that in it bound
I need no other thing,
Wound in mind's wandering
As mummies in the mummy-cloth are wound.

Yeats's own pride and disatisfaction with *The Tower* may have grown from his belief that there was a deathfulness in its very perfection. *The Winding Stair* (1933) would move beyond the accomplishment of *The Tower* toward exploration of physical passion and assertion of commitment to the temporal world.

More than one-third of the poems that Yeats wanted to appear in the definitive edition of his lyrics were printed in the three last books of his career: *The Winding Stair* (1933), *A Full Moon in March* (1935), *Last Poems* (1939). The last fifteen years of his life, though developing from his massive prior work, composed a creative outburst of energy without parallel in English letters. He was in those last years freed of some of the monetary troubles that had plagued him throughout his life, and he was no longer compelled to do editing and reviewing in order to maintain his household. His long association with the Abbey Theatre that had consumed much of his powers had come to an end, and though he continued writing plays he was not absorbed with details of management and personnel and policy. All his force could then be devoted to the lyric.

These last years are his most brilliant. The versatility of the verse is as astonishing as its variety. He moves from poems expressing his own personal attachments to persons and places to poems in which his own being is seen as a representative social and historical being. He turns then to poems where the historical and the eternal meet, moving through a series of levels of being to an ultimate assertion of values. He imagines himself as a country slut who enacts 'the black mass of Eden,' celebrating her own physicality. He assumes one mask and then another, becoming a dramatist in an extended series of lyrics that shows what he takes to be the redeeming feminine qualities. He writes simple brief songs and in a moment of folly undertakes the writing of violent marching songs for the Irish blue shirts. He praises aesthetic ignorance and explores the intellectual problems of the Irish Protestant Ascendancy of the 18th century. His imagination moves restlessly over all the subjects and figures that he has treated, and he both perfects his technical abilities and returns to forms that he had explored earlier and abandoned, so that some of his most compelling poems are ballads.

So too with the major symbols of his poetry; the sun and

moon, the bird, especially the swan, the tree, the four elements, are examined freshly, and some of them are eventually dropped from the poetry, so that the swan virtually disappears in the last two books, and the sun and moon lose their symbolic force in the final book. The figures who in his life have become legendary symbols, Maud Gonne, John Synge, his father, John O'Leary, Lady Gregory, are evoked in his memory and looked on for their ultimate meaning. It is a crowded stage, and the tone is steadily dramatic, mainly in the manner of tragic joy that he thought of as the highest and most appropriate emotion for the human condition.

The verse remains traditional and experimental. The forms are those of *The Tower*, meditative poems in decasyllabic lines, with the *ottava rima* a favoured stanza, songs in a stress prosody often making variations on the fourteener so that a line of four main stresses is followed by one of three. The voice thus rendered is capable of enormous range.

And as one looks over the entire body of Yeats's verse, the striking feature is the variety and variability of the poetry, in its forms, its symbols, and its attitudes. For Yeats never remained content with any success; he moved on, questioning his achievement, searching for the more appropriate mode, the fuller articulation of what he took to be his role as poet in the universal drama. These last years are summary, not in the sense that they make up an abstractable and identifiable body of ideas and methods but because they embody this rage toward self-transcendence:

> Grant me an old man's frenzy,
> Myself must I remake
> Till I am Timon and Lear
> Or that William Blake
> Who beat upon the wall
> Till Truth obeyed his call;
>
> A mind Michael Angelo knew
> That can pierce the clouds,
> Or inspired by frenzy
> Shake the dead in their shrouds;
> Forgotten else by mankind,
> An old man's eagle mind.

Nothing is ever settled. The poems in *The Tower* had an air of finality that the succeeding volumes did not have, so that even the final lines of the *Collected Poems* which would become

the epitaph on his grave stone leave the specatator in a condition of anguished balance between life and death:

> Cast a cold eye
> On life, on death.
> Horseman, pass by!

'Between extremities/ Man runs his course.' These lines open
what Yeats thought of as his most typical poem, 'Vacillation.'
The conflict within the poem is basically between the Swords-
man and the Saint, and the poet takes an intermediate position.
Conflict does not end with these primary figures but involves
the tension between remorse and joy, and *The Winding Stair*
as a whole is intent on casting out remorse so that tragic joy
may prevail. One major symbol, that of the divided tree, at once
defines the arena of the poem and illustrates how, in his
maturity, Yeats worked his symbols for all they were worth:

> A tree there is that from its topmost bough
> Is half all glittering flame and half all green
> Abounding foliage moistened with the dew;
> And half is half and yet is all the scene;
> And half and half consume what they renew,
> And he that Attis' image hangs between
> That staring fury and the blind lush leaf
> May know not what he knows, but knows not grief.

The sources for this symbol are several, but the motive for
their use is single, controlled by the poem's whole. The tree is
one of the most often remarked of Yeats's symbols, and
he used it frequently and throughout his career. Its importance
is evident in the drafts of 'Among School Children,' where the
briefly appearing hawthorn tree is asked whether it is all or
the creator of all. The tree is a god-like force, and whether hawthorn, chestnut, or hazel, it has supernatural weight. Like birds,
trees participated in a dual nature, rooted in earth, feeding on
air, organic and fluent, between heaven and earth, self-complete.
From his early studies in Blake and in the cabala, he learned of
the dual trees of life and knowledge, and in the *Mabinogion* he
learned of Peredur's divided tree and cited it in his essay (1897)
on 'The Celtic Element in Literature.' He contemplated the tree
in various forms throughout his lyrics, and he read of the tree
of Attis in *The Golden Bough, Hasting's Encyclopedia of Religion and Ethics*, and Julian's hymn to the Great Mother of
the Gods. The tree of Peredur was composed of two great opposites, moisture and fire, and although in the *Mabinogion* it

merely took its place as one more odd item in the landscape, Yeats, by integrating it in his total understanding of the generic symbol, endowed it with rich connotations. The tree that eventually appeared in the poem was original in the sense that it was a new complex of elements, the pine tree of the priests of Gallus, the trees of life and knowledge, Peredur's tree, and the organic form of the Romantic imagination. Several cultures were thus folded together into the special form required by Yeats's imagination. But the tree has been so taken from its origins that it is no longer theirs. What the poem, under the concentration forced upon it by the limits of stanzaic form, offers is a tree that is ancient, dual, widely distributed in the human imagination, and made up of both mere stupid persistent life and the all-revealing flame of deathless knowledge. The stanza has a wide and deliberately suppressed context that Yeats hopes will in part be widely suggestive; but its function in the poem limits those associations.

This stanza is characteristic of the way in which Yeats, in his late years, used his most intently contemplated images. Even when they are not presented with such elaborateness, they gain from their appearance in other poems. This symbolic structure is related to the drama of the verse as embodied in the dramatic forms of the poet himself and those personae he creates. The result is an interlocking structure of dramatic symbolic lyrics. Each poem has its form and its rich texture, and is in turn enriched by its relation to all the other poems. Nor should the term symbolic indicate that the main texture of the bulk of the poems is so dense and packed as that of the tree of 'Vacillation'. Often the profundity of the verse comes from the very simplicity of statement, as in 'Her Anxiety':

> Earth in beauty dressed
> Awaits returning spring.
> All true love must die,
> Alter at the best
> Into some lesser thing.
> *Prove that I lie.*

> Such body lovers have,
> Such exacting breath,
> That they touch or sigh.
> Every touch they give,
> Love is nearer death.
> *Prove that I lie.*

If the poem were anonymous and isolated from any body of work, its beauty would be clear; related as it is to the other lyrics (twenty-five in all) of love and death in 'Words for Music Perhaps', it takes on wider associations and meanings while retaining its integral power.

And so it is with the body of Yeats's lyric poetry. The poems have their individual vitality, and they have a further vitality when related to the whole of his work and the curve of his career and life. Yeats is not a poet who yields himself entirely through his poems; he remains a man, and a man of a time and place. Much of the power of his work grows from the integrity of his sense of himself as poet and man, and at least part of its reference is to the unity of being that he sought and perhaps achieved only in the marmoreal stillness of the study as the poems revealed themselves to him. He is a poet primarily but also a man of letters. He founded one of the most continuously successful of national theatres, the Abbey, and if only his dramatic writing and criticism had survived, he would have to be reckoned with as a figure in theatrical history. His prose, expository, narrative, and autobiographical, is distinguished in style and both revealing and moving in subject. He lived a life at the centre of the Irish state as it became one of the first nations to reclaim its identity as the colonial structure broke up.

But it is as a lyric poet that he will be remembered. His participation in the movements of modern art, as suggested earlier, makes him seem an eccentric. He wanted always, what too much of modern art denied, a vision of heroic possibility. At the end of his life he wrote an introduction to his collected essays in which he made clear his opposition to much modern poetic theory:

> I have never said clearly that I condemn all that is not tradition, that there is a subject-matter which has descended like that 'deposit' certain philosophers speak of. At the end of his essay upon 'Style' Pater says that a book written according to the principles he has laid down will be well written, but whether it is a great book or not depends upon subject-matter. This subject-matter is something I have received from the generations, part of that compact with my fellow men made in my name before I was born. I cannot break from it without breaking from some part of my own nature, and sometimes it has come to me in super-normal experience; I have met with ancient myths in my dreams, brightly lit; and I

think it allied to the wisdom or instinct that guides a migratory bird.

And he goes on to assert the importance of 'A table of values, heroic joy always . . . and a public theme . . .' That table of values was not to be abstract but realized in the full artistic work. What that meant is suggested by his last letter:

> It seems to me that I have found what I wanted. When I try to put it all into a phrase I say, 'Man can embody truth but he cannot know it'. I must embody it in the completion of my life. The abstract is not life and everywhere draws out its contradictions. You can refute Hegel but not the Saint or the Song of Sixpence.

The work was the realization of the life. The poet would, in carrying out his role, fulfill his destiny and create a new public. He may have succeeded beyond any hope. He is now one of the most widely read poets in English, and his work seems established with the same security as that of Donne or Wordsworth. There have been few poets in any language so varied, intense, and integral as Yeats.

He was, in many ways, a man of his era, in spite of his notorious rejection of much of modern thought and art. He studied and made extensive use of the Cambridge anthropologists, as Joyce and Eliot would after him, and he shared the widely diffused preoccupation with theory of history. He accepted and even advocated the essential isolation of the artist from the dominant norms of the society, and he assumed an irreconcilable conflict between the claims of art and those of mechanistic science. He deplored the idea of progress and sought fresh sources of religious feeling in Eastern thought. Of the major artists of the 20th century, he made the most searching inspection of theory of symbolism, and as early as 1895 he had settled on a syntax and diction that were to set directions for the main writing of the first half of the century, banishing archaism and inversion, striving toward a natural measure that would not violate traditional forms.

Yet he remains an outsider, as if he were the prototypical poet who found himself suddenly in the 20th century and had to shape poems under forbidding conditions. The greatest modern poet would seem less an historical anomaly if he were thought of as a great poet writing in the modern period. He himself thought that his function as critic and poet was to reassert the great criteria that poetry has always lived under.

Describing the poet's function, to be more type than man, more passion than type, a dramatic form in the human imagination, Yeats concluded that '. . . we adore him because nature has grown intelligible, and by so doing a part of our creative power.' As Yeats has.

# BIBLIOGRAPHY

The most comprehensive bibliography of works by Yeats is Allan Wade's *A Bibliography of the Writings of W. B. Yeats*. London, 1958. The following list is highly selective, and stresses the more inclusive and less specialized works; many omissions are made with regret.

## A. Works by Yeats

*Autobiographies* (New York and London, 1953).
*Collected Plays* (New York and London, 1966).
*Collected Poems* (New York and London, 1963). See also *A Variorum Edition of the Poems of W. B. Yeats*, eds. Allt and Alspach (New York and London, 1965).
*Essays and Introductions* (New York and London, 1961).
*Explorations* (New York and London, 1962).
*Letters* (ed. Allan Wade) (London, 1954).
*Letters on Poetry to Dorothy Wellesley* (London and New York, 1964).
*Mythologies* (New York and London, 1959).
*A Vision* (New York and London, 1961).

## B. Biographical and Critical Studies

Bradford, Curtis. *Yeats at Work* (Carbondale, Ill., 1965).
Ellmann, Richard. *W. B. Yeats, The Man and the Masks* (New York, 1948; London, 1949). *The Identity of Yeats* (New York, 1959; London, 1964).
Henn, T. R. *The Lonely Tower* (New York and London, 1965).
Jeffares, A. N. *W. B. Yeats, Man and Poet* (London, 1949). *A Commentary on the Collected Poems of W. B. Yeats* (London, 1968). (Ed.) *In Excited Reverie* (New York and London, 1965).
Kermode, Frank. *Romantic Image* (London, 1957).
Parkinson, Thomas. *W. B. Yeats, Self-Critic* (Berkeley and Cambridge, 1951). *W. B. Yeats, the Later Poetry* (Berkeley and Cambridge, 1964).
Stallworthy, Jon. *Between the Lines* (Oxford, 1963).
Unterecker, John. *A Reader's Guide to W. B. Yeats* (New York, 1964). (Ed.) *W. B. Yeats* (Englewood Cliffs, New Jersey, 1964).
Ure, Peter. *Yeats the Playwright* (New York and London, 1963). *W. B. Yeats* (New York and London, 1965).
Wilson, F. A. C. *Yeats and Tradition* (New York, 1958; London, 1957). *Yeats's Iconography* (London, 1960).

## JAMES JOYCE

*Arnold Goldman, University of Sussex*

'Joyce is *sui generis*: an unique genius whose individuality is paramount, an experimenter in art so thorough that he exhausted what he discovered'; 'Joyce is in an Irish tradition of writers, comic or contemporary like Moore, Yeats and Synge, a writer "under Parnell's star" ';[1] 'James Joyce wrote English, even in *Finnegans Wake*, and his primary place is in the tradition of English fiction.'

Each assertion is in measure true, as is a fourth, perhaps less well attended to, that Joyce is a European writer, who wrote primarily with a tradition of Continental literature in his ears—French, Italian, Norse, Danish, Russian, and German. It was in the steps of Continental writers, more than Irish or English, that he felt himself to be following and it is also against them and their tradition that he should be measured. To the speaker attacking *Finnegans Wake*'s artist-figure, Shem, whose 'lowness creeped out first via foodstuffs',

'Rosbif of Old Zealand! he could not attouch it . . . He even ran away with himself and became a farsoonerite, saying he would far sooner muddle through the hash of lentils in Europe than meddle with Ireland's split little pea'.

## I

Joyce brought himself to the notice of literary Dublin during his undergraduate years at the Royal University (now University College, Dublin) primarily with two lectures, an essay and a polemic. In each he declared his independence of Irish, Anglo-Irish, and English literary currents and his allegiance to the

Continent. In 'Drama and Life', delivered to the university's Literary and Historical Society in January, 1900 (when Joyce was still seventeen), he concluded that the drama of heroism and high deeds was finished:

Life indeed nowadays is often a sad bore . . . Epic savagery is rendered impossible by vigilant policing, chivalry has been killed by the fashion oracles of the boulevards. There is no clank of mail, no halo about gallantry, no hat-sweeping, no roystering! The traditions of romance are upheld only in Bohemia. Still I think out of the dreary sameness of existence, a measure of dramatic life may be drawn. Even the most commonplace, the deadest among the living, may play a part in a great drama. It is a sinful foolishness to sigh back for the good old times, to feed the hunger of us with the cold stones they afford. Life we must accept as we see it before our eyes, men and women as we meet them in the real world, not as we apprehend them in the world of faery.

If it is strange to see a boy of seventeen reading his elders a lesson in severity, in anti-romanticism, it is stranger still that this lesson can be seen in retrospect as the announcement of a lifetime's artistic programme. Joyce's prose sketches, called 'epiphanies', written between 1900 and 1903, contain the first fruits of his intent to capture life 'as we see it before our eyes'. Haloless gallantry and the dramatic life to be drawn 'out of the dreary sameness of existence' are to be found in the stories of *Dubliners* begun in 1904. We will return to these, but we must note first the literary traditions against which Joyce sets himself —not only the novel of romance but the developing Irish literary renaissance, shrewdly glanced at in 'the world of faery' for its traffic with the leprechauns, the 'little people' of folk myth —and the one with which he aligns himself when he says that 'the deadest among the living' have a part to play 'in a great drama'. It is hardly necessary to seek out the paper's direct citation of *The Master Builder*, *The Wild Duck*, *Ghosts* and *Pillars of Society* to feel the impress of Henrik Ibsen behind the phrase about the dead and the living. Joyce had just read Ibsen's latest play—his last as it turned out—whose title makes Joyce's point: *When We Dead Awaken*. Joyce had written to the editor of the prestigious London magazine, the *Fortnightly Review*, asking if he might write an essay on Ibsen for the journal, and undeterred by a polite rejection pressed forward with a long review of 'Ibsen's New Drama' which the *Fortnightly* published on April

1, 1900. (The title means either Ibsen's newest play or all of his plays.)

In his essay Joyce again declared a Continental allegiance, and in sketching a portrait of 'the Master' in Christiana he showed to what, in the world of art, that allegiance was:

> Ibsen's power over two generations has been enhanced by his own reticence. Seldom, if at all, has he condescended to join battle with his enemies. It would appear as if the storm of fierce debate rarely broke upon his wonderful calm. The conflicting voices have not influenced his work in the very smallest degree.

The image is clearly idealized: the eighteen year old Joyce needed such a dispassionate father-figure.[2] It is clear from *Stephen Hero* (the first draft of his quasi-autobiographical novel), from *A Portrait of the Artist as a Young Man* (its final version), and from his early letters that Joyce felt a fierce storm of 'conflicting voices' about his ears, demanding that he conform to their conception of a good Irishman, a good son, a good fellow. He required some defence against these importunities and in the *Portrait* had Stephen Dedalus put it that 'the only arms' he would 'allow' himself to use were 'silence, exile, and cunning'.

Ibsen's stance as an artist was related, in Joyce's essay, to his conception of drama, and particularly to his treatment of character. Joyce singled out 'a curious admixture of the women in [Ibsen's] nature' and related it to the knowledge of women in the plays:

> that he knows women is an incontrovertible fact. He appears to have sounded them to almost unfathomable depths. Beside his portraits the psychological studies of Hardy and Turgénieff, or the exhaustive elaborations of Meredith, seem no more than sciolism.[3] With a deft stroke, in a phrase, in a word, he does what costs them chapters, and does it better.

The disparagement of precisely those English writers then held in highest regard for their portraits of women is characteristic. (Turgenev comes in for a knock as a reflex of a long-standing argument carried on with his brother Stanislaus Joyce over the comparative merits of Tolstoy and Turgenev.[4])

In October 1901, Joyce heard that the Irish Literary Theatre, founded in 1899 with a promise to bring the best in world drama to Dublin, was henceforth to be concerned solely with presenting Irish authors. He was incensed at the treachery—to their own earlier ideals and to *his* ideals and hopes[5]—and wrote a polemical essay titled 'The Day of the Rabblement' in protest. When the university authorities turned down its publication in a new student magazine, Joyce had his polemic printed privately. Rage alternates with contempt in Joyce's language: 'the Irish Literary Theatre must now be considered the property of the rabblement of the most belated race in Europe'. W. B. Yeats, George Moore and Edward Martyn, the theatre's guiding spirits, were artistic traitors, 'shy of presenting Ibsen, Tolstoy or Hauptmann. . . . Earnest dramatists of the second rank, Sudermann, Björnson, and Giacosa, can write very much better plays than the Irish Literary Theatre has staged'. Joyce directs his wrath equally at turncoat intellectuals and the Irish 'rabblement', for her Philistine public opinion, which he also calls '*la bestia Trionfante*', adapting an epithet of the Italian philosopher and heretic Giordano Bruno, burned at the stake by the Inquisition in 1600. 'A nation which never advanced so far as a miracle-play affords no literary model to the artist, and he must look abroad'.

Joyce was, of course, already looking abroad himself, and he would shortly be making his first trip to the Continent, where he was eventually to live, in 'voluntary exile', from 1904 to his death in 1941. Before leaving, however, there were parting shots to deliver in a second paper read before the Literary and Historical Society, wherein he simultaneously disinterred and embalmed the Irish writer James Clarence Mangan. (This time the university magazine, *St Stephen's*, published Joyce's essay.) Mangan, he wrote, 'has been a stranger in his country'. He described Mangan's youthful sufferings, particularly at the hands of the 'gross nature' of his father. (Even close friends like Constantine Curran were kept by Joyce from knowing of his own father's similar grossness.) From this beginning Joyce constructs both an apology for Mangan ('it is only his excesses that save him from indifference') and a careful delineation of his limitations, by which Mangan is made into a sea-mark or warning for Irish writers who remain merely Irish, luxuriating in an exculpatory myth of Irish life whereby 'England' or 'modernism' is made the enemy of beauty, truth and freedom:

> Mangan is the type of his race. History encloses him so straightly that even his fiery moments do not set him free from it.[6] He, too, cries out, in his life and in his mournful verses, against the injustice of despoilers, but never laments a deeper loss than the loss of plaids and ornaments.

Joyce is saying at one and the same time that the very condition of Ireland which kept Mangan from being a great poet and which will keep any other writer from greatness who remains among them also keeps Irishmen from understanding their writers. Before nine months were out, Joyce was off for Paris—as *Finnegans Wake* has it, with a mixed prayer and whoop of joy on his lips : 'Euro pra nobis!'

## II

Joyce wrote some forty 'epiphanies'. These short prose pieces (none more than a page long) are either romantic prose-poems or naturalistic-dramatic fragments. They testify to two sides of his temperament, the one an attempt to escape from or discover through his surroundings a sustaining beauty in life and in the imagination, the other a willingness to descend into the commonplace for revelations, even if these are revelations of the stagnation and paralysis of that life. The expression of each owes more to Continental than English models, both on the romantic-symbolist side (for instance, Maeterlinck—if via Walter Pater) and the naturalistic (e.g. Flaubert's dictionary of clichés). Joyce later used epiphanies as constituents of his longer prose writing. Particularly interesting are those epiphanies which cut somewhat between the romantic and naturalistic and which their recent editors, Robert Scholes and Richard M. Kain, note at one point to have become part of Joyce's nature development of the interior monologues in *Ulysses* :

> Two mourners push on through the crowd. The girl, one hand catching the woman's skirt, runs in advance. The girl's face is the face of a fish, discoloured and oblique-eyed; the woman's face is small and square, the face of a bargainer. The girl, her mouth distorted, looks up at the woman to see if it is time to cry; the woman, settling a flat bonnet, hurries on towards the mortuary chapel.

This is the work of a writer who has set himself to observe 'men and women as we meet them in the real world' : Joyce's brother noted the origin of this description in their mother's funeral in August, 1903 (Joyce had returned from Paris to Dublin in April at the onset of her fatal illness.) Joyce casts no romantic haze over what he sees and finds no obligation to prettify the scene : we must cast our minds back to a time when to note that grief was not spontaneous was thought worse than bad taste in an author.

During his first Continental stay, Joyce had worked at his

collection of epiphanies and on his lyric poems and had read in libraries—all under worsening financial conditions. There was little work to be had as a tutor of English and remittances from a family itself now without funds were small. Oddly, while he was a temperamental 'European' in Ireland, once in Europe his major study was Aristotle, Aquinas and . . . Ben Jonson, rather than modern Continental authors: he was 'steeling himself' in hard schools.

Joyce remained back in Dublin for a year after his mother's death, apparently aimless, but during this time he began both his pseudo-autobiographical novel and a collection of short stories. Though he wrote these in part in alternate sections, with perhaps the more objective stories as a relief from the effort of refashioning more personal material, it will be convenient to discuss them, and his collection of poems, *Chamber Music*, sequentially. (*Stephen Hero* and the epiphanies were posthumous publications).

The thirty-six poems in *Chamber Music* are, at first sight, the most purely English of Joyce's writings. They are for the most part quasi-Elizabethan love lyrics, but the qualification is important. In the *Stephen Hero* manuscript, Joyce had Stephen Daedalus (as he then spelled the name) describe his lyrics thus:

> in his expressions of love he found himself compelled to use what he called the feudal terminology and as he could not use it with the same faith and purpose as animated the feudal poets themselves he was compelled to express his love a little ironically. This suggestion of relativity, he said, mingling itself with so immune a passion is a modern note.

These ironies are part of a 'modern note' which also includes the influence of French symbolist poets like Paul Verlaine, particularly as filtered to Joyce through Arthur Symons' *The Symbolist Movement in Literature* (1899). (Symons helped Joyce find a publisher for *Chamber Music*.) They were written with 'gallic acid', to cite *Finnegans Wake*, 'on iron [i.e. Erin] ore'.

While its 'English' influences lie more in the lyrics of Byrd and Dowland than in the love-sequences of the sonneteers, *Chamber Music* has like the latter an order. The idea of 'mak[ing] his scattered love verses into a perfect wreath', Stephen Daedalus says (in *Stephen Hero*), was suggested to him by Dante's *Vita Nuova*. As William York Tindall has put it,

The thirty-six poems tell a story of young love and failure.

At the beginning the lover is alone. He meets a girl and their love, after suitable fooling,[7] is almost successful. Then a rival intrudes. The hero's devotion gives way to irony and, at last, despair. Alone again at the end, the lover goes off into exile.

('Introduction,' *Chamber Music*, New York, 1954, p. 41)

Joyce's vocabulary is at times un-Elizabethan, and he draws this aspect to our notice the more by using his modernisms as rhyme-words: antiphon/overgone, chant/visitant, is/austerities, moan/alone/Monotone:

## XII

What counsel has the hooded moon
    Put in thy heart, my shyly sweet,
Of love in ancient plenilune,
    Glory and stars beneath his feet—
A sage that is but kith and kin
With the comedian Capuchin?

Believe me rather than am wise
    In disregard of the divine,
A glory kindles in those eyes,
    Trembles to starlight. Mine, O Mine!
No more be tears in moon or mist
For thee, sweet sentimentalist.

The moon (and the priest) inculcate a romance about love to which the girl, a 'sentimentalist', would incline; the lover's irony attempts to disabuse her of the love with 'Glory and stars beneath his feet' and convert her to a sub-lunar love in which she is its true image. The figure is a compliment, and recommends itself to her ego, but we are left in no doubt that its acceptance requires the abandonment of one faith for another, whose authority is the lover. Irony enters the sequence of poems not merely, as Tindall suggests, when 'the hero's devotion gives way', but here as an instrument of his lovemaking itself. Tindall also, after a very sensitive description of the sequence (e.g. p. 60), proceeds to load it with an enormous apparatus of particular 'symbols', which he then turns on as failing to 'communicate':

The trouble with *Chamber Music* is that the form is inadequate for the burden it seems meant to carry. If the girl of these poems, for example, is designed to present Joyce's ideas about women, religion, and imagination, she does the job less satisfactorily than Mrs. Bloom. She lacks the body to embody these suggestions.

(ib., pp. 91–2)

If the girl is *not* 'designed to present Joyce's ideas', the criticism presumably abates somewhat. *Chamber Music* qualifies in part as 'symbolist' poetry not because it contains 'symbols' for 'Joyce's ideas'—Edmund Wilson's comment, in *Axel's Castle*, that 'the symbols of symbolism . . . were metaphors detached from their subjects', is relevant here.[8] That detachment makes symbolist poetry self-reflexive, centripetal and autonomous—little self-sufficient worlds of words—qualities shared to a degree by *Chamber Music*. The interest of Joyce's poems lies not outward, in being the temporary container of 'ideas' ready for categorization, but inward, towards their coherence, tone and modulations. The irony is a part of this centripetality. It includes the irony of the poems' consciousness of *being* poems, and ironies directed at the artist himself, as writer and lover. Here in 'What counsel has the hooded moon', for example, the poet admits how natural to his mistress is the sentimentalizing of love he is trying to combat, and his own lines about the moon have attractions despite the context of disparagement.

*Chamber Music* was virtually complete when, in the Dublin summer of 1904, Joyce wrote what was to be the first story in *Dubliners*, 'The Sisters'. As an immediate model for a partly integrated series of short stories Joyce had George Moore's *The Untilled Field* (1903). Moore had returned to Ireland after many years in Paris and London, and had set up as a pillar of the new Irish literary revival with Yeats, Martyn and Lady Gregory. The title of his stories is a symbol of the condition of Ireland's culture, neither barren nor yet harvestable, but fallow and awaiting its seeding: a complex image of the relation of Ireland's new literary figures to the country. Moore brought to his *Erin ore* Gallic ironies out of Flaubert and de Maupassant, and behind them lay the great Russian short story collections of the mid-nineteenth century, Gogol's St. Petersburg stories. Dostoevsky's *Poor Folk* and Turgenev's *Sportsman's Notebook*.[9] The marriage of Irish material and Continental traditions was thus bearing fruit almost simultaneously in both Moore and Joyce.

Joyce was a keen disparager of Moore's stories, calling them 'damned stupid' and referring to 'that silly wretched book of Moore's' when he read it in November, 1904 In part, his reaction may have been anger at Moore's getting in first, or spoiling it for him, but he was not above learning from Moore, and *The Untilled Field* may have fortified Joyce in turning his 'asides' from his novel into a unified whole. The central figure of many of Moore's stories is the parish priest. At first Moore treats his priests as grotesques, hideously naïve men bent on crushing out

82

any joy of life in their parishes. But gradually they become more sympathetic figures, as Moore realized that through them he could reveal both the irony and the pity of the condition of the country.[10]

In Joyce's *Dubliners* a series of secular figures replaces Moore's priest. Joyce spoke of the plan of *Dubliners* as focusing on the phases of man's life from childhood to maturity. By and large, each story turns on an attempt to burst the bonds of everyday humdrum existence. These attempts are most often thwarted, as when the young boy in 'Araby' arrives at the bazaar only when it is closing, or Eveline cannot tear herself from her promise to her dying mother and seek a life abroad for herself. Other entrapments abound, as when Bob Doran is manoeuvred by Mrs. Mooney in 'The Boarding House' into an unwanted engagement with her daughter. Humiliations, and particularly the humiliation of those who have been attempting to get outside themselves and into communication with others, occur as the plots of 'A Little Cloud', 'Clay', 'A Painful Case' and 'The Dead'. (The sense of the human necessity of communion Joyce shared with his idol Tolstoy—as expressed for instance in 'The Death of Ivan Ilych'—along with a gloomy sense of its unlikelihood of success.) The young boy in 'The Sisters' finds himself accidentally free from the baleful influence of a paralysed and half demented ('too scrupulous') priest: he is about nine years old and can hardly identify the feelings of release he is experiencing. In *Dubliners'* final, and longest story, 'The Dead', a more paradoxical statement of thwarted desire and release from the sufferings of solitariness emerges.

In 'The Dead', Gabriel Conroy, a college teacher with a degree from the Royal University, attends with his wife Gretta the annual party given by his aunts, the Misses Morkan. He is painfully conscious that 'their grade of culture differed from his', and it is particularly his outward-looking, un-Irish bent that comes in for criticism, at all levels:

—And what are goloshes, Gabriel?
—Goloshes, Julia! exclaimed her sister. Goodness me, don't you know what goloshes are? You wear them over your . . . over your boots, Gretta, isn't it?
—Yes, said Mrs. Conroy, Guttapercha things. We both have a pair now. Gabriel says everyone wears them on the continent.
—O, on the continent, murmured Aunt Julia, nodding her head slowly.

Conroy's cultural cosmopolitanism is soon flushed out by Miss Ivors, a devotee of cultural nationalism:

—Well, we usually go to France or Belgium or perhaps Germany [for holidays], said Gabriel awkwardly.

—And why do you go to France and Belgium, said Miss Ivors, instead of visiting your own land?

—Well, said Gabriel, it's partly to keep in touch with the languages and partly for a change.

—And haven't you your own language to keep in touch with—Irish? asked Miss Ivors.

—Well, said Gabriel, if it comes to that, you know, Irish is not my language.

Their neighbours had turned to listen to the cross-examination. Gabriel turned right and left nervously and tried to keep his good humour under the ordeal ...

—And haven't you your own land to visit, continued Miss Ivors, that you know nothing of, your own people, and your own country?

—O, to tell you the truth, retorted Gabriel suddenly, I'm sick of my own country, sick of it!

The events of the evening conspire to shake his complacency in his own 'grade of culture'.

Later, Conroy, much abashed to discover a current of feeling in his wife deeper than any he has created in her and clearly abandoning for the time being his struggle for a Europeanized sensibility, may yet be experiencing a genuine sympathy as he broods over and even identifies himself with her long-dead Irish first love:

Generous tears filled Gabriel's eyes. He had never felt like that himself towards any woman, but he knew that such a feeling must be love.[11] The tears gathered more thickly in his eyes and in the partial darkness he imagined he saw the form of a young man standing under a dripping tree. Other forms were near. His soul had approached that region where dwell the vast hosts of the dead.

In that region, who is to say whether Gabriel's state of mind was positive or negative, whether he was becoming a better man or a worse, transcending himself or merely wallowing in romanticism? In discovering an approach to life and in creating an artistic fabric capable of holding in solution even such apparently contradictory interpretations, Joyce had hit upon his major mode.

This paradoxical composition extends not only to the interpretation of character. It exists as well in the environmental fabric of the fiction in an increasingly clear manner in each of Joyce's books—but it is already making its presence felt in *Dubliners*.[12] The aspect to which I wish to draw attention here Joyce shares in great measure with Anton Chekhov. Commenting on Joyce's early stories, Richard Ellmann wrote, 'The closest parallel to Joyce's stories are Chekhov's, but Joyce said he had not read Chekhov when he wrote them.'[13] What they share is not only what Ellmann calls 'grim exactitude and submerged lyricism", but something altogether more structural.

In *The Irish Writers 1880–1940*, Herbert Howarth has described 'Literature Under Parnell's Star' (his sub-title), i.e., the sense shared by Irish writers from George Moore and Yeats to Synge and Joyce that Ireland after the overthrow and death of its leader Charles Stewart Parnell was in a trough of history. Bereft, even self-bereft, of the leader who seemed to promise them their freedom from England ('Home Rule'), Irish politics and culture appeared to pass into a period of stagnation. In retrospect, given the successful creation of a Republic in the 1920s, the turn-of-the-century years can be regarded as a time of ferment and crisis. While there were those who believed this even at the time, writers—Joyce perhaps foremost—were inclined to depict both the hopelessness and the hopefulness, and to judge each from the standpoint of the other: e.g., from the negative pole hopefulness could seem foolishly impractical and messianic.

When Joyce had written his first story, 'The Sisters', he sent a note to his friend C. P. Curran saying, 'I call the series *Dubliners* to betray the soul of that hemiplegia or paralysis which many consider a city.'[14] Curran has recently complained at Joyce's inability to see the real excitement of the time:

Yeats had already in 1899 written of the intellectual excitement which followed the lull in political life after the Parnell split and of premonitions of things about to happen. When Joyce was writing in 1903–4 these things were in fact happening and all sorts of converging lines were carrying from disparate, newly tapped sources unsuspected energies which in that very decade founded a new school in literature and in the next established a new State. Nothing seemed to me more inept than to qualify the focus of this activity as a hemiplegia or paralysis, however much one might quarrel with its exuberances or fanaticisms.[15]

That Chekhov embodied in his stories and plays a Russia embroiled in similar cross-currents of feeling is patent. There may have been no single Russian Parnell, and the class of people among whom 'boredom and the monotony of life' was mainly felt may have to be translated up a good few notches, but plays like *Three Sisters* of 1900 (remember Joyce's title for his first story),[16] *The Cherry Orchard*, or *Uncle Vanya* display a nexus of nostalgia for a past time of greater hope and civility, stagnation in present circumstance and hope for the future, similar to that found in *Dubliners* (or *Ulysses*, for that matter). In both Joyce and Chekhov, each posture is viewed both with and without sympathy, and it is a matter of continuing controversy as to where lies the bias of each author and his writings.

## III

*Stephen Hero*, more prolix than its final version, shows, for instance, more sympathy with Stephen in its very wording than does *A Portrait of the Artist as a Young Man*. It displays at times an over-eager attempt to enlist us on Stephen's side, or at least to convince us of the importance of his thought and action:

> It must be said simply and at once that at this time Stephen suffered the most enduring influence of his life. The spectacle of the world which his intelligence presented to him with every sordid and deceptive detail set side by side with the spectacle of the world which the monster in him, now grown to a reasonably heroic stage, presented also had often filled him with such sudden despair as could be assuaged only by melancholy versing.[17] He had all but decided to consider the two worlds as aliens one to another . . . when he encountered through the medium of hardly procured translations the spirit of Henrik Ibsen. He understood that spirit instantaneously . . . Ibsen had no need of apologist or critic: the minds of the old Norse poet and of the perturbed young Celt met in a moment of radiant simultaneity.

Despite the special pleading, what Stephen needed Ibsen for is manifest. 'The two worlds' is but one way of putting a split allegiance that many writers, particularly since the dawn of the Romantic movement, have felt within themselves: contrary desires to make their art mirror 'men and women as we meet them in the real world' on the one hand, but on the other, to cause to shine through it some positive commitment to values and imagination. It would not be enough to comment on the shortcomings of one's fictional characters and leave one's own positive values to be passed on to the reader by contagion; somehow one must *find* one's values *within* the fictional world, yet without falsifying it. These values are easier to picture in a world of romance and 'faery' than in a faithful reflection of sordid surroundings. Ibsen, to Stephen and to the young Joyce, seemed to point towards a unified vision of 'two worlds' which were tearing him apart.

There is a great deal in *Stephen Hero* of this sort of commentary upon Stephen, taking its cue from short dramatic exchanges. The alternation, and the swelling of the commentary—apparently even greater in the lost 518 pages which comprised the first part of the novel—provoked Stanislaus Joyce to compare his brother's work to George Meredith's. The comparison was rejected scornfully, but is nevertheless valid, and Joyce seems to have taken it to heart during the process of revision. The passages of comment, we may imagine, kept the 'sordid . . . detail' of Dublin at a manageable distance, and itself instanced a failure of unity in Joyce's vision.

It is customary—and correct—to say that *A Portrait of the Artist* is 'condensed' and 'compressed' from *Stephen Hero*. What is significant, however, is the very different cast Joyce gave the second version by dramatic indirection rather than by assertion. The new presentation, conveying Stephen's debt to Ibsen indirectly, allows us to test and assess the influence. In the final version, Stephen walks from the dreary section of Dublin in which his family now lives to the University, and as he goes he tries to shape his experience into something artistically manageable—not yet by creation of his own, but by recalling writers who affected him and whose art might be a bulwark against ugliness and squalor:

The lane behind the terrace was waterlogged and as he went down it slowly, choosing his steps amid heaps of wet rubbish he heard a mad nun screeching in the nuns' madhouse beyond the wall.
—Jesus! O Jesus! Jesus!
He shook the sound out of his ears by an angry toss of his head and hurried on, stumbling through the mouldering offal, his heart already bitten by an ache of loathing and bitterness. His father's whistle, his mother's mutterings, the screech of an unseen maniac were to him now so many voices offending and threatening to humble the pride of his youth. He drove their echoes even out of his heart with an execration . . .
The rainladen trees of the avenue evoked in him, as always,

memories of the girls and women in the plays of Gerhart Hauptmann . . . His morning walk across the city had begun; and he foreknew that as he passed the sloblands of Fairview he would think of the cloistral silverveined prose of Newman, that as he walked along the North Strand Road, glancing idly at the windows of provision shops, he would recall the dark humour of Guido Cavalcanti and smile, that as he went by Baird's stonecutting works in Talbot Place the spirit of Ibsen would blow through him like a keen wind, a spirit of way-ward beauty, and that passing a grimy marine-dealer's shop beyond the Liffey he would repeat the song by Ben Jonson which begins:

I was not wearier where I lay.

This prose is not as coercive as that of *Stephen Hero* : in being less directly assertive it allows us not only to be critical of Stephen but to be sympathetic as well. We realize how much he needs these analogies, how little he can allow himself to ex-perience directly. He not only will feel these things, he needs to feel in advance that he will feel them. Criticism and sympathy merge as we see how slender a reed 'literature' might be when the likely analogy is one of *weariness*.

For Joyce it was largely a matter of discovering a form which would permit a maximum of the 'youthful pride' and romantic longings (the 'monster') to be conveyed without either com-mitting himself to it wholly or being without sympathy for it. In the *Portrait*, Joyce presents Stephen Dedalus' inspiration— again a 'European' one—in a more allusive and even symbolic manner : on another walk Stephen's surroundings *do* depress him. Dublin becomes for the moment, 'Like a scene on some vague arras, old as man's weariness'. It is old, 'weary' and 'patient of subjection'. But then,

Disheartened, he raised his eyes towards the slowdrifting clouds, dappled and seaborne. They were voyaging across the deserts of the sky, a host of nomads on the march, voyaging high over Ireland, westward bound. The Europe they had come from lay out there beyond the Irish Sea, Europe of strange tongues and valleyed and woodbegirt and citadelled and of entrenched and marshalled races. He heard a confused music within him as of memories and names which he was almost conscious of but could not capture even for an instant . . .

At this point in the novel Stephen has just rejected a proffered life in the Church—and, it soon appears, Roman Catholicism itself. This is a momentous decision for him, reversing the entire previous pattern of his life (and of the novel). Heretofore Stephen has sought to bring 'order' into a life of squalor and confusion, by success in school, by seeking out women to relieve the pressure of sexuality, by total and abject submission to the Church as a refuge from sin. Each attempt, characterized by a turning outward to rely on something outside himself, had failed of its purpose. The offer of a life in 'orders', as a Jesuit priest, is the culminating possibility of discovering security by joining others—and Stephen has just rejected it, for reasons he is himself unable to specify. It is merely 'some instinct . . . stronger than education or piety . . . an instinct subtle and hostile' which 'armed him against acquiescence'. In turning against this ultimate 'order' he realizes that

> His destiny was to be elusive of social or religious orders . . .
> He was destined to learn his own wisdom apart from others
> or to learn the wisdom of others himself wandering among
> the snares of the world.

Shortly thereafter—and importantly *not before* his decision against a life in the Church—Stephen is vouched a vision of his true 'vocation' as an artist. From the 'confused music within him as of memories and names' he is led to the mythic significance of his own name, Dedalus, and to align his fate with that of his namesake, the ancient Greek labyrinth-maker and constructor of wings, whom he calls 'the fabulous artificer':

> Now, at the name of the fabulous artificer, he seemed to hear
> the noise of dim waves and to see a winged form flying above
> the waves and slowly climbing the air. What did it mean?
> Was it . . . a prophecy of the end he had been born to serve
> and had been following through the mists of childhood and
> boyhood, a symbol of the artist forging anew in his workshop
> out of the sluggish matter of the earth a new soaring impalp-
> able imperishable being?

The visionary scene concludes with Stephen's enrapt sight of a girl standing alone on the foreshore of Dublin Bay, a sight which seems to him to be a guarantor of his own artistic faith: 'Her image had passed into his soul for ever . . . To live, to err, to fall, to triumph, to recreate life out of life! A wild angel had appeared to him . . . an envoy from the fair courts of life'. The girl, that is, is a part of the here and now of Stephen's environment which is yet outside of its squalor: a symbol of the unified vision.

Joyce had completed his revision of the *Stephen Hero* manuscript to this point by about 1908. The continuing discouragements of his life abroad, in Pola, Trieste and Rome, make his persistence in thinking of himself as an 'artist' awesome. He had left Dublin in the autumn of 1904 with Nora Barnacle— a Galway girl who had come to Dublin to be a chambermaid— to the surprise of friends and family, who thought it a *mésalliance*. Joyce held a succession of posts as an English teacher in Berlitz schools, but there was never enough money to make ends meet, and he filled his correspondence with agonized appeals for even minute sums of money. At times he worked from 7.30 a.m. to 11.00 p.m., which hardly left time for reading, let alone writing.

A second, powerful cause of discouragement was the failure of *Dubliners* to come to publication despite Joyce's having contracts with two publishers between 1907 and 1913. Each found ways of evading their contractual responsibility, alleging the likelihood of prosecution for libel because, for example, a character utters a disrespectful sentiment about Edward VII, or others use the expletive 'bloody'. Joyce, and some of his friends as well, came to believe that there was something behind the publisher's hesitancy, particularly in the case of the Dublin publisher Maunsell. In the end, Grant Richards, the English publisher who failed to issue the book in 1909, thought better of it in 1914, and *Dubliners* was finally published. No prosecutions ensued, but despite a number of good notices, the book did not then sell in any numbers.

Meanwhile Joyce had returned to revise his manuscript of Stephen Dedalus' university years. This last chapter of the *Portrait* constitutes about a third of the book. It tests at length Stephen's discovery of an artistic faith and his self-reliance. We are shown the inimicality of his family ('Is your lazy bitch of a brother gone out yet?', asks his father), his teachers ('Take Mr. Moonan. He was a long time before he got to the top. But he got there'), other students ('Dedalus . . . I believe you're a good fellow but you have yet to learn the dignity of altruism and the responsibility of the human individual'). Stephen has no more visions to buttress his soul: he must now work out his artistic faith in cold, hard terms and he sets about creating a theoretical foundation in aesthetics for himself, feeling himself to 'require a new terminology and a new personal experience'.

Stephen's new terminology, with its key words *stasis* and *kinesis*, and its three 'Aquinian' requirements for art—*integritas* (wholeness), *consonantia* (harmony) and *claritas* (radiance)—

was, we now know, once part of Joyce's own aesthetic theoriz-
ing. This basis in autobiography should not blind us to their
dramatic significance within the novel, where Stephen's need
for a foothold to reassure himself is so great, and where the
very terms have implications about his own life.

The *Portrait* concludes with Stephen's decision to exile himself from Ireland, no longer to 'serve that in which I no longer
believe, whether it call itself my home, my fatherland or my
church', and with his first attempts to capture 'a new experience' in diary entries. His initial visionary experience fortified
by his aesthetic terminology, he now sets about getting down
on paper the raw materials for literary creation.

## IV

*A Portrait of the Artist as a Young Man* was published serially
in the English magazine the *Egoist* in 1914–15, and in book form
in 1916. Joyce had entered into an extraordinary efflorescence of
creative activity. Within a short time he completed his revision
of the novel, began another, *Ulysses*, and paused momentarily
only to write his play, *Exiles*.[18] In *Exiles*, Richard Rowan, an
expatriate Dubliner, returns with his wife to decide whether
to remain in Ireland and accept a position teaching at the University. As in 'The Dead', a culture-conflict melts into the tension between husband and wife, particularly whether Bertha
will accept being as 'free' as Richard wishes. He wants to live
'in doubt', on principle. He therefore engineers a situation whereby he can no longer be sure whether Bertha has remained faithful to him (though she disappointingly continues to claim she
is, and does not want the 'freedom' he wishes to foist upon her).
The play ends in irresolution, the only sure thing being that
Richard will again leave Ireland for Europe.[19]

Joyce has here turned from the portraiture of 'young manhood' to the tensions of maturity so delicately handled in 'The
Dead'. Richard Rowan is consciously risking what Gabriel Conroy had thrust upon him. The influence of Ibsen can still be
seen throughout.[20] Joyce had written in 1900 that the ten Ibsen
plays from *A Doll's House* to *When We Dead Awaken* consti-
tuted 'an epoch in the history of drama', and both the first and
the last of these live again in *Exiles*, where questions of the
'freedom' of women and of the artist's perhaps inhuman relation to his human 'subject'—a potentially tragic *Pygmalion*—
figure largely.

For in the novel Joyce had already begun he was not only to

return to Stephen Dedalus, back from Paris and in near-despair, but to take on as the book's second focus the marital problems of middleaging Leopold Bloom. Unlike Richard Rowan in *Exiles*, Bloom is only too assured of his wife Molly's infidelity. Almost his first action is to hand her the morning post which, as he suspects, appoints a time of assignation between her and her new lover, Hugh E. ('Blazes') Boylan. Throughout the hours of June 16, 1904, Bloom—though he is often trying to put it from his mind—has to face what to do about this tryst: whether, for instance, to be present at home that day when Boylan arrives, ostensibly to arrange a singing tour of Ireland for Molly. Later in the day, after he has *not* attempted to prevent their meeting, Bloom must decide what to do:

> What retribution, if any?
> Assignation, never, as two wrongs did not make one right. Duel by combat, no. Divorce, not now. Exposure by mechanical artifice (automatic bed) or individual testimony (concealed ocular witness), not yet. Suit for damages by legal influence or simulation of assault with evidence of injuries (self-inflicted), not impossibly . . .

For the moment—for the novel—at any rate, Bloom does none of these, as perhaps the low-keyed tone of the narration already hints. He is equally full of plans to turn Molly's attention away from Boylan, and hopefully back to himself, but these too may come to nothing. What is true is that he 'accepts' the adultery, 'the futility of triumph or protest or vindication'. Joyce's novel throws a considerable weight of sympathy in his favour, but equally it goes to some lengths to make the cuckolded Bloom a laughing-stock.

Stephen Dedalus' problem is perhaps more difficult to identify. He is living seven miles south of Dublin, in a converted military tower overlooking the bay, with two other young men, 'Buck' Mulligan, a medical student, and Haines, an Englishman interested in the Irish cultural revival. There has been a rumpus the night before: 'If he stays on here,' says Stephen of Haines, 'I am off.' Mulligan is to decide, then, but a complicated game ensues (though the participants never acknowledge its existence) as to whether Mulligan can make Stephen choose to leave and thereby avoid the onus of having to put him out. Stephen, however, feels Mulligan is 'usurping' him, driving him out, and he tends further to see Mulligan as a symbol of those Irishmen who play along with their English 'masters'. Worse, he feels that the Irish people themselves turn to their Mulligans as leaders, while their true artists are ignored. Stephen would rather be put out of the tower, to prove that he is hard done by.

Stephen is also brooding on the events of the past year. He refused to pray at his mother's deathbed, refused to make a hypocritical profession of faith so that her last hours could be happy. He is paying a heavy psychological toll, even to feeling he is somehow guilty of her death. (Later, in a drunken stupor he shouts, 'Cancer did it, not I.') Stephen connects his mother's death with his present situation, recalling Buck Mulligan's flippant remark, *O its only Dedalus whose mother is beastly dead*. He sees in this a reflection of his place in the tower and in Dublin, where he has a temporary school-teaching post. We follow Stephen, as we do Bloom, throughout the day, displaying different facets of his relationships with others, contemporaries, the school head, the Dublin literary people. (We discover, for instance, that many of them—but not Stephen—have been invited to George Moore's that evening.)

While most of the chapters in *Ulysses* concern *either* Bloom *or* Stephen, certain of those when both are present bring into clear focus the social and political background of Dublin in 1904. (These chapters carry forward an interest first shown in the stories 'Grace' and particularly 'Ivy Day in the Committee Room'[21] in *Dubliners*, and in the argument about whether the Irish people should have followed Parnell or the Church which ruins the Dedalus family's Christmas dinner in *A Portrait of the Artist*.) Ireland's past is the subject of *Ulysses'* chapter set in the office of a Dublin newspaper—to which Stephen and Bloom come on separate errands—and that past is seen sentimentally through a haze of glorious rhetoric. Ireland's present is involved in the next chapter in which both appear, set in the city streets as a civic and vice-regal procession passes—symbol of Ireland's domination by England, and of her hollowly pompous and cynical co-operation in that domination.

Sentiment for the past, cynicism for the present and, in a third chapter (where Stephen Dedalus, we note, takes no part), bluster in the future. Here, in Barney Kiernan's pub—favourite hangout for frequenters of the Law Courts—Bloom argues with an Irish nationalist, opposing a kind of quietism to patriotic bluster and rant. In a rage, the Citizen (as he is called) attacks Bloom and drives him from the pub: Bloom is a 'Messiah' Ireland won't wear. (In a later chapter, a surrealistic fantasy, Joyce makes Bloom Lord Mayor of the New Bloomusalem: only the people turn on him and his schemes of improvement and send him to a martyr's death!)

Ultimately Bloom and Stephen do meet, and we realise that the encounter of such apparently dissimilar types is something towards which the whole movement of the novel has been tending. After all, one is a young Irish ex-Catholic, ex-student, a poet and a rebel, and the other is a Jewish-born advertising canvasser, whose idea of literary success is to concoct a romantic short story for a pulp magazine. In fact, two of the major techniques of *Ulysses* have prepared us to feel that there is a point to this meeting.

These techniques are first, the presentation of Stephen and Bloom's inner selves by means of interior monologues, and second, by the systematic symbolism and symbolic analogies with which Joyce underpinned the novel.

With both Stephen and Bloom, we can hardly but admire the quickness of their minds. However obsessed, about mother and treachery or about adultery, their thought-processes are interesting and amusing to follow and through them we come to see that they share certain basic attitudes about religion, Ireland and other people's motives, if at very different levels of articulation. Both, for example, are alienated from those around them. Both *notice* things, Stephen more intellectually, Bloom more in terms of his daily observation. If we compare the consciousnesses of others—e.g. Father Conmee or Tom Kernan—with Bloom and Stephen, we see how the latter have more in common with one another than with any of their Dublin acquaintances. Not content with allowing us to make the comparison, Joyce himself at one point, in a chapter where only Bloom is present, intrudes a thought of Stephen's between two of Bloom's. Bloom is deciding to write a titillating note to a woman who answered his advertisement for a secretary (after all, if Molly . . .) , when Joyce cuts across his thoughts with Stephen's thought, 'One life is all. One body. Do. But do', which he had earlier imagined Shakespeare to be thinking at a crucial moment in the playwright's career. 'Done anyhow', continues Bloom, as he decides he will write.

In respect of the novel's symbolic analogies, it was soon apparent (*Ulysses* began appearing in serial instalments in 1918) that a complex association of each part of the novel with Homer's *Odyssey* was involved. Not only was there an analogy of characters—Bloom with Ulysses, Stephen with Ulysses' son Telemachus, Molly with Penelope, Stephen's employer Mr. Deasy with Homer's Nestor—but each chapter was modelled on an Odyssean adventure. Joyce prepared for his friends a whole chart of these analogies.[22] Much of the detail is indeed curious, as when Father Coffey, who appears momentarily in Joyce's 'equivalent' of Homer's 'Hades' chapter, is noted to be *Ulysses'* Cerberus. As a fact about the novel this adds very little, though it is important to understand how far Joyce needed the impulse of brooding on, developing and even parodying other works of literature to create his own. The Homeric analogy provides a ready-made [23] relationship for Stephen and Bloom, one which we may feel, however, that Joyce developed as much ironically as straightforwardly in terms of Telemachus and Ulysses.

Other, non-Homeric specifications in Joyce's chart are equally important clues to the novel's structure, such as the lists of narrative 'technics' (sic) and 'art' (e.g., theology, history, philology, economics) embodied in different chapters. Both these show *Ulysses' encyclopedic* dimensions [24] and are important guides to the thematic interests of particular portions of the novel. These systems of analogy help Joyce to point *Ulysses* away from the domestic and local action towards a plot and situation microcosmically representative of a comprehensive universal creation. The 'arts' of various chapters together suggest a Dublin rendered in a multiplicity of theoretical aspects. Having a different 'technic' for each chapter lends the novel an aura of being a story which is not just to be told in the one possible (or 'best') way, but which can and perhaps should be told in many different ways, even, were there space enough, in an infinity of ways. By the adoption—or partial adoption—of a rigorous schema for *Ulysses*, Joyce was committing himself at least in part to as much concentration on abstract forms of order as on the uniqueness—the 'quidditas' in his earlier formulation—of his chosen situation. For some readers this formal ordering imparts to the novel more coldness and objectivity than they can bear. It is important to note, however, that Joyce employs a number of formal systems (the pseudo-scientific, the depth-psychological, even the straightforwardly hallucinatory) and that to an extent they cancel one another out. Though this was obviously his intention, there are those who criticise *Ulysses* for not asserting the primacy of one mode of vision over all others. The conclusion must be that *Ulysses* is not a novel for those committed to a single explanation of things, nor even for those who believe literature under a short-run obligation to be 'on the side of people'—i.e., warm, sympathetic and understanding of its characters. *Ulysses* is that, but it is other things besides.

After the publication of *Ulysses* in 1922, Joyce committed himself to a second 'epic', a project which was to take him some seventeen years to complete. His difficulties were now no longer financial but concerned his health (glaucoma and associated eye diseases), which incapacitated him for long periods, his daughter Lucia's worsening mental illness, and, in literary terms, the monstrous technical complexity of his new task. For the language of *Finnegans Wake* was to be a further development of the twilight speech of the last chapter of Ulysses, the long, unpunctuated monologue of Bloom's wife Molly as she lies between wakefulness and sleep at the end of the longest day in literature. In this sense the style of *Finnegans Wake* is night-language, the verbal record of a dream-state, and the novel itself a dream-book written in its own kind of 'English', unique and consistent and resembling nothing so much as 'jabberwocky':

> Here, upon the halfkneed castleknocker's attempting kithoguishly to lilt his holymess the paws and make the sign of the Roman Godhelic faix, (Xaroshie, zdrst!—in his excitement the laddo had broken exthro Castilian into which the whole audience perseguired and pursuited him *olla podrida*) outbroke much yellachters from owners in the heall (Ha!) in which, under the mollification of methaglin, the testifighter reluctingly, but with ever so ladylike indecorum, joined. (Ha! Ha!)

The dream-convention is underlined by a plot which makes clear that many if not all of the chapters are being dreamed by the drunken Dublin publican who is the protagonist of the domestic 'level' of the novel. (*Finnegans Wake* carries *Ulysses*' encyclopedic aspect a step further and puts the analogies to the Dublin-based story on a more nearly similar footing with it.) There are also certain characteristic plot-elements of dreams, such as in this quotation, a guilt-fantasy defence of himself by a *testy fighter* (witness and defendant) who yet joins his own *persecutors* and *pursuers*.

*Finnegans Wake*'s language is not entirely bounded by the dream-convention: it is equally a 'world-language' (despite its basis in English). The care with which Joyce worked into its fabric hundreds of words and phrases from dozens of other languages is becoming increasingly clear to scholars. (At the moment there are whole lexicons of Gaelic, German and Scandanavian words which appear in the novel.) Similarly, the *Wake* contains hundreds of allusions to the world's literature, as J. S. Atherton has shown in his *The Books at the Wake* (London and New York, 1960). By way of his early announcements of allegiance to a wider tradition of literature than Irish or English, through the more formalized levies upon Homer and others in *Ulysses*, Joyce had arrived at what Harry Levin, in his *Contexts of Criticism*, has called 'the idea of world literature'. The awesome point is, that this 'idea' is not to be ascribed to a theory of literary history, but to the novel itself : *Finnegans Wake* is world literature.

The *Wake's* basic situation, called by the authors of *A Skeleton Key to Finnegans Wake* the 'monomyth' (after Joyce's use of the word on p. 581), is hardly a plot at all. Each main character has many names, and at different moments the personalities of even these overlap, father with sons and mother with daughter. As the previous quotation shows, the prose always retains an Irish 'lilt' ('kithogue', 'laddo', the pronunciation of *tr* as *thr* in exthro'), and the domestic plot can be specified as once again in Joyce a Dublin one. There seems to have been some scandal concerning the publican, H. C. Earwicker (whose initials, H. C. E., appear buried in hundreds of phrases throughout the book). That is the subject of much of the earlier part of the book, and the events of the evening, night, his dreams and chapters on his family (his wife Anna—her initials A. L. P. are treated similiarly—his children Jerry and Kevin and Issy) comprise the latter portions.

We learn very little for certain about the family, however, for the novel's structure is a development of *Ulysses'* encyclopedic dimension into the cosmic as well, so that the individual Earwicker not only has as his avatar the legendary Finn, but is also related to a host of other 'heroes'. Moreover, the *Wake* takes over and extends from *Ulysses* the subjection of each facet of the plot to nearly endless scrutiny and here, overtly comic contradiction. Every piece of information implicating Earwicker as a criminal is qualified or contradicted, from whether he is the culprit to whether the crime even took place at all—only to find when we become almost certain that blame cannot be proved, H.C.E. attempts a speech of exoneration so lengthy and involved that it is clear he *feels* guilty. (Samuel Beckett was part of Joyce's circle of friends in Paris in these years, and his play *Waiting for Godot* has undoubtedly made this technique of taking away with both hands what the writer creates with his little finger available to thousands for whom *Finnegans Wake* is a closed book.) There are in the *Wake* direct conflicts of both opinion and fact—the novel's characteristic image is the courtroom trial—and indirect ones, particularly in the scarifyingly lengthy scrutiny of documents by imaginary professors, philologists and historians (sometimes the four gospellers themselves, and sometimes the four authors of the Irish *Annals*). The trial—and the bar-room brawl—are the vehicles of the father's relation to his environment, man's to his society. Within the family, the image of conflict is the battle between brothers, symbolically called Shem and Shaun (otherwise Mercius and Justius, Glugg and Chuff, the Gripes and the Mookse, the Gracehoper and the Ondt, Nick and Mick—i.e., the Devil and St. Michael; the connotations of each pairing are not far to seek). The essence of this conflict is most often the tension between artist (or intellectual) and solid citizen; the audience and prize is usually the brothers' sister—as when they compete under the names of Caseous and Burrus for the attention of Margareena. Perhaps the presiding image over all these conflicts is that of a 'wake' itself, that 'all too Irish' event which begins in honour of the dead and in fellowship and moves, lubricated by Irish whiskey and porter, through maudlin sentimentality to a chaotic cataclysm of malice, broken furniture and cracked crowns.

The *Wake* carries further *Ulysses'* tendency to make each chapter an independent 'version' of Dublin life by having each of its chapters becoming a 'little wake' in itself, a miniature of the whole. The first chapter describes the 'pftjschute of Finnegan, erse solid man' and its causes,

> It may half been a missfired brick, as some say, or it mought have been due to a collupsus of his back promises, as others looked at it. (There extand by now one thousand and one stories, all told, of the same.)

The corpse is described as though it were a museum through which we tour, and the fall is retold in various fables and stories. At the chapter's end the supposed dead man, as in the ballad from which Joyce took his title, awakens as whisky is poured inadvertently over him during his wake. Here however, unlike the ballad, the mourners request Finnegan to stay dead: 'You're better off, sir, where you are'. The age of heroes is over, and Finnegan's replacement, Earwicker the bourgeois, has arrived.[25] This pattern is repeated variously throughout the novel. The second chapter takes the story of H.C.E. through to his fall, as the rumours about his misbehaviour spread and become at length a ballad in their turn. The third chapter rehearses this fall more formally as a trial, and in the fourth another trial, apparently of Earwicker's son, under the name of Festy King, mingles with the first. (With the arraignment of 'Festy King' we are drawing close to the kind of ritual death of annual kings in primitive season rites described in anthropological studies like Sir James Frazer's *Golden Bough*. Parts of *The Golden Bough* appeared in the *Fortnightly Review* when Joyce was a student.) Part I of the *Wake* is thus passing from heroic avatar (Finn) to father (HCE) to son.

In Chapter V, the mother (ALP) defends her son and husband in a letter, her 'mamafesta', and this defence of course expands into another version of the 'monomyth'. Others follow, including a chapter of questions and answers, a mime play ('Mick, Nick and the Maggies'), a classroom lesson and its textbooks, an inquest. Plot elements have been decreasing since the arraignment of H.C.E., but now they phase back in to a degree with the third chapter of Book II (the eleventh of the novel's seventeen), which contains suggestions of the domestic plot's now occurring on one particular day. The tendency to have each chapter, and even parts of chapters, be images of the *Wake* itself, continues, however—and begins, at this very point I think, to place great strains upon the reader who has persevered so far into the work. For the method entails a certain repetitiousness when the brilliant devices of mime-play and children's lesson are not followed by others of similar ingenuity. The subject of the novel now becomes the boring 'solid' brother, Shaun, and Joyce may have fallen into that old literary quandary, how to present a dull character without boring the reader. Only Book II, Chapter four, which tells the monomyth in the guise of the Tristan and Isolde story, and the novel's last two chapters, almost sentimentally domestic and then lyrical, have an inner spark otherwise too often lacking in the novel's last seven chapters.

These last two chapters focus first on familial care and concern for the young and on the relations of middle-aged parents and then on the all-accepting embrace of the woman—a more enveloping, forgiving and positive embrace than Molly Bloom's at the end of *Ulysses*. A.L.P. 'accepts' knowing that she has 'let on' (pretended) to herself that all her men were more than they really are :

All me life I have been lived among them but now they are becoming lothed to me. And I am lothing their little warm tricks. And lothing their mean cosy turns. And all the greedy gushes out through their small souls. And all the lazy leaks down over their brash bodies. How small it's all! And me letting on to meself always. And lilting on all the time. I thought you were all glittering with the noblest of carriage. You're only a bumpkin. I thought you the great in all things, in guilt and in glory. You're but a puny. . . . I'll slip away before they're up. They'll never see. Nor know. Nor miss me. And it's old and old it's sad and old it's sad and weary I go back to you, my cold father, my cold mad father, my cold mad feary father. . . .

Anna Livia Plurabelle (A.L.P.), the mother, is here also the river Liffey winding its way through Dublin and out beyond its bay to the 'cold' sea to complete a natural cycle which can but begin again. The cyclic basis of the monomyth points to an image of *Finnegans Wake* as life itself, its subject that 'great creating nature' of which Shakespeare wrote in *The Winter's Tale*.

*Finnegans Wake* builds on itself, telling version after version of its essential story. It builds, as has been said, upon the literature of the world, and upon its sub-literature as well, for Joyce had a genuine and even compulsive interest in the artifacts of popular culture. Buried in a pun in the *Wake* we are as likely to find Mutt and Jeff or Annie Rooney as Hamlet or Don Quixote. These wholesale incorporations have a curious double effect, both of happy tolerance in an authentic comic context and of egregious pretension—as though Joyce is saying he can take anything up into his masterwork, use anything no matter how trivial and, as the Elizabethans might have said, 'eternize' it. It is said of Edmund Spenser, whose Elizabethan epic poem *The Faerie Queene* aspired to be the capstone of its civilization, that he was a poet's poet. Joyce in *Finnegans Wake* is an epic writer's epic writer, levying on the monuments of the past for what J. S. Atherton calls his 'structural books'. Those monuments of world art were even allowed to include Irish ones, *The Book of Kells*, the *Annals*, Swift's *Tale of a Tub*—so tolerant had the mature Joyce become of the country he once said had not 'advanced so far as a miracle-play' in literary models for the artist. The artist who then had to 'look abroad', lived abroad (after visits in 1909 and 1912, Joyce never again set foot on Irish soil), and lived to look back for models.[26] But he continued to look about him for them as well, and in building *Finnegans Wake* not only upon but out of the entirety (to speak metaphorically) of world literature, Joyce was merely completing the process of recognition and adaptation which had begun when the budding artist first discovered that his vocation was to be independent of other people's orders if he was to forge his own, an order which would be 'the conscience' not of himself alone but 'of his race'. That 'race' had diverse origins, for James Joyce had many fathers, and the *Wake* (like the totality of his writing) is the story of his relation to them.

# NOTES

1. See Vivian Mercier, 'James Joyce and Irish Tradition', *Studies*, XLV (1956), pp. 194–218, and Herbert Howarth, *The Irish Writers 1880–1940* (London and New York, 1958).

2. William Archer, Ibsen's translator, passed on to Joyce Ibsen's appreciation of the essay. Joyce wrote Ibsen a long letter in return (see *Letters*, ed. S. Gilbert, Vol. I, pp. 51–2). 'Before Ibsen's letter Joyce was an Irishman', wrote Richard Ellmann, 'after it he was a European' (*James Joyce*, New York, 1959, p. 78).

3. Pretentious superficiality.

4. But in *Stephen Hero*, Stephen has 'read and admired certain translations of Turgenieff's novels and stories'.

5. In the summer of 1901 Joyce had translated Gerhard Hauptmann's *Vor Sonnenaufgang* and *Michael Kramer*. He was undoubtedly hoping for their performance in his translations by the Theatre. He submitted them to Yeats in 1904, and received for reply, 'Nor do I think it very likely we could attempt German work at present. We must get the ear of our public with Irish work' (*Letters*, ed. Ellmann, Vol II, p. 58).

6. See Stephen Dedalus's remark in *Ulysses*, 'History is a nightmare from which I am trying to awake'.

7. A needlessly derogatory phrase.

8. London, 1961, p. 24 (originally published in 1931).

9. The Russian stories were available in both English and French translations by the turn of the century. George Moore wrote an introduction to an 1894 translation of *Poor Folk* and the Constance Garnett translations of Turgenev's works appeared between 1894 and 1899.

10. This becomes clearest in the sequel to *The Untilled Field*, *The Lake* (1905), a deliberately ambivalent portrait of a priest who educates himself from fanticism to 'free thought', abandons his cloth and emigrates to America. Joyce was equally caustic about *The Lake*, which he criticized at length (see *Letters*, II, 154, 162–3), but soon the revised edition of 1906 was drawing from him admiration (ib., 201). Joyce wrote that a story of Anatole France 'suggested . . . The Dead' (ib., 212), but it is possible to see something of the Ireland vs. the Continent theme as coming from *The Lake*.

11. Michael Furey had declared that he did not wish to live without Gretta, who has told Gabriel, 'I think he died for me.'

12. I will not here rehearse the arguments I advanced in *The Joyce Paradox* (London and Evanston, Ill., 1966), to which the reader is referred.

13. *James Joyce*, p. 171. The source is Herbert Gorman's notes.

14. *Letters*, Vol I. p. 55. Hemiplegia—half-paralysis, paralysis of one side.

15. *James Joyce Remembered* (London and New York, 1968), pp. 54–5. Yeats had written, 'The lull in the political life of Ireland has

been followed among the few by an intellectual excitement ... and among the many by that strong sense of something about to happen which has always in all countries given the few their opportunity' (quoted in Curran, pp. 59–60).

16. Each work contains sisters on whose brother all the family's hopes are pinned. In neither are they realized. The quotation is from the first sentence of Chekhov's story 'Ionych' (1898).

17. See Joyce's comment that 'the only book I know like *Stephen Hero* is Lermontoff's *Hero of our Days*', 'a likeness in the aim and title and at times in the acid treatment' of the protagonist (*Letters*, II. iii).

18. Earlier Joyce plays, written in the first years of the century, have not survived. *A Brilliant Career* was read by William Archer in the wake of the Ibsen correspondence.

19. There is little connection between the domestic and cultural themes at the end of *Exiles*, whereas in the finale of 'The Dead' they are merged.

20. Many writers have commented on this, e.g., James T. Farrell, 'Exiles and Ibsen', in S. Givens, ed., *James Joyce: Two Decades of Criticism* (New York, 1948), pp. 95–131.

21. Ivy Day (October 6) commemorates the death of Parnell in 1891.

22. The best reproduction of Joyce's chart is to be found in *A James Joyce Miscellany, Second Series*, ed. Marvin Magalaner (Carbondale, Ill., 1959), between pp. 48 and 49. T. S. Eliot was one of the first to draw attention to Joyce's use of Homer in '*Ulysses*, Order and Myth', *Dial*, LXXV (Nov. 1923), 480–83 (reprinted in Seon Givens, op. cit.). For a recent discussion of the 'Homeric' aspect of *Ulysses* see S. L. Goldberg, *The Classical Temper* (London and New York, 1961), Ch. V.

23. I use the word as it is found in art criticism, associated perhaps first with the work of Marcel Duchamp. See Hans Richter, *Dada* (London, 1965), pp. 88–9.

24. For a general description of the encyclopedic as a fictional genre see Northrop Frye, *Anatomy of Criticism* (Princeton, 1957).

25. Joyce patterned his shifts from a time of the gods to a time of heroes to a time of the bourgeoisie on the cyclic theory of history of Giambattista Vico, an eighteenth-century Italian professor of philology.

26. *Finnegans Wake* contains, however, little in the way of recantation, or palinode. The theme of the provincial brother versus the continentally-oriented brother is one of the book's most important. There is at one point, however, the question 'Was liffe worth leaving?', to which the answer is, 'Nej'.

# BIBLIOGRAPHY

## A. Works by Joyce

*Chamber Music*, ed. William York Tindall (New York, 1954).

*The Critical Writings of James Joyce*, eds. Ellsworth Mason and Richard Ellmann (London and New York, 1959).

*Dubliners* (London, 1967 and New York, 1958).

*Exiles* (London, 1952 and New York, 1951).

*Finnegans Wake* (London and New York, 1964).

*Letters of James Joyce*, Vol. I. ed. Stuart Gilbert (London and New York, 1957); Vols. II and III, ed. Richard Ellmann (London and New York, 1966).

*A Portrait of the Artist as a Young Man* (London, 1956 and New York, 1964).

*Stephen Hero* (London, 1956 and New York, 1955).

*Ulysses* (London, 1960 and New York, 1961).

*The Workshop of Daedalus*, eds. Robert Scholes and Richard M. Kain, (Evanston Ill., 1965). Contains *The Epiphanies*, an early essay of Joyce's titled 'A Portrait of the Artist', and various notebooks and manuscript fragments used in the composition of the *Portrait*; also portions of memoirs by people who knew Joyce as a young man and selected passages from Joyce's 'esthetic milieu'.

## B. Critical Material

Atherton, J. S., *The Books at the Wake* (London and New York, 1960).

Campbell, Joseph and Robinson, Henry Morton, *A Skeleton Key to Finnegans Wake* (London and New York, 1944). A sentence-by-sentence précis of the *Wake*, in 'normal' English.

Curran, C. P., *James Joyce Remembered* (London and New York, 1968).

Eliot, T. S., '*Ulysses*, Order and Myth', *Dial*, LXXV (Nov. 1923). Reprinted in Seon Givens, ed., *James Joyce: Two Decades of Criticism* (New York, 1948).

Ellmann, Richard, *James Joyce* (New York, 1959). The standard modern biography.

Farrell, J. T., 'Exiles and Ibsen', in Seon Givens, ed., *James Joyce: Two Decades of Criticism*.

Glasheen, Adaline, 'Joyce and the Three Ages of Charles Stewart Parnell', in *A James Joyce Miscellany, Second Series*, ed. Marvin Magalaner (Carbondale, Ill., 1959).

Goldberg, S. L., *The Classical Temper, A Study of James Joyce's Ulysses* (London and New York, 1961). (Chapter V : 'Homer and the Nightmare of History.')

Goldman, Arnold, *The Joyce Paradox* (London and Evanston, Ill., 1966). A study of how Joyce developed the structures of his fictions, with emphasis on the 'freedom' imparted to his characters.

Howarth, Herbert, *The Irish Writers, 1880–1940* (London and New York, 1958). A fine study of the social and political background for the main figures of the Irish literary revival, with attention to their characteristic themes.

Joyce, Stanislaus, *My Brother's Keeper* (London and New York, 1958). A memoir of the Joyce brothers in their Dublin years.

Levin, Harry, *Contexts of Criticism* (Cambridge, Mass., 1957), pp. 131–39 and 269–86.

Levin, Harry, *James Joyce: A Critical Introduction* (London and New York, 1960). First published in 1941, this is still the best single introduction to Joyce's work.

Magalaner, Marvin, *Time of Apprenticeship: The Fiction of Young James Joyce* (London and New York, 1959).

Mercier, Vivian, *The Irish Comic Tradition* (Oxford and New York, 1962).

Mercier, Vivian, 'James Joyce and Irish Tradition', *Studies*, XLV (1956).

Symons, Arthur, *The Symbolist Movement in Literature* (London, 1899).

Tysdahl, Björn, *Joyce and Ibsen* (Oslo and New York, 1968).

Wilson, Edmund, *Axel's Castle* (London, 1961 and New York, 1931).

The student is further directed to Robert H. Deming, *A Bibliography of James Joyce Studies* (Lawrence, Kansas, 1964). Further to the present essay, see particularly Section I:B.3. ('Milieu Studies').

## 4

# D. H. LAWRENCE

*John Goode, University of Reading*

It seems blindingly obvious now that Lawrence is a very great novelist and that critics who try to claim otherwise are either exhibitionist or oblivious, yet the first coherent claim for his major status was not made until twenty-five years after his death, by F. R. Leavis. It is not difficult to see why: in two ways, Lawrence is isolated from the mainstream of critical theory which derives from the modern movement. In his last novel, *Lady Chatterley's Lover*, he gives a definition of the value of fiction which exactly places him in relation to his contemporaries:

> It is the way our sympathy flows and recoils that really determines our lives. And here lies the vast importance of the novel, properly handled. It can inform and lead into new places the flow of our sympathetic consciousness, and it can lead our sympathy away in recoil from things gone dead. (IX)[1]

'Sympathy' takes us straight back to George Eliot (see, for example, her essay 'The Natural History of German Life' where she advocates realism on the grounds that it enables an extension of our sympathies). It implies an essentially *secular* view of art, in which creative achievement has no absolute intrinsic value. 'I do write,' Lawrence said in a letter of 1913, 'because I

---

1. Since there is no authoritative edition of Lawrence's novels, references are to the chapter in which the quotation occurs. This is indicated by a Roman numeral in parenthesis after the quotation. Where there is an unbroken series of quotations from one chapter, the reference is given only after the first quotation in the series.

want folk—English folk—to alter, and have more sense'. At the same time, much of his criticism, particularly in the twenties, is directed against didacticism. In 1914, he wrote to Sir Thomas Dunlop: 'You asked me once what my message was. I haven't got any general message, because I believe a general message is a general means of sidetracking one's own personal difficulties.' There is no contradiction: the kind of didacticism Lawrence deplores is that which tries to impose a moral order on experience, not that which, like his own, tries above all to *depose* order and discover instead the meaning for the individual of the flux of life itself. And this makes for the second factor in his dis-orientation from the major impetus of modern art— there is no rage for order, no seeking after values which transcend historical change. In a way which makes Lawrence alien to his major contemporaries, he is a relativist: 'Einstein,' he wrote in 1921, 'isn't so metaphysically marvellous, but I like him for taking out the pin which fixed down our fluttering little physical universe.' To measure the deterioration of modern life or to impose order on its flux by values derived from the past, the cultural tradition, is, for Lawrence to get the dead to bury the dead.

Leavis's definitive evaluation grows precisely out of his recognition of the centrality of the major pre-modern novelists, Jane Austen and George Eliot, for example. This is, without doubt, the right perspective in which to place the achievement of Lawrence against that of T. S. Eliot or James Joyce. It is, however, a very problematic perspective. Significantly, the quotation with which we began is from a novel which is overtly immoral by any standards which are to be derived from 'the great tradition' (we ought not to be surprised that Leavis finds the book intolerable). It explicitly attacks the whole range of moral positives (from duty, to tolerance of other people's weakness) which affirm in any way the relevance of social institutions (from marriage to intelligent conversation). We need to note how positive, in that quotation, is the concept of 'recoil'. Of course, revulsion from what has gone dead is an important effect of George Eliot's fiction too (we recoil from Casaubon as much as from Sir Clifford Chatterley), but it is not a positive function of the novel, equal to its affirmations. Once the discriminations have been made, the effect of *Middlemarch* is to establish large areas of tolerance (for example, for such figures as Cecilia and Sir James).

And the recoil is, throughout Lawrence's work, precisely from those values, values which make for integrity and accommodation, that we find in Jane Austen and George Eliot. In *A Propos of Lady Chatterley's Lover*, Lawrence writes:

This, again, is the tragedy of social life today. In the old England, the curious blood-connection held the classes together . . . We feel it in Defoe or Fielding. And then, in the mean Jane Austen, it is gone. Already this old maid typifies 'personality' instead of character, the sharp knowing in apartness instead of knowing in togetherness . . .

(*Phoenix II*. p. 513)

This was in 1930, and it has its particular context. But it is congruent with much earlier criticism, in that it sees the nineteenth century as an epoch of egoism accommodated, through 'personality', in society, followed by an epoch in which the social institutions of personality have to be destroyed. An important review of 1913, '*Georgian Poetry 1912–1913*', sees that anthology (to which he contributed himself) as an affirmation of life against the nihilism of Flaubert, Nietzsche and Hardy, but sees too that it could only come about because of that nihilism:

The last years have been years of demolition. Because faith and belief were getting pot-bound, and the Temple was made a place to barter sacrifices, therefore faith and belief and the Temple must be broken. This time art fought the battle, rather than science or any new religious faction. And art has been demolishing for us: Nietzsche, the Christian religion as it stood; Hardy, our faith in our own endeavour; Flaubert, our belief in love. Now, for us, it is all smashed, we can see the whole again. We were in prison, peeping at the sky through loop-holes. The great prisoners smashed at the loop-holes, for lying to us. And behold, out of the ruins leaps the whole sky.

The evaluation is carefully historical. If Flaubert and Dostoevsky have to be attacked more vigorously than Jane Austen or George Eliot, it is not because the latter pair are more moral or life enhancing, it is because they are more irrelevant historically—they have been demolished already. Flowers of evil are more valuable than the innerly corrupt cabbages of the self-contained personality.

The only relevance finally of the great tradition is that it is an opposite. In some ways, *Mansfield Park* is a perfect bourgeois novel because the house whose values are affirmed can accommodate personality—Fanny Price is granted integration through the discovery of a role (duty) and the sanctity of a retreat (her private room) in which the inner being can remain un-violated. Such a compact is not possible in Lawrence, and it is to the affirmation of modes of being alien to those which Jane Austen affirmed that we must pay most attention.

## I. 1885–1912

Lawrence was born in 1885 in Eastwood, a small mining village outside Nottingham, the fourth child of a collier. Though his world was industrial, it was not really urban since a little beyond Eastwood there was an unmolested rural world which was as much a part of Lawrence's childhood landscape as the colliery: 'so that the life,' he wrote in later years, 'was a curious cross between industrialism and the old agricultural England of Shakespeare and Milton and Fielding and George Eliot' (*Phoenix* p. 135). To the tension which resulted from this dual environ-ment was added the violent social tension evident in his parents' marriage. Mrs. Lawrence was a Nonconformist with middle-class antecedents whose response to the spontaneous but irre-sponsible world of her husband was a conventional social aspiration realized vicariously through her children. 'I am sure,' Lawrence wrote, 'my mother never dreamed a dream that wasn't well off' (*Phoenix* p. 822). She it was who strove to ensure that he had an education that would displace him from the working class milieu in which he was brought up. But there is a third tension in Lawrence's early life which both derives from that education and through the relationship that he formed in 1901 with Jessie Chambers, and that was the equally bourgeois but 'unconventional' aspiration to a higher plane than social reality; 'a world apart,' Jessie wrote in her memoir, 'where feeling and thought were intense, and we seemed to touch a reality that was beyond the ordinary workaday world'. Lawrence's identity then grows in relation to a threefold anti-thesis, industrial and rural, community and social aspiration, convention and idealism. It makes for a pervasive and complex rhythm in his work between a powerful need for human rela-tionship and an intense dynamic of self-realization.

It is a rhythm made more complex by his specific historical situation. Lawrence's career is at once a tribute to and indict-ment of the Forster Education Act (1870) which definitively established a national system of elementary education. From the Board School which was that Act's creation, Lawrence won a scholarship to Nottingham High School in 1898, but the scholarship was not enough to cover his expenses so that much of the Lawrence family income had to be directed towards providing an education which would separate their child from them. He worked as a clerk for a few months in 1901, but ill health forced him to give up the post. In Autumn, 1902, on the advice of his mother's Congregationalist minister, Lawrence re-entered the educational system as a pupil teacher. Under a scheme set up by the Balfour Education Act of that year, he was, in 1903, drafted to the Pupil Teacher Centre in Ilkeston where he was able to matriculate. For financial reasons, however, he had to defer taking up a place at Nottingham University College for a further year. He got to Nottingham in 1906 and gained his teacher's certificate there two years later. These years are crucial in Lawrence's development. The national education system gave him an opportunity unavailable to previous generations to achieve middle-class status. But it meant much hard work and self denial for an education which an intelligent boy could see was inadequate. In 'Education of the People', an essay Lawrence wrote at the end of the First World War, Lawrence offers a very sharp diagnosis of the contradictions inherent in the system : theoretically, education is about disinterested ideals, but in fact the whole system is geared to the material needs of society so that it is caught hopelessly between sentimentalism and vulgar utilitarianism. Negatively, Lawrence's education taught him the intellectual poverty of the academic mind; positively, it put him in touch with the major intellectual currents of his time, Darwin, Schopenhauer, William James, which displaced him both from the working-class world of his father and the middle-class values, sustained by Christianity, which his mother cherished. It demanded too a kind of integrity which neither these values nor the romantic withdrawal of Jessie Chambers could accommodate. But at the same time, because of her, he was turning towards a profession which the national education system was hardly designed to encourage : he seems to have begun *The White Peacock* in 1906, and, in 1907, he submitted three stories to the *Nottingham Guardian*, one of which, under Jessie's name, was published ('A Prelude'). By the time Lawrence left Eastwood, in 1908, to take up a teaching post at Davidson Road School, Croydon, he was already caught up in the painful process of deracination which is inevitable for the working-class or lower-middle-class intellectual.

Describing his mother's concept of success in an essay of

1929, Lawrence wrote: 'Flights of genius were nonsense—you had to be clever & rise in the world, step by step.' (*Phoenix* II p. 301). Lawrence's London years mocked her wisdom. The step-by-step career at Davidson Road was morally crippling because Lawrence found that the system did not allow him to develop a non-institutional relationship with the boys (the sequence of poems called 'The Schoolmaster' registers his predicament at this time). On the other hand, the flights of genius had some success. Jessie Chambers sent some of his work to Ford Madox Hueffer (later Ford), editor of *The English Review* in 1909. Hueffer did not only publish Lawrence (at first in the November issue) but also introduced him into the literary world. During 1910, Lawrence finished his first two novels, *The White Peacock* and *The Tresspasser* and seems to have had little difficulty in getting them published (in 1911 and 1912 respectively). In June 1911 Martin Secker was asking him for a volume of short stories: as a writer he had arrived. It is not surprising that Lawrence found himself alien to the bourgeois morality of his mother, and, perhaps, the last link with that morality was severed when, in December 1910, she died. In November of the following year, pneumonia forced Lawrence to give up his post at Davidson Road and from then on he never returned to a 'regular' profession. And, as though it were a final dramatic gesture against the world his mother had dreamed of for him, Lawrence met and eloped with the wife of the Professor of Modern Languages at Nottingham, Frieda Von Richthofen, early in 1912. They went to Germany, her homeland, and spent most of the next two years travelling in Europe. Exile was to become the dominant note of Lawrence's life from this point, and by the end of 1912, he had completed the novel that was to present the inevitability and representativeness of that exile and was also his first great work, *Sons and Lovers*.

During these years, as we have seen, Lawrence saw his own role as that of the new affirmer after the total negation of bourgeois morality by Flaubert and Hardy. There was no return to the dualistic 'personality' of Jane Austen and George Eliot. The apart, inner self that their *modus vivendi* relies on ultimately takes refuge in mental consciousness, and this, Lawrence realized, was only destructive since it could only make of the 'inner self' a mirror image of the social being from which it is withdrawn. The inner self might be the antithesis of social being, but this too is just another kind of reflection. The early short stories (all collected in *The Prussian Officer*) affirm a different order of being which can make no compact with the social world but which must either subvert that world or atrophy within it.

This process is most schematically evident in 'The Daughters of the Vicar'. The vicar's family live in a situation which is for them socially degrading: one of the daughters who has 'a proud, pure look of submission to a high fate', marries a clever and wealthy but physically monstrous clergyman in order to create for herself a place in the world within which she can exist unviolated. The second finds herself nursing a lower-class woman through her last illness and through this being forced into physical intimacy with the woman's son, a collier. It is partly a story which affirms the priority of sexual love over class convention, but more it is the dramatic realization of an order of being which class convention will not accommodate. When she finds herself washing the back of the collier she feels 'the almost repulsive intimacy being forced upon her. It was all so common, so like herding. She lost her own distinctness'. Through her relationship with the son she is to find another kind of distinctness, but it is only after the individualism of bourgeois convention has been totally subverted. The new distinctness is one which acknowledges a relationship which the conventional world tries to make merely a function of itself.

But 'class' is only one of the social mediations which Lawrence sees as a destructive force which has to be overcome by a new vitality. A less schematic and more powerful story than 'The Daughters of the Vicar', 'The Christening', presents a world in which the compact between inner and outer worlds is seen in a context of the very idea of family itself. It is hardly a story at all: a collier smitten with locomotor ataxy has three daughters drifting into spinsterhood. One of them has an illegitimate baby, and the clergyman is called to christen it; during the ceremony, the collier speaks a strange prayer rejoicing that the child has no father: 'Aye an'I wish it had been so with my children, that they'd had no father but Thee. For I've been like a stone upon them, and they rise up and curse me in their wickedness'. The family, enacting the will of the father, is well to do and different from 'the common collier folk', but the rise in the world, the transformation of the father's 'pride' into the group identity of social being, has crushed the individuality of the children: 'They had never lived; his life, his will had always been upon them and contained them. They were only half-individuals.' The bastard is only a pathetic gesture at individual assertion (for its mother hates the man who is its father), and it is, paradoxically, at the end, the broken-down father, still exercising his will through his debility, who affirms 'joy in life' —a pride of being not thwarted by the sense of group responsibility. The paradox enables us to see how much more Lawrence is concerned with than simply the realization of the price of conformity. The father's will is not morally condemned: it is simply the unnatural distortion of his pride, his vitality, through the very fact of fatherhood. We are witnessing not the struggle of the emergent individual against the static group, but the inextricable involvement of the emergent individual with the *emergent* group—itself the medium of individual vitality.

Both of these stories illustrate how much the Lawrencean affirmation of vitality demolishes the equilibrium between 'inner' and 'outer' being which is the basis of characterization in the nineteenth century novel, and we ought to cite other stories, 'The White Stocking', 'Odour of Chrysanthemums', 'The Prussian Officer' and 'The Thorn in the Flesh', which, though they have very different immediate concerns, demonstrate the same dramatic realization of the collision between incompatible orders of being. In three of these stories, a new kind of 'self' emerges unmediated by its given role (husband or subordinate, for example) to disrupt a precariously controlled social situation. In the fourth, 'Odour of Chrysanthemums', this naked self, the undamaged body of a collier asphyxiated in the mine, brings to his wife, as she prepares him for burial, the recognition of the gap between her socially conditioned vision of his failure and his 'real' being. This is the moment of her true marriage in which she acknowledges his separateness, but it belongs to death and she has still to go on living. The continuity of the past which was between them is a death-in-life: 'The child was like ice in her womb'. And, although she turns back to life, it is in the knowledge that the reality of her life, 'her ultimate master', is utterly separate from her existence, is death. The recognition has been foreshadowed by her half-conscious gesture of wearing the chrysanthemums her child has torn up: later in the story, she links the flower with the failure of her marriage, but her spontaneous gesture is all that gives life to her drab, defeated appearance, and it binds her to the man's reality.

The awareness registered in these stories is undoubtedly more articulate because both Meredith and Hardy had realized it in their novels. But already, Lawrence has gone much further than they. Because he has a much deeper sense of human *groups* than Meredith, there is never any reduction to a theatrical antithesis between personal vitality and social rigidity. And, unlike Hardy, Lawrence does not find it necessary to dramatize this sense in terms of an already dying society. The great achievement of these stories is that they realize an interaction between the individual and his social context which is both eruptive and diurnal, a salient feature of the modern provincial world. But, of course, the stories necessarily simplify, because although the social order is not rigid, we cannot fully recognize that it is the product not only of changing individuals but also of changing groups. It is only when we turn to the novels that we become aware of a threefold dynamic growing from the relationship between the social order, the human group and the emergent individual.

*The White Peacock* already shows a remarkable grasp of these complexities. Critics from Lawrence himself onwards have habitually regarded it with contempt, and it is undeniable that it is very uneven and, finally, incoherent. But this is because of what Lawrence is trying to do—to use a medium which is essentially that of personal relationships (the declared model was George Eliot) to register forces which are beyond 'personality' and which determine the development not merely of single individuals but also of the human group in which they have their being. So that Lawrence finds it necessary to intersperse the fragmented drama with choric prose-poems, structurally irrelevant set scenes and a vast network of literary allusions. But if the technique is painfully improvised, it looks forward to the later novels in its effort to articulate rhythms which will not be contained in the conscious life of the individual, and it initiates themes which are going to remain crucial throughout Lawrence's work.

The opening chapter impressively announces the overt moral scheme of the novel through the invocation of the drama's setting. Nethermere is a world of somnolence : 'the whole place was gathered in the musing of old age' (Part One, I), and this is emphasized by verbal echoes—'the water slid *sleepily* among them', 'the low red house . . . *dozed* in sunlight.' But if it is a world of the past, the figures in the landscape are young, on the edge of life, and though the central figure, George Saxton, participates in the somnolence of Nethermere, this is seen not as a retreat into the static but a precarious unconsciousness of what life is to be about : 'Your life is nothing else but a doss. I shall laugh when somebody jerks you awake'. The dominating tension of the novel is already before us : the characters, held in the pastoral fixity of Nethermere, belong not to the past but

to the future—awakening will mean separation from the landscape and growth will mean uprooting. So we have, in these
opening pages, beneath the quiet surface, the irritated buzzing
of young bees, some of whom, with the lazy curiosity which is
to be his own destruction, George kills. And later in the chapter,
the other main figure, Letty, whose life is also to be a kind of
ruin, expends her vibrant but trivial energy on a battered piano.
Both George and Letty come into being within the world of the
past, but for both of them it means not nourishment but distortion. Letty summarizes the whole theme of the novel when she
says to George:

> You never grow up, like bulbs which spend all summer getting
> fat and fleshy, but never wakening the germ of a flower. As
> for me, the flower is born in me, but it wants bringing forth.
> (Part One, III)

The flower is a pervasive metaphor of being in Lawrence because it implies both rootedness in a common soil and highly
individual blossoming. But it is an ideal relating only two of the
terms which we have noted in the Lawrencean vision—the group
and the individual. In actuality what relates them is the social
structure which they create between them, and in *The White
Peacock*, the flower of being is distorted because of the social
structure. George is to sink his roots deeper and deeper in the
declining provincial world and to rot inwardly; Letty, whom
George fails to 'bring forth', is to turn outwards to the world of
the industrialist and to become a forced growth taking refuge
in the being of others. Both recoil from the torture which it is
'to each of them to look thus *nakedly* at the other.'

Growth becomes, therefore, deeply implicated with the destruction of the group. George is, in some respects, the representative of the pastoral world of Nethermere. There is, for example,
a straightforward antithesis between his home and the strident
sophistication of the home of Letty's industrialist in 'The Riot
of Christmas': after the cake-making, the reading aloud and the
dance in stockinged feet, we have the high-flown talk with its
allusions to Maeterlinck and the correct and coy kissing under
the mistletoe. And, of course, in terms of the social structure of
the novel, it is the second party which embodies supremacy. In
personal terms, it is so because the will of Letty searches for a
personal role. On the way to the party, the protagonists meet
two boy mineworkers who are reminders that the gaiety which
is to come is paid for by impersonal exploitation; Letty's response personalizes the impersonal: 'Fancy, . . . those boys are

working for me!' (Part One, VIII). A little later, at the party, we explicitly see Letty coming to love Leslie, the industrialist, because the social order he commands gives her an opportunity of playing a role, of masking the naked self in the personalized impersonality of social being: 'Letty was enjoying her public demonstration immensely; it exhilarated her into quite a vivid love for him'. The determinative need to play a social role is not fully explored in terms of Letty's character, and this is one of the faults of the novel, but it is also part of its striking originality. It is clear that it is partly because her vitality demands a more powerful relationship than George can offer her—for if he is a noble peasant, Letty's 'taureau', he is one who is rotting internally because the pastoral world is not the world of youth. Letty's response to his inertia is to escape into social determinism; having confessed to George that dancing with him is 'real', she goes on to justify her engagement to Leslie in these terms: 'I have been brought up to expect it—everybody expected it— and you're bound to do what people expect you to do—you can't help it. We can't help ourselves, we're all chess-men' (Part One. IX). The reality can only be momentary: in the world of the actual, George is impotent. It is not insignificant that Letty is finally thrown on to Leslie by a combination of mechanization and chance—his motor car accident from which, with the false maternal relationship Lawrence saw as characteristic of bourgeois marriage, she has to nurse him. But we cannot separate the mechanization of Letty from the general breaking up of Nethermere. Letty's own family, for example, has a stability made precarious by the death of the father whose corpse lies in a squalid urban backstreet evoked with elaborate realism. After this discovery, the pastoral of the novel is always flawed. The Saxton farm is being ruined by the rabbits with which the Squire infests his estate, and George only stirs himself to contemplate emigrating. This is not simply elegiac, however. Within the pastoral world, there is always a sense of violence underneath the surface: the drowned cat, the hunted rabbits, the mad dog. 'If we move,' says Letty, 'the blood rises in our heel-prints' (Part One, II). The violence is part of the reality, but it remains unassimilated by the characters so that their awakening must also become a turning away. The unassimilated violence is present in Annable, the gamekeeper who stands as a reminder to the main characters of the reality which, in their awakening, they reject. But he can be no more than a reminder because he is only a very literary symbol. In actuality, he is an agent of Nethermere's destruction, since it is his job to protect the rabbits. His commitment to animal vitality is highly self-conscious, and, after his death, his family is reduced to an urban slum. Annable is a bitter joke: what he stands for is not even available to himself. After his death, the novel becomes an exercise in realism, acting out the inevitable distortions of being implicit in the first half. George drifts into a highly sensual marriage, compensates with a momentary socialism and finally collapses into alcoholism, 'like a tree that is going soft'. Letty becomes just a social being. The children of Nethermere, necessarily growing out of the hollow which cannot contain them, have to cast themselves 'each one into separate exile'. It is in this atrophied way that the violence of vitality finds its way into their lives, not through the organic wholeness that Annable stands for. In this novel, becoming is an uprooting: it grows out of the group, but it flowers only in the city, and the flower is rotten, wasteful: 'What did it matter to them what they broke or crushed ... What did it matter, when all the great red apples were being shaken from the Tree to be left to rot.' (Part Two, VII).

*The White Peacock* is finally incoherent, however, because none of the individual characters in the novel are capable of experiencing *subjectively* the full implications of the changes which the novel registers (the first person narrator hardly exists as a character within the novel at all), and it comes to seem over-deterministic. It is not until we reach *Sons and Lovers* that the complexities we have already noted can be made coherent through the extension of consciousness within the protagonists so that they become subjects of these complexities and not merely objects. It is, of course, an autobiographical novel based on Lawrence's own early life, but he was right, I think, to describe it as 'impersonal'. It is impersonal in the sense that the subjectivity portrayed in the novel belongs to the characters and not to the narrator. Paul Morel's experience is fully coherent with the world realized in the novel so that its coincidence with Lawrence's own is only a matter of curiosity. The more so since the subjectivity of Paul is a highly representative one in that it is responsive to the most salient features of the historical world which the novel imitates. Of course, Paul is, like Lawrence himself, very exceptional, but it is only possible to realize the whole truth of a social world in fictional terms through the exceptional man; the character who is realized as 'average' in a novel can only, obviously, embody part of the truth. *Sons and Lovers* is a portrait of the artist as a young man, but the portrait can stand for the landscape of a whole epoch. In the particular case, it is the only way in which the epoch can be recorded since it is an epoch in which the working class emerges not as a *class* but as separate individuals nurtured and uprooted by the new aspirations and opportunities offered by the post-Forsterian 'democracy'.

This is not merely a matter of content but of the very form of the novel. We are to witness the working class boy emerge as the bourgeois hero, and whereas *The White Peacock* fails because Lawrence tries to engraft an impersonal range of experience onto a personal form, *Sons and Lovers* is a great novel because it *transforms* a bourgeois fictional structure. It is a structure in which the education of the hero is achieved by exile from the sanctity of childhood and a search for values 'in the world' which will accommodate his integrity and aspirations. The major instances in English are *Tom Jones* and *Great Expectations*, but in them the hero's exile is external: neither Tom nor Pip have a family. *Sons and Lovers* is a radical transformation because the exile cannot be referred to that particularity; on the contrary, Paul's exile takes place from within the family because the family itself is changing. We are aware, above all, not of personal and moral alienation from a static ideal, but of a series of cultural dislocations which create and demand a particular kind of personal integrity.

The first of the major cultural dislocations is within the marriage of Paul's parents. Mrs. Morel has been drawn into her marriage by the need for an experience which is outside the narrow confines of her puritan upbringing. But it is not simply an atavistic reaction against her father's middle class values: the 'dusky, golden softness' of Morel's 'sensuous flame of life' belongs to his working class vitality but she sees it in terms of expansion, 'something wonderful, *beyond her*' (I), so that as soon as it is seen, socially, as a contraction of possibilities, she becomes alien to their relationship. She can only relate to Morel subjectively, trying to change him into her own image: 'His nature was purely sensuous, and she strove to make him moral, religious. She tried to force him to face things. He could not endure it—it drove him out of his mind'. The verbs, 'strove', 'tried to force' are verbs of an imposed will bent on assimilating their relationship to the social reality, and later in the chapter, we have 'She was almost a *fanatic* with him . . . she tortured him . . . she destroyed him'. Lawrence later felt that he had been unfair to Morel, but the reservations are clearly there. It is not that the novel is unbiased—it cannot be because it is to be about Paul's experience, and Paul is given his identity by his mother—it is that the bias is registered as a socially specific mode of consciousness. For Mrs. Morel's vision of the family is culturally specialized: she sees it as an agent of social mobility. In a significant glimpse into her past, Lawrence relates how she rebuked her middle-class lover, John Field, for not going into the ministry because of his father's pressure to go into business with 'But if you're a *man*?' But she now recognizes that being a man is not enough, and it is significant that she calls Barker, Morel's colleague, more of a man than her husband although he is physically inferior—she can admire Barker for his ability to do his wife's chores when she is in childbirth. She sublimates a primarily physical relationship into a socially efficient one. Of course, Morel *is* a failure and it is to sentimentalize the novel to see him as the embodiment of 'organic' values. Nevertheless through him we are alerted to other possibilities of family life. Paradoxically, the most fully realized moment is immediately after he has been definitively placed in relation to his own family: 'He was an outsider. He had denied the God in him' (IV). The phrase adumbrates a kind of social Calvinism— through his irresponsibility he has cut himself off from grace, from the elect in a world of social mobility (it comes after he has found out that Paul has won a prize). But immediately after this we see him inaugurating a Ruskinian idyll in which he unites the whole family through their participation in craftsmanship. This is followed by Paul's most transparently unfair rejection of Morel during his illness. Lawrence is not being inconsistent here. Morel *can* achieve an organic relationship with his family, but it is only vestigial: through his lack of moral rigour in a world of social hardship, he is beyond redemption. But so too is the kind of familiar order his craftsmanship memorializes, for it is marginal to his real social life as a miner. We are in a world in which the only meaningful social unit is Mrs. Morel's vision of the family.

It is this vision which gives Paul his identity. The process of individuation for Mrs. Morel is through her family. She has her own ways out—significantly through the moral vitality of the chapel and the feminist emancipation of the Women's Guild, but these are only consolatory. The very naming of Paul is an act of self-realization. She takes the baby to the cricket field, a pastoral island in the urban prison of her marriage, and thinks of her child as a future Joseph, an exile who was to save a nation and his own family. Momentarily, she offers him up to the sun, to the impersonal world from whence he came, but immediately she clutches him to her bosom, to the particular individuality of his origin. And she names him Paul, after the only theologian her father had felt sympathy with, so that it means a recommitment to his narrow individualistic values— St. Paul, of course, is not, like Joseph, the hero of social salvation, but of personal salvation. Paul's exile is not to be that of the leader, but of the isolate self. After she has settled Paul in his first job, Mrs. Morel thinks proudly of her two sons: 'Now she had two sons in the world. She could think of two places, great centres of industry, and feel that she had put a man into each of them' (V). 'In the world', in this context, is a cliché of the self-made man, and when Paul tells her about his work, it is like a tale from the *Arabian Nights* to her: she discovers her 'beyond' in the modern social structure, the centre of industry.

Of course, the realization of Paul's relationship with his mother is much more profound than such an analysis suggests. It is not just the product of the social order, it is the creation of a cultural world, a new human group. Soon after Morel has asserted his relatedness through craftsmanship, we have a glimpse of a pastoral communion between Mrs. Morel and Paul when she brings home a small cornflower dish from the market—it is a reminder that Mrs. Morel is not just putting sons into the world, but creating a home for them to return to. But there is a very significant difference between this moment and the vestigial communal sense created by Morel: the latter has to do with work, the former with a possession. It is as though the tenor of the relationship between Paul and his mother were communal, but its inevitable vehicle of expression acquisitive. What most immediately identifies Paul as separate from the environment he confronts, is the class-based social mediation which has been granted to him by his mother's aspiration (Mr. Braithwaite drops his 'h' 's, Mr. Jordan is 'common'). It is this context which we should bear in mind when we consider the quality of their relationship. Inevitably it has been seen as Oedipal, and certainly it is very close: they sleep together, Mrs. Morel fights bitterly to prevent Paul from being taken from her by Miriam, and Paul finally has to kill her to release himself from her possessive will. But the most overtly Oedipal moments in the novel, when they both go to Paul's interview, and when they go for the first time to Leiver's farm are surely too conscious to suggest repression: 'She was gay, like a sweetheart' (V); 'You *are* a fine little woman to go jaunting out with' (VI). Moreover, the language, 'sweetheart', 'jaunting', suggests less sexual love than the *social appearance* of sexual love. And the episodes in which it occurs confirm this: both are scenes in which Paul, through his mother, establishes emancipation from the world of Morel. In the first he is going to get a job which takes him out of the mining community, and, in the second, mother and son are going to re-establish a friendship made through the chapel in the rural world beyond the industrial reality of Bestwood (we note that Mr. Leivers is another of the men Mrs. Morel feels she could have been a good wife to). The texture of Paul's relationship with his mother is one of an intimacy so close that the only adequate means of expression are sexual, but its structure is throughout one of social aspiration. The texture is determined by the distortion of family relationships caused by the cultural dislocation between the working man and his aspiring wife. When Morel is ill because of an accident caused by his own irresponsibility, Paul talks of himself as the man in the house. Later, when Mrs. Morel complains that her husband is giving her less money because Paul is working, Paul grows angry because she still cares about Morel's responsibility when he feels that it is a role that he himself can fill. Whatever quasi-sexual relationship there is between Paul and his mother, is thus determined by the changing structure of the family. The Morel family is neither an organic cultural unit because of the father's inability to establish its unity, nor is it straightforwardly an agent of social mobility because Mrs. Morel cannot establish her own kind of relationship with Morel, and has to replace it first by her relationship with William and then with Paul. And Paul becomes so meaningful because he is able, like Barker and like John Field, to be, for his mother, more than a man—a domestic help-meet (the bread-baking emphasizes this, and when Paul burns the bread it is the first crisis in the break-up of the relationship) and a social success. We shall only make the mistake of devaluating Mrs. Morel if we trivialize her social aspiration with a word like snobbery. Lawrence knows better, and he is able to dramatize the deep inner pressure towards individuation in terms of the social structure with such force that it is right to say, as Keith Sagar puts it, that Paul is 'kindled into life by his mother'. But we shall not make sense of the rest of the novel unless we are aware as well that this does not mean that Mrs. Morel's values are a moral norm. For it is a particular mode of life that she kindles Paul into—one determined by the Congregational Chapel and the bourgeois vitality of her father. And it is a mode that Paul has to grow beyond to rediscover his manhood.

This is a simplifying formula and the process which the novel records involves a more complex evolution than it suggests. In the first place, we have a second cultural dislocation, between Paul and his mother, which is dramatized through his relationship with Miriam, the girl he meets at the farm to which his mother takes him. It is predicted already on their walk to the farm. Paul rhapsodizes over the pit in the distant landscape while his mother remains utilitarian about it. Paul's response is aesthetic and humanist—'There's a feel of men about trucks' (VI)—and it is the kind of romanticism which only those who are already emancipated from the social world of the colliery can afford. The individuality conferred on Paul by his mother and his job takes him beyond both, into the realm of the ideal. The exact process is made clear by a comment on his art: 'From his mother he drew the life-warmth, the strength to produce; Miriam urged this warmth into intensity like a white light' (VII). The distinction here is not very different from the distinction Arnold makes between Hebraic and Hellenic qualities which differentiate middle-class and cultured virtues—the distinction between energy and light. At the climax of the quarrel with his mother about Miriam, Paul overtly defines his estrangement in cultural terms: 'You don't care about Herbert Spencer'. (VIII) Unlike the dislocation between Paul's parents, however, this is not one of class but of generation: 'You're old, mother, and we're young.' The movement from Mrs. Morel to Miriam, and the shift of interest from the work at Jordan's to the pastoral world of the farm, is a development from one phase of middle-class aspiration to another—from a desire for self-realization by 'facing' the world (society) to a desire for self-realization in a world that the self shapes, a movement, in the vocabulary Lawrence knew from Schopenhauer, from will to idea.

It is a move to an inevitable but expendable phase in Paul's individuation. The relationship with Miriam is doomed because it does not release Paul from from his mother's subjectivity but merely offers a rival imposed image, more narrowly subjective because it is more atrophied from reality. Miriam remains coiled up against reality and she uses Paul to mediate with the world without coming to terms with it. In scene after scene we see that Miriam relates only to a specialized image of Paul, always having to make allowance for a 'lower' (physical and societal) self which has nothing to do with her. Finally she has to hand over this lower self to Clara Dawes, and it is after Paul has showered Clara with flowers in a dionysiac ritual which transcends Miriam's dualistic being that Paul begins to grow free of his mother in more than intellectual terms. He takes her to Lincoln Cathedral and there realizes that his 'woman' is old, and cannot share his life any more. At the end of the same chapter (IX), the Morel family disintegrates—Paul's sister gets married, his younger brother finds a sweetheart and Paul begins to feel that he must leave. After this, the novel becomes a painful record of Paul's search for a total self which is neither his mother's nor Miriam's.

Nor Clara's. Through her he finds 'a baptism of fire in passion', but this is a single rite which is unrepeatable and transitional. Their relationship is simply, for Paul, a release from other subjectivities. It involves, above all, a descent from the other-created self into oblivion: 'She wanted to soothe him into forgetfulness' (XIII). During their first walk together, they watch the landscape merge into a one-ness which obliterates all the individual life of Paul into indistinctness. Only an impersonal relationship can release him from personality. But, of course, Clara is a person—'About *me* you know nothing' (XIII)—and as soon as she demands a personal relationship, he has to retreat into the dualism of a day-time world of work, and a night-time of love. The womanliness of Clara gives Paul his manhood, makes possible for him the kind of vitality that had once existed between his parents and that had momentarily flickered up again in the scene immediately before Paul's quarrel with his mother about Miriam as a reminder both of what the parents might have achieved and of what Paul's relationship with Miriam necessarily leaves out of account. But Clara has to return to her husband for a permanent relationship, and, indeed, it is only through her husband that Paul can discover his manhood as an isolate being, Fighting him, he becomes aware of himself as a machine, and after the fight, Lawrence habitually calls him not Paul, but Morel. In a more meaningful sense than before he has become the man in the house, for he has learnt the physical intimacy and separateness which is part of the vitality of manhood but which for the collier is confined to the mine. Clara and Baxter give Paul not a new self, but a knowledge of the impersonality and separateness that a truly self-created being must take account of. Both his mother and Miriam remain to be fully rejected in the closing pages of the novel. And, paradoxically, in releasing himself from their subjectivities through a brutal self assertion, he becomes more nakedly bourgeois than either—a kind of Robinson Crusoe figure, stripped of everything but the shut fist and the clenched mouth, turning his back on the proffered oblivion in his mother's death 'towards the faintly humming, glowing town'. For all that it is a journey towards self discovery, there is no discovery at the end of *Sons and Lovers*, for Paul asserts his selfhood, not like Robinson Crusoe in an unknown land, but in the old world of men and the city: it is merely a renewed determination to go on 'quickly' without the mediating relationships offered by the subjectivities around him. And this takes us to the heart of the Lawrencean moral agony: for in the escape from the dualistic 'personality' which transforms its vitality into an energy within the social machine or tries to hold it apart in mystic evasion, the hero has to recognize more radically his own apartness. The intensity and completeness with which this agony is realized seem to me to make *Sons and Lovers* a very great novel indeed, and although we must see *The Rainbow* and *Women in Love* as necessary progressions following it, it is surely a futile and academic exercise to try to arrange a hierarchy of value between the three.

## II. 1913–1919

The first four years after the elopement with Frieda (whom he married in 1914) are, for Lawrence, years of an amazing creative energy which was richly productive. In January, 1913, he began work on what was to become *The Lost Girl*, but set this aside for 'The Sisters' which was to become both *The Rainbow* (finished in March, 1915) and *Women in Love* (finished in June, 1916, though probably revised thereafter). In addition he wrote some of his greatest stories—'The Prussian Officer', 'Thorn in the Flesh' and 'England My England'—and three of the major prose essays which form the ideological framework of his greatest novels—'A Study of Thomas Hardy' (written 1914), *Twilight in Italy* (written between 1913 and 1915, published 1916), and 'The Crown' (written and published in 1915). These, together with the later essay, *Psychoanalysis and the Unconscious* (1921) repay the careful reading that their rhetoric demands and illuminate sharply the concepts which underly Lawrence's fictional characterization. The sources of the massive impetus of these years are obvious—the effective release from the inhibitions of the past through the relationship with Frieda, the positive strength which seems to have come from that relationship (see the volume of poems entitled *Look! We have Come Through!*), and, more problematically, a sense of the possibility of finding a sympathetic community among the intelligentsia.

By 1914, Lawrence had a wide ranging circle of friends both literary and aristocratic—the Garnetts, Edward Marsh (editor of *Georgian Poetry*), the imagist poets, H. D. and Amy Lowell,

John Middleton Murry and Lady Cynthia Asquith. In the following year, he met Lady Ottoline Morrell who introduced him to E. M. Forster and Bertrand Russell. The importance of this is more than casual. Lawrence spent the early months of 1915 trying to set up a dialogue with Russell which would provide a political solution to the situation precipitated by the war, and later in the year he tried to get going, with Middleton Murry and Katherine Mansfield, a little magazine, *The Signature*. Both efforts were attempts to create a social role within the context of a minority culture. Both failed. By August, 1915, he had quarrelled with Russell and Lady Ottoline: 'they are static, static, static . . . they filch my life for a sensation unto themselves'. On the surface the quarrel was with Russell's liberalism, but not far beneath there is a personal incompatibility which reflects an inescapable class antagonism (made dramatically clear by a disastrous weekend Lawrence spent at Cambridge with Russell and J. M. Keynes). *The Signature* ran only for three issues. The events of 1915 show how little, really, Lawrence could be assimilated into the minority culture to which his becoming a writer inevitably drew him. The story of his later career is partly the story of his cultural marginalization—from the wide circle of 1914–15 to the narrow one of Middleton Murry and Katherine Mansfield, and finally to the bizarre cult-world of Mabel Dodge Luhan and the Honourable Dorothy Brett. And however much this is explained away by Lawrence's 'temperament', it is bound up with his objective insight into the inextricable relationship between the minority culture and the 'mass-civilization' it tries to reject.

1915 was also the year which brought the definitive declaration of war between Lawrence and the bourgeois reading-public. In November, *The Rainbow* was suppressed for indecency. And the years which follow are years of a more insidiously personal persecution. At the end of 1915, Lawrence was lent a house in Cornwall (one of his congenital problems was finding somewhere agreeable to live) and it seems to have been a place he could like. But since, though he was not a conscientious objector, he was openly opposed to the war, and since also he was married to a German, he was suspected of spying and finally, in October, 1917, forbidden to live in Cornwall which, obviously, was strategically important for any potential invasion (the whole traumatic episode is recorded, rather hysterically, in chapter IX of *Kangaroo*). Not surprisingly, as soon as the war was over, Lawrence's first concern was to get out of England. It took him until October, 1919 when he went to Germany.

Because *Sons and Lovers* is about self-discovery, it can have no end, for the only self that can be 'discovered' with finality is the static self of egoism. 'When I assert an identity in the temporal flux, I become like a cabbage which folds over itself in its effort to contain the flux in static individuation.' This image is from 'The Crown', Lawrence's most explicit discourse on the nature of being: 'Whilst I am temporal and mortal,' he writes, 'I am framed in the struggle and embrace of the two opposite waves of darkness and of light' (*Phoenix* II. p. 377). There is an Absolute of being but it is in the consummation of this struggle:

> It is that which comes when night clashes on day, the rainbow, the yellow and rose and blue and purple of dawn and sunset, which leaps out of the breaking of light upon darkness, of darkness upon light, absolute beyond day or night.
>
> (ibid. p. 373)

In time, the Absolute is attainable only as a moment of consummation in relationship. We must, as individuals, recede from the consummation towards the relative eternities of light (love) or darkness (power). And therefore the consummation must be imperfect and what remains of it is the residue, the child—who will also strive towards the meeting of the two waves of the tide. This is an ontology which is discovered after *Sons and Lovers*, but the novel clearly moves towards it: Paul cannot go into the tide of his mother's own recession into darkness; having once reached perfection in love and once in battle, he must turn towards the light-and-darkness of the town. But equally, Lawrence needs to create a new structure to realize fictionally the full implications of this vision of being. *The Rainbow* is both an extension and a re-focusing. From a single family in a particular historical phase, we move to a whole cycle of overlapping generations who live through more than half the nineteenth century. And from biography we move, logically, to the history of *relationships* within that generational cycle.

The rainbow as an image is the symbol of consummated relationship, the perfect arch, different from either of the beings whose relationship creates it, but perceptible in the temporal world only as a transient vision. And it is also out of Genesis, God's covenant to Noah that generation will not cease. There is sensible discussion of its significance both by Arnold Kettle and Keith Sagar. But though it is helpful to keep it in mind, it is necessary to forgo discussion here when there is so much to be said about the basic pattern of the novel. For, I think, it is less than central to the totality of the novel. It does not occur *explicitly* until the visionary rhetoric of the final pages: insofar as it occurs positively, it is in the implicit, inarticulate feeling Tom Brangwen has about his relationship with Lydia Lensky; insofar as it becomes conscious, it is in the *false* arches of Will's Cathedral or Anna's commitment to the arch of daylight, dawn and sunset. Since it is a non-temporal absolute, and since the primary affirmation of the novel is that humans live in time, it can obviously be no more than a point of reference—it cannot be a controlling structural device. And it is to the 'structure' of the novel that we must first be attentive. The difficulty here is that 'structure' as an aesthetic term suggesting architectural unity has little relevance to a novel so much enacting the rhythms of time: we are confronted rather with a process in which the controlling motive is the movement from one generation to another. It is a twofold movement—we can talk, helpfully, of a pattern of change and continuity, but this does not suggest that we are confronted in this novel with two kinds of change. It is better to think of historical change (which enacts the changing environment of man) and evolutionary change (which enacts the changing nature of man). Both establish a dialectic between continuity and change—between, on the one hand, the Brangwen vitality and the coming of urban society, and, on the other, between the constant Brangwen aspiration towards new modes of being and the evolving individuation of the Brangwen vitality. But finally what the novel is about is the relationship between these two changing spheres—a changing world is in collision with changing man.

The first perspective of change is the record of man's vitality being distorted by his entry into the social world. The Brangwens stand not for a social myth, like 'community', but pre-social man, for whom life is fully integrated with the rhythms of nature: 'working hard because of the life that was in them, not for want of the money' (I). The women who face 'outwards to where men moved dominant and creative', express a social aspiration which, though, as Leavis says, it is not ironized since it is a process of becoming more human, is destructive of this integration, for it is less to the *outer* world that they look than the world *beyond*, the world of social consciousness attainable by 'education and experience'. It is experienced as fantasy ('the magic land') by the mind apart from its world and it is a fantasy of self distortion—'she *strained* her eyes to see', 'she *craved* to know'. Knowledge is to be the ultimate destructive agent of Ursula's relationship with Skrebensky: 'she knew him all round, not on any side did he lead into the unknown' (XV).

Moreover, like Mrs. Morel, they enact their aspiration vicariously through their children. But this is not to be the portrayal of aspiration within the social system; it is a brief statement of the Brangwen's entry into the social system. The narrative of the novel begins with historical specificity, the coming of the canal in 1840, and already we have a changed image of the Brangwens—they make money from the trespass across their land; they grow richer by supplying the new town beyond—'they were almost tradesmen'. The land becomes 'property' and the new generation of Brangwens move into society—Alfred becomes a draftsman, crushing the life within him, becoming successful and cultivating a mistress; his brother becomes a butcher and a drunkard and his sister marries a collier. Tom Brangwen is sent by his mother to Grammar School and made to feel 'guilty of his own nature'. As soon as they enter the world, fulfilling the dream of the women, the Brangwens are split beings.

In Tom, the duality can be resolved. It takes the form, merely, of an inherited female need for the 'beyond', and this can be supplied by the 'Polish Lady', Lydia Lensky, who is foreign but alienated from her own world and finds in Tom a stability which enables her to relate again to what is outside her. Thus she can be assimilated into the Marsh Farm, and they finally achieve a rootedness in separation which is the basis of human relationship. Nevertheless it is a limited integration, private and inarticulate. Tom becomes atrophied from the farm world, a gentleman farmer whose only real activity is getting drunk and whose individuality is only finally asserted in death. Lydia never belongs fully to the farm at all, and after Tom's death, she retreats into the world of her past. What is the 'making' of Tom, the confrontation of the unknown, is also the defeat of the Brangwen integration with the land. The duality between inner and outer worlds becomes increasingly insoluble. Anna and Will are only related in their withdrawal from the world, and once they redescend to it, their relationship disintegrates until unity means only predatory victory of one over the other. Both are more specifically social beings than Tom. Will, the son of Alfred, is already urban and his creative vitality is thwarted both by a dualism within himself and by his polarization from Anna. Anna too is unable to create a relationship with the outer world. She finds the Brangwen household constricting because it 'belittles' her, but its very qualities alienate her from the outer social world. She can only relate to society through fantasy: she holds herself aloof from the world around her not, like her mother, because she is prepared to accept the limited horizons of the Marsh Farm in exchange for stability, but because she identifies with high society—the Princess Alexandra. She is drawn to Will because 'he was the hole in the wall, *beyond*·which the sunshine blazed on an outside world' (IV) and when he fails to offer the relationship which will take her beyond the immediate world, she has to cast him off and withdraw into her own pregnancy. The stability she finds in the end is much less inclusive and more private than Lydia and Tom find: it is a retreat into the 'trance of motherhood', to a daylight world. The darkness she leaves to Will who holds it coiled inside him so that it appears only in outbursts of violence against his daughter.

Out of this spirit, Ursula's own relationship to the world grows, and the process of alienation becomes more inexorable and more complex. She recoils from her mother's fecundity, and she recognizes her own apartness because of the treacherous violence of her father. Being alone in her selfhood, Ursula is compelled to seek her being in the outer world from which Anna retracts, and it is a search which discovers no mode of relationship because it has to take place in a world which has institutionalized relationships. The key chapter here is the one describing her life as a schoolteacher, significantly and justifiably entitled 'The Man's World' since it offers a paradigm of the new urban world Ursula has to confront. It is a great chapter because Lawrence does not simplify the issue, as Dickens does in *Hard Times*, by confusing the system with its agents. Even Harby, the odious headmaster who is most fully committed to making the system work is not allowed to become mechanical: 'He seemed to have some cruel, stubborn, evil spirit, he was imprisoned in a task too small and petty for him, which yet, in a servile acquiescence, he would fulfil, because he had to earn his living' (XIII). There is no sentimentalization—Harby the man is not simply separated from Harby the headmaster—but the word 'imprisoned' discriminates the two: his very 'evil spirit', harnessed as it is to the system, is too big for the system, and we have throughout the chapter a sense that there is an ominous gap between the system and the vitality it demands. It is precisely this local greatness which gives the chapter its function in the novel as a whole. For Lawrence is thus able to give us Ursula caught up in the system without destroying her as an established and developing character: Harby is not only her enemy but also her mentor. It is not people that the system mechanizes, but the relationships between people, as the episode with Williams shows. And that is precisely the point towards which the novel has been moving—the increasing separation of the inner being from the relationships by which it forms itself, so that being becomes, in the end, a distorted recoil from relationship. As the Brangwens move into society, and as society moves towards the Boer War, what has, from the beginning, been postulated as the only mode of being which does not falsify relationships, the rhythmic flow of 'blood-intimacy' which realizes the rainbow, has been destroyed.

But Ursula's alienation is not merely the distortion of her vitality through the changing nature of social relationships. If we are content with this perspective, the end of the novel becomes, as S. L. Goldberg argues, less of a diagnosis of the modern world in terms of the vitality which Ursula inherits than a protest against it: the modern world crumbles too quickly before the 'chosen vessel of vitality'. We need to be aware as well of the changing nature of the vitality, of the modes of being in which the protagonists discover themselves, which evolve progressively from generation to generation. And Ursula inherits three developing needs. First, as the third Lensky woman, she seeks in man a mediator with the outer world. For Lydia this means seeking a separate existence which can give her rootedness, and she has to bring Tom to *submit* not to herself, but to the recognition of her own separateness. For Anna, Will is an agent of her relationship with the outer world: it is only *part* of him that she needs and as soon as his agency ceases to be effective she casts him off—we move from submission to defeat, 'Anna Victrix'. Ursula, as we have seen, is compelled to discover herself as an isolate being, and she seeks in Skrebensky an image of what she wishes to become: 'He seemed simply acquiescent in the fact of his own being, as if he were beyond any change or question. He was himself' (XI). And once she has asserted herself against him, she can only destroy him. Submission, defeat, destruction—this is the most obvious evolutionary pattern. But Ursula is also the heir of Tom and Will, and this means that in seeking herself, she must also seek physical identity, the blood intimacy of the male Brangwens. In Tom's case, this means submission to the darkness which he does not understand; in Will's case this means containing the darkness within himself and relieving it through sensuality or violence. For Ursula no such dualism is possible: she is compelled to seek ecstasy, the fulfilment of the physical being within the isolation of her individuation. And this is involved with the third inherited force, that of the female Brangwens. When she is, early on, seeking her 'real self' (the reiterated concept in Ursula's story) she comes across Genesis VI which suddenly refers to the 'Sons of God', and she construes this to mean that there was a race of men other than the sons of Adam: she conceives of herself as one of the beautiful women who was taken by these antediluvian giants. Later, she mocks the Genesis story of the flood on the same grounds as T. H. Huxley, who argued that the flood was merely a local event. This links with the drowning of Tom to whom the flood at the farm has seemed all-engulfing: Tom is not Noah, since he drowns, but he *is* one of the sons of Adam. Her mockery comes after she has met Skrebensky whom she sees as one of the sons of God. The Skrebenskys have come to stand, after Anna's visit, for a reality beyond the suffocating intimacy of the Brangwen farm. Enacting the female Brangwen aspiration to the beyond, Ursula seeks her real being in a mode beyond the Brangwens and ultimately beyond the human.

This is surely why the world in which she is compelled to seeks her identity crumbles before her so quickly. The whole of her relationship with Skrebensky is summed up in their dance at Fred Brangwen's wedding. Like the corn harvest in which Will and Anna come together, this is a moonlight ritual of sexual ecstacy. But whereas the first scene is a rhythmic enactment of sexual vitality in which unity is never quite realized, the second is a scene in which Ursula meets Skrebensky to go *beyond* him to seek out 'pure being' through her relationship with the moon: 'She wanted the moon to fill her, she wanted more, more communion with the moon, consummation' (XI). And she returns to Skrebensky only to destroy him, like a corrosive salt. Ursula takes her being from the moon (a theme which is importantly continued in *Women in Love*), and this is not Lawrencean mystagogy—it is a validated metaphor for the destructive vitality of 'pure being' which emancipates itself from the world of man. Thus the Brangwen vitality becomes not simply the value against which 'modern' life is measured, it is also an agent of that life. Skrebensky is not merely a 'nullity'—he is made a nullity by Ursula's vitality. The continuity between the generations is an evolution towards death and extinction.

It is the relationship between the two processes we have noted that gives *The Rainbow* its coherence. For it means that we have, not a historical novel opposing 'traditional' values to social change, but a complex portrayal of man's descent into history and his evolution towards and beyond the forms of being which that descent encounters. Of course, it is modern history that Lawrence is concerned with, but the novel's enquiry is into

the nature of historical man, and through this into the relationship between 'objective' reality and 'subjective' being. Man is
agent and patient of his own destiny. And the end of the novel
seems to me to be perfectly coherent with the realization of this
relationship. Ursula, pregnant by Skrebensky who has deserted
her for social integration, is surrounded by unseen horses as she
walks in the rain. She climbs a tree to escape them and has a
miscarriage. After a long and obscure illness, she awakes to a
new sense of being, denuded of social reality, like a kernel
which has burst its shell. Looking out from her parents' new
house over the industrial waste land of Beldover, she sees the
corruption of a people bowed down by industrialism. But she
sees too a rainbow arched over the town and feels that it is
arched in the blood of the working people. The horses are clearly the unacknowledged forces of her inner being—the darkness
which had sought and failed to discover the unknown in Skrebensky. But they appear as nightmare, and though, like Tom's
drowning, it is a consummation of her being, it is utterly private.
We have moved into an era in which the 'blood intimacy' of
the Brangwens is buried in the inner being of the isolate self.
But also, by causing the miscarriage, the horses acknowledge
the end of 'generation' and hence the end of the old bases of
personal relationship. Finally, they seem to be 'running against
the walls of time', affirming that is the vitality of change against
the 'Absolute' of 'pure being'. So that they are at once a challenge and an affirmation : a challenge to the absorption of being
in the outer world and to the family as an agent of aspiration
and continuity—an affirmation of new potentials of being in
time. So that the naked kernel of being is able to discover a new
sense of the human group, of relationship beyond the social
order, in the rainbow—'the very iris of my being'. This is not
utopian because it is not a glimpse of a new social order, but an
inward vision of something beyond pure individuality : it is
an image of what the new self needs to create, but the rainbow is
a momentary image, and it presupposes that the deluge will precede it. From this point, Lawrence has to move on from the
portrayal of the creation of social man to the portrayal of the
society he creates moving towards its destiny in destruction.
And this means moving from saga to panorama, and from the
symbol which is a referential covenant to a structural system
of symbols which are the signals of social destiny. The end of
*The Rainbow* takes us straight to *Women in Love*.

It is, in fact, a massive and necessary prelude to *Women in
Love* in that, as a recreation of man's entry into the historical

world, it gives a large temporal perspective to what is to be the final judgement on that world affected by the Brangwen sisters who wait, at the opening, with slightly pretentious boredom to discover a role in the present. *Women in Love* is, in a way that *The Rainbow* cannot be, a historical novel specifically narrating the death of a society. And this means that it is concerned not simply with the coming of social change and the consequent erosion of ethical values (as, for example, a novel by Scott or Balzac might be) but with the death of ways of being, a death precisely caused by the very evolution of vitality that is registered in *The Rainbow*. The best preparation for the study of *Women in Love* is George Dangerfield's history of the years 1910–1914, *The Strange Death of Liberal England*. Dangerfield finds it necessary to talk of the 'neurosis' of a whole society, and his picture is essentially one of institutions dying in the face of an unaccommodated vitality; this is what is happening in *Women in Love*. Gerald, both through the determinant role of his own vitality and through its need to relate to the destructive critical vigour of Gudrun, goes to his death in the navel of the world, and his death, we are made to feel, is an apocalyptic image of the end of the social world which he dominates and by which he is created. But the link with Dangerfield's book is more than one of content: for a historical narrative, its organization is surprisingly spatial—Dangerfield moves rather from one social area to another than through successive points in time. And *Women in Love* has, in its central portions, this sense too—we move from Shortlands to the Café de Pompadour to Breadalby to Beldover and back to Shortlands. Each location contains a part of the society Lawrence is portraying. Again, we are confronted with a transformed nineteenth century form—the panoramic novel—and as a social picture it is bound to be rather static. This is one reason why we cannot separate it from *The Rainbow*—without the temporal prelude of the earlier novel we are likely to look on *Women in Love* as an organism of related moral values, as a 'fable' with social significance. Whereas it is a chronicle of a moment in history.

This means that primarily we should be concerned with the novel's presentation of a world moving to its death, rather than with the moral values with which Lawrence is measuring that world. Although it was written during the war, and although its conception was involved with the sense Lawrence gained from the war of the drift of societal ideologies towards social destruction, it importantly is not a novel *about* the war; it is about the social world which was obliterated by it. It is, that is to say, a novel about a world which has already gone. Its going is recognized to be inevitable, not because of the coming of an external historical event, but because of its inherent characteristics. It is central to Lawrence's purpose to realize this inherentness because his history is not of 'events' but of the evolution of consciousness within a static order. This is why Birkin and Ursula seem so unsatisfactory as representatives of 'normative' values: what they stand for is no real alternative to what is taking place, for the death is inevitable and even desirable. We can see clearly how much Lawrence is concerned to preserve a sense of historical inevitability if we consider *Twilight in Italy* which in many detailed ways is a trial run for the novel. It is a remarkably concrete and vivid record of the erosion of the spontaneous vitality of the Italian soul by the encroachment of Northern efficiency and Northern consciousness. The village players who act Ibsen and Hamlet ('tragedy of the convulsed reaction of the mind from the flesh, of the spirit from the self'), the *padrone* of the Lemon Gardens who frets about his new spring lock, the peasants who go to America and return uprooted and vacant and the Italian exiles in Switzerland who drift into a mechanical anarchism—all these are signs of the coming of a new era of self-consciousness and mechanical dualism to a way of life which has always been of the 'shadow', vital and physical. And there are constant digressions on the corruption of England by the Industrial Revolution. Lawrence's moral attitude is clear, but it exists within a bitter and tenacious recognition that this has to be, not simply because it has happened and is undeniable, but also because it is part of human evolution. The Italian 'soul' is a regression, and, as he says, 'It is better to go forward into error than to stay fixed inextricably in the past'. *Women in Love* maintains the same balance of attitudes: the world of the Criches must go forward to meet its destiny in violent death because of its very vitality.

We can say 'the Crich world' because although the novel is panoramic, the social centres which are established exist as functions of the hegemonic world of Shortlands. Shortlands, the seat of industrial power, determines the dominant modes of consciousness of the novel. It depends on a rigorously imposed order maintained by the kind of vitality exemplified in Gerald's determination to make the Arab mare face the train which frightens her; on, that is, the violent subjugation of physical energy to the machine. But it is also, clearly, a dualistic world. The first generation of Criches simply assimilate their energy into the creation of industrial prosperity, but Gerald's father attempts to mitigate this energy with a hopelessly paralytic philanthropism. As the leader of the third generation, Gerald becomes the agent of power, shaping the family affairs into a highly mechanized efficiency. But not all of Gerald can be absorbed into this creation of his outer being: his is a power which cannot be contained by the outer world, and through him the order of Shortlands comes to be dependent on an underworld of degenerate centres—the darkness of Beldover, the mindlessness of the Pompadour and the dissolution of being into 'talk' which is Breadalby. Thus, in this perspective, *Women in Love* establishes a 'social statics' in which the hegemonic consciousness of industrial power has escape routes into decadence.

But there is too a 'social dynamics' and this is realized by what transforms the novel from panorama to apocalypse—the complex patterns of symbols and symbolic scenes which have been discussed most fully by Leavis. It is impossible, in an essay of this scope, to go beyond what he offers as analysis, but it is necessary to say something about the function of symbolism in *Women in Love*, for Lawrence's kind of symbolism is very different from 'literary' symbolism. He had experimented with a symbolic structure in *The Trespasser* (1912) which moves from a depressing social environment to the Isle of Wight, a landscape in which the main characters act out the implications of their situations in mythic terms. It is clear that Lawrence moves towards symbolism in an attempt to cater for the aspects of self which are not available to a socially defined consciousness (personality). It is not so much a rhetorical device as part of the vision which is being realized. In *Women in Love* we do not have two co-existing levels of reality, the actual and the symbolic, but we have a process in which the actual modulates into the symbolic as it plays out its implications without the defence of social mediation. Again and again there are scenes which begin as panoramic realism and come to focus on symbolic gesture or theme. Thus at the wedding which opens the novel, we have Gerald, at this stage insisting on social conformity, suddenly summoning the guests to the breakfast with a conch shell, which embodies the nature of his vitality—the primitive assertion of tribal domination. Again, at Breadalby, we have a country house party sharply realized in terms of social types and the 'stream of conversation' by which they declare their own abstraction and stagnation. When Hermione, mechanically asserting her will after her defeated attempt to crush the vitality in Birkin, suggests that her guests go swimming, the party resolves itself into a tableau of stagnant pastoralism: 'one wanted to swoon into the bygone perfection of it all' (VIII). But the image recedes in time beyond its human context: 'Don't they look saurian? They are just like great lizards'. It is an image of a primeval world obliterated by evolution. Significantly, it is Gudrun who makes this remark for it is she who is to demolish this escape route for Gerald, as she draws him into the destructive impetus of his own dualism (Gerald has joined the swimmers, but he is fascinated by her destructive criticism of it). Similarly, the Café de Pompadour moves towards its definitive symbol of the African fetish, the disintegration into mindlessness (this is another world which Gudrun finally places and overtakes). This modulation operates too on a personal level—Birkin discovers his image of the relationship he wants with Ursula in his cat's attitude towards the wild female; Gerald and Gudrun recognize their desire for mutual destruction in the violence of the rabbit.

Too much of the symbolism is bound up with the freedom of the characters in the novel for us to think of it as the author's way of giving order to the reality he is imitating. They *choose* their symbolic acts and images as ways of declaring their relationship with the outer world and of indicating the direction of their vitality. The best analogy is perhaps from anthropology. One of the major debates in this field at the turn of the century was the nature of totemism (Sir James Frazer had published two books on the subject in 1887 and 1910; Freud had related the problem of totemism to psychoanalysis in *Totem and Taboo*, 1913). Malinowski in an essay on Frazer writes:

> totemism expresses ritually and mythologically man's selective interest in a number of animal or plant species; it discloses the primitive's profound conviction that he is in body and mind akin to the relevant factors of his environment.
>
> (*Sex, Culture and Myth*, 1963, p. 281)

*Women in Love* is the portrait of a society seeking out the relevant factors of its environment: the characters, especially Gerald, are compelled by the dynamics of their own vitality to break through the static world of contained social consciousness and act out the violence and destruction implicit in the mode of being which gives them their hegemony. The massive coda of the novel discovers the landscape, the new world of frozen mountains, where the society is dominated by Loerke the artist whose work is at once the most extreme product of industrialism and the most conscious satire of it. Gerald has used Gudrun as an escape from the pressure of the external world of Shortlands on the inner vacuum of his being (his first intercourse with her is both a release from consciousness, a kind of masturbation, and a return to the womb), and then, once he has realized that she is no Minette, he tries to assimilate her into his dualism, thinking of her as the wife to whom he will be unfaithful. But through the mountains and through the extreme, corrupt and satiric consciousness of Loerke, Gudrun selects her own, reductive and anti-static kinship with her environment. Loerke is *her* 'totem', and in his defence, she delivers Gerald the blow which sends him to his death. His frozen body is the image of what the consciousness of the world of Shortlands implies.

I have offered an account of the way in which we need to approach the form of *Women in Love*, but it would be simply dishonest of me to pretend to give even the same perfunctory account of its themes as I have tried to do in the discussion of other novels. The overall theme of *Women in Love* is easier to describe than that of *The Rainbow* or even *Sons and Lovers*: it is the study of the dynamic implications of the modes of consciousness created by a static but dying society realized in the sexual relationships which exist within that society. But, of course, what is important is the detailed realization of this theme and that requires a prohibitively extensive analysis. There is an important problem, however, which must be discussed, and this has to do generally with the kind of 'historical' novel *Women in Love* is, and in particular with the structural importance of the relationship between Ursula and Birkin.

A novel which claims to have historical significance, as I think *Women in Love* does, ought to realize an awareness of potential change. Yet we have noted that the sense of development that there is *in* the novel has to do not with historical change but only with the symbolic realization of the *terminus ad quem* of a particular epoch: the future seems to be only an ending. Ursula and Birkin do seem, on the face of it, to be intended to offer an alternative mode of relationship, one which is not only beyond corrupt possessiveness, but also beyond 'love'—that is mutual absorption. Yet nobody has satisfactorily answered Leavis' objections to Lawrence's portrayal of this relationship—that it is a rhetoric of assertion rather than realization, and that it is limited by an overbearing jargon (the chapter called 'Excurse' gives sufficient examples of this). We surely have to admit that this is a very problematic aspect of the novel.

But also, we must recognize how much Lawrence recognizes

the limits of what Ursula and Birkin achieve. Although he is very explicit about their struggle towards a viable relationship, he says very little of their marriage, except to define its limitations. In the first place, Birkin is looking for a more than private relationship: he aspires to be free 'with a few other people', that is to make his relationship with Ursula the basis for a new society. This is linked with his failed desire to achieve a deep relationship with Gerald. It is an unresolved aspiration—Birkin has to give in, at least temporarily, to Ursula's contentment with privacy. Secondly, their first act under the new dispensation is to disrobe themselves of their social being altogether by resigning their educational posts. They opt, that is for exile, not for the kind of regeneration through education which had been glimpsed early in the novel in Ursula's classroom. Finally, Birkin's major consolation for his despair about Gerald is a Darwinian faith that the human race will be totally destroyed and replaced.

These qualifications do not contest the obvious fact that Birkin is close to Lawrence's own view. But they do *place* Birkin in the world which is being destroyed. Nobody can fail to have been struck by Birkin's irresoluteness for much of the novel— the difficulty he has in ending his relationship with Hermione, and the way in which, for all his ideas, he participates in the talk and the social pretence of Breadalby and the Pompadour (Minette revealingly thinks of him in the same group as Halliday). It is significant that Birkin is finally driven out of these groups, by Hermione's violence and Halliday's mockery, rather than by his own decision. Birkin is very much (dramatically if not ideologically) part of the world whose destruction is being enacted. Indeed we must go further and say that the social world which is portrayed is for the purposes of the novel, the *human* world. To escape from it is to escape from humanity.

This enables us to define the quality of the novel which is both its strength and its limit. When we say that *Women in Love* is about the death of a whole society, we must note too that Lawrence's social vision is almost entirely hegemonic. That is to say, the nature of a society defines itself for him by the structures of consciousness created by the classes which dominate it. This has been increasingly true since *Sons and Lovers*— Lawrence's interest has been primarily in those impulses towards self-realization which are the *making* of a social structure. This is recognized, I think, in a small scene in *Women in Love*. Shortly before they leave England, Birkin and Ursula discover a chair in a market which they see as the survival of pre-industrial England, a more productive age. They buy it, but then decide that the continuity with the past it represents is not for them—they must opt out of the world of possessions altogether. So they give it to a poor man and the pregnant girl he is about to marry. They are urban England, subdued and miserable, yet they have also a certain singular vitality which is appealing. It is as though Birkin and Ursula were giving up society but laying a stake in the future by bequeathing their most valuable possession to a class which is not present in the novel except as part of the dualistic world of Shortlands. It is a very slight reminder that there is a humanity beyond the Crich world, although it is one which the Criches hold in their power. And surely this is the right perspective. It would have been quite sentimental for Lawrence to have shown a 'new' humanity *replacing* that of Shortlands. As Birkin says to Ursula, it is not possible to be of the end and of the beginning. Equally, however, we know that it is the end of a *particular* world. And the end must seem to be complete, for it is only possible to conceive of being in terms which are consciously available within human society, and human society is determined by its possessors. The new heaven and the new earth cannot be of this vocabulary. It suggests a vision which is limited, but the vision would be weakened if it were dissipated by Utopian projections.

### III. 1919–1930

From 1919 to 1922, Lawrence stayed on the Continent, largely in Sicily. It is another fruitful phase which includes the completion of *The Lost Girl* (May, 1920) and *Aaron's Rod* (May, 1921) and the writing of two important tales, 'The Fox' and 'The Captain's Doll' (both finished in 1921). He also wrote two important essays on the theory of personality, *Psychoanalysis and the Unconscious* (1920) and *Fantasia of the Unconscious* (1921), the second of his remarkable travelogues, *Sea and Sardinia* (1921) and most of the poems of his best volume, *Birds, Beasts and Flowers*. The pattern of his career is clear at this point: there is a new initiative and a new determination to discover an audience. In January, 1920, we find him refusing to accept an offer of £200 for the rights of *The Rainbow*, partly because 'I believe in my books and their future'. In February, he is impressing on his American agent the urgency of securing a public in America, and, in May, he is looking for an opportunity to serialize *The Lost Girl*. At the same time there is a co-existent despair. In February of the same year, he writes to Amy Lowell, 'Why can't I earn enough, I've done the work'. By May, 1921, the short-lived concern for and faith in a public has evaporated: 'I have *nearly* finished my novel *Aaron's Rod* . . .', he writes to S. L. Koteliansky, 'But it won't be popular.' *The Lost Girl* had sold only 2,300 copies, and *Women in Love* (published in England in 1921) was branded as indecent by the popular press. Lawrence was never a willing cultural martyr, and such alienation was damaging. The preface to *Fantasia of the Unconscious* is an embarrassing attempt to be indifferent to 'the general reader', and the violent, assertive rhetoric of the book contrasts dismally with the lucidity of the earlier essay on psychoanalysis.

This is certainly one factor in the decision to accept a more disastrous exile than that of Europe. In 1922, after a good deal of vacillation between rival invitations to Ceylon and New Mexico, Lawrence sailed east. As soon as he arrived, he disliked Ceylon and moved to Australia. After three months there, he finally arrived in Taos, New Mexico in September to take up an offer of a house by a wealthy American admirer, Mabel Dodge Sterne (later Luhan). There he was based until he finally returned to Europe in September, 1925, but Harry T. Moore has computed that he only stayed there for a total of eighty weeks in those three years. In this tragically unsettled phase, the only major fiction of real merit is 'St. Mawr' which seems to ironize bitterly every character in the story (including, I think, the horse). The novels of these years are simply bad: *Kangaroo* (1923), despite sharp insights into Australian society, is uncontrolled autobiography; *The Boy in the Bush* and *The Plumed Serpent* are barely readable because of a self-indulgent didacticism. The danger signs in Lawrence's alienation had long been evident. In the lonely years at the end of the First World War, in essays such as 'Education of the People' and 'Democracy', we see a tired mind which has a very sharp sense of the problems of modern society reaching desperately for a simple solution. He had found it mainly in a mystic (and mystifying) concept of social leadership. This takes, however, a long time to get into the novels. In *Aaron's Rod* it is a marginal and unrelated theme, in *Kangaroo* it is dominant, but the novel is largely concerned with its rejection. Only in *The Plumed Serpent* does it become programmatic, and that is a novel that Lawrence himself was later to reject. His fictional imagination resisted as long as possible the subjective ideology that his isolation led him to, and it is significant that only when he has cut himself off from the ineluctable reality of Europe can Lawrence fully indulge himself.

Lawrence, it needs to be insisted, found himself in a dilemma that was barely soluble. He recognized, as soon as he left Europe, that exile was dangerous. From Ceylon, he wrote:

> But I do think, still more now I am out here, that we make a mistake forsaking England and moving out into the periphery of life. After all, Taormina, Ceylon, Africa, America—as far as *we* go, they are only the negation of what we ourselves stand for.

He felt also that Australia and America failed to provide the self with any kind of societal reality (of course, he was kept very much on the fringe of American society in the bogus primitivism and opulent bohemianism of Mabel Dodge Luhan's cultural menagerie). At the same time, he couldn't bring himself to encounter the old chagrin of living in England ('But I feel England has insulted me, and I stomach that badly'). So, throughout 1923, we find him making plans to return to Europe, but finally letting Frieda go alone, only joining her at the end of November. And as soon as he is in London, he wants to return to America. He sailed back in March 1924. One reason that he must have been drawn back was simply that in America he had an audience. He wrote to Secker in 1922 that whereas from the sale of the whole of his work in England he was getting about £120 a year, he had been offered, in America $1,000 for the magazine rights of 'The Captain's Doll' alone, and, in the same year, he learnt that *Women in Love* had sold 15,000 copies in America. There is no reason to assume that these sales would have diminished if Lawrence had not lived there, but Lawrence was a writer who was socially responsive enough to be drawn to where he was wanted.

Illness, however, was soon to become the major fact of his life. In Mexico, in February 1925, tuberculosis was definitively diagnosed, and in September he crossed the Atlantic again, this time for good. The next four years, frighteningly restless though they were, see a final creative phase. 'Sun' was written in 1925, *The Virgin and the Gypsy* and 'The Man Who Loved Islands' in 1926, and 'The Escaped Cock' ('The Man Who Died') in 1927–8. *Lady Chatterley's Lover* was begun in October, 1926 and finished in December 1927. It is also a period of great essays— the attack on Galsworthy, 'Pornography and Obscenity' and a moving series of pieces about his home country 'Autobiographical Fragment', 'Nottingham and the Mining Country' and 'Auto-biographical Sketch'. Both the creativity and its particular direction suggest a renewed determination to resume battle with the particular world in which he was so deeply rooted, and whose institutions and culture drove him into exile. And he achieved a kind of victory. *Lady Chatterley's Lover*, though it was privately published, was seized by the police in October, 1928 (and it remained a classic underground book until 1960). In January, 1929, the manuscript of his satiric poems, *Pansies*, was seized by the Post Office (with very doubtful legal justification), and in July, the police carried off thirteen of his paintings from an exhibition in London. Lawrence became the only modern writer to become, like Dickens, a household name.

It is almost inevitable that, after *Women in Love*, Lawrence's work should seem disappointing (though this is a highly relative statement). It is not simply that it would be very difficult for any writer to transcend the achievement of the three novels we have most fully discussed, it is also that the very nature of *Women in Love* demands a progression which inevitably places Lawrence historically. Although, as he himself said, it is a destructive novel, it is not pessimistic because it is so much a novel about the past. You cannot really be pessimistic about the past, only about the future: if, somehow, life goes on, you are compelled to discover a basis for the affirmation of its continuity. This is complicated by the war, which, for Lawrence asserted the pastness of the world he knew, and, despite its horror, granted new hope for a totally new future. And fiction must move from the 'destructive' to the programmatic. Because of the limitations of Lawrence's vision, the programme is full of difficulties.

This is an oversimplifying formula because it suggests that 'the programme' is an imposition of absolute moral values on the world of the novel. Whereas, at least in *The Lost Girl*, it is much more an affirmation of a new centre of vitality which is discovered within the portrayed historical situation. Alvina Houghton is a powerfully realized study in alienation. Externally, she is entirely the product of her father's megalomaniac but trivial business world, and she has to learn first to become an outsider by marrying a theatrical Italian, and second to confront the landscape which has made him, a landscape which is an eternal negation of human effort, before she can realize her own being, not in a futile antithetical struggle with society, but in relation to the 'pre-world' against which man has to assert his significance. She has to be lost to society, and to her own former being in order to discover the reality of human relationships which social institutions disguise. But it is not this thematic coherence which gives the novel its impressiveness; it is simply the density with which Alvina's social world is realized. The petty bourgeois world with its pretentiousness and its commodity-fetishism is so much on top of us, that we recognize Alvina's escape to Italy with Cicio not as a romantic gesture of defiance but as a real necessity—the only way to avoid becoming one of Woodhouse's old maids. If Cicio were not there, he would have to be invented.

And yet here, in its very convincingness, is the problem which confronts us in the later Lawrence. Symbolically, Cicio stands for the masculine force of darkness, the reaffirmed rootedness of being in 'unconscious' sexual relationship. But Cicio is *realized* as something less than what he has to stand for. In the first place, he comes to Woodhouse with the tawdry and absurd 'Red-indian' troop, the Natcha-kee-Tawaras (we do not have to read the novel very closely to see that they are meant to be tawdry and absurd): this means that he is not only the primitive principle of blood consciousness but that he is playing at being such a symbol—his presocial subversiveness is part of his social being. And thus he is almost comically dualistic—if he is capable of taking Alvina out of Woodhouse, he is also capable of being impressed by its affluence, and Alvina is both a social and a sexual 'catch'. This is partly explained by the 'modern education' which makes 'money and independence an *idée fixe*' (X), but we should note that Lawrence recognizes that this is 'more efficacious' than the 'old instinct' which it overlays, and, more importantly, that the old instinct is 'an instinct of the world's meaninglessness'—it is not realized as more than a negation. When we arrive in *his* world, Califano, he becomes a radically diminished symbol: it is not he, but the landscape which creates a new sense of being outside social convention. And the predominant sense that Alvina has is that of a '*lapse* of life' (XV). At the end, Cicio goes off to the war and we are not certain that he will come back. We cannot be sure whether Alvina is lost to society or lost completely. The necessary affirmation of a life apart from social institutions is perilously near to death. Lawrence must inevitably proceed from the negation of *Women in Love* to the discovery of new orders of vitality, but although vitality is *conceptually* clearly defined in 'The Crown' and *Psychoanalysis and the Unconscious*, its realization in *fictional* terms is difficult.

We find it best realized in the stories—in 'The Horse Dealer's Daughter', 'You Touched Me', and 'The Captain's Doll', for example. But this is significant—the short story does not have to confront the problem of the *duration* of what it affirms. Indeed the first two stories just mentioned depend for their whole strength on a tension, at the end, between an unambiguous momentary affirmation of the reality of physical communion and utter doubt about that moment's duration in time. The novel cannot be so ambiguous about duration, and by the nature of Lawrence's concern for human life which is not atrophied by the individualism of bourgeois morality, the durational realization of the new order of vitality must mean that we move from a moral issue to a social one.

The key text here is *Aaron's Rod*, which is a much better novel than is usually thought. Aaron, caught in the dualism of work and family on the one hand, and self indulgent escape on the other, has to break out or rot inwardly. His problem may be, as Moynahan dismissively says, boredom, but boredom can be very complex, and in Aaron's case it involves an integrity which refuses to be absorbed in the conventionally ordered world, a separate self which cannot be held in apartness but which must be responded to in action. The vivid portrayal of his home life in the opening chapters makes us feel that self-exile is the only integrity. The difficulty begins with the exile itself. Unlike Wells' Mr. Polly, Aaron finds no retreat. The only other world is that of his sophisticated patrons, and that is a world as oppressive and as alienating as that of his home. We see this most clearly in the scene in which Sir William Franks ceremoniously displays his medals: we are still in a world of social labels and Aaron, having no label himself, has to look on. He has not escaped, he has only become invisible. The ambiguities of *The Lost Girl* become central, and the very structure of the novel becomes an aimless wandering from set to set. It is as though Aaron's self-discovery and flight to freedom can have no meaning beyond the single act of going away. And this is clearly because there is no social order which can contain the basis of the regenerated human group. The isolate self becomes absolute but not more 'free' in its cutting loose.

The novel works best, I think, if we see it as totally directionless. It then becomes a vivid portrayal of the man of personal integrity picking his way among the ruins of the post-war world. But there is a direction—marginal and unrelated—in that Aaron is vaguely searching for Rawdon Lilly. Lilly, who is an idealization of Lawrence, offers him a relationship which is meaningful outside the social consciousness. But, it is also clear that it is a relationship which is contradictory. At the end of the novel, Lilly is trying to explain that he believes in both the idea of natural superiority and its concomitant idea of submission, *and* that every man is 'a sacred and a holy individual, *never* to be violated' (XX). The ideological difficulty is resolved by a loud explosion from a political bomb which obliterates the conversation. Aaron's flute is broken, his individuality violated. Freedom from social reality is impossible. More than this, Lilly's own mode of relationship is essentially one of violation. Personal sufficiency, he tells Aaron at the end, is not enough: Aaron must submit to some higher being. The message is clear: the emancipated self needs to discover real contact and real community. But dramatically, Lilly cannot offer this new sense of relationship because he is too much a part of the intellectual set in which Aaron discovers his inexorable isolation. The only way in which Lawrence can bring out the possibilities that Lilly is meant to offer is by making him give a sermon at the end: it is crude, but significantly crude—Lilly can only oppose the corrupt intellectual world against which he is meant to offer alternative values with talk, and talk is the safety valve by which the sophisticated world which Aaron has encountered, survives. Lilly is *dramatically* no more meaningful to Aaron's predicament than Sir William Franks, except, that is, in the finite interval of consummated intimacy in Covent Garden when Lilly nurses the sick Aaron back to life. Lilly may be as a character an idealization of Lawrence, but his social importance is assessed with a realism which is inescapable. It leaves Lilly chattering away while the bombs go off.

We are confronted then finally with the incoherence of Lawrence's social vision. Throughout the tales of the period which follows *Aaron's Rod*, we find a more and more lucidly realized sense of the moral relationship between the kind of integrity discovered by Alvina and Aaron and the meaningful human contact within which it can survive. But in the novels, *Kangaroo* and *The Plumed Serpent* especially, we find a desperate but inevitable attempt to envisage fictionally the new society which such a morality demands. In the process, the morality is distorted into propaganda: vitality becomes order. It is not until we reach *Lady Chatterley's Lover* and Lawrence returns again to the historical problem which is his most central concern, the changing consciousness of those who inhabit an industrial society, that we get a real sense of what he was trying to make articulate.

It is a failure, but it remains one of the few really challenging texts about the values inherent in modern society, and the source of its failure is also a source of its strength. Sir Clifford Chatterley is a Gerald who has survived the war, and is thus unmanned, an anachronism whose only motive for survival is an atrophied social will. His own concept of integrity is precisely that of 'personality', the living in apartness which Lawrence finds so nauseating in Jane Austen: 'Isn't the whole problem of life,' he says, 'the slow building up of an integral personality, through the years? living an integrated life?' (V). Such an integrity is entirely mental and, as Connie realizes, 'out of touch' (in all possible ways) with any sense of human community. It is a sterility reflected at one level by the mechanical orderliness of Wragby and the dreary standardization of Tevershall, and at another by the futile talk of Sir Clifford's friends. It is an undeniably powerful realization of a bourgeois mode of being. Lawrence has been criticized for making Sir Clifford a cripple, and thus simplifying the moral situation by a symbolic accident. But, though the physical debility is symbolic, it seems to me to be justifiable in historical terms: his wound is a war wound, and the war was fought in the interests of Sir Clifford's class. He is not sterile because he is a cripple, but a cripple because he is sterile—because, that is, he accepted the role offered him by his class. It does not need demonstrating that in scene after scene, Sir Clifford defines himself as a totally class-conscious being, and as something less than human, so that in this novel about tenderness, we do not find it shocking that Connie feels 'as if he ought to be obliterated from the face of the earth' (XIII). Sir Clifford is of a different species from the humanity that Lawrence is trying to realize in the relationship between Connie and Mellors: he has no more place in their world than a dinosaur, and to feel sorry for Sir Clifford is to be sentimental and not see that he is totally, through his own effort of will, a class product.

What one wonders, on the contrary, is why, if he is such an anachronism, Sir Clifford takes quite so much exterminating. He is so weak and pathetic that though we can believe in his odiousness, it is difficult to believe in his capacity for survival. Many of the scenes in which he appears are brilliantly realized, but they hardly add to one another—Sir Clifford is definitively placed as soon as he appears. Of course, industrialism was not about to disappear in 1928, but we get very little sense of its power within the novel.

The difficulty arises from the ambiguity of Mellors. In a

brilliant review of the novel, in 1929, Edmund Wilson hailed the sexual language Mellors uses as a breakthrough both for Lawrence and for the novelist in general. 'It gets rid,' he wrote, 'of a good deal of the verbosity, the apocalyptic grandiloquence, into which (Lawrence's) subject has so often led him, and it keeps the love scenes human'. This seems to me to be undeniable, as long as we are thinking of the novel as a moral act. The trouble is that the language is part of the social vision because it is not merely the authentic language of sexuality, but also a consciously adopted working-class dialect which is to make the relationship with Connie subversive of Sir Clifford's class hegemony. And in *this* perspective, the language is not a breakthrough but a regression. Mellors adopts dialect not spontaneously but as a conscious atavistic gesture of defiance. And we have to come back again to a point that we have made earlier. For Lawrence, we have seen, the idea of a cultural absolute to measure the impoverishment of the modern world is contradictory: in is using the dead to bury the dead. But in the end, the four-letter words come to have a role remarkably similar to that of the literary tradition in *The Waste Land*. And this applies too to the sexuality itself: it is a retreat to the woods, to a pastoral world, and thus it comes to seem not a social force but a *standard*, absolute but without visible presence in actuality. Mellors himself is an anachronism: 'He was a man in dark green velveteens and gaiters . . . the old style, with a red face and red moustache and distant eyes' (V). And though he is from the working class, as much of his rhetoric is directed against it as it is against the world of Sir Clifford. So that the opposition between himself and Sir Clifford remains a very personal one. Socially it is not very effective. By the end of the novel, the moral values are clearly and explicitly defined in Mellors' letters to Connie, but it is significant that it is letters we have, for the whole situation remains unresolved—they are still apart, and Sir Clifford survives. Connie and Mellors are as impotent socially as Sir Clifford is morally.

It is indeed Sir Clifford who makes the sharpest social affirmation in the novel: 'An individual may emerge from the masses. But the emergence doesn't alter the mass. The masses are unalterable' (XIII). Mellors is effective only as long as he is an individual who has emerged—he cannot challenge the hegemony of the impotent except by getting away. He is, after all, a gamekeeper, a man whose job it is to preserve life for 'fat men' to take again at their leisure. Connie feels that Clifford's remark is 'a truth that killed', and this is devastating—for it places Mellors exactly: he is the lie that heals, the myth of the organic past. We cannot rationalize these limitations by seeing Mellors as another Birkin: Birkin is a social saviour, but this is part of him that is mocked by the novel. His business is not salvation but survival. Mellors, however, has to be more: he stands outside society to offer a direct challenge to its conventions. It is radically limiting that his programme is carried not to society but apart from it.

We are now openly facing the central limitation of Lawrence's hegemonic vision. In *Women in Love*, there is an oddly assertive passage which describes the workers' response to Gerald's cult of efficiency; we are told simply that they accept it because they too worship the machine. It is isolated and structurally unimportant, but this kind of assertive blurring is much more evident in *Lady Chatterley's Lover*. Mellors, for example, laments the industrialization of the working class: 'It's all a steady sort of bolshevism just killing off the human thing, and worshipping the mechanical thing' (XV). In Lawrence, essentially, there can be no conflict of social forces, because all social forces are determined unilaterally by the dominant class—bolshevists are only capitalists. In the case of *Women in Love*, this hardly matters since we are concerned only with the death of society. But in *Lady Chatterley's Lover*, we are confronted with the struggle between the forces which make for death and those which make for life. At the very least, in such a struggle, it seems anachronistic, after the General Strike, to write a novel in which working-class consciousness is merely an extension of bourgeois consciousness, and which might therefore simply be ignored. It makes Mellors' job a simpler one: his values might not stand up so easily to those of a collier's wife. But it makes it also a curiously irrelevant one.

This is, however, to ignore the most interesting character in the novel, Mrs. Bolton. As Sir Clifford's housekeeper, she takes over the role of wife, because she is able to be both slave and *magna mater* to her employer. Her success is primarily a sign of his corrupt infantilism. But Connie too is drawn to her, and when Mrs. Bolton tells her the story of her husband's death in the mine and the loss of physical relationship she endured because of it, Connie feels that she is, like Mellors, 'another passionate one out of Tevershall' (XI). Moreover, it is 'them as runs the pit' that Mrs. Bolton explicitly blames for this loss to her of human contact. When she discovers that Mellors is Connie's lover, she is gratified by the implied social revenge: 'A Tevershall lad . . . My word, that was a slap back at the high-and-mighty Chatterleys!' (X). And her relationship with Sir Clifford is detached and shrewd: 'in some corner of her weird female soul, how she despised him and hated him! . . . The merest tramp was better than he' (XIX). These moments make Mrs. Bolton neither more sympathetic nor more contradictory, but they mean that she is, as much as Connie and Mellors, a challenge to the power of Sir Clifford. And in one way a more effective challenge—they escape him, she takes him over. It is not insignificant that she, rather than Mellors, becomes Connie's source of information about the working people, for, upstart as she is, she is not so much of a class renegade as Mellors. So that if, through Mellors, Lawrence has by-passed the main social issue in the themes with which he is dealing, he creates, through Mrs. Bolton, a fragmentary image of the class conflict to which he tried to become indifferent. The real challenge that Lawrence needed to face in the late twenties, was not that of the class whose inner death he had registered in *Women in Love*, but that of the class from which he came.

There are signs, in the later essays, of a new appraisal of his own society. And we even find him stepping out of the tradition of social thought which dominates English literature from Carlyle to Leavis and takes refuge in a golden age of a pre-industrial 'organic community': in 'Nottingham and the Mining Countryside' he blames the squalor of England not on urbanism but on the attempt to impose the village on industrial society and the failure to build radial cities. It is one crucial index of Lawrence's new engagement with the world in which he had his being. But the real confrontation never came. Lawrence's health had deteriorated steadily since 1925. In 1928, he was forced to go to Switzerland because of his lungs, and in the following year moved to the South of France. He died on March 2nd, 1930, aged 44.

# BIBLIOGRAPHY

## A. Works by Lawrence

(i) *Fiction*. There is no authoritative edition. All the novels are available in Penguin, and all but nine of the stories. *The Phoenix* Edition (London, 1954 onwards) has all the novels except *The Boy in The Bush*, and all but one of the stories. The texts of *The Rainbow* and *The Lost Girl* are incomplete in this edition.

| | | |
|---|---|---|
| *The White Peacock*, | London, | 1911 |
| *The Trespasser*, | „ | 1912 |
| *Sons and Lovers*, | „ | 1913 |
| *The Prussian Officer and Other Stories*, | „ | 1914 |
| *The Rainbow*, | „ | 1915 |
| *Women in Love*, | New York, | 1920 |
| *The Lost Girl*, | London, | 1920 |
| *Aaron's Rod*, | „ | 1922 |
| *England My England* (stories), | „ | 1922 |
| *The Ladybird* (stories), | „ | 1923 |
| *Kangaroo*, | „ | 1923 |
| *The Boy in the Bush*, (with M. L. Skinner), | „ | 1924 |
| *St. Mawr, together with The Princess*, | „ | 1925 |
| *The Plumed Serpent*, | „ | 1926 |
| *The Woman Who Rode Away* (stories), | „ | 1928 |
| *Lady Chatterley's Lover*, | Florence, | 1928 |
| *Sun* (1st unexpurgated edn.), | Paris, | 1928 |
| *The Escaped Cock*, | „ | 1929 |
| *The Virgin and The Gypsy*, | London, | 1930 |
| *Love Among the Haystacks* (stories), | „ | 1930 |

(ii) *Other Works*

*The Complete Poems* ed. Pinto and Roberts. 2 Vols. (London and New York, 1964).

*The Complete Plays* (London, 1965; New York, 1966).

*Three Plays* (introduction by Raymond Williams; Harmondsworth, 1969).

*Twilight in Italy* (London, 1916; New York, 1916).

*Sea and Sardinia* (London, 1923; New York, 1921).

*Mornings in Mexico* (London, 1927; New York, 1927).

*Etruscan Places* (London, 1932; New York, 1957).

(Note, these four travel books are available in both the Penguin and Phoenix editions.)

*Fantasia of The Unconscious* and *Psychoanalysis and the Unconscious*, in one volume (London, 1961; New York, 1960).

*Phoenix* (essays) (London and New York, 1936).

*Phoenix II* (London, 1968; New York, 1967).

*Studies in Classic American Literature*, Mercury Books, London, 1965. (Originally published in 1923).

(iii) *Bibliography*. Warren Roberts: *A Bibliography of D. H. Lawrence* (London, 1963).

## B. Biographical Material

### (i) *Letters*

*The Collected Letters of D. H. Lawrence*, edited by Harry T. Moore, 2 Vols. (London, 1962). (This is by no means complete. Not only are there uncollected letters scattered through various memoirs and periodicals, but the Huxley volume, mentioned below, has many, and important letters not reprinted here.)

*The Letters of D. H. Lawrence*, edited by Aldous Huxley (London and New York, 1932). (Huxley's Introduction is one of the best early essays on Lawrence).

### (ii) *Secondary Material*

*The Intelligent Heart* by Harry T. Moore (Revised Edition, London, 1960; New York, 1962). (The most reliable of the many biographies.)

*D. H. Lawrence: A Composite Biography*, edited by Edward Nehls, 3 Vols. (Madison, Wisconsin, 1957–1959). (A collection of documents, some previously unpublished, from memoirs of Lawrence. Some of it is illuminating, much of it is trivial. It is worth consulting for reference, and a sustained reading of almost any section gives a good idea of the inadequacy and egoism of most of Lawrence's friends and enemies.)

*D. H. Lawrence, A Personal Record* by 'E. T.' (London, 1932; New York, 1936). (This is Jessie Chambers' memoir. It gives a lucid, though of course, subjective account of her relationship with Lawrence. More importantly, it gives us some sense of the kind of cultural milieu in which the adolescent Lawrence found himself.)

## C. Critical Material

### (a) *Books*

F. R. Leavis: *D. H. Lawrence, Novelist* (London, 1955; New York, 1956). The first extended critical assessment of Lawrence by a major critic. It is still the most important book on Lawrence, and it is also Leavis's best work.)

Mark Spilka: *The Love Ethic of D. H. Lawrence* (Bloomington, Indiana, 1955).

H. M. Daleski: *The Forked Flame: A Study of D. H. Lawrence* (London and Evanston, Illinois, 1965). (Although this is rather pedestrian, it makes useful connections between the discursive prose and the fiction, so that it is always worth consulting on particular issues.)

Julian Moynahan: *The Deed of Life: The Novels and Tales of D. H. Lawrence* (Princeton, 1966). (The best critical book on Lawrence since Leavis. Particularly it is good on the novels Leavis underestimates—*Sons and Lovers, The Lost Girl* and *Lady Chatterley's Lover.*)

Keith Sagar: *The Art of D. H. Lawrence* (Cambridge, 1966). (This has a good, detailed chronology and a full bibliography. The criticism is sensible and informative.)

Gamini Salgado: *D. H. Lawrence's Sons and Lovers* (London, 1966).

Colin Clarke: *River of Dissolution: D. H. Lawrence and English Romanticism* (London, 1969).

## (b) Collections

Harry T. Moore and Frederick Hoffman (eds.): *The Achievement of D. H. Lawrence* (Norman, Oklahoma, 1953). (Contains a useful sample of early essays on Lawrence, and above all, Edmund Wilson's review of *Lady Chatterley's Lover.*)

Mark Spilka ed. *D. H. Lawrence: A Collection of Critical Essays* (Englewood Cliffs, New Jersey, 1963). (Notably reprints Marvin Mudrick's essay on *The Rainbow*, and Raymond Williams' account of Lawrence's social thinking.)

*'Sons and Lovers': a Casebook*, ed. Gamini Salgado (London, 1969).

*'The Rainbow' and 'Women in Love': a Casebook*, ed. Colin Clarke (London, 1969).

## (c) *Single essays*

Arnold Kettle: *An Introduction to the English Novel*, Volume Two, (London, 1953) (on *The Rainbow*).

S. L. Goldberg: *'The Rainbow*: Fiddle Bow and Sand' in *Essays in Criticism*, xi (October, 1961).

Frank Kermode: 'D. H. Lawrence and the Apocalyptic Types' in *Continuities* (London, 1968).

Mark Kinkead-Weekes: 'The Marble and the Statue: The Exploratory Imagination of D. H. Lawrence' in *Imagined Worlds*, ed. Maynard Mack and Ian Gregor (London, 1968).

## 5

## T. S. ELIOT

### John Fuller, Magdalen College, Oxford

### I

T. S. Eliot's earliest poetry, preserved in the volume *Poems Written in Early Youth*, is the clearest evidence of the extraordinary intellectual achievement of his mature work and of the justice of his celebrated complaint that 'the situation of poetry in 1909 or 1910 was stagnant to a degree difficult for any young poet of today to imagine.' The poet who was to rescue his art from the effete public-schoolish aestheticism or jingoism of the post-Victorian tradition is ingenuously revealed in this volume in all his hesitancy, and in all the controlled excitement of his discoveries.

The poems are more uneven than in any comparable body of juvenilia from such a respected writer. There is sexual symbolism and disgust in the Swinburnean 'Circe's Palace' (1908), and an interesting absorption in most of the other very early pieces in the symbolic suggestiveness of withered flowers. Such characteristics deepen the literary origins and significance of similar passages from the mature work, and incidentally demonstrate how much Eliot owes to his reading of Dante and the Jacobeans. The Smith Academy Graduation poem and the Harvard Class Ode are unequivocally bad (it can hardly be pretended now that they do not exist) and the earliest poem, the ottava rima 'A Fable for Feasters' (1905) is nearer to Barham than to Byron. There remains, of course, the impact of Laforgue, intriguing in this volume because it shows not only how quickly Eliot's poetry toughened, but just how precarious yet marvellously assured this toughening process really was. 'Nocturne' (1909), 'Humouresque' and 'Spleen' (1910) are rejects of a mode of which 'Conversation Galante' (1909) is the surviving canonical example. The influence was quickly absorbed: 'Portrait of a Lady' (1910) and 'The Love Song of J. Alfred Prufrock' (1911) really feel and ambitiously recreate the nervous angularities which in the juvenilia are merely tentative formulae:

> And Life, a little bald and gray,
> Languid, fastidious, and bland,
> Waits, hat and gloves in hand,
> Punctilious of tie and suit
> (Somewhat impatient of delay)
>     On the doorstep of the Absolute.

('Spleen')

This is so very near to 'Prufrock' that it almost looks like a clue to an allegorical interpretation, until we remember that poem's eloquent actuality and almost unmanageable breadth of symbolical reverberation:

> Shall I part my hair behind? Do I dare to eat a peach?
> I shall wear white flannel trousers, and walk upon the beach.
> I have heard the mermaids singing, each to each.
> I do not think that they will sing to me.

Prufrock is much more than the Pierrot puppet: it would be limiting to relate his predicament in any central sense to the sexual timidity found in the juvenilia, with their failing conversations and schizophrenically self-deprecatory wooers ('the usual debate/ Of love'). The poem's strength lies in the distance it has moved from that point: it has turned from Laforgue's initial attraction of contributing an essentially stylistic sophistication to the adolescent's emotional self-respect; it has deepened the pose into the persona, where there is a more satisfying relationship between fiction and feeling. Here we begin to sense the importance of a serious reading of the Victorians, of Browning, say, and Henry James.

Eliot developed this oblique and metaphorically striking method of dealing with his feelings in poetry almost entirely on his own. Laforgue and the Symbolists he discovered through reading Arthur Symons, for instance, while the impressionistic method of 'Preludes' (1909–11) or 'Rhapsody on a Windy Night' (1911) owes a great deal to Bergson's theories about how memory modifies experience. Eliot was not aware, that is to say, of the Imagist movement, already launched; and it was not until 1914, when he first settled in London and associated with Ezra Pound, that he had much direct experience of what his contemporaries were up to. 'Rhapsody' is an experiment in probing the significance of one's private store of mental images. The 'lunar synthesis' is Eliot's version of the Bergsonian *durée*, that shifting present consciousness in which perception and memory meet. The floors of memory are dissolved in order to achieve the synthesis: the perceptions become images, and the images define consciousness. A similar view of the role of past literature in relation to the modern writer was proposed by Eliot in his essay 'Tradition and the Individual Talent' (1919).

The philosophical rationale of the poem is, however, only a circumstance of its origin, in this case Eliot's attendance at Bergson's lectures in Paris in 1910–11. The poem itself proposes a significant interrelationship between the present (a young man alone amidst the melancholy detritus of the big city) and the past (a lost world of innocence and natural instinct, here represented by the sea). When the poem describes a prostitute's dress as being 'stained with sand' and the corner of her eye twisting 'like a crooked pin', the apparent inconsequentiality of description (the setting is evidently the Paris of the novels of Charles-Louis Philippe) is to be attributed to the power which the world of the sea has in impinging itself upon the young man's consciousness:

> I have seen eyes in the street
> Trying to peer through lighted shutters,
> And a crab one afternoon in a pool,
> An old crab with barnacles on his back,
> Gripped the end of a stick which I held him.

The blind tenacity of a primal form of life here represents with 'imagist' accuracy and power all that Eliot intended by 'the doorstep of the Absolute.' The image reappears in 'Prufrock' in the famous lines:

> I should have been a pair of ragged claws
> Scuttling across the floors of silent seas.

Prufrock's mermaids and the crab's awareness of the offered stick quite clearly then represent the effort to understand what cannot be understood, just as the trapped prostitutes and alienated night-walkers are seeking an embracing vision to release them from the Dantesque hell of the city. This is the essence of Eliot's early poetry, and the fund of imagery used to embody it comes, it would seem, from the childhood circumstances which Eliot has himself described, life in St Louis where he was born, and holidays at Cape Ann, Massachusetts: 'The experience of a child of ten, a small boy peering through sea-water in a rock-pool, and finding a sea-anenome [is] not so simple, for an exceptional child, as it looks' (*The Use of Poetry and the Use of Criticism*, 1933).

It is imagism's prime tenet that emotion must be recreated in the reader, and not merely described for him. Eliot is at least half-way there in his use of private images whose meaning for him is not open to rational investigation, but which together provide a *formula* for the emotion which must be evoked. This formula Eliot in 1919 termed the *objective correlative*, a phrase which now seems as dated as Pound's *vortex*, an exactly contemporary effort to define the same feelings about the irrational in poetry ('The image is not an idea. It is a radiant node or cluster . . . a VORTEX'). The most celebrated instance of Eliot's own application of this irrationality in his imagery occurs in 'Journey of the Magi' (1927) where the water-mill and the six ruffians are drawn from Eliot's personal memories: 'Such memories may have symbolic value, but of what we cannot tell, for they come to represent the depths of feeling into which we cannot peer' (*The Use of Poetry*).

This aversion from the depths of personal feeling is fully justified by Eliot's critical theory of the impersonality of poetry; that the poet has less a personality to express than a medium to perfect 'in which impressions and experiences combine in peculiar and unexpected ways' ('Tradition and the Individual Talent'). But the shift of emphasis seems now of local interest only: we do read Eliot for the personality, and in the *Prufrock* volume particularly for poems like 'Hysteria' (1915), 'La Figlia Che Piange' (1911) or 'Portrait of a Lady' which themselves investigate the precariousness of achieved personality. In 'Hysteria', the laughter of the girl attains a devouringly threatening sexual significance:

> I was drawn in by short gasps, inhaled at each momentary recovery, lost finally in the dark caverns of her throat, bruised by the ripple of unseen muscles.

The point is, of course, that it is the speaker, not the girl, who is hysterical: erotic challenge triggers the anxiety and the sense of dissociation. In 'Portrait of a Lady' a similar reversal, and a liberal use of ironic Laforguean *dédoublement*, allows the Jamesian portrayal of a Boston 'précieuse ridicule' to emerge wholly through the troubled reflections of the boor who cannot rise to her emotional demands.

In comparison with these, the handful of satirical poems in the *Prufrock* volume, written after he had met Pound, and apparently under the influence of the latter's 'Moeurs Contemporaines' (Mr. Hecatomb Styrax and the rest), seem thin indeed. They are mostly portraits from Eliot's New England past, but they are without either the psychological subtlety of the earlier monologues or the imaginative brilliance of the later quatrain poems. Only 'Mr. Apollinax' (1915), a grotesque portrait of Bertrand Russell confounding some American socialities and academics, achieves a satisfying intensity of intention. Eliot had attended Russell's logic class in 1914, though he was at the time much more interested in Bradley's 'finite centres' and objected, in his Harvard doctoral thesis on Bradley, that Russell's Theory of Descriptions dogmatically assumed the existence of a single real world. Even so, the priapic Russell was to be protected from New England prissiness.

A poem also written later than most of the *Prufrock* volume is 'The Death of St. Narcissus' (1912), printed in *Poems Written in Early Youth*). The principal interest of this piece lies in its relation to *The Waste Land*, into which part of it was cannibalized, but its vivid exposition of a relished sense of sin and abasement through masturbation would certainly have enlarged the scope of the earlier volume. In 1917 Eliot was moving in a different direction. For one thing he was forging his reputation as a critic, and moreover the influence of Pound was to take him away from *vers libre* and towards the quatrains of Gautier. Eliot had married in 1915, and from 1917 undertook a tiring job at Lloyd's Bank. The poems collected in *Ara Vos Prec* (1920) show all the signs of a feverish, though controlled, intensity of creativity. The strain was to lead to a breakdown, and the breakdown was to lead to the composition of *The Waste Land* while Eliot recuperated in Margate and Lausanne, but meanwhile it produced the quatrian poems, the most characteristic and unreasonably vilified of all Eliot's work.

## II

The influence of the 1920 poems is undeniable, and possibly Eliot was not to have so great a direct influence again until the period of *Four Quartets*. Poems such as Basil Bunting's 'Villon' or Edgell Rickword's 'Sir Orang Haut-ton at Vespers' are quintessential verse of the twenties, and could hardly have been written without Eliot. Yeats took three of the quatrain poems for the *Oxford Book of Modern Verse* in 1936, yet these are the poems that Grover Smith (a devoted Eliot exegete) finds 'obscure, precious and bombastic', 'in execrable taste', 'merely learnedly clever' and so on. Clearly the poems are nothing if not controversial, and they may be admitted as short on 'real' feeling, in the sense that such feeling comes across in, say, 'La Figlia Che Piange' or 'Marina' (1930), poems by no means personal in the accepted expressive sense. But the cold brilliant quatrain poems are products of a fantastic literary imagination. They are even in a sense by-products of a critical imagination (the critical imagination that he was so powerfully developing in his journalism at the time) and they are thus very close to Eliot's real intellectual interests. If Eliot is an intellectual poet, then he should be revealing himself here.

Their themes (the sensitive lover in a world of hard fact; the common man and the Church; the conflict of body and soul; the aspirations of an heroic past and a sordid present) are treated with a kind of hysterical gravity that never trivialises, even when the allusive irony seems impenetrable or the argument to be lost in mere evocation.

'Burbank with a Baedeker: Bleistein with a Cigar' (1919) seems to propose an extension of the Prufrock persona, the cultured expatriate, representative of a class from whom all initiative has gone. One is reminded, in this context, of Clough's *Dipsychus*, another Venetian poem with a Prufrockian theme of sexual timidity contrasted with the Mephistophelean urgings of an exteriorized Id. Clough's problem (seen above all in his best poem *Amours de Voyage*) is that of how to bring oneself to act. Dipsychus is the divided soul. Like Prufrock's, his division is primarily a psychosexual one expressed in social terms, behind which lies the Victorian obsession with prostitution as the only alternative to marriage. As the Spirit tauntingly remarks:

> If the plebeian street don't suit my friend,
> Why he must try the drawing room, one fancies.

Prufrock's dilemma involves just this kind of conflict (which is also a literary confrontation, as it were, of Charles-Louis Philippe and Henry James) and something like it is also present in 'Burbank'. In Clough's words, it is 'a conflict between the tender conscience and the world.' After all, what real Princess would be seen in a small hotel? 'Volupine' enshrines a professional voluptuousness which the New Englander cannot satisfy. The phrase 'defunctive music' (drawn from Shakespeare's 'The Phoenix and Turtle') suggests a funereal rather than a hymeneal ceremony: Burbank's encounter is a melancholy affair, full of imagery of drained power and elegant unexcitability:

> Defunctive music under sea
> Passed seaward with the passing bell
> Slowly: the God Hercules
> Had left him, that had loved him well.

Contrast with this the swift dramatic appearance of the masterful Klein, glimpsed like a celebrity at a first night:

> The boatman smiles.

> Princess Volupine extends
> A meagre, blue-nailed, phthisic hand
> To climb the waterstair. Lights, lights,
> She entertains Sir Ferdinand

> Klein.

The way the Jewish surname hangs beyond the stanza as an ironic afterthought is an instance of Eliot's instinctive sense of drama: the whole poem is mysterious and mesmerising.

The explicit social point of Burbank's failure and Klein's success, and more particularly of the grotesque Bleistein's confrontation with the Canaletto, is unavoidably here that antisemitic prejudice from which Eliot is so frequently defended. Shakespeare's anti-semitism (which is introduced helpfully into the poem) was largely a matter of unthinking tradition. In 'Burbank', the economic ascendancy of Jewish families in 1919 is a real enough 'fact' lurking behind it. The ironical presence of Sir Alfred Mond (one of the architects of I.C.I.) in 'A Cooking Egg' (1918) is a similar indication of an odd equation of modern capitalism with High Renaissance skulduggery (Mond's companions there are Sir Philip Sidney and Lucretia Borgia). Even the left-wing W. H. Auden in 1935, creating for *The Dog Beneath the Skin* a financier patently based on Mond, automatically and conveniently named him 'Grabstein'. But if one is inclined to take Eliot's gratuitous introduction of sinister Jewish characters into poems like 'Sweeney among the Nightingales' (1918) and 'Gerontion' (1919) as a quaint irrelevance, it is as well to remember such statements of Eliot's as this, made in the year that Hitler came to power:

Reasons of race and religion combine to make any large number of free-thinking Jews undesirable . . . and a spirit of excessive tolerance is to be deprecated.

(*After Strange Gods*, 1933).

This looks more like the prejudice of the St. Louis business world.

We are probably lucky that Eliot's archetypal sensualist, the violent vulgarian Sweeney, came to be represented as a stage Irishman and not as a stage Jew (after all, Bleistein's 'saggy bending of the knees' is very like Apeneck Sweeney 'spreading his knees'). In 'Sweeney Erect' (1919), the civilization of Emerson is punned into an absurd identity with Sweeney seen as a sexually excited ape-man, while the brothel, the razor and the terrified epileptic introduce a new detail and directness in Eliot's portrayal of the underworld. If Prufrock is the tentative romantic, on the doorstep of the Absolute, Sweeney is the putative rapist and murderer :

> Any man might do a girl in
> Any man has to, needs to, wants to
> Once in a lifetime, do a girl in.
>
> (*Sweeney Agonistes*, 1927)

For such a roughneck, the situations he finds himself in are presented with a curious ritualism. 'Sweeney Among the Nightingales' has the grand manner which Yeats admired, but the climax appears to depend almost entirely upon a private image which from other contexts (the suppressed 'Ode' from *Ara Vos Prec*, and lines 196–206 of *The Waste Land*) relates to an intense experience of sexual humiliation.

Humiliation of this kind begins to take an extreme form in the 1920 poems. It is true that the theme was present in 'Prufrock', 'Hysteria' or 'La Figlia Che Piange', but the cringing epileptic of 'Sweeney Erect', the bugbitten honeymooners of 'Lune de Miel' (1917) or the slobbering waiter of 'Dans le Restaurant' (1917) signal a new level of erotic disappointment and disgust. Such feelings are encapsulated in 'Whispers of Immortality' (1918) where the Jacobean poets are compared with twentieth century intellectuals, followers of Bradley perhaps. Webster and Donne were aware of death in life, and apprehended the Unknown through and beyond the flesh. Eliot recreates their sharp sense of the body's precarious pleasure in terms of the prostitute Grishkin (not for the first time do we note that Eliot has an acute nose for female smells) and con-

cludes that even though 'the Abstract Entities/ Circumambul-
ate her charm. . . . our lot crawls between dry ribs/ To keep
our metaphysics warm.' The lure is not taken, and the modern
experience (retreating in disgust from sex) is thus radically
different from the experience of the Jacobeans. In its treatment
of 'thought' and 'sense', the poem obviously relates to Eliot's
notion (put forward in his 1921 essay on the Metaphysical
Poets) of the 'dissociation of sensibility.' The form of the poem
conveniently approximates to the form of Donne's 'The Ecstasie.'

In other 1920 poems Eliot is concerned with the Church as
an institution, and is plainly satirical. The incongruous treatment is signalled by the Popean touches in 'Lune de Miel ('Où
se trouve la Cène, et un restaurant pas cher'). A cheap spaghetti
is just as necessary as Leonardo's *Last Supper*, in other words,
and Eliot lugubriously exposes the caprices of man's spiritual
and bodily appetites by the continued presence in the poem of
the St. Apollinaire, 'vieille usine désaffectée de Dieu', which the
honeymooners never manage to visit.

'The Hippopotamus' (1917) is the only quatrain poem to be
fully rhymed. This, with a line from Cowper, allows the parody
of hymn metre to carry its comparatively simple irony of contrast:

> The hippopotamus's day
> Is passed in sleep; at night he hunts;
> God works in a mysterious way—
> The Church can sleep and feed at once.

Such knock-you-down argument is elaborated with a heavy
dose of theology in 'Mr. Eliot's Sunday Morning Service' (1918)
where the Church's feeding is seen as being based specifically
upon the convenient weakness of the flesh, in particular upon
the sexually guilty adolescent clutching his 'piaculative pence.'
This function of the 'sable presbyters' is compared to the fer-
tilizing of bees, whose role is itself 'blest' because it is like that
of Christ, who acted as intermediary between the divine and
the human. Such mediation should, of course, lead Man to a
contemplation of the divine; but Eliot presents it merely as a
rationalization of the human. The clergy themselves, far from
denying the flesh, are said to be 'polyphiloprogenitive', that is
they are keen on having large families.

What, roughly, was at the back of Eliot's mind in this poem
is the relevance of Christ in a material age. It is worth looking
at more closely as an example of Eliot's intelligence and suggestiveness in these poems. His theme is a radical one, because

161

theologians very early on felt that the whole idea of the Incarnation was (a) contaminating the Godhead with a symbolically sexual act, and (b) paradoxical anyway if the Son was really God. If the Son was God, then he already existed at the time of his conception ('superfetation' means becoming pregnant a second time, before the delivery of the first foetus). Origen was typical of those theologians who felt that the Incarnation affirmed the values of the flesh, and therefore denied it. He also denied the resurrection of the body and castrated himself (which is why he is 'enervate'). He provides a complete contrast to the worldly presbyters who act as 'sutlers', that is act for a metaphorical Lord of Hosts as some kind of steward or quartermaster. They are like the 'religious caterpillars' of the epigraph, the friars in *The Jew of Malta* who are eager to collect Barabas's wealth when they think he is about to turn Christian.

Eliot appears to be faced with an ecclesiastical reality (or a cartoon version of it: the sexual energy of dissenters is a convenient myth comparable to the anti-semitic ideas in these poems) and to contrast with it the vaguest, and yet in a sense the clearest, Christian notion of divinity that he can find: 'the Word'. This is something he returns to in 'Gerontion': what has the 'Word' to do with men? How does it make its demands upon them? Here, as if to cut firmly through to the bed-rock, as it were, of the ecclesiastical superstructure, Eliot introduces the Greek of the Gospel according to St. John:

In the beginning was the Word.

In the beginning was the Word.
Superfetation of τὸ ἕν . . .

The repetition seems to be designed to remind Eliot of what he is saying, as though this were something one could say without really taking in the meaning. And indeed, in the tradition of theological controversy, 'the subtle schools' which are 'controversial, polymath' have overlaid the Word with a miasmal mist of quibbling irrelevancies. This provides a second function for the word 'superfetation', and perhaps a more sympathetic one, for even without accepting the Christian myth we must surely see that the intervention implied in the Incarnation is fruitful, whereas the dissemination of Christ's teaching after his death has only led to conflicting and sometimes untenable positions.

Thus Origen and the Presbyters, representing Church philosophy and Church administration of a probably random choice on Eliot's part (he might have written a poem with the same ultimate point if he had used, say, Pelagius and the Papists) are the extremes which the religious sensibility is faced with in the world. The world itself is like the cracked and overvarnished surface of a Perugino Baptism: it is a wilderness, a waste land perhaps, at the centre of which 'through the water pale and thin/ Still shine the unoffending feet.' That is to say, not only the Word but the Word made flesh can still be imagined in the context of the Holy Trinity, the 'Baptized God', 'The Father and the Paraclete.' And it can be imagined in art, by the perhaps consciously sedate 'Mr. Eliot' who (we are to imagine) is having a Sunday morning bath and is thinking of these things, thinking himself into being Sweeney, shifting from ham to ham. Sweeney knows nothing of Perugino, but 'Mr. Eliot' can relate him to the baptized Christ with an irony which is central to the reasonable conclusion of the poem: we should take the suggestion to be that one's Sweeney nature must be accepted somehow, that one's soul shouldn't 'burn invisible and dim', but must assume the fleshly role even if it is ultimately a purgatorial one. Sweeney is more generous, more natural than Origen, and at least honest in having a Sunday bath rather than grovel before the grasping clergy. But it is a dilemma.

### III

When one turns to 'Gerontion' one finds that a good deal of this rather cool juggling with religious history remains, but has been generalized and turned into a much more profound lament for the inability to believe in anything. When we are told that 'In the juvescence of the year / Came Christ the tiger', the image plays a comparable role to that of the baptised Christ in 'Mr. Eliot's Sunday Morning Service.' It conveys a similarly primitive awareness of the essential dynamism of Christianity, a dynamism which has since been lost. It has been lost by the presbyters, and it has been lost by Mr. Silvero, Hakagawa, Madame de Tornquist, Fräulein von Kulp and by Gerontion himself. The headlong syntax suggests that Christ emerges from the darkness as the Logos turned tiger (Blake's tyger, perhaps) only to be betrayed. He is betrayed not only historically ('flowering judas') but continually in the present, because the devourer is himself devoured: he becomes a sacrament which can be taken casually, 'among whispers', by nominal Christians who are much more interested in worldly things, their porcelain, their Titians, their spiritualism, their sexual adventures. Their movements are sensual, nocturnal and vague, 'caressing', 'bowing', 'shifting': the remarkable unity of atmosphere implies their close proximity, perhaps in a hotel.

If it is a hotel, we may be sure it is a symbolic one. Like Gerontion's 'windy house' we can take it as representative of modern European civilization, without purpose as well as without belief. As in Tennyson's *Maud*, war is seen in this context as energetic, heroic and life-giving, 'fought in . . . warm rain' whereas Gerontion is 'waiting for rain.' *The Waste Land* also contains somewhere within it the kind of call to order that Eliot seems to have in mind here. The subject emerges more specifically in the early thirties, particularly in the unfinished poem 'Coriolan' (1931–2) influenced by St. John Perse, where the existing fragments clearly conflate the Christian hero with a quasi-fascist Leader in a manner not unlike that of Auden's *The Orators*.

If 'Gerontion' is about the loss of purpose and the loss of belief, it is expressed in such insistently erotic language that it is very hard for the reader to keep distinct the private and the public nature of the persona that Eliot has used. Beneath the surface a quite different subject can be glimpsed, a subject that at the climax of the poem reveals itself nakedly, though deliberately:

> I would meet you upon this honestly.
> I that was near your heart was removed therefrom
> To lose beauty in terror, terror in inquisition.
> To have lost my passion: why should I need to keep it
> Since what is kept must be adulterated?
> I have lost my sight, smell, hearing, taste and touch:
> How should I use them for your closer contact?

It is easy enough to see that Gerontion is not simply a persona in the sense that Tennyson's Ulysses is a persona, because he is not given any character. Indeed, at moments when he himself makes generalized poetic statements, it is hard to see him even as a voice. Gerontion's poetry merges with Eliot's:

> What will the spider do,
> Suspend its operations, will the weevil
> Delay? De Bailhache, Fresca, Mrs. Cammel, whirled
> Beyond the circuit of the shuddering Bear
> In fractured atoms.

The mind at work here has seen more than Gerontion has seen. Eliot's problem is similar to that in *The Waste Land*, where

Tiresias (another sexually ambiguous old man) is not only a persona but a unifying consciousness. Eliot had to point this out in a note ('What Tiresias sees, in fact, is the substance of the poem'). This makes 'Prufrock' seem even traditional. 'Gerontion' is naturally much nearer to the kaleidoscopic *Waste Land*, and was nearly part of it. It shares with the later poem its dense conflation of spiritual with sexual failure, its sense of exhaustion and disgust, and its method begins to open up, to make more evocative and elegiac, the intellectual methods of the quatrain poems. The combination of ideas and images in the quatrain poems had been strange and radical : without them the later poems could not have so laconically digested the tissue of allusion and quotation which supports them, and is so very often (as in the quatrain poems) their only structure.

*The Waste Land* (1922) is a highly emotional poem, full of tenderness and anguish. It also exhibits a curious combination of great imaginative poise and uncertain mental control. As a weary and impersonal catalogue of ills it still seems fresh, because of its absolute lack of self-indulgence : where it once seemed arbitrary to the opponents of modernism, now some kind of coherence of feeling strikes us as the salient fact of its organization. Arbitrariness was certainly in the air at the time, and it might appear at this distance of time that the fragmentary method of *The Waste Land* owed something to the contemporary Dadaists, who constructed poems out of newspaper cuttings or words drawn from a hat ('These fragments I have shored against my ruins'). But in an article in Wyndham Lewis's short-lived *Tyro* of 1922, Eliot specifically expressed his suspicions of Dada. His peculiar responsibility to tradition removed him from much meaningful contact with a European avant-garde obsessed with the evils of passéism.

Nor, we gather, was Pound's blue-pencilling responsible for its method. Though Pound cut the poem by about a third, it seems clear that he did not make it a different *kind* of poem. The story is sufficiently detailed in Pound's *Letters*, where there emerges, however, just a slight suggestion that Pound was inclined to regard the poem as a greater whole than Eliot had intended.[1] The early reviews naturally treated the poem as a sequence, a view which has unfortunately been set aside by the later tendency to read it as a discursive structure presented with a riddling obliqueness. It is, in fact, a great Imagist poem, eschewing a conventional texture of 'thought'. It allows the images to represent the emotion directly. Eliot himself said something of the sort when he read the poem at Oxford in 1928 :

Mr. Thomas Eliot was the guest last week-end of Mr. Stead, the Chaplain of Worcester College, and on Saturday evening a small number of fortunate people was invited to hear him read. . . . Mr. Eliot compared his poem to a body stripped of its skin: the 'anatomical' interest is at first more puzzling, but is more unusual and more real.

(Cherwell, 11 February 1928)

The 'skin' here is what readers of post-Victorian poetry expected: the surface meaning, the progression of ideas, the argument. It was never Eliot's intention to provide this, since part of imagism's whole raison d'être was its reaction against stale rhetoric. Indeed, any post-Symbolist poetry (and Eliot was much influenced by the Symbolists) had to take account of their assumption that a poet's beliefs and opinions have no real place in his poetry. If, it was felt, ideas are given primary importance, than the language of poetry begins to take a secondary, purely decorative place. As Pound said:

> Since the beginning of bad writing, writers have used images as ornaments. The point of Imagism is that it does not use images as *ornaments*. The image is itself the speech. The image is the word beyond formulated language.

This very clearly describes *The Waste Land*.

At possibly its simplest level it is a poem of metropolitan angst, with atmospheric roots in the symbolism of *The City of Dreadful Night*:

> Unreal City,
> Under the brown fog of a winter dawn,
> A crowd flowed over London Bridge, so many,
> I had not thought death had undone so many.
> Sighs, short and infrequent, were exhaled,
> And each man fixed his eyes before his feet.
> Flowed up the hill and down King William Street,
> To where Saint Mary Woolnoth kept the hours
> With a dead sound on the final stroke of nine.

('The Burial of the Dead')

Eliot is observing commuters on his way to work at Lloyd's Bank in the familiar twenties' terms of the lifeless and automatic (compare Lang's *Metropolis* or the early choruses of Brecht's *Mahagonny*). The dead sound of the final stroke of nine introduces the death of the commuters' working day, a dehumanization to which echoes of Baudelaire and Dante contribute. The dynamism of the city was predictably to breed a new modernist romanticism which was essentially fatalistic (one thinks of the deaths of James Thomson, Crane or Mayakovsky). Both Eliot and Pound were suspicious of the desire to celebrate the soul of the city in romantic terms. Eliot in particular was too much aware of the significance for him of its pre-industrial past:

> O City city, I can sometimes hear
> Beside a public bar in Lower Thames Street,
> The pleasant whining of a mandoline
> And a clatter and chatter from within
> Where fishmen lounge at noon: where the walls
> Of Magnus Martyr hold
> Inexplicable splendour of Ionian white and gold.
>
> ('The Fire Sermon')

The fishmen are one of the positive symbols of the poem (the river is fruitful) not least by virtue of their association with a church which Eliot describes in a note as having 'one of the finest among Wren's interiors.' The classical ideal of the Augustan age ('Inexplicable splendour of Ionian white and gold') is representative of ordered life in the context of communal belief. The proposed destruction of nineteen city churches, which Eliot mentions in the same note, is symptomatic of the meaningless obliteration of that order. It is material progress opposed to a community of purpose, an interference from the world of Sir Ferdinand Klein. There is, interestingly, more engaged feeling on this subject in the mediocre commissioned play *The Rock* (1934) than there is in much of Eliot's other drama.

Allusions to Ezekiel come early in the poem, and turn up again in the last section: thus the Hebrew captivity is a significant vehicle of the quasi-religious colouring which the poem automatically assumes. But generalized myth is of deeper importance. Eliot develops an ascetic solution to the problems of London's 'dead', and one of its most pervasive means of organization in the poem is the use of the Grail legend, which Jessie Weston in the little book which Eliot acknowledges, had shown to be the surviving record of a ritual phallic religion. The waste land is ruled by the wounded Fisher King, who must be cured by the questing hero being able to ask the right question. The Grail and spear carried by the female Grail-bearer who directs the hero to his initiation, are sexual symbols, representative of the life principle behind the Grail legend. In Eliot's poem, the continued suggestion is that the 'hero' fails to ask the question, and like the Fisher King becomes neither living nor dead :

—Yet when we come back, late, from the Hyacinth garden,
Your arms full, and your hair wet, I could not
Speak, and my eyes failed, I was neither
Living nor dead, and I knew nothing,
Looking into the heart of light, the silence.
                                        ('The Burial of the Dead')

This erotic disappointment is at the heart of many of Eliot's poems, and may be compared with 'Dans le Restaurant', 'La Figlia che Piange' or 'Burnt Norton'. In *The Waste Land* it is supported with a savage insistence by eight or nine vignettes of sexual relationships doomed to failure, vignettes that go beyond the merely dramatic to imply a social and historical range that gives the poem its peculiarly panoramic quality.

It is plain that the sexual death-in-life obsessed Eliot: this is why April is the cruellest month, because Spring, the season of lovers, brings no love. It is in the second half of *The Waste Land* that the consequent renunciation of love begins that is to occupy Eliot's later poetry. Prominent in 'The Fire Sermon' is the ascetic solution. The section ends :

To Carthage then I came

Burning burning burning burning
O Lord Thou pluckest me out
O Lord Thou pluckest
burning

This collocation of Buddha and St Augustine is, as Eliot himself wrily notes, 'not an accident.' Indeed, at the time of writing *The Waste Land* Eliot seriously considered becoming a Buddhist. In his Fire Sermon, Buddha pictured this world as one of unfulfilled desires whose metaphor was fire, the purgatorial element. This happy metaphorical identity allows Eliot to present the disease and its cure in the same terms, and eventually the Christian image predominates. In 'The Hollow Men' (1925), whose motto is 'A penny for the Old Guy', man is prepared for burning in a desiccated state where the unfulfilled desires have been rejected, but nothing has taken their place. The broken syntax of the end of 'The Fire Sermon' is repeated in fragmentary prayer that dissolves in futility :

Between the desire
And the spasm
Between the potency
And the existence
Between the essence
And the descent
Falls the Shadow

*For Thine is the Kingdom*

For Thine is
Life is
For Thine is the

*This is the way the world ends*
*This is the way the world ends*
*This is the way the world ends*
*Not with a bang but a whimper.*

## IV

In Part III of 'Little Gidding', Eliot laid down, with all the precision and dullness of his expository style, that distinction between Immediacy and Possibility which seems to govern the spiritual odyssey of his later period:

There are three conditions which often look alike
Yet differ completely, flourish in the same hedgerow:
Attachment to self and to things and to persons, detachment
From self and from things and from persons; and, growing
    between them, indifference
Which resembles the others as death resembles life.

Symbols representative of these distinctions have been met before in Eliot's poetry (one thinks of the whirlpool and the desert of *The Waste Land*) but in the decade between 'The Hollow Men' and 'Burnt Norton' Eliot begins to stress *attachment* and *detachment* particularly as extremes between which grows *indifference*, which is like death. Something like this indifference governs 'The Hollow Men' where life itself is seen as 'death's dream kingdom', and beyond that death itself as 'death's other kingdom.' The indifference is once again the inability to love, like the quester in 'The Burial of the Dead' ('I was neither / Living nor dead'):

Is it like this
In death's other kingdom
Waking alone

At the hour when we are
Trembling with tenderness
Lips that would kiss
Form prayers to broken stone.

The implication here that erotic vulnerability is linked with the religious impulse (and also with the diversion of emotion into art) takes 'The Hollow Men' a good deal further from those parts of *The Waste Land* which it resembles. The hollow men exist in a purgatorial state, removed from the actual world. Even the generalized situations of the 'Give . . . sympathize . . . control' passage in 'What the Thunder Said' seem highly specific by comparison with the taunting abstracted twilit imagery of the later poem, where the Dantesque symbols of eyes, stars and the multifoliate rose reinforce the purity and simplicity of Eliot's spiritual objectives: they are redolent, as in *Ash Wednesday* (1930), of worship of the Virgin Mary.

Eliot's conception of the movement from attachment to detachment (as described in 'Little Gidding') was much influenced by his reading of the Spanish mystic, St. John of the Cross; Sweeney's murder of Mrs. Porter in the uncompleted parts of *Sweeney Agonistes* (1927) was ironically intended as a commentary on the motto to the play taken from St. John of the Cross: 'Hence the soul cannot be possessed of the divine union, until it has divested itself of the love of created beings.' To kill a whore becomes in the play a paradigm of this process of detachment 'from persons', and 'love of created beings' is seen (as usual in Eliot) either as a romantic impossibility or as an obscene joke. Eliot could very powerfully represent life as a farce. One of his most celebrated lines comes, after all, from *Sweeney*:

Birth, and copulation, and death.
That's all the facts when you come to brass tacks:
Birth, and copulation, and death.

Sweeney later tells his story about a man who killed a girl and kept her in a bath with a gallon of lysol, and describes the man's mental state in terms very reminiscent of 'The Hollow Men':

He didn't know if he was alive and the girl was dead
He didn't know if the girl was alive and he was dead
He didn't know if they both were alive or both were dead

Sweeney is in this sense a hollow man: he has violently and symbolically put sex behind him, but has no desire for the spiritual rebirth which would bring him close to the divine reality described by St. John of the Cross. He has located and seen through the materialism of modern life and the animal motions which are all that he sees behind it in his description of the tedious desert island. The corpse has not begun to sprout.

The play was fitted out with the apparatus of the music-hall and Noh drama, and the quasi-surrealist ending (to be found in Hallie Flanagan's *Dynamo*, 1943) with Father Christmas as *deus ex machina* instead of the Eumenides or God or Mrs. Porter's ghost, somewhat obscures the central importance of Sweeney's developed sensibility here. Sweeney shares not only with the hollow men, but with the Magus and Simeon of the Ariel poems (1927, 1928) a racking perception of the need for spiritual change and an accompanying inability to follow the spiritual quest to its final end. The involvement of spiritual yearning with the need to act seems to suggest the leap of faith of Kierkegaard. 'The Shadow' of 'The Hollow Men' is the abyss over which one leaps, and the latter poem concludes with metaphors of inaction derived from *Julius Caesar* (II. i. 63–5) and from Valéry ('Entre le vide et l'événement pur' from 'Le Cimetière Marin'). The possession of the divine union is hardly envisaged except in terms of the broken images from Dante (the rose, the star, the eye) and the broken fragments of liturgy.

Eliot reached this position at a time when his metamorphosis from a dangerous modernist poet ('a drunken helot' in Arthur Waugh's famous phrase) into a respected man of letters was virtually complete: as editor of the *Criterion* and director of Faber and Gwyer, with his first *Collected Poems* behind him, his authority and reputation was assured. The critical treatment of Eliot in a number of surveys of modern literature published in the late twenties is sufficient indication of this. In a sense, the Eliot of this period is the Eliot that has stuck in the public consciousness, the Eliot of 'Not with a bang but a whimper' and 'Birth, copulation, and death'. It is easy to see that the earlier poetry developed very logically into this infectious nadir of despair. From 'Prufrock' to 'The Hollow Men' one could claim that his primary theme is the vision of death related to a failure of communication in an erotic situation. In more senses than one, Eliot's poetry is the poetry of emotional breakdown. And therefore, despite the sometimes heavy intellectual apparatus, a poetry of emotion. Despite its frequent allusiveness and abstruseness, it is designed to work directly upon the reader: the very lack of argument seems to guarantee its urgency.

But Eliot, always anxious not to repeat himself poetically, had to move on. This is not as cold-blooded as it sounds, because in a sense the psychological development of the poet works in step with the poetic development. The consciousness which controls and adjusts, indeed the very experience, is the same. This is particularly true of Eliot, whose later work begins to carry an air of speculation and uncertainty, and consequently seizes on those parts of experience which *are* understood and builds upon them with a slightly weary air of authority and relieved persuasion. The emotional depths of 'The Hollow Men' are to some degree relieved by the Christian conversion of two years later, and by his tentative and controlled representation of the process of renunciation in the Ariel poems. The later stages of Eliot's spiritual odyssey are familiar, from *Ash Wednesday*'s dark night of the soul to the purging and self-confrontation of 'Little Gidding', and to the ever-present theme of sacrifice in the plays.

## V

It is not a happy story, and it is, of course, dangerously easy to read the poetry from this time onwards almost specifically as spiritual autobiography. A large number of his admirers felt cheated by Eliot's refined orthodoxy and acceptance by the exegetes. The live moment of his real poetic authority passed. A year after his conversion, the first fugitive volume by Auden appeared. Auden was prepared to continue the anatomy of modern society tentatively begun by the early Eliot. Eliot himself was in the conscious process of rejecting the real world as we know it, and the Baudelairean 'possibility of fusion between the sordidly realistic and the phantasmogoric' lost its appeal for him. There have been many complaints about Eliot's development at this time: that he turned from the fictional to the personal, from the satirical to the contemplative, from the prophetic to the mystical. None of these is more telling than the charge of a weakening of language involved in the occasional vein of philosophical pedantry or dependance on liturgical tags, or even in the evocative word-play found suspiciously in 'Landscapes' (1933–4) and disastrously in *Ash Wednesday* (it was the kind of thing found in Gertrude Stein, then popular, and picked up by, say, the early George Barker):

> Against the Word the unstilled world still whirled
> About the centre of the silent Word.

Even so, Eliot's intelligence and mastery are continually in evidence. The metaphorical subjects of the Ariel poems, for instance, are very cleverly handled. 'The Journey of the Magi' (1927) and 'A Song for Simeon' (1928) are historical dramatic monologues of old men who know of the Incarnation but not of the Atonement. They are in a spiritual no-man's-land much like the hollow men, still of this world, but with knowledge of forgiveness. Clearly, this mirrors the poet's spiritual predicament, his effort to achieve the calm of faith. The way that the elements of the Christian myth lurk riddlingly within a symbolic landscape in these poems ingeniously suggests Eliot's own speculative approach to what seems to be more and more inevitable. 'Animula' (1929) is perhaps the least impressive of the series, although its Wordsworthian theme of the soul developing away from God, distracted by the variety of the world, misshapen by time, 'Unable to fare forward or retreat', is clearly central to much of Eliot's later work. In 'Marina' (1930) the infant Christ is metamorphosed into the restored daughter of Shakespeare's *Pericles*:

> What is this face, less clear and clearer
> The pulse in the arm, less strong and stronger—
> Given or lent? more distant than stars and nearer
> > than the eye

Only here does the possibility of Christian faith seem healthily redemptive, fresh as the breath of the sea whose imagery steals into the poem. And possibly we read this mistakenly, possibly it is a form of contrived persuasion on Eliot's part, because however mystical and symbolical Shapespeare's last plays now seem, their essence is just that miraculous human restoration which Eliot can no longer hope for: their symbolism is less Christian than seasonal, and thereby is intimately bound up with human generations. The daughters are real daughters, the fathers real fathers above all.

The probable key to Eliot's later poetry is his estrangement from his first wife, who became mentally ill. *Ash Wednesday* (1930), which was originally dedicated to his wife, is a poem of more positive renunciation of the world than the magus was able to achieve. The first part ambiguously suggests renunciation of both poetry and sex. Much of the imagery involves a deliberate deployment of the courtly love tradition, a Dantesque sublimation which blends with the Christian themes: the Lady of the poem, honouring the Virgin in meditation, blends with the Virgin herself, while the Garden and the Rose, so suggestive of mediaeval love poetry and to reappear in *Four Quartets*, are redolent of an imagined Eden. In the second part, the mystical themes begin to predominate. St. John of the Cross had written of the soul's preparation for ecstacy as an undergoing of trial and torment: the theme of being devoured by an animal relates to this, and implies submission to a death of the senses. The staircase in the third part is a spiritual staircase. The third stanza combines a sexual with a mediaevalized romantic image of the temptation of the world which must be rejected:

> At the first turning of the third stair
> Was a slotted window bellied like the fig's fruit
> And beyond the hawthorn blossom and a pasture scene
> The broadbacked figure drest in blue and green
> Enchanted the maytime with an antique flute.
> Blown hair is sweet, brown hair over the mouth blown,
> Lilac and brown hair;
> Distraction . . .

The image is a familiar one (it may even be connected with Eliot's memories of Jean Verdenal, dedicatee of *Prufrock*, 'coming across the Luxembourg Gardens in the late afternoon, waving a branch of lilac,' as recounted in the *Criterion* Commentary of April, 1934, and appears as early as 'Portrait of a Lady'). The power of this rejected world of lost lilac and lost sea voices is reconsidered in the last part of the poem, and seen as illusory: 'Suffer us not to mock ourselves with falsehood.'

The forms of *Ash Wednesday* seem perilously near to stifling many of Eliot's poetic virtues. Its theme is unyieldingly unsympathetic. A more characteristic wryness and density may be found in 'Five Finger Exercises' (1933) a sequence which probes certain autobiographical and sacramental matters with a deceptive light-heartedness. Eliot continued to write comic poetry and poetry for children in this decade, and his major excursion into the drama was to prove overwhelmingly absorbing to him: these efforts to maintain an open, publicly accessible art were matched by a growing extension of his critical activity into the fields of politics, education and church government. His reactionary social criticism, maintained with astonishing diligence in the editorial pages of the frequently anti-humanist *Criterion*, reached a climax with the ill-fated *After Strange Gods* of 1933. Nor was he shy of lending himself to the demands of church propaganda in a way which unreasonably narrowed his literary magnanimity: *The Rock* (1934) has similarly, and understandably, not been reprinted, although the grandeur of its choruses (later extracted into the *Collected Poems*) evidently had some influence, for instance on Auden's and Isherwood's *The Dog Beneath the Skin* (1935).

Eliot's plays bear a certain similarity to *Four Quartets* in theme. It is clear that his interest in the theatre from the mid-thirties onwards left him free to devote his non-dramatic poetry as much as he possibly could to the internal and speculative. More specifically, Eliot himself admitted that 'Burnt Norton' (1935) originated in lines left over from *Murder in the Cathedral* of the same year, and it is interesting to observe how one of 'Burnt Norton's' key symbols, that of the door into the rose-garden, is used later in *The Family Reunion* (1939) as an image of that spiritual enlightenment which the doomed hero, Harry, can only partially recreate with Agatha and with Mary. We are again reminded in the first part of 'Burnt Norton' of that 'heart of light' (Dante's 'cor dell'una delle luci nuove') which recurs in Eliot's vision. The rose-garden episode is, however, framed rather ponderously by quasi-philosophical speculation on the nature of time. Eliot's poetry is good above all because it is dramatic, and it is not unfair to say that the weak parts of *Four Quartets* are weak where they are furthest from the dramatic.

They are possibly the most deliberately organized of Eliot's poems, and, significantly, the most open to formal exegesis. The later three ('East Coker' 1940, 'The Dry Salvages' 1941, and 'Little Gidding' 1942) deliberately conform to the quasi-musical structure of 'Burnt Norton'. The pattern and subject-matter of the various 'movements' is in each quartet the same, and each is furnished with its predominant season and predominant element, thus being able to suggest thematically a larger illustration of the endless transmutation of the elements described by Heraclitus.

These two mottoes from Heraclitus (now re-attached to 'Burnt Norton', but applied to all the *Four Quartets* in book form) summarize the essentially conflicting states which are explored in these poems. The first may be translated as 'Though the Word is universal, most men live by their own values', and indicates for Eliot the divine Law which men struggle to discover and obey, that condition of Being which is beyond man's attainment except in fragmentary mystical experiences. The second motto may be translated as 'The way up and the way down is the same', and indicates for Eliot the elemental flux of time, that condition of Becoming in which man is continually being subjected to the anxiety of change and uncertainty of desire. A predominant symbol of this flux in *Four Quartets*, and in Eliot's later poetry generally, is the Buddhist wheel turning about its theoretically still centre. This 'still point of the turning world' is to be identified with the spiritual repose which is the objective of the whole mystical quest. It is to be identified with the Logos itself. Thus the wheel is a unified symbol of this central conflict of Becoming and Being.

The most successful parts of *Four Quartets* embody these ideas in terms of real experience, in images of the London Underground, for instance, in 'Burnt Norton' and 'East Coker', or in the air-raid setting of part two of 'Little Gidding':

> In the uncertain hour before the morning
>   Near the ending of interminable night
>   At the recurrent end of the unending
> After the dark dove with the flickering tongue
>   Had passed below the horizon of his homing
>   While the dead leaves still rattled on like tin
> Over the asphalt where no other sound was
>   Between three districts whence the smoke arose
>   I met one walking, loitering and hurried
> As if blown towards me like the metal leaves
>   Before the urban dawn wind unresisting.

Eliot's painful confessional encounter with this largely Yeatsian 'familiar compound ghost' owes much to Dante's *Inferno*, and has an intensity and control which lifts the poem to a satisfying level of poetic, rather than intermittently philosophical, achievement. Here, at last, the 'unreal city' comes into its own, and the essentially autobiographical intent of *Four Quartets* is fully recognized.

In a sense, then, the whole of Eliot's poetry is an ingenious and inventive attempt to find striking though devious ways to express personal feelings in impersonal terms. His supposed dissatisfaction with all this (and that passage in 'East Coker' about the wasted years of poetic effort is hardly true, one would have thought) was publicly expressed at a time when the consolations of faith paradoxically allowed him a greater confessional freedom. But there is no doubt that the reader feels, in the long view, that the emotional spring of Eliot's poetry that he took so much trouble to dam and canalize into an extraordinary system of intellectual irrigation, is, finally, erotic. It is for this reason that the avowed spiritual exploration of *Four Quartets* strikes one at times as being little more than an evasive bluster, more reminiscent of Tennyson's Ulysses than anything else:

Old men ought to be explorers
Here and there does not matter
We must be still and still moving
Into another intensity
For a further union, a deeper communion
Through the dark cold and the empty desolation,
The wave cry, the wind cry, the vast waters
Of the petrel and the porpoise. In my end is my beginning.

('East Coker')

If one compares this with Prufrock's mermaids, one learns more than ever to value Eliot's most distinctive contribution to English poetry: the alert and sensitive irony of a truly critical intelligence.

NOTE

1. The manuscript of *The Waste Land* has recently been made available; Donald Gallup's description of it, 'The "Lost" Manuscripts of T. S. Eliot', *Times Literary Supplement*, November 7, 1968, suggests that Pound's editing was less radical than has been sometimes thought.

BIBLIOGRAPHY

A. Works by Eliot

For Eliot's own work, readers should consult the full and usefully chronological bibliography by Donald Gallup (London, 1970). The poems referred to in my chapter will be found in *Poems Written in Early Youth* (London, 1967) and *Collected Poems 1909–1962* (London, 1963). The plays are included in *Collected Plays* (London, 1962). These three volumes are contained in *The Complete Poems and Plays of T. S. Eliot* (London, 1969). Eliot's criticism is collected in *The Sacred Wood* (London, 1920), *The Use of Poetry and the Use of Criticism* (London, 1933), *Selected Essays* (London, 1951), *Of Poetry and Poets* (London, 1957) and *To Criticise the Critic* (London, 1965).

B. Biographical Material

A valuable biographical summary may be found in Kristian Smidt, *Poetry and Belief in the Work of T. S. Eliot* (London, 1961), pp. 1–33. Herbert Howarth, *Notes on Some Figures behind T. S. Eliot* (London, 1964) is good on Eliot's education and the American background generally, and scattered biographical reminiscences of great interest are collected in *T. S. Eliot: A Symposium*, ed. Richard March and Tambimuttu (London, 1948) and in *T. S. Eliot: The Man and his Work*, ed. Allen Tate (London, 1967).

C. Critical Material

Good critical introductions include F. O. Matthiessen, *The Achievement of T. S. Eliot* (London, 1947), George Williamson, *A Reader's Guide to T. S. Eliot* (London, 1955), Hugh Kenner, *The Invisible Poet* (London, 1959), and Northrop Frye, *T. S. Eliot* (Writers and Critics series; London and Edinburgh, 1963). The most usefully detailed guide is Grover Smith, *T. S. Eliot's Poetry and Plays: a Study in Sources and Meaning* (Chicago, 1956). Students will also find helpful *A Collection of Critical Essays on 'The Waste Land'*, ed. Jay Martin (Englewood Cliffs, New

Jersey, 1968). *'The Waste Land': a Casebook*, ed. C. B. Cox an Arnold P. Hinchliffe (London, 1968), *'Four Quartets': a Casebook*, ed. Bernard Bergonzi (London, 1969), and *T. S. Eliot's Four Quartets, a Commentary* by C. A Bodelsen (Copenhagen, 1966). Collections of critical essays on Eliot include *T. S. Eliot, a Study of His Writings by Several Hands*, ed. B. Rajan (London, 1947), *T. S. Eliot, a Selected Critique*, ed. Leonard Unger (New York, 1948), and *T. S. Eliot, a Collection of Critical Essays*, ed. Hugh Kenner (Englewood Cliffs, New Jersey, 1962).

## 6

## THE NOVEL IN THE 1920's

### Malcolm Bradbury, University of East Anglia

I

Periods in literature, especially short ones like a decade, are not always illuminating units for discussion. A literary scene at any given time contains a variety of generations, directions and aesthetic obsessions; and yet there are decades which invite attention as a decade—periods of social or intellectual ferment when human environment and men's ideas seem to crystallize certain themes and focus on certain propensities for change and debate, periods which remarkably cohere styles, moods, and aesthetic tendencies. Often with such periods it is worth stopping to look at them as a phase, a synthetic point in social and literary history, worth satisfying our feeling that they stand at the centre of development and make us understand it the better. Two recent periods stand out like this in English literature; the 1890's and the 1920's. For in the modern development of English literature the 1920's exist for us now, I think, as a turning point; it is the period when something happens to the fortunes of modernism, when its possibilities and its limitations are so explored as to lead us toward the kind of art we have now. In a series of major works—Joyce's *Ulysses* (1922); Lawrence's later, more symbolist novels; Wyndham Lewis's *Tarr* (1918), *The Childermass* (1928), *The Apes of God* (1930); E. M. Forster's best work *A Passage to India* (1924); Ford Madox Ford's remarkable *Parade's End* tetralogy (1924–1928); the finest novels of Virginia Woolf—many of the best propensities of modernist writing were realized in fiction, continuing and adapting the tradition of experimental fervour which had been remaking fiction from Henry James onward. But the tradition acquires a certain terminal mood over the decade, and the high point is something of an end, as if this era were exhausting itself and a new and more muted one emerging. There is still *Finnegans Wake* to come, but Forster produces no more, Lawrence dies, Virginia Woolf's fiction falls off, and the successors start to renounce modernist experimentalism and undertake their working of the form in a rather different fashion. The critics often identify this redirection as an apostacy of the 1930's; but the development figures in the 1920's too, and really, perhaps, belongs there. For not only does the modernist strain become more terminal; a new kind of modernism, a working prose of the modern, a working acceptance of its conditions and its stuff, starts to emerge, with its own appropriate voices—the vein of comic surreal in Waugh or Huxley, the vein of socio-psychic curiosity of late Forster or Ford. What, in the broad way, happens in the 1920's is the redistribution of the forces of modernism in the face of a different kind of world, a post-war and modernized world, and a consequent challenge to its capabilities and resources. And that, I think, is why the decade seems a crucial decade in letters, and a very modern one. It is a transitional phase, a phase of aesthetic revision, an era that turns us over into our kind of artistic milieu.

What does become of modernism in the 1920's? We usually take modernism to mean the internal stylization of the arts, the distortion of the familiar surface of observed reality, and the disposition of artistic content according to the logic of metaphor, form, or symbol, rather than according to a linear logic taken from story or history. Modernism is that situation where the artist performs as a radical in a particular sense; he is concerned not so much with revolution in the world as with revolution in the word. He is devoted to radicalizing his primary environment, which is that of art itself. Modernism hence has oblique relations with the modern world, and makes an oblique report upon it. In its works, modern history is not really a field for the proper enactment of events or structure; it is rather a contingent and fallen world, stuck in history and time without possessing an order, a structure or a myth. Art must therefore make excursus from it, and so modernism's account of modern experience is perhaps finally of its problems an an aesthetic locale. Modernism in this sense considerably pre-dates the twenties, and most of its radical changes in the realm of the aesthetic and the fictive had taken place long before. The Tradition of the New goes back in England to the turn of the century, and in the novel—which tended to be in England the first form to 'go' modernist—it reaches back a bit further, certainly to Henry James. From the 1890's onward, a succession of movements had laid down a modernist mode, highly various in aesthetics and practice, but manifesting a continuous conviction about cultural dislocation and the need for the new. Gradually, in fact, there was set up the model of an artistic situation in which art was the product of a creative ferment analogous to rebellion in other spheres; in which it was problematically placed, and must struggle to ensure the language, the structure and even the survival of the formal object; in which the artist was socially isolated, in communion not with the contingencies of immediate history, but with some primary and distant artistic utopia, the hints of whose being lay in aesthetic consonance and the epiphanies of formalism, but whose model on this earth was possibly bohemia—the artistic community of peers, at once an emancipated social order and an aesthetic enclave. The critical remaking of the literary tradition in this direction had been pretty well achieved by about 1915, and the historical transition into modernism was by then more or less accomplished, so that it had become one of the inescapable environments of the modern arts. In the novel, more than in any other form, there existed a body of unavoidable performances—the novels of James, George Moore, Conrad, Stephen Crane, early Lawrence, early Joyce—which pointed a direction and an aesthetic tendency. There were a number of explicit statements, by James, Conrad, Ford, and others, suggesting what the aesthetic was. Then there were certain other basic figures who had been established as literary and intellectual influences: the unmaskers of process, like Darwin, Marx, and above all, for the later moderns, Freud; the cyclical historiographers, like Vico and Spengler; the Russian novelists of consciousness, notably Dostoyevsky; and the post-impressionist painters, whose modes were regarded as being adaptable by analogy to literature. The emphasis on technique, or on the perceptual resources of the artist himself as a subjective consciousness; the emphasis on rendering, or the heightened resonance that might be attached to certain observed objects; the emphasis on the tactics of presentation through the consciousness of characters, rather than upon the 'objective' presentation of material; and the emphasis on the medium of art itself as the writer's essential subject-matter—all of these pieties of modernist fiction were established before the twenties.

Indeed one could argue that by the 1920's the heyday of modernism was already past; that its culminating phase was between 1908 and 1915, when London became for a while the international capital of what was after all an international tendency, and drew in writers and modes of writing on a cosmopolitan scale, so producing a new and radical literary environment. By the end of the war, something obviously happened to all that. Paris once again reverted to being the real capital of modernism; Ezra Pound symbolically left England in 1921, complaining that it was finished, or reverting to type. Joyce had lived on the Continent for years, and Ford (disgusted because of the pulling down of Regent Street and the late demobilization of writers—two significant indicators of the spirit in which the English cultivated the arts) also became an expatriate across the channel; and so did Lawrence, equally sure of the demise of England as a cultural environment. All this could suggest that modernism had been a foreign tendency that had visited England briefly and was now going away again. To a point that would be true, since there is a revision toward literary nationalism in the post-war years. But it is surely in the twenties that the real assimilation of modernism into the tradition occurs, to become not so much an intellectual innovation as an intellectual necessity. That was how Virginia Woolf presented it in her famous essay on 'Mr. Bennett and Mrs. Brown': '. . . in or about December, 1910, human character changed,' she said. Which is to say that modernism had not only an aesthetic but an enhanced historical sanction. It was not only the fictive working of human consciousness that was different; consciousness itself, she argued, had changed. The material fabric upon which the 'materialist' novel depended was not stable any more but shifting; Freud had changed not only the world of ideas but the self-knowledge of persons; and modernism was not just a foreign technique but the centre of the new enquiry. The two main aesthetic statements about the novel coming out in England in the nineteen-twenties both assume as much : Percy Lubbock's *The Craft of Fiction* (1921) is post-Jamesian, E. M. Forster's *Aspects of the Novel* (1927) is Bloomsbury with reservations, and both take for granted a modernist norm for fiction.[1] Of course the stylistic availability of modernism now meant that its resources and funds were used by different writers in vastly different ways—but it tends now, in the twenties, to provide the frame in which an acceptable and 'serious' critical discourse can be carried on or a new formalism stated. So if the twenties in some ways seem just to continue the existing tendency—and obviously many of the major works of the decade (*Ulysses, Lady Chatterley's Lover* or *Parade's End* in the novel; *The Waste*

*Land* and middle Yeats in poetry) do go on with developments opened up before the war—there is a change in the environment of modernism. When, in 1937, T. S. Eliot looked back in his review *The Criterion* over the literary achievements of the century, he felt that the pre-war period was devoted to a critical energy, the remaking of the tradition, and the post-war to productive consolidation. And though in fiction (unlike poetry) many of the great new works did appear pre-war, there is a clear truth in this. The twenties caught many of the highest energies and excitements of the new tendencies: even if these now divided out between expatriate bohemias and English Bloomsburies. And, in moving forward, modernism also began to exhaust itself—a development which can in part be explained as a natural evolution in the literary tradition, but which also has much to do with history, and the way the 1920s suffered and met a new stage in modern society which led it toward our own kind of social, political and intellectual situation.

## II

Now a full generation past, the 1920's is a period we look back on with some ambivalence. It is the first clearly modern decade we have behind us—an age of conspicuously modern styles in life; an age positively beyond Victorianism, signalling its arrival with the symbolic publication of Lytton Strachey's mocking *Eminent Victorians*; an age organized round modern communications, modern production and consumption, represented by a modern political spectrum. It is also behaviourally modern—its conduct is that of men emancipated and exposed by the forces of a *gesellschaft* society, that modernized and urban-centred environment, secular, mobile, heterodox, in which experience is constantly varied, society seems less like a community than an impersonal crowd, men are constantly compelled to create and recreate their identities, their aspirations, their values. The decade's temper of revolt and emancipation—the urge toward freer behaviour, the fascination with the forces below or outside the currents of English middle-class civilization, the struggle of young against old, the self-assertion through styles and fashions, the appeal to the temporary, the hedonistic, the sensational—is the temper of an era exploring a new social environment, one we are still exploring. The old order is, in the 1920's, still very much alive, the sense of ambivalence sharper, and the revolt is very much the revolt of a single class, the bourgeoisie.

And this is markedly an a-political decade, channelling its progressivism into personal rather than public reform, into behavioural politics rather than social utopianism. All of this gives the decade a distinctive temper *as* a decade, and makes it historically dateable. This distinctiveness is further sharpened by the fact that the period begins and ends with an apocalyptic moment. It begins with the end of the First World War, with all the sense of social and psychic shock implied by that, all the distancing from past history it enforced, all the sensations of starting anew in a changed environment it prompted. The decade itself tended to see the war as a point of initiation, leaving at a distance the earlier world, producing a cultural 'jump.' And it revels in and is obsessed by its own newness, its severance from past experience, its new manners and social mixes. Equally it ends with another structural transformation: the slump that followed the American Great Crash of 1929–1931. If the twenties tended to mythicize and moralize the war, and see it as the product of a false idealism and positivism, then the thirties tended to moralize and mythicize the slump; this was the price of the twenties as the war was the price of Victoria and Edward—the cost of the gay a-political cynicism, of living on borrowed time and unpaid debts, of refusing to look deep into the structure on which this middle-class emancipation was built. Orwell called it 'a period of irresponsibility such as the world has never before seen,' and there is probably still an element of this sort of opprobrium in our own evaluation of the era.

In short, if the twenties is the first self-evidently modern decade we have behind us, it is also one that seems spared some of our primary concerns, with historico-political analysis, with the exploration of the tendencies at work beneath its surface. There is an insistent element in modern interpretation of the modern which says that politics is a primary way of looking at reality and knowing it, and not to be political is not to know, is to have an insufficient alliance with coming history. The twenties is very much open to this sort of charge—though, in fact, politics is only one form of interpretation or even of action, and we narrow the term too much if we apply it only to parties and to ideologies. Sensitivity to fashion (making new roles and identities, finding new communities and reference groups, discovering fresh forms of sensibility) is a radical enterprise too, is also a way in which change occurs. But style can quickly date and also seem faintly immoral; hence the view that the twenties is in its life and its arts a period only of personal sensibility, a period when the mind explored itself and the modern without really understanding, without sinking deep into the substructure. And hence the familiar cliché about the twenties—it was stylish, modish, hedonist, flapperish, a phase when the modern was all such fun. The arts of the period are marked with all of this, and we are apt to find them, like the decade, modern but dated. Yet there is surely a connection between the age's passionate interest in style and its high artistic productivity. For its intensified styles in life, its exploration of new manners, new tastes and fashions, new identities sought in the quickening flux of modern history, are linked with the accelerated mood of aesthetic exploration in the arts, with style in a more literary sense. The era is one of proliferating expression at all levels; the new fashions, the new music, the new amusements, the new media are all part of a general explosion of innovative expression. The politics of personal consciousness are often finally a matter for the arts, and there is a way in which the artist in the twenties seems to explore more of the decade's primary experience than, say, the politician or the revolutionary intellectual. The arts of the time, concerned in new ways with exploring new structures and orders in consciousness, mental states below consciousness, and the subjective apprehension of experience and history, are participating in activities essential to the decade; they are part of the new cultural economy of the twenties, its new disposition of the forces of personal relationships, sexuality, motive and identity. To this extent, then, the arts of the twenties tend not only to report the modern, but also to enact it. Yet at their most serious they do so obliquely; with that terminal strain of structure and language which is not so much modern as modernist. And modernism, as we have seen, is something other than an explicit response to modern life; it is an aesthetic disquiet before the modern, a crisis-awareness in the field of the arts. What happens, then, when the modern and modernism converge?

## III

One important element of modernism in the 1920's was its deepening distrust both of history and progressivism, the 'twilight of the gods' feeling that Orwell linked with the absence of a proper politics. As I have said, this mood was there in earlier modernism, but the war obviously sharpened it and changed it. Above all, the war gave modernism a specific event to be apocalyptic about. It had long been presenting modernity as a revolutionary state of transition, and the times as times of change; but it had not, so to speak, pinned down the point of change, the turn in the cycle which was also the point of lapse into experience. The war, a clear moment of severance, social, intellectual, moral, experiential, questioning established forms of idealism and hope, challenging an onward and upward view of history, disillusioning the intellectual middle-class and also initiating them into the experience of change and exposure, could positively confirm the modern as a state of cultural crisis. Hence the famous comments of Henry James's letter of 1915 to Howard Sturgis, about the war: 'The plunge of civilization into this abyss of blood and darkness by the wanton feat of those two infamous autocrats' he wrote 'is a thing that so gives away the whole long age during which we have supposed the world to be, with whatever abatement, gradually bettering, that to have to take it all now for what the treacherous years were all the while really making for and *meaning* is too tragic for any words.' James himself perhaps overlooks the extent to which a new historiography, apocalyptic and pessimistic, recognizing transition, anarchy and the destructive element, had been part of a lot of modernism and part of the symbolist typology even of his own fiction; his own distinction between 'clumsy life at her stupid work' and the artistic construct, taking its own distinctive order from the artist's technique and 'fine consciousness', itself implies the symbolist conviction that history and society do not give a sense of reality or a linear logic. But this can be viewed positively or negatively; the symbolist endeavour can be a joyous expansion of the powers of art, or the exposure of internal failure in history, politics and the social fabric—the 'realities' of much preceding fiction. Earlier modernism had been finally most concerned with the establishment of an *art* of fiction. The twenties tended toward the latter view; the large progressive element in earlier modernism (its obvious symbol is that of the Nietzschean or Lamarckian superman who will evolve to reunite man and society in a new world) darkens. For the war gives the new era, but not the new man; it gives revolution or apocalypse, but that is more ending than beginning, and leaves man more lost than renewed. The transition into the modern has occurred, yes; and modern man is initiated, is beyond innocence, is dispossessed of former meanings and orders. But this is not an internal growth; it is a product of the 'unreasonable wound' of war, and produces disillusion, a sense of living between disaster and disaster.

This change in the historical typology produces a change in

modernism, and gives a different kind of fictional construct in the writing of the 1920's. Joyce and Lawrence must lie outside the scope of this essay; but in the later work of both it is embodied; and Lawrence can here be used briefly as a convenient example, because (as several critics, and notably Frank Kermode, have pointed out lately) his fictional typology is often drawn straight from apocalyptic symbolism and thought. For Lawrence, the war is the obvious end of something ('The world is gone, extinguished'; 'it was in 1915 the old world ended'; 'Europe is in a slow flux of destruction', he writes in his war-time letters) but also a beginning, a phoenix rebirth ('I know we shall all come through, rise again and walk healed and new in a big inheritance here on earth'). But in the post-war novels the notion of the last days rather than the first ones gets stronger, culminating in *Lady Chatterley's Lover* (1928). Set in a 'tragic age' in which men live among the ruins with new little habits and new little hopes, the book is dominated by the 'bruise of the false inhuman war', which creates a thin, modern, post-cataclysmic sensibility which can only look to the next cataclysm—the bad time that Mellors says is coming in the book's last pages. This theme of the double cataclysm is recurrent—very much so in Huxley and Waugh, for example. And of course it throws attention onto the nature of the modern world itself, the crisis stage which becomes an isolated and separated era of existence. The fictions of the time often begin by indicating a primal transition *into* change—a point before which all experience is prelapsarian and innocent, after which all experience is aware yet cursed—and then go on to treat a universe of continuous flux and change without discernible direction. The past being gone, men *must* enact their lives within the modern; but they as much as the novelist are implicated in a world in which time no longer progresses, in which history is—as Stephen Dedalus says—'a nightmare from which I am trying to awake.'

The problem of structuring and mythologizing a modern history which is (in the words of T. S. Eliot's famous comment on *Ulysses*) 'an immense panorama of futility and anarchy' is the primary one of the art of the twenties. To a point, one can see that writers are seeking to know and internalize their decade, to live through its exposed and initiated consciousness, to seek a frame appropriate to its existence. So one order in the fiction enacts itself through the novelties of the age—its new generational sense, its exotic pleasures, its urbanized and modernized ferment, its orgies and its despairs. Immersion in the present, that kind of giving up of self to the intensifying pace of history that Scott Fitzgerald identifies in his 'Crack-Up' essay as his own way of proceeding, is one possible artistic mode; it can produce the smart exoticism of a Michael Arlen, the febrility of a Ronald Firbank, the mixture of comic involvement and satirical detachment we have in Huxley or Waugh. The sense of flux and provisionality can themselves become elements of the characters, as they do for Calamy in Aldous Huxley's *Those Barren Leaves*:

'I don't see that it would be possible to live in a more exciting age,' said Calamy. 'The sense that everything's perfectly provisional and temporary—everything, from social institutions to what we've hitherto regarded as the most sacred scientific truths—the feeling that nothing from the Treaty of Versailles to the rationally explicable universe, is really safe, the intimate conviction that anything may happen, anything may be discovered—another war, the artificial creation of life, the proof of continued existence after death—why it is all infinitely exhilarating.'

'And the possibility that everything may be destroyed?' questioned Mr Cardan.

'That's exhilarating too,' Calamy answered, smiling.

Yet in most of the novelists of the twenties there is an attempt to show that this provisionality and contingency are historically novel and put a painful strain upon art, on apprehension and order. The feeling of surveying an existence without essence, a continuum without a structure, runs deep in the art and gives it a sense of internal strain—a certain terminal quality in the writing which reveals that it is attempting to reach toward the limits of language, the ultimate possibilities of form, the extreme of an aesthetic order beyond time and history.

So the fiction of the twenties is pulled two ways—between witnessing to the modern as an extraordinary spectacle, a new historical environment; and standing aside to give history, seen as an inferior order, an aesthetic consonance of some sort. The novelist's dilemma—and out of the dilemma the twenties made a major art—is suggested by the distinction Forster makes in *Aspects of the Novel*; the novel is, he says, a mixed form, and exists between two simultaneous obligations, to 'the life in time and the life by values.' By making the two things discrete, he suggests that values are no longer in time; life in time refers to human individuals and causal sequences (Forster associates this with 'plot'), while life by values is partly the life of the denser human consciousness, but more finally the realm of art itself, that element of aesthetic compactness in a fiction which is orderly and transcends the normal world of the human (Forster associates this with 'rhythm'). This sharpens an old distinction —the disposition of the novel both to realism and poetry had long been recognized—but Forster here really suggests that the temporal and moral worlds are not contiguous, yet must meet for novels to be made. That suggests an ironic mode of fiction; it limits the possibilities of moral heroism in time, or in progress through history. The age's characteristic epic becomes anti-heroic, the epic of contingency, as in *Ulysses*; or else the novel becomes lyrical, the lyric of personal consciousness, as in the novels of Virginia Woolf; or realism becomes a comic species, a type of the surreal, as in Huxley or Waugh. But gradually the assimiliation of Freud and Marx brings positivism back into the novel, substituting a psychological or political utopianianism for the aesthetic one. By the thirties this had come about, and a new and less aesthetically corrugated phase in the novel begins.

## IV

Apart from Joyce and Lawrence, treated in separate essays in this volume, the two most obviously important novelists of the twenties are E. M. Forster and Virginia Woolf. Both writers are associated with Bloomsbury—that vague yet influential social and intellectual entity against which Lawrence protested, and which served as a typically native equivalent for Montparnasse : as an aesthetic clearing house, a publishing centre, a forum for taste. Like many of those associated with it, both Virginia Woolf and Forster were direct heirs of the late Victorian intelligentsia; Virginia Woolf's father was Leslie Stephen, and Forster's family background lay in the atmosphere of evangelical, upper-middle class reform. Bloomsbury was self-consciously emancipated and avant garde, but it took its inheritance fairly seriously, and its modernism was never the modernism of extremes. Forster, born in 1879, published four of his five novels in the Edwardian period, and many of his critics have wanted to identify him as essentially a late-Victorian writer. This is, I think, a mistaken as-sessment, but it is not hard to see how it comes about; Forster's humanism, his belief in art as a species of the liberal social intelligence, his 'romantic' contrasts between the spontaneous passions and social restraint, and his socio-moral vein in the novel, his emphasis on solid social realities, on manners and *mores*, associate him with pre-modernism. Virginia Woolf, born in 1882, published her first novel in 1915, and her eighth and last twenty-six years later in 1941, and on the face of it is very much the more 'modernist'. She belongs emphatically to that species of novelists of consciousness that developed out of the ferment of psychological thought at the end of the nineteenth century, when environmentalism and positivism were challenged by men like William James and Henri Bergson. It was William James, in his *Principles of Psychology* (1890), who, in stressing that reality was not an objective given but was perceived subjectively through consciousness, gave the phrase we associate with her kind of fiction; arguing that the mind is not a mirror of matter, but is active and is a stream or flux with its own movement and structure, he said: 'A "river" or a "stream" are the metaphors by which it is most naturally described. In talking of it hereafter, let us call it the stream of thought, of consciousness, or of subjective life.' This emphasis on the stream of consciousness is the basis of a new subjectivist psychological novel, which is what Mrs Woolf writes; and for this, along with Joyce, Dorothy Richardson and Katherine Mansfield, she clearly has a significant place in the modernist history of forms. Then, too, her literary sensibility was clearly very much shaped in the environment of aesthetic upheaval that took place in Bloomsbury after Roger Fry organized the Post-Impressionist Exhibition of paintings in 1910. Yet if Forster is in many ways indebted to the romantic tradition in the novel, she, like most of Bloomsbury, is clearly indebted to Pater and late Victorian aestheticism. Her novels are prose-poems conducted by means of rhythm and symbols, and reaching finally toward a self-consciously poetic illumination. She admired Forster's work, but her objection to it was that it was 'extremely susceptible to the influence of time,' and was hence divided between realism and poetry; Forster admired hers but complained that her novels lacked density, tended to stand in poetry and reached out toward the world—'she is always stretching out from her enchanted tree and snatching bits from the flux of daily life as they float past, and out of these bits she builds novels.' All of this seems to give the modernist advantage to Virginia Woolf, and yet finally *A Passage to India*, Forster's one novel of the 1920's, seems to me one of the great modern novels, while no one single novel of Virginia Woolf's seems to get beyond the feminine fragility of her sensibility, even though three of her novels, written in the late twenties and early thirties —*Mrs. Dalloway* (1925), *To the Lighthouse* (1927) and *The Waves* (1931)—are major achievements.

*A Passage to India* (1924), Forster's fifth and last novel, is a book dominated by one of the great intimations of the modern multiverse, the echo in the Marabar caves which levels all meanings to one, declares that 'Everything exists; nothing has value.' But beyond that is a symbolist cohesiveness which seeks to unite the book, to make it into a resonant unity. It is the one work of Forster's that embodies deeply and intensely the neo-symbolist preoccupations|he sets out three years later in *Aspects of the Novel*, and behind it runs an oblique debt to Proust, who clearly elaborated for Forster the idea of 'rhythmic' composition as a modernist substitute for a linear plot. To this extent, *Passage* comes out of a different environment from Forster's four previous novels, which appeared between 1905 and 1910, though many of the themes of these, and the bias towards a socio-moral type of fiction, still remain. Forster's first three novels were social comedies with 'romantic' moral implications, set in a relatively stabilized social world in which the bearers of the Forsterian virtues—the virtues of the developed heart, of spontaneous passion, of trust in the imagination—battle with the armies of the benighted, who 'follow neither the heart nor the brain.' The fourth, *Howards End* (1910), differs—for though it is still conducted within a mode of social comedy that has an outlet toward the world of the unseen and the visionary, it turns on a sense of a new historical acceleration. It is a 'Condition of England' novel, contrasting and trying to connect the worlds of the new businessmen (the Wilcoxes, masters of the world of 'telegrams and anger') and the new intellectuals (the Schlegels, concerned with seeing things 'whole'). Something is happening to England; a new 'civilization' of luggage advancing, the 'red rust' of urbanization spreading over the countryside; even a potential clash between the world imperialisms. Forster distrusts the historical process and appeals against it, to the visionary 'sense of space' that replaces the 'sense of flux' in the novel's central figure, Margaret Schlegel. But if the question of the book is a romantic one (can society, like a good man, 'live in fragments no longer'?), it is located deeply in a modernizing world. Forster's conclusion is ironic; it turns on a symbolic gesture toward a spiritual ideal, but insofar as that ideal lives in time it lives in the image of agrarian England—and *that* can exist in the future beyond the book only by a 'weakness of logic' in history. This means that the book's most valued centres can be given spiritual and moral validity, but not historical justification; and unity can only be a symbol. This is the theme that returns, with even greater force, in *A Passage to India*.

This, too, is a social comedy, concerned with manners and morals and life in time. The setting, densely given, is India, the time the 1920's, the period that of the British Raj; and here again are the two groups of the earlier novels, differently disposed—now it is the rationalist, ruling British and the more spiritual and mystical Indians. Once again there are the moral heroes committed toward human contact and connection; this is Forster's 'humanism,' and this gives him his human plot, his occasions for the comedy of manners and morals, his opportunities for acute historical and political observation. The story of Adela Quested and Mrs. Moore, who come out from England to see the 'real India'; of the strange violations that come to both of them in the Marabar caves; of the public trial of the Indian Aziz, accused of assaulting Miss Quested; and of its consequences in the realm of personal, social and political life—all of this is set in a social and moral world densely registered, deeply populated, and heavily analysed, with a due sense of its reality and its importance. Indeed Forster's social, political and historical observation is fuller and finer than it has ever been before, his responsiveness to individual persons and occasions deeper. He creates a larger and more complex society in this novel than in any other, with a human cast of thousands, disposed into religions and hierarchies, duties and roles. This is a traditional species of the English novel but Forster manages it for superb comedy of manners and morals; even if his direction is finally to question society and manners, to show, as he had always shown, that the private life is prior to its forms and orders. The demands of historical realism are therefore great; Forster is trying to give us the feeling of a whole country and of the many orders of problem that exist within it. His English are the Empire-building upper-middle class, whose power depends on their capacity to preserve and even exaggerate the rational and judicial norms of their civilization; their task is 'to do justice and keep the peace,' save for those in positions of more independence who can concern themselves with other realities. His Indians (or rather the Anglicized ones who can come within the social orbit Forster creates, though many others are there too in the background) have more goodwill, but live by discontinuity and muddle, and they too are divided—by religion, by caste. The privileges of social comedy enable Forster to move freely between the worlds, playing off each against the other and employing the comic muse to suggest that men, like it, may move more freely among the forms they have created.

And a large part of the action is about that—about the need for 'goodwill plus culture and intelligence' for which Fielding stands, or that capacity to see the 'essential life' beyond the social forms with which Mrs. Moore moves toward the real India. This theme is so deeply there that some critics have seen the novel as one which seeks this unity, human and spiritual, and achieves it; a novel which reaches, through the capacity to see the universe large, to an international and spiritual over-view. All that *is* there; but is it the novel? For there is, first of all, something ambiguous about the over-view. By shifting his world from Europe to India, Forster is inevitably less concerned with those contradictions *within* western culture that have been his theme before, and much more with a total challenge to that culture. Moreover, the tendency of the book is toward a cultural and spiritual eclecticism so vast that it must have nihilist implications. In *Howards End* Mrs. Wilcox can stand, however precariously, for unity—of the various Englands, the various needs of society and of vision. In *Passage* much more has to be faced—a multiplicity of incompatible civilizations; the physical and spiritually drained landscape of India itself; the relativistic relation between all things (races, creeds, social hierarchies) the country throws up. Mrs. Moore stands in her lifetime for the nullity of a divisive land, a country the opposite of the potentially 'romantic' England of *Howards End*. After her death, her influence persists and this mysterious survival seems the opposite of her vision of emptiness; even so, it hardly scatters it. The book speaks for human reconcilement and for that devotion to the personal which gives both sound relationships with others and a sense of the power of the unseen; but it does this in a world placed and limited by a primitive, primal universe, 'older than all spirit,' emancipated from time and history, independent of the human and manifesting meaninglessness, which is also indifference and evil. So Forster confronts his moral heroes, and therefore the values which we usually take to be his own, with a challenge more profound than he has even given them, a challenge to the significance of human relations and human endeavour. Hence the many spiritual collapses—Mrs. Moore's possession by the horrific echo, Fielding's withdrawal into incompleteness, Adela's retreat from India—we meet on the way; hence the failure of any one person in the novel to see its universe whole. If there is unity, it is a unity so vast that no man may master it; it must take the form of a wholeness beyond and outside the earth—or of the unity which art can give to itself.

The strength of *A Passage to India* comes from Forster's comic vision of human muddle, a muddle that can comprehend what he calls, in *Aspects of the Novel,* 'the immense richness of material which life provides.' This gives him access to the contingent world in all its contingency, to the realism of the novel which demands that everything should be included. But inclusion is also the formal problem of the book; as the English missionaries suggest, someone, something, must be excluded from the gathering, or we are left with nothing. Forster's attempt in the novel is precisely to recognize those orders which normally are excluded, those elements in mankind and in nature which are beyond being envisioned. The novel persistently presses onward toward fullness, with a profound moral power. There are the expanding circles of men : 'And there were circles even beyond these—people who wore nothing but a loincloth, people who wore not even that, and spent their lives knocking two sticks together before a scarlet doll—humanity grading and drifting beyond the educated vision, until no earthly invitation can embrace it.' There are the circles of things, which reach even beyond heavenly invitations : the missionaries find their heaven will take in mammals but not wasps, and even Godbole, when including the wasp, cannot include the stone it is on. Only nature includes all; but does nature *mean*? It seems not; Forster is post-romantic, and the universe is a cipher rather than a speaking voice, is solipsistic rather than a divine intimation— like the hollow boulder which 'mirrors its own darkness in every direction infinitely.' And then above it are the circles of the sky : 'Beyond the sky must not there be something that overarches all the skies?', and is that something a meaning or a silence? Forster simultaneously indicates both total multiplicity and total unity, with two voices for each of these orders : comedy for muddle, poetry for mystery. Comedy and poetry share the book between them in perpetual interplay, proliferating muddle yet manifesting formal order. The human world may be unredeemable, yet Forster venerates and sanctifies those who seek to redeem it; the universe may be incomprehensible, yet he supports those who seek to comprehend it. To do that, he is both social novelist and symbolist, a rare and precarious combination, yet one which he carries to the point of a major fictional triumph. Forster's is finally a dualistic world : he *is* 'materialistic', as Virginia Woolf says, in his conviction that life in time and within the social frame is what we normally live by, and that states of vision are rare, incomplete, and not notably redemptive; and he is aesthetic or poetic in his sense that the material world must be framed by a visionary sense, an awareness of the multiplying unseen. But conveying the powers of that is something that, he accepts, lies beyond the life of men in time; it is a power that has to do with art, which by at once being inclusive and rebarbative can create a sense of wholeness, order and completeness.

Virginia Woolf's conviction that Forster failed to irradiate his world with that sense of aesthetic timelessness which was, for her, the basis of life as well as poetry therefore constitutes a real difference between them. Indeed her own evolution as a novelist—after a couple of tentative starts in *The Voyage Out* (1915) and *Night and Day* (1919)—is towards a different formal species. The histories of English literature usually take her to be an imaginative contemporary of Proust and Joyce, interested in the same kind of formal experiment; and indeed she often comes out as the best modern example we have of the native experimental novelist. The other major figures are cosmopolitan and expatriate, but she fought the battle on native grounds, using Bloomsbury for Montparnasse and exploring, as no other purely English novelist succeeded in doing, the formal resources of the new kind of novel. So, in his brilliant study of European realism, *Mimesis*, Erich Auerbach can take her as his central representative of the forms of modernist realism, and *To the Lighthouse* affords him a happy distillation of the most important procedures and typologies it employs—the disappearance of the objective narrator, and of objective reality conveyed as something generally valid and recognizable; the use of the subjective consciousness to present a multiple impression of what is perceived; the use of a contrast between 'interior' and 'exterior' time and the presentation of the interior life through a random association 'neither restrained by a purpose nor directed by a specific subject of thought'; and the deliberate cutting away of the significance of large exterior events, like staple events in history or even the deaths of characters. After reading Auerbach's chapter on her, it would be impossible not to grant that she was deeply and seriously involved in a revolution in the novel—that major change in form that accelerates between about 1913 and 1920, when a new species of psychological novel emerges. By that time the Paterian novel of impressions and 'quickened, multiplied consciousness' had become part of the modernist stock, the classic figure in that development being of course Henry James. But—under various new assumptions about the evaluation of experience through consciousness, and in the spirit of the expanding revolt against scientific positivism and rationalism, particularly apparent in the growing emergence of psychology as a study—the form now revealed an obvious extension of resource and technique. In 1913 the first two volumes of Marcel Proust's eight-volume *Remembrance of Things Past* came out; in 1915, when Mrs. Woolf's own first book was published, the initial volume of Dorothy Richardson's twelve-volume novel called *Pilgrimage* appeared; and the following year saw book publication of Joyce's *A Portrait of the Artist as a Young Man*. All these were simultaneously psychological *and* experimental novels; their importance formally lies in the conjunction of the two things. In all, in quite different ways, the structure is gained through orders taken from psychological as opposed to historical time; and hence the focus lies in the operation of the subjective consciousness of one of several characters, the crises and discoveries of the action being a form of psychic growth or awareness, or else simply a living through of that continuum in the mind which decreates chronological time and objective reality, working rather by random stimuli and synchronic associations. This kind of novel gives us therefore an intermittent and dislocated universe, in which life becomes stuff and the flickering impulses of the mind toward registration, assimilation and order produce a new type of aesthetic structure, a new sort of historiography of mental content, a new experimentalism.

Virginia Woolf's fiction obviously distils, to a remarkable degree, the possibilities afforded the novelist by his release from traditional views of time and identity. In the two famous aesthetic statements we have from her—the essays 'Mr Bennett and Mrs Brown' and 'Modern Fiction'—she puts the stress on those two major aspects of the 'new' novel which, running together, make it so technically spectacular; its revolutionary nature, and its realism of consciousness. So the famous statement in 'Modern Fiction':

if a writer were a free man and not a slave, if he could write what he chose, not what he must, if he could base his work upon his own feeling and not upon convention, there would be no plot, no comedy, no tragedy, no love interest or catastrophe in the accepted sense, and perhaps not a single button sewn on as the Bond Street tailors would have it. Life is not a series of gig lamps symmetrically arranged; but a luminous halo, a semi-transparent envelope surrounding us from the beginning of consciousness to the end. Is it not the task of the novelist to convey this varying, this unknown and uncircumscribed spirit, whatever aberration or complexity it may display, with as little mixture of the alien and external as possible?

These two essays add up to an important general plea for a new timbre in the novel, yet at the same time they are turned very much in the direction of her own distinctive interpretation of the new fiction—a version which suggests that what makes the 'modern' novel is not a new and more psychological way of understanding and ordering human experience, but a new and more poetic way of rendering it. The new technique is realistic, she says, and is faithful to life and the novelist's feeling about it; but it is also highly selective, cutting out extraneous materials in the interests of giving us a purer impression of the varying 'spirit' in life. For many of her contemporaries, the sense of contingency and disorder the new novel of consciousness sought to convey was a simultaneous consequence of a lesion in history —the collapse of a community which meant the collapse of a traditional art—and of the discovery of new orders in consciousness which gave a potentially new basis for myth. Their experimentalism is witness to the strain of finding structure and language in a demythicized age; it speaks to the deep sense of multivalency that had come into the arts after the questioning of determinist realism. But in turning to consciousness they turned to the insights of a new concern in psychology, which, while not seeing man as free again, suggested that the realm of consciousness had its own independent forces and powers. This gave the novel a heightened aestheticism, a new emphasis upon form and symbol and the powers of language itself to create an independent kingdom of force; it also gave a new emphasis upon the techniques of tapping those systems of power which existed below the realms of the conscious ego. So for Joyce, 'stream of consciousness' affords a way to another world of motifs and orders, an archetypal mythology; for Lawrence too, concerned with his own very different version of the novel of consciousness, the problem was to break down the stable ego in order to explore the energies and gestures of the unconscious and the symbolic history this made. Both, that is, were seeking to make fiction a version of psychic history. But for Virginia Woolf the experimental novel of consciousness is very explicitly an emancipation, a utopia of the novel in which the writer, freed from the kingdom of necessity and moving into the kingdom of light, is no longer bound by onerous conventions prescribed by tradition and the reader. Neither the novelist nor the consciousness in which he deals is conditioned, socially or psychologically; and the essential effect of the new novel is to release the lyrical intensities of the form.

In short, for Virginia Woolf consciousness is intuitive and poetic rather than subterranean or mythopoeic; it is the creative energy of the self which makes its own subjective time, its Bergsonian *durée*, out of the connective tissue linking the immediate moment with the past. The flux has no marked social origin—in *Mrs. Dalloway* there is an inference that the city has to do with these fleeting and multiple impressions, but there is no similar suggestion in *To the Lighthouse* or *The Waves*—and, with whatever Bloomsbury and Bergsonian additions, the essential sensibility harks back to Pater:

> While all melts under our feet, we may well grasp at any exquisite passion, or any contribution to knowledge that seems by a lifted horizon to set the spirit free for a moment, or any stirring of the senses, strange dyes, strange colours, and curious odours, or work of the artist's hands, or the face of one's friend. ('Conclusion' to *Studies in the History of the Renaissance*)

This is why, of course, Virginia Woolf's novels impress us not for their realism, not even their psychological realism, but for their sensibility. She is only relatively interested in the psychological continuum, or in the individual identity. The novel of consciousness really affords her the opportunity of a lyrical impressionism, a fiction of intensified sensitivity and fine sensations; and it is rendered usually through a sensitive supra-consciousness that works in association with the characters but which is the narrator's own, dominating and unifying the action. So, commonly in her novels, consciousness is permitted to shift not only temporally (backwards and forwards in time) and spatially (from this place to that) in the individual ego, but from character to character; while the characters often share a common focus in relation to an external symbol—like the lighthouse or the waves. Though the novelist remains in the same condition of immediate responsiveness as the characters, knowing little more than they, sharing their bewilderment and wonder, and though the events all remain essentially internal, the stream of consciousness is finally the emancipated associative flow of the novelist herself (who can function as an independent source of reflection in the absence of any character whatsoever, as in the 'Time Passes' interlude in *To the Lighthouse*). And consciousness so does more than apprehend the flux and contingency of life, that 'incessant shower of innumerable atoms' she speaks of in the 'Modern Fiction' essay; it is also concerned with poetic intimations, moments of vision, 'little daily miracles, illuminations, matches struck unexpectedly in the dark' (*To the Lighthouse*), and trembles persistently on the brink of a revelation. She can and does create the flux in its terrifying enormity —so Septimus Smith in *Mrs. Dalloway*, dislocated by the war, accepts that 'it might be possible that the world itself is without meaning'; so Eleanor at the end of *The Years* recognizes that the atoms that 'danced apart and massed themselves' might hardly compose an identity, 'what people called a life'—but the flux is also the context for a sensitized appreciation of the essences in things. Time, in her work, often tapers to a point and distils, in the direction of Mrs. Ramsay's intimation in *To the Lighthouse*:

> there is a coherence in things; a stability; something, she meant, is immune from change, and shines out (she glanced at the window with its ripple of reflected lights) in the face of the flowing, the fleeting, the spectral, like a ruby; so that again tonight she had the feeling she had once today, of peace, of rest. Of such moments, she thought, the thing is made that endures.

This is symbolist, though Virginia Woolf sees these intimations, as her characters do, from within time, so that they are never absolute. Even so, the repeated hints of a pattern which traces its mystery in the universe, the repeated suggestion that the flux is potentially a world of broken forms mirroring true forms in a world beyond, is the basis of Mrs. Woolf's charged and highly iconographic style of discourse. In *To the Lighthouse* and *The Waves*, her two most evidently symbolist novels, lighthouse and waves are really symbols *about* symbols; the lighthouse's brief pulses, the faint and evanescent patterns left by the waves, are both rhythmic and temporary, resonant and incomplete. They are recessive forms from a vaguely suggested world beyond, like the momentary glimpses we are given, often rather archly, of things as essences, 'single, distinct':

> It seemed now as if, touched by human penitence and all its toil, divine goodness had parted the curtain and displayed behind it, single, distinct, the hare erect; the wave falling; the boat rocking which, did we deserve them, should be ours al-

ways. But alas, divine goodness, twitching the cord, draws the curtain; it does not please him; he covers his treasures in a drench of hail, and so breaks them, so confuses them that it seems impossible that their calm should ever return or that we should ever compose from their fragments a perfect whole or read in the littered pieces the clear words of truth. For our penitence deserves a glimpse only; our toil respite only. (*To the Lighthouse*.)

Hence her characters live between flux and pattern; and because the novels themselves are patterned and rhythmic she inevitably validates most of those characters who have an aesthetic and symbolist propensity of her own sort. In so doing, she not only tends to poeticize modernism, but also to feminize and domesticate it. In *To the Lighthouse*, for example, the male world is represented as materialist, historicist, philosophical, public, and this is a system of assessment and identity repudiated by the book, which celebrates the female world in which sensitivity, intuition, beauty and domesticity unite. The men who 'negotiated treaties, ruled India, controlled finance' are excoriated and protected by sensibilities, notably Mrs. Ramsay's, attuned to higher matters —who, like the author, are never won over by the claims of history, abstract ideas, or the objective existence of things, mental crudities belonging to the 'fatal sterility' of the male. Because of this, the essential form of her novels, whatever the complexities of their pattern, is always finally the domestic novel of sensibility; and hence, I think, there is something inescapably limited about the matter of consciousness with which she deals, something too easily got about the states of 'rapture' and completeness she conveys. Her method, unlike that of Joyce or Forster, prescribes a large cutting away of much modern experience in the interests of keeping her fictional world intact. Her novels not only have an aesthetic; they are *about* the aesthetic view of life, and challenge themselves much less than do Forster's or Ford's.

*To the Lighthouse* is probably her best novel, but there is something unsolid and aloof about its achievement; it is as if its deliberated perfection of form cannot quite be substantiated with the materials of life in which the book must deal. Its two episodes, an evening and a morning ten years apart, split by an interlude which focuses those ten years of history into tiny parentheses, describe a world with Mrs. Ramsay in it and a world without her. Thematically, the book deals with a number of matters fundamental to Mrs. Woolf's works: the relation of male to female, of intellect to intuition, the difference between the isolation of pure thought and the social and humane quality of living, like Mrs. Ramsay, 'in beauty.' Mrs. Ramsay, a reconciling force and an invigorating one, is a unified sensibility :

> Mrs. Ramsay, who had been sitting loosely, folding her son in her arm, braced herself, and, half turning, seemed to raise herself with an effort, and at once to pour erect into the air a rain of energy, a column of spray, looking at the same time animated and alive as if all her energies were being fused into force, burning and illuminating (quietly though she sat, taking up her stocking again), and into this delicious fecundity, this fountain and spray of life, the fatal sterility of the male plunged itself, like a beak of brass, barren and bare.

With her beauty and her 'capacity to surround and protect,' with 'her raptures of successful creation,' she is idealized in the novel; but the images by which she, as well as her raptures, are rendered are decorative, shaped, fine; they are complex metaphors, drawing upon but never *realizing* the iconography of romanticism : trees, fountains, rain, waves. These 'iconographic' moments run through the novel; Charles Tansley seeing Mrs. Ramsey's beauty plain, Lily Briscoe seeing human thought as a scrubbed kitchen table in a tree, Mr. Ramsey going to 'a spit of land which the sea is slowly eating away, and there to stand, like a desolate sea-bird, alone,' facing the dark of human ignorance. The book is full of such moments of gazing, of contemplation, of rapture; moments coming so little out of the action and so much out of the emphasis of the writer. The characters, stopping to admire one another, to venerate one another, and particularly to worship or recall Mrs. Ramsay's 'knowledge and wisdom,' seem able to do so because so little else can happen in their universe, because they inhabit a world in which this is a norm of human activity and relationship, its basic human obverse being the sense of loneliness and isolation. The world of the novel is scarcely penetrable from outside, by the real as opposed to the stylized contingencies of life. And as for the novel as a whole, that too is a total metaphor, shaped and fined, ending as it does with the last brush-stroke to Lily Briscoe's picture, which is in effect the signal for the total filling out of the composition. It ends *as* a composition, entire and of itself; and so while the flux may be the flux of consciousness, it moves inevitably toward a coherence, not of the human mind of the characters but of aesthetic composition. So pattern seems, finally, the pattern of art as artifice, and this limits the ultimate scale of her modernism, though of course it doesn't limit its absorbing interest. Her work is at bottom crystalline and complete, a fiction that refines the tradition but does not *make* a tradition on which successors can draw.

## V

Ford Madox Ford, on the other hand, is surely one of the novelists who, by seeing modernism as a craft or a technique, has made its manners and ways available to a whole generation of successors. For Ford, modernism was less a subject-matter or an art of aesthetic completeness than an enabling refinement of form that was very variously disposable. Like Forster, he really derives from the earlier, pre-war generation of novelists, though he comes out of a rather different context. A friend of Stephen Crane, Henry James, and Joseph Conrad (with whom he collaborated on two novels), he was very much a part of that self-consciousness about the art and craft of fiction, that stress on technique, which permeated the earlier phase of modernism in the novel. Then between 1908 and 1911 he edited the remarkable *English Review*, where he first printed D. H. Lawrence and Wyndham Lewis. In the early twenties he moved to France and edited the expatriate magazine *transatlantic review*, which printed Gertrude Stein, Joyce, and Hemingway. Now Ford had a second lease of life as a writer, and it went along with a fascinating change in his fiction, a change which was also to bring to a culmination his best powers. In part his expatriation might be regarded as a cause, though the change is already apparent in the remarkable force of *The Good Soldier* (1915), a highly lucid, composed and tight psychological novel of sexual relationships. But it comes to a peak in the four novels that comprise *Parade's End* (1924–1928), a loose and panoramic sequence which is focused in the war, though it indirectly deals also with the half-decade before it. The novel crystallizes the era previous to the twenties in a whole vision, taking its force from the viewpoint the new decade provides upon a past which Ford had already several times explored at closer hand. But the sequence is not only the distillation of a period, but also of an art—the art of a writer who had assimilated but never before made so potent the aesthetics of a particular tradition in modernism.

We might say that in some ways the tradition behind Ford is consonant with that of Virginia Woolf, or Proust, or other contemporaries concerned with the creation of a new intensity of rendering in fiction. But at the same time Ford is fairly close to the Edwardian novel (there are certain marked resemblances between *Howards End* and the sequence) and in other ways to the more realistic epical-historical vein of nineteenth century fiction. The novelist Ford is closest to is Conrad, writing on whom he says many things that clearly apply to his own work. Ford's name for the kind of writing he valued was 'impressionism,' but he uses the term in rather a different way from Virginia Woolf. An experience is, as for Virginia Woolf, composed of 'various unordered pictures,' and the artistic recreation of it demands not an evocation of a single stated reality observed by the writer and registered as a fact with the reader, but an impression (or as Ford would say a 'constatation') rendered by recognizing the shifting matter consciousness becomes aware of, when it experiences, when it recalls, when it tells. This also involved, for Ford, the notion of the aloof or detached narrator, presenting the novel 'without passion,' and with a guiding selectivity. To a considerable extent, all this is consonant with Virginia Woolf's aesthetics, but there are marked variations (variations that in fact made Ford's fiction very much more available than Virginia Woolf's, and in a way much more representative). For the point of Ford's technique was less that it should predetermine the experience dealt with by the novelist than that it should answer to it, enable it to exist. For Ford, the subject-matter of a novel was—he used a word of James's—an 'affair,' presented by oblique techniques to the point of maximum intensification and effect. And behind that view lies another of Ford's aesthetic convictions—his belief that art's task is registration, and that that means registering the temper of the age. So *Parade's End* is panoramic, and in a way Virginia Woolf's novels could never be, not even *The Years*. Ford in fact sustains many of the interests of the nineteenth-century novel, in the public life, in the social web, in 'history.' The sequence is specifically involved in historical events and it takes its temper and forms its needs according to the telling of a history; the selected spots of time in which each chapter or section is focused usually bear some essential relation to a major historical moment, and the theme of the sequence is 'the world as it culminated in the war.' The techniques, then, are techniques for presenting large-scale dispositions of time, of characters, of moods and insights, of bringing the large and the small into relation—all this in the interests of giving not only a sense of psychological verisimilitude but social accuracy. Indeed *Parade's End* is an historical allegory with a psychological centre, a 'Condition of England' novel in which the primary centre of registration is an individual who, nonetheless, *enacts* history.

So Ford saw the sequence's central character, Christopher Tietjens, as the focal point of numerous forces, a man with a full awareness of history and society and capable of responding to these: 'I seemed to see him stand in some high places in France during the period of hostilities taking in not only what was visible but all the causes and all the motive powers of infinitely distant places.' Tietjens—the Yorkshire Tory, the representative of a line of feudal and ministerial inheritance, a man of 'clear Eighteenth-century mind,' passionate and enduring, agonized and unexpressionless, a man living out an old code in all its contradictions to its last possible conclusion—is the focus of this historical world; he draws it together and surveys it, and he also suffers from it and for it. The whole novel-sequence turns on his power to experience, survey and suffer so many forces from so many sources—the result being, in fact, one of the most agonized and agonizing historical novels ever written. But to convey the fullness of experience around Tietjens, experience both detailed and incidental and vast and systematic, Ford has to create a complex realism, a sense of the fullness and complexity of life in history and time. And to do this he produces, within the confines of the realistic novel, the novel of story, a remarkable literary intensity. This is the point of attention for his experimentalism—his experiments, his use of time-shift, of oblique narrative at ironic distance, of 'progression d'effet' or intensification through sequence, are craft-devices rather than self-conscious art-devices. Ford held that a novelist should express his temperament but not, in an explicit sense, his values or prejudgements; he should stand above and beyond while yielding as far as he could to the logic of his material. The result is that Ford's fiction at its best, as here, is a fiction of inexorable thoroughness, filled with a vast and complex web of experience, persistently intensified by every means Ford had at his disposal. Ford's purpose is not to master his material, to bring it into a total metaphor or symbol as Virginia Woolf sought to do, but to handle it, as fully as possible. And in that respect he is closer to epical modernists like Proust or Joyce. On the other hand, he catches history just at the point before total disunity sets in, before art comes to seem the only possible means of giving any order to history at all. The book indeed combines two aesthetics, one drawing on the epicality of nineteenth century fiction, the other drawing on the crafts of modernism; and it therefore succeeds in carrying a public theme—that of dramatizing, in

Ford's phrase, 'the public wants of a decade'—and a private theme—the psychological history of Christopher Tietjens—side by side. The novel is both a social and a psychological history, concerning both the world external to the individual and the individual's assimilation of event and process.

Ford is able to manage this because he takes as the centre of his 'affair' a character who can unite within himself the public and private lives, while at the same time living out this responsibility as an unbearable strain—a strain so unbearable that Ford seems to suggest that this is the last time a man of his kind could even envision mastering the two realms of experience. Tietjens is a member of the 'governing classes,' and as he himself notes 'Our station in society naturally forms rather a close ring' so that a small central cast of characters, recurring in different roles, provides Ford with a large social mythology. Tietjens, linked by kinship and friendship with government, military and literary circles, is deeply conscious of his role in a caste, though as a Yorkshire feudalist he is also distanced from its values; he feels obliged both to live by its codes and yet in certain details or through certain weaknesses to transgress them, and to carry experience from the past and the future into his response to the present. He is therefore both the explorer of the culture, a culture in radical change, and its scapegoat. This theme, of a cultural apocalypse and a tragic yet faintly absurd hero, gives the theme of the entire novel. Tietjens is in a very specific way the last of his line, the last Christian gentleman, the last just inheritor to his estates, the man hoping to take 'the last train to the old Heaven.' His is a sacrificial, even a suicidal, heroism; his chivalric notion of male nobility and of human nobility is threatened by social change, the transforming nature of war, and the shifting relationship between the sexes; and three wars—social war, world war, sex war—are intricately related together in the novel. Ford's hero is then a figure of romance caught at the point of historical extinction; after him there will be no more parades, no more glories, no more men who 'do not', no more such squirearchial aristocrats. To some extent he is presented as an absurd figure with a perverted creed, and we may argue about how much he softens in the novel and adapts to self-knowledge. But certainly he sees the contradictions in himself, as he lives through the code he believes in yet seeks to reach beyond it, as he masochistically sustains his own identity yet radically questions the society he lives in.

Certainly, in Ford's allegory of change, Tietjens's agony precedes the war; it is not the war that is the basic solvent of society, but rather the strains in the body politic and the mind of men which make war almost a necessary purgatory. The agony is indeed there from the novel's beginning; in particular it comes from a false, unhappy marriage Tietjens has contracted with an unfaithful wife, Sylvia. This 'chivalric' act—Sylvia, with whom he has not had relations, is apparently pregnant—inevitably throws the Tietjens heritage into doubt from the start, and Tietjens sustains the chivalry by refusing to divorce Sylvia when she begins to deceive him. In her turn Sylvia—one of the most frightening immoralists in all literature—is devoted to an endless assault on Tietjens's chivalry, attempting to bring him down to human scale, to bring him to heel, to bring him to bed. The same assault on the chivalric disposition—caught in a distilling symbol in the moment when General Campion's car hits the horse Tietjens is driving—is intensified as the action moves from the relatively secure world of 1912 to the world at war; a war presented as a war of mismanagement, bureaucracy, politics and red tape where the forces threatening the hero are less the enemy he is fighting than his own government, the leaders of his own army and Sylvia, symbolically entrenched with the General's party in France. But at the same time the war turns the cycle and begins, in a dark and bleak way, to lead toward a new life for Tietjens. He collapses toward madness but then manages, with the help of Valentine Wannop— the 'New Woman' figure, suffragette and pacifist, with whom he has long been in love—to cut himself off from his own past, to find a life beyond agony and purgation. The tree at Groby is felled; but Tietjens lives on, with the curse of ancestry lifted from his shoulders. This is all very explicitly a fable of an historical irony, a story of a change which is inevitably a disaster, for Tietjens's evolution is also a moment of historical lapse into a lesser world. The age of the aristocrat gives way to that of the bureaucrat, the age of the chivalric gives way to the age of the mechanical, the age of values and convictions gives way to the world of valuelessness—but Tietjens has suffered enough for history and finally (like Guy Crouchback in Evelyn Waugh's *Sword of Honour*, the equivalent fable for the Second World War) he forgoes the epic pilgrimage and makes his settlement.

Tietjens's ironic position in history is supported by the irony of the novel itself. For Ford's technique of 'aloofness', derived from Flaubert, is not only an art of effective registration but a condition of moral and evaluative distance. However much the sequence may seem lovingly to evoke an old England in which a residue of eighteenth century *mores* and values survives, Ford stands historically beyond all that, in a stance of detachment apparent from the opening words of *Some Do Not* . . . onward:

> The two young men—they were of the English public official class—sat in the perfectly appointed railway carriage. The leather straps to the windows were of virgin newness; the mirrors beneath the new luggage racks immaculate as if they had reflected very little; the bulging upholstery in its luxuriant, regulated curves was scarlet and yellow in an intricate, minute dragon pattern, the design of a geometrician in Cologne. The compartment smelt faintly, hygienically of admirable varnish; the train ran as smoothly—Tietjens remembered thinking—as British gilt-edged securities. . . .

And the two young men, administrators of the world ('If they saw a policeman misbehave, railway porters lack civility, an insufficiency of street lamps, defects in public services or in foreign countries, they saw to it either with nonchalant Balliol voices or with letters to the *Times*, asking with regretful indignation, "Has the British This or That come to *this?*" '), are located in an historical distance and put at an artistic remove, as throughout the novel Ford registers both through his characters and beyond them. The whole novel, working as it does by a technique of chronological distillation which suddenly intensifies and makes symbolic particular foci of consciousness and particular points in time, works, therefore, by presenting it characters in the light of a long, oblique vision—which is a way of withdrawing from an historical to a technical structure. Ford does of course attempt social history, but the gradual reduction of the novel toward the experience of individual consciousnesses parallels Tietjens' own withdrawal from the historical and social centre; all that can be left is a kind of authorial remoteness. For if, as Tietjens learns, modern history is not a form for action but a form for suffering, then the artist himself must withdraw from it. What is so striking about the sequence is that it so fully concerns itself with external as well as internal events as to make manifest the conditions bringing about this kind of style. It has a real as opposed to an implied historical dimension; it can and does deal in event as well as artistic metaphor; but it leads the way toward a tactic of 'fictional indifference,' a withdrawn irony, which is one of the hallmarks of much twenties writing. Ford's 'modernism' of technique is therefore an oblique or ironic species of realism, a way of dealing in history and event without direct celebration of it. And his detachment is not finally a withdrawal into the province of art but a separation from his hero through technique—the strategy of much post-modernist fictional art.

## VI

This sort of irony has fed pervasively into modern fiction, then, and has made much modern art, as Ortega y Gasset has said, an art of *observed* as opposed to *lived* reality. Ortega has called this a 'dehumanization' of art and pointed out that its characteristic modes are irony or comedy. And indeed the comedy of absurdity or satirical indifference does play an important part in the formal evolution of the decade. We often tend to see comedy in terms of its moods of enjoyment or mockery rather than as a vision; yet one of its powers is precisely that of immersing itself in the immediate and prevailing world without taking responsibility for it, without granting it a full reality. This is a different kind of comedy from that we saw in *A Passage to India*, where the comic function is largely to mediate, to sympathize, to grant to reality reality's due—even though, certainly, reality is a species of muddle. But there is in the comic writing of the twenties another voice: that which responds very specifically to the modern as a modern, but then sees its nature and ways as a kind of farcical absurd. The three most important figures here are Wyndham Lewis, Aldous Huxley and Evelyn Waugh (with Ronald Firbank as an interesting fringe case); and what all have in common is that in their different ways they are fascinated by the modern social and intellectual performance— but fascinated through a sense of abstracted involvement that withdraws from its value or real importance. What marks their powers is not simply their way of grasping at contemporary experience—the experience of an urban, modern *gesellschaft* society, particularly in its urban bohemian centres—though they do that with remarkable success; but in their mode of authorial displacement, their sense of the contingent nature of contemporary action, their sense of a lost logic running through society and history. In all this they begin to move beyond the 'classical' element in modernism—though Wyndham Lewis speaks specifically out of that—towards an acceptance of the world beyond reason and control, a world of what Waugh calls 'galvanized and translated reality.' So in all of them there is a sense of an historical lesion, a lapse in human order, a 'gap in the continuity of consciousness,' to take a phrase from *Lady Chatterley's Lover*, a transference into a wounded and post-war age.

In all there is certainly an implied rationalism or classicism, disdaining what it half-enjoys but clearly unable to return to absolute satirical security. And in all there is a species of comedy turning not on compassion (though that is not always absent), or social discovery of virtue; but a transliteration into conditioned farce, in which metaphors of apocalypse, indifference, mechanism, generational struggle abound to create a world in which all heroism is lost, all quests suspect, all virtues unestablishable.

Of these three writers, Wyndham Lewis is closer to modernism than the other two, and perhaps for that reason most explicit about his methods and assumptions. Lewis was born in 1882, educated at the Slade School and then as an artist in Munich and Paris, and he returned to London in 1909, the most receptive time, when it was opening up to the new movements. Ford took him up as a writer for the *English Review*; then with Pound he moved, through the neo-classicist argument, toward Vorticism, with its celebration of the energetic centre locked in art. He started *Blast*, a magazine of immediately pre-war explosion, and was in many ways an obvious product of these heady days of movements, of an avant garde that sought links across the arts (Lewis was painter and writer), of international intellectual inheritances. But from the war onward he conducts a singularly independent career, simultaneously promoting and attacking avant garde radicalism, and it is perhaps this that drives him toward satirical acerbity. The paradox subsists at the heart of his work—an art of the mechanical, it contains a profound protest against mechanism, mass-society, the dehumanization of man and of art; an art of indifference, it assaults indifference as the apostacy of true energy of selfhood; an art of tragic vision, its primary tone is that of satire and comedy. Lewis's deep neo-classicism is obviously a modernized poetic. So his sense of comedy turns on a double conviction—of the eternal ridiculousness of man, and of his particular *modern* absurdity as he converts himself, in a post-rationalistic age, toward a 'wild body.' 'The root of the comic,' he tells us in *The Wild Body* (1927), 'is to be sought in the sensations resulting from the observation of a thing behaving like a person. But from that point of view all men are necessarily comic; for they are all things, or physical bodies, behaving like persons.' That is the broad Bergsonian view of comedy (*Le Rire*), and Lewis applies it both as a fictional method and as a philosophy. Bergson's view was that laughter occurs when the *élan vital* of man is absent or deliberately arrested, producing a momentary anaesthesia of the heart in the observer. Lewis obviously accepts this and even extends it into a critique of Bergson's own romanticism, by applying the broad concept particularly to contemporary history. So the wild Kriesler in *Tarr* is a comic machine-man who is operated by a spasmodic romanticism; indeed Lewis suggests that it is precisely in the state of romantic intensity that man is most mechanized (the wild body), and that only through art and intellect can man escape from the comic predicament. So, in the prologue to *Tarr*, he describes Tarr's function in the book as to 'exalt Life into a Comedy, when otherwise it is, to his mind, a tawdry zone of half-art, or a silly Tragedy.'

All of this means that Lewis is capable of operating superbly between a Bergsonian comic indifference and a very contemporary satiric disgust. In *Tarr*, an assault on pre-war Parisian bourgeois-bohemia, written during the war and published in 1918; in *The Childermass* (1928), an abstract epical comedy of ideas set on an arid steppe on the threshold of heaven (later extended into the *Human Age* sequence of the 1950's); in *The Apes of God* (1930), a social comedy of ideas directed against English Bloomsbury-bohemia in the twenties—in his work of the twenties, then, he maps out a satirical intention that is in part immersed in the changing age, and is in part remote from it. He explicitly rejects 'fiction from the inside' (the interiorized novel of Joyce or Stein) on the grounds that it intrinsically romanticizes, and comments: 'The *external* approach to things (relying on the evidence of the *eye* rather than of the more emotional organs of sense) can make "the grotesque" a healthy and attractive companion. . . . Dogmatically, then, I am for the Great Without, for a method of external approach.' In many ways his is essentially a psychological fiction, but it is psychology rendered comic by withdrawal and by the techniques of *grotesquerie*. Hence Lewis's distinctive prose constantly jogs from within to without, with the drift of the comic *reductio* always working toward a sense of mechanism, as in *Tarr*:

> Tarr possessed no deft hand or economy of force: his muscles rose unnecessarily on his arm to lift a wine-glass to his lips: he had no social machinery at all at his disposal and was compelled to get along as well as he could with the cumbrous one of the intellect. With this he danced about it is true: but it was full of sinister piston-rods, organ-like shapes, heavy drills. . . .

In *The Childermass*, where the satirical intention is intensified, this often goes away from the specific occasions of a realized comedy toward satire of ideas, or apologue. But the balance returns in *The Apes of God*, a grand vision of the twenties, where Lewis balances comic detachment and satiric disgust. Focusing on mock-bohemia and the artistic amateur, the 'general rabble that collects under the equivocal banner of ART' (these are the Apes who are, in Lewis's vision, bringing art in society to its end by confusing it with life), he can be much more explicit about the social and structural sources of the mechanism and the romanticism he attacks. England is a culture 'dead as mutton,' trapped in the 'insanitary trough' between the wars, its social and intellectual and artistic decline going hand in hand. Lewis gets good comedy out of this, as in a superb passage on the General Strike, but also a savage satire that fully enjoys its disgust—as in this passage, describing the aged Lady Fredigonde Follett, an obvious symbol for the whole culture, rising from her chair:

> The unsteady solid rose a few inches, like the levitation of a narwhal. Seconded by alpenstock and body-servant (holding her humble breath), the escaping half began to move out from the deep vent. It abstracted itself slowly. Something imperfectly animate had cast off from a portion of its self. It was departing, with a grim paralytic toddle, elsewhere. The socket of the enormous chair yawned just short of her hindparts. It was a sort of shell that had been, according to some natural law, suddenly vacated by its animal. But this occupant, who never went far, moved from trough to trough— another everywhere stood hollow and ready throughout the compartments of its elaborate mental dwelling.

If Lewis is capable of this kind of force, and of the intelligence needed to hold such episodes as part of a coherent vision, he can at times become quirky, quaint and shrill. Even so, his contribution to modern comedy and satire is immense, and it shows the links between the comic and the late development of modernism. Like Eliot and Pound, Lewis maps a general social transition of *mores* and values and tests this against the arts as a species of intelligence and purity. But because art is seen as *in* society, his attention turns into it, fully and elaborately, and his species of technique so becomes an important register of his age. In his work, the new style both expresses the needs of modernity and seeks to control certain aspects of it; it seeks to open out new energies while deploring most of those that are released. If this is classicism, it is classicism of a new kind, a radical classicism that reveals as well as seeks to contain the new experiences at work in the world. In his writings, the human world is the centre of sickness; but there are independent energies, in indifference and art, which can provide continuation, and which allow the satirical and comic energies he manifests to live.

Some of the same themes recur in the work of Aldous Huxley, particularly in the four key novels of the twenties—*Crome Yellow* (1921), *Antic Hay* (1923), *Those Barren Leaves* (1925) and *Point Counter Point* (1928)—which represent an entire phase in his work. But Huxley, though capable of the same satirical vision, rarely directs it specifically against the social objects he sees; rather at the wearisome condition of general humanity. Both writers, certainly, deal with the fate of intellect and culture in an environment where the props and stays ensuring their survival seem threatened; but Huxley releases, so to speak, the forces of freedom more thoroughly in order to survey them. His work, too, is comedy of ideas in a universe dichotomized between intellect and passion; but the essential difference is finally that Huxley recognizes himself to be one of the order of persons he is satirizing—the new artist-intellectuals—and so manifests a greater degree of involvement and even guilt. He also comes from the literary generation successive to Lewis's—he was born in 1894 and comes to literary notice with the emergence of a new, university-educated fashionable intelligentsia at the end of the war. But from *Crome Yellow* on he recognizes his involvement in the post-war world and hence knows his own sources in culture and art as insecure. And each of his books is a web of multiplied parables or narratives that establish ways of saying so. Frequently they start with the brilliant cultured surface of the intellectual and social smart set, and then penetrate beneath to the boredoms, discomforts and animal passions that stir there. Though the novels often seem narrow in locale—he uses the device of the English or Italian country-house party familiar in the novel of ideas from Peacock onward—his world is essentially urban and sophisticated, with a collapsing aristocracy and a traditional middle-class intelligentsia somewhere in the background, manifesting their withdrawal or their half-extinction. At the centre, usually, are a group of new semi-bohemian, but upper-middle-class artists, writers, intellectuals, living in a 'pointless landscape' and conducting ineffective but modern sexual liaisons. The cast is often large enough for Huxley to follow out a multiplicity of stories, sometimes supplemented by stories within stories that recall the past. And most of these stories are illuminations of the fact that his characters are men of an idea, attempting to cohere passion within reason, and generally not succeeding. Two basic types recur: the sensitives who, while sympathetically presented, usually fail, and the arrogantly insensitive who frequently succeed, in those areas of love and self-fulfilment with which most of his actions are concerned. As a result, his novels are largely novels of *in*action, for his scrupulous, devastating analysis leaves us with a masochistic withdrawal from action. At the same time, the novels also turn on the emptying out of the centre from any dream, hope, or institution, and hence have an apparent air of cynicism, a suggestion of universal failure.

In fact, however, the author's own cynicism and detachment are very much part of the matter for analysis. The embarrassment of the novelist's feeling that his own ideas and assumptions are themselves a sterile or incomplete view of life comes out most clearly in *Point Counter Point*, where the writing of novels of ideas becomes part of the theme, and where the character of Philip Quarles is the novelist's self-surrogate. But this element runs through all the twenties novels, starting in *Crome Yellow* with the figure of Dennis, the sensitive writer conscious of the loss of a real infinite to feed upon:

> 'I make up a little story about beauty and pretend that it has something to do with truth and goodness. I have to say that art is the process by which one constructs the divine reality out of chaos. Pleasure is one of the mystical roads to union with the infinite—the ecstacies of drinking, dancing, love-making. As for women, I am perpetually assuring myself that they're the broad highway to divinity. And to think I'm only just beginning to see through the silliness of the whole thing!'

Behind the lost divinity, though, lies a world of inevitable chaos, if also of inevitable freedom from ideals. The mind is left to its own convulsions—to intellectual hobbyhorses, a sense of cultural loss, a vague hope of aristocratic withdrawal or of a new élite's emerging—while the body is left to the basic human satisfactions or to pullulating animalism. As part of the supersession of art and intellect, Dennis ends the novel driving off to the station in a hearse, while over all its action lies the vague promise of apocalyptic last days, caught in the figure of the iron Mr. Bodiham. Huxley plays the consequent ironies both ways, showing the follies of idealism and the vices of animalism. As the twenties progress, and as Huxley shifts his scene more directly into the world of the urban intelligentsia, the mood of disillusion get more clearly stated, the sense of what Lawrence found in *Point Counter Point*, a theme of the 'slow suicide of inertia,' increases, and a vision of man as the Freudian hypocrite, a creature of self-delusion farcically posturing in the role of a sublime and civilized being while really seeking to fulfill simple and often gratuitous passions, grows. But for Huxley the modern is a species of evolution as well as a matter for excellent comedy and farce, and so his world of parties, free love, adulteries, revolutionary and reactionary passions and the boredom of 'disillusion after disillusion' is an intense experiencing of the time. The cultural and moral passions both expose, and are exposed by, the new freeing of repressions, the new sorts of men and women, the new freedom and freshness of vision of the post-Freudian as well as the post-war universe. The artist, here, is deeply implicated in the modern not only as an art-form but as an enveloping experience. 'Living modernly's living quickly,' says Lucy Tantamount in *Point Counter Point*, 'You can't cart a wagonload of ideals and romanticisms about with you these days.' Huxley's fictional world is one in which this view may produce a sense of yearning loss; it is certainly one in which it is taken for granted. And if the consequence is that intelligent man is left in a comic predicament, in an historical void, then Huxley sees that as inescapable, such is the contemporary historical acceleration. The result is hardly cynicism, but a complex blend of involvement and disgust. He is satirically savage, but not satirically secure; his novels are a continuous, tentative intellectual inquiry into new forces as well as a species of ironic detachment. Indeed, the desperation and absurdity of the characters is not at a total distance; it touches the novelist as well.

If Huxley undercuts his fictional frame in this way, Evelyn Waugh restores it with a grand completeness that makes his work a superb example of pure modern comedy. The internal world of the action is very close to Huxley's, and Waugh has in his early work—particularly his two novels of the twenties, *Decline and Fall* (1928) and *Vile Bodies* (1930)—a full and thorough response to the details and moods, passions and instincts, manners and mores of accelerating modernity. His Bright Young Things are less intellectual than Huxley's; and such ideas as they may possess are a matter only for comic attention. They are, rather, metropolitan, smart, fashion-centred, a set or a herd rather than a community; but they still derive from a similar type of historical and social change. Behind their world is a vast historical collapse, a shift from an agrarian to a metropolitan society, from permanence to impermanence. Waugh is sometimes seen as a nostalgic writer, but this is to mistake him; his essential vision is a modern one, in which the illogicality of history is granted and there are no restitutions to be had. Instead all that is left is a world of shadows that can be treated comically because it is a matter for little concern. Waugh does in fact create a genuine sense of anguish in his characters, particularly in the later books, and often a purgatorial relation between ideals and life as offered. But at the same time he does face the modern in history by enacting it comically, comedy being the species proper to the principles of energetic depravity Waugh sees at work in the world; one may sense the agony within the author without ceasing to see that he is urging us beyond it. Comedy is the voice appropriate to a world without any notable salvations to offer, and may indeed have its own salvations— So Paul Pennyfeather, in *Decline and Fall*, is finally protected by a comic good fortune that takes away his identity but allows him survival.

*Decline and Fall* is in fact a kind of modern *History of Tom Jones* in which the realm of comic fortune sustains the characters in an otherwise anarchic world; but whereas Tom learns to take his place within a world of order, Paul Pennyfeather, the 'intelligent, well-educated, well-conducted young man,' who is allowed to exist in the novel only as a shadow, can revert only to his state of simple innocence away from the Big Wheel which turns the world. At the beginning of the book, Paul is taken out of that state when he is unjustly sent down from college; he then suffers a succession of other injustices, largely at the hands of the Metropolitan smart set, into whose hands he has got by spending a 'very modern night of love' with Margot Beste-Chetwynde. The lesson he learns is that he has not the hard powers of survival which fit him for the modern fray, those comic powers that Margot and the unkillable Grimes possess, powers which Waugh explicitly links with the Dionysian and anarchic dimensions of comedy, and had best not try to learn from life, since its lesson will be total cynicism. Waugh creates this theme with a fine comic stylization; the novel takes place in a 'devised' comic universe in which the laws of probability are slightly suspended, where special codes of comic fortune and misfortune work, where comedy's wild laws have precedence over hopes, values, ideals. Hence the survival power of Waugh's main metropolitan characters, who are associated with a primitive survival-mechanism which enables them to be without seeking to become. But *Decline and Fall*, with its Gibbon overtones to the title, is the last book which suggests that there is anywhere to withdraw to. With *Vile Bodies*, we shift to a more totally urban world, one in which all hopes, values, traditions, permanence belong to the past and exist only to be violated. Waugh once again takes a riotous pleasure in the world of accelerating 'faster, faster,' a world of motor-races, flimsy marriages, brief affairs, parties ('those vile bodies')—a world where, as Huxley's Lucy Tantamount said, 'Living modernly's living quickly.' At the same time the acceleration comes to take on the style of a herd-suicide, and it all ends in an explicit apocalypse on the biggest battlefield in the history of the world. This surrealistic intrusion into history is consonant with the mode of the whole novel, which uses a flickering and filmic technique to catch a succession of manners and moments out of the twenties, and demands that we accept not its accuracy but its imaginative truth. And Waugh shows the acceleration as an unstoppable process; the characters may yearn for stability, and they feel that things cannot go on like this much longer, but it is a feverish fun even if the overtones are ominous, and stability is not to be had. To this extent Waugh sees in the 'radical instability of the world-order' a social and political source, and in passingly suggesting the inadequacies of the politicians and the older generation he does show the Bright Young Things as trapped in a socio-political situation which demands and compels this bright, dangerous and unreal behaviour from them. Waugh changes his universe from book to book, and his own relation to it; but despite his unconcern and his comic detachment he does take the neuroses and dissonances of society as his own at least as far as enacting them as matters of observation and experience. What his comic remoteness provides is a vision of what he knows and even enjoys as a profoundly contingent universe. As in the work of Nathanael West (a writer Waugh resembles in several respects), the dominant style is that of grotesque, a parodic distortion of the insubstantiality of modern civilization, which lacks true images, true quests, true centres of value. In this world the only mode of survival is a comic self-sufficiency, which is what Waugh gives to some of his characters, and also to his own way of telling. It is Waugh's sense of anarchy which makes his comedy, and it is a comedy of apocalypse. Indeed the modern may not only *end* in an absurd apocalypse on the battlefield of *Vile Bodies*; in some sense it already *is* that apocalypse, as the last days seem to work themselves out in the stuff and *mores* of twenties society.

## VII

By the end of the twenties, it would then seem, there had
been a considerable remaking of modernism as this decade of
the modern began to be assimilated into art, as a generation of
post-modernist writers emerged, and as the hopes of a new
liberation through the arts and the advanced relationships that
seemed to accompany them came to be thrown into question.
It is possible to see this as the end of modernism in England,
for certainly the obvious and conspicuous elements of creative
ferment are less evident in the writings of the end of the decade.
But the art of the late twenties does not divest itself of the
problems of modernism, or even its sense of artistic expansion.
Rather it intensifies an element that was always there in modernism, an awareness of the grotesque, a capacity for irony and
detachment in the writer, a dehumanization of art; or else it
emphasizes what was also there in obverse, the element of
irrationalism, of psychic flux and flow, of immersion in the
forces of the unconscious. Certainly, though, the purity of the
aesthetic stasis begins to be left behind by the end of the nineteen-twenties, as modernism more and more comes to mean an
encounter with the newly modern world. In short, the artistic
expectancy of modernism seems radically to darken, the luminous symbol to recede, the joyous freedom of art itself to become
constrained. The decade was a time of ambivalence about modernism, just as it was ambivalent about most other things. The
writing of the age is marked by all sorts of potentialities for
radical ferment, by feelings that this is a new age, artistically,
intellectually, socially, one in which a new cultural stimulus
is possible. Yet this is coupled, in much of the work that specifically responds to the decade, with a sense that a new barbarism, a new and uninvited degree of social dislocation, a new
kind of human exposure has come about. The fervour for the
new time accelerates in the twenties in many ways, as the new
generation finds a buoyant independence given it from old
moralities, the old family-centred society, the old codes and
responsibilities. All that is very much there in the decade; in
the liberated note of Virginia Woolf's art or the fascination with
the new young in Huxley or Waugh. Yet if we look at the most
important writers of the period, we can hardly say that theirs
is a joyous view of the age.

Indeed we may say that, if one of the results of modernism
was an abstracting of social or psychological stability and of

material reality from the novel, in the interests of creating what Virginia Woolf would call a less 'material' reality, a less solid emphasis on history, then the approach itself seems to become problematic as, more and more, history curdles the problem by doing the same thing of itself. If in fact there is, as I have suggested, some community of style and typology among the best writers of the decade, then it would seem that the drift of style and structure is toward the ironic and parodic, the bias of the typology toward a sense of double cataclysm; while the new relationships, the new forms of consciousness towards which art is undoubtedly disposed become matters for sharpened unease. In discovering technique, modernism seemed also to have discovered an empty centre to experience which it was left to the twenties to explore as an historical fact.

## NOTE

1. The third important statement about fiction is C. H. Rickword's 'A Note on Fiction', which appeared in two parts in *The Calendar of Modern Letters* in 1926. But what that marks is the transition of modernism into literary criticism of the novel.

## BIBLIOGRAPHY

Sean O'Faolain, *The Vanishing Hero: Studies in the Novelists of the Twenties* (London, 1956).

The following studies of particular novelists are of value:

*E. M. Forster*

Frederick C. Crews, *E. M. Forster: the Perils of Humanism* (London, 1962).
K. W. Gransden, *E. M. Forster* (Writers and Critics: Edinburgh and London, 1962).
Wilfred Stone, *The Cave and the Mountain* (Stanford, 1966).
Lionel Trilling, *E. M. Forster* (London, 1944).
Malcolm Bradbury (ed.), *Forster: a Collection of Critical Essays* (Engelwood Cliffs, New Jersey, 1966).
Malcolm Bradbury (ed.), *A Passage to India: a Casebook* (London, 1970).

*Aldous Huxley*

John Atkins, *Aldous Huxley* (London, 1956).
Peter Bowering, *Aldous Huxley: A Study of the Major Novels* (London, 1969).

*Wyndham Lewis*

Hugh Kenner, *Wyndham Lewis* (London, 1954).
Geoffrey Wagner, *Wyndham Lewis* (London, 1957).
William H. Pritchard, *Wyndham Lewis* (New York, 1969).

*Virginia Woolf*

Erich Auerbach, *Mimesis* (Princeton, 1953).
Joan Bennett, *Virginia Woolf* (Cambridge, 1945).
E. M. Forster, *Virginia Woolf* (Cambridge, 1941); reprinted in *Two Cheers for Democracy* (London, 1951).
A. D. Moody, *Virginia Woolf* (Writers and Critics: Edinburgh and London, 1963).

See also pp. 48 and 276 for material on Ford Madox Ford and Evelyn Waugh.
Three books on the novel published during the twenties are all of

considerable relevance to this discussion. They are Percy Lubbock, *The Craft of Fiction* (London, 1921), E. M. Forster, *Aspects of the Novel* (London, 1927), and Edwin Muir, *The Structure of the Novel* (London, 1928). See also Virginia Woolf, *A Writer's Diary*, ed. Leonard Woolf (London, 1959). There are some valuable contemporary discussions of the literature of the twenties in *Towards Standards of Criticism*, selected from the *Calender of Modern Letters* by F. R. Leavis (London, 1933). Aspects of fiction are also discussed in William Van O'Connor (ed.) *Forms of Modern Fiction* (Minneapolis, 1948), David Daiches *The Novel and the Modern World* (Chicago, 1960) and Frank Kermode, *The Sense of an Ending* (New York and London, 1967) and *Continuities* (London, 1968).

## 7

## ASPECTS OF THE NOVEL 1930–1960

### Stephen Wall, Keble College, Oxford

In 1930 just over 4,000 books of fiction were published in Britain; about half of these were new titles, the rest being reprints and new editions. In that year fiction formed 27 per cent of the total book production. Except for the inevitable plunge during the war of 1939–1945, the numbers of novels published annually did not fluctuate greatly during the next thirty years: there were 4,222 titles (including 2,353 reprints) in 1939; 3,871 titles (1,463 reprints) in 1951; 4,209 titles (1,820 reprints) in 1960. However, the proportion of books of fiction to the total number of published books declined steadily after the war. In 1940, they formed 34 per cent of the total; in 1950, 22 per cent; and in 1960, 18 per cent. Even so, according to the figures in *Whitaker's Cumulative Book List*, (which appears annually and from which these totals have been taken), it can be calculated that the number of new novels published during the years between 1930 and 1960 was in the region of 60,000.

A great many of these will have been intended as ephemeral entertainment—crime stories, adventure stories, romances, and so on—and only a small proportion of books in this category could survive literary consideration. But even a small proportion of so large a total amounts to a formidable body of respectable work, and it is obvious that no account of it can be both adequate and short. What the following pages try to offer is a brief indication of some of the qualities of a few of the novelists whose work has remained in circulation and may well survive.

All the writers described in this chapter have contributed

something distinctive to the continuing life of the novel, but they are not by any means the only novelists of the period under consideration for whom this could be claimed. Some familiar names do not appear here because their work seems to have been overrated, but more have not found a place simply because there was no room. Discussions of recent literature can easily dwindle into mere *catalogues raisonées*, and it seemed better to attempt—however briefly—that more detailed description and analysis for which summary epithets and cursory annotation are no substitute. In any case, a complete review of a field as crowded as the figures already given indicate is unlikely to be within one critic's competence, and selectivity is probably a condition of his survival. Indeed, surveys which claim to offer a comprehensive history of recent fiction may encourage a premature orthodoxy by the very selections that they are, in fact, making.

The volume of academic commentary on contemporary novels is now so great that instant consecration has become dangerously possible. All literary judgements, no doubt, are interim in nature, but they ought to be particularly so when the works in question have yet to demonstrate their resilience under new historical conditions and changing literary climates. When we try—as we should—to say why certain novelists are important and valuable to us in the present, we should not speak of them as if they had already taken on the established aspect of the past. It is the more important to resist any authoritarian impositions of judgement when they cannot represent the consensus of opinion over a period of time. In this chapter, no special legitimacy is claimed for the selection of subjects for discussion, and any local judgements made in the course of it make no pretence to finality.

As far as the heroic generation of modernism is concerned, a wide measure of agreement has of course become established: whatever one's personal attitude towards, say, Joyce or D. H. Lawrence, it is accepted that they are 'there', that our literary consciousness has been deeply affected by them, that they have become, in a word, classics. That sort of status cannot yet be confidently said to belong to the novelists considered here. Few —perhaps none—of them were or are possessed of the kind of literary genius that by its nature does not occur often. Nevertheless, the best work of the novelists of this period was deeply felt and finely executed, and it justified the continuance of the novel as the dominant literary form of the time.

## Samuel Beckett (b. 1906)

The only one of the novelists now to be reviewed to have direct links with modernism was Samuel Beckett. His novels only became widely circulated after the success of his plays *Waiting for Godot* and *Endgame* in the 1950's, but his first book of fiction —a collection of stories encouragingly titled *More Pricks than Kicks*—had appeared in 1934. His first published novel was *Murphy* (1938), which received slight attention; *Watt* was written during the German occupation of France, but did not appear until 1953. His later novels were first composed in French, and were subsequently translated by Beckett himself and others. The French *Molloy* came out in 1951; its English version followed in 1955. *Malone meurt* (1951) and *L'Innomable* (1953) formed a trilogy which was completed in English by *Malone Dies* (1956) and *The Unnamable* (1958). *Comment C'Est* dates from 1961; *How It Is* appeared in 1964. As John Fletcher and others have shown, the English versions can often involve considerable revision of the original French texts, and they can certainly be considered as re-creations rather than mere translations.

Samuel Beckett was born near Dublin in 1906, went to teach at the École Normale Supérieure in Paris in 1928, and abandoned an academic career three years later. Beckett became an associate of James Joyce, but while his work continues the modernist tradition of radical innovation in form, its increasingly painful content is quite contrary to Joyce's celebratory and affirmative attitudes. Indeed, while Joyce tried to ingest into his fiction ever larger areas of experience, Beckett has taken the opposite course of an increasing exclusiveness; in his latest works human beings are reduced to disembodied voices.

Already in *Murphy* many of the traditional assumptions and techniques of fiction are mocked and subverted. Murphy is a 'seedy solipsist' who, after a pleasantly inactive period living on the immoral earnings of Celia, finds a congenial refuge in a mental hospital, the Magdalen Mental Mercyseat. Murphy envies the patients, and thinks of them 'not as banished from a system of benefits but as escaped from a colossal fiasco', and is encouraged by 'the absolute impassiveness of the higher schizoids, in the face of the most pitiless therapeutic bombardment'. The other characters in the novel are presented with much comic vitality and even, in the case of Celia, with some tenderness. Some of Beckett's ruling pre-occupations begin to emerge: the confused mental processes of Mr. Kelly, for example, are an early sign of Beckett's obsession with the state of senility. Even the natural world of *Murphy* amusingly anticipates that state of run-down later to become general:

> The sheep were a miserable-looking lot, dingy, close-cropped, undersized and misshapen. They were not cropping, they were not ruminating, they did not even seem to be taking their ease. They simply stood, in an attitude of profound dejection, their heads bowed, swaying slightly as though dazed ... they seemed one and all on the point of collapse.

*Murphy* is full of philosophic references and obscure scholastic jokes, but in this novel as in its successors it is important to resist the temptation to treat these as clues to a conceptual, 'real' meaning. Ultimately, Beckett's novels are explorations of areas of experience with which philosophy is powerless to cope. Not that his characters—who, however destitute, often have about them the relics of what was once a good education —do not sometimes take a mordant pleasure in such beguiling though futile intellectual disciplines as mathematical calculation; counting, as one of them exclaims, is 'one of the few pleasures in life'.

*Watt* is particularly haunted by the possibilities of series, and is pre-occupied with the meticulous contemplation of contingencies. But its scrupulous analyses never lead to firm conclusions, and are in any case applied to utterly arbitrary situations. Watt spends much of his time in the service of Mr. Knott trying to deduce a few comforting laws from the apparently random nature of his employer's activities, but the results, as Beckett laconically says, 'were meagre':

> One of the first things that Watt learned by these means was that Mr. Knott sometimes rose late and retired early, and sometimes rose very late and retired very early, and sometimes did not rise at all, nor at all retire, for who can retire who does not rise? What interested Watt here was this, that the earlier Mr. Knott rose the later he retired, and that the later he rose the earlier he retired. But between the hour of his rising and the hour of his retiring there seemed no fixed correlation, or one so abstruse that it did not exist, for Watt.

Much of the novel is taken up with similarly inconclusive speculations in which the unreliability of all information and the impenetrability of all occurrences are paradoxically presented in prose of the greatest lucidity and elegance.

Such enquiries help to pass the time—the one thing of which

225

Beckett's characters have more than enough—but they cannot protect them or us from the Swiftian precision with which human misery is catalogued. The members of the 'fortunate family' of Lynch include

> . . . Tom Lynch, widower, aged eighty-five years, confined to his bed with constant undefined pains in the caecum . . . his only surviving daughter May Sharpe, widow, aged sixty-two years, in full possession of all her faculties with the exception of that of vision. Then there was Joe's wife née Doyly-Byrne, aged sixty-five years, a sufferer from Parkinson's palsy but otherwise very fit and well . . .

The ennumeration of disability remorselessly accumulates for ever three pages. Beckett does more justice to such woes in his novels than in his plays, and the violence and obscenity they contain are a sign of the courage with which he has faced the intensity of human distress. The fascinating loquacity of Beckett's heroes should not distract us from the appalling nature of their situations, or the cruelty of which they show themselves capable.

Molloy's story takes up half the novel named after him, and he presents it with a verbal force that contrasts with his physical decline. Probably the nearest character in the novels to the tramps or *clochards* of *Waiting for Godot*, he is engaged in a quest for his mother—although in view of his own advanced years the possibility of his mother's still being extant seems remote; at any rate, he does not find her. Molloy spends some time in permutations of the *Watt* type—how to transfer sixteen stones from one pocket to another in a satisfying order, for instance—but he is increasingly pre-occupied with the problems created by the shortening and stiffening of his legs. Molloy's stoic resilience in the face of disabling and disgusting handicaps is noble in its way, but he is not allowed the benefit of any sentiment. He is capable, even in his decrepit state, of shocking violence. When he meets a stranger in the forest who tries to detain him, Molloy knocks him down with a crutch.

> Seeing he had not ceased to breathe I contented myself with giving him a few warm kicks in the ribs, with my heels . . . I carefully chose the most favourable position, a few paces from the body, with my back of course turned to it. Then, nicely balanced on my crutches, I began to swing, backwards, forwards, feet pressed together, or rather legs pressed together, for how could I press my feet together, with my legs in the

state they were? But how could I press my legs together, in the state they were? I pressed them together, that's all I can tell you. Take it or leave it . . . I swung, that's all that matters, in an ever-widening arc, until I decided the moment had come and launched myself forward with all my strength . . . I rested a moment . . . took up my position on the other side of the body and applied myself with method to the same exercise. I always had a mania for symmetry.

In *Malone Dies* the truculent pedantry and Irish inflections of Molloy's manner modulate into a style with a greater emotional range and flexibility. Malone, a reincarnation of Molloy (each Beckett hero has relations of some kind with his predecessors), is lying on what he is quite sure is his death-bed. While waiting for his demise, he starts to tell himself some stories; intended to be soothing, Malone's fitfully pursued fictions finally coalesce into a conclusion of frightening power, and the book ends as Malone ends. It is what he had earlier looked forward to as 'no ordinary last straw'. Malone's stories are partly parodies of standard types of narrative, and as such he finds them agonizingly tedious, but, as he says, 'there's no use indicting words, they are no shoddier than what they peddle'. Other topics which keep Malone just going are speculations about the room he is in and the nature of those responsible for its minimal services, and stray personal memories. Some of these are recalled in language of an almost Wordsworthian simplicity and intensity:

When I stop, as just now, the noises begin again, strangely loud, those whose turn it is. So that I seem to have again the hearing of my boyhood. Then in my bed, in the dark, on stormy nights, I could tell from one another, in the outcry without, the leaves, the boughs, the groaning trunks, even the grasses and the house that sheltered me. Each tree had its own cry, just as no two whispered alike, when the air was still. I heard afar the iron gates clashing and dragging at their posts and the wind rushing between their bars. There was nothing, not even the sand on the paths, that did not utter its cry. The still nights too, still as the grave as the saying is, were nights of storm for me, clamorous with countless pantings.

However, Malone is very ready sardonically to depreciate such lyricism, and there is generally in Beckett's later novels a constant struggle between the gratuitous beauty and power that he cannot help giving to his prose, and the increasing intransigence of his attempts to present 'nothing . . . with the utmost formal distinctness' (the phrase occurs in *Watt*). One of Beckett's reasons for turning to French was the feeling that it would be easier to write in it 'without style', but in fact the distinction of his language has proved impossible to suppress; the authority of his style has played a large part in making his vision of life and its accompanying metaphors so influential.

*The Unnamable* is probably the most painful of Beckett's works. The Unnamable's situation is one of extreme isolation, immobility, and anguish; he weeps continually. He disowns Beckett's earlier heroes:

> All these Murphys, Molloys and Malones do not fool me. They have made me waste my time, suffer for nothing . . . I thought I was right in enlisting these sufferers of my pains. I was wrong. They never suffered my pains, their pains are nothing, compared to mine, a mere tittle of mine, the tittle I thought I could put from me, in order to witness it.

The struggle of words against the implacable silence, the compulsion to say words 'as long as there are any' under intolerably encapsulated conditions, lead *The Unnamable*, as Beckett himself realized, to 'complete disintegration'. However, *How It Is*—where the language has broken down into short paragraphs of panted phrases run together and issuing from a grovelling world of mud and darkness—illustrates those powers of linguistic recovery which the author so deeply distrusts. Despite its extreme austerity, this book remains an astonishing, even if hardly rewarding, example of what can be salvaged by that 'literature' whose seductions Molloy once congratulated himself on resisting.

## *Graham Greene* (b. 1904)

Graham Greene is probably more widely read than any comparable novelist of his generation, and he is one of the few contemporary English writers with a world reputation. His serious works have continually been interspersed with what he calls his 'entertainments', but nearly all his novels involve the use of popular narrative formulas acceptable to a large audience. His first published work, *The Man Within* (1929), although uncharacteristically historical, was about a man on the run, and he was followed by a succession of fugitive heroes in such novels as *A Gun for Sale* (1936) and *The Power and the Glory* (1940). The spy story, the crime novel, and the political thriller lie behind both an 'entertainment' such as *The Confidential Agent*

(1939) and more ambitious books like *Brighton Rock* (1938) and *The Quiet American* (1955). A common theme links both the priest's compassion for his flock in *The Power and the Glory* and Scobie's pity in *The Heart of the Matter* (1948) with Rowe's mercy-killing in *The Ministry of Fear* (1943), a war-time melodrama. Seen retrospectively, the entertainments sometimes look like sketches for later and weightier works: *Our Man in Havana* (1958), a comedy of corruption in Cuba, was followed by *The Comedians* (1966), a much grimmer account of oppression in Haiti.

Many of Greene's novels have been filmed (with particular success in the case of *The Third Man*), and his narrative technique has much in common with cinematic methods: compare, for instance, *Stamboul Train* (1932) with the film *The Lady Vanishes*, or consider the Hitchcockian opening of *The Ministry of Fear*, in which an apparently reassuring fête in a London square turns sinister. Another attraction has been the widely dispersed nature of Greene's fictional backgrounds. His books are rather more likely to be set in Sweden, Mexico, the Congo, Saigon or Cuba than in Brighton or London. Greene has been an inveterate traveller, and he also has the good journalist's gift for being on the scene just before the crisis breaks. *The Quiet American* so remarkably anticipates the problems of the American presence in Vietnam that it has kept its topicality for over a decade. Some of his earlier novels vividly catch the atmosphere and public anxieties that now seem so characteristic of the 1930's. His books have a natural continuity with the world of headlines and newsreels.

The popular elements in Greene's novels have been deployed in a thoroughly professional way; his narratives are usually straightforward and involve a good measure of action and suspense. Admittedly, the time-scheme in *The Quiet American* is complex, but perhaps Greene counted on a familiarity with the highly sophisticated use of flashbacks found in films. In any case the action, though dislocated, all leads to the resolution of the simple question raised at the outset: how and why did Alden Pyle, the quiet American, come to die? Greene's prose style is one in which tendencies to morbid lyricism and to aphorism are toughly reined back in the interests of readability. Greene's novels, in short, do not—by their literary manners—insinuate that they ought to be read in a highbrow state of mind.

Greene's novelistic efficiency has ensured an easy and successful reception for a fictional world that is, in fact, intensely personal, even obsessive. This world is instantly recognizable, and is sometimes insisted on to the point of self-parody. Physically, it is shabby, sweaty and squalid (Greene's evocation of dreary pleasures taken in third-rate hotels is sometimes remicent of the atmosphere of another 'cinematic' writer, Simenon). The world of Greene's entertainments probably owes a good deal to Conrad's *The Secret Agent*. Metaphysically, this world is utterly fallen—one which might have been created, as the Manicheans believed, by the devil. Only God's compassion, however, could be equal to a state of such general misery. The nature of the connection in Greene's mind between the wretchedness of life and the love of God is clearly made in a well-known passage from *The Heart of the Matter*, which is set in British West Africa:

> Nobody here could ever talk about heaven on earth. Heaven remained rigidly in its proper place on the other side of death, and on this side flourished the injustices, the cruelties, the meannesses that elsewhere people so cleverly hushed up. Here you could love human beings nearly as God loved them, knowing the worst: you didn't love a pose, a pretty dress, a sentiment artfully assumed.

Greene's preference for places where what he feels to be the residual conditions of life are sharply exposed has probably had much to do with his choice of such subjects as the persecution of priests in Mexico in *The Power and the Glory*, an African leper-colony in *A Burnt-Out Case* (1961), and the brutal tyranny of the Duvalier regime in Haiti in *The Comedians*. Nevertheless, the vision holds bad nearer home, as Pinkie, the boy-gangster hero of *Brighton Rock*, insists:

> '. . . it's the only thing that fits. These atheists, they don't know nothing. Of course there's Hell, Flames and damnation,' he said with his eyes on the dark shifting water and the lightning and the lamps going out above the black struts of the Palace Pier, 'torments.'

Graham Greene became a Catholic before he began publishing novels, and he is unusual among English writers in that in his work Catholicism is the normal faith of his characters. His own religious pre-occupations, however, are continually in evidence, partly reflected in situations that almost become personal clichés: the recurring figure of the priest who has lost his *amour-prêtre*; the nagging problem of marital breakdown and the impossibility of divorce. Greene is not didactic; he seems to use Christian terms to express, even to justify, a temperament whose bias was established well before his conversion—as his autobiographical essays, 'The Lost Childhood' and 'The Revolver in the Corner Cupboard' make clear. Behind his work lies a persistent sense of loneliness and homesickness, of a boredom so fixed that it becomes synonymous with despair. 'He felt the loyalty we all feel to unhappiness—the sense that that is where we really belong' (*The Heart of the Matter*). And however much this feeling may be construed theologically as an apprehension of 'perfect evil walking the world where perfect good can never walk again' ('The Lost Childhood'), it involves Greene's characters in fates that are doctrinally difficult to resolve. Several of them choose sin, choose damnation, out of pity and as a demonstration of human solidarity. As the whisky-priest—a corrupted man who has betrayed his office—says, in *The Power and the Glory*:

'. . . Why do you think I tell people out of the pulpit that they're in danger of damnation if death catches them unawares? I'm not telling them fairy stories I don't believe myself. I don't know a thing about the mercy of God: I don't know how awful the human heart looks to Him. But I do know this—that if there's ever been a single man in this state damned, then I'll be damned too . . . I just want justice, that's all.'

Scobie, the hero of *The Heart of the Matter*, dies in mortal sin since he commits suicide, but his motives include a compassionate desire to stop giving pain—to his wife, to his mistress, and to Christ. Will he be damned for his 'loyalty' to 'unhappiness'? Father Rank says to his widow '. . . don't imagine that you—or I—know a thing about God's mercy.' The epigraph to this novel, taken from Péguy, reflects the emphasis of Greene's thinking during the middle period of his career: 'Le pécheur est au coeur même de chrétianité . . .' (the sinner is at the very heart of Christianity).

Such doctrinal open-endedness leaves these novels accessible to both Catholic and non-Catholic audiences. In *The End of the Affair* (1951), however, the theological argument is more insistent: the narrator's affair with a married woman is ended when, during an air-raid, she begs God for his survival. Her prayer is answered (as Scobie's prayer for the peaceful release of a suffering child is answered in *The Heart of the Matter*), and the lover's rival thus becomes God—to whom he is consequently forced to yield some reluctant recognition.

With *The Quiet American* and its successors, Greene has seen the theme of commitment to human wretchedness more in moral and political terms. His heroes have been in the mould of Fowler in that novel—a not particularly sympathetic news-man living in Saigon, whose initial position is one of detach-ment:

> 'I'm not involved. Not involved,' I repeated. It had been an article of my creed. The human condition being what it was, let them fight, let them love, let them murder, I would not be involved. My fellow journalists called themselves correspon-dents; I preferred the title of reporter. I wrote what I saw: I took no action—even an opinion is a kind of action.

Fowler's non-partisan position is eroded partly by his hatred of the suffering caused by war, partly by his disgust at Alden Pyle's infatuation with naive political abstractions which makes him indifferent to such suffering, and partly by the quiet Ameri-can's attempt to marry his Vietnamese mistress. Fowler becomes as engaged as Pyle, and is implicated in his death; as one of the character says, 'Sooner or later, one has to take sides. If one is to remain human.' In *The Comedians* Brown, another unsym-pathetic narrator and the owner of a decaying hotel in Haiti, is finally driven by the intolerableness of the suffering around him into small, shabby gestures of commitment.

One of the Comedians is Major Jones (his rank, like the rest of his history, is doubtful), the latest in a long line of drifters and failures; Minty in *England Made Me* (1935) and Harris in *The Heart of the Matter* are others. They show a pathetic loyalty to the old school and the miseries of their adolescence, and they represent a further modulation of Greene's nostalgia for un-happiness. Their presentation is largely comic, and Greene's humour—generally sardonic though latterly more urbane—has been under-rated. Even the quiet American, mainly offered as an example of the lethal properties of innocence, is also a figure of a grim sort of fun.

To share the joke, however, the reader has to side with the narrator, and most of Greene's novels are in fact or in effect written in the first person. While this assists narrative concen-tration and intensity, it also inhibits the fictional possibilities of relationships. The egoism of many of his heroes is not the less for being freely confessed and deplored. Greene's heroes, like the novelist himself, present enclosed and private landscapes as if they really were the public, accessible world.

*Evelyn Waugh* (b. 1903–d. 1966)

Evelyn Waugh's reputation as a writer offering a new type of heartless comedy was established by his first novel *Decline and Fall* (1928), and confirmed by its successors *Vile Bodies* (1930) and *Black Mischief* (1932). As a comedy of manners, *Vile Bodies* provides a definitive version of the life-style of the 'Bright Young Things' of the 1920's who—encouraged by gossip columns in the popular press—restlessly pursue novel social situations which they will fabricate rather than do without. A slight plot concerns the ineffectual efforts of the hero to lay his hands on enough money to marry—efforts to which his fiancée hardly contributes more than bored acquiescence. The book proliferates rather than progresses : few of Waugh's novels, in fact, have a strong forward movement. At the end of *Vile Bodies* a perfunctory attempt is made to suggest the holocaust that its trivial generation will provoke and deserve, but in the actual conduct of the book Waugh preserves the ferocious detachment common in his early work.

*Decline and Fall* is a more successful exercise in this terse manner, in which clipped dialogue (a smart idiom of the period also to be found in Anthony Powell's *Afternoon Men* and the earlier plays of Noel Coward) is accompanied by an ostensibly neutral exposition. A strong authorial presence nevertheless makes itself felt through offensive inflections of tone, damaging asides, and sudden, gratuitously cruel swerves of plot. Paul Pennyfeather, the extremely light-weight hero of *Decline and Fall*, is a modest, serious young man who has the misfortune to be debagged by dining-club drunks in his Oxford college. Sent down, he teaches at a dubious private school in Wales, and then becomes tutor to one of the boys and fiancé of his flagrantly rich mother, Margot Beste-Chetwynde. In his innocence, Paul fails to realize that she is deeply involved in the South American White Slave traffic, and he suffers for her misdeeds in the Egdon Heath Penal Settlement. He is soon retrieved and returns under a light disguise to his old and unsuspecting college.

Paul is certainly an innocent encountering the wickedness of the world, but the world of *Decline and Fall* is too fantastic and arbitrary to serve any coherent satirical purpose, nor has Waugh at this stage a sufficiently defined attitude to his material on which any radical critique could be based. The novel is animated by grotesque characters whose monstrousness is made acceptable by their intense energy and resilience, and by

233

Waugh's success in finding for them appropriate idioms of speech. Such 'dynamic' figures as Captain Grimes or Mrs. Beste-Chetwynde (in later novels Lady Metroland) totally evade moral considerations; indeed, Waugh clearly takes pleasure in their predatory exploitation of social anarchy. Any sympathy theoretically available to Paul as the hero is neutralized by the author's mockery of his spinelessness—consider the feebleness of Paul's response to his entirely unjust conviction: 'His sentence of seven years' penal servitude was rather a blow'.

Paul is said to be a 'static' character, and it is best for him to keep out of things—an inaction to which Waugh's later heroes often find themselves condemned. Like them he is caught between allegiance to an inherited code and the practices of a changed world in which it appears anarchronistic and inapplicable:

He had 'done the right thing' in shielding the woman: so much was clear, but Margot had not quite filled the place assigned to her, for in this case she was grossly culpable, and he was shielding her, not from misfortune nor injustice, but from the consequence of her crimes; he felt a flush about his knees as Boy Scout honour whispered that Margot had got him into a row and ought jolly well to own up and face the music. As he sat over his post-bags he had wrestled with this argument without achieving any satisfactory result except a growing conviction that there was something radically inapplicable about this whole code of ready-made honour. . . . On the other hand was the undeniable cogency of Peter Beste-Chetwynde's 'You can't see Mamma in prison, can you?' The more Paul considered this, the more he perceived it to be the statement of a natural law.

The unthinking cynicism and brittle hedonism of London society is presented much more severely in *A Handful of Dust* (1934). Tony Last is the complacent inheritor of Hetton Abbey, an extreme example of the Victorian Gothic country house in which each bedroom is named after an Arthurian character. Brenda, his Guinevere, develops a fondness for a superfluous London drone called Beaver, and spends an increasing amount of time in town with him. When her son is accidentally killed she feels she has no further ties with Hetton which she never could stand anyway, and asks for a divorce. Tony adopts the Victorian solution for disappointed love and sets off to discover a lost city in South America, where he is finally trapped and permanently confined by the sinister half-caste Mr. Todd, who insists on

234

interminable readings from Dickens. In England, Tony is presumed dead; Brenda re-marries—though not to Beaver—and some energetic cousins take over and develop Hetton.

Brenda and her London circle are shown as unspeakably selfish and her lover is clearly hopeless, but Waugh seems to have a more ambiguous attitude to Tony. The whole affair is, as one of the chapter titles indicates, 'Hard Cheese on Tony'; he genuinely suffers for the specious diversion of others. At the same time, Tony is insensitive to others because he is too deeply sunk in the dream of English Gothic for which Hetton is the romanticized scene. When his marriage breaks up, he feels that

A whole Gothic world had come to grief . . . there was now no armour glittering through the forest glades, no embroidered feet on the green sward; the cream and dappled unicorns had fled . . .

The legendary city he later seeks in the jungle is

. . . Gothic in character, all vanes and pinnacles, gargoyles, battlements, groining and tracery, pavilions and terraces, a transfigured Hetton, pennons and banners floating on the sweet breeze, everything luminous and translucent . . . a tapestry landscape filled with heraldic and fabulous animals and symmetrical, disproportionate blossom.

But this 'transfigured Hetton' can only provide sanctuary for him in delirium. Waugh views Tony's 'delight and exultation' in what Hetton stands for with much sympathy, but metes out a savage punishment to him for so foolishly trusting such an anachronism. The remarkable tension and economy of style in *A Handful of Dust* suggests that Waugh was deeply involved in and baffled by this *impasse*.

A similar dilemma reappears in a later novel, *Brideshead Revisited* (1945), but it is there handled with much less discipline. In this novel Waugh's Catholicism was explicit and expounded for the first time, although he had been received into the Roman church in 1930. It brought him a wider audience at the price of increased critical hostility from those unsympathetic to the novel's religious and class allegiances. According to Waugh himself, the theme of *Brideshead Revisited* is 'the operation of divine grace on a group of diverse but closely connected characters'; the connections intended to reveal this significance are between Charles Ryder, the narrator, and various members of the family of the Marquis of Marchmain. One son, Sebastian, is Ryder's friend at an indulgently remembered Oxford (which seems nearer to Max Beerbohm's *Zuleika Dobson* than to any recollectable reality); a married daughter, Julia, is later Ryder's mistress and might have become his wife had not the unexpectedly 'good death' of Lord Marchmain recalled her to Catholic obedience and duty.

The Brideshead family and house present in its most caressed form Waugh's consoling myth of a Catholic aristocracy, but even in this novel, written during the war in a mood of unbridled nostalgia (Waugh later admitted that he 'piled it on rather'), the cult of the ancestral house cannot protect its inmates from the modern world, although it may bring them nearer to God. However, Waugh concedes this point so reluctantly that it can hardly be said to be fairly made.

The trilogy, *Sword of Honour*—made up of *Men at Arms* (1952), *Officers and Gentlemen* (1955), and *Unconditional Surrender* (1961)—is an extended treatment of the experience during the second world war of another upper-class, Catholic hero. Guy Crouchback incredulously asks someone else if he seriously believes that God's Providence concerns itself with the perpetuation of the English Catholic aristocracy, but the tendency of the trilogy is to affirm that, among other things, it does. Crouchback, demoralized by the collapse of his marriage and living idly in Italy, sees the call to arms in 1939 as a crusade against the modern age and an opportunity to regain the honour of his forbears. The war disappoints him, however; he sees serious action only twice. He takes part in the ragged evacuation of Crete, and is involved in an unsatisfactory mission to Jugoslavia. Through various accidents he is reconciled to his wife, and assumes responsibility for her child by a cowardly ex-hairdresser called Trimmer, who has been built up by propaganda as a war hero. This act of charity is real, but it is limited and private; it seems all that the world will allow. Not that Guy grasps opportunities for heroism with much vigour: for all his decency he is a debilitated as well as an obsolete figure, and is often over-shadowed by other characters. Even so, only Apthorpe in *Men at Arms* has the old comic vitality of Waugh's earlier grotesques. The humour of the barbarous Brigadier Ritchie-Hook, for instance, is forced and juvenile, and such characters as Trimmer (the name, as often in Waugh, is facilely suggestive) have an almost allegorical thinness. The function of the writer Ludovic, too, seems not to have been clearly envisaged by the author.

The large ambitions of *Sword of Honour* are undercut by its narrow sympathies. Its occasionally truculent and essentially defensive attitudes are too much the product of impatience and discomfort for its successes to be other than local. *The Loved One* (1948), a savage farce about Californian burial rites, was a reminder that Waugh wrote better within clear formal limits and in a consistent tone of aggressive distaste.

The last novel in which members of Waugh's pre-war repertory appeared was *Put Out More Flags* (1942), but in the same year he published a novel-fragment under the title *Work Suspended* which interestingly seems to predict his inability to come to settled terms with a world transformed by war and social change. Although it leaves narrative ends untied, the two parts of *Work Suspended* are remarkably self-sufficient. In the first, 'A Death', the narrator—a self-satisfied writer of high-class detective stories—recalls his relationship with his father, who represents a world that died in 1939. In the second part, he falls in love with his friend's pregnant wife; he responds in a confused way to the birth of her baby a few days before the outbreak of war. This narrator is unusually independent of the novelist, and the work holds a poised sense of possibilities rare in an author whose presence is normally so assertive—even when his attitudes remain ambivalent.

*Anthony Powell* (b. 1905)

Although Anthony Powell's first novel *Afternoon Men* (1931) has some clear affinities with Evelyn Waugh's early fiction, and although their subsequent work often deals with similar social milieux, their essential attitudes are very different. *Afternoon Men* is a comedy, largely conducted in trite dialogue, of raffish behaviour and enervated morals on the bohemian fringe of London society; although comparable with *Vile Bodies* or *A Handful of Dust*, its tone and manner are more deeply impersonal. The novel makes no judgement on the life its depicts, but is rather an exercise in a style in which laconicism, ironic understatement, and moral neutrality are the main features.

In the five comedies which Powell published during the 1930s there are some signs of the mature interests and techniques later to be embodied in his post-war novel sequence, *The Music of Time* : *Afternoon Men* appropriately begins with a party, a social occasion of the type that Powell was often to use later; *From a View to a Death* (1933) has a hero who sees himself as a man of the will in a way that anticipates subsequent characters; and the narrator of *What's Become of Waring?* (1939) shows signs of developing the characteristic tone of *The Music of Time's* presenter, Nicholas Jenkins. But when Powell inaugurated this series of novels with *A Question of Upbringing* in 1951, it became clear that—whatever the continuities between it and his previous fiction—he was now working on an entirely different scale.

By 1968 nine volumes of *The Music of Time* had appeared. It reflects the course of Nicholas Jenkins's life but it is not in any strict sense a chronicle, being a discontinuous narrative, often discursive in manner and always selective in its episodes. It does, however, follow a roughly chronological order : *A Question of Upbringing* takes place at school (not named but apparently Eton) and at Oxford University in the 1920s; in *A Buyer's Market* (1952) and *The Acceptance World* (1955) Jenkins has moved to London and is working for a publisher; the next two novels —*At Lady Molly's* (1957) and *Casanova's Chinese Restaurant* (1960)—explore various circles in London during the 1930s; Jenkins works for a time in the film business, marries, and becomes established as a writer. In *The Kindly Ones* (1962) war begins to loom largely, and the trilogy, *The Valley of Bones* (1964), *The Soldier's Art* (1966), and *The Military Philosophers* (1968) deal with Jenkins's experiences in the army (and can thus be compared with Waugh's *Sword of Honour*).

Powell's procedure and to some extent his manner recalls Proust's *A La Recherche du Temps Perdu*, but the degree to which *The Music of Time* imitates the French work can easily be exaggerated (the important French influence, if any, could well be Stendhal). Apart from its clear relation to the English tradition of social comedy and its native tendency to present every man in his humour, Powell's work is conspicuously pragmatic and unphilosophical in its approach to memory and time. The emphasis is not on Jenkins's private life and interior feelings, but on his response to the proliferating and often recurring series of characters with whom he comes at various times into contact. At first, in *A Question of Upbringing*, Jenkins is shown in relation to three of his school contemporaries—Stringham, Templar, and Widmerpool. They reappear at intervals in the novels that follow : Stringham, for instance, declines into alcoholism after the collapse of his marriage and his failure in business, is then cured and is surprisingly discovered serving as a mess waiter in the army. Templar, like Widmerpool, goes into the city without attending university; in *The Acceptance World* Jenkins has a love affair with Templar's wife. Widmerpool, without being specially liked by Jenkins, dogs his life throughout, turning up at all sort of junctures. But these characters are elsewhere superseded by others with which Jenkins becomes friendly, by family acquaintances of long standing, and by connections forced on him by circumstances. As the sequence proceeds, one strand of relationship is added to another until a remarkable sense of social fabric is created.

As Jenkins's experience accumulates it continually obliges him to reconsider persons and situations which, formerly seen from one point of view, have later to be reviewed in the light of fresh information. The original estimate of Widmerpool, for example, based on the derisive treatment he received at school, has to be radically revised when important men in the city (such as Sir Magnus Donners) speak of him with respect. Stray remarks or chance encounters will reveal unsuspected facets of the past: in *The Kindly Ones* Jenkins stumbles on the reasons behind Jean Templar's behaviour during their affair ten years earlier. Jenkins constantly contrasts attitudes and opinions, bringing remembered judgements to bear on new evidence. The need for such modification is the justification for the fastidious finesse of Powell's style—a style which nevertheless sometimes gets trapped in a Micawberish orotundity.

Such complex correlations are achieved by leaving out much that is normally included by novelists who have contracted what P. G. Wodehouse once called 'the saga habit'. The historical background of *The Music of Time*—the slump, the Spanish civil war, and so on—has usually to be inferred from its effect on individual persons; even the second world war is obliquely treated. The author provides no discernible political or religious perspective (although he is obviously affected by his literary pursuits and upper-class affiliations). Ideas generally appear as aspects of character. Even physical description is severely restricted. Jenkins's own life has to be understood as a mere premise to the narrative; he further justifies the absence of any treatment of his married life by claiming that so complex a subject simply cannot be written about, that it 'finally defies definition' (*Casanova's Chinese Restaurant*).

One of the achievements of *The Music of Time* is its creation of a plausible and multifarious fictional world without apparent recourse to authorial omniscience. The reader's knowledge does not outstrip Jenkins's, and although Jenkins is clearly highly observant and socially at ease with a wide range of people, he is not endowed with an unnatural degree of penetration or prescience. We encounter the other characters as they affect Jenkins, but his sensitivity as a recording medium, his alertness to nuance and implication, make the discipline that Powell imposes on himself viable. Jenkins's honesty with himself and his acknowledgement of how much remains unknown prompts many passages like this:

> However, when it became clear that Eleanor did not much like him, I found myself, I hardly knew why, assuring her that Widmerpool, at school and in France, had always been quite an amiable eccentric; though I could not explain, then or now, why I felt his defence a duty; still less why I should have arbitrarily attributed to him what was, after all, an almost wholly imaginary personality: in fact one in many respects far from accurate. At that time I still had very little idea of Widmerpool's true character: neither its qualities nor defects.
>
> (A Buyer's Market)

Such reflections and such admissions inspire a certain kind of trust.

Jenkins may be in some ways a colourless character, but he has an encouraging sense of the density and the inscrutability of other people; he does not shrink from 'the difficulty of understanding, even remotely, why people behave as they do' (*At Lady Molly's*). He accepts the limitations imposed by his own point of view because he feels it is in the nature of things and in the nature of narrative art; after attempting to describe Jean Templar, Jenkins comments:

> But descriptions of a woman's outward appearance can hardly do more than echo the terms of a fashion paper. Their nature can be caught in a refractive beam, as with light passing through water: the rays of character focused through the person with whom they are intimately associated. Perhaps, therefore, I alone was responsible for what she seemed to me.

However, Jenkins does not rely solely on his own observation, and he gathers what he can by collating the opinions of others and by using his connections. (Sillery, the Oxford don who ceaselessly tries to establish personal links which may later be of use to him, in some ways parodies Jenkins's activities). It is a logical consequence of Powell's design that his novels should often concern themselves with social occasions—the first half of *A Buyer's Market*, for instance, is almost entirely devoted to the events of one festive evening. Such assemblies, besides providing opportunities for technical *tours de force* on the author's part, allow Jenkins to observe shifting patterns of relationship under revealing conditions. In one of its aspects, *The Music of Time* is gossip given the condition and status of art (it is appropriate that Anthony Powell should also have written a study of John Aubrey, the 17th century hoarder of anecdote and scandal).

Jenkins's curiosity is wide, but he is especially interested in those who attack life by the exercise of the will, although a quite opposite type—illustrated by such men as the witty, articulate, but indecisive composer Moreland—is personally more congenial to him. The novel-sequence offers a rich collection of egoists : Widmerpool is the prime example, but Uncle Giles, Erridge, and J. G. Quiggin are among many others. Widmerpool's career shows a classic pattern of over-reaching; each time he appears to be scaling some new peak of power or social acceptibility—handicapped as he is by pompous manner and piscine appearance—some unlucky and often ludicrous accident sets him disastrously back. But Jenkins is continually surprised to find, later, that Widmerpool has risen undiminished from humiliation—indeed, there is a suggestion that Widmerpool almost welcomes it. At any rate, he has the rubbery resilience of a true comic creation, although his upward striving takes on less amusing and more sinister aspects as he grows older and more powerful.

Widmerpool's disasters and his over-all development show Powell's integration of the slow-burning comic episode of which he is master (Widmerpool's discomfiture at the Walpole-Wilson dance in *A Buyer's Market*, for instance), with his larger intentions. He remarks, in *A Question of Upbringing*, on 'the general tendency of things to be brought to the level of farce even when the theme is serious enough'. His characters are obliged to dance to the music of time, but they cannot control their steps since they must act out their own natures, without regard for general pattern or decorum. What is serious to them may be absurd to the spectator, but he is, in his turn, bound to appear in an equally vulnerable light to others. The tentative nature of Jenkins's observations and judgements are therefore essential to the whole conduct of *The Music of Time*. Strict adherence to his own point of view is balanced by an open-mindedness that gives the other characters their freedom.

*Joyce Cary* (b. 1886–d. 1957)

The energy and stamina so evident in Joyce Cary's novels were characteristic of the author. In 1920, after six years as a colonial administrator, Cary settled in Oxford in order to write; *Aissa Saved*, his first novel to be published, did not appear until 1932. It followed over a decade of false starts, experiments, and unfinished works (the manuscript fragments of the uncompleted *Cock Jarvis* run to about a million words). By the time of his death, Cary had published fifteen novels—several of them drawing on his African experience—and his last work, *The Captive and the Free*, appeared posthumously in 1959. But even these published novels represent only a fraction of the fiction that Cary actually wrote, since their final form was the result of selective editing from a much larger body of material. Cary himself described his methods:

> I do not write, and never have written, to an arranged plot. The book is composed over the whole surface at once like a picture, and may start anywhere, in the middle or at the end . . . I should think I write about three times the material that finally appears in any book, that is to say, for a novel of about 100,000 words I write at least 300,000. This is of course a fearful waste, and I have tried to avoid it, but it seems to me the only way in which I can get the kind of form I want, a certain balance and unity within a given context.

One of the results of this perversely heroic procedure is the consistency of texture apparent in Cary's best work. In such cases as *A House of Children* (1941)—a largely autobiographical novel recalling Cary's childhood in Northern Ireland—a steadily maintained retrospective tone is valuable. It is similarly important to the success of *Charley Is My Darling* (1940)—a study of the havoc caused by a war-time London evacuee in the West Country—that the child's perspective be consistently conveyed. But the 'balance and unity' of which Cary speaks is particularly vital to the two trilogies which form his most substantial achievement, since these two series of first-person narrations by radically differentiated characters are recorded throughout in idioms appropriate to their varied natures. Habits of syntax, patterns of association, turns of phrase and idiosyncrasies of vocabulary are all adjusted to suit and express each protagonist in turn, and Cary's methods clearly helped him—perhaps at the cost of some inflexibility—to sustain these impersonations without flagging.

The first trilogy consists of *Herself Surprised* (1941), *To Be a Pilgrim* (1942), and *The Horse's Mouth* (1944). As well as being richly achieved 'characters', the narrators of each of these novels also stand for fundamental aspects of human nature as Cary came to conceive it. In *Herself Surprised* Sara Monday surveys her checkered progress from a young country-bred kitchenmaid to an elderly if still vigorous house-keeper convicted of fraud. She marries the gentleman of the house where she is in service, shocks the respectable neighbourhood with the loud vulgarity of her behaviour, runs off with Gulley Jimson, an artist who comes to paint her husband's portrait, and ends as the servant and mistress of Thomas Wilcher, a retired lawyer. Although —like Defoe's heroines—she is theoretically penitent, Sara is much more assertive than apologetic. Her sentiments are closer to those of Chaucer's Wife of Bath: 'Unto this day it dooth myn herte boote/ That I had had my world as in my time'. Driven forward 'in the fury of my life'. Sara admits that 'I gave myself up to the sweet world', but because she means no harm she is constantly surprised at the turns her life takes as it responds to the demands of her nature. Sara has a superficial sense of religion and morality, but her behaviour is dictated by the female principle itself, which has little to do with either. As Cary himself commented, 'Her morals were the elementary morals of a primitive woman, of nature herself, which do not change'. Her domestic, nest-building character is constantly kept in view not only by her actions and her comments on them, but also by the kind of imagery she almost too invariably employs:

> The sun was so bright as a new gas-mantle—you couldn't look at it even through your eyelashes, and the sand so bright gold as deep-fried potatoes. The sky was like washed-out Jap silk and there was just a few little clouds coming out on it like down feathers out of an old cushion; the rocks were so warm as new gingerbread cakes and the sea had a melty thick look, like oven glass.

Gulley Jimson, the narrator of *The Horse's Mouth*, responds to Sara's life force as the artist that he essentially is. Some of his nude paintings of her, made in their early days, hang in national art galleries; in the period covered by *The Horse's Mouth*—the last stages of Gulley's life—Sara remains the Eve in his vast designs. Nevertheless Gulley has had to free himself from Sara in order to maintain the artist's independence from the domestic ties with which she was always seeking to bind him, and in the end he is responsible for her death.

Gulley continues to paint up to his own last moments, and resorts to unscrupulous shifts and dodges in order to keep creating. Such episodes as Jimson's occupation and wrecking of the tasteful flat of some titled connoisseurs are presented as farce, and have the orgiastic character which can also be seen in the celebrations of the African clerk Mister Johnson, in the novel named after him, and in the exploits of Charley Brown, in *Charley Is My Darling*. Both of them resemble Jimson in their attempts to mould the external world into the shapes suggested by their imagination. Gulley realizes himself in actions that are increasingly extreme, and this, coupled with the furious pace and agressiveness of the prose of *The Horse's Mouth*, gives the novel an astonishing momentum. Gulley's final act is to attempt a huge mural of the Creation on a wall that is about to collapse. This climactic episode dramatizes the conception of creativity underlying the whole novel, and which is indeed central to Cary's thought.

Jimson continually quotes William Blake, and his own paintings in his last phase may be thought of as aggrandized variations of Blake's visionary works:

> ... I took Blake's Job drawings out of somebody's bookshelf and peeped into them and shut them up again. Like a chap who's fallen down the cellar steps and knocked his skull in and opens a window too quick, on something too big.

For Gulley, Blake's poem 'The Mental Traveller' provides a symbolic account of his relations with Sara. And like Blake, Cary himself tended to see the world in dualistic terms; the title of his last novel, *The Captive and the Free*, was first formulated during the 1920s.

Gulley Jimson is a free man because he trusts absolutely, and at whatever cost to himself and others, in the creative imagination, even though—socially speaking—such an attitude must lead to anarchy. Wilcher, the narrator of *To Be A Pilgrim*, is his opposite: a man bound by tradition and memory, haunted by the evangelical certainties to which his sister sacrificed herself, longing to make some supreme gesture of faith for which he can never summon up enough courage. His deepest impulses are to conserve, and this gives him a sensitivity to English traditions and the historical past that neither Gulley nor Sara possess, but they also inhibit his self-realization. Yet Wilcher too, at the end, comes, in theory at least, to accept the necessity of change, which he characteristically expresses in Bunyanesque terms of pilgrimage. He writes to Sara:

> With you I can make a new life, and unless life be made, it is no life. For we are the children of creation, and we cannot

escape our fate, which is to live in creating and re-creating. We must renew ourselves or die . . . We are the pilgrims who must sleep every night beneath a new sky, for either we go forward to the new camp, or the whirling earth carries us backwards to the one behind. There is no choice but to move . . .

Yet Wilcher is bound by his nature to aspire to rather than to achieve freedom. He is a more complex and divided character than Sara or Gulley, and *To Be A Pilgrim* is accordingly the most subtly organized novel in the first trilogy—especially in its handling of time.

All three protagonists are in various ways eccentric, and it might be felt that Cary jeopardizes the serious acceptance of the fundamental principles they represent by expressing them through persons that are strongly humoured, if not grotesque. But it could also be argued that Cary has learnt the lesson of Dickens, and knows that the exaggerated presentation of characters can guarantee their authenticity when their energy is great enough to make them irresistible. When we say that such characters are larger than life, we mean that they are too big for most novels. In this trilogy, however, Cary's theme was large enough to accomodate the excessive vitality it contains.

The protagonists of the second trilogy are presented with more modification and emerge, perhaps, with less clarity. The pattern of two men fighting for opposing principles of life and also over a woman recurs : Nina, who tells her story in *Prisoner of Grace* (1952), was the first wife of Chester Nimmo, whose early life is recalled in *Except the Lord* (1953), and later married the soldier James Latter, the father of her children and the narrator of *Not Honour More* (1955). Nimmo is a Protestant politician with a spell-binding presence but, in the interests of effective power, he has to stoop to manoeuvre and deception. Latter sees such deviousness as simply crooked, and believes in the simple maintenance of truth, by violence if need be. The whole truth of their inter-relations has to be established by correlating the three separate accounts, and they are less self-sufficient as individual novels than the earlier trilogy.

*The Moonlight* (1946) is another attempt to build a novel round three representative lives; Victorian notions of duty conflict with modern ideas of sexual emancipation. *A Fearful Joy* (1949) chronicles the eventful life of Tabitha Baskett, who passes through a number of historically significant environments; again the interest lies in the struggle between the inevitability of change, resistance to change, and the satisfaction of the imagination in change. The pace of *A Fearful Joy* (written, like some other novels by Joyce Cary, in the rarely used historic present tense) is extremely reckless, and its headlong career from the late Victorian age to post-war society must pay some price in superficiality. Its last page, however, in which the elderly Tabitha is seized with laughter at the sight of a square child yelling its head off in the park—a laughter so profound that it strains her heart—powerfully strikes a characteristically affirmative note. This capacity for joy and this confidence in the world distinguishes Joyce Cary from most of his contemporaries and is typical of his almost anachronistic vigour.

## Henry Green (b. 1905)

Like most of his work, Henry Green's second novel *Living* (1929) adopts an unconventional approach to its subject. It deals with life in a Birmingham factory, and with the lives of those who work in the factory whether as craftsmen or managers, but it is not in any self-consciously sociological sense a study of industrial conditions. It clearly reflects the author's own experience of working in the family firm of which he later became managing director ('Henry Green' is the pseudonym of Henry Vincent Yorke), but the novel is almost disconcertingly free from any philosophy of labour, capital, and industrial relations. The characters may have social attitudes that are true to type, but for the author the world of *Living* is 'given'.

In fact, Henry Green's characters are like the novels in which they appear in that they seem to have remarkably little speculative life; religion does not even cross their minds, and their politics have to be inferred; they are not troubled by abstract notions and hardly by moral principles. Henry Green is primarily a novelist of states of feeling, and with his essentially lyrical quality goes a refusal to consider many of the implications of his material. He approaches situations and events, towards which most writers would have felt obliged to define and display their attitudes, in a curiously oblique manner. *Party Going* (published in September 1939, the month the Second World War broke out) could be—and has been—considered as a portrait of a society in decay, an allegory of an *ancien régime* condemned by its own triviality. The story, which is no more than an episode, concerns the congregation of a party of smart, young and rich people held up by fog at a London railway terminus, prior to their departure for a continental holiday. They retire to the station hotel from which they can survey the waiting crowds below. But although a summary of the novel might make it seem simply a critique of the irresponsible rich, in the book as written, satire is only one element, and not a dominant one, in a complex of modes. The reflections of Alex, waiting in the station hotel, are typical of the novel's tempered judgements:

> Here he pointed his moral. That is what it is to be rich, he thought, if you are·held up, if you have to wait then you can do it after a bath in your dressing-gown and if you have to die then not as any bird tumbling dead from its branch down for the foxes, light and stiff, but here in bed, here inside, with doctors to tell you it is all right and with relations to ask if it hurts. Again no standing, no being pressed together, no worry since it did not matter if one went or stayed, no fellow feeling, true, and once more sounds came up from outside to make him think they were singing, no community singing he said to himself, not that even if it did mean fellow feeling.

In *Party Going* wealth not only separates the few from the many and encourages idle, boring lives; it also produces the beauty of women like Amabel, 'sanctified' by celebrity.

*Concluding* (1948) can also be seen as prophetic. It is set in the future in a state home for girls who are to be trained as servants, and follows a day in the life of Mr. Rock, once a scientist of great reputation and now living in retirement in a cottage on the institution's estate. But although it may well incorporate Green's own feelings about the dangers of official regimentation and resentment at the intrusion of public organizations into what ought to remain inviolable areas of private life, the novel is not a tract for its times in the sense that its contemporary, Orwell's *1984* was meant to be. Where it is not imaginatively self-sufficient, *Concluding* is not so much a warning against state intervention as a celebration of the individual's ability to survive and evade it.

In Green's wartime novels—*Caught* (1943), *Loving* (1945), and *Back* (1946)—the war exists as a premise to the action, or peripheral to it. *Caught* reflects Green's own experience in the Auxiliary Fire Service during the bombing of London, but the blitz —although forming an impressive climax to the novel—does not dominate the book, however deeply it affects some of the characters. The wider issues of the war are not discussed. *Loving* is set in Ireland, a neutral country in which the war seems remote, and although the hero and heroine return to England at the end of the book, we are told that 'they lived happily ever after' (the use of the formula is an indication of the novel's affinities with fairy-tale). *Back* deals with the difficult return of a disabled prisoner of war to civilian life, but the problems of his life are resolved in an essentially private way.

Henry Green's last two novels to date, *Nothing* (1950) and *Doting* (1952), are a return to the 'society' material of *Party Going*, but technically they are distinguished by a rigorous, even doctrinaire, abdication of authorial comment, and are conducted largely in dialogue. It is left very much to the reader what attitude he adopts to the superficial life their characters lead. In *Concluding* was partly a study in youth and age, these two comedies consider youth and middle-age, but they remain innocent of generalizable notions.

In all his books, Green observes a degree of neutrality towards class unusual in an English writer, and remarkable in one with such a wide social range. He has been strikingly successful in suppressing social or moral side-effects in his fiction; we are induced to consider his subjects on his terms. The main means of enforcing this acquiescence is the markedly individual and often idiosyncratic quality of the prose. Green's language has been analysed at length by Edward Stokes in his useful study of the novelist. Green's writing is saved from affectation and factitious elegance by its closeness to the diction of ordinary life, but it is given a peculiar quality partly by syntactical distortions and odd constructions, and partly by an extremely suggestive use of image and symbol. In *Living* a studied use of imagery—often conceits, in fact—is juxtaposed with heightened transcriptions of common-place chat. Here the heroine, Lily Gates, is with her boy-friend at the cinema :

> Later her head was leaning on his shoulder again, like hanging clouds against hills every head in this theatre tumbled without hats against another, leaning everywhere.

On the next page, however, she is presented thus :

> This girl Lily Gates went shopping with basket and by fruiterer's she met Mrs. Eames who stood to watch potatoes on trestle table there. Mrs. Eames carried her baby. Lily Gates said why Mrs. Eames and oh the lovely baby the little lump. She said she saw prices was going up again. She put finger into baby's hand and sang goo-goo.

The omission of definite articles is a constant feature of the style of *Living*, and although the reader comes to accept it easily enough, it indicates a certain self-consciousness of literary intention; Green's later works are evidently composed with great verbal care, but they are also more relaxed. He continues to use as a basis a disingenuously simple style combining colloquial phrases with a fastidiousness quite foreign to their origin, but he adds to this a battery of more elaborate effects. Such passages as this paragraph from *Concluding* do have a narrative function, but they seem also to owe much of their presence to the aesthetic pleasure they give to their author:

> Her grandfather, again in difficulty on account of the treacherous light, but glad of his escape, waded much as though the moon had flooded each Terrace six inches deep. For the spectacles he used seemed milk lensed goggles; while he cautiously lifted boots one after the other in an attempt to avoid cold lit veins of quartz in flagstones underfoot because these appeared to him like sunlight that catches in sharp glass beneath an incoming tide, where the ocean foams ringing an Atlantic.

*Concluding* is unusually rich in scenes like this which have an almost Romantic suggestiveness, and it may partly have been a sense that his writing was becoming too lush that made Green turn to the banal exchanges of *Nothing* and *Doting*. This elaborate, idiosyncratic prose tends to be associated with those moments in his novels when everyday reality becomes invested with a dream-like or hallucinatory quality, becomes a landscape of mythical properties, like the station in *Party Going* or the cemetery in *Back*.

Green's fascination with the possibilities of style is accompanied by a use of symbolism that often seems as much fanciful as earnestly thematic. His most persistent symbols are birds: pigeons in *Living* and *Party Going*; peacocks and doves in *Loving*; starlings in *Concluding*. The pigeons in *Living* are the kind trained by fanciers to return home, and there is an obvious analogy between them and Lily Gates's attempted elopement— but the birds are put to other subtler uses, and their successors in later novels have functions that are less easy to define. Such symbols are also counter-pointed among themselves: the pigeon that kills itself flying into a balustrade at the beginning of *Party Going* is off-set by the gulls that fly away from London out to sea. These birds parallel the situation of the characters, hoping to escape, but frustrated by fog—and perhaps doomed too, since the railway station they wait in is associated with death, burial and the underworld. But such natural life is also true to its own rhythms and keeps its arbitrary spontaneity, and reflects Green's pleasure in what is unpredictable and chancy.

The delicacy of Green's effects is helped by his tendency to restrict the action of his novels in space and time: the activities of *Party Going* only occupy a few hours; those of *Concluding*, one day; the minimal plot of *Loving* all takes place in a Irish country house and its grounds. Henry Green is much less interested in the development of a character over a period of years than in shorter passages of intense experience. However, his novels can survive the conventional test of providing memorable characters. Such men as Mr. Craigan in *Living*, Charley Raunce the Butler in *Loving*, and Mr. Rock in *Concluding*, emerge with a surprising solidity despite Green's evasion of normal methods of description and analysis. The hero of *Caught*, Richard Roe, is less coherently presented than Charley Summers of *Back*: both of them have been shocked by their war experience, but Summers's trauma and recovery are more single-mindedly considered. He benefits too from the simple but powerful symbolism in *Back* which associates his dead love Rose with the roses growing where she is buried, and the 'light of roses' that the pink shade of the bedside lamp spills over the body of Rose's half-sister to whom Charley finally transfers his love at the end of the book. The conclusion of *Back* is a both dazzling and moving example of the kind of effect which justifies the idiosyncrasy of Henry Green's writing.

## Ivy Compton-Burnett (b. 1884 d. 1969)

Ivy Compton-Burnett belongs to that rare kind of novelist who finds out early what her subject is and how she can deal with it, and remains strictly within the limits suggested by that understanding. The exceptionally even tenor of her fictional way between *Pastors and Masters* (1925) and her eighteenth novel *A God and His Gifts* (1963) exposes her to the charge of resting content with repetitive variations on unduly idiosyncratic themes. However, there are local, if minor, differences of emphasis and method, and although all the novels operate within the same assumptions and form a remarkably consistent canon, some of them are clearly better than others.

The manner of a Compton-Burnett novel is immediately recognizable. It is conducted largely in dialogue. Characters are described on their first appearance; the author provides them with minimal stage directions, makes it clear what tone is being used, and narrates such essential but always few actions as cannot be mediated through or deduced from conversation. But the essential activity of these books is in their speech—speech, moreover, in an idiom shared by all the characters. There is no attempt to give each person an individual dialect, although some do achieve a certain personal shading of the prevailing tone. This community of discourse is given some plausibility by the fact that the major characters are normally drawn from a tightly-knit family group to which only closely related outsiders have access, but Miss Compton-Burnett is not much concerned with verisimilitude. The expressive possibilities of her dialogue have been helpfully indicated by Robert Liddell, in his enthusiastic introduction to her work:

> Her idiom sometimes approximates to what one might actually say if one were in the character's skin and situation, but also to what one might think of saying and bite back; to what one might afterwards wish one had said; to what one would like other people to think; and to what one would like to think oneself.

The characters in these novels speak with a lucid precision which can mobilize and reveal strong feelings despite the apparent restrictiveness exercised by the unfailingly 'polite' tone. They self-consciously manipulate their language as a medium of defence or aggression, and the reader of Ivy Compton-Burnett needs to develop an acute ear for the nuances by which emotion is betrayed, hatred directed, or hypocrisy unmasked. Apparent complaisance can indicate underlying dissent, gallantries become the vehicle of unremitting venom, self-depreciation may be the camouflage of self-sacrifice. Abstract discussion serves as well as the consideration of practical issues to reveal the nature of the speakers:

> 'What is Truth?' said Aubrey. 'Has Justine told us?'
> 'Truth is whatever happens to be true under the circumstances,' said his sister, doing so at the moment. 'We ought not to mind a searchlight being turned on our inner selves, if we are honest about them.'
> 'That is our reason', said Mark. ' "Know thyself" is a most superfluous direction. We can't avoid it.'
> 'We can only hope that no one else knows,' said Dudley.
> 'Uncle, what nonsense!' said Justine, 'You are the most transparent and genuine person, the very last to say that.'
> 'What do you all really mean?' said Edgar, speaking rather

hurriedly, as if to check any further personal description.

'I think I only mean', said his brother, 'that human beings ought always to be judged very tenderly, and that no one will be as tender as ourselves. "Remember what you owe to yourself" is another piece of superfluous advice.'

'But better than most advice,' said Aubrey, lowering his voice as he ended. 'More tender.'

In this passage, from near the beginning of *A Family and A Fortune* (1939), the various views taken are characteristic of the persons advancing them. The way in which Dudley protects the delicate generosity of his sympathies by a light cynicism is entirely congruent with the manner in which he subsequently sacrifices his own happiness to his brother's. When Justine exclaims that he 'can't always play second fiddle', Dudley serenely replies 'Yes, I can. . . . It is a great art and I have mastered it', and the novel shows that he is as good as his word. His apparently disparaging remarks about human nature—'Of course, people are only human. . . . But it really does not seem much for them to be'—have to be understood in the light of his disinterested actions.

It would be a mistake to think of I. Compton-Burnett's novels as simply conversation pieces (although it is true that the vice of her manner is to fall into aimless verbal quibbling). The dialogue arises from strong situations and has to cope with violent events. Melodramatic happenings are an essential part of both her technique and her vision. In *Men and Wives* (1931) a tyrannical mother attempts to commit suicide; after her return from a mental home, one of her sons murders her rather than let her re-establish the oppressive old regime (by a typical irony, however, the victim gets her way posthumously). In *Manservant and Maidservant* (1947) an over-bearing father is allowed by his two sons to walk onto a dangerous bridge without their warning him, and he is killed. In *More Women than Men* (1933) a girl with pneumonia is fatally exposed to the cold by the woman who wants her out of the way. In *Elders and Betters* (1944) Anna Donne destroys the will in which Aunt Sukey leaves her money to the family which has given her a home, and illegally preserves the one by which she herself profits even though it is clearly the product of an aberrant impulse. Anna then drives her Aunt Jessica to suicide so that she can marry Jessica's son. These crimes, like others in Ivy Compton-Burnett's novels, are unvisited by retribution; their perpetrators often end up with a marked improvement in their prospects.

At its best, the dialogue in these books is a convincing projection of the characters who turn out to be capable of such deeds, and our knowledge of their acts gives a sinister dimension to the words they speak. Anna Donne's doctrine that 'we should always accept wills without any question, because they are a kind of message from someone who is dead' comes with a shocking dissimulation from one who has herself fraudulently frustrated a dying wish; what she offers as a defence of her conduct acts as a judgement on it. It should be admitted that the dialogue does not always show character in action as well as it does in Anna's case. The sections in *Elders and Betters* where she resists suggestions that she should make over her inheritance to those for whom it was intended, and her later demoralization of Jessica, have a dramatic momentum which comes from a sense of conflicting wills deeply engaged. The weakness of the Compton-Burnett method becomes apparent when the dialogue retreats too far from action in the directions of report, commentary, and aside.

The subtle effects available to the speakers in these novels derive partly from their close knowledge of their auditors—their own families and their close associates. The familial emotions are what interests Miss Compton-Burnett most. *Parents and Children* (1941) proves that she is quite capable of keeping a clear grip on the complex ramifications of feeling in a family of nine children who live with their parents in the house of their grandparents, attended by nannies and governesses. Neville, its youngest member, is touchingly portrayed. The eldest daughter exclaims 'Dear, dear, the miniature world of the family! All the emotions of mankind seem to find a place in it', and she thus indicates the justification behind the drastic economy on Miss Compton-Burnett's *dramatis personae*. Dudley, at the end of *A Family and A Fortune*, comes to the conclusion that has continually sustained his creator:

> I can't be shut away from family life; it offers too much. To think that I have lived it for so long without even suspecting its nature! . . . It will be a beautiful family talk, mean and worried and full of sorrow and spite and excitement. I cannot be asked to miss it in my weak state. I should only fret.

Ivy Compton-Burnett's novels are set in a time—the last decade or so of the nineteenth century—when the family was a much stronger unit, as well as commonly a larger one, than it now normally is. (In an often quoted remark, the author has said that she does not feel that she has a real or organic knowledge of life later than about 1910). Whether or not the domestic tyranny, the suppressed violence, and the latent incestuousness in her novels accurately reflect the under-side of high Victorian respectability, it is clear that she has built on what she feels she knows with a discipline comparable to Jane Austen's. Three or four families in a country village is the very thing she works on. Miss Compton-Burnett's wit and social comedy suggest further affinities between the two writers: Dominic Spong, the pompous family lawyer in *Men and Wives*, is in the tradition of Mr. Collins; Fulbert Sullivan's absence abroad and his sudden return are not unlike Sir Thomas Bertram's in *Mansfield Park*; and only too many Compton-Burnett characters could claim connections with Mrs. Norris. But apart from the fact that, as Pamela Hansford Johnson reminds us, 'the novels of Miss Compton-Burnett are *terrible*', they may well have been as much influenced by the tradition of Victorian family novels (as written, for instance, by Charlotte Yonge and Mrs. Henry Wood), as by Jane Austen, or, for that matter, Henry James.

Ivy Compton-Burnett is, nevertheless, an original; she has created certain new if limited kinds of fictional effect by the tenacious practice of idiosyncratic conventions. This makes her work predictable: when one of her families assembles at the beginning of the day, we come to know well what kind of scene will follow—indeed, she may fairly claim to have added a new terror to the English breakfast. Gerard Manley Hopkins once wrote that it was the vice of distinctiveness to become queer, and Ivy Compton-Burnett's writing can become gratuitously odd, and sometimes slips into self-parody. The uncompromising rigour of her manner, the socially exclusive nature of her actors, and the continuous concentration she demands have limited her appeal, but for sympathetic readers her novels have not only seemed admirable but have been found to be addictive.

## Elizabeth Bowen (b. 1899)

The best novels of Elizabeth Bowen belong to a persistent, widely-used fictional tradition in which a tense, even tremulous sensibility is combined with an awarenesss of the large moral implications of private actions, and with an inability to resist occasions of social comedy based on polite assumptions. This kind of novel is not always the result of much formal self-consciousness on the author's part; to many recent English novelists a loose amalgam of sensitivity to mood and place,

254

observation of manners, and moral scrutiny has seemed the obvious combination to adopt. Elizabeth Bowen has clearly given thought to her medium; her 'Notes on Writing a Novel', reprinted in her *Collected Impressions* (1950), indicate an attitude toward the novel form very similar to that of Henry James—as conveyed, for instance, in his 'The Art of Fiction' (1884). James's influence on such writers as Elizabeth Bowen has often been deeper than that of Jane Austen, to whom they have tended to look back as the founding mother of their mode. Virginia Woolf's highly-strung attempt to catch the 'myriad impressions' received by 'an ordinary mind on an ordinary day' has also had a lasting influence on the texture of novels written within this tradition. Elizabeth Bowen's work shows the direct or diffused effect of all these models, but it has its own individual distinction.

Her first three novels, *The Hotel* (1927), *The Last September* (1929), and *Friends and Relations* (1931), are slighter than their three successors : *To The North* (1932), *The House in Paris* (1935), and *The Death of the Heart* (1938), which form the most satisfactorily achieved part of her work. Their themes are related without being repetitive and, in *The Death of the Heart* at least, are handled with great assurance. They are commonly and correctly said to present the confrontation between innocence and experience, but any suggestion of an arid allegorical encounter would be insensitive to the sensuous and intuitive nature of their characters' experience.

*To the North* uses the classic device of the double heroine (put to such various uses in *Sense and Sensibility*, *Vanity Fair*, *Howards End*, and *Women in Love*). Cecilia Summers, a young widow, lives with her sister-in-law Emmeline. Cecilia does not take to Markie, a rising barrister, but Emmeline does, and the novel counter-points the course of their love affair with Cecilia's coming round to the secure if unexciting Julian. Emmeline's feeling for Markie is so intransigently selfless that his egocentricity finds it oppressive, and the novel ends tragically for them. Emmeline's unworldliness—contrasted with Cecilia's inability to survive happily outside some sort of social swim—gives her emotions an intensity which others find unnerving, and she is forced into an intolerable isolation. Markie's 'idea of the heart was hazy', and his incomprehension of Emmeline anticipates the hostility innocence arouses in *The Death of the Heart*.

The social comedy of *To the North* (the gaucheness of the school-girl Pauline, the inquisitive rectitude of Lady Waters) is muted in its immediate successors. *The House in Paris* is perhaps too unremittingly sombre, but there is a finer adjustment in *The Death of the Heart*, where clear comic possibilities are ironically roped in to assist the main, serious concerns of the book. *To the North* also establishes Elizabeth Bowen's command over scene as the correlative of feeling. Emmeline and Cecilia live in St. John's Wood—a part of London which, with the neighbouring Regent's Park, Miss Bowen has made very much her own—but Emmeline's country week-ends and the trip to Paris during which she and Markie become lovers also show this novelist's power to convey the intensity of a character's emotion by a hyper-sensitive response to the physical world around her. It can be argued that in Miss Bowen's less successful novels environment is too often required to under-write personal feeling; however, this much-practised technique is also effective in the sequences in *The House in Paris* which take place at Boulogne and at Hythe on the English coast.

*The House in Paris* presents the helplessness of innocence before experience in one of its most obvious forms: the vulnerability of children before the passions of adults. Leopold is the offspring of a brief affair between Karen, a girl from a respectable English background, and Max, the French fiancé of an old friend of hers. Leopold is adopted by others; at the age of eleven he is summoned to meet his mother in Paris, but she does not turn up. The present situation—Leopold's visit—is presented in two sections between which the past which led to it is recalled (Miss Bowen seems fond of three-part structures of this kind). Leopold's hapless state is poignantly conveyed, but the design of *The House in Paris* involves much retrospective exposition—again more diplomatically handled in *The Death of the Heart*. The strength of the book lies in its lucid recognition of the devastation caused by the curious impersonality of passion.

*The Death of the Heart* is Elizabeth Bowen's most secure presentation of the lonely desolation of innocent immaturity wounded by the shifty compromise of the worldly. Portia is the adolescent half-sister of Thomas Quayne, and comes to live with him when her mother dies. She and Thomas's wife Anna cannot get on satisfactorily: Portia's naïve watchfulness is felt by Anna as a standing critique of the admittedly thin, compromised quality of her life and marriage. Portia's love for Eddie, an unreliable and egocentric young man in Thomas's office, is handicapped by her feeling that there must be some clue to adult behaviour that she has not grasped. Like Emmeline in *To the North*. Portia's love is too honourable to be self-seeking; it is a suspended, end-stopped state uninterested in mere gratification. The paradoxical effect of her generosity is destructive:

> Innocence so constantly finds itself in a false position that
> inwardly innocent people learn to be disingenuous. Finding
> no language in which to speak in their own terms they resign
> themselves to being translated imperfectly. They exist alone;
> when they try to enter into relations they compromise falsi-
> fyingly—through anxiety, through desire to impart and to
> feel warmth. The system of our affections is too corrupt for
> them. They are bound to blunder, then to be told they cheat.
> . . . Their singleness, their ruthlessness, their one continuous
> wish makes them bound to be cruel, and to suffer cruelty. The
> innocent are so few that two of them seldom meet—when
> they do meet, their victims lie strewn all round.

As Miss Bowen later remarks, 'Happy that few of us are aware
of the world until we are already in league with it'.

The moral argument of *The Death of the Heart* is conducted
more explicitly than in its predecessors, as if the issues involved
had by now become fully defined for the author, but it is made
powerful by the clarity of its characterization and the logic of
its plot. Portia is given an extra degree of authenticity by the
reproduction in the novel of extracts from her girlish diary, the
contents of which so upset Anna; innocence is given a convincing interior life. Moreover, Portia's friend Lilian attracts to herself the more gawkily absurd aspects of adolescent behaviour,
leaving Portia free to be treated with the maximum intensity.
The organization of the novel shows much care: such details
as the connection between Anna's objection to the hotel habits
that Portia has picked up during her wandering life with her
mother, and the hotel-like impersonality of the Quayne household are encouraged to tell. Portia's relationships with the house-
keeper Matchett and with Major Brutt—a drifting old acquaintance who insists in turning up—are both touching in
themselves, and integrated with the larger necessities of the
novel. Portia's final flight to the Major in his Kensington hotel—
justified to her by her sense that they are 'the same', both homeless and both laughed at—is a poignant final irony, since the
Major has to act according to the unfeeling dictates of what is
called common sense, even though he perceives how inade-
quately it meets the desperation of Portia's case.

Elizabeth Bowen's later novels do not show either this intensity or this degree of control. *The Heat of the Day* (1949) again
concerns betrayal. Robert Kelway betrays his country during
the war, and allows his love affair with Stella Rodney to proceed

in her ignorance of his treachery. The truth is forced out by an enigmatic security agent called Harrison. Their relationship is presented as the product of history—'Their time sat in the third place at their table'—and is created and ended by forces outside themselves. Nevertheless, both Kelway and Harrison need more plausible motivation than Miss Bowen provides for them, and the Jamesian obliquity with which they are treated weakens the force of their relationship with Stella. *The Heat of the Day* does give a memorable picture of war-time London, even if the short stories collected by Miss Bowen in *The Demon Lover* (1945) leave a sharper impression of the particular quality of life at that time.

*A World of Love* (1955) takes place in an Irish country house, and *The Little Girls* (1964) partly at the English sea-side just before the first World War. Both are presented with Elizabeth Bowen's characteristically elegant evocativeness, but also involve an increase of mannerism with little extension of range. The nostalgia by which both are strongly affected is hostile to the moral urgency that marked the work of her middle period.

## Angus Wilson (b. 1913)

Angus Wilson first became known as the author of *The Wrong Set* (1949) and *Such Darling Dodos* (1950), two volumes of short stories which rely greatly on a talent for malicious imitation and exposure. His ear for the ways in which speech and reference give away class awareness and cultural pretension, his insight into the corrupt and self-deceiving motives of small social actions, and his ability to make vividly recognizable environments precipitate violent crises, enabled him to bring to the short story a novel aggressiveness. It seems clear that this sort of tone was partly due to some disturbances in Angus Wilson himself. 'Raspberry Jam', the first story he wrote, is both grotesque in its characters and horrific in its conclusion, and was written, according to the author, 'in feverish excitement' after his recovery from a period of personal breakdown. A similar energy also informs the stories in which the characters are mocked and discomfited. In 'Crazy Crowd', for instance (from *The Wrong Set*), the Cockshott family cultivate what are supposed to be 'interesting' and even lovable eccentricities, but their 'integrity' and 'warmth' (in Wilson's early work such qualities seem to ask for enclosure between suspicious commas) are revealed as egoism of the most rampant kind. At this period Wilson's facility in mimicking the performances people put on to impress others but which involuntarily disclose their infatuation with the self gave his work unusual force.

*Hemlock and After* (1952), Angus Wilson's first novel, retains many of the qualities of his short stories. In fact, short narrative units still came more naturally to him than longer flights, and many of the book's episodes—despite a fairly elaborate plot—seem relatively self-contained studies of widely-dispersed environments. Minor characters are picked off with a sniper's precision and economy:

> One barrister's wife said, 'I don't think I could have borne it if they'd made that terrible hotel and built those dreadful suburban villas. Can't you imagine them—Mon Repos, Wee Nook, and all the other horrors.'
>
> 'Betjeman's paradise,' laughed Mrs. Rankine, who was literary.

The last three words take care of *her* (if not of Mr. Betjeman too). Both *Hemlock and After* and its successor *Anglo-Saxon Attitudes* (1956) offer a continuous exhibition of those contemporary manners which set the teeth on edge: we are shown cultural snobbery, food snobbery, travel snobbery; middle-class philistinism and nordic feyness; left-wing wishful thinking and the bogus sincerity of popular political commentators; academic crankiness and mindless proletarian violence; theatrical bitchiness and homosexual malice.

The initiation of Bernard Sands, the hero of *Hemlock and After*, into the homosexual world—presented by Angus Wilson with a candour that was new at the time—is the essential stage in the process of self-discovery with which the novel is basically concerned. Sands is a distinguished middle-aged author who has successfully negotiated a new scheme for helping younger writers. But his achievement is, for him, undermined by an increasing unease about his own motives—brought to a crisis when he is involuntarily excited by the arrest of a young homosexual for importuning—and by a growing awareness of evil around him, particularly in the revolting form of Mrs. Curry. Mrs. Curry is laconically described in the cast list at the beginning of the novel as 'a lady of many interests'; she prattles continually about love and comfyness, and the listener must take her remarks as either

> a pretty, playful expression of some general beauty in human nature and the world around, or else (as) a statement of such extreme obscenity that the mind reeled before it. Mrs. Curry's words could never be taken in any ordinary sense.

Her activities include such gestures towards 'a bit of love in this crazy old world' as procuring and pornography. The disgust which Wilson was adept at arousing is fittingly directed at this monstrous person, even if her grotesque vitality pushes the novel strongly in the direction of melodrama.

The balance between such strong if simplified external presentation, and the complex, interior analysis of Bernard's self-distrust was not easy for Wilson to hold; here as elsewhere in his work he attempts to accommodate a plausible if barbed review of the contemporary world with more symbolic manifestations, with creatures of fantasy. But although Wilson's novels have been constructed with increasing care, the kind of creative force associated with such nightmares as Mrs. Curry has dwindled; there has been a certain loss of energy for which the novelist has tried to compensate by steadiness of application.

*Anglo-Saxon Attitudes* shows the first results of this diligence. Around Gerald Middleton's buried awareness of an archeological fraud Wilson groups a large number of scenes of English life in which representativeness plays as large a part as idiosyncrasy. The effect is panoramic and the method largely Victorian; the influence of Dickens is felt not only in the general design but also in the portrayal of such a Gampish character as Mrs. Salad, a former ladies' cloakroom attendant. With a cast of nearly forty actors, Gerald's own situation is not treated with enough intensity for it to occupy a commanding rather than a linking position, and although he resolves his own crisis more confidently than Bernard Sands does, he remains grey by comparison.

Angus Wilson's third novel, *The Middle Age of Mrs. Eliot* (1958), marks a further determined effort to widen his range. Meg Eliot's struggles to reconcile herself to widowhood after the arbitrary death of her husband and to discover sufficient resources in herself to enable her to carry on alone are given detailed and prolonged attention. The heroine is perhaps the most successful of Wilson's studies in self-realization, and certainly her development is presented with much generosity of feeling. But the forces making for this new sympathy inhibit the energies formerly available for hostile caricature, and the actual conduct of the novel tends to be flaccid. Wilson's world has become more congenial, at the cost of being more enervated. The presiding genius behind *The Middle Age of Mrs. Eliot* —Wilson is very conscious of his relations with English fictional tradition—is not Dickens, but George Eliot (whose work is often mentioned). However, Angus Wilson is understandably unable to revive the moral strenuousness of her vocabulary in a modern situation. When, after a period of living with her quietist brother, Meg Eliot comes to the decision to leave him, she says

'You feel that apart, cut off from the world, you can live a life that, by not harming, helps the world. I've wanted to persuade myself into it because it soothed me; but for me the only way I can feel of use is to keep my curiosity, to be with people—yes, even awful people . . . It's no denial of your truth, but for me the only sense is to assert one's faith in people by living among them. I'm quite a silly person, David, really.'

Such language shows understanding and even wisdom, but it lacks the dimensions of moral dignity within the reach of Maggie Tulliver or Dorothea Brooke.

A warmer account of self-recovery is given in *Late Call* (1964), in which Sylvia Calvert, a manageress of second-rate hotels, tries to adjust to a new life with her headmaster son in a 'new town'. She finds the well-equipped house and the theoretically 'progressive' ethos hard to get used to, and Wilson sensitively records the small details of daily life that loom largely in a state of distress. Sylvia is a women of less education than Meg, and the author only just escapes a patronizing attitude to her tastes, even if his clearly humane intentions do prevail in the end. Her son Harold is less generously treated. A new variation of a recurring type in Wilson's work—the humanly inadequate liberal of benevolent principle and self-deceiving practice—Harold is seen with a hostility that seems willing to wound yet—for thoroughly creditable reasons—afraid to strike. In Wilson's earlier days he would have been dealt with ruthlessly; now, the balance between authorial animus and a more understanding empathy is uneasy.

The dangerous complacency of reasoning people when faced with natural forces which they under-estimate forms part of the subject of *The Old Men at the Zoo* (1961), which is set in an 'utterly improbable' near future. Simon Carter, the narrator, fails to reconcile his administrative gifts and his consequent involvement in the world of power with his talents as a naturalist, and the decline that follows is clearly meant to have a general and admonitory application. Carter's situation—poised between engagement in the world and withdrawal from it—reflects one of the underlying motifs in Wilson's fiction, but the novelist does not move at ease within his persona. If we are to take *The Wild Garden* (Angus Wilson's informative lectures on his own work) as a guide, the symbolism of *The Old Men at the Zoo* derives (as the crises of Sands, Middleton and Meg Eliot derived) from Wilson's personal experience, but it is doubtful if the public projection of it has been clearly focussed.

The range of Wilson's themes and character-types is more limited than this documentary breadth of view might lead one to suppose, and *No Laughing Matter* (1967) presents in the form of a family chronicle some familiar figures. Nevertheless, the experimental form of this long novel and its willingness to take novelistic risks are encouraging signs of Angus Wilson's refusal to be content with self-imitation, and of his continued efforts to do justice to individual existences in the context of a wider public life.

## William Golding (b. 1911)

*Lord of the Flies* (1954) was William Golding's first novel, and it remains his best known; indeed, its academic success has been extraordinary. The novel has a strong narrative appeal for young audiences, and it lends itself to interpretation with seductive ease. The fact that the doctrines which tend to emerge from the practical criticism of this text are theologically impeccable and morally wholesome makes its attractiveness, from the pedagogic point of view, all the greater. When the value of the avalanche of exegesis brought about by the educational explosion of the 1950's and 1960's comes to be considered calmly. the celebrity of *Lord of the Flies* is likely to make it a test case.

Since its material and attitudes are consistent with Golding's later novels, which show an uncompromising austerity and make no concessions to easy accessibility, the wide currency of *Lord of the Flies* is in a way surprising. But among the special factors operating in its favour is the benefit it derives from being a later variation of a myth introduced into fiction by one of the first novels, *Robinson Crusoe*. Defoe, of course, was immensely confident of his hero's ability to survive his isolation, and this optimism is echoed, with much greater complacency, by the immediate source of *Lord of the Flies*: R. M. Ballantyne's Victorian boys' story, *The Coral Island* (actually referred to on Golding's last page). Golding's book is a refutation of Ballantyne's jolly account of the missionary fun had by his British lads on a Pacific island, but it is still an exercise in a convention which not only children's books show to be vigorously alive.

Ballantyne had no doubt that, even when left to their own devices, his boy-heroes would show the moral and spiritual soundness of their upbringing. Golding—who has been a schoolmaster and portrays the manners and idioms of English school-boys with great fidelity—uses his children as the presenters of 'the end of innocence, the darkness of man's heart', and one of the larger questions his novel provokes is how far it is satisfactory, or simply fair, to use the potential savagery of boys as an indication of the innate depravity of man.

Although Golding himself has taken a highly allegorical view of *Lord of the Flies*, its local, particular, and physical life is firmly imagined. When the boys are dropped, in some atomic holocaust, from the air onto the island, it naturally seems to them like a dream realized: the beaches, the lagoon, the jungle have a 'strange glamour'. Ralph and Piggy discover a shell or conch which they use to summon the others by blowing into it. Whoever holds the shell has the right to speak at their assemblies. Much later, the destruction of the conch accompanies the 'fall through the air' of Piggy, always the advocate of reason and science. The shell obviously becomes symbolic of those forces in the boys which try to maintain the processes and standards of civilization. Nevertheless, the conch is made very real as a beautiful object; Mark Kinkead-Weekes and Ian Gregor rightly remind us that

> Physical realities come first for Golding and should stay first for his readers. Other meanings are found in and through them, as the man-breath passes through the shell-spiral to emerge as a signal. But we must not translate the shell into the signal.

Golding is able to write virtually the whole novel in terms of the boys' consciousness because he has such a secure apprehension of those physical sensations which form so large a part of childhood experience. The boys' division into tribes, their nightmares, their taboos, their retreat behind the mask of paint, their final capitulation to the ritual of hunting that they have evolved —these retrogressive steps towards barbarism owe something to the modern study of primitive peoples, but a great deal more to the vivid factualness of both the boys and the place they find themselves in. Each step of the backward path—and much of the story's power comes from the convincing graduation from initial delight to final terror—is conveyed through the kind of experience natural to the actors. Such obvious interventions by the author as the descent onto the island of a dead parachutist (who, according to Golding, signifies 'history') are rare.

However, one character does seem under undue pressure from the novel's argument. Only Simon has the courage to face both the idol the boys have set up and the stinking corpse of the parachutist. He doesn't believe in 'the beast' : 'maybe it's only us'. When he tries to bring the good news that the parachutist is not to be feared (i.e. he tries to deliver man from history), he is martyred as he cries out 'something about a body on the hill'. Simon's intense sensibility and his fainting fits help to make his religious insights plausible, but the feeling that he is 'special' because he is to a unique degree the vehicle of the novelist's doctrine remains. Simon's sea-burial, however, does show how remarkably Golding can make physical descriptions yield metaphysical implications :

> The water rose further and dressed Simon's coarse hair with brightness. The line of his cheek silvered and the turn of his shoulder became sculptured marble. The strange, attendant creatures, with their fiery eyes and trailing vapours, busied themselves round his head. The body lifted a fraction of an inch from the sand and a bubble of air escaped from the mouth with a wet plop. Then it turned gently in the water.
>
> Somewhere over the darkened curve of the world the sun and moon were pulling; and the film of water on the earth planet was held, bulging slightly on one side while the solid core turned. The great wave of the tide moved further along the island and the water lifted. Softly, surrounded by a fringe of inquisitive bright creatures, itself a silver shape beneath the steadfast constellations, Simon's dead body moved out towards the open sea.

*The Inheritors* (1955) involves a greater exercise of the physical imagination because its characters live more completely at the level of animal sensation. Barely evolved from the animal state and keeping many of the sensory faculties since lost to *homo sapiens*, they are his immediate predecessors : Neanderthal man, referred to in the novel simply as 'the people'. Technically, this novel is Golding's greatest *tour de force*, since he successfully negotiates the problem of conveying the consciousness of creatures only on the brink of thought. Again, the exactness with which he registers primary sensations becomes an essential part of his subject :

> Lok's nose opened automatically and sampled the complex of odours that came with the mist.
>
> He squatted, puzzled and quivering. He cupped his hands over his nostrils and examined the trapped air. Eyes shut, straining attention, he concentrated on the touch of warming air,

seemed for a moment on the brink of revelation. . . . He let the air go and opened his eyes. . .

He frowned at the island and the dark water that slid towards the lip, then yawned. He could not hold a new thought when there seemed no danger in it.

Lok has to face the challenge of the 'new men', whose resourcefulness, intelligence and social organization so far outclass his own. Behind this opposition of species lies a clear allegorical significance: *The Inheritors* is a fable of the Fall. 'The people' do not live a paradisal existence exactly, since the conditions of life in the ice age are hardly temperate; but they have, initially at any rate, the qualities of innocence. They possess a natural piety, will not themselves kill for food, think no harm of the 'new men', and live for and within their own group with a touching selflessness.

Nevertheless, Lok is fascinated by the new men; he watches the coupling of two of them—its private pleasure-hunting contrasts with the frank and sociable sexuality of the people—with astonishment and excitement. Towards the end of the novel, Golding suddenly abandons the Neanderthal point of view, and after transitional and objective passage, adopts that of the new men. Lok becomes simply 'the red creature', and this violent change of perspective is curiously desolating: the loss of innocence is enforced on us by the deprivation of a consciousness which we have shared intimately.

This terminal peripety is used in all Golding's first three novels. The sudden intrusion of the naval officer and the 'trim cruiser' at the end of *Lord of the Flies* is a shock effect designed to make the reader jump the gap between the boys' tragedy and the adult world. At the end of *Pincher Martin* (1956) there is a casual remark which forces us to re-assess the whole novel: 'He didn't even have time to kick off his sea-boots'. Martin's struggles to survive on a barren mid-Atlantic rock are suddenly seen as an illusion of his own creation; what they really show is the refusal of a soul to accept judgement or the reality of a God who judges.

The purgatory of *Pincher Martin* again relies on Golding's remarkable gift for presenting the physical sensations of isolated human beings pushed up against the back wall of existence, but it also reveals the less convincing side of his talent: his uneasiness with social relationships. In *Free Fall* (1959) too, Golding's mythic tendencies are embarrassed by the representation of modern society. *The Pyramid* (1967) presents an attractive and understanding study of recollected village life, but this modest success involves the sacrifice of mythic pretensions (and may indicate a change of direction in Golding's work). Only in *The Spire* (1964) is there a satisfactory accommodation of private vision with a sense of community. Jocelin, Dean of a mediaeval cathedral very like Salisbury, causes a dizzyingly high spire to be erected on a structure that gives every sign of having foundations that are too insecure to support it. Whether this enterprise and what it costs in human lives and suffering is the product of faith or vainglory is an ambiguity that Jocelin has to struggle with. His reflection that motives are corrupt ('There is no innocent work'), is put against his mystical vision of the appletree. *The Spire* is more difficult to reduce to thesis than Golding's earlier novels, but the experience it offers is as intense.

*Lawrence Durrell* (b. 1912)

Lawrence Durrell's *The Alexandria Quartet* was one of the more spectacular successes of post-war English fiction, and gave its author an immediate and international reputation. Durrell was previously known as a poet and a writer of topographical studies of Mediterranean subjects; he had also published four novels, one of which—*The Black Book* (1938)—had appeared in Paris and was not available in England. Durrell has never lived in England for very long, and the attention paid to the *Quartet* abroad as well as at home was partly due to its freedom from anglo-saxon provincialism—a freedom that the novelist advertises by many jaunty asides deriding English inhibitions. The experimental pretensions of these four novels were also treated more seriously by some continental critics than by literary opinion at home, which has not tended to be welcoming and sympathetic to radical innovations of form in recent fiction. Durrell was rather seen as in the tradition of other deracinated English writers to whose heads the Mediterranean has gone, and was praised as an heir to Byron or denigrated for wallowing in the footsteps of Norman Douglas.

The *Quartet* consists of four books: *Justine* (1957), *Balthazar* (1958), *Mountolive* (1958), and *Clea* (1960). All of them are marked by a prose which cultivates the maximum level of sensation; the writing assaults the imagination with an almost physical impact:

Streets that run back from the docks with their tattered rotten supercargo[1] of houses, breathing into each others' mouths,

266

keeling over. Shuttered balconies swarming with rats, and old women whose hair is full of the blood of ticks. Peeling walls leaning drunkenly to east and west of their true centre of gravity. The black ribbon of flies attaching itself to the lips and eyes of the children—the moist beads of summer flies everywhere; the very weight of their bodies snapping off ancient flypapers hanging in the violet doors of booths and cafes. The smell of sweat-lathered Berberinis, like that of some decomposing staircarpet. And then the street noises: shriek and clang of water-bearing Saidi, dashing his metal cups together as an advertisement, the unheeded shrieks which pierce the hubbub from time to time, as of some small deli-cately-organized animal being disembowelled.

The method may ultimately be Dickensian, but the writing gives the impression of operating without restraints; the sensibility is uncensored. The style may at times become what Durrell him-self has called 'too juicy', but it is capable of considerable local effectiveness. When a man is dying in hospital, the narrator describes how 'one of his hands came running over the counter-pane like a frightened rat to grope for mine'; the great ball in *Balthazar* offers 'dancers swaying like wet washing in a high wind, the saxophones wailing like a litter of pigs'. The prose is most notably under full pressure during the description of some of the set-pieces which occur throughout the *Quartet*—the duck-shoot at the end of *Justine*, the fish-drive at the beginning of *Mountolive*, the ride in the desert of Nessim and Narouz, the under-water swimming in *Clea*. This physical strenuousness takes place in an exotic environment, and the effect on an English temperament can be powerful; the diplomat Mountolive reflects that 'His sensations recalled nothing he had ever known, were completely original'.

The chief beneficiary of the sensuality of Durrell's prose is the city of Alexandria itself, to whose various and changing aspects —as it was in the late 1930's and during the war—he recurs with fascinated frequency. Durrell's Alexandria is essentially an open city, where any variety of religion, any permutation of sex, and any trend of speculation is not only permitted but almost en-joined. It is a city where 'a hundred little spheres which religion or lore creates . . . cohere softly together like cells to form (a) great sprawling jellyfish'; it is 'an anarchy of flesh and fever, of money-love and mysticism' where many races cohabit. Durrell more than once maintains that character is a function of place, and thus character in Alexandria must be an extremely open question. In fact, the *Quartet* proceeds on the assumption that character is neither fixed nor predictable, and Alexandria is a place where the range of human possibility can be shown in peculiarly naked and even ruthless conditions.

Two further factors encourage Durrell's refusal to subscribe to the notion of a stable ego: the fact that the 'central topic' of the *Quartet* is 'an investigation of modern love', and the fact that 'the form of the novel' is based on the relativity proposition' (see the Note to *Balthazar*). An epigraph to *Justine* quotes from the letters of Freud: 'I am accustoming myself to the idea of regarding every sexual act as a process in which four persons are involved'. As far as the *Quartet* is concerned, this must be taken as a conservative estimate. Darley, a teacher and writer and the narrator of *Justine* and *Clea*, is progressively in love with Justine, Melissa, and Clea; Mountolive first loves Nessim's mother and later Pursewarden's sister; Pursewarden is loved by Justine, and loves Melissa and his own sister, and so on. Pursewarden's assertion that 'Everything is true of everybody' comes to seem a reasonable inference. But it is not only true because the psyche is 'as completely unsubstantial as a rainbow' and only becomes coherent when the truest form of attention, love, is paid to it. The paying of attention is itself subject to the laws of relativity: 'Our view of reality is conditioned by our position in space and time—not by our personalities as we like to think' argues Pursewarden; 'Thus every interpretation of reality is based upon a unique position. Two paces east of west and the whole picture is changed.' (*Balthazar*).

The actual structure of the *Quartet* is an attempt to put this theory into fictional practice. In *Justine* Darley, having retired to a Greek island, recalls his Alexandrian experience and in particular his love affair with Justine, the wife of the wealthy Copt, Nessim. He sees Nessim's behaviour as largely due to his jealousy of Justine, and although Darley is aware of her flamboyant reputation, he does not on the whole question the genuineness of her love for him. But he later receives from his friend Balthazar a commentary on *Justine* which forms the basis of the book named after him. This proposes many new interpretations of what Darley has recorded and adds much new information of which Darley was unaware. It becomes clear, for instance, that Justine was in fact using her affair with Darley as a screen to hide from Nessim her pursuit of Pursewarden. In *Mountolive*—narrated in the conventional third person—we realize that Nessim's odd behaviour was really due to the critical stage he had reached in a political intrigue, in which Justine was his accomplice. In these three novels time is, theoretically, stayed; the relation between the different accounts they offer is spatial. *Clea*, however, is a true sequel; but even here some 'Workpoints' are added to suggest that the whole 'word continuum' could be extended indefinitely.

The effect of this organization is to offer a novel form of suspense. The gradual emergence of the principal characters as they are revealed by different witnesses encourages the idea that the accumulation of evidence will finally allow us to establish what Justine or Nessim or Pursewarden was *really* like. Pursewarden first appears as someone on the fringe of Darley's acquaintance who has inexplicably left him some money. Pursewarden gradually assumes a more central position, and by *Clea* we are offered what seem to be the real motives behind his suicide. This tendency in the *Quartet* conflicts with what a fully rigorous application of the relativity proposition would surely imply; its characters do in the end assume the kind of recognizable personality that Durrell has suggested is an illusion. Moreover, the fact that *Mountolive* is objectively narrated by the novelist with access to what is sometimes called a God's eye view, implies that the account of events given there has more authority than the versions offered by characters immersed in them.

As an experiment, *The Alexandria Quartet* may lack the intellectual rigour to be seen, for example, in some of the *nouveaux romans* written in France, but its form provides a convenient container for Durrell's various talents and interests. His natural forte is the episode, and his temperament favours violent shifts of tone. The structure of the *Quartet* allows his writing to be fragmentary without becoming dispersed, and permits the juxtaposition of lyric intensity with aphoristic conversation and indecent farce. The restlessness and robustness which compromise the *Quartet* as a formal design are the foundation of its fictive life. Comic and symbolic modes meet in the friendship between Scobie—an absurd but vividly and even touchingly realized old seaman who has settled in Alexandria because of what he darkly refers to as 'tendencies'—and Clea, the painter who cannot paint well until her hand has been mutilated and replaced by an artificial one. The elasticity of the general scheme allows both satirical sketches of diplomatic life, and the horrific experience of a British ambassador in a house of child prostitutes. It suits Durrell because, as V. S. Pritchett suggested, he is as much a raconteur as a novelist.

Romance, intrigue, mythic suggestiveness, and bawdy comedy re-appear in *Tunc* (1968), the first part of a two-decker novel. In this case the central notion of the work—an inquiry into the nature of culture and the possibilities of individual freedom within and without a culture—is more strictly related to the local life of the novel. The highly erogenous zone of Alexandria is deserted for episodes in various parts of Europe, but the pressure of the thesis makes them less centrifugal than their predecessors in the *Quartet*. Whether the consequent loss of energy is adequately compensated for by the greater integration of the action probably depends on how convincing Durrell's organizing concept of culture is felt to be.

## Iris Murdoch (b. 1919)

Iris Murdoch's first novel *Under the Net* (1954) shows some signs of the influence of Beckett's *Murphy* and perhaps also of its dedicatee, Raymond Queneau; since she is by profession a philosopher it is not surprising that its thought has connections with Sartre (of whom she has written a study) and Wittgenstein. Its originality is nevertheless considerable, and it contains the first presentation of ideas and principles that have continued to underlie Miss Murdoch's work. She is a prolific writer (which has not always been to her advantage in a critical climate which sometimes seems unreasonably suspicious of abundance and energy), and between *Under the Net* and *Bruno's Dream* (1969) published twelve novels.

The mode of comic picaresque in which *Under the Net* is conducted has subsequently been abandoned by its author, but it is used there with much confidence. Jake Donoghue, the narrator, ekes out a precarious living as a translator. He becomes involved in such bizarre incidents as the kidnapping of a rather *passé* film-star dog, a political rally on a film set of ancient Rome, and a series of philosophical conversations at a centre for research into the common cold. The novel also follows his relationship with two sisters, Anna and Sadie—the first of many significant siblings—and with Hugo Belfounder, the first of a line of figures possessed of mysterious authority. Surprising and often fantastic incidents, and a patterned structure of relationships which lead to discoveries and realignments, have remained the basis of Iris Murdoch's procedure.

*Under the Net*, however, is more academic than its successors, since it explicitly debates those notions later absorbed into the novelist's creative methods; they then become implicit in the action, rather than extrapolatable comments on it. Jake's conversations with Hugo are about the relationship between language and reality. Hugo's position, according to Jake, is that language is contaminated by theory, that

> all theorizing is flight. We must be ruled by the situation itself and this is unutterably particular. Indeed it is something to which we can never get close enough, however hard we may try as is were to crawl under the net . . . Only the greatest men can speak and still be truthful. Any artist knows this obscurely; he knows that a theory is death, and that all expression is weighted with theory.

For most, such an argument must lead to silence, and Hugo is associated in the novel with such non-verbal activities as fireworks and mime. But the writer is bound to try to crawl 'under the net' of theoretical description to get as close as possible to truth as it is actually experienced, and Miss Murdoch's novels are all attempts to do this. In the process they may refer to already formulated concepts (she certainly does not share Hugo's contempt for them), but she is not a philosophical novelist in the sense that her fictions are designed to demonstrate such concepts; her books do not follow the example of Sartre's *La Nausée*. On the contrary, she reposes a sometimes reckless trust in her imagination, and her strong impulse towards pattern and form is more exploratory than didactic.

Part of her intention is an attempt to restore an awareness of the human personality as something substantial, mysterious and impenetrable. In an important 'polemical sketch' entitled 'Against Dryness' (published in *Encounter*, January, 1961), Iris Murdoch complained that 'we have been left with far too shallow and flimsy an idea of human personality'; in her view, 'what we require is a renewed sense of the difficulty and complexity of the moral life and the opacity of persons'. We also need to be reminded of the irreducibility of the physical world over which we think to exert a facile control. In her novels, homage is often paid in both minor and major incidents to a reality that is outside the characters and cannot be deformed by them. The author's interest in unlikely mechanical problems is possibly a playful acknowledgement of a similar attitude. It follows too that however symbolical her novels become—and they are full of intriguing objects and radiant artefacts (especially pictures)—these physical realities are supposed in the last analysis to remain beyond interpretation.

It is in love that we have the most acute sense of the otherness and rewarding mystery of someone else, and all Miss Murdoch's novels are love stories. They sometimes approach being so in the more sentimental sense, and *The Sandcastle* in particular has been criticised as novelettish. But more often the elaborate series of relationships that the characters experience is seriously aimed at discovering new aspects of human possibility and of finding new ways of presenting the density and variousness of human nature. Some readers, it should be added, find the complications of plot thought necessary to this end go beyond what is reasonable or credible.

*The Bell* (1958) and *A Severed Head* (1961) display in different ways many of the most interesting features of Iris Murdoch's imaginative vocabulary, and illustrate the extremes of her range. *The Bell* begins with a fine narrative security—'Dora Greenfield left her husband because she was afraid of him. She decided six months later to return to him for the same reason'—and the novel is convincingly paced throughout. Elsewhere, as in *The Unicorn* (1963), narrative momentum can be dissipated by the complexities of the story's later developments. The physical setting of *The Bell* is also 'lived-in' to an unusual degree—far more known and felt by the reader than, say, the Dorset country house in *The Nice and the Good*.

Imber Court is a Palladian Gloucestershire mansion with a convent in its grounds. It is used by a small half-lay, half-religious community made up of people who have too strong an attraction to the spiritual life to live happily in the world, and not enough vocational tenacity to embrace the discipline of withdrawing from it. Michael Meade's situation is characteristic of this uneasy state : he has long hoped to become a priest, but inability to resist a romantic kind of homosexual feeling finally puts it out of the question. Not the least of *The Bell's* merits is the generous understanding with which Michael's emotional life is treated. To Imber comes Dora, a feckless young women with no religious sense; she is an artist, if anything. She feels at a disadvantage with the community because of her unsatisfactory relations with her husband. When another guest discovers an old bell lying on the bed of a lake, she attempts to exploit its recovery : 'In this holy community she would play the witch'.

The bell is a beautiful object, and Dora acknowledges its aesthetic authority in a way similar to her reaction to a picture by Gainsborough seen in the National Gallery. Most of the characters are related to the bell in one way or another, but it means different things to each of them; it is not a symbol which can be satisfactorily glossed in a phrase. The bell itself has a legend engraved upon it: '*Vox ego sum Amoris*. . . . "I am the voice of love" '. It is the ambiguity of this voice that disturbs Michael; his love of the sacred is shackled by his love for the profane. He comes to realize that, as the Abbess says, 'all our failures are failures in love'. But the Abbess also adds that 'the way is always forward, never back', and this resilience is endorsed by the end of the novel itself. Dora's schemes and Michael's affections have had a catalytic effect on Imber and the community has collapsed, but both of them prepare to continue their lives with an enhanced sense of their identity. The conclusion of *The Bell* achieves that respect for contingency which Iris Murdoch has spoken of as desirable. Dora's personality is presented with a freedom and a density that is rarer in Miss Murdoch's fiction than her theoretical writings might lead one to suppose. As Dora rightly reflects, early on in the book, 'How very much, after all, she existed; she, Dora, and no-one should destroy her'.

The construction of *A Severed Head* is formalized and choreographic, its prevailing tone witty and 'civilized'—even if part of its meaning is concerned with what lies beyond urbanity. Six persons—Martin Lynch-Gibbon, a wine merchant; his wife Antonia; his brother Alexander, a sculptor; his mistress, Georgie; Antonia's psychiatrist, Palmer; and Palmer's half-sister, Honor—are deployed in permutations of alliance that involve each of them with at least one and generally two of the others. Martin makes a dazing series of discoveries until a conclusion is reached which embodies what those revelations have taught him about himself. As an enquiry into the nature of love, *A Severed Head* is more cerebral and analytical than is usual in Iris Murdoch's later work—it is probably her most Freudian novel. Yet even this book witnesses the author's attempts to find for herself new modes for the imaginative understanding of personality, and reflects her lament for 'the general loss of concepts' that the present age has suffered. Martin talks to Alexander while he is in the early stages of modelling a clay head. Alexander complains that

> 'We don't believe in human nature in the old Greek way any more. There is nothing between schematized symbols and caricature. What I want here is some sort of impossible

liberation. Never mind. I shall go on playing with it and interrogating it and perhaps it will tell me something.'

'I envy you,' I said. 'You have a *technique* for discovering more about what is real.'

'So have you,' said Alexander. 'It is called morality.'

I laughed. 'Rusted through lack of practice, brother.'

The playing and interrogation that Alexander speaks of are comparable with the author's fictional activities.

Like several of her books, *A Severed Head* can easily give the impression of being an obscure game the author is playing with herself. But the type of novel that she has so energetically continued to try to write is one which will not rely on exhausted and easily apprehended views of human nature, She has also tried to accept the challenge of form inherent in most art while trying to resist the tendency of form to diminish the freedom of her characters. Her attempts to accommodate the imagination she trusts, the patterns which attract her, and the concepts that are important to her, may have been intermittently successful, but the implications of her work may turn out to be as important as its achievement.

NOTE

1. Durrell misuses this word, which properly means a person overseeing a cargo. *Ed.*

BIBLIOGRAPHY

A. General Studies

Allen, Walter : *Tradition and Dream* (London, 1964).
Bergonzi, Bernard : *The Situation of the Novel* (London, 1970).
Burgess, Anthony : *The Novel Now* (London, 1967).
Fraser, G. S. : *The Modern Writer and his World* (London, 1964).
Gindin, James : *Post-war British Fiction* (Cambridge, 1962).
Karl, Frederick R. : *A Reader's Guide to the Contemporary English Novel* (London, 1963).
Kettle, Arnold : *An Introduction to the English Novel*, Vol. II (London, 1953).
McCormick, John : *Catastrophe and Imagination*. An interpretation of the recent English and American novel (London, 1957).

B. Studies of individual novelists

Coe, Richard N. : *Beckett* (Writers and Critics, Edinburgh and London, 1964).
Cohn, Ruby : *Samuel Beckett: the Comic Gamut* (New Brunswick, New Jersey, 1962).
Fletcher, John : *The Novels of Samuel Beckett* (London, 1964).
Kenner, Hugh : *Samuel Beckett: a critical study* (New York, 1961; London, 1962).
Bloom Robert : *The Indeterminate World: a study of the novels of Joyce Cary* (Philadelphia, 1962).
Mahood, M. M. : *Joyce Cary's Africa* (London, 1964).
Wolkenfeld, Jack : *Joyce Cary: the Developing Style* (London and New York, 1968).
Wright, Andrew : *Joyce Cary: a Preface to his Novels* (London and New York, 1958).
Burkhart, Charles : *I. Compton-Burnett* (London, 1965).
Liddell, Robert : *The Novels of I. Compton-Burnett* (London, 1955).
Fraser, G. S. : *Lawrence Durrell: a study* (London, 1968).
Moore, Harry T. (ed.) : *The World of Lawrence Durrell* (Carbondale, Southern Illinois, 1962).
Kinkead-Weekes, Mark and Gregor, Ian : *William Golding: a critical study* (London, 1967).
Stokes, Edward : *The Novels of Henry Green* (London, 1959).

Allott, K. and Farris M.: *The Art of Graham Greene* (London, 1951; New York, 1963).

Pryce-Jones, David: *Graham Greene* (Writers and Critics, Edinburgh and London, 1963).

Byatt, A. S.: *Degrees of Freedom: the Novels of Iris Murdoch* (London, 1965).

Bradbury, Malcolm: *Evelyn Waugh* (Writers and Critics, Edinburgh and London, 1964).

Carens James, F.: *The Satiric Art of Evelyn Waugh* (Seattle, 1966).

Stopp, F. J.: *Evelyn Waugh: Portrait of an Artist* (London, 1958).

Halio, Jay L.: *Angus Wilson* (Writers and Critics, Edinburgh and London, 1964).

## 8

## ENGLISH POETRY, 1930–1960

### G. S. Fraser, University of Leicester

### I

Two very great poets, W. B. Yeats and T. S. Eliot, were flourishing in this period, but each has been given a separate chapter in this book, so their later work will not be dealt with here. It should be remembered, however, that Eliot particularly was very helpful to poets of a younger generation. As a director of Faber and Faber, he was largely responsible for that firm's publication, in their twenties, of poets like Auden, MacNeice, and Spender, and he also published poems and reviews by them in his magazine, *The Criterion*. In his political, social and religious views he was at an opposite pole from most of the poets who began to become famous in the 1930s, but he never allowed his extra-literary beliefs to distort his literary judgement. It used to be said that he had a direct influence on them technically, and Louis MacNeice, in a volume of tributes to Eliot published on his sixtieth birthday, said that what fascinated him in *The Waste Land* and Eliot's other early poems was the idea of playing Hamlet behind the gasworks—the fusion, in other words, of the grand style and of sordid urban imagery. Yet Eliot's style was an exceedingly individual one, repeating and varying from beginning to end with intensifying skill and poignancy a rather narrow range of dominant emotions and key images. None of the young poets of the 1930's whom he encouraged had his peculiar immediacy of atmosphere.

Though Yeats was even further away, in his romantic and aristocratic view of life from the poets of the Auden group than Eliot, and though he felt that he was not a 'modern' poet in theirs or Eliot's sense, his direct influence can be much more widely traced. The metre and the tone of Auden's 'i September, 1939' is that of Yeats's 'Easter 1916', with the same ironies, the same modulations from the colloquial to the sublime. C. Day Lewis, a poet like Louis MacNeice of Irish ancestry, often echoes Yeats in his early work; MacNeice is less reminiscent, but there are some similarities of cadence and tone, which perhaps come mainly from an Anglo-Irish intonation and from that peculiar fusion, or juxtaposition, of bleakness and swaggering gaiety which is part of the Anglo-Irish temperament. MacNeice, also, before the great period of Yeats scholarship had set in, published a study of Yeats in 1942 which is interesting as being written 'this side idolatry.' Yeats himself was also willing to learn from younger poets and Richard Ellmann traces the influence of Auden's abrupt clipped rhythms in such a play as *Paid on Both Sides* in Yeats's short dramatic masterpiece *Purgatory* (a play, incidentally, which Auden reviewing Yeat's posthumous *Last Poems and Plays* found 'worthless').

A more important influence on the young poets of the 1930's than either Eliot or Yeats was, however, Hopkins. Hopkins had died in 1889, a selection of his poems edited by his friend Robert Bridges came out in 1918, but took ten years to sell out. A new edition with an enthusiastic introduction by Charles Williams came out in 1930, and the note of buoyancy and hope in Hopkins, his enthusiastic and loving particularity of observation, the vigour of his stress rhythms, appealed deeply to a young generation of poets, spiritually tired of both what seemed to them the defeatism of *The Waste Land* and the unreal posings of Yeats: they might not share Hopkins's faith, but they responded immediately to his ardour. It is clear from Yeats's remarks on Hopkins in his preface to the *Oxford Book of Modern Verse* and from Eliot's cavillings in *After Strange Gods* that the two older poets had been introduced to the great Christian poet of nature too late to digest him into their systems or, perhaps, even to hear his rhythms properly. Of poets fairly recently dead, there are strange echoes in the early Auden of Kipling and Newbolt (Orwell even described Auden as a 'gutless Kipling'). The poetry of the Auden group never, in fact, in the 1930's reached a mass audience, but the poets did aim at a popular appeal. Auden, as he showed in his excellent *Oxford Book of Light Verse* and in the anthology he edited with John Garrett, *The Poet's Tongue*, shows a learned interest and sound taste in the ballad and folk-song tradition, in nursery rhymes, in comic and colloquial verse. Older poets like Yeats, whose last volume is more full of ballad refrain poems than any even of his most youthful ones, and, in a very different way, Robert Graves, had shared this feeling for the popular roots of poetry; and Eliot himself was very much aware, as *Sweeney Agonistes* shows, of the attractiveness of strong blues beats and syncopation.

What was new in the reachings out of the 1930's poets to this traditional or contemporary popular tone, to ballads or cabaret songs, was that it was uncondescending. It sought at least to reach out directly to a popular audience in that audience's own terms; even what might be called the mythology of the Auden group, the fascination with spies, airmen, explorers, and so on, the note of daunting ominousness, owed something to boys' weeklies, to sub-literary figures like Sexton Blake, Dixon Hawke, and Ferrers Locke, though it owed as much, of course, to Auden's fascination with northern things, bleak Icelandic landscapes, the curtness of the saga style. The poets of the 1930's tend to be discussed too exclusively in terms of the social and political crises of that decade, and of ideas, the ideas, for instance, of Marx and of Freud or Groddeck. Certainly Auden, MacNeice, Day Lewis and Spender were poets very much pressed upon by external affairs. But they were never, though they might sometimes wish to appear so, mere journalists or propagandists in verse. What lasts in their poetry is not topical, even the urgently and honourably topical, but the personal and the universal. It was Auden himself, at the end of a decade in which he had been seen by many as a spokesman for the Left, who, in his great elegy for Yeats, said both that in comparison with a poet's mastery of language the oddity of his opinions or the element of absurdity in his life are unimportant: and that (except, and it is a very important exception, in the psyche) 'Poetry makes nothing happen.' Poetry does make some things happen: when Yeats in old age asked himself remorsefully,

> Did that play of mine send out
> Certain men the English shot?

the historian's answer would probably be a qualified 'yes': it was one factor. The poetry of the 1930's that we associate with Auden and his group was, far more than Yeats's poetry, a poetry of protest and warning. If it had never been written, the external history of the 1930's would probably be exactly what it is. Poems like MacNeice's magnificent 'Eclogue for Christmas' or Auden's elegies for Yeats and Freud have their lasting value, not as practical political or social acts, but as profound criticisms of a culture.

## II

The period covered by this brief study divides, with rather unusual neatness, into three sections. During the 1930's, a period of social and political disaster,.and of cultural shoddiness, the poet typically saw himself as a man, like Wilfred Owen, with a duty to warn. The point was clearly put by Michael Roberts in his introduction to the famous anthology of 1932, *New Signatures* :

> The poet is in some ways, a leader : he is a person of unusual sensibility, he feels acutely emotional problems which other people feel vaguely, and it is his function not only to find the rhythms and images appropriate to the everyday problems of normal human beings, but also to find an imaginative solution to their problems, to make a new harmony out of strange and apparently ugly material.[1]

This paragraph is important not only as defining the central attitudes of a good many of the young poets of the 1930's, but as defining the themes, even the topics, of some of their best poems. MacNeice's *Autumn Journal*, for instance, is essentially a long self-examination, a very honest one, by a poet who is wondering whether he is playing the role that Roberts has assigned to him. Intellectually tougher, more frankly a hedonist, basically more sceptical and more individualistic than most of his contemporaries, MacNeice, the son of a Church of Ireland clergyman who became a Bishop, is nevertheless nagged by a conscience which is not precisely a religious conscience but the conscience of social puritanism. Again and again, the poets of the Auden group are being tempted by the private life, the pastoral landscape, Venusberg, something childish and very natural, and rejecting it : the group and its harsh social purposes must be primal. Complacent regressiveness must be avoided as must self-pitying introspection. The world must be seen with synoptic insight 'as the hawk sees it or the helmeted airman.' England is a country where nobody is well and the poet is the stern healer, down on funk, self-deception, self-regard. Strangely, this terror of regressiveness has its own obviously regressive side.

The poets of the 1930's had not been directly affected by the great slump and by massive unemployment, but they came from that section of the middle classes, the fixed-income professional classes, that feels such crises quite acutely in an indirect way. Throughout the thirty years of this study the value of the pound sterling, in what it can buy in necessaries and simple luxuries, has been steadily falling. The tradition of what one may call the class of professional public servants in this country has always been an austere one. In the 1930's, perhaps already in the late 1920's, it was becoming still more austere. Stephen Spender expresses this well in his autobiography:

> We lived in a style of austere comfort against a background of calamity. Little of our money seemed spent on enjoyment, but went on doctors or servants, or on maintaining a style of life.[2]

MacNeice, Rex Warner, Day Lewis, Geoffrey Grigson were all sons of Anglican clergymen: Auden also had clergymen in his family though his father was a Professor and a Medical Officer of Health in the Midlands; Christopher Isherwood's father was a retired Army colonel. Spender's father was a distinguished Liberal journalist, but his working life had latterly coincided with the decline of the Liberal Party in the years after the First World War. Spender is an interesting example of how the family traditions of these poets gradually caught up on their rebelliousness. His little prose book, written for Victor Gollancz's Left Book Club, was called *Forward from Liberalism*, but his verse play *Trial of a Judge* shocked his new Communist friends by the belief it inculcated in truth and justice as absolute values. The liberal judge who would not bow to realpolitik was his hero, just as a similar character, ineffective but scrupulously honourable, was the hero of Rex Warner's allegorical novel, *The Professor*. It is easy to see, also, in Auden's poems and plays of the 1930's foreshadowings of his definite Christian stance from the 1940's onwards, which are also perhaps attitudes lingering on from a Christian upbringing. Day Lewis's ability, in the 1930's, to absorb the tone of stronger poets like Auden and Yeats was to modulate, after the 1940's, sometimes as in *An Italian Visit* in humorous pastiche, more often in admiring direct imitation, towards an attempt to revive the manners of the nineteenth-century poets he most admired, Hardy and Browning. Oddly enough, Louis MacNeice, who was the most sceptical of these poets about complete transformations of society, about what might be called visionary or apocalyptic Marxism, was to remain throughout his working life the most consistently socially engaged. He started as just left of centre, and remained firmly left of centre to the end. He had taken a first in Greats at Oxford, taught Greek in Birmingham and then at Bedford College in the University of London, and his long historical perspective gave him a sense that, if utopia never comes, neither is any social disaster final. His individualism was a very critical and responsible individualism; his zest for life, combined with a deep sense of life's loneliness, variety and precariousness, never made him feel inclined to give up the struggle.

Because they so closely reflected the concern of the ordinary intelligent man in the 1930's with the slump, unemployment, the invasion of Abyssinia, the Spanish Civil War, the fear of Hitler, the hope that Soviet Russia might prove a bulwark against Hitlerism, these four poets, Auden, MacNeice, Day Lewis, and Spender have rather unfairly dominated discussions of the poetry of the 1930's, and their own later work, except Auden's, has perhaps not had enough critical discussion. The Nazi-Soviet pact of August 1939 made them see that some of their hopes, at least, were illusory, and perhaps led to Auden's bitter lines in '1 September, 1939':

> As the clever hopes expire
> Of a low, dishonest decade . . .

Looking at them in retrospect, one can see that one at least, Auden, was a major poet; MacNeice, in skill, intelligence, and honesty, was nearly a major poet; Day Lewis was a most versatile craftsman, fluent and sincere, but cursed by the inability ever to find a voice that was quite his own; Spender was an uneven poet, his gift primarily lyrical, or a gift for the subjective impression of mood. His best poems of the 1930's are those where the earnest, oratorical social conscience is least in evidence; poems about the Spanish Civil War where the horror of war, and the loss of a friend, matter more to him than the justice of the cause: poems about the break-up of his first marriage, moving for their honest expression of rancour, anguish, jealousy, emotions which a semi-Marxist 'group' morality should theoretically despise.

Monroe K. Spears in the most thorough of a number of good studies that have been written of Auden's poetry compares him, in stature and the nature of his gift, to Dryden. The comparison is apt in several respects. Like Dryden, Auden is a copious poet, like Dryden he is in easy command of every verse form to which he sets his hand; as in Dryden's case, we admire his vigour but do not feel that he is always equal to himself. Dr. Johnson contrasting Dryden with Pope noted that Pope is always trying to write as well as he can; Dryden is not, because he knows he can always write well. The vigour and fire of Auden's mind carries us through certain loosenesses, roughnesses, eccentricities, faults of taste and tone. Like Dryden, he is, though sometimes in a mode of allegory or fable, primarily a poet of discourse. He writes, that is to say, poems about love, or love poems for imagined simplified characters, rather than love poems of his own: he writes poems discussing religion, like Dryden's *Religio Laici*, which has something in common with Auden's *New Year Letter*, rather than personal devotional poems, or poems exploring personal religious experience, like Eliot's *Ash Wednesday* or Hopkins's or Donne's religious sonnets. Purely personal shame, sorrow, and repentance are not for him poetically interesting unless they can be given a universal or aphoristic form. Like Dryden he is a poet of learned inventiveness but also, when it is appropriate, of coarse, direct and racy language. He is unlike Dryden in having created in his early poems a myth-world, the private mythology described by Christopher Isherwood in *Lions and Shadows*, and in the obscurity of his early work, *Poems* (1930) and *The Orators* (1932). The early poems were often put together from fragments of different poems, the fragments that Christopher Isherwood had admired: the obscurity is less in the detail than in the structure as a whole, and in the fact that, in the early work, the application of the detail, to his own state or to the contemporary world, is left very much to the reader. By the time of his last volume of the 1930s, *Another Time*, Auden, however, had learned to construct poems that were coherent wholes in themselves; that presupposed wide reading and alert intelligence in the reader, but did not trouble him with opaque private allusions. From 1940 onwards, Auden lived mainly in the United States, taking his holidays in Italy or in Austria. He developed a new interest in music, writing libretti for operas, and his early interest in the strictness of the saga style was replaced by an amused and affectionate regard for Southern baroque. To some of his English admirers, the later poems sometimes seemed to have lost the bite, directness, and sheer Englishness of the early work, and their experiments in language could seem frivolous. But looking back on his work as a whole one sees a steady gain in power and wisdom, a remaking of the self.

MacNeice's career was very different. Where Auden was a poet of intuition and feeling—feeling of a generalized rather than personal sort—and of insight often mounted on fantasy, MacNeice was a poet of thought, of quick cleverness, and remarkably vivid sensations. He was uncertain of his intuitions;

his feelings were puzzling and painful to him, and this very lack of certainly both about his deepest feelings and about what could be the grounds of faith gives his poems of the 1930's a peculiar awkward honesty in a propagandistic age. MacNeice's *Autumn Journal* might claim to be the most honest longish poem of the 1930's; compared with Auden's ambitious, and at moments rhetorically magnificent, *Spain* it has the questioning, clumsy, and piercing note of Arthur Hugh Clough as contrasted, say, with the deep-booming organ voice of Tennyson. Auden had a larger, more vigorous and more ranging mind but MacNeice a more painfully self-questioning one. The comparison with Clough does not hold, however, all the way through. MacNeice was a much more technically adroit poet, flashingly witty and vividly aware of the transient richness of the world; 'Euston, the smell of soot and fish and petrol', 'the moment cradled like a brandy glass.' In his middle years, after the Second World War, he concentrated on longish poems which sometimes, like *Autumn Sequel*, gave an effect of alert improvisation masking a deep staleness or tiredness. But his last two volumes of poems, *Visitations*, and *The Burning Perch* (which came out in the year of his death, 1963), showed a renewed mastery of the short poem, less vivid in detail but more unified in shape than his early short poems, and often bleakly piercing in their sense of the ominousness of life. He died in his early fifties when, perhaps, like Yeats at the same age, he may still have had his greatest years ahead of him.

### III

Though Auden and his group aimed at a wide audience, they never, in the 1930's, quite achieved this. Their poetry even at its most direct, even in its imitations or parodies of popular modes like the ballad, unconsciously presumed a cultural background in the reader not dissimilar to their own, a background of intellectual and to some degree of social privilege. Their Leftism was of a kind that members of the literary and social Establishments, from Virginia Woolf to Sir Harold Nicolson, could easily come to terms with. There was nothing wild or Villonesque about their backgrounds; they had professional qualifications, the social adaptability of the professionally educated, and, however much they may have consciously deplored it, a sense of social security, of being part of the recognized set-up. Another group of young poets of the 1930s, Dylan Thomas, George Barker, David Gascoyne were genuinely Villonesque, did live from hand to mouth, had roots or contacts that if not (as in Barker's case) properly working-class, were near this. Oddly enough, these poets were much less political than the Auden group, much more directly lyrical; the early poetry of all three can be seen as springing out of the rich frustrations of adolescent sexuality and an intoxication, rather like the intoxication of the young Keats, with words, Edith Sitwell, a poet rather similar in temperament, saw nothing to admire in the work of the Auden group, but hailed Dylan Thomas's second volume, *Twenty-Five Poems* (1936) as a masterpiece. Though Dylan Thomas's politics, in so far as politics interested him at all, were orthodoxly and sanely Leftish, he similarly aroused the admiration of a powerful poet of the Right, the South African, Roy Campbell, who was ostracized for his long poem (one of his least successful poems) in praise of General Franco, *Flowering Rifle*, and who, in 1946, was to launch an attack on the composite poetic orthodoxy of the 1930s in his volume *Talking Bronco*. Campbell invented a composite character called 'MacSpaunday' (a fusion of the names MacNeice, Auden, Spender, and Day Lewis) as a symbol of a verbal anti-Fascist crusader who, when it came to the push, would not risk his life for his beliefs. But he did not satirize Dylan Thomas. In Thomas's direct lyrical energy he, like Edith Sitwell, perhaps saw a poetic bias akin to his own.

Thomas's poems were to achieve a very wide popularity and a very wide influence. On his sadly early death in 1953, his *Collected Poems*, which came out in the previous year, had already sold ten thousand copies, a very large sale even for the work of a famous poet. Yet his poems are extraordinarily difficult, if one thinks, that is, of the task of understanding a poem as involving producing a prose paraphrase of it. There are several guides to Thomas's poetry, most of which content themselves with loose associative paraphrase. The later poems, those in *Deaths and Entrances* (1946) and the poems written after that and included in the *Collected Poems* are easier to give an account of, but still not very easy. The most useful book about the poet is Ralph Maud's *Entrances to Dylan Thomas's Poetry* which seeks to explain the poems not by paraphrase but by a study of poetic method, of Thomas's way of balancing up emotionally negative and emotionally positive words and images so that each poem can be thought of as a pattern of pluses and minuses, a kind of equation. But it may be generally helpful to say that Thomas's poems are celebrations not statements, and that they celebrate an ambiguous cosmic process in which life and death, birth and death, man and nature, creation and destruction are seen as mutually necessary to each other, and their images (like Shakespeare's King Lear, Thomas thinks in images, not concepts) mutually imply each other. Blake's line 'Joy and grief are woven fine' is perhaps the best short clue to what Thomas is after. There is a development in his poems; it is the earlier ones that are mainly concerned with the splendour and mess of cosmic process, the later and clearer ones are touching recollections, often, of 'angel infancy', of a lost Edenic innocence, echoing certain moods of Wordsworth and Henry Vaughan. The great tolling voice of the poet breaks down, in any case, the intellectual reserves of the reader; Thomas's poems exist essentially as sound patterns and are not perhaps complete on the page, need his own voice to complete them. It was a voice of hypnotic power. Its message was that of a bard, if not that of a prophet. The poems are full of Biblical imagery and Thomas's closest poetic confidant, the distinguished Welsh poet, Vernon Watkins, saw Thomas as essentially Christian; William Empson, an admirer, though not so close a personal friend, saw the message as being one of what he called 'pessimistic pantheism.' Thomas's religiousness was, in fact, unlike Eliot's, say, not the sort of religiousness that can translate itself into intellectual formulae; it was above, or below, dogma. But it is as a poet not of religious thought but of the raw and awesome experience that makes religiousness that he will be remembered; a poet in his own formulation working up through a warring dialectic of images from darkness to light. His poems, though extremely individual, are oddly impersonal or unegotistic. As a person, he was a great comic performer, and this side of him comes out in his short stories, *Portrait of the Artist as a Young Dog*, and in his poetic radio play in prose, *Under Milk Wood*—a transformation of the small Welsh town by the sea, Laugharne (Llaregub in the play) where he spent his happiest and most fruitful times. His grim death, his brilliant but drunken and desperate performances in America, the legend of the poet who was always drunk, imitation of the weakest and most imitable aspects of his work by poets with none of his talent, the fecklessness about money which in fact went with an ability to put skill and industry into many things (film scenarios, broadcast scripts, radio performances, public readings) have obscured the meticulous care that he put into his poetry proper, his 'craft or sullen art.' Bad memorial poems, an indiscreet and hysterical memoir by his widow, John Malcolm Brinnin's blow-by-blow account of the *dégringolade* in which Brinnin acted as impresario, none of these things have helped Thomas's posthumous reputation; but his correspondence with Vernon Watkins shows us the true poet and what was best in the real man.

George Barker's first book *Thirty Preliminary Poems* came out in 1933, a year before Dylan Thomas's *18 Poems*; both were published by David Archer's Parton Press. David Archer should be mentioned as a very benevolent man who did much to keep the poorer poets (poorer in wealth) of the 1930s and later going. He had a poetry bookshop, and my memory of my only visit to it is that I found two rare and reasonably valuable books, John Crowe Ransom's *God Without Thunder* and an English translation of Léon Daudet's memoirs, long out of print. I would gladly have paid a pound each for them, but Archer insisted on my having them as a gift. To one young poet, who visited his bookshop frequently, he always gave, when the poet was leaving, a box of matches. The poet, who did not smoke, would throw it away after leaving the shop. The fourth or fifth time after receiving the box, he opened it, either out of curiosity or because a friend in a pub asked him for a light. It contained a five-pound note. Run on these principles, Archer's bookshop ultimately had to close, but he will have his reward in heaven. He stands in my mind for an element of kindness, of charity, which redeems the fecklessness of London bohemian life.

A digression, but one that suggests an atmosphere. Dylan Thomas, George Barker, David Gascoyne, W. S. Graham, poets whose names point to a broadly romantic reaction against the clinical strictness of the young Auden's influence, were all friends of Archer's. It has been George Barker's misfortune to be generally compared with Dylan Thomas, and generally to his detriment. The comparison is inept. In that bohemian London world of the 1930's and after, Dylan Thomas was a natural innocent and victim, Barker had the toughness, cockiness and ruthlessness not only to survive but to thrive—the toughness and ruthlessness of a cockney Irishman. There are three disparate elements in his poetry, a Keatsian lushness of imagery, a Byronic or Villonesque gift for mockery and confession, in a flip off-hand style, and, in some short poems, a simple old-fashioned lyricism, suggesting Tom Moore or Moore's Victorian imitators. More crudely, there is in Barker a poet of 'sensations rather than thoughts', a wide boy, and a concert-platform singer. These three strands of talent never quite fuse, and in each of his modes Barker exhibits what could be called a brilliant bad taste: Geoffrey Grigson has lambasted him, rather in the manner of *Blackwood's* on Keats, in an essay whose title is taken from a line of Barker's: 'How Much Your Acrobatics Now Me Amaze!'

The imagery is brilliant but also often flashy; the ear for verbal music is rich but greedy for coarse clashes and sonorities; the simple singer warbles, is aware of his audience, is a little too throaty. There is poetry everywhere, but there are few poems satisfactory as wholes. The basic themes are a Roman Catholic sense of guilt and a wild sexuality, on which the sense of guilt impinges. *The True Confession of George Barker*, of 1950, a Villonesque testament which Barker's usual publishers were too squeamish to bring out, is the most impressive sustained poem.

David Gascoyne, who wrote in the late 1930's the first English book on Surrealism, and who experimented in his early work with the Surrealist method, moved on to write a kind of visionary poetry, at once radically revolutionary and Christian, a vision of what he called in a fine poem of the 1940's the 'Christ of Revolution and Poetry' and was to go on to Blakean visions of modern London as a city of the damned. He combines an intense and high-strung poetic temperament with a surprising occasional gift for good-natured parody, or satire, and his diction at its best has the purity of a poet seeking to get beyond diction, beyond mere 'art', to the language of an angry and bewildered prophet. W. S. Graham, a rather younger man than any of these, was handicapped quite early on by the label 'the Scottish Dylan Thomas.' He is an extremely conscious and cerebral poet, resembling Dylan Thomas only in the meticulous care (a single long poem will sometimes take him years) with which he builds up his verses, and in the fact that his poems are, by conscious intention, untranslatable into prose. He has lived as much, or more, among painters than poets and his most famous volume *The Night Fishing* (1955) recalls, especially in its title poem, the fusion or compromise in much modern painting between the abstract and the near-figurative. He puts, he has said, word upon word, like brick upon brick, working at abstract problems of movement and structure. The words, it might be said, in their relations, their shocks against each other, or quieter juxtapositions, become the main items in the poem: words chosen not like Dylan Thomas's for associativeness but for a tight self-identity, a muscular separateness. A poet's poet, rather than a poet for the common reader, his difficult intentions and painful and slow honesty in carrying them out have aroused the respect of all craftsmanlike readers. Though communication, except of an abstract structural pattern, is not his purpose, his character and background, working-class Greenock, the sea, fishing boats, a certain defiant and bony sturdiness, a demand to be listened to, express themselves in these poems.

I may seem to be lingering too long on the 1930's but that was a more seminal decade than the 1940's or 1950's: much that is best in the final twenty years of our survey seems to me to come out, either by reaction or direct or indirect imitation, of the 1930's. I have dealt with the Auden group, and with some young poets who might be thought of as in general reaction against it. All the poets of the Auden group had been to Oxford. Cambridge in the 1930s also produced poets of distinction, notably William Empson, Ronald Bottrall (whom F. R. Leavis in *New Bearings in English Poetry* thought the most promising young poet of the period), Kathleen Raine, and Charles Madge. Of these, Empson is the most famous, but more so, perhaps, as a critic than a poet. As an undergraduate, working under I. A. Richards, he drafted a dissertation which was to become his famous first book of criticism, *Seven Types of Ambiguity*. Critics of a traditional type, like John Sparrow, had attacked 'modern' poetry precisely for something like ambiguity, the difficulty of arriving at a settled judgement about the modern poet's attitudes or feelings, and the unnecessary intellectual puzzles he set the reader. Empson's book suggested that all or very much good poetry of the past, if read carefully enough, has the same sort of difficulty, sets the same sort of puzzles, and that one main power of poetic language (as distinguished, for instance, from the language of expository prose) is that, whether or not the poet consciously intends it, it can hold in solution attitudes and beliefs that might seem to be not easily compatible with each other, or even flatly to contradict each other. Puns and quibbles, as in Shakespeare, deliberate sophistries, as in Donne, can be the instruments of very serious poetry. In the United States particularly, Empson's approach caught on and critics like Allen Tate and Cleanth Brooks looked for Donne-like qualities, for 'paradox' and 'tension', even in poets like Wordsworth or Keats where one could not expect to find such qualities. Empson, as a critic, like his mentor I. A. Richards, no doubt, owed a great deal to Eliot's early essays on Metaphysical poetry and on the rich and puzzling language of Jacobean dramatists like Tourneur.

Empson's first volume is often, indeed, reminiscent of Donne, both in the tortured ingenuity of its conceits and quibbles and in the note of despairing passion which echoes through it. *Poems* came out in 1935. Empson's second volume, *The Gathering Storm*, written after an experience of teaching in Japan and then China, during the Japanese invasion, was still difficult, but more hopeful and sturdy, and certainly more social, in its tone. Having seen how the great civilizations of the Far East have managed to survive disasters greater than Western Europe had in 1940 experienced for centuries, Empson's attitude to the Second World War was a stoically and ironically courageous one. The tone of this volume suggested less Donne than Restoration poets like Rochester, Dryden, and Marvell in his political satires. There were experiments in terza rima, with a hanging line left at the end of a poem, and in villanelle with a constant ringing of the changes on the sense of the refrain, which were to have a great, if belated, influence on young poets coming into notice in the 1950's, like John Wain. More important still was to be the influence of Empson's tone, dry, flat, throw-away, matter-of-fact, though masking and mastering a great body of inner pain. Perhaps the central tension or paradox of Empson's own poetry, its central ambiguity, is our sense of extraordinary ingenuity combined with a plain man's blunt and direct attitudes, and appetites, these attitudes and appetites themselves undermined by a Buddhistic sense (in the Far East, Empson had been greatly impressed by Buddhist art) that all striving and craving partakes of illusion. Empson's ingenuity is in the end the least important part of his poetic equipment; the passion, the conviction in the voice, the courage with which he struggles with a sense of pain, fear, and dereliction, these are the most important parts.

Ronald Bottrall has suffered a great deal from Leavis's backing him, in the 1930's, as the most promising of what were then the younger poets. He has combined a copious production of poetry with a successful career as a British Council administrator and teacher, but very few critics would say that Leavis's hopes have been fulfilled. Bottrall in his early work was much influenced by Pound, whose first thirty *Cantos* he reviewed for *Scrutiny*. Some of the early work resembled the *Cantos*, other parts of it, social-satirical examinations of the London literary scene, had the note of *Mauberley*. In a sense, Bottrall had learned the lesson of the Master all too well. The new appetite for poetry in the 1930's was not for allusive obliqueness but for a certain directness of emotional impact, which is, for instance, however difficult his thought-structure is, one of the obvious qualities of Bottrall's friend Empson. Bottrall's career, also, encouraged a kind of cosmopolitanism in his poetry, an evocation of the history, thought and atmosphere of foreign places, and it was just this cosmopolitanism that the young poets of the

1950's, the 'Movement' generation, were reacting against; they rediscovered Empson, so very sturdily English even when he is writing about China, but ignored Bottrall. He has had bad luck in two decades, but this intelligent, copious, uneven poet could bear restudying.

Of the other Cambridge poets I have mentioned, Charles Madge in the 1930's showed most technical promise; he wrote some brilliant poems in quatrains, of a lucid eighteenth-century elegance, and one very splendid sonnet, 'The sun of whose terrain we creatures are.' He had a quality, rare among his contemporaries, or direct eloquence, his quatrains almost recalling Gray's in their poise, but without an effect of pastiche or frigidity. He got caught up, however, in a social movement of the time, a kind of amateur mass sociology called 'Mass Observation'—observations by masses of people rather than of them—and was to end up as a Professor of Sociology. The title of one of his volumes was *The Father Found* and in a reading of his poems which I once attended he explained that the Father was, or turned out to be, Society. In the early 1950's he published some poetry in a new style, modelled a little on Pound's *Cantos*, in Peter Russell's magazine *Nine*. It was interesting, but had not the authority of the early work, and has not been collected. All one can say, with a sigh, is that the gain of social studies has been poetry's loss.

Though Kathleen Raine was a Cambridge contemporary of these poets (and, indeed, for a time was married to Charles Madge), she is not really of their school, and would say today that she considers the whole 'modern' attitude to poetry a mistake. She studied the natural sciences at Cambridge and her poetry is marked by a vivid sense of natural process, a knowledge of botany and geology, for instance, but, as with Blake, on whose symbolism she has done much scholarly work, this 'vegetative universe' has become for her merely a veil before, or an inadequate symbol for, a real and eternal world of Platonic forms, the world of what Blake and Coleridge called the Imagination. For her, as for Coleridge, the poetic imagination (what Coleridge called the Secondary Imagination) is a reflection, or recreation, in the poet's soul of the Primary Imagination, the creative power of God. She would now call herself a Christian Platonist, and this seems to her to be the tradition also of the English poets she most admires, Spenser, Milton, Blake, Shelley, and Yeats. With its deliberate exclusion of 'mere human emotion' (which was a good enough subject, for instance, for Chaucer and Shakespeare), Miss Raine's world may seem to some readers a very etherial one; but the purity of her diction, the clarity of her imagery, and her perfect ear should make her seem to the candid reader, even if he cannot share her philosophy. one of the finest lyrical and meditative poets of our time.

## V

I have said that the period we are considering falls very neatly into three sections. The first was the 1930's, a decade dominated by political and economic crisis, by the threat of war; the imagination of the poet, or of some leading and influential poets, tended in that decade to be at the mercy of external forces, the poetic conscience directed to public issues. The Second World War, strangely enough, slackened that sense, for the young poet, of the primacy of politics. Young men in the army found themselves defending a social system about which they felt a great scepticism against a system, that of Nazi Germany and its satellites, which was positively evil. And one effect of life in the forces, of course, is to impress upon poets the values of the private life, home surroundings, family affections, things which the Auden group had, on the whole, reacted against. Three young poets of considerable talent, Keith Douglas, Alun Lewis, and Sidney Keyes all died in their twenties in that war, Douglas in Normandy, Keyes in North Africa, Lewis in India. Keyes and Douglas had both begun to make a reputation in Oxford as undergraduates before they enlisted. Lewis, a Welsh schoolteacher, who had done research in history, had written some poetry before the war but had published little. His poetry was less 'literary', more uneven in technique, but also perhaps less protected by the sophistications of technique than that of the other two. It aroused the interest and sympathy of Robert Graves who found in Lewis's fusion of the themes of love and death, and in his awareness of the mysteries of the Welsh mythological tradition, something akin to the poetic philosophy which he was working out himself, during the war, in *The White Goddess*. The poet of the recent past whom Lewis most admired, and to whom perhaps he owed most, was Edward Thomas, whose great poetic gifts had been released by the First World War, which gave him a leisure to write which as a hard-working literary journalist he had never enjoyed. The concept of a 'war-poem' is a very ambiguous one. Lewis wrote about the loneliness of soldiers, but he could also write about the loneliness of Welsh miners. When he went to India, the poverty and dignity of a peasant society which has watched so many armies passing, and has turned back to till its poor soil, moved him deeply. The pity of the human condition, our wish for death as a sort of sleep, the memory and reality of distant love in dreams, these were the topics that moved him, and the war was at most a pretext.

Lewis is very much a 'human' poet, Keyes was very much a 'literary' one. Like his Oxford friend, John Heath-Stubbs, he had turned away from the influence of Auden, towards the Romantic tradition, which was embodied for him in Wordsworth, in Coleridge, in Yeats, in Rilke, in the modern German romantic cinema. He had had a very lonely childhood, and his deepest emotions sprang from books, rather than people; he fell unhappily in love in Oxford with a German girl, a refugee from Hitler's Germany, but this love in its very hopelessness smacked also of the literary romantic tradition. His careful diction and rhythms arouse admiration but seem to put a veil between the reader (perhaps between the poet also) and the poet's more faltering, more hesitant, more spontaneous emotions. Even in the poems written on active service, the scene is never objectively described; Keyes used myth and history to refer to it obliquely. He was socially very successful at Oxford, producing plays, making many friends, writing for and helping to edit *Cherwell*, he was a good soldier, yet the impression he leaves is that of a solitary; one for whom the brute items of the external world do not exist unless they can become part of his vocabulary of symbols. There is, however, a real if frail distinction in his verse, and had he lived he might have broken out of his enclosed world.

I have a certain vested interest in Keith Douglas, the first edition of whose *Collected Poems*, which came out in 1951, I helped to edit. This edition came out too late to cash in on the vogue for war poetry and too early to appeal to an interest in the Second World War as past and over, as history. It was not till the beginning of the 1960's that a fine poet, Ted Hughes, by a brilliant broadcast and a fine selected edition put Douglas really on the map, preparing the way for a comprehensive edition of his verse and prose. Douglas was the hardest, toughest, most masculine of these three poets, the only one who could be described as a 'natural soldier', the only one who wrote poems, as the poets of the First World War did, dealing with the actual experience of combat. When I met him during the war, when I helped to edit him, what moved me was the extraordinary poise and maturity of so young a man, the gallantry and courage which, however, did not imply any false romanticising of war: though the external, objective approach, which he needed in order to steady his nerves, might give a careless reader a false impression of emotional, not merely technical, hardness. Re-reading him from the standpoint of middle age, I am more aware of an element of brittleness and precariousness in the poise, of the strain that he is enduring, of how deeply life (not only the war) had hurt him. This new awareness of his youth, his vulnerability, the fine face he was putting on things, enhances rather than diminishes my sense of his achievement as a man and a poet. He was, I think, the only one of these three poets, who, had he lived, might have become a great poet, and a leader and model for younger men.

One fine poet of war, who survived, and who is unjustly neglected, is the Scottish poet Hamish Henderson. His *Elegies for the Dead in Cyrenaica* suffered, perhaps, like Keith Douglas's *Collected Poems*, from coming out a few years after the war was over. They are vigorous poems in a loose free verse, with a technique of juxtaposition and association, that owes something to Pound, something perhaps to the later work in English free verse, of the doyen of Scottish poets, Hugh MacDiarmid. They evoke the skirling of the pipes, the Highland rage for combat, but also the pathos and homeliness of the private's life. A Scottish Nationalist, and a Marxist, a firm believer that the deep and healthy roots of all culture are in the common people, Henderson has devoted his great gifts in recent years not to original composition but to collecting on tape all the variants that survive of Highland and Lowland Scottish ballad, lament, and folk-song.

## VI

Much of the best new poetry of the Second World War period was, however, written by civilians. In Cairo, in particular, three poets, Lawrence Durrel, Bernard Spencer, and Terence Tiller. wrote poems which evoked with peculair vividness both the splendour and misery of the Egyptian scene; Durrell and Spencer wrote poems also about mainland Greece where they had been working before the fall of Crete. The magazine which they edited in Cairo, *Personal Landscape*, had very high standards, compared to many other wartime poetry magazines, and published some of the work of Keith Douglas. All three writers had a peculiar elegance of craftsmanship, and Durrell and Spencer had a peculiar sensibility to light and landscape, which gave their work a certain family likeness; there was in their poetry also a sense of play, of art as a game—in Auden's sense, 'a serious game'—which was unusual in wartime poetry. Tiller, though a very patient craftsman, was perhaps of the three the most sombrely morally engaged, the least merely 'aesthetic' poet: but Durrell and Spencer were also commenting on life, though perhaps rarely rawly and directly on life, but more on life as embodied in the images which Egypt and Greece embodied of the grandeur and decay of the Mediterranean roots of Western culture. Durrell was to become the most famous of these poets (though his fame as a poet has never matched his fame as a novelist), but Bernard Spencer, unjustly neglected during his lifetime—his *Collected Poems* came out a year or two after his tragically early death in 1963—seems to me to have had a purer, if less various and copious, gift. Work as a B.B.C. producer for the Third Programme has prevented Tiller, in recent years, from producing as many new poems as his admirers would wish. These poets had a slightly younger disciple, Alan Ross, now editor of the *London Magazine*. Ross, who served in the Royal Navy during the war, was not one of the Cairo circle, but after the war gave an admiring broadcast talk on their work, and his own poems, mainly arising out of his travels in Italy and Africa, have something of the combination of terseness, visual exactness, and a sad and balanced sense of history, which he admired in the Cairo group. It should be admitted that to some critics poetry of this sort, because depending on the attraction of the exotic, because not rooted in native English experience, appears precious and derivative; I have heard it described as 'picture-postcard poetry', but, though tart and amusing, the description is unfair.

One should mention along with these poets of the Mediterranean two poets born in Greece, who have written very distinguished work in English, Demetrios Capetanakis and Constantine Trypanis. Capetanakis died young but his one volume, sympathetically introduced by his friend John Lehmann, has a peculiar mature poised sadness that recalls the great Alexandrian poet, Kafavis or Cavafy. Trypanis was born in the island of Chios, but, coming of a wealthy family, had an English governess. He taught at Oxford for many years, but is now at Chicago. His poems, which have been highly praised by W. H. Auden, are remarkable for the elliptical precision with which they evoke Greek landscape and history. His longest, most recent, and most ambitious poem, *Elegies for a Glass*

*Adonis*, is essentially an elegy for a culture that has petrified or, in his own image, vitrified, and gathered dust: an elegy for a seed that has not died to be reborn. In most ages, a poet writing in a language not his own is at a disadvantage. In our age, when native taste in language is uncertain, when English like American poets are always uneasy about their own idiom, a foreign poet writing in English may gain by handling the language with an old-fashioned simple correctness and purity.

## VII

I would like now to break the so far strictly chronological pattern of this survey by considering a number of poets who began to attract wide attention after 1945, but some of whom had been writing for many years, and all of whom would consider the poetic activity as essentially 'timeless.' Edwin Muir, a poet born in the Orkneys and brought up, from his 'teens onwards, in the slums of Glasgow, had made a living throughout the 1920's and 1930's as a critic and translator of great writers in German like Mann, Broch, and Kafka. During the war he worked for the British Council in Edinburgh, and later in Prague and Rome. He became Warden of Newbattle Abbey, a residential adult education college near Edinburgh, and finished off his public career as visiting professor of poetry at Harvard. He had been writing and publishing volumes of poems since the 1920's, and his *The Story and the Fable* of 1940 (revised and expanded in the 1950's as *Autobiography*) had been recognized as a small masterpiece. It was not till his younger friend J. C. Hall edited the first edition of his *Collected Poems* in 1951, however, that the full scope of his poetic gift was generally recognized.

Muir's gift as a poet, as the title of the first version of his autobiography suggests, was essentially that of a fabulist. The three greatest influences on his poetry were probably the ballads, still a living oral tradition in the Orkneys of his youth, Heine, and Wordsworth. Though a master of simple stanza forms and of a clear and dignified blank verse he is not in any sense a 'modernist' in diction or technique, or, except in a very profound and hidden sense, a modernist in topic or themes. It seemed to him that the stuff of good poetry is perennial and that the great innovators of this country, Pound, Eliot, and the others, had created a revolution only on the surface of poetry, had twisted, as it were, the shape of the waves; the deep sea swell underneath was still the same. His poetry is not, however, divorced

296

from his often raw and painful personal experience. In one of his most ambitious and successful long poems, 'The Labyrinth', though the fable is the fable of Theseus, though the Cretan labyrinth is contrasted with the Aegean islands on which the Gods look down, the reader of his autobiography knows also that the labyrinth is the slum streets of Glasgow, in which the young Muir wandered endlessly, and the Aegean islands are the Orkneys of his childhood, bare, treeless, but still carrying on a timeless tradition of pastoral, the unchanging lives of farmers and fishermen, ruled by the unchanging circuit of the seasons. A fine and sombre poem, 'The Horses', imagines a moment when our mechanical and destructive civilization has at last killed itself, and mysteriously great horses come to lead the men who survive back to that natural agricultural life. In the title of one of his finest short poems, Muir had 'one foot in Eden'; his poems are more than merely archetypal because he had the other foot planted on earth and because he recognizes, like Wordsworth, that sorrow and the Fall and the fading of the vision into the light of common day are not all loss, they enrich our sympathies, enrich 'the human heart.'

There are a number of other poets who tend to group in one's mind with Edwin Muir, because their vision of life is broadly or precisely a Christian one, because their handling of metre and diction is 'traditional' rather than 'modern', and because their attitudes to what poetry does are timeless or perennial rather than historical. Vernon Watkins, the friend and confidant of Dylan Thomas, read modern languages at Cambridge, but chose to take a job as a bank-clerk in Swansea so that he could devote all his best energies to poetry. He had a house on the beautiful Gower peninsula looking out over cliffs on a wonderful sea-scape of fretted rocks, indented bays, and often wild and high waves, seabirds battling against the wind, and an ever-changing pattern of clouds and colours in the sky. These elements he wove slowly into long poems of musical modulation, in which, as in Henry Vaughan's poems and as sometimes in Wordsworth, the changing and mysterious light of the sky, in particular, became for him an emblem, perhaps an example, of God's brooding presence in the world and to the soul. He could write, however, poems of another sort: quatrains of a Landorian elegance, that sometimes risked a Landorian frigidity: a strangely personal and intimate poem in which, in a dream, he meets his dead friend Dylan Thomas: an easy, gay, conversational poem in which he records, with extraordinary felicity and vivacity, the talk of Yeats. Watkins's output was not large, he would take years to get a poem to his liking from the germ through successive drafts to a publishable version, and he scorned the sort of criticism which attempted (as a survey like this must) to tie down the manner and tone of a poem to a particular historical period. He died in 1967, shortly after retiring from his banking post, caught by a heart-attack, while resident poet at an American college, in the middle of a vigorous set of tennis. Into his sixties Watkins retained the athletic vigour of a young man, not only physically, but in the suppleness and energy of his verse.

Another Welsh poet who stands more or less outside the time pattern, or period fashions, is R. S. Thomas, an Episcopalian clergyman, with a parish in the hill country of North Wales. Though exact and detailed in his recording of natural scenery, Thomas is not a nature mystic like Watkins, and, like Crabbe, he dislikes the pastoral sentimentalities of the tourist's eye view of Wales. He knows that the sheep, so pleasantly dispersed on the hill side, have fluke or foot-rot; that the life of small farmers in these pleasant white-washed plain little houses is often mean and grinding; he knows, from his pastoral care, that envy, hate, meanness and malice flourish as much in small hamlets as in big towns, and that 'honest poverty' is not always an ennobling influence on human nature. North Wales is much more nationalistic than South Wales (the Gower peninsula, from which Watkins came—and Watkins's name is very English—is a kind of enclave of Welshmen of ancient English speech and descent). Thomas is a nationalist, bitter about the tourists who sprawl with their caravan sites along the north coast of Wales, or about the English intellectuals who rent and refit derelict cottages, and the 'Elsan culture.' But his sense of the beauty of his country, and his compassion as a Christian priest for his parishioners, conquer a certain tendency in him towards an almost Swiftian bitterness, a dour realism like Crabbe's. His diction is an admirably clear and plain, his rhythms are not those of song but of precisely modulated speech.

One might mention along with Thomas an English poet, now in his eighties, of Scottish birth and education, but for many years a clergyman in the home counties, Canon Andrew Young. Young had been known for many years as a writer of short and exact nature poems (he is a distinguished amateur botanist, who has written a delightful book about his hobby, *A Prospect of Flowers*) that combine their precision of observation with a pleasant fancifulness, like that of a minor metaphysical. His long poem, *Out of This World and Back*, starts in his country parish and explores the afterworld, before getting back home.

The plain exactness of the introduction carries on to the visionary part of the poem, and gives it a peculiar sort of authenticity. Though comparatively neglected by critics, *Out of This World and Back* is one of the best long-short or short-long poems of our time. Another poet who does not fit into any categories easily is Basil Bunting, a Northumbrian poet in his sixties, the only really distinguished English disciple of Ezra Pound. He is a first-rate technician but his *Collected Poems*, obscurely published in 1950 in Texas, were almost ignored in England (in *Nine* I wrote the only English review). *Collected Poems*, with some additions, has recently been published in this country as *Loquitur*. Bunting's recent long poem *Briggflats*, with a Northumbrian setting, and some use of Northumbrian dialect, has been highly praised by Cyril Connolly.

One other writer is apt for mention here, because, like Bunting, he owes a great deal to Ezra Pound. David Jones is a Londoner, of Welsh ancestry, who fought through the First World War. His *In Parenthesis* (1937), which won the Hawthornden prize, is a kind of epic of that war, partly in cadenced prose, partly in long versicles which might be described indifferently as free verse or liturgical prose. He is probably better known as an artist, visionary painter, engraver, masterly letterist than as a writer; in his patient craftsmanship combined with visionary strangeness he is, as an artist, broadly of the school of Blake but, unlike Blake, he is both a Roman Catholic and a passionately accurate archaeologist, so his vision, unlike Blake's, is an orthodoxly Christian one. *The Anathemata* (1952) is a work much more difficult for the ordinary reader than *In Parenthesis*. One critic, David Blamires, has said :

It shares the qualities of chronicle, epic, drama, incantation and lyric and is at the same time none of these and more than all put together. The poet himself defected in his own description of it as 'fragments of an attempted writing', and yet this does contain a necessary truth. He is right to call it an attempt—an attempt at a vision of Britain; and the fragments are inevitable, since the knowledge of one man must be fragmentary, though he may possess the perception of essentials and the things that will stand for others and be the light shining in darkness. Each poet seeks to recreate the world in his own image, that part of the world that he sees, but the overwhelming number, especially at present, confine themselves to the fraction, the aspect, the minute detail of life on which they put the imprint of their vision. What

distinguishes the *Cantos* or *Finnegans Wake* or *Ulysses* and
*The Anathemata* is the fact that are attempts to depict a
*universum*; they represent a totality including the whole of
history.[3]

*The Anathemata* cannot be judged or even summarily described in a survey of this length: merely, with great respect,
called attention to.

A work that rasises some puzzles of the same sort as *The
Anathemata* is the very long poem, itself only the beginning
of an even longer one, by the doyen of Scottish poets, Hugh
MacDiarmid, *In Memoriam James Joyce*, which came out in
1955. A lively correspondence in *The Times Literary Supplement* in 1965 revealed that a number of passages in this long
work were pieces of prose by other writers (some of them long
anonymous articles in *The Times Literary Supplement* itself)
which Mr. MacDiarmid had transposed into a Poundian free
verse. Any poem attempting to 'depict a *universum*' must, like,
Pound's own *Cantos*, contain some passages of allusion and con-
cealed quotation but what worried critics was that in reflective
passages, in what seemed his own most intimate self-communings, Mr. MacDiarmid in *In Memoriam James Joyce* was in fact
transcribing—giving them, no doubt, by breaking them up into
a sort of verse, a new cadence or a new solemnity—the reflections and self-communings of other people. Yet it may be that
by lifting some words of mine, rearranging their typographical
setting, and putting them in the context of his own words, a
poet makes them his own. Eliot makes lines of Shakespeare or
Dante or Cavalcanti his own: can one absorb and transform
in the same way whole pages of somebody else's expository
prose?

MacDiarmid had made his early reputation by lyrical, comic
and satirical poems in a revised Lowland Scots. There, a young
admirer of his, Iain Crichton Smith, thinks, his real genius lay.
His mistake, in later years, has, Crichton Smith thinks, been
to attempt to use poetry for purposes of communication and
persuasion for which prose is much more efficient, to sacrifice
the god of poetry to the idol of the idea. I am not quite sure
about this. I find myself in the later MacDiarmid much that is
obstinately tedious, and passionately one-sided, in what is
possibly a typically Lowland Scottish way, but also plenty of
other passages that have a cantankerous life or a raw and
moving immediacy, presenting the hesitant process of thinking
rather than the moulded results of thought.

## VIII

The poets I have been dealing with in the last section were either too individual by nature or too ambitiously and experimentally individualistic to have a very direct technical effect on the work of younger poets. One poet, who again thinks of poetry as timeless, as a 'pre-historical or post-historical' activity but who has had a great influence on younger poets is Robert Graves. I would count Graves and Auden (Auden very much admires Graves, Graves tends to dismiss Auden as a 'synthetic' poet) as the two most fertile, intelligent and variously gifted poets of English birth surviving today. For Graves, true poetry is Muse poetry, poetry written out of love for the Muse, who is the White Goddess, representing Birth, Love, and Death, a feminine image of the fertility of Nature. She dominated the early Mediterranean world, as the Cretan lady with birds in her hat and snakes in her hands shows, as the Cycladic goddesses show, and for Graves all went wrong when the Olympians supplanted her, when the upstart mouse-god Apollo enslaved her votaries, the Muses. Graves's theory of poetry owes something to Nietzsche's epoch-making essay *The Birth of Tragedy*, which distinguished between the roots of tragedy in Dionysian orgy, dancings and sacrifices, and the Apollonian distancing which turned this bloody and ecstatic raw material into art. Though in theory Graves dismisses Apollonian distancing, in practice his great influence on younger poets, the almost universal admiration now felt for him, springs at least largely from his neatness, control, and delicacy as a verse craftsman, as well as from the attraction of his sardonic personality, that of an English eccentric of the old type, and from the quirky humour he displays in his comic poems, these 'satires and grotesques' he devises for wits rather than for the appreciation of fellow poets. The poems are also, I think, profoundly moving because the mythic overlay does not disguise the deeper personal layer of experience from which they spring: shell-shock, terror, and depression, after the first World War: the tensions of a difficult marriage with Nancy Nicholson and a difficult poetic and critical partnership with the American poet, Laura Riding: the growing serenity and happiness of his later years, married to a much younger wife, attracting younger admirers, a new serenity coming to him in age. The poems of the seven years between *Collected Poems, 1959* and *Collected Poems, 1965*, which comprise about the last third of the second volume, are the happiest Graves has written. But even his most painful earlier poems are, in an aesthetic sense, happy since they shape the way in which the reader takes the poem towards that 'overplus of pleasure' which Wordsworth saw was necessary for poetic satisfaction. The only two important hostile criticisms of Graves that I know of pounce on this point. In 1939 in *Twentieth Century Verse*, the editor of that magazine, Julian Symons, said that he thought Graves was skilful but overrated: there was an underlying raw material that could be called 'Graves' but it was too easily turned into pleasing and innocuous stuff that could be called 'poetry.' (Auden, and Graves himself in the dedicatory poem introducing *Collected Poems, 1959*, have both recognized neatness and facility as this poet's danger). In the 1950s, Philip Hobsbaum similarly in *Time and Tide* wished to dismiss Graves as a 'pastoral' poet, who pleased but could not deeply or disturbingly move. To me, he does seem disturbing, moving, and almost in spite of himself, 'modern', in a way that Muir or Watkins or Andrew Young, for instance, are not. He moves in that psychological realm of traps, ambivalences, ironies and tensions, 'ambiguous gifts', which is the distinctively 'modern' realm. He does not appeal, as Muir and Watkins and David Jones appeal, to Kathleen Raine; his vision and his appetites are too earthy, his White Goddess myth is all too far from her own Christianized neo-Platonism. She agrees with me, however, that he 'keeps up the language.'

## IX

I have dealt with the war poets of the Second World War and with what might be called the 'Cairo school' of Durrell, Spencer, and Tiller. The years between 1945 and 1953 were a period in which older poets like Graves and Muir enhanced their reputation but in which new poets of a younger generation seemed far to seek. The period with its rationing and drabness, with the introduction of the Welfare State, was one of social justice but aesthetic meagreness. Young poets who had shown promise in the war years tended to dry up. Too many lesser poets, in little magazines, wrote in a loose and vague evocative style, drawing on the weaker aspects of Dylan Thomas or George Barker. The slightly factitious general interest in poetry which a war in this century always produces ('Where are the war poets?') died down. The death of Dylan Thomas in 1953, however, was the signal for a crystallizing of attention round a number of younger poets, who had been appearing in the Fantasy Press pamphlets published by Oscar Mellor at Oxford and in the subscription volumes produced by Reading University School of Art. The first novels of two of them, John Wain and Kingsley Amis, aroused much interest and drew attention also to their poetry, and to the poetry of their friends. In 1956, Robert Conquest gathered these poets into a anthology *New Lines*, and in his introduction gave them something like a programme: the contributors were Kingsley Amis, Robert Conquest, Donald Davie, D. J. Enright, Thom Gunn, John Holloway, Elizabeth Jennings, Philip Larkin, and John Wain.

An article in *The Spectator* (October 1, 1954) dubbed this group of writers, 'The Movement.' The name, in retrospect, seems slightly inept; what was common to these poets was not so much any forward-looking or dynamic quality as a kind of call to order. They reacted against the Poundian kind of experimentalism, against both Dylan Thomas and his imitators, against the political Marxian Utopianism of the 1930's, against the ambitious emotional gesture and the large subject. Several of them had taken First class honours degrees in English at Oxford or Cambridge. As contrasted socially with the Oxford and Cambridge poets of the 1930's (who had tended to take poor degrees) they represented the academic type of mind, with its quality of balance, and its limitation of dryness and cautiousness. Socially, they were different: grammar school boys who had won scholarships; of the lower middle class rather than, like Spender or Auden or MacNeice, of the lower upper class; suspicious of metropolitan slickness, with its tendency to confuse social viability with literary merit—suspicious of what then began to be widely called (Amis's friend Henry Fairlie gave the phrase its currency) 'the Establishment.' All these writers were also, with the exception of the one women poet among them, Elizabeth Jennings, who was a devout Roman Catholic, atheists or agnostics. Their aesthetic aims were clarity and honesty, the avoidance of obfuscation, the poem as an instrument for the rational control of feeling. They believed in regular metre, strict stanza forms, clearness of communication, the provision of motives, rational motives, for the emotions a poem expresses. Though highly literate, and though their poems (several of them were university teachers of English) tended often to have a kind of donnish allusiveness, they were suspicious of 'literariness' in poetry, in the sense of any attempt to revive a romantic 'high style.'. Some disliked poems about foreign places or about philosophical ideas. Their immediate sources and influences were various, but not ever the main sources and influences of high 'modernism': not Pound, or Eliot, or even Yeats. Elizabeth Jennings owed much to the clarity and vision of Edwin Muir. Philip Larkin admired very much Hardy, Edward Thomas, John Betjeman, and R. S. Thomas. Donald Davie produced a useful anthology of the late Augustans. William Empson, about whose poetry John Wain had written excellently, was a strong influence, though fairly soon sloughed off, on the early Wain, and Wain's second volume *A Word Carved on a Sill* had a title taken from a poem by Robert Graves. A copious and talented older poet, Roy Fuller, who had begun writing in the late 1930's as a disciple of Auden's and who continued to express in his verse and prose the attitudes of a wry and disabused but not renegade Marxian, found these attitudes congenial, and was to be included in Conquest's second anthology, *New Lines II*, in 1963. The poetry of the 'Movement' as a whole was a poetry of moderation and rationality, a poetry which aimed at prose virtues, which viewed with distaste undisciplined squads of emotion. The attitudes behind it were humanly admirable (Hitlerism was an awful example of what undisciplined, unexamined emotions can do). The danger, often admirably overcome, was that of a certain tiredness, flatness, and tepidity. Roy Campbell's epigram 'On Some South African Novelists' has been cited *ad nauseam*, but it does come in aptly here:

> You praise the firm restraint with which they write—
> I'm with you there, of course:
> They use the snaffle and the curb all right,
> But where's the bloody horse?

Nearly all this poetry, in fact, had the plainness and honesty of prose; the question that critics asked was whether it did not have also, too often, the prosiness. Did it skim the ground, but with strong wings? Or did it merely walk along the ground, and had it wings at all? Could it fly if it tried to? There was also a moral question; was this poetry, much of it written by university lecturers and librarians, the work of a new élite, a group comfortably off on the whole, not wanting to change its world *very* radically—it was odd how these enemies of the Establishment so rapidly became pillars of it, quietly supplant-ing the older generation on the Third Programme, in the Sunday reviews, and in the literary weeklies—and could the poetry of Philip Larkin, for instance, be fairly summed up, as a radical poet of the Left, Christopher Logue, summed it up, as 'genteel belly-aching'? On a rather different level, could not the fear of destructive and irrational emotion become a poetically destructive 'fear of feeling', a paralysing dread of the Dionysian violence, the wild dance, which lies at the primitive roots of poetry? For A. Alvarez, the 'Movement' was cursed by the traditional English curse of primness, reticence, niceness, what he summed up as 'gentility.'

Alvarez, introducing a Penguin anthology of new poetry, contrasted a finely modulated poem of Philip Larkin's about horses at grass with the rough vigour of another poem about horses— less satisfactory as a whole—by Ted Hughes. Hughes had no connection with the 'Movement' but some ties with a slightly younger association of poets, the 'Group'. The roots of the Group were in Cambridge rather than Oxford, and at Cambridge one of its leading members, Philip Hobsbaum, had attacked the 'Movement' fiercely in the magazine *Delta* for being smooth, gutless, and beset by clichés. In London, he gathered round himself young poets who, at regular meetings, subjected the work of one of their number to close and detailed criticism, looking for rough energy, for what Dr. Leavis calls 'rootedness' rather than smoothness, and when Hobsbaum departed to Sheffield to study under William Empson, the Group met in the Chelsea house of Edward Lucie-Smith—whose own elegant and subdued poems were, ironically enough, very 'Movementish.' Hughes who, though not officially a 'Group' poet, was the sort of person the group admired, who wrote magnificently about birds and animals, was a poet of fierce, one-sided, driving emotion, not at all a poet of rationality and balance; the most obvious influences behind his work were D. H. Lawrence and poets of the First World War like Rosenberg and Owen. Another poet who had loose associations with the Group was David Holbrook, famous for his work on the use of poetry in educating culturally deprived children, and for the fierce neo-puritanism of his general cultural comments. Though both sets of poets avoided overt political commitment, the 'tone of voice' of the 'Movement' on the whole was liberal-conservative, that of the 'Group' radical in an ideologically uncommitted way. One other influence on the Group was the American vogue for 'confessional' poetry, starting off with Robert Lowell's *Life Studies* (1959) and reaching its climax, in this country, in the last poems, written shortly before her death in 1963, of the American-born poet Sylvia Plath, the wife of Ted Hughes. Thom Gunn, though very much of the 'Movement' in his clarity of diction and syntax, was more akin, in some ways, to Hughes in his fascination with restlessness, the dominating impulse, and adolescent violence. Gangs of leather-jacketed American motor-cyclists, in the James Dean and Marlon Brando tradition, provided him with striking images. But he studied under Yvor Winters, the great reactionary critic and formalistic-moralistic poet, at Stanford and so presented violence and lust always at a certain cool evaluating distance. Poets like Philip Hobsbaum himself, or like George MacBeth (a useful friend to young poets as a Third Programme poetry producer) got the violence and pain into the texture of their verse. Hobsbaum wrote about being a fat man, about losing his teeth, about mistaking the lavatory steps in a pub for a flat grille because of his astigma-tism; MacBeth was one of a number of poets who began to feel it necessary to relive in imagination the horrors of Hitlerism, identifying themselves often with the torturers rather than the tortured. Peter Redgrove was another often powerful young poet whose obsession was with negative emotions, with the ugly as an aesthetic category. It was between these two poises of spectatorial withdrawal and immersement *dans la boue* that English poetry seemed cautiously balanced at the end of the 1950's. Of the poets I have mentioned, Philip Larkin was the most generally respected; Ted Hughes and Thom Gunn were found by young readers the most exciting.

As I draw to the end of this survey, I have preferred to give a general picture of the scene and its directions rather than to give summary assessments, as I have done earlier of Auden, Graves, or Muir, of poets of whom some, in a different context, fully deserve such assessments. The late fifties are still very near to us; Larkin, Hughes, Gunn have no doubt all still their major work to do. A word, by way of epilogue, about the scene in the 1960's. What nobody could have clearly foreseen in the late 1950's was a movement away from the concept of poetry as literature towards a concept of poetry as popular perfor-mance, as a group activity, though there were hints of this already in the 1950's in the San Francisco Beats and, in this country, in Christopher Logue's experiments with poetry and jazz. A generation is now growing up that will get its first idea, not of poetry exactly but of the poetic, from the words of Bob Dylan's songs or of the Beatles' 'Eleanor Rigby' rather than from the printed page. As poetry becomes an audio-visual art the idea of the permanence of the poem may disappear. To young Americans, I have heard Leslie Fiedler say, Robert Lowell is now a historical figure, like Longfellow. The old distinctions, he added, and discriminations—I suppose between the transient and the permanent, the valuable and the worthless, the public and the private—must be swept away. While one side of poetry is becoming immersed, then, in the performatory arts, another, in the growth of interest in what is called concrete poetry, is being assimilated to purely visual patterning, to the graphic arts, to decoration. The whole traditional idea of what a poem is, of what (or whom) it is for, is radically under question. To one brought up in that old tradition, however, the history of these thirty years of English poetry—thirty years also of very rapid change in the political status and social structure of Great Britain—will seem a worthy period. Not as 'great' a period as the period of innovation, of great solitary figures like Yeats, Eliot, and Pound earlier in the century: but a period of poetic resource and honesty against a background of continual and unassuaged social anxiety.

## NOTES

1. Michael Roberts, preface to *New Signatures* (London, 1932).
2. Stephen Spender, *World Within World* (London, 1951), p. 137.
3. *Agenda*, David Jones Special Issue, V (1967), 101–102.

## BIBLIOGRAPHY

### A. General Critical Works

F. R. Leavis. *New Bearings in English Poetry*, (London, 1932). This looks back at the poetic revolution of the nineteen-twenties, and makes suggestions about the possible future development of English poetry, some of which were withdrawn in the second edition (1950).

Francis Scarfe. *Auden and After* (London, 1942). A journalistic but informative survey of the poetic personalities and movements of the thirties. It can be supplemented by Stephen Spender's autobiographical volume, *World within World* (London, 1951), Julian Symons' *The Thirties* (London, 1960), and D. E. S. Maxwell, *Poets of the Thirties* (London, 1969).

Derek Stanford. *The Freedom of Poetry* (London, 1948).

A. Alvarez. *The Shaping Spirit* (London, 1958). The American edition is called *Stewards of Excellence*.

G. S. Fraser. *Vision and Rhetoric* (London, 1959).

Anthony Thwaite. *Contemporary English Poetry* (London, 1959).

M. L. Rosenthal. *The New Poets* (New York, 1967).

Ian Hamilton (ed.). *The Modern Poet* (London, 1968).

### B. Studies of Particular Poets

*W. H. Auden*

Richard Hoggart. *Auden* (London, 1951).

Joseph Warren Beach. *The Making of the Auden Canon* (Minnesota, 1957).

Monroe K. Spears. *The Poetry of W. H. Auden* (New York, 1963).

Barbara Everett. *Auden* (Writers and Critics, Edinburgh and London, 1964).

Monroe K. Spears (ed.). *Auden: a Collection of Critical Essays* (Engelwood Cliffs, New Jersey, 1964).

John Fuller. *A Reader's Guide to W. H. Auden* (London, 1970).

*Robert Graves*

J. M. Cohen. *Robert Graves* (Writers and Critics, Edinburgh and London, 1960).

Douglas Day. *Swifter Than Reason* (Chapel Hill, 1963).
Michael Kirkham. *The Poetry of Robert Graves* (London, 1969).

## Hugh MacDiarmid

K. D. Duval and Sidney Goodsir Smith (eds.). *Hugh MacDiarmid: a Festschrift* (Edinburgh, 1962).
Kenneth Buthlay, *Hugh MacDiarmid* (Writers and Critics, Edinburgh and London, 1964).

## Edwin Muir

P. H. Butter. *Edwin Muir* (Writers and Critics, Edinburgh and London, 1962).
—— *Edwin Muir: Man and Poet* (Edinburgh, 1966).

## Dylan Thomas

Elder Olson. *The Poetry of Dylan Thomas* (Chicago, 1954).
T. H. Jones. *Dylan Thomas* (Writers and Critics, Edinburgh and London, 1963).
Ralph Maud. *Entrances to Dylan Thomas's Poetry* (London, 1963).
Constantine Fitzgibbon. *The Life of Dylan Thomas* (London, 1965). The authorized biography.
E. W. Tedlock (ed.). *Dylan Thomas: the Legend and the Poet* (London, 1960). Miscellaneous reprinted essays.
C. B. Cox (ed.). *Dylan Thomas: a Collection of Critical Essays* (Engelwood Cliffs, New Jersey, 1966).

## C. Anthologies

Michael Roberts (ed.). *New Signatures* (London, 1932) and *New Country* (London, 1933). These two collections helped to popularize the Auden group; in *The Faber Book of Modern Verse* (London, 1936) Roberts exemplified the poetic attitudes of the time, both by his selection and his introduction. In *Poetry of the Thirties* (Penguin: Harmondsworth, 1964) Robin Skelton provides an excellent retrospective survey of the period.
J. F. Hendry and Henry Treece (eds.). *The White Horseman* (London, 1940). An anthology of the 'neo-apocalyptic' romantic movement that briefly flourished in the war years. Retrospective surveys are provided by Ian Hamilton in *The Poetry of War 1939–1945* (London, 1965) and Robin Skelton in *Poetry of the Forties* (Penguin: Harmondsworth, 1968).
Ian Fletcher and G. S. Fraser (eds.). *Springtime* (London, 1953). An eclectic anthology which included early work by many of the Movement poets, who were more substantially represented in *New Lines*, edited by Robert Conquest (London, 1956).
A. Alvarez (ed.). *The New Poetry* (Penguin: Harmondsworth, 1962).
Philip Hobsbaum and Edward Lucie-Smith (eds.). *A Group Anthology* (London, 1963).
Robert Conquest (ed.). *New Lines II* (London, 1963).
John Press (ed.). *A Map of Modern English Verse* (London, 1969).

## 9

## ENGLISH DRAMA 1900–1960

### G. K. Hunter, University of Warwick

It is difficult to fit drama into the 'periods' that literary history presupposes, if we think of it as reaching its fulfilment in the theatre rather than the study—and surely we must do this. For drama differs from literature in a number of important ways. Theatrical experience is more closely related to social life than is the experience of books. A play which fails, fails more catastrophically than does a book, in terms of money and in terms of reputation. An avant-garde theatre is more difficult to sustain than a little magazine; the *garde* has to be much larger; for the work being promoted involves the understanding co-operation of many different people, author, backer, producer, designer, actors, not to mention the audience. The rise and fall of literary fashions is more hectic (especially in the modern period) than the movement of theatrical taste. The theatre tends to demand what its audiences are used to, the conventions that they already understand, the moral or social judgments that they automatically endorse; often change can enter here only by way of imperceptible modifications. The English society of the first half of the twentieth century has been very reluctant to deny its Victorian inheritance; and standard theatrical fare has reflected this conservatism. We should notice the extraordinary persistence throughout the period of plays about upper-middle-class adultery, constructed in the form of the so-called 'well-made-play'.[1]

The year 1900 can only be made significant for the student of the theatre by noting that it marked the end of Ibsen's career as a writer. Up to this point the direct impact of Ibsen on the English theatre had, however, been rather negative. The nineties had seen various attempts to 'liberate' the English theatre from its position of slavish assent to Victorian morals. J. T. Grein's 'Independent Theatre' (1891–97), G. B. Shaw, William Archer and other advanced figures, had promoted productions of *Rosmersholm*, *A Doll's House*, and (most spectacularly) *Ghosts* (in 1891). The critical reaction to this last play ('an open drain, a loathsome sore unbandaged, a dirty act done publicly' etc.) had made it quite clear that the English public was not ready for Ibsen.

Three years later Miss A. E. F. Horniman (disposing, curiously enough, like Grein, money made out of tea) spent £4,000 promoting a season of such 'modern' plays as W. B. Yeats's *The Land of Heart's Desire* and Shaw's *Arms and the Man*. Miss Horniman did not recover much of her money; but went on, undeterred, to become one of the great benefactors of twentieth-century drama, founding the first provincial repertory theatre —the Gaiety in Manchester—and assuming responsibility for the Abbey Theatre in Dublin.

There was another way of reaching the public, however, besides losing money. In 1891 Shaw had responded to the failure of Ibsen on the English stage by publishing *The Quintessence of Ibsenism*; and later in the decade he began to print his own plays, to reach a reading public even if he could not command a theatre audience. The route was not so strange to Shaw. He had begun by writing novels; the vast stage-directions in his plays reveal his kinship with the Dickensian art of comic caricature, though his interest is in intellectual rather than visual caricature. Take the entry of Hector Malone in *Man and Superman*:

Hector Malone is an Eastern American; but he is not at all ashamed of his nationality. This makes English people of fashion think well of him, as of a young fellow who is manly enough to confess to an obvious disadvantage without any attempt to conceal or extenuate it. They feel that he ought not to be made to suffer for what is clearly not his fault, and make a point of being specially kind to him. His chivalrous manners to women, and his elevated moral sentiments, being both gratuitous and unusual, strike them as perhaps a little unfortunate; and though they find his vein of easy humor rather amusing when it has ceased to puzzle them (as it does at first) they have had to make him understand that he really must not tell anecdotes unless they are strictly personal and scandalous, and also that oratory is an accomplishment which belongs to a cruder stage of civilization than that in which his migration has landed him . . .

(and so on for another sixty-seven lines).

Shaw was never to succeed wholly in detaching himself from the perspectives that the novel, the dominant art form of his age, imposed on his writing. An even more obvious example of this is the epilogue to *Pygmalion*: 'the rest of the story need not be shewn in action . . . etc.' where it is clear that the dramatist has allowed the novelist to take over the story that he no longer wishes to handle.

The theatre that Shaw was trying to promote was a theatre of dissent, of argument and of questioning. The late Victorian theatre had been in the main a theatre of social affirmation. Even though a play like *The Second Mrs. Tanqueray* (1893) by Sir Arthur Pinero (1855–1934) might, in the shadow of Ibsen, titillate its audience with the possibility of defending 'the woman with a past', and blaming the man-of-the-world for her failings, in the end Paula Tanqueray must be shown denying the possibility of living through such revaluations. Female purity—that central virtue of the Victorian domestic scene— is reaffirmed. The woman with a past must retire, either from 'Society', as in comedies like Oscar Wilde's *Lady Windermere's Fan* (1892), or from life, as in tragedies like *The Second Mrs. Tanqueray*.

The theatre of dissent did not achieve any real foothold in London till the famous Barker-Vedrenne seasons at the Court Theatre in 1904–1907. Harley Granville-Barker (1877–1946) had been asked in 1904 to produce *Two Gentlemen of Verona* for Mr. Vedrenne, the manager of the Court Theatre. He agreed, if Vedrenne would permit him to produce also six matinée performances of Shaw's *Candida*. Out of this arrangement grew a prolonged series of afternoon performances, not only of *Candida*, but of ten Shaw plays, Barker's *The Voysey Inheritance*, Ibsen's *Hedda Gabler* and *The Wild Duck*, Galsworthy's *The Silver Box*, of three Euripides plays, translated by Gilbert Murray, and a whole range of avant-garde works. The performances were given only on afternoons in the first year, but later evening performances were added.

The reason for the choice of the Court Theatre for this venture points to its precariousness. This theatre, in Chelsea, could not command the same rental as the West-End houses. The same economic argument explains the afternoon performances: actors could play there at the higher reaches of their art and still make money by evening performances elsewhere. The nature of the audience is uncertain. Sir Francis Burnand says that 'the female element predominates over the inferior sex as something like twelve to one. The audience had not a theatre-going but rather a lecture-going, sermon-loving appearance'. On the other hand we should remember that Edward VII —not a notably sermon-loving monarch—commanded an evening performance of *John Bull's Other Island*, and laughed so much, it is said, that he broke his chair. Perhaps we may best guess the nature of the audience from the nature of the plays they preferred—Shaw above all, and *Man and Superman* above the other Shaw plays. Clearly these were people happy to identify themselves with Jack Tanner and Ann Whitefield, not so attached to traditional social attitudes that they resented paradoxes pointed at them, but not so detached from them that the jokes were irrelevant. It seems reasonable to suppose that the tastes which supported Norman Shaw's later architecture, garden suburbs, Richard Strauss's opera, female emancipation, impressionist paintings (even the post-impressionist exhibition of 1910) also supported the Barker-Vedrenne seasons.

Other features of the new theatrical mode seemed even more obvious at the time. The Barker-Vedrenne management was in conscious revolt against the Victorian actor-manager system. Great stress was laid on the team-work involved; on the willingness of the 'star' of one performance to play a minor role in the next, and so on the change from 'astonishment' to 'truth' as the emotional effect aimed at. The scenery was also notably spare (for economic as well as aesthetic reasons); the absence of museum reproductions ('real silver inkstands') threw more weight on the quality of the actual speaking. Scenery aimed at the broad 'harmony of colours and agreeable lights and shadows'. In this, of course, Barker was in key with the stylistic movement headed by Edward Gordon Craig (1872–1966) who was already far more influential on the Continent than in England, and was to continue so.

The whole mode of production also calls to mind the relationship between Barker and William Poel (1852–1934), who was already changing the notion of Shakespearian staging from the cluttered methods of Beerbohm Tree to a more 'Elizabethan' stress on simplicity and speed, with fidelity to the *spirit* of the play rather than the letter. Poel both produced and acted in the Court Theatre.

Throughout this minor revolution the theatre remained, as it was to remain throughout the period of this article, a middle-class institution. It may well be that this is an essential characteristic of the modern theatre. At any rate the drama of social conscience remained intensely aware of its middle-class audience. It aimed its fascinations chiefly at those involved in the status quo, but who at the same time were worried about the morality of the status quo. The relationship of Shaw's plays with the established way of life is nicely parallelled by their relationship with the 'well-made-play' type of structure. Shaw made a great display of his contempt for the well-made play, for Pinero and Sardou, but his own plays often relied on the 'well-made' structure to chart the individual's struggle against society. *Mrs. Warren's Profession* is skilfully organized as a series of 'well-made' revelations, quite in the manner of Scribe.

*Mrs. Warren's Profession*, and Shaw's plays in general, differ from those of his predecessors in the valuation given to the views put forward by the play. Pinero had allowed Society to win, as in any theatre of reality it must; Shaw organizes his denouements as paradoxical conversations which allow the best talker to win; and the best talker in Shaw is the individual least bound by fixed social conventions—usually the emancipated 'modern' woman. If the Victorian domestic ethos is based on the purity of womenhood, and the need for its protection, Shaw is able to stand this on its head by making the pure young woman the spokesman for emancipation, rationalism, unconventionality—Vivie Warren with her cigars and actuarial competence, Margaret Knox (in *Fanny's First Play*) who realizes that the exultation of a prayer meeting leads naturally to a fracas with the police, Ellie Dunn (in *Heartbreak House*), Major Barbara. And not only does Shaw use the 'pure' girl to express unconventional truths; he gives the defence of the proprieties to those with least moral status—to Mrs. Warren, to Boss Mangan and the Burglar (in *Heartbreak House*), to Mr. Knox (in *Fanny's First Play*).

The most obvious pleasure in Shaw's plays is that provided by a dazzling virtuosity in handling paradox; in this Shaw is the obvious heir of Oscar Wilde. If Shaw's wit has worn a little thin, this is largely because its pleasures depend on some residual sense of shock when standard values and expectations are inverted. When the standard really changes the paradox may seem laboured, the targets over-easy. But England has hung on to its sense of the sustaining truth of the Victorian social proprieties far longer than might have seemed possible. The violent end to Edwardian calm proposed by the Great War, and endorsed in poetry and in painting, was not accepted in the

English theatre. In the years when Pound and Eliot and Joyce were revolutionizing the modes of perception in other art-forms, and when Brecht and Pirandello were casting their shadows over the future of European drama, the English theatre could only offer a new play by Sir James Barrie (1860–1937) about female purity defeating existence: how a child-bride (Mary Rose) escapes into a never-never land and becomes a winsome ghost without ever becoming an adult woman; or a play by Galsworthy (1867–1933) on late-Victorian social problems, or by Somerset Maugham (1874–1965), elegantly balancing cynicism and sentimentality on the subject of social-register adulteries.

Continental innovations, even of the previous century, were still unacceptable to the general public. When Chekhov's *The Cherry Orchard* was produced in London in 1924, Henry Arthur Jones, still one of London's major playwrights, wrote that the play gave him 'the impression of someone who had entered a lunatic asylum and taken down everything the lunatics said'. The Great War did in fact produce one major English play, and this is a play written curiously enough in the 'madhouse' manner of Chekhov. Shaw's *Heartbreak House* is called 'a fantasia in the Russian manner on English themes'; but in fact it is no more truly Chekhovian than *Mrs. Warren's Profession* is truly Ibsenite. What Chekhov gave to Shaw was the courage to abandon his usual rationalism, his usual doctrinaire paradoxes, in favour of a poetic indeterminacy, a great cry of horror and despair to match the occasion of its birth. *Heartbreak House* is a play in which the brilliant conversation does not simply lead to youthful squibs at the expense of established sense, but to a genuine vision of a world which civilized conversation can adorn but never save:

> I tell you, one of two things must happen. Either out of that darkness some new creation will come to supplant us as we supplanted the animals, or the heavens will fall in thunder and destroy us.

'Heartbreak House' is England, the Edwardian England of house-parties and privilege, of the alliance between civilizing great ladies, wealthy men and natural leaders, displaying the effortless superiority of self-conscious aristocracy: 'charming people, most advanced, unprejudiced, frank, human, unconventional, democratic, and everything that is delightful to thoughtful people'—and now bombed, burgled and (more serious) steered on to the rocks:

*Shotover*. The Captain is in his bunk, drinking bottled ditch-water; and the crew is gambling in the forecastle. She will strike and sink and split. Do you think the laws of God will be suspended in favor of England because you were born in it?

*Hector*. Well, I don't mean to be drowned like a rat in a trap. I still have the will to live. What am I to do?

*Shotover*. Do? Nothing simpler. Learn your business as an Englishman.

*Hector*. And what may my business as an Englishman be, pray?

*Shotover*. Navigation. Learn it and live; or leave it and be damned.

*Heartbreak House* may be Shaw's greatest play; but it is not an English *Cherry Orchard*; for the symbols it uses are too fantastic to have the force of Chekhov's. The cherry orchard in Chekhov's play is not only a symbol, but is also an actual piece of real estate; Captain Shotover's ship-house, his poop, his rum, his navigation are fantasy only. The play was, one need hardly add, a crashing failure when first produced in 1921.

The witty reduction of Establishment proprieties forms the staple of most comedy in the next two decades—but (with the decline of Edwardian idealism and gravity) on a basis of farce rather than serious comedy like *Heartbreak House*. Noel Coward (b. 1899) begins, seriously enough, in *The Vortex* (1924), with melodrama. As usual, the play is concerned with the lives of wealthy idlers; but now (in the twenties manner) the idlers are artists *manqués* not leaders *manqués*. Their wit is bitchiness rather than social paradox, their superiority conveyed by their sensibility rather than their intelligence. We are asked, as audience, to feel envy and admiration at the dazzle of high life; but it is now high-life which has no social consequence and which could have no social consequence. Coward's great theatrical skill in the structure of farce has made much of this world and he has continued to dazzle audiences with witty adulteries into the present day, when it might seem that colour supplements had taken over his rôle.

The well made, mainly realistic, play continued to decline with gentle self-indulgence throughout the twenties and thirties and forties. The minor talents of James Bridie, J. B. Priestley and Terence Rattigan sustained an image of the London theatre as a place of efficiently organized routine escapism, of well-bred paradox and parlour revolution. In the late thirties Priestley began to experiment with disruptions of the time-sequence and this introduced a thread of expressionism into the commercial stage, but a thread only. One has the impression of a period of theatrical stagnation and complacency; with little protest from inside the country and little disturbance from outside. In the thirties the German Expressionist drama and the Russian experimental theatre were suppressed. The deeply French theatre of Giraudoux or Cocteau could exert little or no influence. O'Neill's plays flickered briefly over the West End and created a distasteful impression of meaningless violence. Even the world of the film, which in the earlier years of the century seemed to offer a genuinely international art-form sharply focussed on social realities, and with technical pressure to devise a truly modern style—even the film collapsed in the thirties into a routine of Hollywood stereotypes. None the less, one has the feeling that the film had drained away much of the creative energy that might have roused the British theatre from its post-Ibsen torpor.

As late as 1950 Harold Hobson, surveying the past year in the British Council's *Year's Work in the Theatre*, made the point that

> As one might have expected, the shortage of new dramatists continues . . . Dramatic history suggests that our expectations ought to be modest. Our present school of drama, based on realism and the social conscience, has flourished for more than fifty years. The span of time between *The Second Mrs. Tanqueray* and *The Winslow Boy* is, theatrically speaking, enormous. Our characteristic contemporary drama is in its extreme old age. Instead of expecting it to put forth new shoots, we should be honourably digging its grave.

With this as an epitaph it might seem that we should pass over the period of the two wars without further ado. But the post-Ibsenite theatre of realism and social conscience does not completely exhaust the British theatrical scene, though it very nearly does so. The best dramatists of the period, including Ibsen himself, have shown a constant awareness of the see-saw relationship between external social realism or 'naturalism' and the poetry or dream of inner life. Most have sought to find a point of balance between these pressures and all have failed to find anything like security of balance, though single balanced instances can be found. I have already mentioned *Heartbreak*

*House* which, if it is Shaw's greatest play, is only so by virtue of its capacity to escape from either preaching or sentimentality into something like poetry.

The other dramatist who should be mentioned in this connection is Sean O'Casey (1880–1964), but before we turn to O'Casey perhaps we should look at J. M. Synge (1871–1909) who presents the problem of Celtic 'poetry' in a simpler form. And Synge, fortunately enough, has placed an acute statement of the problem I am discussing before his *The Playboy of the Western World* (1907):

> All art is collaboration; and there is little doubt that in the happy ages of literature, striking and beautiful phrases were as ready to the story-teller's or the playwright's hand as the rich cloaks and dresses of his time . . . This matter, I think, is of importance, for in countries where the imagination of the people, and the language they use, is rich and living, it is possible for a writer to be rich and copious in his words, and at the same time to give the reality, which is the root of all poetry, in a comprehensive and natural form. In the modern literature of towns, however, richness is found only in sonnets, or prose poems, or in one or two elaborate books that are far away from the profound and common interests of life. One has, on one side, Mallarmé and Huysmans producing this literature; and on the other, Ibsen and Zola dealing with the reality of life in joyless and pallid words. On the stage, one must have reality, and one must have joy.

Synge's plays represent, it has been claimed, the poetry of the real speech of Irish peasants. On the other hand it must be pointed out that his plays contain elaborately stylized actions, in which a life simplified by art is presented for our sophisticated nostalgia.

The early Irish audiences of *The Playboy* objected that the peasants depicted were untrue because they were not pious enough; I think we can see today that a different form may be given to this objection. The peasants in Synge are not 'true' in any sense; they are literary fictions, like the language imputed to them—a language made up, no doubt, of elements that really occurred, but made up into a state of chemical purity that is quite remote from anybody's real speech. One can see why W. B. Yeats (1865–1939) approved of Synge and promoted his plays. What Yeats himself was to seek in the 'noble plays', the Noh plays of Japan—ritualized expression of aristocratic feelings— Synge found in the simple emotions of his peasantry. O'Casey's language is less totally simplifying than Synge's; but still may be thought over-decorative for the function it serves in the plays. There is still, even in the language of *Juno* and *The Plough and the Stars*, an invitation to indulgent condescension, and sentimentality about the magic of Celtic speech.

This too-easy appeal of Celtic magic has continued to exercise a rewarding fascination: Brendan Behan's *The Hostage* (1958) draws on O'Casey's mode without any of O'Casey's drive towards general truth. Dylan Thomas's 'play for voices', *Under Milk Wood* (1953) is more purely literary. It has, however, been a great success, on stage and on television, no less than on the radio (for which is was designed) and on record. Part of the appeal it makes is due to this same sense of a simplified golden world of Celtic peasants spouting poetry at the drop of a penny.

O'Casey is a greater problem than any of these because he is a greater dramatist—probably the only dramatist of the first half of the century (other than Shaw) likely to be remembered at the end of the second half. Unlike Synge's, his plays are complex enough to seem representative of real existence, especially those by which he is generally remembered—*Juno and the Paycock* of 1924, and *The Plough and the Stars* of 1926. These are often called 'realistic'—they are certainly more realistic than O'Casey's later plays—but they depend heavily for their effect on the unrealistic language he gives to his characters, the repetitions and incantations by which they control their relationship to one another. It was a long time before dramatists saw the possibility of using language in this way outside the special Celtic milieu.

These plays of O'Casey's are like Chekhov's in their bitter-sweet intertwining of tragedy and comedy. The comedy comes from pretentiousness—especially in the peacocking and good-for-nothing, self-regarding men (like 'Captain' Boyle or Peter Flynn) whose adaptation to environment depends on this comic self-deception. The tragedy is more especially that of the women —urban peasant women caught in a political struggle they are not committed to and are not responsible for, but which crushes them none the less.

The tragedy of unavailing maternal protest, against war and heroism and self-sacrifice, found a human-sized and therefore articulable context in the Dublin slums. The same feelings, when felt about the Great War, seem to have been too large for theatrical expression. Not until R. C. Sherriff's *Journey's End* of 1928 did the War come home to London audiences, and then only in terms of public-school sentimentalities and Boys' Own Paper heroism. *Journey's End* neither sought nor achieved any new expression or new style of sensibility to correspond with its newness of subject-matter. That the public was not ready for theatrical methods more appropriate to the civilization-crushing process of the War is indicated by the fate of O'Casey's *The Silver Tassie*. In the same year as *Journey's End* began its phenomenal career, Yeats, as director of the Abbey Theatre, rejected *The Silver Tassie* in terms which made it clear that the generalized subject matter and the dispersed 'series of almost unrelated scenes' were added together as two faults, not as cause and effect. Yeats, the proponent of the remote and the hierarchical, could not bear the propagandist and opinionated pacificism that *The Silver Tassie* represented. And what Yeats, from one angle, rejected in 1928, London rejected, no doubt from another angle, when *The Silver Tassie* was produced there in 1929, the year in which the printed form of *Journey's End* clocked up at least twelve impressions.

*The Silver Tassie* mixes the 'realism' of the first three O'Casey plays—the stylized quasi-poetry of the Dublin tenements—with a second act in France employing the full panoply of German expressionist theatre : chanted choruses, ritual recitations, interpolated songs and ballads, symbolic scenery, and characters chosen to represent dehumanized humanity lost in a world of monstrous forces :

> *Croucher (resuming).* And I prophesied, and the breath came out of them, and the sinews came away from them, and behold a shaking and their bones fell asunder, bone from his bone, and they died, and the exceeding great army became a valley of dry bones.
>
> *The voice from the monastery is heard, clearly for the first half of the sentence, then dying away towards the end :* Accendat in nobis Dominus ignem sui amoris, et flammam aeternea caritatis.
>
> *A group of soldiers come in from fatigue, bunched together as if for comfort and warmth. They are wet and cold, and they are sullen-faced. They form a circle around the brazier and stretch their hands towards the blaze.*
> *1st Soldier.* Cold and wet and tir'd.
> *2nd Soldier.* Wet and tir'd and cold.
> *3rd Soldier.* Tir'd and cold and wet.
> *4th Soldier.* [*very like Teddy*]. Twelve blasted hours of ammunition transport fatigue!

*1st Soldier.* Twelve weary hours.

*2nd Soldier.* And wasting hours.

*3rd Soldier.* And hot and heavy hours.

*1st Soldier.* Toiling and thinking to build the wall of force that blocks the way from here to home.

*2nd Soldier.* Lifting shells.

*3rd Soldier.* Carrying shells.

*4th Soldier.* Piling shells.

These expressionist techniques were, no doubt, appropriate to a Germany culturally ravished by war. But the English theatre remained resistant to their effects till the mid-fifties. The English theatre between the wars seems to reflect a society which has re-formed its ranks and is making a brave effort to pretend that nothing much has happened. Of course, some minority tastes reflected these foreign events. The repertory of the tiny Gate Theatre, exempted as a 'club' from censorship, was boldly modernist; but no effective English dramatist seems to have been inspired by its exhibitions. The poetic dramas of W. H. Auden (b. 1907) and Christopher Isherwood (b. 1904),—especially *The Dog Beneath the Skin* (1935), *The Ascent of F6* (1936), *On the Frontier* (1938)—reflect the close acquaintance of the authors with post-war art in Germany; Auden and Isherwood are, presumably, the first English Brechtians. The Group Theatre, which Auden helped to found in 1932, together with the director Rupert Doone and the scene designer Robert Medley, aimed to convey analysis of contemporary society through forms derived from the music-hall; and the plays they performed in their most famous season—at the Westminster Theatre in 1935 (Auden's *The Dance of Death*, Auden and Isherwood's *The Dog Beneath the Skin*, Eliot's *Sweeney Agonistes*)—reflect these aims very obviously. The Eliot playlet I shall return to. The work of Auden and Isherwood differs from Eliot's by its greater reliance on parody and on song, and its greater commitment to thoroughgoing Freudian Marxism.

The decline in O'Casey's acceptability, when he ceased to make 'Irish character' the excuse for his non-realism, left the problem of 'poetic theatre' in the hands of amateurs. The last period in which straight poetry had enjoyed any real esteem in the theatre was in the reign of the Victorian and Edwardian actor-managers, who had seen the grandoise expressions of poetry as entirely appropriate to their sumptuous and spectacular methods of production. Stephen Phillips's plays (*Herod* [1902] *Paolo and Francesca* [1902] etc.) mark the end of this particular use of poetry, though the production in 1923 of the *Hassan* of James Elroy Flecker (1884–1915) gave it a brief return to glory. In truth, the spectacular powers of the cinema had overtaken those of the theatre, and films like *Intolerance* (1916) or *Ben Hur* (1926), or any score of Biblical 'epics', made the splendours of Beerbohm Tree seem laboured and ineffective. If poetry were to return to the theatre it would have to be under very different auspices.

The problem of what poetry would be appropriate to a modern theatre exercized over a long period the most brilliant critical mind of the century—T. S. Eliot. Eliot saw that the poetic plays of nineteenth century poets—Keats' *Otho the Great* (1819), Shelley's *The Cenci* (1819), Browning's *Stafford* (1837), Swinburne's *Chastelard* (1860), Tennyson's *Beckett* (1879) (they all wrote them!)—were not serious as poetic *drama*; for in them the poetry did not at all affect the structure, but existed only as a Shakespearian wash applied to a structure thought out in prose. The obvious example of this view of poetic drama is to be found in the collaboration of Keats and his friend Charles Brown. Brown tells us how they worked:

'I engaged to furnish him with the fable, characters and dramatic conduct of a tragedy, and he was to embody it into poetry. The progress of this work was curious; for, whilst I sat opposite to him, he caught my description of each scene, entered into the characters to be brought forward, the events, and everything connected with it. Thus he went on, scene after scene, never knowing nor inquiring into the scene which was to follow until four acts were completed.'

Eliot saw that a truly poetic drama would have to be one in which the poetic vision affected radically the whole structure of the play:

It is possible that what distinguishes poetic drama from prosaic drama is a kind of doubleness in the action, as if it took place on two planes at once.

Poetry would have to provide 'a figure in the carpet', a pattern below the level of plot and character. The search for a drama which would fulfil these conditions led Eliot inevitably towards the idea—seductive in this period—of 'ritual':

I say the perfect consummation of the drama, the perfect and ideal drama is to be found in the ceremony of the mass.

Elsewhere he speaks of his desire to make drama as formalized as 'the dance, including its highest forms—the ballet and the mass . . . (for is not High Mass—as performed, for instance, at the Madeleine in Paris—one of the highest developments of dancing)'.

In the same period W. B. Yeats was moving in the same direction, and his 'plays for dancers' are purer and more arcane versions of dramatic ritualism than are Eliot's plays. Yeats gave little thought to a public theatre:

> We must make a theatre for ourselves and our friends and for a few simple people who understand from sheer simplicity what we understand from scholarship and thought.

Eliot remained aware of the theatre as a place which, if it was to have any importance, required a public more representative than this. He was also aware of ritual as providing no simple answer:

> Of what value is it to 'revive' the Sword Dance, except as a Saturday afternoon alternative to tennis and badminton for active young men in garden suburbs?

Dramatic effect depends on conventionalities and stock responses and a general idea of entertainment. Only then will 'the ideal medium for poetry . . . and the most direct means of social usefulness [be in] the theatre'.

> What I should like to do is this; that the people on the stage should seem to the audience so like themselves that they would find themselves thinking 'I could talk in poetry too'. Then they are not transported into an unaccustomed artificial world; but their ordinary, sordid world is suddenly illuminated and transfigured.

Eliot's early poetry dwell on a world of futile idlers, measuring out their lives in coffee spoons, as in Maugham's or Coward's plays—characters unable to detect any figures in their carpets, but still hankering for significance, for

> the awful daring of a moment's surrender.

In Eliot's early poetry surrender is something that will not come, for what could it be that one would surrender to? It is only on the verge of conversion that the lurking unknown becomes focussed enough to be dramatized. In *Sweeney Agonistes* (1932) the 'real world' of an established convention—the tough murder-story (it was originally to be called 'Wanna go home, Baby?')—

is juxtaposed against the terror of death and the unknown. But there is no plot in *Sweeney*; renunciation remains a possibility, but cannot be an action. The play remains a fragment, 'an observation' (like the *Prufrock* poems).

In *Murder in the Cathedral* (1935) the desire to renounce social inanity ('living and partly living') becomes at last a positive action, since in Christian terms renunciation need no longer be equated with loss:

> action is suffering
> And suffering action. Neither does the agent suffer
> Nor the patient act. But both are fixed
> In an eternal action, an eternal patience.

Martydom is the special case of renunciation which is heroic action. The play in its celebration of martydom is able to reveal both the transfigured meaning, which is martyrdom, and the sordid world of the knights for whom this is a political opportunity or a murder mystery: 'Who killed the Archbishop?' (Originally the title was to be *The Archbishop Murder Case*.)

The plays which follow try to carry the heoism of renunciation into a world more modern and more 'ordinary' than that of *Murder in the Cathedral*, for an audience less committed to the rituals of transfigured meaning than the Canterbury Cathedral audience of his first play:

> Such experience can only be hinted at
> In myths and images. To speak about it
> We talk of darkness, labyrinths, Minotaur terrors.
> But that world does not take the place of this one.
> Do you imagine that the Saint in the desert
> With spiritual evil always at his shoulder
> Suffered any less from hunger, damp, exposure,
> Bowel trouble, and the fear of lions,
> Cold of the night and heat of the day, than we should?

The real world, offered with increasing obviousness in *The Family Reunion* (1939), *The Cocktail Party* (1950), *The Confidential Clerk* (1953) and *The Elder Statesman* (1958), succeeds (alas) only in conquering the illumination of myths and images that Eliot can provide. The Greek myths behind the plays (the *Oresteia*, the *Alcestis*, the *Ion*, the *Oedipus Coloneus*) do not exert any commanding relevance to make their real worlds mythic; and the verse, designed to be inconspicuous, succeeds drably in being just that.

Eliot's search for a poetry which can be organic, not decorative, to the dramatic action seems in the light of subsequent experience to have been too self-consciously concerned with 'poetry' and 'dramatic action' as separate entities conceived in largely nineteenth century terms, and requiring to be manipulated into a common framework. Eliot's early perception that 'our problem should be to take a form of entertainment and subject it to a process which would leave it a form of art. Perhaps the music hall comedian is the best material', is not a perception he was able to act upon. Perhaps the magisterial deliberation with which he makes the suggestion gives a reason why. In any case it was not until *Waiting for Godot* (Paris 1953) that the suggestion came to full fruition, and then by a strange and circuitous route.

The obvious influence on Samuel Beckett (b. 1906) is James Joyce (whose disciple he was from 1928 onward). Joyce's writings, by the time Beckett was working with him, were very remote from any possible theatre. Joyce had clearly abandoned by *Ulysses* (1922) the structural coherence of a 'plot' designed to discipline the episodes, making them no longer simply the route by which we follow characters through a social crisis to a resolution, but matters of independent interest. By the time of *Finnegans Wake* (1939) he was not even concerned with 'characters' in the traditional sense; but with the density of generalized experience, piled vertically on the single moment of apprehension rather than drawn out in the time-horizontal of plot. Fantasy, unintelligibility, circularity, giddiness—these are recurrent characteristics of *Finnegans Wake*. Beckett is able to dramatize these by seeing (what Joyce had already seen but not dramatized) the ways in which such features are essential parts of the audience's life already, in popular culture, in comics, strip-cartoons, stray conversations, music-hall turns. *Waiting for Godot* secures its hold on entertainment by abandoning the external realism of Eliot's Cocktail Parties and concentrating on the realism of puzzlement, the realism of half-understanding, the realism of non-communication in isolated individuals, the tiny rituals with which we pass the time, with which we *wait* (whether for Godot or the next bus).

This concentration on the quality of the individual's passive bewilderment in the face of modern society may indeed be seen as the characteristic which binds together much of the 'new drama' that has revolutionized the English theatre since 1956.

*Endgame* (*Fin de Partie*) which followed *Godot* in 1957 is Beckett's most elaborate play, though even more bleak than its predecessor and slightly less accessible. Its 'action' shows the

325

bringing of the will into conformity with a world finally denuded of meaning; its characters are either blind and imobilized or cowed and helpless, or else (like the parents, Nagg and Nell) survive, legless, in dustbins, reduced to such basic utterance as 'I want me pap'. The vision of the end-game of the world in this play has the power of a total commitment to its truth, a total integrity of purpose. Elsewhere Beckett's austere genius has led him to so rigorous a purging of superfluities that his material has become almost too pure to be visible. In *Krapp's Last Tape* (1958) we are down to one man and a tape-recorder. In *Happy Days* (1961 New York, 1962 London) we have two characters, both buried in sand. In *Act Without Words* even the luxury of language is dispersed with.

Eliot had focussed on the heroism of renouncing the world; Beckett deals rather with the failure to get even to the point where there is enough freedom to make the gesture of renunciation, so that *Waiting for Godot* ends not even with a whimper, but with:

> *Vladimir.* Well? Shall we go?
> *Estragon.* Yes, let's go.
> *They do not move.*

Godot came to London in August 1955 and produced the familiar theatrical emotions of outrage and bewilderment. The ten years since the end of the second war had not served very effectively to prepare London audiences for this new art. At first, indeed (as may be seen from Harold Hobson's remark quoted above, p. 317) it seemed as if the theatrical reaction to the Second World War would be identical to that following the First—a closing of the ranks and 'back to normalcy' movement. The repertories of the early post-war years rings with the names of the past and their current imitators—Priestley, Coward, Shaw, Rattigan, Maugham, Emlyn Williams. The only novelties came from France. Sartre, Anouilh and Cocteau gave an impression of galvanic intellectual and rhetorical activity to a stage that had been without these qualities since the heyday of Shaw. And Christopher Fry and John Whiting seemed to be trying to match the imported product with English wares, rhetoric with rhetoric, pretension with pretension.

Theatrical production may be thought to have shown the onset of new concepts in this period more clearly than did the new plays. The commercial production of Shakespeare (especially at Stratford-on-Avon) was gathering strength to pick up the fifty-year-old suggestions of Poel, Granville-Barker and Edward Gordon Craig. The growth of the Apron-stage, the decline of elaborate scenery and, in consequence, the ending of long intervals while stage-hands hammer and shift elaborate sets—these combined to give a new fluidity, a new scope for symbolism, a new mode of attacking the audience. Arena staging came not only to be talked about but even engaged in.

It is often said that it was the production of John Osborne's *Look Back in Anger* at the Royal Court Theatre on 8th May 1956 that marked the emergence of 'the new drama'; but this is clearly a simplification. A number of factors appear to converge. The English Stage Company opened at the Royal Court Theatre in April 1956 (showing Angus Wilson's *The Mulberry Bush* and Arthur Miller's *The Crucible* before *Look Back in Anger*), with the specific aim of establishing a 'writer's theatre' (which in the context must mean 'a young writer's theatre'). As I have already said, *Waiting for Godot* came to London in August 1955. Ionesco's *The Bald Prima Donna* was staged in 1956—*The Lesson* had been given as a curtain-raiser in 1955. Brecht's Berliner Ensemble came to London in 1956; and Brecht's ideas began to have wide currency.

Of all these new elements, Osborne's play may seem to be least novel. But its social content was obviously explosive at this point. Jimmy Porter, of working-class origin, educated at a red-brick (or rather 'white-tile') University has married above himself, and his relationship with Alison, his wife, a well-bred young lady, is one of brawling discontent. The brilliantly verbalized and vaguely focussed 'anger' of the play realized many contemporary frustrations. The Labour government of 1945, the decline in *rentier* incomes, the hang-over from wartime equality of effort, the boom in classless forms of science and technology—these had seemed to promise a post-war class-free Britain. But the Labour government fell, Attlee became an Earl, the Establishment could be seen refurbishing its image. It became clear that the class-struggle required anger no less than legislation, as much effort to retain the qualities of working-class life as to control the means of production. 1956 was a vintage year for the anger of the individual demonstrator, the year of the Hungarian rising, and of the Suez adventure. Richard Hoggart's *The Uses of Literacy* (1957) provides one celebrated document of the new a-political or even anti-political concern with the culture of the working-class. The rather mechanical exploration of 'slumming' and 'provincialism' in John Wain's *Hurry On Down* (1953) and Kingsley Amis' *Lucky Jim* (1954) was beginning to yield richer social observation in such books as John Braine's

*Room at the Top* (1957) and Alan Sillitoe's *Saturday Night and Sunday Morning* (1958). D. H. Lawrence's opposition of the irrational, the instinctive and the tender as against the poised, the conceptual, the correct, of knowing how to feel against knowing how to behave, provides an important framework for this whole way of writing.

*Look Back in Anger* has its strength in the sharp contrasts of value that it sets up, and in the rhetoric that Osborne is able to summon to express his oppositions. Its weakness is in its plot-structure, the implication that at the end the action has been resolved in some way. For it hasn't. Osborne's next play (and to my mind his best play)—*The Entertainer* (1957)—avoids these expectations of linear development. Archie Rice, the music-hall 'entertainer', moves through the cycle of his 'turns' and ends, as he began, with his sleazy integrity, his acceptance of what he has become, his rejection of gadget-happy Canada—and with nothing else.

Osborne (b. 1929) has continued to be obsessed with the individual-in-a-mess, whose *mess* is indeed the special condition of his being intensely alive, set against those whose cut-and-dried competences brand them as cut and dried-up individuals. Of his later plays perhaps *Inadmissible Evidence* (1964) is the strongest statement of this central theme.

Proof that *Look Back in Anger* was a symptom of liberation rather than a cause may be found in the flood of plays, most of them in different and more advanced modes, that poured forth in the next few years, changing the whole theatrical scene. Among dramatists whose names are now household words it is extraordinary how many began successful playwriting in 1957. This was the year in which Harold Pinter wrote *The Room*, his first (already characteristic) play; this the year of John Arden's first play, *Soldier, Soldier*. This is the year when Alun Owen wrote *Two Sons* for radio—subsequently enlarged into television *No Trams to Lime Street* (1959). In 1957 The English Stage Company produced N. F. Simpson's *A Resounding Tinkle*. By 1958 Arnold Wesker had written *The Kitchen* (first version) and *Chicken Soup with Barley* was performed in the same year. In 1956 Joan Littlewood and the Theatre Workshop settled in the Theatre Royal, Stratford (E. London). In 1958 Henry Livings, working with the company on Behan's *The Quare Fellow*, wrote *Jack's Horrible Luck*. In the same year the Stratford ensemble produced Shelagh Delaney's *A Taste of Honey*. By 1960 many of the major works of Wesker, Pinter, Osborne, Arden had already been produced. One other significant date ought to be mentioned. Edward Albee was first performed in 1959 when *The Zoo Story* was staged in Berlin.

Of these new dramatists Wesker and Shelagh Delaney are most like Osborne in their concern for a realistic social setting, though both are anxious to use the setting as a metaphor for the pressures any society can exert on struggling and largely resourceless (therefore usually proletarian) individuals, whose capacity for caring, for tenderness and for mess are the only guarantees they have of their own vitality. It is the weakness of both these authors, however, to remain largely locked inside their social outlook. The point they want to make seems stronger than the theatrical life they create to make the point; and sympathetic though the point may be, it is not enough to sustain a career in the theatre.

Harold Pinter (b. 1930) seems to be the most extraordinarily gifted of the new English playwrights. Pinter is a good instance of the folly of setting up opposing schools of 'Absurd' and 'Kitchen Sink' drama, for though 'Absurd' in the absence of motivations, the inconsequentiality of development in his plays, Pinter is a realist in so far as he projects the actual speech patterns of real people evading (as real people usually do) the logic of events. The first effect he made on at least one spectator was of an unbearable accuracy of observation, simultaneously hysterically funny and hysterically horrifying; and the enormous success of *A Night Out* on radio and television in 1960 (the highest ratings of its week) presumably reflects this:

*Albert*: I can't go down to the cellar, I've got my best trousers on, I've got a white shirt on.
*Mother*: You're dressing up tonight, aren't you? Dressing up, cleaning your shoes, anyone would think you were going to the Ritz.
*Albert*: I'm not going to the Ritz.
*Mother* [suspiciously]: What do you mean, you're not going to the Ritz?
*Albert*: What do you mean?
*Mother*: The way you said you're not going to the Ritz, it sounded like you were going somewhere else!
*Albert* [wearily]: I am.

The imprisonment of the individual inside his modes of speech, the sheer clutter of verbal forms, as of technical objects, gives a crazy poetry to much that Pinter has written, a poetry in which fantasy and reality are inextricably intertwined. His 'weakness' (when set against a purist like Beckett) is a tendency

329

to seek to explain. *The Caretaker* centres on the mutually exclusive fantasies of Aston (about to build a shed), Mick (about to redecorate the flat) and Davies (about to go to Sidcup to get his papers) and is brilliantly effective in these terms. It seems to be a mistake to explain further, as Pinter has done, with his story of Aston's insanity and his treatment in the mental hospital. The power of his plays is less concerned with how people come to be thus and more with the fact that they are thus, and together.

The bewildered individual, struggling to cope with the world, appears in other dramatists in other modes: in the bolshy-fantasies of Henry Livings, where the individual escapes into short-term comic dream-lives; among the gormless rustics in David Rudkin's *Afore Night Come* (1962) where we have an attempt to create the blood and soil significance of a ritual murder in the world of helicopters and pesticides.

John Arden's Sergeant in *Sergeant Musgrave's Dance* (1959) reflects a different kind of individual bewilderment—the bewildered logic of the individual who claims to understand the history he is enacting, but whose world remains more complex than his logic seems to allow. Arden (b. 1930) is clearly one of the most gifted, but also one of the most puzzling of the younger English dramatists. He seems to owe little or nothing to his contemporaries; but there is an obvious debt to the historical plays of Bertold Brecht in nearly all his work.

Brecht's *Galileo* (Zurich 1945) and *Mother Courage* (written 1939; Zurich 1941) have opened up for several dramatists the rather tired genre of the history play so that it can take account of the pressures of social development on the individual who seeks to live for himself (herself). Brecht's didactic aims made these plays a mixture of explicit historiography (facts and figures) with evocations of folk-life (ballads, fables, demonstrations), and individual self expression.

Too many English history-plays have been mere escapes from present pressures into a romanticized freedom from all pressure —'Gordon Daviot's' *Richard of Bordeaux* (1932), a weakened retelling of Shakespeare's *Richard II*, comes to mind; or Christopher Fry's *The Lady's Not for. Burning* (1948), an effectively distanced fantasy in self-indulgently quirky language. Even Shaw's *St. Joan* (1924) suffers from a sentimentalized view of History. Brecht's Marxist tying of the past into the process that explains the present has made this escape route more difficult. Joan Littlewood and the Stratford (East) ensemble have taken to the Brechtian 'method' with great gusto; and their ballad recreation of the First World War, *Oh What a Lovely War* (1963), has attracted large audiences (sometimes, it seems, for nostalgic rather than doctrinaire reasons). In *Sergeant Musgrave's Dance* the vaguely nineteenth-century past is clearly meant to reflect on labour versus capital struggles of the contemporary world; Osborne's *Luther* (1961) is, like other Osborne heroes, a rebel against social corruption, who is at the same time the victim of his own physical and psychic process—a martyr with bowel trouble cut almost precisely to Eliot's specification, as Eliot's St Thomas à Beckett was not. Robert Bolt's *A Man for All Seasons* (1960) exhibits a more parlour-Brechtian technique, with 'Common Man' making comments from a disenchanted objective position on the life and death of St. Thomas More.

It may be proper to end on a more practical note, since (as I pointed out in the first paragraph of this essay) the theatre is so heavily dependent on practical support. And this is one of the areas where the English theatre has changed most radically in the last few years. The growth of the radio and the television play has made drama (and especially one-act drama) financially attractive to would-be writers in a way it has not been in the recent past. Moreover, the kitchen-sink or proletarian-fantastic tone of much that has been successful suggests that the capacity to document experience (in prison, on a building-site, as a prostitute or con-man) may be more important than a command of literary form. The range of people who write plays has grown enormously.

Changes in the financing of the general cultural world are also important to the would-be-writer. There has been increasing direct support for experimental art. The expanding universities have supplied both an audience and a ferment of relevant ideas. The theatre department at Bristol (the first in the country) has clearly been of crucial importance in the careers of both Arden and Pinter. Seasons of foreign drama in London or at international festivals (like the Edinburgh Festival) make for a rapid dissemination of avant-garde experiments. And television difuses a sense of these novelties into every home, where a thousand may scoff, but one can learn. It seems obvious that the theatre of the future will have to work its passage in a world dominated by television; but, conversely, the television dramatist will undoubtedly continue to feel a need for the personal confrontations that only the theatre can provide.

## NOTE

1. 'The well-made play' is difficult to define positively, for the use of the phrase has mainly been in polemic—to describe a kind of play that 'advanced' playwrights did not wish to associate with. It is usual to point to the works of Eugène Scribe (1791–1861), Dumas *fils* (1824–1895) and Victorien Sardou (1831–1908) as central examples of the style; but it is probably wrong to assume that their plays are shallow only because they are well-made. The basic aims of the well-made play are, I assume, to hold the audience in the same kind of rapt attention as melodrama, but without departing from probable modes of realistic existence in a conventional society. The intrigue is, in consequence, of central importance; which should be so skilfully disposed that we are led on from a state of initial ignorance through increasing intensity of confrontations (ideally, expected confrontations—the so-called *scènes-a-faire*) to a complete and satisfying resolution. It is obviously difficult to balance the conflicting claims of theatricality and realism without collapsing into farce or melodrama, but it is not clear that this collapse is a necessary consequence of being 'well-made'.

BIBLIOGRAPHY

The British Council published *The Year's Work in the Theatre*
for the three years 1948–1951. It has also issued two other
relevant pamphlets: *Drama Since 1939* by Robert Speaight
(1947) and *Drama 1945–1950* by J. C. Trewin (1951).
J. C. Trewin published at the same time a fuller survey: *The
Theatre Since 1900* (London, 1951).
For the European and theoretical background see John Gassner,
*Direction in Modern Theatre and Drama* (New York, 1965).
H. K. Moderwell, *The Theatre of Today* (New York & London,
1914; 1927), gives a good account of the new methods of staging
developed between 1890 and 1900.
For the English Theatre down to 1914 see *The Victorian Theatre* by
G. Rowell (London)—with a splendid bibliography.
For Poel see Robert Speaight, *William Poel* (London, 1954).
On Granville Barker see C. B. Purdom, *Harley Granville Barker*,
(London, 1955).
On the Barker-Vedrenne season see Desmond MacCarthy, *The Court
Theatre 1904–1907* (London, 1907).
Martin Esslin, *The Theatre of the Absurd* (London, 1962; Harmonds-
worth, 1968). Catalogues the European, English and American
fortunes of the various kinds of drama to which the label
'absurd' might be applied.
John Russell Taylor, *Anger and After* (London, 1962; Harmondsworth 1963). Describes the 'new' drama in Britain between 1955
and the year of publication.
John Russell Taylor, *The Rise and Fall of the Well-made Play* (London, 1967). Deals with the tradition of conventionally good
playwriting from Scribe to Rattigan.

Dates of plays are those of first *public* performance. Performance in London unless otherwise specified.

| | |
|---|---|
| 1893 | Pinero, *The Second Mrs. Tanqueray*. |
| 1894 | Miss Horniman sponsors a London season of modern drama. |
| | Poel founds the Elizabethan Stage Society. |
| 1895 | Wilde, *The Importance of Being Ernest* |
| 1899 | The London Stage Society founded (lasted till 1939). |
| | Irish Literary Theatre (later Abbey Theatre) founded in Dublin. |
| 1902 | Stephen Phillips's *Paolo and Francesca*. |
| 1903 | Synge, *The Shadow of the Glen* (Dublin). |
| 1904 | Barrie, *Peter Pan*. |
| | Synge, *Riders to the Sea* (Dublin). |
| 1904–1907 | Barker-Vedrenne productions at Court Theatre. Shaw, *Man and Superman, John Bull's Other Island, Candida, Captain Brassbound's Conversion, Major Barbara*, etc., etc. Barker, *The Voysey Inheritance*, Galsworthy, *The Silver Box*. Ibsen, Hauptmann, Schnitzler, etc., etc. |
| 1905 | Gordon Craig's essay *The Art of the Theatre* published. |
| 1906 | Pinero, *His House in Order*. |
| 1907 | Barker, *Waste*. Shaw, *Caesar and Cleopatra*. |
| | Synge, *The Playboy of the Western World* (Dublin). |
| | Miss Horniman founds the Manchester Repertory Company. |
| 1909 | Pinero, *Mid-channel*. |
| | Galsworthy, *Strife*. |
| 1910 | Galsworthy, *Justice*. |
| | Barker, *The Madras House*. |
| | Shaw, *Misalliance* |
| 1911 | Shaw, *Fanny's First Play*. |
| 1912 | Houghton, *Hindle Wakes* (Manchester). |
| 1913 | Shaw, *Androcles and the Lion*. |
| | Opening of Birmingham Repertory Theatre. |
| 1914 | Shaw, *Pygmalion*. |
| 1916 | Brighouse, *Hobson's Choice* (Manchester). |
| 1919 | *The Cabinet of Dr. Caligari* (German expressionist film). |
| 1921 | Maugham, *The Circle*. |
| | Shaw, *Heartbreak House*. |
| 1922 | Galsworthy, *Loyalties*. |
| 1923 | O'Casey, *Shadow of a Gunman* (Dublin). |
| | Maugham, *Our Betters*. |
| 1924 | Shaw, *Back to Methuselah* (Birmingham, 1923). |
| | Shaw, *St. Joan* (New York, 1923). |
| | Coward, *The Vortex*. |
| | O'Casey, *Juno and the Paycock* (Dublin). |

| 1925 | Shaw, *Mrs. Warren's Profession* (Birmingham). |
| 1926 | O'Casey, *The Plough and the Stars.* |
| 1928 | Sherriff, *Journey's End.* |
| 1929 | O'Casey, *The Silver Tassie.* |
| | Shaw, *The Applecart.* |
| | Maugham, *The Sacred Flame* |
| 1930 | Yeats, *The Words upon the Window-pane* (Dublin). |
| 1931 | Bridie, *The Anatomist.* |
| 1933 | Priestley, *Laburnum Grove.* |
| 1935 | Eliot, *Murder in the Cathedral* (Canterbury) |
| | Greenwood, *Love on the Dole.* |
| | Auden and Isherwood, *The Dog Beneath the Skin.* |
| 1937 | Auden and Isherwood, *The Ascent of F6.* |
| | Priestley, *Time and the Conways.* |
| 1938 | Auden and Isherwood, *On the Frontier.* |
| | Yeats, *Purgatory.* |
| 1939 | Eliot, *The Family Reunion.* |
| 1941 | Coward, *Blithe Spirit.* |
| 1946 | O'Casey, *Red Roses for Me.* |
| | Fry, *A Phoenix too Frequent.* |
| | Rattigan, *The Winslow Boy.* |
| 1947 | Priestley, *The Linden Tree.* |
| 1948 | Fry, *The Lady's Not for Burning.* |
| 1949 | Eliot, *The Cocktail Party* (Edinburgh). |
| 1955 | Beckett, *Waiting for Godot.* |
| 1956 | Osborne, *Look Back in Anger.* |
| | Behan, *The Quare Fellow.* |
| 1957 | Beckett, *Endgame.* |
| | „ *All that Fall* (broadcast by B.B.C.). |
| | Osborne, *The Entertainer.* |
| | Simpson, *A Resounding Tinkle.* |
| 1958 | Beckett, *Krapp's Last Tape.* |
| | Behan, *The Hostage.* |
| | Delaney, *A Taste of Honey.* |
| | Wesker, *Chicken Soup with Barley* (Coventry). |
| | Pinter, *The Birthday Party* (Cambridge). |
| 1959 | Arden, *Sergeant Musgrave's Dance.* |
| | Wesker, *Roots* (Coventry). |
| | Owen, *No Trams to Lime Street* (television). |
| | „ *The Rough and Ready Lot.* |
| | Pinter, *A Slight Ache* (broadcast by B.B.C.). |
| 1960 | Pinter, *The Dumb Waiter* (Berlin, 1959). |
| | Arden, *Soldier, Soldier* (television). |
| | Pinter, *The Night Out* (television). |

## 10

## POPULAR READING: THE NEW 'SENSATION NOVEL'

Andrew Bear, Centre for Contemporary Cultural Studies,
University of Birmingham

The main tradition of writing about popular fiction, which is characterized by contempt for the literature itself and by a deep concern for the state of society, has its roots in the nineteenth century. As Raymond Williams has shown, many literary intellectuals were disturbed by certain trends in the emerging industrial civilization, and it came to be widely believed that new forms of mass entertainment were playing a part in the dehumanization of the whole environment. Wordsworth made the connection at the beginning of the century:

> For a multitude of causes, unknown to former times, are now acting with a combined force to blunt the discriminating powers of the mind, and, unfitting it for all voluntary exertion, to reduce it to a state of almost savage torpor ... To this tendency of life and manners the literature and theatrical exhibitions of the country have conformed themselves. The invaluable works of our elder writers . . . are driven into neglect by frantic novels, sickly and stupid German Tragedies and deluges of idle and extravagant stories in verse.

Coleridge, a few years later, turned explicitly to the new habit of reading novels:

> I will run the risk of asserting, that where the reading of novels prevails as a habit, it occasions in time the entire destruction of the powers of the mind ... it produces no improvement of the intellect, but fills the mind with a mawkish and morbid sensibility, which is directly hostile to the cultivation, invigoration and enlargement of the nobler faculties of the understanding.

A similar association between an attack on a new medium

of popular entertainment and a major critique of society itself had been present in the earlier controversies about the stage in the sixteenth and eighteenth cnturies, and it is still to be observed in the attack on television at the present time. In Victorian England, however, it had a special force, for it was felt that the unprecedented *quantity* of novels was a new and alarming development. The great reviews are full of complaints that 'literature' was coming to mean 'novels'. The period was actually described as the 'age of Novels', and at the end of the century a writer for *Blackwood's Magazine* (1898) echoed the widespread concern when he referred to the 'overwhelming and ever-increasing preponderance of fiction'. Inevitably, then, the new reading habit was identified as an at least partial cause of the 'corruption of the times'. In 1895 the *Contemporary Review* claimed that novels were placing 'civilization itself' in danger, and other strong views were expressed:

> But that such reading [of novels] as at present prevails has, by reason both of its quality and quantity, has [sic] led to a deterioration of the human species, physically, mentally, and morally, we entertain no doubt; nor do we see how, unless the vicious habit be somehow corrected, the race can escape from being ultimately divided into two sections, the members of one of which will be little removed from invalids, and the members of the other scarcely distinguishable from *crétins*.
>
> *Temple Bar* (1874)

This tradition has survived, with remarkably little modification, to the present day. Modern writers make a far more rigid distinction than the Victorians did between 'popular' and 'serious' fiction—'The cleavage between the popular and the serious novel constantly increases'—but while the latter has been reserved for more respectful treatment, those novels which reach a large audience are still condemned as both a symptom and a cause of cultural disintegration.

The most influential carrier of the tradition seems to have been Q. D. Leavis' famous study *Fiction and the Reading Public* (1932). Like the Victorian writers quoted, Mrs. Leavis was not interested in popular fiction for its own sake—she claimed that the ordinary methods of literary criticism 'can necessarily take no heed of the majority of novels'—but she argued that they were of great cultural significance:

> this body of writing has exerted an enormous influence upon the minds and lives of the English people; till recently it has

337

superseded for the majority every other form of art and amusement; and it forms the only printed matter beside newspapers and advertisements which that majority reads; from the cultural point of view its importance cannot be exaggerated.

Her interest was in the combined social effect of popular novels as a 'class' of fiction, and in what their numerical preponderance over 'significant works of fiction' (defined as the novels of Lawrence, Woolf, Joyce, Powys and Forster) revealed about the state of civilization. The author's low opinion of popular novels themselves emerges clearly in passages such as this:

> it is a peculiarity of this last generation that a consistent selection by the majority of the 'worst' novels ('worst' by consensus of the critical minority) has created a state exactly contrary to what the Martian or innocent eighteenth-century observer might expect, so that 'best seller' is an almost entirely derogatory epithet among the cultivated.

Mrs. Leavis further remarked that it is often impossible to read ordinary popular novels 'without forfeiting one's self-respect'. The effect of novel reading on members of the reading public was to:

> work upon and solidify herd prejudice and to debase the emotional currency by touching grossly on fine issues,

while the 'enormous sales' of novelists like Marie Stopes offered 'convincing proof of the incapacity of the twentieth century to manage its emotional life for itself.' In another passage, the effect of reading popular fiction, and the danger of becoming 'addicted' to it, was further defined:

> The form of self-indulgence specified here accounts for the immense success of novels like *The Way of the Eagle*, *The Sheik*, *The Blue Lagoon*, a more detrimental diet than the detective story in so far as the habit of fantasying will lead to maladjustment in actual life.

The main assumptions carried by this tradition of criticism seem to be: that it is all much the same; that it is necessarily bad in immediately obvious ways; that it gets worse as time goes by; that its inevitably harmful effects may be specified in general terms; that it directly reflects the state of civilization; and that certain identifiable characteristics of both content and effect will be common not only to most popular novels, but to the other popular arts as well. The various elements in the critique have been combined in different ways, but the basic approach is usually recognizable. A modern American writer, for instance, has emphasized the similarities between all the major forms of popular art:

American popular art can now offer soap opera from cradle to grave . . . America's unfunny comics become one with the popular novel, the radio serial, the 'Hollywood' movie, and much TV drama. The ingredients are common to all: the milieu of the upper middle class . . . the cliches of American romantic love, the continual sexual titillation . . . the straight nosed, firm chinned heroes—and all of them are directed towards the wish fulfilments of a mass audience.

K. E. Eble, *The American Scholar* (1958–59)

At about the same time, an English writer stressed the harmful effects and the state of contemporary civilization:

Where popular reading is concerned . . . there would seem to be some evidence of a decline in quality. Certainly, popular reading matter of the twentieth century has demonstrated a distressing poverty in the imaginative life of the people . . . the various forms of popular literature—crime or love stories —are to be condemned . . . because the attitudes they involve in important matters of human relationship and moral choice are obstructive to finer or more subtle responses. The expectations about human behaviour aroused by the ordinary work of popular fiction or magazine story involve grossly oversimplified stereotypes which, to addicts, must to some extent interfere with their ability to understand those with whom they have to live in close personal contact, as in family life . . . there is a good deal of evidence to suggest that the cinema and television foster a kind of escapist day-dreaming which is likely to be emotionally exhausting and crippling to apprehensions of the real world.

G. H. Bantock in *The Modern Age* (Volume 7 of the *Pelican Guide to English Literature*)

David Holbrook has particularly emphasized the state of contemporary culture:

The truth is that our adult culture at large nowadays is a desert, an impoverishment, a disgrace . . . the vast spiritual impoverishment of the modern world . . . the spreading psychic spinelessness, inculcated by the pressures of the phantasy-

projection industry . . . Now, even among intelligent undergraduates, the spineless phantasy has overcome natural good
sense, and even youthful idealism. Some of them will tell you
that Ian Fleming is a very good writer!

There, the implicit judgement of Ian Fleming is inseparable from
the judgement of modern society: the one confirms the other.
Mr. Holbrook also makes the assumption that all the popular
arts may be discussed and dismissed together. In this particular
essay he was reviewing Hall and Whannel's *The Popular Arts*,
in which the authors had claimed that some popular writers are
better than others. Mr. Holbrook protested strongly that there
could be no point in such an undertaking:

> There is little point in discriminating, as Hall and Whannel
> do, between pop and pop . . . Raymond Chandler they choose
> as better than Mickey Spillane because he shows by his ironic
> asides that he knows what he is doing. I see no value in such
> 'discriminations': if we are to have muck, let's have outright,
> sheer muck, rather than muck that pretends, by snobbery or
> irony, to be superior.
>
> *The Use of English* (1966)

For those interested in the study of popular reading, there are
by now a number of reasons for doubting the adequacy of the
familiar critical tradition just outlined.

The first is the characteristic tone of contempt, and the effect
which this has had on the criticism itself. It is difficult to see
how a work of any kind is to be read accurately if the critic is
to approach it convinced that he is dealing with muck or that
the very act of reading will somehow force him to forfeit his
self-respect. Richard Hoggart has described the feelings aroused
by listening to popular music and watching television:

> Who can listen to a programme of pop songs, or watch *Can-
> did Camera* or *This is Your Life*, without enduring a compli-
> cated and complex mixture of attraction and repulsion, of
> admiration for skill and scorn for the phoney, of wry ob-
> servations of similarities and correspondences, of sudden re-
> minders of the raciness of speech, or of the capacity for
> courage or humour, or of shock at the way mass art can
> 'process' anything, even our most intimate feelings.
>
> *The American Scholar* (1964)

That seems to offer a more reasonable approach to popular
literature, and is certainly more in accord with my own re-

sponse to many of the popular novels I have read. One doesn't want to assert, of course, that *The Cruel Sea* or *A Town Like Alice* or *Goldfinger* are unjustly neglected masterpieces, works of art of a high order. Even so, they have an interest of their own, but more than this, if it is true that such works are of great cultural significance, it is hard to see how that significance will be revealed if the critic is to approach them with a completely closed mind. I do not share Mrs. Leavis's view that the ordinary methods of literary criticism 'can necessarily take no heed of the majority of novels'. I would argue, to the contrary, that the full meaning of even the most mundane work will remain obscure *unless* the ordinary methods of literary criticism—attention to detail and structure, comparison, sympathetic involvement—are applied to it as they would be in the reading of those novels which command a different kind of respect.

The second problem is raised by the complex of social and psychological assumptions which lies behind almost all discussions of the artifacts of popular culture. It is even difficult to be sure, in many cases, whether the judgements of modern society condition the judgements of popular fiction, or vice versa. One view is that the popular literature of a period offers a direct *reflection*—a kind of mirror image—of the actual social and moral situation, and another is that the popular literature is itself a *causal factor* in the creation of the conditions described. These closely related assumptions touch on delicate and complex issues, and the immediate problem is whether the strong sense of moral urgency (and the tendency to strong language) so apparent among the writers quoted is really compatible with the difficulty of the questions involved. The twin hypotheses, that popular literature 'reflects' society and/or 'affects' people, are *hypotheses* after all and not proven facts. Mr. Holbrook has stated extremely what is implicit elsewhere—that all popular literature is 'muck' and modern society a 'desert'—but to express such judgements is not to establish that the two are interdependent.

It is a fact, however, that we know very little about the English book-reading public at the moment—its size and social composition—and even less about the psychological process of reading fiction. It is an odd and unfortunate situation, but the large body of professional research relating to television has no counterpart in studies of the novel. It may be useful, however, to abstract a summary picture of the reading public as it has been presented in literary criticism, and compare this tentatively with the sketchy evidence actually available. On the question of audience size, the nineteenth century view that novel reading had become a majority activity seems to have persisted: the *quantity* of fiction remained its most alarming feature. Mrs. Leavis quoted with approval the Minister of Education (1927), 'Nearly everyone in this country already has the [reading] habit, and has it very badly', and she herself described fiction as 'the chief or only form of art that the general public encounters', 'the typical reading of a people', 'the leisure of the majority', and referred to 'the hold it has on the present generation'. The last point raises the separate question of the reading *process*, and here too the picture seems fairly clear: people may develop a 'craving' for fiction, become 'addicted' to it, read habitually, compulsively and uncritically, take what they read very seriously in a search for 'compensation' or 'identification', become 'escapist', 'maladjusted', unable to 'face facts', until finally, in Mrs. Leavis's phrase, they are 'living at the novelist's expense'.

As for the latter, there is no direct modern evidence of any kind available. No one, it seems, has ever set out to explore carefully the way people respond to fiction. Quite basic things are unknown—whether people read all books in the same way, whether the typical level of involvement is as high as that predicted above, whether the circumstances under which a book is read make any difference, whether individual personality factors come into it, whether age, sex, or education can be crucial variables, and so on. The indirect evidence from studies of the use of television, however, suggests that the picture is too simple. It is likely that any readers who could reasonably be called 'addicts' will form a tiny, disturbed minority, and probable that a variety of personal and social factors play a part not only in the selection of books, but in the perception of the same book by different readers. Furthermore, the level of detachment is likely to be fairly high even among the unsophisticated (cf. the phrase 'it's only a story'). The last point has recently been discussed, in two important articles, by D. W. Harding.[1] He deplored the 'pseudo-psychology' that has had free reign in so many discussions of the reading process, and even cast doubt on the familiar concept of 'identification', arguing that the reader is far more likely to approach a book in the role of 'onlooker' than as a totally involved 'participant'.

Evidence on the first question of the number of readers in relation to the total population is also difficult to obtain, but once again, what there is does not support the view described. To some extent it is a matter of perspective. Certainly a very large number of novels are sold every year—more than at any other time in history—yet now that television and the modern popular press have demonstrated what a 'mass medium' can really be like, the novel has begun to appear relatively unimportant. Over 90 per cent of the British public live in homes equipped with television, and it is estimated that the average adult spends eighteen hours viewing every week.[2] Audiences of thirty or forty million have been known for a single television programme, and it is probable that even the non-commercial B.B.C. regards one million as the minimum audience required to justify transmission. Publishers do not reveal sales figures, and there is no way of knowing how many people read a book once it is placed in a library, so no comparable evidence is available for novels. It is certain, however, that very few novels ever sell one million copies (total population fifty-two million), which may be further compared with the daily sales (4,844,000 in 1965) of the *Daily Mirror*.

One notices, too, that complaints about the misuse of the reading 'habit' have been replaced, especially among teachers, by the worry that many children are reluctant to read *books of any kind*. Ironically enough, research designed partly to find out whether television caused people to stop reading books has highlighted the fact that vast numbers didn't read them in the first place. In samples taken in London and Birmingham, William Belson found that only 38 per cent and 30 per cent respectively expressed themselves 'quite' or 'very' interested in 'reading books of fiction', while 25 per cent and 32 per cent respectively expressed themselves 'not interested'. This hardly suggests a pattern of uniform, nation-wide addiction to novels. But this concept of 'addiction' has always raised problems—how many novels must a person read in a year to qualify? It has been found in the United States that about three-quarters of the population do not read one book of any kind in a month, that about half the population do not read one a year, and that the 'high' reading minority (defined as four or more books a month) constitutes only 7 per cent of the total population. Even *before* the spread of television:

> Of the five major public media of communication, book reading is the most limited in terms of total population. Almost everybody listens to the radio or reads a newspaper, but only one person in four reads a book a month.
>
> Lester Asheim

Beside this, we need to place the finding, confirmed both in

England and the United States, that the coming of television did not cause a significant permanent decrease in the amount of book reading. Other media, notably comics, radio and film suffered major declines, but book reading, estimated from sales and public library circulations, changed relatively little. (This statement is based on the assumption that the decline of suburban lending-libraries and the book clubs was more than compensated by the rising sales of paperbacks.) In other words, it cannot be argued that changes wrought by television resolve these conflicting pictures of the reading public. If it is considered, furthermore, that 25 per cent of the American public reads one book a month, but only 7 per cent one a week, the concentration of those who read *more* than one a week must be in something like 3 per cent or 4 per cent of the population. I have never seen it so defined, but I would have thought that an 'inordinate addiction' to fiction must mean more than one book a week.

There are some indications that English people read more than Americans, but nothing to suggest a really radical difference. In all probability, the proportion of absolute non-readers is lower, but the very heavy readers similarly concentrated in a small minority. A recent nation-wide survey found that 53 per cent of the sample had not visited a library in the preceding four weeks, and the results in general confirm Belson's finding that between 20 per cent and 30 per cent of the population never or rarely read books of any kind. Studies of children's reading confirm this, and similarly show the heavy readers as a very small minority. This is probably relevant, as it is widely believed that the years of childhood are crucial in determining how much a person will read in later life. One recent study estimated that heavy readers formed a one-in-ten minority of schoolgirls, and only 12–14 per cent of the samples of children taken for the Nuffield television study were found to have read six or more books in the preceding month. On the other hand, all studies of reading known to me have shown the importance of class and education as variables: book readers as a group are not representative of the population, but come very largely from the reasonably well-educated, upper and middle-class sectors. Bernard Berelson's summary description of the reading public in the United States is perhaps an over-correction of the traditional picture, but it has its usefulness:

the so-called concentration of the audience is higher for book reading than for the other media. About 10 per cent of the adult population does 70 per cent of the book reading. Within the book reading group itself (as defined) [one book a month] 20 per cent of the readers do 70 per cent of the reading. Thus a relatively small group of people accounts for a large share of the reading. Nor does the tremendous sale of quarter books contradict this point: 10 per cent of the buyers are responsible for 80 per cent of the sales.

The addicted reader, it seems, is more a maverick than a member of the herd.

\*　　\*　　\*

There are various ways in which the unmanageable mass of popular fiction may be reduced for the purposes of discussion. In the present essay it will be useful to consider a number of 'overall bestsellers', by which is meant those few books which achieve really massive sales, and appear to break the boundaries of the normal reading public. These books, presumably, sell in excess of all others because they catch the attention of the large groups of occasional readers in the population. There are not very many of them, and in the absence of reliable figures their identification must to some extent be a matter of instinct. But they do exist, and it seems to me that a number of novels which have dominated the market in the period since the war may represent something new and possibly significant in popular fiction. It is to these novels that I propose to re-apply the the nineteenth century term 'sensation novel'.

According to figures available from America,[3] the six overall bestselling novels for the whole of the twentieth century are *Peyton Place*, *In His Steps*, *God's Little Acre*, *Gone With the Wind*, *Lady Chatterley's Lover*, and *The Carpetbaggers*. The authors who clearly dominate a more complete list of overall bestsellers are Mickey Spillane, Ian Fleming, Grace Metalious, Harold Robbins, and Erskine Caldwell. The old religious novel *In His Steps* and *Lady Chatterley's Lover* are special cases, which means that four post-war authors have become the prodigies of American publishing: Caldwell, whom they resemble, is the only writer from an earlier period to have survived on this scale, and his position actually rests on the sales of modern paperback reprints. Otherwise, only *Gone With the Wind* is unassailable. It will therefore be worth analysing the features

345

which these books share, because they appear to represent a new direction in popular reading. Nor does there seem much doubt that the same four recent writers are similarly important on the English market: Fleming and Spillane obviously are, Pan Books are known to have established a record with their first paperback reprinting of *Peyton Place*,[4] and the Four Square edition of *The Carpetbaggers* which I have lists eighteen reprints between February and October of 1964. There is sufficient evidence here to make possible the identification of a trend (it is not the only one, of course), in which Ian Fleming is unquestionably the most important English representative.

There is some measure of agreement about the main qualities of the 'typical' bestseller of earlier generations. Arnold Bennett, for instance, once described how he went about writing fiction that would sell:

> I put in generous quantities of wealth, luxury, feminine beauty, surprise, catastrophe and genial incurable optimism.

Mrs. Leavis found many examples of similar advice in the 'how to write fiction' manuals produced in the inter-war period. Their main import, she argued, was that the writer should 'set the reader up with a comfortable frame of mind'. This, clearly, points to the kind of fiction which K. E. Eble, in the passage quoted earlier, called 'soap opera', and Mrs. Leavis recognized it as a *typical* quality of bestsellers:

> What these highly popular novelists have won their reputation by, in fact, is the terrific vitality set to turn the machinery of morality. In a novel by Marie Corelli, Hall Caine, Florence Barclay, Gene Stratton Porter, the author is genuinely preoccupied with ethical problems, whatever side attractions there may be in the way of unconscious pornography and excuses for day-dreaming . . . These novels will all be found to make play with the key words of the emotional vocabulary which provoke the vague warm surges of feeling associated with religion and religion substitutes— *e.g.* life, death, love, good, evil, sin, home, mother, noble, gallant, purity, honour.

Cheering, uplifting, moral—attractive but recognizably ordinary people triumphing against adversity. These are the qualities indicated, and there is no doubt that the analysis held true of many bestselling novels in the years after *Fiction and the Reading Public*, for example in famous ones like *Anthony Adverse*, *Good-Bye Mr. Chips*, and *National Velvet*. Even in the post-war period, P. N. Furbank[5] identified qualities related to these as still the most characteristic features of the bestseller. He defined the three main ones as the 'congratulation system', the use of 'romantic disproportion', and the 'dependence on nostalgia', and he saw Nevil Shute as 'perhaps the most characteristic post-war best-seller'. Other important modern bestselling authors whose work might also be described in this way are Morris West and Taylor Caldwell, one of whose novels, *Tender Victory*, has been described as:

> a charming inspirational novel . . . A heart-warming story of how an American pastor brings five orphaned war-victims back from Europe, and makes a normal home for them . . . She can handle scenes of violence with masculine assurance, but the best scenes in the book are the compassionate ones. It is a good book; I mean good, not in the aesthetic, but in what is more important, the moral sense.

This is an extremely generalized picture, of course, but it does offer a basis of comparison for discussing the group of great bestsellers named. Less than ten years after Mr. Furbank wrote, Nevil Shute no longer looks so central.

Nicholas Monsarrat's *The Cruel Sea* (1951) is an interesting example of a novel which has much in common with the familiar 'uplifting' bestseller, yet in important ways it anticipates the trend towards sensationalism. An odd aspect of its reputation is that it has often been recommended as stirring reading for young people, but it seems to have been thought that this function would be best served if the book was read in the 'expurgated' edition which was still on sale until very recently. There are two main emphases in the novel. One is the realistic narrative of the Battle of the Atlantic, and the other, which may be called the theme, concerns the concept of 'dedication' and the moral effects of the war on Ericson and Lockhart, the two central characters. In one passage, the *Compass Rose* picks up the under-water echo of a German submarine, and Ericson is forced to make a decision:

> The place where the U-boat lay, the point where they must drop their charges, was alive with swimming survivors.
>
> The Captain drew in his breath sharply at the sight. There were about forty men in the water, concentrated in a small space: if he went ahead with the attack he must, for certain, kill them all. He knew well enough, as did everyone on board, the effect of depth-charges exploding under-water . . .

Now there were men instead of fish and seaweed, men swimming towards him in confidence and hope . . . And yet the U-boat was there, one of the pack which had been harrassing and bleeding them for days on end, the destroying menace which *must* have priority, because of what it might do to other ships and other convoys in the future . . .

All right, then, thought Ericson, with a new unlooked-for sense of brutality to help him : all right, we'll go for the U-boat. With no more hesitation he gave the order . . . and having made this sickening choice he swept into the attack with a deadened mind, intent only on one kind of kill, pretending there was no other.

Clearly, as Mrs. Leavis noted of earlier bestsellers, Monsarrat is 'genuinely preoccupied with ethical problems' : indeed, the slightly stagey quality of the scene derives precisely from the reader's feeling that it has been engineered in order to make the ethical problem explicit. But it is necssary to take account of the whole passage :

Mercifully the details were hidden in the flurry and roar of the explosion; and the men must all have died instantly, shocked out of life by the tremendous pressure of the sea thrown up upon their bodies. But one freak item of the horror impressed itself on the memory. As the tormented water leapt upwards in a solid grey cloud, the single figure of a man was tossed high on the very plume of the fountain, a puppet figure of whirling arms and legs seeming to make, in death, wild gestures of anger and reproach. It appeared to hang a long time in the air, cursing them all, before falling back into the boiling sea.

When they came back to the explosion area . . . it was as if to some aquarium where poisoned water had killed every living thing. Men floated high on the surface like dead goldfish in a film of blood. Most of them were disintegrated, or pulped out of human shape. But half a dozen of them, who must have been on the edge of the explosion, had come to a tidier end : split open from chin to crutch, they had been gutted as neatly as any herring. Some seagulls were already busy on the scene, screaming with excitement and delight. Nothing else stirred.

What can one say, as a literary critic, about writing like this? One notes the seriousness of the intention, the deep moral concern. Yet is it not true that the writing is more alive, has more imaginative power, in the second part than in the first? The purpose of the later paragraphs, obviously, is to communicate the human enormity of what Ericson has done, to say something about the nature of decision making and of moral responsibility under war-time conditions. But is that, in fact, what the reader responds to? Would it not be more true to say the description of the area of destruction engages the imagination so forcefully that all else, even the ostensible point of the whole passage, is overwhelmed? But it is not overwhelmed by the author making 'play with the key words of the emotional vocabulary', as Mrs. Leavis found in Hall Caine and others. Indeed, almost the opposite: if anything, there is a kind of playing-down. The effect comes, for instance, in the choice of image and detail—the 'puppet figure of whirling arms and legs', or the deliberate understatement of 'a tidier end', and the analogy (picking up a number of earlier references to fish) of the 'aquarium' with its 'dead goldfish'. There is, too, a peculiar force in the concrete physicality of 'split open from chin to crutch', the gruesome incongruity of the seagulls screaming with 'delight', and in the unexpectedness of 'neatly gutted as any herring', which immediately picks up the three image-threads of fish, food, and tidiness.

This is writing that comes very close to the bone, and it contrasts with the less lively use of language in the first paragraphs—'drew in his breath sharply', 'sickening choice', 'deadened mind'. It cannot be said that Monsarrat is exploiting horror for its own sake, and yet the effect is to arouse physical sensation, rather than emotional or moral involvement either with Ericson himself or with the victims of the explosion. And these are precisely the kinds of passages that one remembers from *The Cruel Sea*, not simply because of the situations, but because at these points the writer is more creatively engaged with words than elsewhere: here, he can seek and find sudden associations and create unforgettable images. The moral issues are less engaging, less well developed, not because they are presented perfunctorily, certainly not because they are ignored, but because the raw physical force of the descriptive prose overpowers all else, and leaves one with a memory of the book which is tactile rather than moral or emotional.

What is emerging here is a new form of 'sensation novel', and its emergence is intimately connected with certain developments of physical realism which have been observable in popular fiction over the last thirty years or so. The change has been most marked, and most remarked upon, in the field of crime fiction, but as the example of *The Cruel Sea* indicates, the trend now extends into other areas as well. Passages which work as the one above now form the imaginative centres not only of crime novels, but also of the middle ground of popular fiction —'strictly best-seller country'—as is suggested by the immense success of *Peyton Place* and *The Carpetbaggers*, which are obstensibly studies of social character.

This has been remarked often enough, but comment has usually been restricted to complaints that popular fiction is less 'moral' than it used to be. That is true, of course—it is one aspect of the permissive society and loosening censorship— but it is doubtful whether it is the main point. Rather, it can be said that novels are now available that offer the reader a quite different range of experiences and satisfactions, a quite different *reason for reading*, than has been common in the past. In important respects, some of the great bestsellers of the post-war period have approached the conditions of pornography— defined here as physical sensation divorced from other considerations—and generalizations about them derived from the 'soap opera' kind of novel have become irrelevant. The experience offered may be described, in Richard Hoggart's phrase, as 'sensation-without-commitment', but it is no longer a quality restricted to the pulp and semi-underground novelettes which he described in *The Uses of Literacy*. It now has a place in the mainstream of popular fiction.

Harold Robbins' *The Carpetbaggers* is the clearest case of a massively popular novel with these characteristics. The absence of moral concern in contrast to even *The Cruel Sea* is marked in passages like this. Jennie Denton, one of the main characters, is nurse to an old man who is dying of cancer:

He opened his eyes and looked at her. The terror had gone from them and a deep, wise calm had taken its place. He smiled slowly. 'All right, Jennie,' he whispered, looking into her eyes. 'Now!'

Her eyes still fastened to his, she reached behind her for a syrette. Automatically she found the sunken vein and squeezed the syrette dry. She picked up another. He smiled again as he saw it in her hand. 'Thanks, Jennie,' he whispered.

She bent forward and kissed the pale, damp forehead. 'Good-by, Charlie.'

He leaned back against the pillow and closed his eyes as she

plunged the second syrette into his arm. Soon there were six
empty syrettes lying on the cover of the bed beside him. She
sat there very quietly, her fingers on his pulse, as the beat
grew fainter and fainter. At last, it stopped completely. She
stared down at him for a moment, then pressed down the
lids over his eyes and drew the cover over his face.

She got to her feet, putting the syrettes into her uniform
pocket as she wearily crossed the room and picked up the
telephone.

It is an unimportant episode, only loosely related to the main
story, yet Charles Standhurst, the old man, is one of the most
vivid of the minor characters, and the brief patient-nurse relationship between these two has a simple, direct human appeal.
Therefore the absence of any pressure in the writing precisely
at the point where one would expect it—at the moment of
death, let alone the question of euthanasia—is particularly striking. The writer's interest is not in the moral sphere at all : the
scene is introduced not as in *The Cruel Sea* to raise a 'problem',
but simply for its own sake.

One could say of this that it represents the fruition of the
naturalists' dream that the novelist should become a 'steno-
grapher', or that Robbins has become the ultimate Hemingway.
But of course the author could not hope to maintain interest at
the length of *The Carpetbaggers* if all scenes were like that. The
result is that the scenes chosen for emphasis must be 'strong' in
themselves, with the stress falling on physical detail : the 'realistic' conventions adopted allow for little else. The final effect
is a massive, almost continous assault on the senses, quite unlike
anything previously available in widely distributed fiction. If
the sensation is strong enough, even plausibility may be
sacrificed :

They made love for the last time on the floor, lying next to
a dead man. In the morning, Anne-Louise Pluvier calmly
turned him over to the police.

Inevitably, the book became a mere patchwork of sensational
scenes from which all interest other than the physical is rigorously excluded. But it has a raw, disturbing force which the
completely straight, understated style of narration makes
immediately available :

He burst through the door and came to a stop in surprised
shock, his eyes widening in horror. His father hung tied to
the centre post, his mouth and eyes open in death, the back

of his head blown away by the .45 that had been placed in his mouth and fired.

Slowly Max's eyes went down to the floor. There was a shapeless mass lying in a pool of blood, which bore the outline of what had once been his mother.

In the aftermath of that scene, the reader follows the young man as he inflicts revenge in kind on the three men who had murdered his parents.

In English popular fiction, the most important representative of this trend in popular reading is Ian Fleming, and his work may best be considered by comparing it briefly with that of an earlier writer who used the same basic conventions.

Leslie Charteris, author of the long series of 'Saint' novels, has written:

> I have been trying to make a picture of a man. Changing, yes. Developing, I hope. Fantastic, improbable—perhaps. Quite worthless, quite irritating, if you feel that way. Or a slightly cockeyed ideal, if you feel differently.
>
> *The First Saint Omnibus* (1939)

This compares interestingly with a comment by Raymond Chandler:

> down these mean streets a man must go who is not himself mean, who is neither tarnished nor afraid. The detective in this kind of story must be such a man. He is the hero, he is everything. He must be a complete man and a common man yet an unusual man. He must be, to use a rather weathered phrase, a man of honour . . .
>
> *The Simple Art of Murder* (1950)

It has often been remarked that the 'new' thriller writers, like Fleming, lack the kind of ethical framework implied in those comments. One needs to be very careful with this observation, however. None of the older English crime novelists, like E. W. Hornung, or John Buchan, or Leslie Charteris himself, were good writers *because* they maintained, or professed, a particular ethical ideal. There are any number of high principles in dull books, and not a few of these are by the authors named. The moral issue is further complicated in the discussion of crime fiction because many of the most famous heroes belong in the 'Robin Hood tradition'—the amateur adventurer opposing evil out of a personal sense of righteousness—and it has been maintained that *all* such books are necessarily pernicious because they immorally assert the right of the individual to act, and even to kill, by taking the law into his own hands. From this point of view, James Bond is actually more 'moral' than the others because he acts only as an official representative of the British Government.

A more profitable approach to the thriller is suggested by Bernard Bergonzi's phrase 'affective superstructure'. In fact, the genre is built on a set of very firmly established conventions which have changed little since the days of Raffles. The thriller is based on violence and adventure, on the pursuit and destruction of villain by hero, with the added interest of the hero's relationship with the heroine who, again by convention, is nearly always present. The most important differences between the new and the traditional thriller is in the way writers have exploited these basic conventions, in the changing points at which the reader feels that the writer's imagination has been most actively engaged.

If one takes the case of Mickey Spillane, for instance, the imaginative focus is clearly physical violence—in shooting or beating scenes, where the writing takes on a raw, tactile strength as in some of the passages quoted earlier. If, on the other hand, one considers the novels of Leslie Charteris, it is clear that the writer is *not* similarly engaged at these points. The same scenes occur, as they must in all thrillers, but they are developed with much greater reticence. At the climax of *The Saint in Miami* (1941; one of the Second World War stories), for example, there is both a shooting and a beating. The first is described:

> March might have thought that he could cover everyone in the room in a split second; but he was wrong. Friede only nodded, slightly and unhurriedly, to another guard who was half-way behind March. A revolver shocked the room twice with its expanding thunder . . .

> Simon's frosted blue eyes settled again on Captain Friede as the Nazi looked up from a body that finished jerking a mere instant after it sprawled on the floor.

The second, even more briefly:

> The captain walked calmly around the room, testing the bonds of Hoppy Uniatz, Karen Leith, Peter Quentin, Patricia Holm, and lastly—with especial care—the Saint.

> Then he hit the Saint six times across the face, with icy calculation.

Those passages show a kind of withdrawal before the fact, a

deliberate avoidance of physical specificity, which is typical. Sexual scenes are treated at a similar distance, even in recent stories. From *The Saint in the Sun* (1963):

> 'I know. How can I thank you?' She reached out and took his right hand in both of hers. 'Only to tell you my heart will never forget.'
>
> With an impulsively dramatic gesture, she drew his hand to her and placed it directly over her heart. The fact that a somewhat less symbolic organ intervened did not seem to occur to her, but it imposed on him some of the same restraint that a seismograph would require to remain unmoved at the epicentre of an earthquake.
>
> 'Don't I still have to earn that?' said the Saint, with remarkable mildness.

The point is not that the Saint is a 'moral' man—plainly he is not—but his sexual activities are not one of the things Charteris chooses to write about.

Charteris is unusual among thriller writers, because his 'affective superstructure' is actually comedy. There is violence, sex, pursuit—all the conventional scenes, but the distinctive notes are struck in the gallery of minor comic characters (Hoppy Uniatz, Inspector Teal), in the Saint's oratorical outbursts on one subject after another, or in the constant verbal play, either among the characters or in the author's frequent intrusions. Now, perhaps, it all seems a little Wodehousean (and has been radically altered for the modern television series), but the distinctive moments in a Saint novel come at points like this:

> The writer, whose positively Spartan economy of verbiage must often have been noted and admired by every cultured student, recoils instinctively from the temptation to embellish the scene with a well-chosen anthology of those apt descriptive adjectives with which his vocabulary is so richly stocked. The pallor of flabbergasted faces, the glinting of wild eyes, the beading of cold perspiration, the trembling of hands, the tingling of spines, the sinking of stomachs, the coming and going of breath in little short pants—all those facile clichés which might lure less ruggedly disciplined scribes into the pitfall of endeavouring to make every facet of the situation transparent to the most nitwitted reader— none of these things, on this occasion at least, have sufficient enticement to seduce him.
>
> *The Saint Goes On* (1934)

354

In one of his many interviews Ian Fleming said:

> I write for warm-blooded people in railway trains, aeroplanes
> and beds . . . I aim for total stimulation of the reader all the
> way through, even to his taste buds.

The affective superstructure of Fleming's novels, in contrast to
those of Leslie Charteris, is physical sensation divorced from
other considerations. He was, more consistently and probably
more consciously than the other bestselling authors mentioned,
a sensation novelist within the terms of my definition.

Much has been written about Fleming, and many theories
have been proposed to explain the distinctive nature of his
novels. It has been variously suggested that his was a sex-and-
violence formula indistinguishable from Spillane's, that his
special appeal derived from a leavening of good British snobbery, that the true 'Fleming Effect' came from the knowing
use of brand names and technical information (Kingsley Amis),
and that the whole thing was a parody, a brilliant send-up of the
familiar thriller conventions.

The last is the most interesting, and has been well argued
by Martin Dodsworth:

> . . . important is the extravagant absurdity of the situations.
> Although . . . irony is quite lacking in the narration, there is
> an irony of situations: the comedy lies in telling a story of
> glaring implausibility with an absolutely straight face . . .
> we cannot help laughing—but it would be fatal if Mr. Flem-
> ing laughed too.
>
> *The Twentieth Century* (1958)

There is clearly some justice in that, but my own view is that
some of the implausible situations are described with a sensual
relish that precludes or overwhelms the impulse to laugh. A
test-case would be the chapter called 'The Long Scream' in *Dr.
No*, where Bond is forced to undertake a fantastic journey
along a tunnel which has been specially designed to torture the
human body beyond endurance. At each stage, the physical
agony, the effort, and the fear are described in evocative detail.
Improbable as it may be, is the first impulse really to laugh
when, for instance, the tunnel walls are heated almost red-hot
—'No! He must drive on, screaming, until his flesh was burned
to the bone'? Surely the point is that plausibility simply isn't
relevant. As in pornography—and as in *The Carpetbaggers*, for
that matter—physical sensation is the whole purpose of the

passage, and once the reader becomes involved at this level, all other possible responses are temporarily overpowered.

This relates to Fleming's own concept of 'total stimulation', which points to a feature of his novels which seems not to have been commented upon. This author differs from the other sensation novelists in having created a totally sensual, largely tactile, verbal universe. Physical stimulation is built into the texture of the writing and the structure of the stories, so that part of the effect is analogous to that described by Steven Marcus (in *The Other Victorians*) as 'Pornotopia'. Fleming found a way of maintaining the pressure, of maintaining the assault on the senses, so that in reading his stories, one is more aware of a total, continuous experience, than of the rather disjointed succession of individually disturbing scenes, as in Spillane or Robbins.

Much can be taken as read. Fleming obviously dwells on concrete physical details in his scenes of violence, his heroines are always potently erotic figures, and the vividness of the actual sexual encounters has often been remarked. But the concept of 'total' stimulation implies more than this—the famous scenes of eating and drinking, for instance ('even to his taste buds'). One notices, too, how many completely irrelevant, but individually strong scenes, are packed into the narrative: the erotic dances in *Live and Let Die* and *The Man With the Golden Gun*, the fight between the gypsy women in *From Russia, With Love* (the chapter is called 'Strong Sensations'), and the various closely described massage scenes.

Fleming also had a characteristic way of handling scenes of violence:

Mary Trueblood swivelled sharply on her chair. A man stood in the doorway . . . There was a gun in his hand. It ended in a thick black cylinder. Mary Trueblood opened her mouth to scream. The man smiled broadly. Slowly, lovingly, he lifted the gun and shot her three times in and around the left breast.

*Dr. No*

That seems to me horrifyingly evocative, partly in familiar ways, but there are two special features. The first is the stress on the absolutely amoral, professional efficiency of the killer ('slowly, lovingly'; 'smiled'), and the second, that this person is a completely unexpected intruder in an atmosphere of normality and calm. Fleming was one of the few crime writers who introduce the incidental victims to the reader before they are killed—which itself heightens the impact—and they are often innocent, unprepared, and defenceless. The girl in the scene quoted had been described contentedly carrying out a routine task. Other examples of this kind of thing are the killing of the old couple in *For Your Eyes Only* as they were watching birds in their garden, of Strangways in *Dr. No* as he was looking forward to his game of cards, and of the Italian pilot (not so innocent, certainly) in *Thunderball* as he was thinking happily of the future. The same methods incongrously applied to the killing of fish in 'The Hildebrand Rarity' suggest that this was a conscious verbal technique.

The Fleming landscape can have special features too. This describes the opening of an underground hide-out in 'From a View To a Kill':

> The dark aperture broadened until Bond could see the roots of the bush running into the earth . . . In a moment the two segments stood apart and the two halves of the rose bush, still alive with bees, were splayed widely open . . . A head and shoulders appeared, and then the rest of the man.

A host of minor verbal devices maintain the effect, often in unexpected ways, as with phrases like 'whipped at his senses' or the sudden application of the word 'obscene' to objects that had not previously seemed so. Similarly, 'His fingers played with the controls as delicately as if they were the erotic trigger points of a woman'. At other times the casual thoughts of the character will turn in a sensual or erotic direction, for instance in Bond's frequent anticipatory speculations about the bed-time potential of the heroine, or:

> In his imagination he could already hear the deep bark of the Savage. He could see the black bullet lazily, like a slow flying bee, homing down into the valley towards a square of pink skin. There was a slight smack as it hit. The skin dented, broke and then closed up again leaving a small hole with bruised edges. The bullet ploughed on, unhurriedly, towards the pulsing heart—the tissues, the blood-vessels, parting obediently to let it through.
>
> *For Your Eyes Only*

Unexpectedly again, the hero and heroine sometimes adopt a variation of the sexual position in order to protect themselves from danger. They do so, for example, crushed between the seats of a crashing aeroplane in *Goldfinger*, under a falling cliff and up an air vent in *Moonraker*, and when tied, 'stripped naked', behind a moving ship in *Live and Let Die*:

> Their bodies were pressed together, face to face, and their arms held round each others' waists and then bound tightly again. Bond felt Solitaire's soft breasts pressed against him. She leant her chin on his right shoulder.

At least one of the characters is aware of the situation:

> 'I didn't want it to be like this,' she whispered . . .

In such cases, of course, no one explanation is ever final. The conflicting definitions of the 'Fleming Effect', however, at least show that these apparently simple and often despised forms of fiction present their own critical problems. The further step of interpreting their cultural significance is even more complex, and at the moment it seems necessary to say that any serious attempt in this direction must await further research.

There seems little doubt that the emergence of what I have called the new 'sensation novel' is connected with certain widely recognized changes in our expectations about moral behaviour, a point which may be emphasised if we consider the near certainty that many of these novels, particularly those by Spillane, Fleming and Robbins, would not have escaped censorship had they been published thirty years earlier. Similar tendencies are obvious in other media, notably films and magazines. But here, unavoidably, one faces an impenetrable entrenchment of conflicting attitudes and ideologies: some will see corruption of mind and manners where others see an important new freedom, and it is clear that the moral controversy over fiction has become unprofitable.

On the other hand, some other lines of enquiry, potentially at least, seem more open. One is the theory, put forward by Marshall McLuhan, that we are moving from a print-orientated culture towards one in which visual and tactile experience has become more important. The new sensation novels, as defined here, may be seen as productions which, although using language, stand at the farthest possible remove from literature itself. The 'hot' medium of fiction, it may be said, is being 'cooled' as the electronic age produces the kind of entertainment that it needs. But the most important questions, as D. W. Harding has argued, are those about which we know least of all. Literary criticism, regardless of the quality of the material to which it has been applied, has always been concerned with 'content analysis', and never with 'response analysis', so that we have virtually no systematic knowledge of the ways in which people actually *use* the fiction that is available to them. Nor do we know with any certainty which people read which novels, or under what circumstances. Yet these are basic questions, and until at least some of the answers are forthcoming speculation based on the analysis of content alone will remain as partial and unsatisfactory as it has always been in the past.

# NOTES

1. 'Psychological Processes in the Reading of Fiction', *British Journal of Aesthetics*, ii, (1962), 133–47. 'Considered Experience: The Invitation of the Novel', *English in Education*, i, (1967), 7–15.

2. The main sources of information for this and the following paragraphs are to be found in the bibliography.

3. Alice Payne Hackett, *70 Years of Best Sellers 1895–1965* (New York, 1967).

4. 'Hard Facts About Soft Covers', *The Author*, 71 (1961) 4.

5. 'The Twentieth-Century Best-Seller', *The Pelican Guide to English Literature: The Modern Age*, ed. B. Ford (Harmondsworth, 1961).

Amis, Kingsley, *The James Bond Dossier* (London, 1965 : New York, 1965).

Barzun, Jacques, 'Meditations on the Literature of Spying', *The American Scholar*, xxxiv, (1965), 167–78.

Belson, William A., *The Impact of Television* (London, 1967).

Furbank, P. N., 'The Twentieth-Century Best-Seller', *The Pelican Guide to English Literature: The Modern Age*, ed. B. Ford (Harmondsworth, 1961).

Hackett, Alice Payne, *70 Years of Best Sellers 1895–1965* (New York, 1967).

Hall, Stuart and Whannel, Pady, *The Popular Arts* (London, 1964 : New York, 1965).

Harvey, John, 'The Content Characteristics of Best Selling Books', *Public Opinion Quarterly*, xvii, (1953), 91–114.

Himmelweit, Hilde T. et al., *Television and the Child* (London, 1958).

Hofstadter, Beatrice K., 'Popular Culture and the Romantic Heroine', *The American Scholar*, xxx, (1961), 98–116.

Hoggart, Richard, *The Uses of Literacy* (London, 1957 : New York, 1958).

Lane, M. J. and Furness-Lane, K. A., *Books Girls Read* : Report of a Survey Conducted by the Society of Young Publishers (London, 1967).

Leavis, Q. D., *Fiction and the Reading Public* (London, 1932).

Marcus, Steven, *The Other Victorians* (New York, 1965 : London, 1966).

Mott, Frank Luther, *Golden Multitudes* (New York, 1947).

Orwell, George, 'Raffles and Miss Blandish', 1944 (extensively reprinted).

Rosenberg, Bernard and White, David Manning eds., *Mass Culture: The Popular Arts in America* (Glencoe, Illinois, 1957).

Schramm, Wilbur ed., *Mass Communications in America* (Glencoe, Illinois, 1957).

# LITERARY CRITICISM IN ENGLAND IN THE TWENTIETH CENTURY

## David Lodge, University of Birmingham

There are many ways of categorizing and distinguishing literary critics, according to their methods and principles: theoretical and descriptive, historical and anti-historical, moral and formal, intentionalist and affective, impressionistic and analytical, Oxford and Cambridge, and so on. I shall have recourse to some of these terms in the course of this essay. But it may help to introduce some order into the extraordinarily complex and crowded scene of modern literary criticism to begin with a loosely sociological categorization—to begin by asking of any particular critic: in what context was he writing, for what audience, and to what implicit or explicit purpose?

I suggest that there are three main kinds of critic (and thus of criticism) in the period. The first is the academic, who is attached to a university or similar institution, who writes usually for an implied audience of fellow-academics and/or students, and for whom literature is in some sense a 'subject', a body of knowledge, and the study of it a 'discipline'. The second kind is the creative writer whose criticism is mainly a by-product of his creative work. He is less disinterested than the academic, more concerned to work out in the practice of criticism the aesthetic principles of his own art, and to create a climate of taste and opinion favourable to the reception of that art. He writes in the first place for fellow-artists, but as there are never very many of these he has to draw on a wider audience, either the academic one, or the 'general reader'. The latter is primarily served by the third kind of critic, for whom it is difficult to find a satisfactory name. After considering and rejecting 'professional', 'journalist', 'man of letters', I have decided to call him the 'freelance'. This kind of critic has usually had an academic training and often begins with ambitions to be a creative writer. He may achieve some minor distinction as the latter, but, whether by inclination or default, most of his energies go into the writing of criticism, characteristically in the form of magazine articles and reviews. Sometimes he becomes an editor or literary editor himself. He may borrow from the first kind of critic a sense of literature as a body of knowledge, and from the second kind a sense of the most creative possibilities in contemporary writing, both of which he is in a position to make available to a wider public. Or he may identify primarily with his audience, representing himself as their defender against the pedantries of academe and the subversions of the avant garde. But his basic commitment is, perhaps, most often to the world of books as a way of life: to the pleasures of reading and to the inexhaustible fascination of the literary world—the rise and fall of reputations, the interweaving of trends and movements, the alliances and rivalries, feuds and conspiracies.

Examples of the first kind of critic are: George Saintsbury, I. A. Richards, F. R. Leavis, C. S. Lewis; of the second, Henry James, Robert Bridges, T. S. Eliot, D. H. Lawrence; of the third, Middleton Murry, Lytton Strachey, Cyril Connolly, John Lehmann. Obviously the compartments are not water-tight. It is not uncommon for one man to combine two of these roles. Both academics and creative writers use freelance media for their criticism on occasion, while creative writers and freelancers are sometimes invited to address academic audiences. In the last ten years or so this fluidity has become very marked, and there are now quite a large number of critics who combine all three roles; that is, they are academics concerned with teaching and research who are also actively involved in creative writing and regular contributors to newspapers, magazines and broadcasting. In this way the academy has come to dominate criticism and to exercise an ever-increasing influence over the production of literature. Such a literary situation (which has in many ways gone further in America) is unprecedented and, in the eyes of many, sinister. It is certainly one of the most important consequences of the revolution in criticism that is the subject of this essay.

If the academic critic is the dominant type at the moment, he is also the most recent—he scarcely exists before this century. Most of the important English critics before this period were of the second type: Sydney, Dryden, Johnson, Wordsworth, Coleridge, Arnold. Arnold, to be sure, shifted in the course of his career from being a poet-critic to being a prototype academic critic, and modern academic criticism rightly reveres him as a father-figure. The third type, the freelance, emerged towards the end of the seventeenth century when social and economic changes, including the spread of literacy and the development of publishing and journalism, created an audience which required or accepted his services. In histories of criticism, which are naturally concerned with seminal ideas and authoritative *oeuvres*, the freelance is inevitably neglected, for his work is bound to be ephemeral, if not derivative. In a survey as compressed as the present one this neglect can hardly be remedied, but it is as well to remember that the freelance can have a considerable day-to-day influence on the literary public, and thus on writers. That the freelances were failing in this respect was one of the most insistent refrains of academic and creative critics in the twenties and thirties. If one does not hear this complaint so often nowadays, it may be because things have improved; or because academics and creative writers, having largely taken over literary journalism, have only themselves to blame for its inadequacies.

Of the many attempts to formulate the 'function of criticism' T. S. Eliot's 'the elucidation of works of art and the correction of taste' has perhaps the best chance of general acceptance, being flexible enough to admit a great many different approaches, but firm enough to give definition. As applied to English literature, criticism in this sense existed in a fairly fragmentary and casual form until the end of the nineteenth century, and occupied a relatively insignificant part of intellectual life. Since that time, the study of English literature has become a dominating element in the humanities, and the elucidation of works and the correction of taste have been carried out with unprecedented industry and rigour. The two developments which, more than any other, helped to bring about this revolution in criticism were the Modernist movement in literature and the rise of English studies in the universities.

In the first two decades of this century both English studies and Modernism were looking for a new poetic and a new sense of tradition. In the twenties they collaborated to find both these things, but since the collaboration was based on a partial misunderstanding, it did not survive for very long, and the academic and creative critics drew apart again. This divergence was accelerated by a complex of other factors. Modernism lost its impetus, got lost in politics, or emigrated. Academe was riven by internecine strife, which could be crudely described as a war between scholars and critics, between Oxford and Cambridge, between those who would interpret Eliot's definition broadly and those who interpreted it narrowly. Eventually the dust settled and a kind of truce was declared (the termination of *Scrutiny* in 1953 might be said to mark this point). But by this time the initiative had passed to America. That is how I see the outlines of the story, and I shall try to fill in the detail as best I can in the space available.

I begin with the rise of English studies. Looking around at the large and flourishing English departments in our universities today, and at the formidable industry of scholarship, criticism, and textbooks they maintain, it is difficult to believe that as an academic subject of any consequence English is scarcely older than the century. Oxford did not establish an Honours School of English until 1893, Cambridge until 1917. English literature was taught before this in Scotland, at the University of London and at the provincial universities founded throughout the nineteenth century. But given the almost total hegemony of Oxford and Cambridge, English could not become a respectable—or respected—subject of study until it was adopted by the ancient universities. They were not anxious to welcome it, and to this day there are colleges that discourage it. However, once the ancient universities admitted English they immediately became, by the nature of the social and educational system, its main custodians. Until very recently nearly all significant academic critics of English literature were educated at Oxford or Cambridge; and if by any chance a bright young man took his first degree at a provincial university, he was likely to be taught by a graduate of Oxbridge, and to be sent there as a post-graduate. Only London managed to recruit from its own ranks on any considerable scale, and since London followed for the most part an austere version of the Oxford syllabus and approach, this had no significant effect on criticism. Only since the last war has the dominance of Oxford and Cambridge been seriously challenged, and then not by any identifiable rival School.

The main pressure from outside on Oxford and Cambridge to start an English Honours course was educational in its motives. Throughout the nineteenth century, and well into the twentieth, pupils at the best schools studied literature almost exclusively in Latin and Greek, (with some excursions into the foreign vernaculars) as they had done in the eighteenth, seventeenth

365

and sixteenth centuries. At that earlier point in time there had been the good reason that most books of information were written in Latin, but the practice survived the obsolescence of Latin as a learned tongue and acquired a new rationale as being providentially the best discipline for the youthful mind. As literacy and education developed, however, the narrowness and exclusiveness of this system became more and more apparent. Romantic and post-romantic critics of culture and society stressed the importance of literature as a reservoir of humanizing values with which to counteract the materialistic influences of the industrial revolution, the growth of science and the erosion of orthodox religion (Arnold being a representative figure here). The classics were not, as a rule, taught with this kind of emphasis, and in any case they were not available to the mass of the literate population. Hence the vernacular literature came to occupy a more and more important place on the lower levels of the educational system, as a kind of 'poor man's classics', but without any corresponding reinforcement on the higher levels. It was in the name of such reinforcement that Oxford was petitioned to initiate a School of English. But, as David Palmer has shown,[1] it was welcomed at Oxford, if it was welcomed at all, by a party who were primarily interested in early English as a specialized subject for linguistic research, increasing Oxford's stake in that expansion of historical philology which is such a striking feature of nineteenth-century European scholarship; while it was opposed by dons with a vested interest in more traditional disciplines as being a soft option (the smear still sticks) likely to encourage (particularly in its literary aspects) crammers and dilettantes. In consequence, when, after much intrigue and argument, the Honours School was finally established, it was saddled with a syllabus that had a forbiddingly large philological component and was heavily biased towards older literature. It did not nourish the educational possibilities of English nor promote the development of English criticism. The result was that in its first few years the new School nearly died from lack of student enrolment and difficulties in recruiting staff. The credit for rescuing it and making it, within twenty-five years, the second most popular School in the university is generally accorded to Sir Walter Raleigh, Professor of English from 1904 to 1922, who succeeded in liberalizing the syllabus to allow students to take half their papers in literature from Shakespeare to 1830 (this terminal date has recently been brought forward to 1945). The language versus literature controversy, however, continued to haunt English studies at Oxford and elsewhere, merging into the later war of Scholars and Critics, and its rumbles may still be heard occasionally. It had the unfortunate effect of discouraging a specifically critical interest in earlier literature, and of instilling in the 'literary' student a hostility to systematic language study which ultimately retarded the development of critical analysis.

The main argument of those who opposed the introduction of English as an Honours subject at Oxford, and fought to keep it, once admitted, in the thrall of philology, was that it was insufficiently factual to be either teachable or examinable. Since (it was assumed) no special skills were needed to read literature in the native modern vernacular, the study of such literature must inevitably degenerate into the having of opinions about it, and opinions of this kind could, or should, not be taught as if they were facts, were not independently discoverable by immature minds, and could not in any case be satisfactorily displayed or tested within the conventions of a written examination. There is much cogency in all these arguments, and occasional cries of disillusionment are still heard from English academics as their force strikes belatedly home. It is in fact the premise on which they are based that is wrong, but it was some time before this was discovered, and documented by I. A. Richards. Their immediate effect was to throw the literary academics on to the defensive. One way of making the study of literature more factual was by stressing literary *history*, particularly the tracing of 'influences' and of the connections between an author's work and his life. In the absence of a critically informed sense of literary tradition, however, such literary history was easily trivialized. A more reliable defence manoeuvre was to take a leaf from the classicist's book (most of the early English dons had a classical education) and go in for editing. There were hundreds of English classics that no one had bothered to edit properly, and the new 'science' of bibliography arose conveniently to give the English academic an impeccably 'objective' occupation and an excuse for postponing criticism.

Sometimes the best form of defence was thought to be attack —a display of bravado in enthusiastic celebration of the uplifting delights of literature, in elaborate flights of rhetorical fancy that lifted opinions beyond the range of rational enquiry, in disarming confessions of amateurism, manly acknowledgements that there were more important things in life than literature. In this way a kind of orthodoxy—an improvized poetic and literary tradition of diluted Romanticism—developed, which has been amusingly parodied by Cyril Connolly, recalling his schooldays at Eton just before the First World War:

'There is a natural tradition in English poetry . . . Chaucer begat Spenser, Spenser begat Shakespeare, Shakespeare begat Milton, Milton begat Keats, Coleridge, Shelley, Wordsworth, and they begat Tennyson who begat Longfellow, Stevenson, Kipling, Quiller-Couch and Sir Henry Newbolt. There were a few bad boys whom we do not talk about—Donne, Dryden, Pope, Blake, Byron, Browning, Fitzgerald who wrote *The Ruba'iyat of Omar Khayyam* and Oscar Wilde who was a criminal degenerate. Chaucer is medieval but coarse, Spenser is the poet's poet . . . a poem is good either because it is funny . . . or because it makes you want to cry. Some funny poems make you want to cry . . . that is because you are not a healthy little boy. You need more Character. The best poems have the most beautiful lines in them; these lines can be detached, they are purple passages and are Useful in Examinations. Gray's Elegy is almost all Purple Patch, and so is the *Ode to a Nightingale,* especially

> Magic casements, opening on the foam
> Of perilous seas, in faery lands forlorn.

When you come to a purple patch you can tell it by an alarm clock going off, you feel a cold shiver, a lump in your throat, your eyes fill with tears, and your hair stands on end.'[2]

The actuality behind this parody may be sampled in the World's Classics selection of *English Critical Essays* (First Series) edited by Phyllis M. Jones. Many of the contributors had done useful work in editing or literary history but, with the exception of W. P. Ker, their criticism was characterized by, to quote E. M. W. Tillyard, 'gossiping, often highly metaphorical description and unspecific praise.'[3] Here are a few representative quotations:

Saintsbury on the Grand Style:

But the grandeur of its grandeur when it is grand!

Sir Edmund Chambers on Matthew Arnold:

I hope I speak to impenitent Victorians like myself who still find in that bygone verse the cool refreshment which it breathed upon its first readers, in days which seemed to Matthew Arnold feverish enough, although they were far less feverish than ours. *Virgilium vidi tantum.* I have a boyhood's image of an Olympian figure, moving somewhat aloof on the outskirts of an Ambleside garden party; and it was in the week in which I first came up as a freshman that Arnold paid his last visit to Oxford, staying with Thomas Fowler of genial memory, in my own college of Corpus, and took his last walk in the happy coombes of Hinksey.

J. A. Chapman on Wordsworth and Literary Criticism:

> 'Then music with her silver sound—why "silver sound"? why "music with her silver sound"?—What say you Simon Catling?'                                        (*Romeo and Juliet*)

> That is 'chough's language, gabble enough'; but does not professional criticism go about saying of poetry, why 'silver sound'? Why 'music with her silver sound'? to the best of its ability, when there is really no answer? There are things that a man can know *enough*, and these are what Wordsworth will write of.

This anthology, published in 1933, was a conservative selection. By this date the critical revolution was well under way, but it finds little representation here. In the defensive note of Chambers and Chapman we see the old guard's resistance to the new (their contributions are dated 1932 and 1931 respectively). 'Why "silver sound"? why "music with her silver sound"?' was indeed just the kind of question in which I. A. Richards and his disciples at Cambridge were interested (and Wordsworth too, incidentally).

At Cambridge, the introduction of an English Honours School had been even more bitterly resisted and longer postponed than at Oxford, but when it eventually came in 1917 the philological and antiquarian bias of the Oxford syllabus was avoided. The revized English Tripos of 1926 (which still obtains with some modifications), allowed the student to spend most of his time on English literature after 1350. This syllabus was a somewhat heterogeneous one, including papers on Life, Literature and Thought, Tragedy, the English Moralists, and Practical Criticism. The character of the degree as a whole, therefore, was likely to be determined by the imprint of the most influential teachers, and the most influential teacher of this period was I. A. Richards. He was largely responsible for making Cambridge the academic centre of the critical revolution that had already started in the world of contemporary letters.

I shall spend less time on Modernism than on the rise of

English Studies, because the story is more familiar, and is covered in various ways by other essays in this volume.

It is generally agreed that the Modern movement in literature, characterized by formal experiment, logical discontinuity, anti-rationalism, subjectivism, symbolism, eclectic mythologizing, radical questioning of accepted values and passionate commitment to art as an autotelic activity, was the product of European Romanticism; that it was largely suppressed in Victorian England, but re-imported there towards the end of the nineteenth century from the Continent of Europe as the English literary world became more cosmopolitan. In major artists like James, Conrad and Yeats, modernism was assimilated and domesticated to great advantage, but it was also taken up by inferior talents, and got confused with the life-styles of the Decadence and the doctrine of art-for-art's-sake. Consequently it fell into disrepute, a process that reached its climax in the traumatic scandal of Oscar Wilde's trial for homosexual offences in 1895. The result was a revulsion against aestheticism in the English literary public, a reversion to Victorian standards of moral health and direct relevance to 'life', which received reinforcement from the imperialistic patriotism of the time. Kipling and Newbolt were the most popular poets of the period, though serious lyric poetry was accorded respect if, like Bridges's, it observed the conventional post-romantic criteria of 'beauty' in poetic diction and subject matter. The Georgian poets provided an appearance of innovation without really disturbing the current orthodoxy. In the novel, Wells, Bennett and Galsworthy broke new ground in matter rather than form, while James and Conrad were neglected and Joyce could scarcely get his work published.[4]

This, very roughly, was the literary situation in England in the years immediately preceding the First World War, a situation which a number of avant-garde writers, notably Ezra Pound and T.S. Eliot, set about revolutionizing under Pound's banner, 'Make it new'. Their first manoeuvre was to establish media for their work and criticism sympathetic to it. Thus began a Golden Age of 'little magazines' which lasted well into the twenties: Ford Madox Hueffer's *English Review* and A. R. Orage's *The New Age* appeared in 1908; J. Middleton Murry's *Rhythm* in 1911; *The New Freewomen*, later called *The Egoist* in 1913; Wyndham Lewis's *Blast* in 1914; *The Signature* in 1915; *Form* in 1916; *Art and Letters* in 1917; a redesigned *Athenaeum* under Middleton Murry in 1919; *The Criterion* edited by Eliot in 1922; the *Adelphi*, again under Murry, in 1923; *The Calendar of Modern Letters* in 1925. These little magazines did not of course present a united front; they provided forums for different groups of writers, and often quarrelled among themselves, but between them they published the work, creative and critical, of most of the significant writers in the contemporary avant-garde: Eliot, Pound, Joyce, Lewis, Virginia Woolf, T. E. Hulme, D. H. Lawrence, Katherine Mansfield, Aldous Huxley, Robert Graves, the Sitwells, Herbert Read, E. M. Forster and many others. Of them all, the man who emerged as leader in the twenties was T. S. Eliot. He not only established himself as the most accomplished and revolutionary poet of the period; he also provided modern literature with a new poetic and a new concept of literary tradition.

Towards the end of his life, Eliot commented:

> The best of my *literary* criticism—apart from a few notorious phrases which have had a truly embarrassing success in the world—consists of essays on poets and poetic dramatists who have influenced me. It is a by-product of my private poetry-workshop; or a prolongation of the thinking that went into the formation of my own verse.[5]

Eliot is, then, a typical example of the poet-critic who writes primarily for fellow-poets. But as I suggested earlier, such critics will normally try to enlarge their audience, by drawing in either the academics or the general reader. The criticism of Yeats, also a quest for a new poetic and a new tradition, never acquired the kind of currency Eliot's did, partly because Yeats never captured an equivalent audience. Most creative critics turn to face the general reader; but Eliot very definitely inclined in the other direction. The subjects on which he wrote in his early essays, characteristically Elizabethan and Jacobean dramatists and poets, were usually too esoteric for the general reader, and assumed a kind of interest and knowledge that was most likely to be found in the expanding schools of English. It was not surprizing that he got a hearing in these quarters, because, as I have suggested, there, too, the need for a new poetic and a new tradition was keenly felt. The connection was made at Cambridge rather than Oxford because the infant English School at the former was less entrenched in conservatism, and in I. A. Richards it had a brilliant and influential teacher who was sympathetic to Eliot's views. Tillyard has recalled that Eliot

> was the man really responsible for introducing into Cambridge a set of ideas that both shocked and satisfied. I cannot think of anyone else who counted in this way . . . Richards

was Eliot's friend, helped substantially in getting his poetry and criticism recognized, and was no advocate of the less eminent exploiters of the poetic tradition against which Eliot had turned . . .[6]

By 1926, according to James Reeves, the freshman at Cambridge was handed *Poems 1909–1925* and *The Sacred Wood* (1920) in much the same spirit as 'the stranger who enters an Anglican Church at service time is handed two books, *Hymns Ancient and Modern* and *The Book of Common Prayer*.'[7] The analogy is perhaps more than superficially apt: it has often been observed that, true to Arnold's prophecy, literature has become the religion of the twentieth century, with criticism its theology; and Cambridge has done much to bring this about. But I anticipate.

T. S. Eliot is discussed at length elsewhere in this volume, and I shall only try to indicate here the kind of influence he had on the general development of criticism in the century. When one turns up the early essays today, the alleged centrality of this influence is not immediately apparent. They seem, especially in comparison with the modern criticism which claims descent from him, somewhat slight, oblique, diffident, almost dilettante at times, and signally lacking in that 'analysis' which has become the hallmark of modern criticism. It seems that Eliot insinuated his revolutionary ideas under cover of a very skilful pastiche of the contemporary style of polite letters. This policy, in marked contrast to Ezra Pound's brashness, no doubt facilitated his access to 'Establishment' journals like the *Times Literary Supplement*. Pound is reputed to have said to him : 'Let me throw the bricks through the front window. You go in at the back door and steal the swag.'

We must, therefore, be alert to pick up in Eliot's criticism the traces of ideas that were to be absorbed and explored and systematized by later critics. For instance, one of the main claims of modern criticism is to have established what may be called a 'cognitive' theory of literature; that is a concept of the work of literature as an object of public knowledge, containing within itself the reasons why it is so and not otherwise, stating a meaning that is to be found in the work and not outside it, except insofar as it assumes a knowledge of the language in which it is written, and of the universe that language describes. As these qualifying clauses imply, it is a tricky concept, and one difficult to maintain in an absolute form; but it is a valuable ideal for the preservation of critical hygiene. Since the literary work is basically a linguistic utterance belonging to a communication process from author to reader, an examination of its meaning cannot eliminate an awareness of or speculations about its expressive source, and must originate in a personal response. But when the critic bases his interpretation and evaluation *primarily* on either the origins of the work (eg. the writer's life, expressed intentions, historical context, etc.) or alternatively on his own subjective responses to the work, he risks committing what two modern critics have called the intentionalist and affective fallacies.[8] Attacks on both these fallacies are to be found in two of Eliot's earliest essays.

'Tradition and the Individual Talent' (1919) attacks by implication most versions of the intentionalist fallacy. A narrow historicism is dismissed by pointing out that in literary matters tradition is not a fixed and immutable order, but 'an ideal order . . . which is modified by the introduction of the new (the really new) work of art.' The historical sense 'involves a perception, not only of the pastness of the past, but of its presence.' (Eliot is speaking of the poet, but critics were not slow to apply the dictum to criticism to justify concerning themselves with what a poem means *now*, rather than attempting to reconstruct what it meant *then*.) The romantic-expressive theory of poetry which encouraged biographical interpretations of literature is countered by a theory of the 'impersonality' of the poet:

> The progress of an artist is a continual self-sacrifice, a continual extinction of personality . . . the more perfect the artist, the more completely separate in him will be the man who suffers and the mind which creates . . . The poet's mind is in fact a receptacle for storing up numberless feelings, phrases, images, which remain there until all the particles which can unite to form a new compound are present together . . . we must believe that 'emotion recollected in tranquillity' is an inexact formula. For it is neither emotion, nor recollection nor . . . tranquillity. It is a concentration, and a new thing resulting from the concentration, of a very great number of experiences which to the practical and active person would not seem to be experiences at all; it is a concentration which does not happen consciously or of deliberation.

In 'The Function of Criticism' (1923) Eliot disposed of the affective fallacy, rather more polemically, for he clearly regarded it as the more pernicious:

> *fact* cannot corrupt taste; it can at worst gratify one taste—
> a taste for history, let us say, or antiquities, or biography—

under the illusion that it is assisting another. The real corrupters are those who supply opinion or fancy.

Having defined the function of criticism in the words quoted earlier, Eliot declares that 'criticism, far from being a simple and orderly field of beneficent activity from which imposters can readily be ejected, is no better than a Sunday park of contending and contentious orators who have not even arrived at an articulation of their differences.' Criticism ought to be 'the common pursuit of true judgement'; it cannot be so as long as critics rely on their own subjective responses, the 'Inner Voice' (a phrase of Middleton Murry's) uncontrolled by any shared principles. 'Why have principles, when one has the Inner Voice? If I like a thing, that is all I want; and if enough of us, shouting all together, like it, that should be all that *you* (who don't like it) ought to want.'

The polemical strategy of this essay is based on an elaborate analogy in which Classicism, Catholicism, legitimate political authority and the common pursuit of true judgement are contrasted with Romanticism, Nonconformism, Whiggery and affective criticism, to the grave disadvantage of the latter set. When in 1928 Eliot made it clear that he held this analogy literally and in earnest, declaring himself 'a classicist in literature, royalist in politics and Anglo-Catholic in religion,'[9] he dismayed many of his admirers in the literary and academic worlds, most of whom were, if not romantics, liberal or socialist in political sympathies and agnostic or heterodox in religious matters. But by that time he had, as well as indicating the lines along which a cognitive theory of literature might evolve, redefined the English poetic tradition; giving prominence to Elizabethan and Jacobean poetic drama, and to the Metaphysical poets, correcting bardolatry (see the essay on *Hamlet* [1919]) casting doubt upon the achievement of Milton, seriously undermining the reputation of the Romantic and post-romantic poets and justifying the character of modern poetry.

Of course this is a simplification and an overstatement. No man can carry out a critical revolution single-handed. To take one example, it would be absurd to say that Eliot 'discovered' Donne and the Metaphysicals. A kind of 'underground' interest had been growing through the nineteenth century, and if anyone deserves credit for 'discovering' them it was Sir Herbert Grierson, who edited Donne in 1912, and whose anthology of *Metaphysical Lyrics and Poems of the Seventeenth Century* (1921) occasioned Eliot's famous essay 'The Metaphysical Poets'. But there seems little doubt that it was this short essay, in which the phrase 'dissociation of sensibility' was first used to define a degeneration in English poetry after the seventeenth century, that really excited the attention of poetry readers, and turned it in a significantly new direction—combined, of course, with evidence of the lively possibilities of the metaphysical vein in Eliot's own verse. 'Dissociation of sensibility' was no doubt one of those phrases (another was 'objective correlative') whose success later embarrassed Eliot. But their success was not surprising. Criticism at this time stood in need not only of a new poetic and a new tradition, but also of a new vocabulary. This brings us back to academic criticism, to Cambridge, and to I. A. Richards.

As has been noted earlier, most of the first English dons were recruited from Classics, and the traces of this education are to be seen everywhere in their work. I. A. Richards was exceptional in having read Moral Sciences (in ordinary parlance, philosophy) at Cambridge. He brought to English studies an unusual aptitude for logical thought, and an interest in aesthetics, psychology and semantics. His first book was *The Foundation of Aesthetics* (1922) written in collaboration with C. K. Ogden and James Wood, and his second *The Meaning of Meaning* (1923) again with Ogden. His first book of specifically literary theory was *The Principles of Literary Criticism* (1924), a book of which, though its arguments have been largely discredited, and in many cases abandoned by Richards himself, it would be difficult to exaggerate the importance.

Richards begins in the spirit of Eliot's 'The Function of Criticism' :

A few conjectures, a supply of admonitions, many acute isolated observations, some brilliant guesses, much oratory and applied poetry, inexhaustible confusion, a sufficiency of dogma, no small stock of prejudices, whimsies and crotchets, a profusion of mysticism, a little genuine speculation, sundry stray inspirations, pregnant hints and random *aperçus*; of such as these . . . is extant critical theory composed.

This situation was particularly regrettable because 'the arts are our storehouses of recorded values . . . The arts, if rightly approached, supply the best data for deciding what experiences are more valuable than others.' Criticism, to become a useful and intellectually respectable discipline must adopt the rigorous methods of scientific enquiry (though literature itself, as a mode of knowledge, is the antithesis of science). This is to be done by applying the new 'science' of psychology—psychology is invoked to provide an objective theory of value.

Experience is characterized by appetencies and aversions. Satisfying an appetency is 'good', and the more we can satisfy, the better. The main problem of life is how to satisfy one appetency without frustrating another: 'the best life is that in which as much as possible of our possible personality is engaged . . . without confusion.' Literature can educate us in this process, through its special way of using language.

> A statement may be used for the sake of the *reference*, true or false, which it causes. This is the *scientific* use of language. But it may also be used for the sake of the effects in emotion and attitude produced by the reference it occasions. This is the *emotive* use of language . . . Poetry affords the clearest example of the subordination of reference to attitude. It is the supreme form of emotive language.

These are some of the salient points of *Principles*. It will be seen that they both contrast with and complement Eliot's views. Whereas Eliot was primarily concerned with the writing of poetry, Richards is primarily concerned with its reception. His motive is educational, as the phrase 'storehouse of recorded values' makes clear. The shadow of Matthew Arnold falls over both writers: Just as we can trace Eliot back to the Arnold of the Preface to *Poems* (1853), so we can trace Richards back to the Arnold of 'The Study of Poetry' (1888), where he said:

> The future of poetry is immense, because in poetry, when it is worthy of its high destinies, our race, as time goes on, will find surer and surer stay. There is not a creed which is not shaken, not an accredited dogma which is not shown to be questionable, not a received tradition which does not threaten to dissolve. Our religion has materialized itself in the fact, in the supposed fact; it has attached its emotion to the fact, and now the fact is failing it. But for poetry the idea is everything.

This quotation stands as the epigraph to Richards's *Science and Poetry* (1926). It is worth remembering, as Tillyard does,[10] that as a philosophy student at Cambridge, Richards came under the influence of G. E. Moore, and thus of the modern anti-metaphysical anti-idealist philosophical tradition, which Moore to a large extent started. In this perspective, all non-verifiable statements, about God, the universe, the soul, etc. are what Richards calls 'pseudo-statements', and poetry is full of them.

For centuries they have been believed; now they are gone, irrecoverably; and the knowledge which has killed them [*i.e. science*] is not of a kind on which an equally fine organization of the mind can be based ... The remedy ... is to cut our pseudo-statements free from belief, and yet retain them, in their released state, as the main instruments by which we order our attitudes to one another and to the world.

It might seem that Richards, here, is risking the error that Eliot perceived in Arnold—'so conscious of what, for him, poetry was *for*, that he could not altogether see it for what it is.' But Richards also makes his point in a way which gives it a quite different emphasis: 'It is not what a poem says that matters, but what it *is*.' This seems much closer to the Symbolist doctrine of the aesthetic autonomy of the poem which Eliot inherited and developed, and which is epitomized in the often-quoted lines of Archibald McLeish:

> A poem should not mean
> But be.

And this is the central puzzle and paradox of Richards' criticism, that from it two quite different kinds of critical approach could be (and were) derived: (1) an essentially moral criticism which placed emphasis on the value of poems for the reader in organizing and evaluating experience for him, and (2) an essentially formal criticism which saw the nature and complexity of the organization as a value in itself.

Consider, for example, Richards' preference for a poetry of 'inclusion' rather than 'exclusion', i.e., a poetry which through its complex organization, and supremely thorough metaphor, brings into play and reconciles a wide variety of possible attitudes to experience, thus being invulnerable to 'ironic contemplation', because such irony has been anticipated and built into the structure and texture of the poem. We can see how this preference derives from the psychological theory of value, but it is possible to adopt the former without adopting the latter. This in fact is what William Empson and the American 'New Critics' did: thus terms like 'ambiguity', 'irony', 'paradox', 'tension', 'complexity', 'richness of texture' became the accepted words of approval in criticism that had little or nothing of Richards's affective theory of value in it.

Furthermore, one can see how Richards's theories fitted in with Eliot's precept and practice. Metaphysical poetry and the poetry Eliot was writing was manifestly a 'poetry of inclusion'

('When a poet's mind is perfectly equipped for its work, it is constantly amalgamating disparate experience' he wrote in 'The Metaphysical Poets'); just as the nineteenth-century poetry he disfavoured was a poetry of exclusion even at its best—'the ordered development of comparatively special and limited experience,' as Richards put it. The impersonality of the poet was also common ground. Though Richards based his theories on psychology, he emphatically dissociated himself from the Freudian kind of psychoanalytical criticism that focusses attention on the personal sources of the poem: 'What concerns criticism is not the avowed or unavowed motives of the artist . . . Whatever psychoanalysts may aver, the mental processes of the poet are not a very profitable field for investigation.' This is very much in accord with the anti-intentionalism of 'Tradition and the Individual Talent'. Richards's theory of value was essentially affective, as we have seen, but he avoided the cruder kind of subjective impressionism castigated by Eliot in 'The Function of Criticism' by practising and preaching a kind of critical analysis which had some pretensions to objectivity—what came to be known as 'Practical Criticism'.

Richards's book of that title drew directly on his teaching experience at Cambridge in the twenties. Over several years he regularly distributed copies of various short unidentified poems, and invited his students to comment freely; then he would lecture on the poems and the responses they had evoked. The object of the exercise was to get students to give an honest and independent reading to poetry undistracted by prejudices and received ideas. What emerged, however, was that the majority of the students—not all students of English, but the most intelligent and articulate of their age group—when deprived of the usual props and directives, were largely incapable of either understanding or discriminating judiciously between what they read. The first half of *Practical Criticism* (1929) documents this experiment, and the second half suggests how the situation can be improved, proposing and defining a technical terminology for the analysis of poetry (e.g. the break-down of Meaning into Sense, Feeling, Tone and Intention) and identifying characteristic obstacles to good reading (e.g. Irrelevant Associations and Stock Responses, Sentimentality and Inhibition).

The book had a very great influence. Practical Criticism as a way of teaching and testing students of literature, already well established at Cambridge by Richards himself, was gradually adopted by other universities, and by schools and training colleges, and it remains to this day in one form or another a staple of literary education. The terminology, style and criteria of Richards's own analysis passed into general currency. The book had a further influence on criticism which was in many ways unfortunate; it tended to encourage an anti-historicism in many ways as narrow and restrictive as the traditional 'Eng. Lit.' historicism, with its apparatus of received opinions, which it aimed to correct, leading to the extreme position that historical knowledge was completely irrelevant to the reading of literature. So there is some justice in George Watson's comment that no 'poetry was ever written for the purpose to which Richards applies it' in *Practical Criticism*, and that his experiment proved only that 'unhistorical reading is bad reading.'[11] However, it was Richards's disciples who abused the method rather than Richards himself. And the historical issue is perhaps not quite as simple as Watson suggests. As regards the pedagogical aspect: experience suggests that had Richards's students been provided with dates and authors they would not have read the poems markedly better—their inadequacies would merely have been more difficult to detect. As regards the application to criticism: while it is true that we must read historically, we can never read *totally* historically: we can never totally recover the universe of discourse to which works of the past originally belonged, and the effort to do so can inhibit our sense of the 'presence of the past' and hence of the richness of meaning the poem can legitimately have for us. Hence a concentration on a poem's internal organization rather than its historical context can yield illuminating results. A case in point is William Empson, Richard's most brilliant pupil. Here is his commentary on Shakespeare's metaphor for leafless woods, 'Bare ruined choirs, where late the sweet birds sang':

> the comparison is sound because ruined monastery choirs are places in which to sing, because they involve sitting in a row, because they are made of wood, are carved into knots and so forth, because they used to be surrounded by a sheltering building crystallized out of the likeness of a forest, and coloured with stained glass and painting like flowers and leaves, because they are now abandoned by all but the grey walls coloured like the skies of winter, because the cold and Narcissistic charm suggested by choir-boys suits well with Shakespeare's feeling for the object of the Sonnets, and for various historical and sociological reasons ('for oh, the hobbyhorse is forgot' and the Puritans have cut down the Maypoles), which it would be difficult now to trace out in their proportions . . .

It is obvious that Empson uses his historical sense to great advantage here, but does not allow it to dominate his reading. The *specifically* historical suggestion is held back until the end of the analysis, and is offered most tentatively. A more scholarly commentator might begin with this item, and regard it as the only hard fact in the analysis.

The story of the genesis of *Seven Types of Ambiguity* (1930) from which this quotation is taken, as related by I. A. Richards[12] is well-known, and a nice illustration of the fruitful interaction between the progressive creative writers and academics at this period. Empson began the work as an undergraduate under Richards's supervision, but his interest in the approach had first been excited by a little book by two young poets, Robert Graves and Laura Riding, called *A Survey of Modernist Poetry* (1927) in the course of which they analysed Shakespeare's sonnet, 'The expense of spirit in a waste of shame' revealing the very great number of 'interwoven meanings' it contained, and equating this density of meaning with value. Encouraged by Richards, Empson began exploring the possibilities of this approach, demonstrating through analysis that 'the machinations of ambiguity are among the very roots of poetry' (itself a somewhat ambiguous, or perhaps merely inelegant, formula).

Though Richards's self-deprecating account makes Graves and Riding appear Empson's main inspiration, his own influence is clear. Empson's 'ambiguity' is only a refinement of Richards's 'emotive'—an attempt to define the special character of literary language in a way which stresses the quality of 'inclusiveness'. Richards himself had observed in *Science and Poetry* that 'most words are ambiguous as regards their plain sense, especially in poetry.' The criterion of ambiguity also tended to support the revised poetic tradition of Eliot. Shakespeare and the Metaphysicals yielded choice examples of rich ambiguity, sustained in vivid metaphor and witty argument. The Romantic poets yielded ambiguities only of a vague and unsatisfactory kind. 'It is not clear what is *more deeply interfused* than what,' Empson irreverently remarked of a famous passage in *Tintern Abbey*.

*Seven Types* is a witty, intelligent and stimulating book, and its success was deserved. As its influence, and that of Richards, Eliot and, later, Leavis, permeated criticism more and more widely, however, a reaction set in, even among sympathizers, which asked, among other things, whether this kind of criticism was not too exclusive in its criteria, whether it did not revise the literary tradition simply by elevating poets who were amenable to its methods, and demoting those who were not. There is some truth in this objection, but two qualifications need to be made. Firstly, these critics did not trick the literary public into changing its right mind—they articulated a massive change of taste and sensibility which had all kinds of social, cultural and historical causes. Secondly, after all the just objections have been registered and concessions made, many of the basic principles and methods of these critics remain valid and useful. To cite one example; the most notorious victim of the critical revolution was Milton, but some of the most persuasive recent defences of Milton (e.g. Christopher Ricks's *Milton's Grand Style* (1964) and Stanley Fish's *Surprised by Sin* (1967) have stressed his skilful exploitation of—of all things—ambiguity. With this mention of the Milton controversy, however, a consideration of F. R. Leavis can no longer be postponed.

Asked to name the greatest English literary critic of this century, most qualified observers would reply 'Leavis', even if some of them added '*hélas*'. It is, however, difficult, if not impossible to give an adequate account of his achievement in a survey such as this. It is not an achievement that can be reduced to a number of seminal ideas, because Leavis is not a deeply original thinker, and has, out of strong conviction, deliberately avoided the field of literary theory. For him, criticism is not discussible in the abstract, but only in the reader's engagement with an actual text. His own engagement with texts, however, cannot be adequately represented by a few quotations, because it assumes magnitude only when experienced in his total *oeuvre*. There is, to be sure, a characteristic Leavisian style and tone—

Here there appear to be possibilities; a situation is partly realized in an urgent and supple idiom, and there appears to be a reserve of meaning which might eventually make itself apparent. But as one reads on one discovers that the qualified success of this and later poems depends upon ambiguity— that when a point is reached at which a definite formulation of an attitude or an issue is made, one is confronted with a shallow commonplace, something vaguely defined in terms of 'love', 'beauty', or 'good—

or—

It must be plain at once that such impressiveness as Johnson's poem has is conditioned by an absence of thought. This is poetry from the 'soul', that nineteenth-century region of specialized poetical experience where nothing has sharp definition and where effects or 'profundity' and 'intensity' depend upon a lulling of the mind. The large evocativeness begins in the third stanza, so that we needn't press the question whether 'clings' in the second . . . is the right word : we know that if we have lapsed properly into the kind of reading the poem claims such questions don't arise . . .

—but this style and tone have proved fatally easy to imitate without maintaining the pressure of Leavis's kind of intelligence and sensibility. The first of the above quotations is in fact not from Leavis,[13] but I think that out of context it might easily be attributed to him. It is only in context that Leavis's distinction as a critic can be fully appreciated. All that can be done here is to indicate the way in which his work relates to the critical revolution already described, and the special character he gave to its continuation. And this will involve reference not only to F. R. Leavis himself, but also to his wife Q. D. Leavis, and the enormously influential journal *Scrutiny* which they helped to start in 1932, and which Leavis for the most part edited until its termination in 1953.

As we have seen, the principal leaders of the critical revolution were T. S. Eliot and I. A. Richards. According to R. C. Townsend, it was Leavis's destiny to consolidate the revolution by reconciling the ideas of its two progenitors. But Townsend acutely points to the difficulty of the undertaking :

hoping that the study of English could enrich and discipline men's sensibility, Cambridge found in Eliot's criticism the means by which this might be accomplished; but in assimilating his criticism, they had to ignore the intentions behind it and ignore his scepticism about the teaching of literature.[14]

It is not surprising, therefore, that in the course of his career Leavis drew further and further apart from Eliot (and eventually from Richards too, though less painfully).

The initial attempt at reconciliation, however, is evident in Leavis's first book, *New Bearings in English Poetry* (1932). He describes it in his Prefatory Note as 'largely an acknowledgement, vicarious as well as personal, of indebtedness to a certain critic and poet' [i.e. Eliot] and deferential allusions to Richards are scattered through the text and footnotes. As the book's title suggests, it is essentially a defence, mainly conducted through detailed commentary, of modernist poetry, principally of Eliot, but also of Hopkins and, with more qualifications, of Yeats and Pound. References to earlier poetry confirm the revised poetic tradition of Eliot :

The mischievousness of the nineteenth-century conventions of the 'poetical' should by now be plain.

If the poetic tradition of the nineteenth century had been less completely unlike the Metaphysical tradition, Mr. Yeats might have spent less of his powers outside poetry.

There is no pressure in [Milton's] verse of any complex and varying current of feeling and sensation; the words have little substance or muscular quality: Milton is using only a small part of the resources of the English language.

Leavis also strikes an Arnoldian note more firmly than either Eliot or Richards in his insistence on the connection between the vitality of poetry, the degree of discriminating encouragement it gets, and the health of culture and society as a whole. Modernist poetry appeared on a literary scene 'in which there were no serious standards current, no live tradition of poetry, and no public capable of informed and serious interest.' It was inevitable, therefore, that poetry like *The Waste Land* was esoteric in its appeal:

> that the public for it is limited is one of the symptoms of the state of culture that produced the poem. Works expressing the finest consciousness of the age in which the word "highbrow" has become current, are almost inevitably such as to appeal only to a tiny minority. It is still more serious that this minority should be more and more cut off from the world around it—should, indeed, be aware of a hostile and overwhelming environment.

This idea of representing an enlightened minority embattled by forces of cultural decadence inimical to the preservation of standards and the nourishment of creative achievement, was to become increasingly insistent in the criticism of Leavis and those associated with him.

*Revaluation* (1936) was designed as a complement to *New Bearings*, exploring the revised tradition that had served as a background to the earlier book, following 'The Line of Wit' through English seventeenth-century poetry as far as Pope, and concluding with a critical reappraisal of Wordsworth, Shelley and Keats. The hostile essay on 'Milton's Verse' in this volume acquired considerable notoriety. Coinciding with Eliot's 'A Note on the Verse of John Milton' of the same year, it provoked a Milton Controversy which continued well into the fifties, and is not entirely defunct today. Both Leavis and Eliot (who was to withdraw many of his criticisms in his British Academy Lecture of 1947) concentrated their attack on the artificiality and expressive limitations of Milton's language, contrasting it unfavourably with, for example, Shakespeare's. Later, in other hands, the focus shifted to Milton's failure to resolve the human and intellectual issues raised by his themes.[16] Those critics who rallied to the defence of Milton, such as C. S. Lewis and E. M. W. Tillyard, were for the most part, historical and scholarly in their orientation and justified Milton by an appeal to literary convention and religious tradition. Milton thus became a major battleground of the war between the Scholars and the Critics (there is of course a certain distortion in this nomenclature favourable to the latter party, who coined it). The result was a steady growth in Milton studies which was ultimately to the advantage of scholarship, criticism and Milton; but there were moments when Milton seemed only the pretext for personal and ideological conflicts.

Other battlegrounds included Shakespeare and Jane Austen. In Shakespeare studies, the mission of the new criticism was to wrest the Bard from the clutches of editors, annotators, historians of Elizabethan stage conventions, and pre-eminently from that nineteenth-century tradition culminating impressively in A. C. Bradley's *Shakespearean Tragedy* (1904) which discussed Shakespeare's characters as if they were characters in realistic fiction, if not real people. Empson had teased the annotators in *Seven Types*, finding delicate ambiguities where they saw only textual cruces. A more representative figure in this field was L. C. Knights, one of the regular contributors to *Scrutiny*, and for a time a co-editor, the title of whose article 'How Many Children Had Lady Macbeth?' acquired considerable currency as an example of the classically inappropriate question to ask of a work of imaginative literature. Against the Bradleyean approach, Knights and other *Scrutiny* critics recommended regarding Shakespeare's plays as dramatic poems, whose meaning was communicated through language, and especially iterative patterns of imagery. This approach had been independently and brilliantly initiated by Wilson Knight in books like *The Wheel of Fire* (1930) and *The Imperial Theme* (1931), and exploited critically the possibilities of a book of a much more 'scholarly' character, Caroline Spurgeon's *Shakespeare's Imagery and What It tells Us* (1935). Out of this line of Shakespeare criticism was to develop later a fruitful criticism of prose fiction, playing down its narrative and mimetic qualities and concentrating attention on patterns of imagery and symbolism as keys to thematic meaning. In 1947 *Scrutiny* began a series of articles entitled 'The Novel as Dramatic Poem.'

Jane Austen had always been a favourite home of the gossiping, appreciative criticism of the 'pre-revolutionary' type, and *Scrutiny* set itself to dispel the myth of 'gentle Jane Austen', the 'instinctive and charming' (Henry James's curious misdescription) First Lady of English Letters. In a series of closely argued articles, Mrs. Q. D. Leavis emphasized Jane Austen's painstaking, dedicated craftsmanship by speculating that the major novels went through several drafts before she was satisfied with them, a process that could be traced back to the early minor works.[18] Another characteristic *Scrutiny* article which achieved greater notoriety was D. W. Harding's 'Regulated Hatred: an aspect of the art of Jane Austen'.[19] So far from being a gentle, consoling artist, comfortably endorsing the values of her own *milieu*, Jane Austen, Harding argued, was in many ways fiercely hostile to that *milieu*, and writing was her way of 'finding some mode of existence for her critical attitudes.'

Perhaps it is timely to observe here that the critical revolution I have been describing was not unresisted. Oxford was largely opposed to it, with exceptions like F. W. Bateson, whose *English Poetry and the English Language* (1934) was a useful extension of the new ideas. And it was far from being triumphant at Cambridge. 'Q'—Sir Arthur Quiller-Couch—whose critical approach was not unlike Raleigh's, was Professor of English Literature until 1944. E. M. W. Tillyard, who had been an ally of Richards in the early days, was not temperamentally at home in the critical revolution, and began to have doubts about its educational effects.[20] F. L. Lucas, Fellow of King's, made a contribution to *Cambridge University Studies* (1933) the occasion of a somewhat ungenerous attack on I. A. Richards and Mrs. Leavis's *Fiction and The Reading Public*. The lines of battle were complicated, but may be studied in the pages of *Scrutiny*.[21]

As Richards and Empson left Cambridge for America and China respectively, and the critical revolution in England passed more and more into the custody of Leavis and *Scrutiny*, the alliance of the twenties between the academics and the literary avant-garde also began to break up. The avant-garde itself was fragmented between Bloomsbury, the increasingly conservative T. S. Eliot and his sympathizers, and the young Marxist-orientated writers of the thirties (Auden, Isherwood, Stephen Spender, Day Lewis). With none of these groups could Leavis communicate. He never wavered in his regard for Eliot's early criticism, and his admiration for Eliot's verse was not diminished by its increasingly religious preoccupations. But a dogmatic Christianity was no more acceptable to him than a dogmatic Marxism, and he regarded Eliot's patronage of the Auden-Spender group in the *Criterion* as a cynical betrayal. *Scrutiny* described itself as 'liberal'[22] but it was a very different kind of liberalism from that of the Bloomsbury group, whose values, life-style and criticism (Strachey, Virginia Woolf and Forster tended to write a smarter, more sophisticated and satirical version of the old appreciative musing-in-the library tradition) were antithetical to everything Leavis stood for.

What Leavis and *Scrutiny* stood for in the widest sense was the preservation through literature and the study of literature of certain life-enhancing values which were located in something called the 'organic community,' that is, the agrarian socio-economic system that preceded the Industrial Revolution, and survived in a few isolated pockets till the end of the nineteenth century, to be totally submerged in the mechanized mass society of the twentieth century. In the organic community, so the theory ran, labour was not alienated but a fulfilling exercise of genuine craftsmanship, life and death were made meaningful by an instinctive connection with the soil and the rhythm of the seasons, and if most of its members were illiterate they nevertheless had their own folk art and a richly expressive oral tradition which nourished the roots of higher culture. The connection made between these ideas and criticism is illustrated by Denys Thompson, writing in an early issue of *Scrutiny* :

> An understanding of this life will help to explain how Shakespeare's use of language differs from Milton's, in what way the idiom of the newspaper and best seller and advertising is destructive of fine language and of fine living, and why, since English traditional culture is dead, it is of the first importance that tradition should be sustained through literature.

Leavis himself does not draw the equations quite as baldly as that, but the assumptions are always there. In *Culture and Environment* (1933) he collaborated with Thompson to write a kind of textbook (intended primarily for schools) designed to inculcate the values of the organic society and to train discrimination and resistance in the face of contemporary civilization, particularly as expressed through popular literature, journalism and advertising. The authors draw freely for inspiration and documentation on Q. D. Leavis's *Fiction and the Reading*

*Public* (1932), a pioneering but somewhat tendentious study arguing that a homogeneous and vital literary culture in seventeenth and eighteenth-century England was destroyed by the growth of literacy, and its commercial exploitation, culminating in a polarization of majority and minority tastes in the twentieth century, and a consequent collapse of standards. One of the (mostly leading) questions appended to *Culture and Environment* as exercises is:

> 'The best novel I've read this week is *Iron Man.*' What kind of standards are implied here? What would you judge to be the quality of the 'literature' he reads, and the reading he devotes to it?

Despite its naivety and tendentiousness, most of the targets of *Culture and Environment* are well-selected (with the exception of jazz, of which the authors show a characteristically insular misunderstanding) and the book undoubtedly did more good than harm. But the underlying concept of the organic community is open to serious question. Though offered as history, it is nearer to myth. As Raymond Williams has observed, 'If there is one thing certain about the organic community, it is that it has always gone.' For Leavis and Thompson it was last seen in the late nineteenth century by George Bourne, from whose books *Change in the Village* and *The Wheelwright's Shop* they quote extensively. But Williams says he could reconstruct it from his own childhood in the thirties, while at the other end of the scale it had already passed for Goldsmith in *The Deserted Village*. It is, in fact, a variation on that nostalgia for a pastoral paradise which runs all through the history of culture, but acquires a special urgency and poignancy in post-industrial civilization (there are many versions of it in nineteenth-century literature); and while it has value as a myth, it does not, as Williams observes, encourage the constructive and beneficial transformation of that civilization.

This cultural aspect of Leavis's thought does much to explain the character of his literary criticism. It explains why, inheriting the mantle of Richards at Cambridge, he chose to display the moral and educational side of that reversible garment rather than the formalist side. His influence was most deeply felt by those whom he personally taught, on whom it was often charismatic, and he characteristically offered his criticism as the by-product of his teaching, not as the product of 'research'. He is deeply, and honourably, committed to the study of literature as a 'humane centre' in education, a self-sufficient discipline, yet one which trains discrimination in non-literary experience. His attacks on scholars and literary historians are motivated less by a belief that their approach is factually ill-founded, than by a conviction that it threatens to deprive literature of the only real life that it has—in the hands of living readers—by diverting them to the pursuit of a 'context' which is in any case best discovered from the literature itself.[23] The historical approach to literature tends inevitably towards relativity in judgement by proposing a special set of criteria for each work; and Leavis's opponents have argued that this is not only fairer to the literature than applying a single set of norms to a diversity of books, but educationally more valuable, since it encourages the student to enjoy as wide a range as possible of literary experience, and equips him with the knowledge that must precede a true judgement.[24] But Leavis has always believed that 'some authors are better than others', and that establishing such preferences is the very life-blood of criticism.

He has, however, persistently refused to be drawn into an abstract statement and defence of his 'norms'. In a critical exchange in *Scrutiny*[22] provoked by *Revaluation*, René Wellek, a distinguished American literary theorist and critic more eclectic than either Leavis or his English adversaries, pointed out this evasion, and suggested that it weakened the force of Leavis's criticism. Leavis did not entirely disown the 'norms' which Wellek attributed to him, (and they are as good a description as anyone has given), but he argued:

> Has any reader of my book been less aware of the essential criteria that emerge than he would have been if I had laid down such general propositions as: 'poetry must be in serious relation to actuality, it must have a firm grasp of the actual, of the object, it must be in relation to life, it must not be cut off from direct vulgar living, it should be normally human ...'? If, as I did, I avoided such generalities, it was not out of timidity; it was because they seemed too clumsy to be of any use. I thought I had provided something better. My whole effort was to work in terms of concrete judgements and particular analyses: 'This—doesn't it?—bears such a relation to that; this kind of of thing—don't you find it so?—wears better than that', etc.

Leavis has made the same point on many occasions. Judgement must be personal, but it aspires to be more than personal by drawing another reader into a dialogue in the form, 'This is so, is it not?' to which the constructive reply is 'Yes, but ...' It must be noted, however, that if the implied norms are not acceptable, or felt to be too narrow (this is the second part of Wellek's objection) the answer may have to be: 'No, not at all,' and the critical dialogue is abruptly terminated. The effectiveness of Leavis's critical method, therefore, depends on the analysis confirming the implied norms rather than the norms underwriting the analysis. The procedure requires a very delicate balance between criteria of formal excellence and of moral or spiritual excellence, for it is generally easier to reach agreement on the former than on the latter. It seems to me that in his later criticism Leavis often lost this balance, especially as his interest shifted from poetry to the novel, which lends itself more readily to moral criticism. Paradoxically, this shift of attention—which was reflected in the editorial policy of *Scrutiny*—was perhaps his most original contribution to the continuation of the critical revolution.

Since the novel has been the dominant literary form at all cultural levels for the last one hundred and fifty years, it seems odd, at first sight, that the critical revolution was so late in turning its attention to that form (nearly all the seminal early books were concerned with poetry or poetic drama). But on reflection several explanations suggest themselves. Eliot was a poet, and Richards's theories—both about literary value and about the special character of literary language—could be most conveniently illustrated from poetry, and short lyric poetry at that. Furthermore, if we trace their thinking back through Symbolism and Edgar Alan Poe to the English Romantics, we find a similar bias: Wordsworth, Coleridge and Shelley were poets, and the kind of claims they made for literature emphasized its transcendental qualities rather than the mimetic ones cultivated in the novel—art as a lamp rather than a mirror.

To Henry James the novel was, or ought to have been, both mirror and lamp. 'The only reason for the existence of a novel is that it does attempt to represent life'—but this representation could only be genuinely illuminating if controlled by an exacting concern for aesthetic form. Indeed, in 'The Art of Fiction' (1884) he described the formal organization of a novel with precisely that emphasis on the *organic* principle that is such a constant feature of Romantic poetics:

A novel is a living thing, all one and continuous, like any other organism, and in proportion as it lives it will be found, I think, that in each of its parts there is something of each of the other parts.

In his criticism—in essays, reviews and the superb Prefaces to the New York edition of his novels—James defended and explored his high conception of the art of fiction with an intelligence and eloquence which make him indisputably the first major critic of prose fiction in English. But his wisdom fell largely on deaf ears. He was indeed *cher mâitre* to a number of young novelists, but his quarrel with one of them, H. G. Wells, who was enjoying a much greater success both popular and literary, illustrates very vividly the resistance that the cosmopolitan 'art-novel', which James represented, met in England in the first decade of the century.

One of James's main contributions to criticism of the novel was to make writers and critics more conscious of the aesthetic and moral significance of narrative method—the 'point of view' from which a story is told. His own preference was for experience reflected through the consciousness of one or more created characters, rendered in the flexible medium of third person narrative but observing the limitations of human knowledge in actuality—a method which he believed gained both in verisimilitude and aesthetic consistency over the omniscient method favoured by most of the nineteenth-century masters. Out of James's precept and practice, his friend and admirer Percy Lubbock constructed a theory of *The Craft of Fiction* (1921). 'The whole intricate question of method, in the craft of fiction, I take to be governed by the question of the point of view—the question of the relation in which the narrator stands to the story' Lubbock wrote. He made great play with the terms 'picture' and 'drama'—the former covering all that in fiction has to be described by a narrator—for instance, scenery, physical appearance, events—and the latter covering the dialogue and confrontation of characters as they might appear on a stage. He concluded that the Jamesian method is the ideal one because it reconciles the two methods—it 'dramatizes the picture by dramatizing the narrator.'

*The Craft of Fiction* was a pioneering work which commanded considerable respect in the forties and fifties, especially in America, when the James revival was at its height, and it is always worth reading. Its great deficiencies as a poetics of the novel are an excessive prejudice in favour of James's techniques, and an almost complete absence of quotation and analysis in critical discussion. In this last respect Vernon Lee's *The Handling* of *Words and Other Studies in Literary Psychology* (published 1923, but including work published much earlier) seems more deserving of the epithet 'pioneering'. In the course of this book Vernon Lee (her real name was Violet Paget, and she was another friend of James's) subjects a number of randomly-selected passages from novels to verbal analysis as 'close' and sensitive as anything that was to be found in novel criticism until very recently. Her interest in analysis and her general theory of literary communication seem to anticipate Richards in many ways, but his references to her are somewhat slighting, as are those of the Leavises. She seems to be one of the unacknowledged prophets of modern criticism.

It has often been remarked that E. M. Forster is the most traditional of 'modern' novelists, and something of the same ambivalence is perceptible in his critical book *Aspects of the Novel* (1927), originally delivered as the Clark Lectures at Cambridge. In his depreciation of the importance of narrative ('Oh dear, yes, the novel must tell a story') and his concept of 'rhythm' (that is, a pattern of reiterated symbols or motifs that enables an aesthetic and thematic ordering of fictional events) he showed himself to be in accord with the tendencies of modern fiction. But he is critical of James and Lubbock:

> for me the whole intricate question of method resolves itself not into formulae but into the power of the writer to bounce the reader into accepting what he says . . . Logically *Bleak House* is all to pieces, but Dickens bounces us, so that we do not mind . . . Critics are more apt to object than readers . . .

The point is a fair one, and has been usefully explored since,[27] but the tone is not encouraging to critical investigation. Neither is the kind of emphasis Forster gives to the 'life' dimension of fiction—

> The intensely, stiflingly human quality of the novel is not to be avoided . . . if it is exorcized or even purified, the novel wilts, little is left but a bunch of words—

for the record shows that this kind of assertion is commonly made to deride formal experiment and formal analysis.

Exceptions to this rule occur when 'humanity' or 'life' are seen not as fixed absolutes but as changing phenomena with which form must keep pace. This was the burden of Virginia Woolf's famous modernist manifesto, 'Modern Fiction' (1919) in which she attacked Wells, Bennett and Galsworthy, seeing in the formal properties of their old-fashioned 'realism' an obsolete vision of reality. 'Is life like this? Must novels be like this?' she asked, and went on to answer her own question in terms very much in the spirit of Henry James:

> Look within and life, it seems, is very far from being 'like this.' . . . the mind receives a myriad impressions—trivial, fantastic, evanescent, or engraved with the sharpness of steel. From all sides they come, an incessant shower of innumerable atoms . . . life is a luminous halo, a semi-transparent envelope surrounding us from the beginning of consciousness to the end.

This is obviously a programme for Virginia Woolf's own novels; but with certain rather prim reservations (later to become more emphatic) she also commends on these grounds the fiction of James Joyce, then appearing in the *Little Review*. When the completed *Ulysses* was finally published in 1922, Eliot saluted its elborate use of myth (in which respect, indeed, it resembled *The Waste Land*) as a magnificent adjustment of form to life:

> Instead of narrative method, we may now use the mythical method. It is, I seriously believe, a step towards making the modern world possible for art . . .

Another writer belonging indisputably but awkwardly to the Modernist movement, holding utterly different views of 'life' from Virginia Woolf, and of myth from T. S. Eliot, but making considerable play with both terms, was D. H. Lawrence. Again, only a brief indication of how he fits into the general picture is possible here. In retrospect, he seems to have had almost as much influence on criticism of the novel as Eliot did in the field of poetry, though the two could scarcely have been more different in their conceptions of the critic's role. The opening paragraph of Lawrence's essay on Galsworthy is the antithesis of 'The Function of Criticism' (and its rapid acceleration from argument to polemic is entirely characteristic):

> Literary criticism can be no more than a reasoned account of the feeling produced upon the critic by the book he is criticizing. Criticism can never be a science: it is, in the first place much too personal, and in the second, it is concerned with values which science ignores. The touchstone is emotion, not reason. We judge a work by its effect on our sincere and vital emotion, and nothing else. All the critical twiddle-twaddle about style and form, all this pseudo-scientific classifying and analysing of books in imitation-botanical fashion, is mere impertinence and usually dull jargon.

(A good way of determining any critic's principles, incidentally, is to get him to read this passage and to note when he stops nodding approval, or starts shaking his head.)

Affective critics are usually the most extreme anti-intentionalists, and so it is with Lawrence: 'Never trust the artist, trust the tale.' This slogan has been adopted by many critics who would perhaps hesitate to endorse the sentence which follows it: 'The proper function of the critic is to save the tale from the artist who created it.'[28] Lawrence is telling us to *distrust* the artist, to ignore not only the intentions expressed before or after writing the work, but also the intentions manifest in the work itself. While it has remote affinities with Platonic theories of artistic inspiration, such a critical position was scarcely possible prior to Freud, depending as it does on the assumption that our deepest and truest motives for behaviour, including artistic creation, are hidden from our own consciousness.

Little has been said so far about the influence of psychology on modern criticism, partly because, in England, this has been pervasive but rarely explicit or fully developed. It is rather surprising, for instance, to find Tillyard saying of his early Cambridge days, 'When it came to the type of practical criticism to which I tended, I expect I was influenced by the sort of Freudianism that was then in the air.' Yet the passage is a revealing one:

> As there is a mind below the surface mind, so, if you begin to dwell intently on the richer kind of poetry, something more than a surface meaning is likely to be revealed. And that other meaning was likely to be more important.[29]

Empson has acknowledged the influence of Freud on *Seven Types*, though he describes it as one that tended to lead him away from verbal analysis. There seems to be an interesting paradox here: Freudian psychoanalysis in one way tended to encourage 'practical criticism': one can draw an analogy between scepticism about a patient's avowed motives and anti-historicism in literary studies, between the depth-analysis of dream-symbolism and the probing of verbal ambiguities in poetry. In other words, both seem to be 'anti-intentionalist'. But taken further, the Freudian approach to literature tends towards a somewhat reductive theory of *unconscious* intention, derived from general theories about human behaviour, or from particular evidence about the writer's life and psyche. This kind of (often second-hand) Freudianism gave a new look to literary biography (e.g. Lytton Strachey), but was anathema to critics like I. A. Richards, as we have seen. As a systematic critical method it never really caught on in England. Ernest Jones's Oedipal interpretation of *Hamlet* (1910) is an exception, and that, significantly, was first published in America, where the literary mind has been more sympathetic to Freud's ideas. D. W. Harding, one of the regular contributors to *Scrutiny*, is an academic social psychologist, but his literary criticism (see for instance the essay on Jane Austen cited above) displays a thorough domestication of psychological insights to the orthodox manner of the new criticism, and in this he is, I think, representative.

The ideas of Jung have been a little more generously acknowledged, for a number of reasons. His attitude to imaginative writers was more respectful than Freud's, and the critical application of his ideas less reductive and deterministic. The notion of the new criticism; and in this he is, I think, representative. themes and images tied in with the anthropological study of culture that took root in England more quickly than psychoanalysis, beginning with Sir James Frazer, and continuing with Gilbert Murray and a group of anthropologists at Cambridge led by F. M. Cornford who were well placed to influence literary criticism. The scholarly study of primitive myth and ritual also appealed deeply to the Modernist movement in literature, coming as it did at a time when Christianity, disinfected of its magical element by nineteenth-century rationalism, seemed no longer available as a source of poetic symbolism. The early work of Eliot is a case in point. The notes to *The Waste Land* acknowledge the influence of Frazer's *The Golden Bough* (1890–1915) and Jessie Weston's *From Ritual to Romance* (1920), an application of Frazer's ideas to medieval Grail legends. The title of *The Sacred Wood* is evidently taken from Frazer's introduction to his great work. In 1934 Maud Bodkin published *Archetypal Patterns in Poetry: Psychological Studies of Imagination*, in which she attempted to explain the enduring and mysterious power of certain literary works—*Hamlet, The Ancient Mariner, Kubla Khan* and the *Divine Comedy*, among others—by applying Jungian and anthropological insights to the affective responses evoked by such literature. This book has become something of a classic of modern criticism, but its initial impact was slight, according to Stanley Hyman,[30] especially in England. Perhaps the reason is that even in Miss Bodkin's sensitive hands, archetypal criticism does not lend itself to that kind of comparative evaluation of literary works which became the special interest of the critical revolution in England. Jung himself pointed out that it is not necessarily the 'best' books which exhibit the archetypes most strikingly.

A heterodox assimilation of psychological theories of all kinds is clearly visible in D. H. Lawrence, but this strain in his criticism was to have most influence in America, particularly as transmitted via *Studies in Classic American Literature* (1924). In England, his more immediate impact was in defining the moral element in literature, especially prose fiction:

> The business of art is to reveal the relation between man and his circumambient universe at the living moment . . . And morality is that delicate, for ever trembling and changing balance between me and my circumambient universe, which precedes and accompanies a true relatedness . . . The novel is the highest example of subtle inter-relatedness that man has discovered. Everything is true in its own time, place, circumstance, and untrue outside of its own time, place, circumstance . . . If a novel reveals true and vivid relationships it is a moral work, no matter what the relationships may consist in . . . The novel is the perfect medium for revealing to us the changing rainbow of our living relationships. The novel can help us to live, as nothing else can: no didactic Scripture, anyhow.

These quotations are taken from 'Morality and the Novel', an essay first published in *The Calendar of Modern Letters*, a short-lived little magazine that Leavis greatly admired, and which in a sense was the model for *Scrutiny*. The appeal of Lawrence's ideas for Leavis is obvious: they affirmed the moral value of literature, and hence of literary study, without tying it down to a specific dogma or ethic—the ideal solution for the secularized puritan conscience. Furthermore Lawrence's celebration, in essays and novels, of the primitive and instinctual impulses in human nature, and his outraged criticism of modern industrialized society, could, squinted at from a certain angle, reinforce the idea of the 'organic community'. It is not surprising, therefore, that in Leavis's later criticism Lawrence came to occupy much the same position—both as a source of ideas and as a criterion of literary achievement—that Eliot had held in his earlier criticism.

In *The Great Tradition* (published 1948, but largely a collection of articles published in *Scrutiny* from 1937 onwards), Leavis 'revalued' the English novel tradition even more drastically than he had the poetic tradition. 'Jane Austen, George Eliot, Henry James, Conrad, and D. H. Lawrence: the great tradition is there.' The influence of Lawrence himself is evident in the criteria of election to this tradition: 'the major novelists not only change the possibilities of art for practitioners and readers . . . they are significant in terms of that human awareness they promote; awareness of the possibilities of life.' In practice the latter point receives far more emphasis than the former. The later phase of Henry James, for instance, in which he was most obviously changing the possibilities of art, is seen as a regrettable decline in his achievement. The novelists in the great tradition are 'all very much concerned with "form" but their essential claim to greatness is that they are all distinguished by a vital capacity for experience, a kind of reverent openness before life, and a marked moral intensity.' Leavis had travelled a long way from the declaration of intent in the introduction to *New Bearings*: 'I have endeavoured to confine myself as strictly as possible to literary criticism, and to remember that poetry is made of words.' There is extensive quotation in *The Great Tradition*, and intelligent commentary, but little analysis of the novelist's verbal art. In *D. H. Lawrence, Novelist* (1955) the quotations get longer, the commentary becomes more hectoring.

*The Great Tradition* intensified the polarization of English critics into admirers and opponents of Leavis, amounting sometimes to obsession on both sides. It was not so much the positive valuations he advanced that did this—the high estimates of Jane Austen, George Eliot, Henry James, Conrad and Lawrence met with general agreement, if not always on the same grounds—but the exclusiveness of the Great Tradition, the dismissal (in effect if not in intention) of the entire eighteenth-century novel, of Dickens (with the exception of *Hard Times*)[31] of Flaubert and of Joyce, not to mention 'the ruck of Gaskells and Trollopes and Merediths.' Taking a detached view, we can see that this exaggerated scale of value, with its dramatic peaks and abysses, is an integral part of Leavis's critical temper, an essential way, for him, of generating intellectual energy in himself and a quickened response in his audience. But he laid himself open, in this way, to the old objection against treating opinions as if they were facts; and the animus which he has provoked is in large part a tribute to the extent of his influence.

This in fact is a paradox which always confronts us in considering the work of Leavis and the critics closely associated with him. As one reads through the files of *Scrutiny*, and the various public utterances that have followed the demise of that journal, the note of isolation, of frustration and persecution grows more and more insistent, the idea of representing a disregarded minority becomes more and more personalized, the 'enemy' becomes more and more numerous and specific: the Auden-Spender 'gang', the academic establishment, the metropolitan literary 'racket', the BBC, the British Council, the *T.L.S.*, Mr. Alan Pryce-Jones, Sir Charles Snow. Yet over the same period the status and influence (the *real* status and influence, not the false kind they profess to despise) of Leavis and *Scrutiny* in the educational and literary communities has grown steadily. They have left an indelible mark on cultural life in Britain and the Commonwealth,[32] and if this was not always in exactly the way they intended, such is the usual fate of ideas and an inevitable part of growth. For example, though Leavis himself disapproves of *Lady Chatterley's Lover* and the B.B.C., no one can doubt that the acquittal of the former and the consolidation of the latter in the face of commercial broadcasting—two of the most significant events in recent British cultural life—owed a great deal to the work of Leavis.

In this last connection, two names immediately occur as examples of critics who are clearly indebted to Leavis, but who have significantly extended his kind of approach to literature and culture; Raymond Williams and Richard Hoggart. The finely written evocation of working-class life in the first part of Hoggart's *The Uses of Literacy* (1957) might be described as an attempt to locate and describe an 'organic community' as an observed actuality rather than as a literary or historical myth, and with a controlling awareness of the alternative dangers of sentimentality and condescension. In the second part of the book, a critical survey of 'mass art' (popular songs, magazines, cheap fiction, etc.) purveyed to the working class in conditions of post-war affluence, *Scrutiny*'s concern for 'standards' and moral objections to the commercialization of culture are obvious influences; but again Hoggart's critique is more open-minded and positive, as is implied in the second part of his general conclusion: that the working classes have tended to 'lose, culturally, much that was valuable and to gain less than their new situation should have allowed.' Since *The Uses of Literacy* Hoggart has advocated a still more tolerant and systematic application of literary-critical methods and principles to materials normally summoned to the bar of critical judgement for instant condemnation, on the assumption that the remedy for a fragmented culture is a common one, not an élitist one.

The same assumption, worked out much more explicitly and idealogically, informs the criticism of Raymond Williams. In the Foreword to *Culture and Society 1780–1950* (1958) Williams wrote: 'We live in an expanding culture, yet we spend much of our energy regretting the fact, rather than seeking to understand its nature and conditions.' The book is an attempt at such understanding through the investigation of the 'cultural debate' that literary intellectuals have generated and sustained since the end of the eighteenth century in response to the changes brought about by the Industrial Revolution, the growth of democracy and the development of the mass media. A skilful blend of cultural history, literary criticism and committed argument, *Culture and Society* was followed by *The Long Revolution* (1961), a knottier, more fragmentary and speculative work, with more obvious political designs upon the reader.

Williams's insistence that all significant human activity, including art, is communal—'Reality in our terms is that which human beings make in common, by work or language'—is clearly Marxist in derivation; but his concern, both in judging literature, and in suggesting lines of social development for the future, is with the reconciliation of the claims of the individual and society, presenting them not as opposed absolutes, but as different aspects of the same entity. Thus in truly 'realistic' novels, 'Every aspect of the personal life is radically affected by the quality of the general life, yet the general life is seen at its most important in completely personal terms.' In this way Williams's thought incorporates the revolutionary dynamic of Marxism without appearing to endorse that brutal subordination of the individual to society that has been the least attractive feature of Marxism in political practice. He is probably the most influential figure in the current revival of Marxism as a basis for political and literary thinking.

Like psychoanalysis, Marxism has rarely been applied in English literary criticism in any systematic way—or not, at least, to any great effect. Christopher Caudwell was the nearest thing to a first-class Marxist critic England produced between the wars, and he was killed in the Spanish Civil War before he had a chance to fulfil his promise, or to resolve the conflict between his basically symbolist aesthetics and his Marxist view of history.[33] A similar conflict, between Marxism and the orthodoxies of the new criticism, is discernible in the work of Arnold Kettle, one of the few academic critics to have remained loyal to Marxism.[34] The politically-conscious thirties threw up a great deal of Marxist-orientated criticism from creative and freelance critics, but little of it has survived. The Second World War, and disillusionment with Stalinism, quenched what spirit it had. Stephen Spender has become a chronicler and defender of the Modernism he once reacted against in the name of political engagement.[35] W. H. Auden has published in his expatriate period criticism of great wit, elegance and suggestiveness,[36] but it seems to exist in a curious vacuum of self-communing, undirected towards any identifiable audience, and thus only fortuitously contributing to the ongoing debate criticism must be. Of all this generation of English writers, George Orwell has the best record for keeping his head through the political storms of the thirties; and his influence—his identification with the underprivileged, his concern for the preservation of truth and decency in public life, his readiness to give serious attention to every kind of literature from Shakespeare and Dickens to Boys' Weeklies—is evident in the work of Raymond Williams and still more of Richard Hoggart.

The cultural criticism associated with Williams and Hoggart has perhaps been the only genuinely new trend to emerge in English criticism since the War capable of attracting a substantial following.[37] On the whole, the picture has been one of consolidation, the emergence of a sensible pluralism in critical method, but with undertones of disillusionment with the critical revolution and uncertainty about how to proceed. As I suggested at the outset, academe has strengthened its hold on the world of letters, and in the fifties initiated its own creative movement (called, very academically, 'The Movement') in which the shop-soiled remnants of modernism left over from before the War were despatched, and the virtues of wit, common-sense, provinciality and dry-eyed moral decency cultivated. But the excitement was comparatively short-lived, and of late enquiring minds have been looking more and more towards America, whither both Modernism and modern criticism seemed to have emigrated. In the late thirties, forties and fifties the seminal ideas of Richards, Eliot, Empson and the other critics of the 'revolution' in England, were adopted, explored and systematized, with rather more intellectual adventurousness than they were in England, under the banner of the 'New Criticism'. And the challenges that have been made to the New Criticism—Chicago neo-Aristotelianism, the varieties of myth criticism and psychoanalytical criticism, comparative literature, applied linguistics—as well as the best work along more traditional lines —literary history, history of ideas, literary biography—have appeared predominantly in America. Thus there has been a reversal of roles between English and American criticism since the last war: England, once the exporter of seminal ideas, has become, with good or ill grace, primarily an importer.

There is one respect in which English criticism continues to have the edge over American criticism: it is on the whole (we can all think of exceptions) generally better written in the sense of being more readable. The point is not a trivial one: it reveals a good deal about the development of English criticism in the twentieth century.

I have described this development in terms of a 'revolution' against a tradition of appreciative belletrism, but there is a sense in which the revolution could be described as a corrective continuation of that tradition. The continuity exists in what linguists would call the 'register' of criticism, that is, its characteristics as discourse, as determined by the assumed relationships between critic, text and reader. This, despite all the variations of personal style, has remained remarkably uniform throughout the century, and has been common to all of the three kinds of critics I began by distinguishing. It might be described as a register of persuasion or polite conversation rather than of exposition.

English criticism has traditionally been modelled on conversation. Much of it has been presented in the form of conversation or dialogue (Jonson's Conversations with Drummond, Dryden's *Essay of Dramatic Poesy*, Johnson in Boswell, Coleridge's Table Talk, Oscar Wilde's 'The Decay of Lying'); but the mode of the English 'essay' and the English lecture, which were the main vehicles of criticism through the eighteenth and nineteenth centuries, was also the mode of a heightened and one-sided conversation. The dangers inherent in this mode—dangers of self-indulgence, loose thinking, and irrelevant gossip—have been pointed out often enough. And the new criticism did much to correct these vices, substituting logical rigour, close attention to the text and exacting standards of relevance. But the extent to which the conversational model persisted may be seen by comparing the ways in which analysis developed in England and America respectively. For the further analysis is taken, the more difficult it becomes to maintain the register of conversation or persuasion: it becomes necessary at a certain point to use technical jargon, statistics, diagrams, numbered categories, all of which belong to the register of scientific exposition. In Richards' early work there was a tendency in this direction, but it was subsequently exploited in America. In England, Richard's approach was, if anything, tamed and domesticated to the native conversational mode. The often-remarked tortuousness of Leavis's prose style, for instance, is the result not of wilful obscurity or insensitivity, but of a tremendous effort to organize the maximum amount of data in a discourse that will not lose its personal and almost intimate character, using every device of imagery, syntactical inversion, elegant variation and parenthesis. It is an enormously difficult undertaking, and the strain of it shows in every line. Empson carried it off marvellously in *Seven Types*, but when in *The Structure of Complex Words* (1951) he attempted a more systematic and scientific kind of verbal analysis, it significantly collapsed under the eccentricity and incomprehensibility of its methodology. Eliot was never much interested in analysis, and made an Olympian version of the English conversational mode his own, with consummate skill.

This mode persists in English criticism through every possible variation of critical purpose and personal style; in, for instance, C. S. Lewis's urbane, good-humoured kind of common-sense historicism, in Raymond Williams's earnest, sometimes ponderous groping for vital connections between abstract concepts, in Richard Hoggart's characteristic blend of abstraction and racy idiom, in the epigrammatic brilliance of Frank Kermode's cosmopolitan eclecticism.

I think the quality of English criticism that I have tried to identify here is a more inclusive one than the 'amateurism' which is sometimes attributed to it, though there are no doubt connections between the two. There are certainly links to be made with the empirical tradition of English philosophy, inimical to grand theory, with the compactness of the English literary world, and with the traditional stress on undergraduate teaching in British universities. Taking all these factors together, it is not surprizing that the extension of the critical revolution as a mode of *knowledge* has been carried on largely in America, where, for historical and ethnic reasons, quite different conditions obtain; or that critics in England, including Eliot himself, have expressed misgivings about that extension, and hence come to question the principles of the revolution itself[38]

As with all such issues, the rights and wrongs of the matter are not easy to determine. Criticism differs from literature in that it can develop as well as change, and the possibilities for growth seem more promising in America than in England. On the other hand, criticism loses its *raison d'être* when it loses contact with an audience, and in its inherited grasp of this principle, English criticism has much to contribute in the increasingly cosmopolitan and collaborative enterprise of criticism.

1. David Palmer, *The Rise of English Studies* (London, 1965). For a more light-hearted, but often acute account of the same subject, see Stephen Potter's *The Muse in Chains* (London, 1937).

2. Cyril Connolly, *Enemies of Promise* (London, 1938).

3. E. M. W. Tillyard, *The Muse Unchained* (London, 1958).

4. An excellent account of this literary situation, particularly as it affected poetry, is to be found in C. K. Stead's *The New Poetic* (London, 1964).

5. 'The Frontiers of Criticism', *On Poets and Poetry* (London, 1957).

6. Tillyard, *op. cit.*

7. Quoted by R. C. Townsend in 'The Idea of an English School: Cambridge English', *The Critical Survey* (Winter, 1967), a most lucid and informative study of the subject.

8. W. K. Wimsatt and Monroe C. Beardsley, *The Verbal Icon* (Lexington, Ky., 1954),

9. *For Lancelot Andrews* (London, 1928).

10. Tillyard, *op. cit.*

11. George Watson, *The English Critics* (Harmondsworth, 1962).

12. In *Furioso* (Spring, 1940), quoted by Stanley Edgar Hyman, *The Armed Vision* (New York, 1948).

13. The first quotation is from R. G. Lienhardt, 'Auden's Inverted Development', and the second from F. R. Leavis, 'Thought and Emotional Quality', both in *Scrutiny* XIII (1945).

14. R. C. Townsend, *op. cit.*

15. The poetry of Gerard Manley Hopkins, remarkably experimental for its time, was not generally known until Robert Bridges published his edition of 1918, and in the 1920's Hopkins became a modern poet by adoption.

16. See A. J. A. Waldock's *Paradise Lost and its Critics* (London, 1947).

17. Reprinted in L. C. Knights' *Explorations* (London, 1946).

18. Q. D. Leavis, 'A Critical Theory of Jane Austen's Writings', in four Parts, *Scrutiny* X (1941/2) and XII (1944).

19. *Scrutiny* VIII (1940).

20. Tillyard, *op. cit.*

21. See especially the articles collected under the general headings, 'The Cambridge Tradition', 'Literary Culture', 'The Literary World' and 'Critics' in the very useful *A Selection from Scrutiny*, ed. F. R. Leavis (Cambridge, 1968), and Dr Leavis's 'Retrospect' in Vol. XX of the 1963 reprint of *Scrutiny*.

22. F. R. Leavis, 'Retrospect of a Decade', *Scrutiny*, IX (1940).

23. The exchange between F. R. Leavis and F. W. Bateson, 'The Responsible Critic', *Scrutiny*, XIX (1953) is particularly revealing in this respect.

24. See, for example, Helen Gardner, *The Business of Criticism*,

(London, 1959); C. S. Lewis, *An Experiment in Criticism* (London, 1961), and Graham Hough, *The Dream and the Task: Literature and Morals in the Culture of Today* (London, 1963).

25. 'Literary Criticism and Philosophy', *Scrutiny*, V (1936/7) and VI (1937/8). Leavis's reply is reprinted in *The Common Pursuit* (1952).

26. See *Henry James and H. G. Wells: A Record of their Friendship, their Debate on the Art of Fiction, and their Quarrel*, edited by Leon Edel and Gordon N. Ray (London, 1958).

27. Notably by Wayne Booth, *The Rhetoric of Fiction* (Chicago, 1961).

28. D. H. Lawrence, *Studies in Classic American Literature* (London, 1924).

29. Tillyard, *op. cit.*

30. Hyman, *op. cit.*

31. Dr Leavis has subsequently revised this estimate, in Dickens's favour.

32. A missionary spirit was inherent in Leavis's approach to English Studies, and was carried into schools, training colleges and universities, as well as into criticism and literary journalism, by those whom he taught—either directly at Cambridge, or indirectly through his publications. It is noteworthy, however, that Leavis's influence in America has been very much smaller than that of Eliot, Richards or Empson, if one is to judge by the slight attention given to him in American surveys of modern criticism such as Hyman's *The Armed Vision* and W. K. Wimsatt's and Cleanth Brooks's *Litrary Criticism: a short History* (London, 1957).

33. Caudwell's two critical books were *Illusion and Reality* (London, 1937), and *Studies in a Dying Culture* (London, 1938).

34. See Arnold Kettle, *An Introduction to the English Novel* (i, London, 1951 and ii, 1953).

35. See Stephen Spender, *The Struggle of the Modern* (London, 1963).

36. See W. H. Auden, *The Dyer's Hand* (London, 1963).

37. It has been usefully described and contrasted with American trends in Martin Green's essay 'British Marxists and American Freudians', in *Innovations* ed. Bernard Bergonzi (London, 1968).

38. In 'The Frontiers of Criticism' (1956), Eliot said: 'These last thirty years have been, I think, a brilliant period in literary criticism, both in England and in America. It may come to seem, in retrospect, too brilliant.' See also Graham Hough, *The Dream and the Task*; John Holloway, 'The Critical Intimidation' in *The Charted Mirror* (London, 1960); and George Steiner, 'To Educate Our Gentlemen' in *Language and Silence* (London, 1967).

# INDEX

The principal references to an author or topic are shown in
bold type

Isherwood, C., 175, 281, 283, 321, 385; *Lions and Shadows*, 283

James, H., 24, 26, 27–28, 31, 32, 154, 158, 180, 182, 196, 203, 204, 254, 255, 363, 370, 385, 389–90, 391, 392, 395, 396; *The Wings of the Dove*, 27; *The Ambassadors*, 27; *The Golden Bowl*, 27; 'The Figure in the Carpet', 32; 'The Art of Fiction', 255, 389
James, W., 110, 191; *Principles of Psychology*, 191
Jennings, Elizabeth, 303–4
*Jew of Malta*, 162
John, St., 162
John of the Cross, St., 171, 174
Johnson, L., 36
Johnson, S., 282–83, 363, 400
Jones, D., 299–300, 302; *In Parenthesis*, 299; *The Anathemata*, 299–300
Jonson, B., 80, 400
Joyce, J., 10, 17, 18, 19, 22, 31, 41, 42, 44, 45, 72, **75–105**, 107, 182, 183, 190, 191, 196, 197, 198, 203, 205, 210, 223, 315, 325, 338, 370, 392, 396; *Chamber Music*, 80–82; *Dubliners*, 41, 76, **82–86**, 90, 93; *Exiles*, 91; *Finnegans Wake*, 75, 79, 80, **96–101**, 181, 299, 325; *A Portrait of the Artist as a Young Man*, 41, 43, 77, **86–91**, 93, 197; *Ulysses*, 19, 79, 86, **91–96**, 99, 180, 183, 190, 299, 325, 392; 'Araby', 83; 'The Boarding House', 83; 'Clay', 83; 'The Day of the Rabblement', 78; 'The Dead', 83–84, 91; 'Drama and Life', 76; 'Grace', 93; 'Ivy Day in the Committee Room', 93; 'A Little Cloud', 83; 'A Painful Case', 83; 'The Sisters', 83, 85
Joyce, S., 77, 79, 87

Kafka, F., 17, 43, 296
Keats, J., 287, 289, 322, 383; *Otho the Great*, 322
Ker, W. P., 368
Kermode, F., 17, 22, 401
Keyes, S., 292–93
Keynes, J. M., 125

Kierkegaard, S., 171
Kipling, R., 31–33, 36, 278, 370; *Departmental Ditties*, 31; *Plain Tales from the Hills*, 31; 'Without Benefit of Clergy', 32; 'Mrs. Bathurst', 32; *Puck of Pook's Hill*, 32–33; 'The Islanders', 36
Knight, W., 384; *The Wheel of Fire*, 384; *The Imperial Theme*, 384
Knights, L. C., 384
Koteliansky, S., 140

Laforgue, J., 25, 43, 153, 154
Larkin, P., 19, 37, 303, 304, 305–6
Lawrence, D. H., 9, 10, 18, 21, 22, 24, 25, 35, 44, 45, **107–152**, 180, 181, 182, 183, 190, 198, 203, 215, 223, 305, 328, 338, 363, 371, 392–93, 395, 396; (fiction) *Aaron's Rod*, 19, 139, 140, 144–45; *The Boy in the Bush*, 140; *England My England*, 19; *Kangaroo*, 125, 140, 145; *Lady Chatterley's Lover*, 106, 141, 142, **145–49**, 183, 209, 345, 397; *The Lost Girl*, 34, 124, 139, 140, **142–44**; *The Plumed Serpent*, 140, 145; *The Prussian Officer*, 111; *The Rainbow*, 43, 124, 125, **127–33**, 137, 139; *Sons and Lovers*, 111, **117–24**, 126, 137; *The Trespasser*, 111, 135; *The Virgin and the Gypsy*, 141; *The White Peacock*, 35, 110, 111, **114–18**; *Women in Love*, 10, 35, 124, 131, **132–139**, 140, 142, 143, 148, 149, 255; 'The Captain's Doll', 139, 141, 144; 'The Christening', 112–13; 'The Daughters of the Vicar', 112; 'The Fox', 139; 'The Horse Dealer's Daughter, 144; 'The Man Who Died', 141; 'The Man Who Loved Islands', 141; 'Odour of Chrysanthemums', 113; 'The Prussian Officer', 113, 124; 'A Prelude', 110; 'St. Mawr', 140; 'The Schoolmaster', 111; 'Sun', 141; 'The Thorn in the Flesh', 113, 124; 'You Touched Me'; (other writings) *Apropos of*

410

411